Northern Tanzania Safari Guide

Serengeti • Kilimanjaro • Zanzibar

the Bradt Travel Guide

Philip Briggs
Chris McIntyre

edition
4

www.bradtguides.com

Bradt Travel Guides Ltd, UK
The Globe Pequot Press Inc, USA

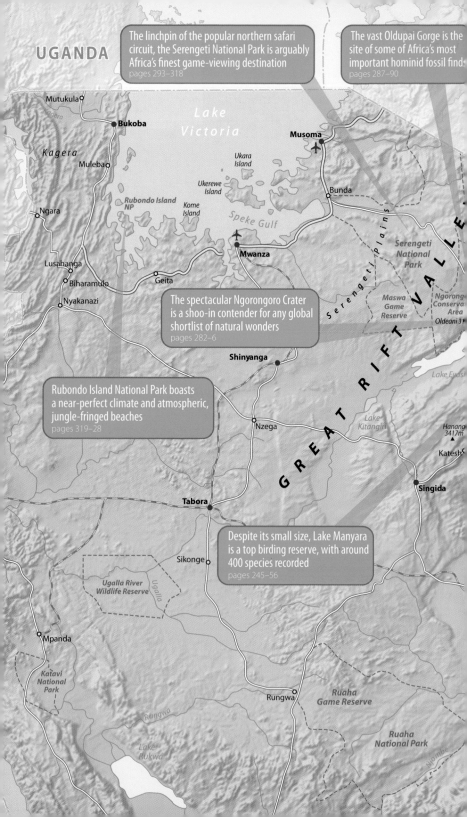

UGANDA

The linchpin of the popular northern safari circuit, the Serengeti National Park is arguably Africa's finest game-viewing destination
pages 293–318

The vast Oldupai Gorge is the site of some of Africa's most important hominid fossil find
pages 287–90

Lake Victoria

Mutukula

Bukoba

Kagera

Muleba

Ukara Island

Musoma

Bunda

Ukerewe Island

Ngara

Rubondo Island NP

Kome Island

Speke Gulf

Mwanza

Serengeti Plains

Serengeti National Park

Lusahanga

Biharamulo

Geita

Nyakanazi

The spectacular Ngorongoro Crater is a shoo-in contender for any global shortlist of natural wonders
pages 282–6

Maswa Game Reserve

Ngorong Conserva Area

Oldeani 3

Lake Eyasi

Shinyanga

Rubondo Island National Park boasts a near-perfect climate and atmospheric, jungle-fringed beaches
pages 319–28

Lake Kitangin

Hanang 3417m ▲

Nzega

Katesh

G R E A T   R I F T   V A L L E

Singida

Tabora

Despite its small size, Lake Manyara is a top birding reserve, with around 400 species recorded
pages 245–56

Sikonge

Ugalla River Wildlife Reserve

Ugalla

Mpanda

Katavi National Park

Rungwa

Rungwa

Ruaha Game Reserve

Lake Rukwa

Ruaha National Park

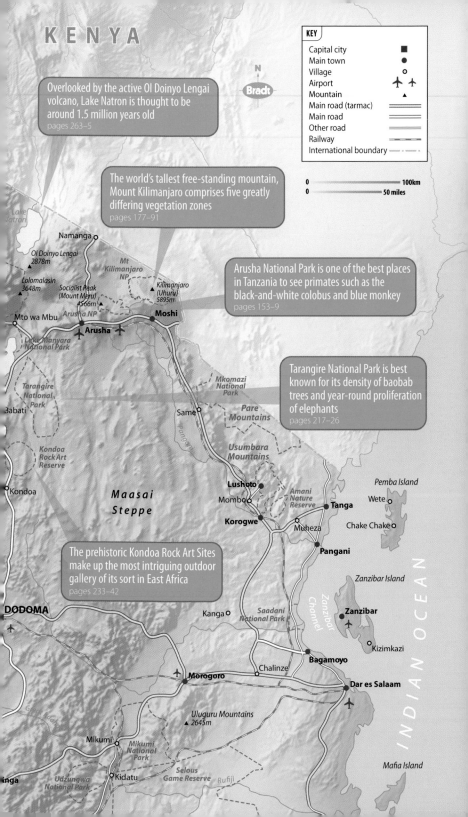

K E N Y A

KEY

Capital city	■
Main town	●
Village	○
Airport	✈ ✈
Mountain	▲
Main road (tarmac)	══════
Main road	═══════
Other road	───────
Railway	╫╫╫╫╫╫
International boundary	∙∙∙∙∙∙

Overlooked by the active Ol Doinyo Lengai volcano, Lake Natron is thought to be around 1.5 million years old
pages 263–5

The world's tallest free-standing mountain, Mount Kilimanjaro comprises five greatly differing vegetation zones
pages 177–91

Arusha National Park is one of the best places in Tanzania to see primates such as the black-and-white colobus and blue monkey
pages 153–9

Tarangire National Park is best known for its density of baobab trees and year-round proliferation of elephants
pages 217–26

The prehistoric Kondoa Rock Art Sites make up the most intriguing outdoor gallery of its sort in East Africa
pages 233–42

N

Bradt

0   100km
0   50 miles

Lake Natron

Namanga

Ol Doinyo Lengai 2878m

Lolomalasin 3648m

Socialist Peak (Mount Meru) 4566m

Mt Kilimanjaro NP

Kilimanjaro (Uhuru) 5895m

Arusha NP

Moshi

Mto wa Mbu

Arusha

Lake Manyara National Park

Tarangire National Park

Babati

Mkomazi National Park

Pare Mountains

Same

Kondoa Rock Art Reserve

Kondoa

Maasai Steppe

Usumbara Mountains

Lushoto

Mombo

Korogwe

Amani Nature Reserve

Muheza

Tanga

Wete

Chake Chake

Pemba Island

Zanzibar Island

Pangani

DODOMA

Kanga

Saadani National Park

Chalinze

Bagamoyo

Zanzibar Channel

Zanzibar

Kizimkazi

Morogoro

Dar es Salaam

Uluguru Mountains 2645m

Mikumi

Mikumi National Park

inga

Udzungwa National Park

Kidatu

Selous Game Reserve

Rufiji

Mafia Island

INDIAN OCEAN

Pangani

Northern Tanzania in colour

left   The Ngorongoro Crater is a mesmerising safari experience — made all the more spectacular by the striking backdrop of the 600m-high crater wall
pages 282–6

below   Lake Manyara National Park is a compact but ecologically varied area known for its tree-climbing lions, plentiful giraffes and prodigious birdlife
pages 245–56

above The annual migration of over a million blue wildebeest forms one of Africa's great natural spectacles pages 298–9

right Tarangire National Park is best known for its density of trees and year-round proliferation of elephants pages 217–26

below The montane forests of Usambara are alive with the raucous squawking of hornbills and the banter of monkeys pages 196–211

above left Stone Town's Anglican Cathedral stands on the site of a 19th-century slave market. Pictured, a sculpture of slaves chained in a pit page 349

above right Nungwi is the centre of Zanzibar's dhow-building industry; generations of skilled craftsmen have worked on the beach outside the village page 366

below Zanzibari locals descend on a beach for a game of sunset football

AUTHORS

Philip Briggs is a travel writer specialising in Africa. Raised in South Africa, where he still lives, Philip first visited East Africa in 1986 and has since spent an average of six months annually exploring the highways and back roads of the continent. His first Bradt Travel Guide, to South Africa, was published in 1991, and he has subsequently written Bradt guides to Tanzania, Uganda, Ethiopia, Malawi, Mozambique, Ghana, Rwanda, Somaliland and East African wildlife. Philip has contributed to  more than a dozen other books about Africa, and his work regularly appears in magazines such as *Africa Geographic*, *Travel Africa* and *Wanderlust*. He also acts as an advisor to specialist tour operator Expert Africa, helping to develop their programmes.

Chris McIntyre went to Africa in 1987, after reading Physics at Queen's College, Oxford. He taught with VSO in Zimbabwe for almost three years and travelled extensively, before writing his first guidebook in 1990. He has since written Bradt guides to Namibia, Botswana and Zambia; co-authored (with his wife, Susan) the last four editions of Bradt's *Zanzibar*; and the previous editions of *Tanzania* and *Northern Tanzania*.

Since the late 1990s, Chris has also run the specialist tour operator, Expert Africa. Here he leads a team of dedicated Africa addicts – based in London, Cape Town, San Francisco and New Zealand – who provide impartial advice and guidance on great safaris to sub-Saharan Africa, including Tanzania. He can be contacted on e chris.mcintyre@expertafrica.com.

PUBLISHER'S FOREWORD   *Hilary Bradt*

Over 30 years ago George and I spent two fruitless days trying to hitchhike through the Serengeti. We were also bitten to distraction by mosquitoes in Mto wa Mbu ('River of Mosquitoes') and arrested in Tabora because, the official said, it was illegal to take photographs in Tanzania without a permit. George sourly wrote in *Backpacker's Africa* (1977): 'We hope someday it will all come together and be the most enlightened and productive country in Africa, but that's not going to happen for a while.' It's happened. The northern safari circuit in Tanzania is widely considered to be the best in East Africa, with an excellent infrastructure and some of the friendliest and most welcoming people in Africa. Philip once wrote: 'I've visited most corners of Tanzania ... and I have to confess that were my time in the country limited to a couple of weeks, then my first priorities would undoubtedly be the Serengeti, Ngorongoro and Zanzibar. They are very special places.' In this book, Philip has been able to indulge himself – and his fans – with the detailed descriptions that these special places deserve.

Fourth edition June 2017   First published February 2006

Bradt Travel Guides Ltd
IDC House, The Vale, Chalfont St Peter, Bucks SL9 9RZ, England
www.bradtguides.com
Print edition published in the USA by The Globe Pequot Press Inc,
PO Box 480, Guilford, Connecticut 06437-0480

Text copyright © 2017 Philip Briggs
Zanzibar chapter copyright © 2017 Chris McIntyre and Susan McIntyre
Maps copyright © 2017 Bradt Travel Guides Ltd; includes map data © OpenStreetMap contributors
Town maps content copyright © 2017 Philip Briggs
Project Manager: Laura Pidgley
Cover image research: Joe Collins

ISBN: 978 1 78477 037 2 (print)
e-ISBN: 978 1 78477 501 8 (e-pub)
e-ISBN: 978 1 78477 402 8 (mobi)

British Library Cataloguing in Publication Data
A catalogue record for this book is available from the British Library

Photographs All photos by Ariadne Van Zandbergen unless otherwise stated
Front cover Lion cub, Serengeti National Park
Back cover A group of Maasai men dancing at a traditional *manyatta*; Elephants walking in Serengeti National Park
Title page Tree-climbing leopard, Serengeti National Park; Dhow at sunset off the coast of Zanzibar; Balloon safari in Serengeti National Park

Maps David McCutcheon FBCart.S; colour relief base by Nick Rowland FRGS

Typeset by Ian Spick, Bradt Travel Guides
Production managed by Jellyfish Print Solutions; printed in India
Digital conversion by www.dataworks.co.in

CONTRIBUTORS

Ariadne Van Zandbergen, who took the photographs in this book and did much of the research for the sections on Kilimanjaro and Ol Doinyo Lengai, is a Belgian-born freelance photographer who first travelled through Africa in 1994–95 and now lives in South Africa. Her photographs have appeared in numerous travel and wildlife guides, coffee-table books, magazines and newspapers, and she runs her own website (*www.africaimagelibrary.com; see ad, below*).

Susan McIntyre is co-author of Bradt's *Zanzibar*. She has worked in public relations for the travel industry since 1999, and created media campaigns for tourist boards worldwide before focusing on some of southern Africa's finest independent safari camps and boutique hotels. Susan continues to travel and to advise on Expert Africa's programme of trips to the Zanzibar archipelago and the Seychelles, with an increasing interest in adventurous family travel, thanks to the young McIntyres.

Emma Thomson (*www.ethomson.co.uk*), former Commissioning Editor at Bradt Travel Guides, is a freelance writer and Fellow of the Royal Geographical Society. She has spent time living with Rangi, Chagga and Maasai communities in Tanzania and is a trustee of Serian UK, a registered charity that supports Monduli Juu's Noonkodin Secondary School, which provides shelter and education to FGM runaways. Emma is also the author of Bradt's award-winning *Flanders* guide.

Richard 'Woody' Wood has travelled to every corner of Tanzania over the 14 years he has lived and worked in the country. He has slept under the stars at Lake Tagalala, fished the Kilombero River, motorbiked across the remote Katavi Plateau, sailed by dhow along the Swahili Coast, climbed Mount Kilimanjaro five times, paddled a dugout up the Great Ruaha, trekked up Ol Doinyo Lengai, and scuba dived off the coast. The director of Wild Thing Safaris, he is now settled in Usa River with his wife, daughter and son, but relishes every opportunity to get out to the back of beyond 'where all the good stuff happens'!

AUTHOR'S STORY *Philip Briggs*

We go back a bit, Tanzania and I. Our first stilted encounter was back in 1986, when as a nervous novice traveller heading from Kenya to Zambia, I'd heard so much about the nightmarish black market, appalling public transport and obtuse officials that I decided to nip through Tanzania in less than a week, stopping only to catch my breath in the spectacularly rundown port of Dar es Salaam.

Two years later, I returned to Tanzania on a less intimidated footing, and followed a more adventurous route that incorporated side trips to somnambulant Tanga and the fabulous ferry ride down Lake Tanganyika. But I guess the real romance began in 1992, when I spent four unforgettable months bussing the length and breadth of Tanzania to research what would become the first dedicated guidebook to this extraordinarily diverse – and at the time vastly underrated – country.

Updating duties have recalled me to Tanzania regularly since then, and every time I'm struck afresh at how much it has blossomed over the course of our acquaintance. The Tanzania I first encountered in 1986 was seemingly stuck in inextricable economic decline, with every aspect of its infrastructure – from roads and public transport to electricity and water supplies – tottering on the verge of collapse. Meanwhile, manufacture had ground to a standstill – simply tracking down a warm beer in Dar was an exercise that could take on epic proportions.

Back then, tourist facilities, such as they existed, were barely functional. And an insane fixed exchange rate ensured that travel was dominated by a risky black market. Had anybody then suggested that Tanzania might one day rank as the most diverse, friendliest and arguably the best safari destination anywhere in Africa, I'd have thought they were insane.

And how wrong I'd have been … for today, more than 30 years on, that's exactly what Tanzania is!

FEEDBACK REQUEST AND UPDATES WEBSITE

At Bradt Travel Guides we're aware that guidebooks start to go out of date on the day they're published – and that you, our readers, are out there in the field doing research of your own. You'll find out before us when a fine new family-run hotel opens or a favourite restaurant changes hands and goes downhill. So why not write and tell us about your experiences? Contact us on ☎01753 893444 or e info@bradtguides.com. We will forward emails to the authors who may post updates on the Bradt website at www.bradtupdates.com/northerntanzania. Alternatively you can add a review of the book to www.bradtguides.com or Amazon.

Acknowledgements

PHILIP BRIGGS

I received an enormous amount of assistance from within the safari industry during the course of researching all editions of this book, as well as earlier editions of the Bradt guide to *Tanzania*, and I would like to express my gratitude to the many safari companies and airlines that have helped ferry us around the country, and to the myriad lodges, hotels and camps that have accommodated us over the years – this would be a poor guidebook indeed were it not for the support and hospitality that has made it possible for me to explore the region so thoroughly.

I am also indebted to my wife, travel companion and photographic collaborator Ariadne Van Zandbergen; to my co-author Chris McIntyre, his wife Susan McIntyre and the staff of Expert Africa (in particular James Denny and Richard Trillo); to Richard 'Woody' and Hannah Wood for updating the Moshi and Arusha chapters; to my parents Roger and Kay Briggs for shuttling us to and from O R Tambo Airport so many times I've lost count; and to various Bradt staffers past and present, notably Tricia Hayne, Adrian Phillips, Emma Thomson and Laura Pidgley.

CHRIS MCINTYRE

Primarily my thanks go to Philip Briggs, my co-author, for kindly allowing me to have a modest input into what was his creation and has always been his book. Then to numerous people in Tanzania, mostly on the islands, who I know will forgive me for only crediting them properly in the Zanzibar book.

In the UK, thanks especially to James Denny, Lyndsey Marris and Richard Trillo. All are African experts in their own right; all work closely with me at Expert Africa; and all got involved with extensive research trips – contributing significantly to various sections of this text. Finally, my love and thanks to my wife, Susie, who undertook the lioness' share of our hard work, on the islands and back in the UK, as she pulled together a detailed and comprehensive update to our Zanzibar book, which forms the basis of the Zanzibar section in this guide.

Contents

LIST OF MAPS

KEY TO MAP SYMBOLS

——·—·—	International boundary	♀	Bar
	Tarred roads (town plans)	✕	Restaurant, etc
	Tarred roads (regional maps)	⌷	Café
	Other roads (regional maps)	☆	Nightclub/casino
------	Tracks/4x4 (regional maps)	@	Internet access
	Railway	†	Church/cathedral
----------	Footpath	☾	Mosque
--▲--	Pedestrian ferry & route	☿	Sikh temple
✈ ✛	Airport/airstrip	⊞	Cemetery
☐	Railway station	∴	Archaeological site
⊟	Bus station	⌂	Cave
⛽	Filling station/garage	※	Viewpoint
✕—✕	Gate/barrier	∭	Waterfall
🛈	Tourist information	♧	Woodland feature
⛬	Museum	▲	Summit (height in metres)
⊞	Important/historic building	○	Spring/waterhole
$	Bank/ATM/bureau de change	●	Other place of interest
⊠	Post office		Crater/escarpment
⊞	Hospital/clinic	⚘	Sports facility
✚	Pharmacy		Glacier
⌂	Hotel/inn/guesthouse etc		Marsh
⋀	Campsite		National park
⬧	Resthouse/hut		Forest park/reserve
			Urban market
			Urban park

Introduction

Tanzania is a statistician's dream. Within its borders lie Africa's highest and fifth-highest mountains, the world's largest intact volcanic caldera, what is widely agreed to be Africa's greatest national park, as well as the lion's share of the continent's most expansive lake. Yet this vast East African country also boasts a litany of evocative place names to touch the heart of any poet: Kilimanjaro, Serengeti, Ngorongoro Crater, Oldupai Gorge, Lake Victoria, Zanzibar, the Indian Ocean, the Great Rift Valley, the Maasai Steppes ...

More remarkable still is that this enviable list of landmarks – with the exception of offshore Zanzibar – is concentrated within a mere 10% of the country's surface area abutting the border with Kenya. And here too, bookended by Lake Victoria in the west and Kilimanjaro in the east, a bloc of contiguous national parks, game reserves and other conservation areas forms what is almost certainly the most expansive safari circuit in Africa, and arguably the finest.

At the heart of this near-pristine ecosystem lies the Serengeti National Park and adjacent Ngorongoro Conservation Area, possibly the most publicised pair of game reserves in the world. And justifiably so: the Serengeti Plains host Africa's greatest wildlife spectacle, the annual migration of perhaps two million wildebeest and zebra, while also supporting remarkably dense populations of predators such as lion, cheetah, leopard and spotted hyena. The floor of the spectacular Ngorongoro Crater is if anything even more densely packed with large mammals, and is the best place in East Africa to see the endangered black rhino.

Less celebrated components of this safari circuit include Lake Manyara and Tarangire national parks, the former protecting a shallow but expansive lake on the Rift Valley floor, the latter a tract of dry acacia woodland notable for its innumerable ancient baobabs and dense elephant population. Then there is the caustic expanse of alkaline water known as Lake Natron, breeding site to millions of flamingos. There is East Africa's most active volcano, the fiery Ol Doinyo Lengai. There is remote Lake Eyasi, its hinterland home to the region's last remaining hunter-gatherers. Dotted amid the savannah, there is jungle-covered Rubondo Island on Lake Victoria, lush montane forest in Arusha National Park, and sodden groundwater forest rising from the shores of lakes Duluti and Manyara. And, when the clouds lift, towering above the twin safari capitals of Arusha and Moshi stand the jagged peaks of Mount Meru and the even taller Kilimanjaro itself.

In short, northern Tanzania is the Africa you have always dreamed about: vast plains teeming with wild animals; rainforests alive with cackling birds and monkeys; Kilimanjaro's snow-capped peak rising dramatically above the flat scrubland; colourful Maasai guiding their cattle alongside fields of grazing wildebeest; perfect palm-lined beaches lapped by the clear warm waters of the Indian Ocean stretching as far as the eye can see – all supported by a tourist infrastructure that has recovered from an immediate post-independence economic free-fall to rank as one of the finest anywhere in Africa.

Northern Tanzania has always boasted an incomparable natural abundance and these days it is serviced by a selection of genuinely world-class game lodges, bush camps and beach resorts. But travel isn't simply about ticking off the sights in comfort. When you spend time in a country, your feelings towards it are determined more than anything by the mood of its inhabitants. I have no hesitation in saying that, on this level, my affection for Tanzania is greater than for any other African country I have visited. Tanzania is an oasis of peace and egalitarianism in a continent stoked up with political and tribal tensions, its social mood embodying all that I respect in African culture. Its people, as a rule, are polite and courteous, yet also warm and sincere, both among themselves and in their dealings with foreigners.

The one thing I can say with near certainty is that you will enjoy Tanzania. Whether you decide to stick to the conventional Serengeti–Ngorongoro–Zanzibar tourist circuit or strike out to the more offbeat likes of lakes Natron and Eyasi; whether you visit the mysterious rock art of Kondoa or track to the breathless peak of Kilimanjaro, you will find Tanzania to be a truly wonderful country.

ATTENTION WILDLIFE ENTHUSIASTS

For more on wildlife in northern Tanzania why not check out Bradt's *East African Wildlife*. Go to www.bradtguides.com and key in NTANZWILD20 at the checkout for your 20% discount.

HOW TO USE THIS GUIDE

AUTHORS' FAVOURITES Finding genuinely characterful accommodation or that unmissable off-the-beaten-track café can be difficult, so the authors have chosen a few of their favourite places throughout the country to point you in the right direction. These 'authors' favourites' are marked with a ✳.

MAPS
Keys and symbols Maps include alphabetical keys covering the locations of those places to stay, eat or drink that are featured in the book. Note that regional maps may not show all hotels and restaurants in the area: other establishments may be located in towns shown on the map.

Grids and grid references Several maps use gridlines to allow easy location of sites. Map grid references are listed in square brackets after the name of the place or sight of interest in the text, with page number followed by grid number, eg: [103 C3].

Part One

GENERAL INFORMATION

Background Information

GEOGRAPHY

The bulk of East Africa is made up of a vast, flat plateau rising from a narrow coastal belt to an average height of about 1,500m. This plateau is broken dramatically by the 20-million-year-old Great Rift Valley, which cuts a trough up to 2,000m deep through the African continent from the Dead Sea to Mozambique. The main branch of the Rift Valley bisects Tanzania. A western branch of the Rift Valley forms the Tanzania–Congo border. Lakes Natron, Manyara, Eyasi and Nyasa/Malawi are all in the main rift, Lake Tanganyika lies in the western branch, and Lake Victoria lies on an elevated plateau between them.

East Africa's highest mountains (with the exception of the Ruwenzori Mountains in Uganda) are volcanic in origin, created by the same forces that caused the emergence of the Rift Valley. Kilimanjaro is the most recent of these: it started to form about one million years ago, and was still growing as recently as 100,000 years ago. Mount Meru is older. Ngorongoro Crater is the collapsed caldera of a volcano that would once have been as high as Kilimanjaro is today. The only active volcano in Tanzania, Ol Doinyo Lengai, rises from the rift floor to the north of Ngorongoro.

SIZE AND LOCATION The United Republic of Tanzania came into being in 1964 when Tanganyika on the African mainland united with the offshore state of Zanzibar, the latter comprising the Indian Ocean islands of Unguja (Zanzibar) and Pemba. It lies on the East African coast between 1° and 11°45'S and 29°20' and 40°35'E, and is bordered by Kenya and Uganda to the north, Rwanda, Burundi and the Democratic Republic of Congo to the west, and Zambia, Malawi and Mozambique to the south. The country extends over 945,166km² (364,929 square miles), making it one of the largest countries in sub-Saharan Africa, covering a greater area than Kenya and Uganda combined. To place this in a European context, Tanzania is more than four times the size of Britain, while in an American context it's about 1.5 times the size of Texas.

CAPITAL Dodoma was earmarked as the future capital of Tanzania in 1973. It has subsequently displaced Dar es Salaam as the official national capital, and is also where all parliamentary sessions are held. Some government departments, however, are still based in Dar es Salaam, which remains the most important and largest city in the country, and is the site of the main international airport, many diplomatic missions to Tanzania, and most large businesses. The main commercial centre and unofficial safari capital of northern Tanzania is the town of Arusha at the southern base of Mount Meru.

CLIMATE

Tanzania on the whole has a pleasant tropical climate, but there are large regional climatic variations across the country, influenced by several factors, most significantly elevation. The hottest and most humid part of the country is the coast, where daytime temperatures typically hit around 30°C on most days, and are often higher. The high level of humidity exaggerates the heat on the coast, and there is little natural relief at night except from sea breezes – for which reason town centres often feel a lot hotter than nearby beaches.

Low-lying areas such as the Rift Valley floor, in particular the Lake Nyasa and Lake Tanganyika areas, are also hot, but far less humid, and thus more comfortable. At elevations of 1,000m or higher, daytime temperatures are warm to hot, and above 2,000m moderate to warm. Most parts of the interior cool down significantly at night, and montane areas such as the rim of the Ngorongoro Crater or Marangu on the foothills of Kilimanjaro can be downright chilly after dark. Alpine conditions and sub-zero night-time temperatures are characteristic of the higher slopes of Mount Meru and especially Kilimanjaro.

Tanzania is too near the Equator to experience the sort of dramatic contrast between summer and winter experienced in much of Europe or North America. The months between October and April are marginally hotter than May to September. In Dar es Salaam, for instance, the hottest month is February (average maximum 32°C; average minimum 23°C), and the coolest month is July (28°C; 18°C). Insignificant as this difference might look on paper, the coast is far more pleasant in the cooler months, while highland towns are far chillier.

Virtually all of Tanzania's rain falls between November and May. The rainy season is generally split into the short rains or *mvuli*, over November and December, and the long rains or *masika* from late February to early May. This pattern of two rainy seasons is strongest in coastal areas and in the extreme north around Arusha, where there is relatively little rainfall in January and February. Even then, there are years when the rain falls more continuously from November to May than is indicated by average rainfall figures. In many other parts of the country, figures suggest that rain falls fairly consistently between mid November and mid April.

For climate charts, see page 72.

HABITATS AND VEGETATION

The bulk of Tanzania is covered in open grassland, savannah (lightly wooded grassland) and woodland. The Serengeti Plains are an archetypal African savannah: grassland interspersed with trees of the acacia family – which are typically quite short, lightly foliated and thorny. Many have a flat-topped appearance. An atypical acacia, the yellow fever, is one of Africa's most striking trees. It is relatively large, has yellow bark and is often associated with water. *Combretum* is a genus of trees typical of many savannah habitats. The dry savannah of central Tanzania can be so barren during the dry season that it resembles semi-desert.

Woodland differs from forest in lacking an interlocking canopy. The most extensive woodland in Tanzania is in the miombo belt, which stretches from southern and western Tanzania to Zimbabwe. Miombo woodland typically grows on infertile soil, and is dominated by broad-leafed brachystegia trees. You may come across the term 'mixed woodland': this refers to woodland with a mix of brachystegia, acacia and other species. Many woodland habitats are characterised by an abundance of baobab trees.

True closed-canopy forest covers less than 1% of Tanzania's surface area, but is the most diverse habitat ecologically, with the forests of the Usambara, for instance, containing more than 2,000 plant species. Most of the forest in Tanzania is montane, associated with the Eastern Arc Mountains and other tall mountains. On the northern safari circuit, the habitat is represented by the montane forests of Kilimanjaro, Meru, Ngorongoro Crater rim and various lesser mountains, as well as the groundwater forests around Lake Duluti and in Lake Manyara. The lowland forests found in the extreme west of the country have strong affinities with the rainforests of Congo.

Other interesting but localised vegetation types are mangrove swamps (common along the coast, particularly around Kilwa) and the heath and moorland found on the higher slopes of Kilimanjaro and Meru.

HISTORY

Tanzania has a rich and fascinating history, but much of the detail is highly elusive. Specialist works often contradict each other to such an extent that it is difficult to tell where fact ends and speculation begins, while broader or more popular accounts are commonly riddled with obvious inaccuracies. This is partly because there are huge gaps in the known facts; partly because much of the available information is scattered in out-of-print or difficult-to-find books; and partly because once an inaccuracy gets into print it tends to spread like a virus through other written works. For whatever reason there is not, as far as I am aware, one concise, comprehensive and reliable book about Tanzanian history in print.

The following account attempts to provide a reasonably comprehensive and readable overview of the country's history. It is, to the best of my knowledge, as accurate as the known facts will allow, but at times I have had to decide for myself the most probable truth among a mass of contradictions, and I have speculated freely where speculation seems to be the order of the day. My goals are to stimulate the visitor's interest in Tanzanian history, and to give easy access to information that would have greatly enhanced my formative travels in Tanzania. Many of the subjects touched on in this general history are given more elaborate treatment elsewhere in the book, under regional history sections or in tinted boxes.

PREHISTORY OF THE INTERIOR The part of the Rift Valley passing through Ethiopia, Kenya and northern Tanzania is almost certainly where modern human beings and their hominine ancestors evolved. The two most common hominine genera on the fossil record are *Australopithecus* and *Homo*, the former extinct for at least a million years, and the latter now represented by only one species – *Homo sapiens* (modern man). The paucity of hominine fossils collected before the 1960s meant that for many years it was assumed that *A. africanus* (the most common Australopithecine in the fossil record) evolved directly into the genus *Homo* and was thus man's oldest identifiable ancestor.

This linear theory of human evolution became blurred when Richard and Mary Leakey, who were excavating Oldupai Gorge in northern Tanzania, discovered that at least two *Australopithecus* species had existed. Carbon dating and the skeletal structure of the two species indicated that the older *A. robustus* had less in common with modern man than its more lightly built ancestor *A. africanus*, implying that the *Australopithecus* line was not ancestral to the *Homo* line at all. This hypothesis was confirmed in 1972 with the discovery of a two-million-year-old skull of a previously undescribed species *Homo habilis* at Lake Turkana in Kenya, providing conclusive evidence that *Australopithecus* and *Homo* species had lived alongside each other for at least one million years. As more fossils have come to light, including older examples of *Homo erectus* (the direct ancestor of modern humans), it has become clear that several different hominine species existed alongside each other in the Rift Valley until perhaps half a million years ago.

In 1974, Donald Johansen discovered an almost complete hominine skeleton in the Danakil region of northern Ethiopia. Named Lucy (the song 'Lucy in the Sky with Diamonds' was playing in camp shortly after the discovery), this turned out to be the fossil of a 3.5-million-year-old Australopithecine of an entirely new species dubbed *A. afarensis*. Lucy's anatomy demonstrated that bipedal hominines (or rather semi-bipedal, since the length of Lucy's arms suggest she would have been as comfortable swinging through the trees as she would have been on a morning jog) had evolved much earlier than previously assumed.

In the 1960s it was widely thought that humans and apes diverged around 20 million years ago. More recent molecular studies indicate that modern man and chimpanzees are far more closely related than previously assumed, and that the two evolutionary lines diverged from a common ancestor between eight and six million years ago. The Afar region of Ethiopia has yielded the world's oldest undisputed hominine *Ardipithecus kadabba* (thought to be around 5.5 million years old). More controversial candidates for the title of the world's oldest known hominine fossil include the seven-million-year-old *Sahelanthropus tchadensis*, discovered in Chad in 2001, and the arboreal *Orrorin tugenensis*, which lived in Kenya about six million years ago and might represent a common ancestor of chimpanzees and hominines.

The immediate ancestor of modern man is *Homo erectus*, which appeared about 1.5 million years ago. *Homo erectus* was the first hominine to surmount the barrier of the Sahara and spread into Europe and Asia, and is credited with the discovery of fire and the first use of stone tools and recognisable speech. Although modern man, *Homo sapiens*, has been around for at least half a million years, only in the last 10,000 years have the African races recognised today more or less taken their modern form. Up until about 1000BC, East Africa was populated exclusively by hunter-gatherers with a physiology, culture and language similar to the modern-day Khoisan (or Bushmen) of southern Africa. Rock art accredited to these hunter-gatherers is found throughout East Africa, most notably in the Kondoa-Irangi region of central Tanzania.

The pastoralist and agricultural lifestyles that were pioneered in the Nile Delta in about 5000BC spread to parts of sub-Saharan Africa by 2000BC, most notably to the Cushitic-speaking people of the Ethiopian Highlands and the Bantu-speakers of West Africa. Cushitic-speakers first drifted into Tanzania in about 1000BC, closely followed by Bantu-speakers. Familiar with Iron Age technology, these migrants would have soon dominated the local hunter-gatherers. By AD1000, most of Tanzania was populated by Bantu-speakers, with Cushitic-speaking pockets in areas such as the Ngorongoro Highlands.

There is no detailed information about the Tanzanian interior prior to 1500, and even after that details are sketchy. Except for the Lake Victoria region, which supported large authoritarian kingdoms similar to those in Uganda, much of the Tanzanian interior is too dry to support large concentrations of people. In most of Tanzania, an informal system of **ntemi** chiefs emerged. The ntemi system, although structured, seems to have been flexible and benevolent. The chiefs were served by a council and performed a role that was as much advisory as it was authoritarian. By the 19th century there are estimated to have been more than 200 ntemi chiefs in western and central Tanzania, each with about 1,000 subjects.

The ntemi system was shattered when southern Tanzania was invaded by **Ngoni** exiles from what is now South Africa, refugees from the rampantly militaristic Zulu Kingdom moulded by Shaka in the early 19th century. The Ngoni entered southern Tanzania in about 1840, bringing with them the revolutionary Zulu military tactics based on horseshoe formations and a short stabbing spear. The new arrivals attacked the resident tribes, destroying communities and leaving survivors no option but to turn to banditry. Their tactics were observed and adopted by the more astute ntemi chiefs, who needed to protect themselves, but had to forge larger kingdoms to do so. The situation was exacerbated by the growing presence of Arab slave traders. Tribes controlling the areas that caravan routes went through were able to extract taxes from the slavers and to find work with them as porters or organising slave raids. This situation was exploited by several chiefs, most notably Mirambo of Unyamwezi and Mkwawa of the Uhehe, charismatic leaders who dominated the interior in the late 19th century.

THE COAST TO 1800 There have been links between the East African coast and the rest of the world for millennia, but only the barest sketch of events before AD1000 is possible. The ancient Egyptians believed their ancestors came from a southerly land called **Punt** and in about 2500BC an explorer called Sahare sailed off in search of this mysterious place. Sahare returned laden with ivory, ebony and myrrh, a booty that suggests he had landed somewhere on the East African coast, most likely in the north of present-day Somalia (but possibly further south). There is no suggestion that Egyptian boats traded regularly with Punt, but they did visit it again on several occasions. Interestingly, an engraving of the Queen of Punt, made after an expedition in 1493BC, shows her to have distinctly Khoisan features. The Phoenicians first explored the coast in about 600BC. According to the 1st-century *Periplus of the Ancient Sea* they traded with a town called Rhapta, which is thought to have lain upriver of a major estuary, possibly the Pangani or the Rufiji Delta.

Bantu-speakers arrived at the coast about 2,000 years ago. It seems likely they had trade links with the **Roman Empire**: Rhapta gets a name check in Ptolemy's 4th-century *Geography*, and a few 4th-century Roman coins have been found at the coast. The fact that the Romans knew of Kilimanjaro, and of the great lakes of the interior, raises some interesting questions. One hypothesis is that the coastal Bantu-speakers were running trade routes into the interior and that these collapsed at the same time as the Roman Empire, presumably as a result of the sudden dearth of trade partners. This notion is attractive and not implausible, but the evidence seems rather flimsy. The Romans could simply have gleaned the information from Bantu-speakers who had arrived at the coast recently enough to have some knowledge of the interior.

Historians have a clearer picture of events on the coast from about AD1000, by which time trade between the coast and the Persian Gulf was well established. The earliest-known Islamic buildings on the coast, which stand on Manda Island off Kenya, have been dated to the 9th century AD. Items sold to Arab ships at this time included ivory, ebony and spices, while a variety of oriental and Arabic goods were imported for the use of wealthy traders. The dominant item of export, however, was **gold**, mined in the Great Zimbabwe region, transported to the coast at Sofala (in modern-day Mozambique) via the Zambezi Valley, then shipped by local traders to Mogadishu, where it was sold to the Arab boats. The common assumption that Swahili language and culture was a direct result of Arab traders mixing with local Bantu-speakers is probably inaccurate. KiSwahili is a Bantu language, and although it did spread along the coast in the 11th century, most of the Arabic words that have entered the language did so at a later date. The driving force behind a common coastal language and culture was almost certainly not the direct trade with Arabs, but rather the internal trade between Sofala and Mogadishu.

More than 30 Swahili city-states sprung up along the East African coast between the 13th and 15th centuries, a large number of which were in modern-day Tanzania. This period is known as the **Shirazi era** after the sultans who ruled these city-states, most of whom claimed descent from the Shiraz region of Persia. Each city-state had its own sultan; they rarely interfered in each other's business. The Islamic faith was widespread during this period, and many Arabic influences crept into coastal architecture. Cities were centred on a great mosque, normally constructed in rock and coral. It has long been assumed that the many Arabs who settled on the coast before and during the Shirazi era controlled the trade locally, but this notion has been questioned in recent years. Contemporary descriptions of the city-states suggest that Africans formed the bulk of the population. It is possible that some African traders claimed Shirazi descent in order to boost their standing both locally and with Shirazi ships.

In the mid 13th century, probably due to improvements in Arab navigation and ship construction, the centre of the gold trade moved southward from Mogadishu to the small island of Kilwa. Kilwa represented the peak of the Shirazi period. It had a population of 10,000 and operated its own mint, the first in sub-equatorial Saharan Africa. The multi-domed mosque on Kilwa was the largest and most splendid anywhere on the coast, while another building, now known as Husuni Kubwa, was a gargantuan palace, complete with audience courts, several ornate balconies and even a swimming pool.

Although Mombasa had possibly superseded Kilwa in importance by the end of the 15th century, coastal trade was still booming. It came to an abrupt halt in 1505, however, when the **Portuguese** captured Mombasa, and several other coastal towns, Kilwa included, were razed. Under Portuguese control the gold trade collapsed and the coastal economy stagnated. It was dealt a further blow in the late 16th century when a mysterious tribe of cannibals called the Zimba swept up the coast to ransack several cities and eat their inhabitants before being defeated by a mixed Portuguese and local army near Malindi in modern-day Kenya.

In 1698, an Arabic naval force under the Sultan of Oman captured Fort Jesus, the Portuguese stronghold in Mombasa, paving the way for the eventual Omani takeover of the coast north of modern-day Mtwara. Rivalries between the new Omani and the old Shirazi dynasties soon surfaced, and in 1728 a group of Shirazi sultans went so far as to conspire with their old oppressors, the Portuguese, to overthrow Fort Jesus. The Omani recaptured the fort a year later. For the next 100 years an uneasy peace gripped the coast, which was nominally under Omani rule, but dominated in economic terms by the Shirazi Sultan of Mombasa.

SLAVERY AND EXPLORATION IN THE 19TH CENTURY The 19th century was a period of rapid change in Tanzania, with stronger links established between the coast and the interior as well as between East Africa and Europe. Over the first half of the 19th century, the most important figure locally was **Sultan Seyyid Said of Oman**, who ruled from 1804 to 1854. Prior to 1804, Britain had signed a treaty with Oman, and relations between the two powers intensified in the wake of the Napoleonic Wars, since the British did not want to see the coast fall into French hands. In 1827, Said's small but efficient navy captured Mombasa and overthrew its Shirazi sultan, to assert unambiguous control over the whole coast, with strong British support.

Having captured Mombasa, Sultan Said chose Zanzibar as his East African base, partly because of its proximity to Bagamoyo (the terminus of a caravan route to Lake Tanganyika since 1823) and partly because it was more secure against attacks from the sea or the interior than any mainland port. Said's commercial involvement with Zanzibar began in 1827 when he set up a number of clove plantations there, with scant regard for the land claims of local inhabitants. Said and his fellow Arabs had come totally to dominate all aspects of commerce on the island by 1840, the year in which the sultan permanently relocated his personal capital from Oman to Zanzibar.

The extent of the East African **slave trade** prior to 1827 is unclear. It certainly existed, but was never as important as the gold or ivory trade. In part, this was because the traditional centre of slave trading had always been West Africa, which was far closer than the Indian Ocean to the main markets of the Americas. In the early 19th century, however, the British curbed the slave trade out of West Africa, leaving the way open for Said and his cronies. By 1839, over 40,000 slaves were being sold from Zanzibar annually. These came from two sources: the central caravan route between Bagamoyo and the Lake Tanganyika region, and a southern route between Kilwa Kivinje and Lake Nyasa.

The effects of the slave trade on the interior were numerous. The **Nyamwezi** of the Tabora region and the **Yua** of Nyasa became very powerful by serving as porters along the caravan routes and organising slave raids and ivory hunts. Weaker tribes were devastated. Villages were ransacked; the able-bodied men and women were taken away while the young and old were left to die. Hundreds of thousands of slaves were sold in the mid 19th century. Nobody knows how many more died of disease or exhaustion between being captured and reaching the coast. Another long-term effect of the slave trade was that it formed the driving force behind the second great expansion of KiSwahili, which became the *lingua franca* along caravan routes.

Europeans knew little about the African interior in 1850. The first Europeans to see Kilimanjaro (Rebmann in 1848) and Mount Kenya (Krapf in 1849) were ridiculed for their reports of snow on the Equator. The Arab traders must have had an intimate knowledge of many parts of the interior that intrigued Europeans, but, oddly, at least in hindsight, nobody seems to have thought to ask them. In 1855, a German missionary, **James Erhardt**, produced a map of Africa, based on third-hand Arab accounts, which showed a large slug-shaped lake in the heart of the continent. Known as the Slug Map, it was wildly inaccurate, yet it did serve to fan interest in a mystery that had tickled geographers since Roman times: the source of the Nile.

The men most responsible for opening up the East African interior to Europeans were **David Livingstone**, **Richard Burton**, **John Speke** and, later, **Henry Stanley**. Livingstone, who came from a poor Scots background, left school at the age of ten, and educated himself to become a doctor and a missionary. He arrived in the Cape in 1841 to work in the Kuruman Mission, but, overcome by the enormity of the task of converting Africa to Christianity, he decided he would be of greater service opening up the continent so that other missionaries could follow. Livingstone was the first European to cross the Kalahari Desert, the first to cross Africa from west to east and the first to see Victoria Falls. In 1858, Livingstone stumbled across Africa's third-largest lake, Nyasa. Later in the same year, on a quest for the source of the Nile funded by the Royal Geographical Society, Burton and Speke were the first Europeans to see Lake Tanganyika, and Speke continued north to Lake Victoria. Speke returned to the northern shore of Lake Victoria in 1863 and concluded – correctly, although it would be many years before the theory gained wide acceptance – that Ripon Falls in modern-day Uganda formed the source of the Nile.

Livingstone had ample opportunity during his wanderings to witness the slave caravans at first hand. Sickened by what he saw – the human bondage, the destruction of entire villages, and the corpses abandoned by the traders – he became an outspoken critic of the trade. He believed the only way to curb it was to open up Africa to the three Cs: Christianity, commerce and civilisation. Though not an imperialist by nature, Livingstone had seen enough of the famine and misery caused by the slavers and the Ngoni in the Nyasa area to believe the only solution was for Britain to colonise eastern Africa.

In 1867, Livingstone set off from Mikindani to spend the last six years of his life wandering between the great lakes, making notes on the slave trade and trying to settle the Nile debate. He believed the source of the Nile to be Lake Bangweulu (in northern Zambia), from which the mighty Lualaba River flowed. In 1872, while recovering from illness at Ujiji, Livingstone was met by Henry Stanley and became the recipient of perhaps the most famous words ever spoken in Africa: 'Dr Livingstone, I presume.' Livingstone died near Lake Bangweulu in 1873. His heart was removed and buried by his porters, who then carried his cured body over 1,500km via Tabora to Bagamoyo, a voyage as remarkable as any undertaken by the European explorers.

Livingstone's quest to end the slave trade met with little success during his lifetime, but his death and highly emotional funeral at Westminster Abbey seem to have acted as a catalyst. Missions were built in his name all over the Nyasa region, while industrialists such as William Mackinnon and the Muir brothers invested in schemes to open Africa to commerce (which Livingstone had always believed was the key to putting the slavers out of business).

In the year Livingstone died, **John Kirk** was made the British Consul in Zanzibar. Kirk had travelled with Livingstone on his 1856–62 trip to Nyasa. Deeply affected by what he saw, he had since spent years on Zanzibar hoping to find a way to end the slave trade. In 1873, the British navy blockaded the island and Kirk offered Sultan Barghash full protection against foreign powers if he banned the slave trade. Barghash agreed. The slave market was closed and an Anglican church built over it. Within ten years of Livingstone's death, the volume of slaves was a fraction of what it had been in the 1860s. Caravans reverted to ivory as their principal trade, while many of the coastal traders started up rubber and sugar plantations, which turned out to be just as lucrative as their former trade. Nevertheless, a clandestine slave trade continued on the mainland for some years – 12,000 slaves were sold at Kilwa in 1875 – and even into the 20th century, only to be fully eradicated in 1918, when Britain took control of Tanganyika.

THE PARTITIONING OF EAST AFRICA The so-called **scramble for Africa** was entered into with mixed motives, erratic enthusiasm and an almost total lack of premeditation by the powers involved. Britain, the major beneficiary of the scramble, already enjoyed a degree of influence on Zanzibar, one that arguably approached informal colonisation, and it was quite happy to maintain this mutually agreeable relationship unaltered. Furthermore, the British government at the time, led by Lord Salisbury, was broadly opposed to the taking of African colonies. The scramble was initiated by two events. The first, the decision of King Leopold of Belgium to colonise the Congo Basin, had little direct bearing on events in Tanzania. The partitioning of East Africa was a direct result of an about-face by the German premier, Bismarck, who had previously shown no enthusiasm for acquiring colonies and probably developed an interest in Africa in the hope of acquiring pawns to use in negotiations with Britain and France.

In 1884, a young German metaphysician called **Carl Peters** arrived inauspiciously on Zanzibar and then made his way to the mainland to sign a series of treaties with local chiefs. The authenticity of these treaties is questionable, but when Bismarck announced claims to a large area between the Pangani and Rufiji rivers, it was enough to set the British government into a mild panic. Britain had plans to expand the Sultanate of Zanzibar, its informal colony, to include the fertile lands around Kilimanjaro. Worse, large parts of the area claimed by Germany were already part of the sultanate. Not only was Britain morally bound to protect these, it also did not want to surrender control of Zanzibar's annual import–export turnover of two million pounds.

Despite pressure put on the British government by John Kirk, angry that his promises to Barghash would not be honoured, there was little option but to negotiate with Germany. A partition was agreed in 1886, identical to the modern border between Kenya and Tanzania. (You may read that Kilimanjaro was part of the British territory before Queen Victoria gave it to her cousin, the Kaiser, as a birthday present. This amusing story, possibly dreamed up by a Victorian satirist to reflect the arbitrariness of the scramble, is complete fabrication.) In April 1888, the Sultan of Zanzibar unwillingly agreed to lease Germany the coastal strip south of the Umba River. Germany mandated this area to Carl Peters's **German East Africa Company (GEAC)**, which placed agencies at most of the coastal settlements north of Dar es Salaam. These agents demanded heavy taxes from traders and were encouraged to behave high-handedly in their dealings with locals.

The GEAC's honeymoon was short. Emil Zalewski, the Pangani agent, ordered the sultan's representative, the Wali, to report to him. When the Wali refused, Zalewski had him arrested and sent away on a German war boat. In September 1888, a sugar plantation owner called **Abushiri Ibn Salim** led an uprising against the GEAC. Except for Dar es Salaam and Bagamoyo, both protected by German war boats, the GEAC agents were either killed or driven away. A horde of 20,000 men gathered on the coast, including 6,000 Shambaa who refused to relinquish their right to claim tax from caravans passing the Usambara. In November, the mission at Dar es Salaam was attacked. Three priests were killed and the rest captured. The coast was in chaos until April 1889 when the Kaiser's troops invaded Abushiri's camp and forced him to surrender. The German government hanged Abushiri in Pangani; they withdrew the GEAC's mandate and banned Peters from ever setting foot in the area.

The 1886 agreement only created the single line of partition north of Kilimanjaro. By 1890, Germany had claimed an area north of Witu, including Lamu, and there was concern in Britain that they might try to claim the rich agricultural land around Lake Victoria, thereby surrounding Britain's territory. Undeterred by the debacle at Pangani (and with a nod and a wink from Bismarck), Carl Peters decided to force the issue. He slipped through Lamu and in May 1890, after a murderous jaunt across British territory, he signed a treaty with the King of Buganda entitling Germany to most of what is now southern Uganda. This time, however, Peters's plans were frustrated. Bismarck had resigned in March of the same year and his replacement, Von Kaprivi, wanted to maintain good relations with Salisbury's government. In any case, Henry Stanley had signed a similar treaty with the Baganda when he passed through the area in 1888 on his way from rescuing the Emin Pasha in Equatoria.

Germany had its eye on Heligoland, a small but strategic North Sea island that had been seized by Britain from Denmark in 1807. To some extent, German interest in Africa had always been related to the bargaining power it would give them in Europe. In 1890, Salisbury and Von Kaprivi knocked out the agreement that created the modern borders of mainland Tanzania (with the exception of modern-day Burundi and Rwanda, German territory until after World War I). In exchange for an island of less than 1km² in extent, Salisbury was guaranteed protectorateship over Zanzibar and handed the German block north of Witu, and Germany relinquished any claims it might have had to what are today Uganda and Malawi.

The word 'tribe' has fallen out of vogue in recent years, and I must confess that for several years I rigorously avoided the use of it in my writing. It has, I feel, rather colonial connotations, something to which I'm perhaps overly sensitive having lived most of my life in South Africa. Some African intellectuals have argued that it is derogatory, too, in so far as it is typically applied in a belittling sense to non-European cultures, where words such as 'nation' might be applied to their European equivalent.

All well and good to dispense with the word tribe, at least until you set about looking for a meaningful substitute. Nation, for instance, seems appropriate when applied in a historical sense to a large and cohesive centralised entity such as the Zulu or Hehe, but rather less so when you're talking about smaller and more loosely affiliated tribes. Furthermore, in any modern sense, Tanzania itself is a nation (and proud of it), just as are Britain and Germany, so that describing, for instance, the modern Chagga as a nation would feel as inaccurate and contrived as referring to, say, the Liverpudlian or Berliner nation.

It would be inaccurate, too, to refer to most African tribes in purely ethnic, cultural or linguistic terms. Any or all of these factors might come into play in shaping a tribal identity, without in any sense defining it. All modern tribes contain individuals with a diverse ethnic stock, simply through intermarriage. Most modern Ngoni, for instance, belong to that tribe through their ancestors having been assimilated into it, not because all or even any of their ancestors were necessarily members of the Ngoni band who migrated up from South Africa in the 19th century. And when the original Bantu-speaking people moved into present-day Tanzania thousands of years ago, local people with an entirely different ethnic background would have been assimilated into the newly established communities. Likewise, the linguistic and cultural differences between two neighbouring tribes are often very slight, and may be no more significant than dialectal or other regional differences within either tribe. The Maasai and Samburu, for instance,

GERMAN EAST AFRICA The period of German rule was not a happy one. In 1891, Carl Peters was appointed governor. Peters had already proved himself an unsavoury and unsympathetic character: he boasted freely of enjoying killing Africans and, under the guise of the GEAC, his lack of diplomacy had already instigated one uprising. Furthermore, the 1890s were plagued by a series of natural disasters: a rinderpest epidemic at the start of the decade, followed by an outbreak of smallpox, and a destructive plague of locusts. A series of droughts brought famine and disease in their wake. Many previously settled areas reverted to bush, causing the spread of tsetse fly and sleeping sickness. The population of Tanganyika is thought to have decreased significantly between 1890 and 1914.

It took Peters a decade to gain full control of the colony. The main area of conflict was in the vast central plateau where, led by **Mkwawa**, the Hehe had become the dominant tribe. In 1891, the Hehe ambushed a German battalion led by Emil Zalewski. They killed or wounded more than half of Zalewski's men, and made off with his armoury. Mkwawa fortified his capital near Iringa, but the Germans razed it in 1894. Mkwawa was forced to resort to guerrilla tactics, which he used with some success until 1898, when he shot himself rather than face capture by the Germans.

Germany was determined to make the colony self-sufficient. Sugar and rubber were well established on parts of the coast, coffee was planted in the Kilimanjaro share a long common history, are of essentially the same ethnic stock, speak the same language, and are culturally almost indistinguishable. Yet they perceive themselves to be distinct tribes, and are perceived as such by outsiders.

A few years ago, in mild desperation, I settled on the suitably nebulous term ethno-linguistic group as a substitute for tribe. Clumsy, ugly and verging on the meaningless it might be, but it does sound impressively authoritative, without pinning itself exclusively on ethnicity, language or culture as a defining element, and it positively oozes political correctness. It's also, well, a little bit silly! Just as Tanzanians are unselfconscious about referring to themselves as black and to *wazungu* as white, so too do they talk about their tribe without batting an eyelid. For goodness sake, at every other local hotel in Tanzania, visitors are required to fill in the 'Tribe' column in the standard-issue guesthouse visitors' book. And if it's good enough for Tanzanians, who am I to get precious about it?

More than that, it strikes me that even in an African nation as united as Tanzania certainly is, the role of tribe in shaping the identity of an individual has no real equivalent in most Western societies. We may love – or indeed loathe – our home town, we might fight to the death for our loved ones, we might shed tears when our football team loses or our favourite pop group disbands, but we have no equivalent to the African notion of tribe. True enough, tribalism is often cited as the scourge of modern Africa, and when taken to fanatical extremes that's a fair assessment, yet to damn it entirely would be rather like damning English football, or its supporters, because of the actions of a fanatical extreme. Tribalism is an integral part of African society, and pussyfooting around it through an overdeveloped sense of political correctness strikes me as more belittling than being open about it.

So, in case you hadn't gathered, Tanzania's 120 ethno-lingual-cultural groupings are tribes for this edition of the guide, a decision that will hold at least for as long as I'm expected to fill in my tribe – whatever that might be – every time I check into a Tanzanian guesthouse.

region, a major base for settlers, and cotton grew well around Lake Victoria. The colony's leading crop export, sisal, was grown throughout the rest of the country. In 1902, Peters decided that the southeast should be given over to cotton plantations. This was an ill-considered move: the soils were not suitable for the crop and the scheme was bound to cause great hardship. It also led to the infamous and ultimately rather tragic **Maji-Maji rebellion**, which proved to be perhaps the most decisive event in the colony during German rule.

Carl Peters was fired from the colonial service in 1906. He believed his African mistress had slept with his manservant, so he flogged her close to death then hanged them both. After that, the German administration introduced a series of laws protecting Africans from mistreatment. To the disgust of the settler community, it also created an incentive-based scheme for African farmers. This made it worth their while to grow cash crops and allowed the colony's exports to triple in the period leading up to World War I.

When war broke out in Europe, East Africa also became involved. In the early stages of the war, German troops entered southern Kenya to cut off the Uganda Railway. Britain responded with an abortive attempt to capture Tanga. The balance of power was roughly even until **Jan Smuts** led the Allied forces into German territory in 1916. By January 1918, the Allies had captured most of German East Africa and the German commander, Von Lettow, retreated into Mozambique. The war disrupted food production, and a serious famine ensued. This was particularly devastating in the Dodoma region. The country was taken over by the League of Nations. The Ruanda-Urundi District, now the states of Rwanda and Burundi, was mandated to Belgium. The rest of the country was renamed Tanganyika and mandated to Britain.

TANGANYIKA The period of British rule between the wars was largely uneventful. Tanganyika was never heavily settled by Europeans so the indigenous populace had more opportunity for self-reliance than it did in many colonies. Nevertheless, settlers were favoured in the agricultural field, as were Asians in commerce. The Land Ordinance Act of 1923 secured some land rights for Africans, otherwise they were repeatedly forced into grand but misconceived agricultural schemes. The most notorious of these, the **Groundnut Scheme** of 1947, was an attempt to convert the southeast of the country into a large-scale mechanised groundnut producer. The scheme failed through a complete lack of understanding of local conditions; it caused a great deal of hardship locally and cost British taxpayers millions of pounds. On a political level, a system of indirect rule based around local government encouraged African leaders to focus on local rivalries rather than national issues between the wars. A low-key national movement called the **Tanganyika Africa Association (TAA)** was formed in 1929, but it was as much a cultural as a political organisation.

Although it was not directly involved in World War II, Tanganyika was profoundly affected by it. The country benefited economically. It saw no combat so food production continued as normal, while international food prices rocketed. Tanganyika's trade revenue increased sixfold between 1939 and 1949. World War II was a major force in the rise of **African nationalism**. Almost 100,000 Tanganyikans fought for the Allies. The exposure to other countries and cultures made it difficult for them to return home as second-class citizens. They had fought for non-racism and democracy in Europe, yet were victims of racist and non-democratic policies in their own country.

The dominant figure in the post-war politics of Tanganyika/Tanzania was **Julius Nyerere** (1922–99). Schooled at a mission near Lake Victoria, he went on to university in Uganda and gained a Master's degree in Edinburgh. After returning to Tanzania in 1952, Nyerere became involved in the TAA. This evolved into the more political and nationalist **Tanganyika African National Union (TANU)** in 1954. Nyerere became the president of TANU at the age of 32. By supporting rural Africans on grassroots issues and advocating self-government as the answer to their grievances, TANU gained a strong national following. By the mid 1950s, Britain and the UN were looking at a way of moving Tanganyika towards greater self-government, although over a far longer time-scale than TANU envisaged. The British governor, Sir Edward Twining, favoured a multi-racial system that would give equal representation to whites, blacks and Asians. TANU agreed to an election along these lines, albeit with major reservations. Twining created his own 'African party', the UTC.

In the 1958 election, there were three seats per constituency, one for each racial group. Electors could vote for all three seats, so in addition to putting forward candidates for the black seats, TANU indicated their preferred candidates in the white and Asian seats. Candidates backed by TANU won 67% of the vote; the UTC did not win a single seat. Twining's successor, Sir Richard Turnball, rewarded TANU by scrapping the multi-racial system in favour of open elections. In the democratic election of 1960, TANU won all but one seat. In May 1961, Tanganyika attained self-government and Nyerere was made prime minister. Tanganyika attained full **independence** on 9 December 1961. Not one life had been taken in the process. Britain granted Zanzibar full independence in December 1963. A month later the Arab government was toppled and in April 1964 the two countries combined to form Tanzania.

TANZANIA At the very core of Tanzania's post-independence achievements and failures lies the figure of Julius Nyerere, who ruled Tanzania until his retirement in 1985. In his own country, where he remains highly respected, Nyerere is called *Mwalimu* – the teacher. In the West, he is a controversial figure, often portrayed as a dangerous socialist who irreparably damaged his country. This image of Nyerere doesn't bear scrutiny. He made mistakes and was intolerant of criticism – at one point Tanzania had more political prisoners than South Africa – but he is also one of the few genuine statesmen to have emerged from Africa, a force for positive change both in his own country and in a wider African context.

In 1962, TANU came into power with little policy other than their attained goal of independence. Tanganyika was the poorest and least economically developed country in East Africa, and one of the poorest in the world. Nyerere's first concerns were to better the lot of rural Africans and to prevent the creation of a money-grabbing elite. The country was made a one-party state, but had an election system that, by African standards, was relatively democratic. Tanzania pursued a policy of non-alignment, but the government's socialist policies and Nyerere's outspoken views alienated most Western leaders. Close bonds were formed with socialist powers, most significantly China, who built the Tanzam Railway (completed in 1975).

Relations with Britain soured in 1965. Nyerere condemned the British government's tacit acceptance of the Unilateral Declaration of Independence (UDI) in Rhodesia. In return, Britain cut off all aid to Tanzania. Nyerere also gave considerable vocal support to disenfranchised Africans in South Africa, Mozambique and Angola. The ANC and Frelimo both operated from Tanzania in the 1960s.

Nyerere's international concerns were not confined to white supremacism. In 1975, Tanzania pulled out of an Organisation of African Unity (OAU) conference in Idi Amin's Uganda saying: 'The refusal to protest against African crimes against Africans is bad enough … but … by meeting in Kampala … the OAU are giving respectability to one of the most murderous regimes in Africa.' Tanzania gave refuge to several Ugandans, including the former president Milton Obote and the current president Yoweri Museveni. Amin occupied part of northwest Tanzania in October 1978, and bombed Bukoba and Musoma. In 1979, Tanzania retaliated by invading Uganda and toppling Amin. Other African leaders condemned Tanzania for this action, despite Amin having been the initial aggressor. Ousting Amin drained Tanzania's financial resources, but it never received any financial compensation, either from the West, or from any other African country.

At the time of independence, most rural Tanzanians lived in scattered communities. This made it difficult for the government to provide such amenities as clinics and schools and to organise a productive agricultural scheme. In 1967, Nyerere embarked on a policy he called **villagisation**. Rural people were encouraged to form *Ujamaa* (familyhood) villages and collective farms. The scheme met with some small-scale success in the mid 1970s, so in 1975 Nyerere decided to forcibly re-settle people who had not yet formed villages. By the end of the year 65% of rural Tanzanians lived in Ujamaa villages. In many areas, however, water supplies were inadequate to support a village. The resultant mess, exacerbated by one of Tanzania's regular droughts, ended further villagisation. Ujamaa is often considered to have been an unmitigated disaster. It did not achieve what it was meant to, but it did help the government improve education and healthcare. Most reliable sources claim it did little long-term damage to agricultural productivity.

By the late 1970s Tanzania's economy was a mess. There were several contributory factors: drought, Ujamaa, rising fuel prices, the border closure with Kenya (to prevent Kenyan operators from dominating the Tanzanian safari industry), lack of foreign aid, bureaucracy and corruption in state-run institutions, and the cost of the Uganda episode. After his re-election in 1980 Nyerere announced he would retire at the end of that five-year term. In 1985, Ali Hassan Mwinyi succeeded Nyerere as prime minister. Nyerere remained chairman of the **Chama Cha Mapinduzi (CCM)**, the party formed when TANU merged with the Zanzibari ASP in 1975, until 1990.

Under President Mwinyi, Tanzania moved away from socialism. In June 1986, in alliance with the IMF, a three-year Economic Recovery Plan was implemented. This included freeing up the exchange rate and encouraging private enterprise. Since then Tanzania has achieved an annual growth rate of around 4% (in real terms). Many locals complain that the only result they have seen is greater inflation. In 1990 attempts were made to rout corruption from the civil service, with surprisingly positive results.

The first multi-party election took place in October 1995. The CCM was returned to power with a majority of around 75% under the leadership of Benjamin Mkapa, who stood down in December 2005 following the country's third multi-party election. This, once again, was won by the CCM, which polled more than 80% of the 11.3 million votes under its new leader, Jakaya Kikwete. The CCM retained power under the 60-year-old Kikwete in the 2010 election, but with a vastly reduced majority, polling only 63% of the vote amongst the 42% of registered voters who turned out for the election. The main beneficiary of this significant electoral shift was the conservative **Chama cha Demokrasia na Maendeleo (CDM, popularly known as Chadema)**, meaning Party for Democracy and Progress, whose leader Dr Willibrord Slaa took 27% of the vote. This trend continued in the 2015 presidential election, which was won by the new CCM candidate John Magufuli, but by a further reduced majority of 58.5% as opposed to the 40% of the vote garnered by the CDM under Edward Lowassa, who had served as prime minister during the first three years of Kikwete's first presidential term.

Widespread corruption is among the main reasons cited for the electoral swing away from the CCM, and this problem has been tackled head on by President Magufuli since he took power in July 2015. The new president's intent to curb wasteful government spending was signalled by the cancellation of expensive Independence Day celebrations, the reduction of costs associated with the state dinner that marks the opening of parliament by 90%, a ban on first-class air travel by ministers, and the reduction of the cabinet from 30 to 19 ministries. Magufuli has also come down strongly on corruption, and allocated a far greater proportion of the budget to heathcare, education and other grassroots spending. Countered against this, Magufuli has quickly acquired a reputation for impulsiveness, one epitomised by the unexpected and immediate implementation of 18% VAT on tourist-related services in July 2016, and he has also displayed a low tolerance for criticism and freedom of speech. It remains to be seen whether the new broom's reformist or repressive tendencies will win out, but either way, it seems likely that the upstart CDM will emerge as a serious contender for the next elections, which are due in 2020.

As Africa experiences its sixth decade of post-colonialism, much of the continent suffers from the same tribal divisions it had at the time of independence. Tanzania is a striking exception to this generalisation, and hindsight demonstrates that Nyerere's greatest achievement was the tremendous sense of **national unity** he created by making KiSwahili the national language, by banning tribal leaders, by forcing government officials to work away from the area in which they grew up, and by his own example. True, Tanzania remains one of the world's least-developed countries, but most sources agree that the economic situation of the average Tanzanian has improved greatly since independence, with unusually high economic growth shown over the past 15 years, as have adult literacy rates and healthcare. Furthermore, Tanzania has thus far navigated the tricky path from British colony to independent state to socialist dictatorship to free-market democracy with remarkably little internal conflict and bloodshed. This long history of adaptability, tolerance and stability should stand the country in good stead as the CCM faces an increasingly meaningful challenge to its half-century of total political dominance.

GOVERNMENT AND POLITICS

The ruling party of Tanzania since independence has been **Chama Cha Mapinduzi (CCM)**. Up until 1995, Tanzania was a one-party state, under the presidency of Julius Nyerere and, after his retirement in 1985, Ali Hassan Mwinyi. Tanzania has

ADMINISTRATIVE REGIONS

Region	Capital	Population (millions)	Area (km²)	Number of districts
Arusha	Arusha	1.7	37,576	7
Dar es Salaam	Dar es Salaam	4.4	1,393	3
Dodoma	Dodoma	2.1	41,311	7
Geita	Geita	1.7	20,054	5
Iringa	Iringa	0.9	35,503	5
Kagera	Bukoba	2.5	25,265	8
Katavi	Mpanda	0.6	45,843	3
Kigoma	Kigoma	2.1	37,040	8
Kilimanjaro	Moshi	1.7	13,309	7
Lindi	Lindi	0.9	66,046	6
Manyara	Babati	1.4	44,522	6
Mara	Musoma	1.7	21,760	7
Mbeya	Mbeya	2.7	60,350	10
Morogoro	Morogoro	2.2	70,799	7
Mtwara	Mtwara	1.3	16,707	7
Mwanza	Mwanza	2.7	9,467	7
Njombe	Njombe	0.7	21,347	6
Pemba North	Wete	0.2	574	2
Pemba South	Chake Chake	0.2	335	2
Pwani	Kibaha	1.1	32,547	7
Rukwa	Sumbawanga	1.0	22,794	4
Ruvuma	Songea	1.4	63,670	6
Shinyanga	Shinyanga	1.5	18,900	5
Singida	Singida	1.4	49,341	6
Tabora	Tabora	2.3	76,151	7
Tanga	Tanga	2.0	26,808	10
Zanzibar North	Mkokotoni	0.2	470	2
Zanzibar South	Mkoani	0.1	854	2
Zanzibar Urban	Zanzibar	0.6	230	2

1

held five multi-party elections since 1995, with the CCM winning them all – the first two under President Benjamin Mkapa, the next two under President Jakaya Kikwete, and the most recent under John Magufuli. The president and unicameral National Assembly of Tanzania are elected concurrently by popular vote, with 264 of the 393 seats in the National Assembly being elected directly, while 113 are allocated to women chosen by their parties (proportionate to each party's share of the electoral vote), another ten are nominated by the president, five are selected by the Zanzibar House of Representatives, and there is also one ex-officio Attorney General. The National Assembly is led by a prime minister, who is appointed by the president along with the cabinet. Twenty-one parties contested the 2010 election, and since then the CCM has held 252 seats on the National Assembly, the **Chama cha Demokrasia na Maendeleo (CDM)** has 70 seats and the Civic United Front has 42. The other two seats are split between two minor parties.

ADMINISTRATIVE REGIONS Tanzania is divided into 29 administrative regions, each with a local administrative capital. These are listed in the box on page 17 with population figures based on the most recent national census, undertaken in 2012.

ECONOMY

Immediately after independence, Tanzania became one of the most dedicated socialist states in Africa, and its economy suffered badly as a result of a sequence of well-intentioned but misconceived or poorly managed economic policies. By

TRADITIONAL MUSICAL INSTRUMENTS

Tanzania's tribal diversity has meant that a vast array of very different – and, for that matter, very similar – traditional musical instruments are employed around the country under a bemusing number of local names. Broadly speaking, however, all but a handful of these variants can be placed in one of five distinct categories that conform to the classes of musical instrument used in Europe and the rest of the world.

The traditional music of many Tanzanian cultures is given its melodic drive by a *marimba* (also called a *mbira*), a type of instrument that is unique to Africa but could be regarded as a more percussive variant of the familiar keyboard instruments. The basic design of all marimbas consists of a number of metal or wooden keys whose sound is amplified by a hollow resonating box. Marimbas vary greatly in size from one region to the next. Popular with several pastoralist tribes of the Rift Valley and environs are small hand-held boxes with six to ten metal keys that are plucked by the musician. In other areas, organ-sized instruments with 50 or more keys are placed on the ground and beaten with sticks, like drums. The Gogo of the Dodoma region are famed for their marimba orchestras consisting of several instruments that beat out a complex interweave of melodies and rhythms.

The most purely melodic of Tanzanian instruments is the *zeze*, the local equivalent to the guitar or fiddle, used throughout the country under a variety of names. The basic zeze design consists of between one and five strings running along a wooden neck that terminates in an open resonating gourd. The musician rubs a bow fiddle-like across the strings, while manipulating their tone with the fingers of his other hand, generally without any other instrumental accompaniment, but the mid 1980s, Tanzania ranked among the five poorest countries in the world. The subsequent swing towards a free-market economy, making the country more attractive to investors, has resulted in dramatic improvement, and Tanzania today – while hardly wealthy – has managed to ascend out of the list of the world's 20 poorest countries. Indeed, with a GDP of US$5 billion in 2015, it now has the eighth-largest economy in Africa, and ranks 83rd in the world. The mainstay of the economy is agriculture, and most rural Tanzanians are subsistence farmers who might also grow a few crops for sale. The country's major exports are traditionally coffee, cotton, cashew nuts, sisal, tobacco, tea and diamonds. Tanzania is also now the third-largest gold producer in Africa (after South Africa and Ghana), and a unique gem called tanzanite is of increasing importance to the export economy. Zanzibar and Pemba are important clove producers. The tourist industry that practically collapsed in the mid 1980s has since grown steadily, and now contributes around 13% of GDP and accounts for 11% of jobs countrywide. Over the past few years, around one million visitors per year have generated up to US$5 billion annually in foreign revenue, a fiftyfold increase since 1990!

PEOPLE

The total population of Tanzania stood at 44.9 million in the most recent census undertaken in 2012, and is now estimated at around 52 million. The most densely populated rural areas tend to be the highlands, especially those around Lake Nyasa and Mount Kilimanjaro, and the coast. The country's largest city is Dar es Salaam,

sometimes as part of an orchestra. Less widespread stringed instruments include the zither-like *enanga* of the Lake Tanganyika region and similar *bango* and *kinubi* of the coast, all of which are plucked like harps rather than stroked with a bow, to produce more defined melodic lines than the zeze.

The most important percussive instrument in African music is the drum, of which numerous local variations are found. Almost identical in structure and role to their European equivalent, most African drums are made by tightly stretching a membrane of animal hide across a section of hollowed tree trunk. A common and widespread type of drum, which is known in most areas as a *msondo* and is often reserved for important rituals, can be up to 1m tall and is held between the drummer's legs.

Percussive backing is also often provided by a variety of instruments known technically as idiophones. Traditionally, these might include the maraca-like *manyanga*, a shaker made by filling a gourd with dry seeds, as well as metal bells and bamboo scrapers. A modern variant on the above is the *chupa*: a glass soda bottle scraped with a piece of tin or a stick.

Finally, in certain areas, horned instruments are also used, often to supply a fanfare at ceremonial occasions. These generally consist of a modified animal horn with a blowing hole cut into its side, through which the musician manipulates the pitch using different mouth movements.

Readers with an interest in traditional music are pointed towards an excellent but difficult-to-locate booklet, *The Traditional Musical Instruments of Tanzania*, written by Lewis and Makala (Music Conservatoire of Tanzania, 1990), and the primary source of this boxed text.

In this book, I've made widespread use of taxonomic terms such as genus, species and race. Some readers may not be familiar with these terms, so a brief explanation follows.

Taxonomy is the branch of biology concerned with classifying living organisms. It uses a hierarchical system to represent the relationships between different animals. At the top of the hierarchy are kingdoms, phyla, sub-phyla and classes. All vertebrates belong to the animal kingdom, phylum Chordata, sub-phylum Vertebrata. There are five vertebrate classes: Mammalia (mammals), Aves (birds), Reptilia (reptiles), Amphibia (amphibians) and Pisces (fish). Within any class, several orders might be divided in turn into families and, depending on the complexity of the order and family, various sub-orders and sub-families. All baboons, for instance, belong to the Primate order, sub-order Catarrhini (monkeys and apes), family Cercopithecoidea (Old World monkeys) and sub-family Cercopithecidae (cheek-pouch monkeys, ie: guenons, baboons and mangabeys).

Taxonomists accord every living organism a Latin binomial (two-part name) indicating its genus (plural genera) and species. Thus the savannah baboon (*Papio cyenephalus*) and hamadrayas baboon (*Papio hamadrayas*) are different species of the genus *Papio*. Some species are further divided into races or sub-species. For instance, taxonomists recognise four races of savannah baboon: yellow baboon, olive baboon, chacma baboon and Guinea baboon. A race is indicated by a trinomial (three-part name), for instance *Papio cyenephalus cyenephalus* for the yellow baboon and *Papio cyenephalus anubis* for the olive baboon. The identical specific and racial designation of *cyenephalus* for the yellow baboon make it the nominate race – a label that has no significance other than that it would most probably have been the first race of that species to be described by taxonomists.

Taxonomic constructs are designed to approximate the real genetic and evolutionary relationships between various living creatures, and on the whole they succeed. But equally the science exists to help humans understand a reality that is likely to be more complex and less absolute than any conceptual structure used to contain it. This is particularly the case with speciation – the evolution of two or more distinct species from a common ancestor – a gradual process that might occur over many thousands of generations and lack for any absolute landmarks.

Simplistically, the process of speciation begins when a single population splits into two mutually exclusive breeding units. This can happen as a result of geographic isolation (for instance mountain and lowland gorillas), habitat differences (forest and savannah elephants) or varied migratory patterns (the six races of yellow wagtail intermingle as non-breeding migrants to Africa during the northern winter, but they all have discrete Palaearctic breeding grounds). Whatever the reason, the two breeding communities will share an identical gene

whose population, estimated at around 4.5 million, exceeds that of the country's next ten largest towns combined. Other large towns with populations exceeding 250,000 are Mwanza, Arusha, Dodoma, Mbeta, Morogoro and Tanga. There are roughly 120 tribes in Tanzania (see box, pages 12–13), each speaking their own language, and none of which exceeds 10% of the country's total population. The most numerically significant tribes are the Sukuma of Lake Victoria, Haya of northwest Tanzania, Chagga of Kilimanjaro, Nyamwezi of Tabora, Makonde of the Mozambican border area, Hehe of Iringa and Gogo of Dodoma.

pool when first they split, but as generations pass they will accumulate a number of small genetic differences and eventually marked racial characteristics. Given long enough, the two populations might even deviate to the point where they wouldn't or couldn't interbreed, even if the barrier that originally divided them was removed.

The taxonomic distinction between a full species and a sub-species or race of that species rests not on how similar the two taxa are in appearance or habit, but on the final point above. Should it be known that two distinct taxa freely interbreed and produce fertile hybrids where their ranges overlap, or it is believed that they would in the event that their ranges did overlap, then they are classified as races of the same species. If not, they are regarded as full species. The six races of yellow wagtail referred to above are all very different in appearance, far more so, for instance, than the several dozen warbler species of the genus *Cisticola*, but clearly they are able to interbreed, and they must thus be regarded as belonging to the same species. And while this may seem a strange distinction on the face of things, it does make sense when you recall that humans rely mostly on visual recognition, whereas many other creatures are more dependent on other senses. Those pesky cisticolas all look much the same to human observers, but each species has a highly distinctive call and in some cases a display flight that would preclude crossbreeding whether or not it is genetically possible.

The gradual nature of speciation creates grey areas that no arbitrary distinction can cover – at any given moment in time there might exist separate breeding populations of a certain species that have not yet evolved distinct racial characters, or distinct races that are on their way to becoming full species. Furthermore, where no conclusive evidence exists, some taxonomists tend to be habitual 'lumpers' and others eager 'splitters' – respectively inclined to designate any controversial taxon racial or full specific status. For this reason, various field guides often differ in their designation of controversial taxa.

Among African mammals, this is particularly the case with primates, where in some cases up to 20 described taxa are sometimes lumped together as one species and sometimes split into several specific clusters of similar races. The savannah baboon is a case in point. The four races are known to interbreed where their ranges overlap but they are also all very distinctive in appearance, and several field guides now classify them as different species. The olive baboon, for instance, is designated *Papio anubis* as opposed to *Papio cyenephalus anubis*. Such ambiguities can be a source of genuine frustration, particularly for birdwatchers obsessed with ticking 'new' species, but they also serve as a valid reminder that the natural world is, and will always be, a more complex, mysterious and dynamic entity than any taxonomic construct designed to label it.

LANGUAGE

More than 100 different languages are spoken across Tanzania, but the official languages are KiSwahili and English. Until recently, very little English was spoken outside of the larger towns, but this is changing rapidly and visitors can be confident that almost anybody involved in the tourist industry will speak passable English. KiSwahili, indigenous to the coast, spread through the region along the 19th-century caravan routes, and is today spoken as a second language by most Tanzanians.

RELIGION

Christianity is the dominant religion of the interior, also accounting for about 35–40% of the total population of Tanzania. Among the more common denominations are Roman Catholic, Lutheran, Anglican and Methodist. Tanzanians of Islamic and Christian persuasion generally live side by side without noticeable rancour, though both are often uncomfortable with the concept of atheism.

Islam has had a long history on the coast and islands of Tanzania as evidenced by the presence of numerous ruined medieval mosques, some of which date back to the 12th century or earlier. It remains the main religion along the coast, and it also has a stronghold in inland towns such as Ujiji and Tabora, which were founded by Arabic traders along the 19th-century caravan routes. It has been estimated that around 35% of Tanzanians follow Islam today, though no exact figures are available. Around 85% of the Islamic population is Sunni.

Traditional **animist** beliefs are followed by most other Tanzanians, in particular the Nilotic-speaking pastoralists of the Rift Valley. The Maasai traditionally worship a dualistic deity, Engai, who resides in the volcanic crater of Ol Doinyo Lengai, while Aseeta, the God of the Datoga, is said to live on Mount Hanang. Many practising Muslims or Christians in Tanzania concurrently adhere to traditional beliefs and will consult local healers and spiritualists in times of ill health or misfortune.

2

Tanzania Wildlife Guide

MAMMALS

More than 300 mammal species have been recorded in Tanzania, a list that includes about 80 so-called large mammals. For most first-time safari-goers, a major goal is to tick off the so-called 'Big Five' – and even if doing so isn't a priority when you first arrive in Tanzania, conversations with lion-obsessed driver-guides and with other travellers are likely to make it one. Ironically, given its ubiquity in modern game-viewing circles, the term 'Big Five' originated with the hunting fraternity and it refers to those animals considered to be the most dangerous (and thus the best sport) back in the colonial era, namely lion, elephant, buffalo, leopard and black rhino. Of these, the first three are likely to be seen with ease on a safari of any significant duration. Leopards are more elusive, with the most reliable site in Tanzania being the Serengeti's Seronera Valley. The only parts of Tanzania where the black rhino remains reasonably visible are the Ngorongoro Crater and Mara River region of the northern Serengeti, but it is also present in a few other reserves.

In the listings that follow, an animal's scientific name is given in parentheses after its English name, followed by the Swahili (Sw) name. The Swahili for animal is *mnyama* (plural *wanyama*); to find out what animal you are seeing, ask '*Mnyama gani?*'

CARNIVORES This order of meat-eating mammals is represented in Tanzania by more than 30 species. These include cats such as the regal lion, along with dogs and jackals, hyenas and various smaller carnivores such as mongooses, otters and genets.

Cats

Stealthy, secretive and inscrutable, the cats of the family Felidae are the most efficient killers among the carnivores, and the most strictly carnivorous. All cats conform to a similar anatomical plan to the familiar domestic tabby, the main physical difference between various species being coat pattern and size.

Lion (*Panthera leo*) Sw: *simba*. Shoulder height: 100–120cm; weight: 150–220kg. Africa's largest predator, the lion is the one animal that everybody hopes to see on safari. It is a sociable creature, living in prides of five to 20 animals (sometimes more) and defending a territory of between 20km² and 200km². Lions hunt at night, and their favoured prey is large or medium antelope such as wildebeest and impala. Most of the hunting is done by females, but dominant males normally feed first after a kill. Rivalry between males is intense, and battles to take over a pride are frequently fought to the death, for which reason two or more males often form a coalition. Young males are forced out of their home pride at three years of age, and male cubs are usually killed after a successful takeover. When not feeding or fighting, lions are remarkably indolent – they spend up to 23 hours of any given day at rest – so the anticipation of a lion sighting is often more exciting than the real thing. Lions naturally occur in any habitat but desert and rainforest, and once ranged across much of the Old World, but these days they are all but restricted to the larger conservation areas in sub-Saharan Africa (one remnant population exists in India). Essentially terrestrial, they seldom take to trees in most of their range, but this unusual behaviour is observed quite regularly in Lake Manyara and parts of the Serengeti National Park. Recent surveys indicate that Tanzania might host around 50% of the world's surviving free-ranging lions, and the Serengeti and the Ngorongoro Crater are arguably the best places in Africa to see these charismatic beasts.

Leopard (*Panthera pardus*) Sw: *chui*. Shoulder height: 70cm; weight: 60–80kg. The powerful leopard is the most solitary and secretive of Africa's large cat species. It hunts using stealth and power, often getting to within 5m of its intended prey before pouncing, and it habitually stores its kill in a tree to keep it from hyenas and lions. The leopard can be distinguished from the superficially similar cheetah by its rosette-like spots, lack of black 'tear marks' and more compact, powerful build. Leopards occur in all habitats, favouring areas with plenty of cover such as riverine woodland and rocky slopes. There are many records of individuals living in close proximity to humans for years without being detected. The leopard is the most common of Africa's large felines, found throughout Tanzania, yet a good sighting must be considered a stroke of fortune. One relatively reliable spot for leopard sightings is the Seronera Valley in the Serengeti. An endemic race of leopard did occur on Zanzibar, although recent research suggests that it is probably extinct on the island, and that the handful of local reports of leopard sightings were probably the result of confusion with the African civet and introduced Java civet.

Cheetah (*Acinonyx jubatus*) Sw: *duma*. Shoulder height: 70–80cm; weight: 50–60kg. This remarkable spotted cat has a greyhound-like build, and is capable of running at 70km/h in bursts, making it the world's fastest land animal. It is often seen pacing the plains restlessly, either on its own or in a small family group comprising a mother and her offspring. A diurnal hunter, favouring the cooler hours of the day, the cheetah's habits have been adversely affected in areas where there are high tourist concentrations and off-road driving is permitted. Males are territorial, and generally solitary, though in the Serengeti they commonly defend their territory in pairs or trios. Despite superficial similarities, you can easily tell a cheetah from a leopard by its simple spots, disproportionately small head, streamlined build, diagnostic black 'tear marks', and preference for relatively open habitats. Widespread, but thinly distributed and increasingly rare outside of conservation areas, the cheetah is most likely to be seen in savannah and arid habitats such as the Serengeti Plains (where sightings are regular on the road to Seronera) and the floor of the Ngorongoro Crater.

Serval (*Leptailurus serval*) Sw: *mondo*. Shoulder height: 55cm; weight 12–15kg. Smaller than but with a similar built to a cheetah, the largely nocturnal serval has black-on-gold spots giving way to streaking near the head. It is widespread and quite common in moist grassland, reed beds and riverine habitats, but tends to be very secretive. The Serengeti is probably the best place in Africa for serval sightings.

Caracal (*Felis caracal*) Sw: *simbamangu*. Shoulder height: 50cm; weight: 15–20kg. The caracal resembles the lynx with its short tail and tufted ears. It is a solitary hunter, feeding on birds, small antelope and livestock, and ranges throughout the country favouring relatively arid savannah habitats. It is nocturnal and seldom seen.

African wild cat (*Felis sylvestris*) Sw: *chapaku*. Shoulder height: 35cm; weight: 2.5–4.5kg. Ranging from the Mediterranean to the Cape of Good Hope, the African wild cat is similar in appearance to – and probably ancestral to – its domestic namesake. Like the caracal, it is common, but nocturnal, and infrequently seen. Though not threatened as such, the African wild cat regularly breeds with feral domestic cats and there are concerns its genetic pool is becoming increasingly diluted where the two regularly interact.

Leopard

Cheetah

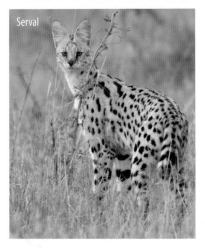
Serval

Caracal

African wild cat

Dogs Five species of canid present in Tanzania: the endangered African wild dog; the insectivorous bat-eared fox; and three species of jackal.

African wild dog (*Lycaon pictus*) Sw: *mbwa mwitu*. Shoulder height: 70cm; weight: 25kg. Also known as the African hunting dog or painted dog, the wild dog is distinguished from other African canids by its large size and cryptic black, brown and cream coat. Highly sociable, living in packs of up to 20 animals, the wild dog is a ferocious hunter that literally tears apart its prey on the run. Threatened with extinction as a result of its susceptibility to diseases spread by domestic dogs, it has become extinct or very rare in several areas where it was formerly abundant, for instance in the Serengeti and most other reserves in northern Tanzania. The global

population of around 6,000 wild dogs – an increase of 50% since the turn of the millennium – is spread across much of eastern and southern Africa, but the Selous Game Reserve is the most important stronghold (estimated population 1,300) and Ruaha National Park also hosts a viable population. The one place in northern Tanzania where wild dogs have been reintroduced is Mkomazi National Park, where a recently reintroduced population is thriving, though seldom seen by visitors. Wild dogs have been reported denning in Loliondo annually since 2008, and scattered sightings in Tarangire, Lake Manyara and the northern Serengeti suggest that this endangered creature is gradually recolonising the northern safari circuit.

Bat-eared fox (*Otocyon megalotis*) Sw: *bweha masikio*. Shoulder height: 30–35cm; weight: 35kg. This small, silver-grey insectivore, unmistakable with its huge ears and black eye-mask, is most often seen in pairs or small family groups during the cooler hours of the day. Associated with dry open country, the bat-eared fox is quite common in the Serengeti and likely to be encountered at least once in the course of a few days' safari, particularly during the denning season (November and December).

Black-backed jackal (*Canis mesomelas*) Sw: *mbweha*. Shoulder height: 35–45cm; weight: 8–12kg. The black-backed (or silver-backed) jackal is an opportunistic feeder capable of adapting to most habitats. Most often seen singly or in pairs at dusk or dawn, it is ochre in colour with a prominent black saddle flecked by a varying amount of white or gold. It is one of the most frequently observed small predators in Africa south of the Zambezi, and its eerie call is a characteristic sound of the bush at night. It is the commonest jackal in most Tanzanian reserves.

Side-striped jackal (*Canis adustus*) Sw: *mbweha*. Shoulder height: 35–50cm; weight: 8–12kg. More cryptic in colour than the otherwise very similar black-backed jackal, this species has an indistinct pale vertical stripe on each flank and a white-tipped tail. Nowhere very common, it is distributed throughout Tanzania, often favouring miombo woodland, but most likely to be seen in the southern reserves.

Common jackal (*Canis aureus*) Sw: *mbweha*. Shoulder height: 40–50cm; weight: 8–14kg. Also known as the Eurasian or golden jackal, this is a predominantly Eurasian and North African species whose range extends as far south as the Serengeti and Ngorongoro. It is cryptically coloured but relatively pale with a black tail tip, and is the most commonly seen jackal inside Ngorongoro Crater, thanks to its relatively diurnal habits. A genetic study published in 2015 suggests that the African population of common jackal is actually a separate species from its Eurasian counterpart, and is more closely related to wolves than to other jackals.

Hyenas Hyenas are characterised by their bulky build, sloping back, brownish coat, powerful jaws and dog-like expression. Despite looking superficially canine, they are more closely related to mongooses and bears than to cats or dogs. Contrary to popular myth, hyenas are not exclusively scavengers: the spotted hyena in particular is an adept hunter capable of killing an animal as large as a wildebeest. Nor are they hermaphroditic, an ancient belief that stems from the false scrotum and penis covering the female hyena's vagina.

Spotted hyena (*Crocuta crocuta*) Sw: *fisi*. Shoulder height: 85cm; weight: 70kg. Sociable and fascinating to observe, the spotted hyena lives in loosely structured clans of about ten animals, led by females who are stronger and larger than males. It is the largest hyena, distinguished by its blotchily spotted coat, and it is probably the most common large predator in eastern and southern Africa. It is most frequently seen at dusk and dawn in the vicinity of game reserve lodges, campsites and refuse dumps, and is likely to be encountered on a daily basis in the Serengeti, Ngorongoro Crater and many other reserves.

Striped hyena (*Hyaena hyaena*) Sw: *fisi miraba*. Shoulder height: 65–75cm; weight: 45–50kg. A predominantly North African species, the striped hyena is pale brown with several dark vertical streaks and a striking off-black mane. It occurs alongside the spotted hyena in dry parts of Tanzania, but is far scarcer and more secretive.

Aardwolf (*Proteles cristatus*) Sw: *fisi ndogo*. Shoulder height: 40–50cm; weight: 10–15kg. This very secretive insectivore looks like a smaller striped hyena, being not much bigger than a jackal. It occurs in low numbers in drier parts of Tanzania.

Spotted hyena

Striped hyena

Aardwolf

© J L Klein & M L Hubert/FLPA

31

African civet

Civets, mongooses and mustelids

African civet (*Civettictis civetta*) Sw: *fungo*. Shoulder height: 40cm; weight: 10–15kg. This stocky, long-haired, rather feline creature of the African night is primarily carnivorous, feeding on small animals and carrion as well as fruit. It has a similarly coloured coat to a leopard or cheetah, and this is densely blotched with large black spots becoming stripes towards the head. Civets are widespread and common in many habitats, but very rarely seen. The smaller and slenderer **tree civet** (*Nandinia binotata*) is a very seldom-seen arboreal forest animal whose dark-brown coat is marked with black spots.

Mongooses Sw: *nguchiro*. Several mongoose species occur in Tanzania, though some are too scarce and nocturnal to be seen by casual visitors. The largest, with a shoulder height of up to 40cm, is the **white-tailed mongoose** (*Ichneumia albicauda*) a widespread solitary nocturnal predator easily identified by its bushy white tail. More common is the diurnal and highly sociable **banded mongoose** (*Mungos mungo*; shoulder height: 20cm), which is dark brown except for a dozen black stripes across its back, and occurs in family groups in most wooded habitats and savannah. The **dwarf mongoose** (*Helogale parvula*) is a diminutive (shoulder height: 7cm) and highly sociable light-brown mongoose often seen in the vicinity of termite mounds, particularly in Tarangire National Park. The more solitary **marsh mongoose** (*Atilax*

Dwarf mongoose

paludinosus) is large (shoulder height: 22cm), has a scruffy-looking brown coat, and is widespread in the eastern side of Africa where it is often seen in the vicinity of water. The **slender mongoose** (*Galerella sanguinea*) is as widespread and also solitary, but it is very much smaller (shoulder height: 10cm) and has a uniform brown coat and black tail tip.

Genet (*Genetta spp*) Sw: *kanu.* Shoulder height: 20–40cm; weight: 1.5–3kg. Often but erroneously referred to as cats, the members of this taxonomically controversial genus are all very similar in appearance: low-slung, slender, with a grey to golden-brown coat marked with black spots, and an exceptionally long ringed tail. Most likely to be seen on nocturnal game drives or scavenging around game reserve lodges, the **large-spotted genet** (*G. tigrina*) is golden brown with very large spots and a black-

tipped tail, whereas the **small-spotted genet** (*G. genetta*) is greyer with rather small spots and a pale tip to the tail.

Honey badger and other mustelids Sw: *nyegere.* Shoulder height: 30cm; weight: 12kg. Also known as the ratel, the **honey badger** (*Mellivora capensis*) is a black mustelid (member of the weasel family) with a puppyish face and grey-to-white back. It is an opportunistic feeder best known for its symbiotic relationship with a bird called the greater honeyguide, which leads it to a beehive, waits for it to tear the nest open, then feeds on the scraps. It is among the most widespread of African carnivores, but it is thinly distributed and rarely seen. Several other mustelids (mammals of the weasel family) occur in the region, including the **striped polecat** (*Ictonyx striatus*), a common but rarely seen nocturnal creature with black underparts and bushy white back, and the similar but much scarcer **striped weasel** (*Poecilogale albinucha*). The **Cape clawless otter** (*Aonyx capensis*) is a brown freshwater mustelid with a white collar, while the smaller **spotted-necked otter** (*Lutra maculicollis*) is darker with white spots on its throat.

Honey badger

PRIMATES The forests of Africa support somewhere between 60 and 100 primate species (taxonomic ambiguities make it impossible to be more exact), but diversity is far lower in the savannah habitats associated with most safari destinations. Despite this, western Tanzania is one of the best places in the world to track chimpanzee, while baboon and vervet monkey are common in most safari reserves, and the montane forests of the coast support several endemic monkey species.

Chimpanzee (*Pan troglodytes*) Sw: *sokwe-mtu*. Standing height: 100cm; weight: up to 55kg. This distinctive black-coated ape, along with the bonobo (*Pan paniscus*) of the southern Congo, is more closely related to humans than to any other living creature. The chimpanzee lives in large troops based around a core of related males dominated by an alpha male. Females aren't firmly bonded to their core group, so emigration between communities is normal. Primarily frugivores (fruit-eaters), chimpanzees eat meat on occasion, and though most kills are opportunistic, stalking of prey is not unusual. The first recorded instance of a chimp using a tool was at Gombe Stream in Tanzania, where modified sticks were used to 'fish' in termite mounds. In West Africa, chimps have been observed cracking open nuts with a stone and anvil. In the USA, captive chimps have successfully been taught sign language and have created compound words such as 'rock-berry' to describe a nut. A widespread rainforest resident, the chimpanzee is thought to number 200,000 in the wild. In Tanzania, chimps are indigenous to the forested shore of Lake Tanganyika, where they can be tracked on foot in Mahale Mountains and Gombe Stream national parks (the latter the site of the original research centre founded by primatologist Jane Goodall in the 1960s). In northern Tanzania, an introduced (but to all intents and purposes wild) population can be visited on Rubondo Island in Lake Victoria.

Olive baboon

Baboon (*Papio* spp) Sw: *nyani*. Shoulder height: 50–75cm; weight: 25–45kg. This powerful terrestrial primate, distinguished from any other monkey by its much larger size, inverted U-shaped tail and distinctive dog-like head, is fascinating to watch from a behavioural perspective. It lives in large troops that boast a complex, rigid social structure characterised by matriarchal lineages and plenty of inter-troop movement by males seeking social dominance. Omnivorous and at home in almost any habitat, the baboon is the most widespread primate in Africa, frequently seen in most Tanzanian game reserves. There are several species of baboon in Africa, regarded by some authorities to be full races of the same species. Two species are present in Tanzania: the **olive** or **anubis baboon** (*P. anubis*), which is the darker and hairier green-brown baboon found in the west, and the **yellow baboon** (*P. cynocephalus*), a more lightly built and paler yellow-brown race whose range lies to the east of the Rift Valley.

Vervet monkey (*Cercopithecus aethiops*) Sw: *tumbili*. Length (excluding tail): 40–55cm; weight: 4–6kg. Also known as the green or grivet monkey, the vervet is probably the world's most numerous monkey and certainly the most common and widespread representative of the *Cercopithecus* guenons, a taxonomically controversial genus associated with African forests. An atypical guenon in that it inhabits savannah and woodland rather than true forest, the vervet spends a high proportion of its time on the ground and in most of its range could be confused only with the much larger and heavier baboon. However, the vervet's light-grey coat, black face and white forehead band should be diagnostic – as should the male's garish blue genitals. The vervet is abundant in Tanzania, and might be seen just about anywhere, not only in reserves.

Red-tailed monkey

Patas monkey (*Erythrocebus patas*) Sw: unknown. Length (excluding tail): 75–85cm; weight: 7–12kg. This localised terrestrial monkey is larger and spindlier than the vervet, with an orange-tinged coat and black forehead stripe. Essentially a monkey of the dry northwestern savannah, the patas occurs in low numbers in the Mbalageti River region of the western Serengeti. It is very fast on the ground, attaining speeds of up to 55km/hour.

Blue monkey (*Cercopithecus mitis*) Sw: *kima*. Length (excluding tail): 50–60cm; weight: 5–8kg. This most variable of African monkeys is also known as the samango and Sykes' monkey, or the diademed or white-throated guenon. Several dozen races are recognised, divided by some authorities into more than one species. Taxonomic confusion notwithstanding, *C. mitis* is the most common forest guenon in eastern Africa, with one or another race occurring in just about any suitable habitat. Unlikely to be confused with another species in Tanzania, the blue monkey has a uniformly dark blue-grey coat broken by a white throat, which in some races extends all down the chest and in others around the collar. It lives in troops of up to ten animals and associates with other primates where their ranges overlap. It is common in Arusha and Lake Manyara national parks and in many forest reserves.

Red-tailed monkey (*Cercopithecus ascanius*) Sw: unknown. Length (excluding tail): 35–45cm; weight: 3–5kg. This small brown guenon has white whiskers, a red tail, and a distinctive white heart-shaped mark on its nose. In Tanzania, it is primarily restricted to western forests in the vicinity of lakes Tanganyika and Victoria.

Blue monkey

Patas monkey

© Thomas Struhsaker

Sanje mangabey (*Cercocebus sanjei*) Sw: unknown. Length (excluding tail): 50–65cm; weight: 7–9kg. Essentially a west African monkey, this shaggy forest-dwelling relative of the baboons is represented by two extremely isolated populations in East Africa: one in Tanzania's Udzungwa Mountains and another along Kenya's Tana River. Both are classified as full species by most authorities.

Kipunji monkey (*Rungwecebus kipunji*) Sw: unknown. Length (excluding tail): 85–90cm; weight: 10–16kg. Discovered as recently as 2003, this large and critically endangered Tanzanian endemic is confined to the forests of the Udzungwa and Mount Rungwe.

© Tim Davenport/WCS

Black-and-white colobus   Angola colobus   Red colobus

Black-and-white colobus (*Colobus guereza*) Sw: *mbega mweupe*. Length (excluding tail): 60–70cm; weight: 10–16kg. This beautiful jet-black monkey has bold white facial markings and beard, a long white tail and in some races white sides and shoulders. Almost exclusively arboreal, it is capable of jumping up to 30m, a spectacular sight with fluffy white tail streaming behind. Several races have been described, and most authorities recognise more than one species. The black-and-white colobus is a common resident of forests in Tanzania, often seen in the forest zone of Kilimanjaro, in Arusha National Park, and along the Grumeti River as it flows through the Western Corridor of the Serengeti.

Angola colobus (*Colobus angolensis*) Sw: *mbega mweupe*. Length (excluding tail): 60–70cm; weight: 10–16kg. Although it is very similar in appearance to the black-and-white colobus, the Angola colobus differs in having a more streamlined and darker tail and no white on the beard. Both species are subdivided into a number of races, and the assignment of some is controversial, but three Tanzanian populations, those of the Eastern Arc Mountains (including the Usambara), southern highlands, and Lake Tanganyika forests, are now generally regarded to be Angola colobus.

Red colobus (*Procolobus badius*) Sw: *kima punju*. Length (excluding tail): 60cm; weight: 10kg. The status of this variable monkey is again controversial, with between one and ten species recognised by different authorities. Most populations have black on the upper back, red on the lower back, a pale tufted crown and a long-limbed appearance unlike that of any guenon or mangabey. Four populations are known in East Africa, of which two live in isolated pockets in Tanzania, and are regarded by some authorities to be full species. The first of these is **Kirk's red colobus** (*P. kirkii*), which is endemic to Zanzibar Island, where it is readily observed in the Jozani Forest in the east. The endemic **Uhehe red colobus** (*P. gordonorum*) is a fairly common and conspicuous resident of the Udzungwa Mountains in southern Tanzania.

Galagos (bushbabies) (*Galago* and *Otolemur* spp) Sw: *komba*. Length (excluding tail): up to 45cm; weight: up to 500g. This taxonomically controversial family (see box, page 215), distantly related to the lemurs of Madagascar, is widespread in Tanzania, where around a dozen species in two genera are recognised. Most commonly seen, and easily identified due to their size, are the three species of **greater galago** (*Otolemur* spp). They occur all along the eastern side of Africa and produce a terrifying scream so loud you'd think it was emitted by a chimpanzee or gorilla. The **lesser bushbabies** of the genus *Galago* are more widespread and common but less readily seen, though they can sometimes be picked out by tracing the cry to a tree and shining a torch or spotlight in its general direction to look for its large eyes.

ANTELOPE AND OTHER BOVIDS The most characteristic mammals of the African savannah are antelope, with more than two dozen species present in Tanzania alone, ranging in size from the ox-like eland to the diminutive duikers. Taxonomists place antelope in the order Bovidae, along with cattle, buffalos and goats, as well as the deer, from which they most obviously differ in having permanent horns rather than seasonal antlers.

Large antelope
Roan antelope (*Hippotragus equinus*) Sw: *korongo*. Shoulder height: 120–150cm; weight: 250–300kg. This handsome horse-like antelope is uniform fawn-grey with a pale belly, short decurved horns and a light mane. It could be mistaken for the female sable antelope, but this has a well-defined white belly, much larger horns and is more brown in facial markings. The roan is widespread but thinly distributed in

southern Tanzania, though rare in the north, with one small population known to occur (yet seldom seen) in the Serengeti.

Sable antelope (*Hippotragus niger*) Sw: *pala hala*. Shoulder height: 135cm; weight: 230kg. The male sable is jet black with a white-striped face, underbelly and rump, and long decurved horns. Females are chestnut brown with shorter horns. One of the main strongholds for Africa's sable population is the miombo woodland of southern Tanzania. It also occurs further north in Saadani National Park, but is virtually absent from northern Tanzania's safari circuit.

Oryx (*Oryx gazella*) Sw: *choroa*. Shoulder height: 120cm; weight: 230kg. This regal, dry-country antelope is unmistakable with its ash-grey coat, bold black facial marks and flank strip, and unique long, straight horns. The **fringe-eared oryx** (*Oryx beisa callotis*) is the only race found in Tanzania, where it is most common (though still scarce) in Mkomazi and Tarangire national parks, and the Lake Natron region.

Waterbuck (*Kobus ellipsiprymnus*) Sw: *kuro*. Shoulder height: 130cm; weight: 250–270kg. The waterbuck is easily recognised by its shaggy brown coat and the male's large lyre-shaped horns. The Defassa race of the Rift Valley and areas further west has a full white rump, while the eastern race has a white 'U' on its rump. The waterbuck is frequently seen in small family groups grazing near water in all but the most arid of game reserves in Tanzania.

Blue wildebeest (*Connochaetes taurinus*) Sw: *nyumbu*. Shoulder height: 130–150cm; weight: 180–250kg. This rather ungainly antelope, also called the brindled gnu, is easily recognised by its dark coat and bovine appearance. The superficially similar buffalo is far more heavily built. Immense herds of blue wildebeest occur on the Serengeti Plains, where the annual migration of more than a million heading into Kenya's Maasai Mara forms one of Africa's great natural spectacles. There are also significant wildebeest populations in the Ngorongoro Crater and Tarangire.

Blue wildebeest

Coke's hartebeest (*Alcelaphus buselaphus cokii*) Sw: *kongoni*. Shoulder height: 125cm; weight: 120–150kg. Hartebeests are ungainly antelopes, readily identified by the combination of high shoulders, a sloping back, red-brown or yellow-brown coat and smallish curved horns in both sexes. Numerous races are recognised, all of which are generally seen in small family groups in reasonably open country. The race found in Tanzania is Coke's hartebeest, which is common in open parts of the Serengeti and Ngorongoro.

Topi (*Damaliscus lunatus*) Sw: *topi*. Shoulder height: 125cm; weight: 120–150kg. Basically a darker version of the hartebeest but with with striking yellow lower legs and straighter horns, this widespread but thinly and patchily distributed antelope, also known as the tsessebe, occurs alongside the much paler Coke's hartebeest in Serengeti National Park, where it is common.

Common eland (*Taurotragus oryx*) Sw: *pofu*. Shoulder height: 150–175cm; weight: 450–900kg. Africa's largest antelope, the common eland is light brown

Coke's hartebeest

Topi

Common eland

in colour, sometimes with a few faint white vertical stripes. It has a somewhat bovine appearance, accentuated by the relatively short horns, square frame and large dewlap. It is widely distributed in East and southern Africa, and small herds may be seen almost anywhere in grassland or light woodland. The eland is fairly common in Serengeti and Mkomazi national parks, but difficult to approach closely.

Greater kudu (*Tragelaphus strepsiceros*) Sw: *tandala*. Shoulder height: 140–155cm; weight: 180–250kg. In many parts of Africa, the greater kudu is the most readily observed member of the genus *tragelaphus*, a group of medium to large antelopes characterised by the male's large spiralling horns and a dark coat generally marked with several vertical white stripes. It is very large, with a grey-brown coat and up to ten stripes on each side, and the male has magnificent double-spiralled horns. A widespread animal occurring in most wooded habitats except for true forest, the greater kudu has been rare in most of Tanzania and Kenya since it was all but wiped out by a rinderpest epidemic in the late 19th century. However, small numbers do persist in Tarangire and Ruaha national parks.

Lesser kudu (*Tragelaphus imberbis*) Sw: *tandala ndogo*. Shoulder height: 95–105cm, weight 60–100kg. The thinly distributed and skittish East African species largely restricted to arid woodland. In Tanzania, it often occurs alongside the greater kudu, from which it can be distinguished by its smaller size, two white throat patches and greater number of stripes (at least 11). Nowhere common, it is most likely to be encountered in Tarangire, Ruaha and Mkomazi national parks.

Greater kudu

Lesser kudu

Sitatunga

Sitatunga (*Tragelaphus spekei*) Sw: *nzohe*. Shoulder height: 75–125cm, weight 50–120kg. This semi-aquatic antelope, notable for its specially adapted splayed hooves, is a widespread but infrequently observed inhabitant of African swamps from the Okavango in Botswana to the Sudd in South Sudan. Tanzania's Rubondo Island is one of the few places where it is readily observed. It is among the most sexually dimorphic of African antelopes. The tall and hefty male, with its large horns and shaggy fawn coat, is all but unmistakable in its habitat. The smaller female might be mistaken for a bushbuck (see below) but is much drabber.

Medium and small antelope

Bushbuck (*Tragelaphus scriptus*) Sw: *pongo*. Shoulder height: 70–80cm; weight: 30–45kg. This attractive antelope, a member of the same genus as the kudu and sitatunga, shows great regional variation in colouring. The male is dark brown, chestnut or, in parts of Ethiopia, black, while the much smaller female is generally pale red-brown. The male has relatively small, straight horns for a *Tragelaphus* antelope. Both sexes have similar throat patches to the lesser kudu, and are marked with white spots and sometimes stripes. One of the most widespread antelope species in Africa, the bushbuck occurs in forest and riverine woodland throughout Tanzania, where it is normally seen singly or in pairs. It tends to be secretive and skittish except where it is used to people, so it is not as easily seen as you might expect of a common antelope.

Thomson's gazelle (*Gazella thomsonii*) Sw: *swala tomi*. Shoulder height: 60cm; weight: 20–25kg. Gazelles are graceful, relatively small antelopes that generally occur in large herds in open country, and have fawn-brown upper parts and a white belly. Thomson's gazelle is characteristic of the East African plains, where it is the only gazelle to have a black horizontal flank stripe. It is common to abundant in the Serengeti and surrounds.

Grant's gazelle (*Gazella granti*) Sw: *swala granti*. Shoulder height: 75–95cm; weight: 35–75kg. Occurring alongside Thomson's gazelle in many parts of East Africa, the larger Grant's gazelle has a brown rather than black side stripe and comparatively large horns. It is common in the Serengeti but might be seen as far south as Ruaha National Park, which represents the most southerly part of its range.

Bushbuck

Thomson's gazelle

Grant's gazelle

Gerenuk (*Litocranius walleri*) Sw: *swala twiga*. Shoulder height: 90–105cm; weight: 35–50kg. This uncharacteristic gazelle is an arid-country species of Ethiopia, Kenya and northern Tanzania, similar in general colour to an impala but readily identified by its very long neck (the Swahili name translates as 'giraffe gazelle') and singular habit of feeding from trees standing on its hind legs. Nowhere common in Tanzania, the gerenuk is present in small numbers in Mkomazi, Tarangire, West Kilimanjaro and the Loliondo area.

Impala (*Aepyceros melampus*) Sw: *swala pala*. Shoulder height: 90cm; weight: 45kg. This slender, handsome antelope is superficially similar to some gazelles, but in fact belongs to a separate family. Chestnut in colour, the impala has diagnostic black and white stripes running down its rump and tail, and the male has large lyre-shaped horns. One of the most widespread antelope species in sub-equatorial Africa, the impala is normally seen in large herds in wooded savannah habitats, and it is one of the most common antelope in many Tanzanian reserves. Mixed impala herds typically comprise an alpha male and a vast harem of females and their offspring. Also common, unsurprisingly, are all-male bachelor herds.

Reedbuck (*Redunca* spp) Sw: *tohe*. Shoulder height: 65–90cm; weight: 30–65kg. The three species of reedbuck are all rather nondescript fawn-grey antelopes generally seen in open grassland near water. The **mountain reedbuck** (*R. fulvorufula*) is the smallest and most distinct, with a clear white belly, tiny horns and an overall grey appearance. It has a broken distribution, occurring in mountainous parts of eastern South Africa, northern Tanzania, Kenya and southern Ethiopia. The **Bohor reedbuck** (*R. redunca*) is found in northern Tanzania, whereas the **southern reedbuck** (*R. arundinum*) occurs in southern Tanzania.

Klipspringer (*Oreotragus oreotragus*) Sw: *mbuze mawe*. Shoulder height: 60cm; weight: 13kg. The klipspringer is an agile antelope that's normally seen in pairs and is easily identified by its dark, bristly grey-yellow coat, slightly speckled appearance and unique habitat preference. Klipspringer means 'rock jumper' in Afrikaans, while the Swahili name means 'rock goat', both apt names for an antelope that occurs exclusively in mountainous areas and rocky outcrops. It is found throughout Tanzania, and is often seen around the Lobo Hills in the Serengeti and the Maji Moto area in Lake Manyara.

Steenbok (*Raphicerus campestris*) Sw: *tondoro*. Shoulder height: 50cm; weight: 11kg. This rather nondescript small antelope has red-brown upper parts and clear white underparts, and the male has short straight horns. It is probably the most commonly observed small antelope in Africa, though it has a broken range, and is absent from southern Tanzania despite being common in the north of the country and in southern Africa. Like most other antelopes of its size, the steenbok is normally encountered singly or in pairs and tends to 'freeze' when disturbed.

Oribi (*Ourebia ourebi*) Sw: *taya*. Shoulder height: 50–65cm; weight: 12–20kg. This widespread but uncommon grassland antelope looks much like a steenbok but stands about 10cm higher at the shoulder and has an altogether more upright bearing. It might be seen in almost any grassy habitat, usually in groups of two or three, but isn't very common anywhere in Tanzania.

Kirk's dik-dik (*Madoqua kirkii*) Sw: *digidigi*. Shoulder height: 35–45cm; weight: 6–8kg. Smaller than the steenbok and easily identified by its large white eye-circle, this adorably dainty antelope has a range focused primarily on Tanzania and Kenya. Usually seen in pairs in dry woodland, it is particularly common in Arusha and Ruaha National Parks.

Common duiker (*Sylvicapra grimmia*) Sw: *nysa*. Shoulder height: 50cm; weight: 20kg. This anomalous duiker holds itself more like a steenbok and is the only member of its family to occur outside of forests. Grey or grey-brown in colour, it is most easily separated from other small antelopes by the black tuft of hair that sticks up between its horns. It occurs throughout Tanzania, and tolerates most habitats except for true forest and very open country.

Forest duikers (*Cephalophus spp*) Sw: *nsya*. Duikers are small to diminutive antelope with slightly hunched backs and a preference for forest undergrowth, where they are less often seen than they are heard crashing through the undergrowth. The **red duiker** (*C. natalensis*) is the most likely of Africa's 12–20 'forest duikers' to be seen by tourists. It is deep chestnut in colour with a white tail and, in the

Red duiker

case of the East African race *C. n. harveyi* (sometimes considered to be a separate species), a black face. The **blue duiker** (*C. monticola*) is easily told apart from the red duiker by its greyer colouring and much smaller size. The all-but-endemic **Abbott's duiker** (*C. spadix*) is a relatively large duiker, as tall as a klipspringer, and is restricted to a handful of montane forests in Tanzania, including those on Kilimanjaro and the Usambara, Udzungwa and Poroto mountains. The endangered **Ader's duiker** (*C. adersi*) is thought to be restricted to forested habitats on Zanzibar Island, where as few as 1,000 animals may survive, most of them in the Jozani Forest.

African buffalo (*Syncerus caffer*) Sw: *nyati*. Shoulder height: 140cm; weight: 700kg. Frequently and erroneously referred to as a water buffalo (an Asian species), the African buffalo is a distinctive ox-like animal that lives in large herds on the savannah and occurs in smaller herds in forested areas. Common and widespread in sub-Saharan Africa, herds of buffalo are likely to be encountered in most Tanzanian reserves and national parks. The best places to see large buffalo herds in Tanzania are the Ngorongoro Crater floor and Katavi National Park.

African elephant

OTHER LARGE UNGULATES

African elephant (*Loxodonta africana*) Sw: *tembo*. Shoulder height: 2.3–3.4m; weight: up to 6,000kg. The world's largest land animal, the African elephant is intelligent, social and often very entertaining to watch. Female elephants live in close-knit clans in which the eldest female plays matriarch over her sisters, daughters and granddaughters. Mother–daughter bonds are strong and may last for up to 50 years. Males generally leave the family group at around 12 years to roam singly or form bachelor herds. Under normal circumstances, elephants will range widely in search of food and water, but when concentrated populations are forced to live in conservation areas, the damage they cause to trees can have a serious environmental impact. Elephants are widespread and common in habitats ranging from desert to rainforest and, despite heavy poaching, they are likely to be seen on a daily basis in most of Tanzania's larger national parks.

Black rhinoceros (*Diceros bicornis*) Sw: *kifaru*. Shoulder height: 160cm; weight: 1,000kg. This is the more widespread of Africa's two rhino species, an imposing, sometimes rather aggressive creature that has been poached to extinction in most of its former range and now has a global population of around 4,000. Contrary to its name, it has smooth grey skin, and is no darker in colour than the extra-limital white rhino (whose name is a derivative of the Dutch *weit* (wide), a reference to the square lips that enable it to crop grass so efficiently). Also known as the hook-lipped rhino, the black rhino occurs in many southern African reserves, but is now very localised in Tanzania, where it is most likely to be seen in the Ngorongoro Crater.

Hippopotamus (*Hippopotamus amphibius*) Sw: *kiboko*. Shoulder height: 150cm; weight: 2,000kg. Characteristic of Africa's sizeable rivers and lakes, this large, lumbering animal spends most of the day submerged, but emerges at night to graze. Strongly territorial, herds of ten or more animals are presided over by a dominant male who will readily defend his patriarchy to the death. Hippos are abundant in most protected rivers and water bodies, and they are still quite common outside of reserves, where they kill more people than any other African mammal.

Giraffe (*Giraffa camelopardalis*) Sw: *twiga*. Shoulder height: 250–350cm; weight: 1,000–1,400kg. The world's tallest and longest-necked land animal, a fully grown giraffe can measure up to 5.5m high. Quite unmistakable, the giraffe lives in loosely structured herds of up to 15, though herd members often disperse and are seen singly or in smaller groups. Formerly distributed throughout East and southern Africa, the giraffe is now more or less restricted to conservation areas, where it is generally common and easily seen.

Common zebra (*Equus burchelli*) Sw: *punda milia*. Shoulder height: 130cm; weight: 300–340kg. This attractive striped horse is common and widespread throughout most of East and southern Africa, where it is often seen in large herds alongside wildebeest. The common zebra is the only wild equine to occur in Tanzania, and is abundant in most conservation areas, especially the Serengeti where the population may be as high as half a million.

Warthog (*Phacochoerus africanus*) Sw: *ngiri*. Shoulder height: 60–70cm; weight: up to 100kg. This widespread and often conspicuously abundant resident of the African savannah is grey in colour with a thin covering of hairs, wart-like bumps on its face, and rather large upward-curving tusks. Africa's only diurnal swine, the warthog is often seen in family groups, trotting off briskly with its tail raised stiffly (a diagnostic trait) and a determinedly nonchalant air. Two other swine species are present but seldom seen in Tanzania. The bulkier, hairier and browner **bushpig** (*Potamochoerus larvatus*) is as widespread as the warthog, but it's infrequently seen due to its nocturnal habits and preference for dense vegetation. Larger still, weighing up to 250kg, the **giant forest hog** (*Hylochoerus meinertzhageni*) is a primarily West African rainforest species known from a few highland forests in northern Tanzania, but the chance of a sighting is practically non-existent.

SMALL MAMMALS

Aardvark (*Orycteropus afer*) Sw: *muhanga*. Shoulder height: 60cm; weight: up to 70kg. This singularly bizarre nocturnal insectivore is unmistakable with its long snout and huge ears. It occurs practically throughout the region, but sightings are extremely rare, even on night drives.

Ground pangolin (*Smutsia temminckii*) Sw: *Kakakuona*. Length: up to 35cm; weight 1.5–3kg. Also known as Temminck's pangolin, this widespread but very secretive nocturnal insectivore is known for its distinctive armour plating and tendency to roll up into an artichoke-like ball when disturbed. Individuals might be seen almost anywhere in Tanzania, but sightings are a once-in-a-lifetime event!

Cape porcupine (*Hystrix africaeaustralis*) Sw: *nungu*. Length: up to 80cm (excluding tail); weight up to 30kg. These common but infrequently seen nocturnal rodents are covered in long black-and-white quills that protect them from predators. They occasionally betray their presence by rattling as they walk.

Rock hyrax (*Procavia capensis*) Sw: *pimbi*. Shoulder height: 20–30cm; weight: 4kg. Rodent-like in appearance, hyraxes are more closely related to elephants. The rock hyrax and similar **bush hyrax** (*Heterohyrax brucei*) are often seen sunning in rocky habitats and become tame when used to people, for instance at Seronera and Lobo lodges in the Serengeti. The less common **tree hyrax** (*Dendrohyrax arboreus*) is a nocturnal forest creature, often announcing its presence with an unforgettable shrieking call.

Elephant shrew Sw: *sange*. These rodent-like nocturnal creatures look like miniature kangaroos with elongated noses. A number of species are recognised, but they are mostly secretive and nocturnal, so rarely seen. The smaller species are generally associated with savannah habitats, but the much larger sengis or 'giant' elephant shrews are resident in the Eastern Arc and other coastal forests.

© J L Klein & M L Hubert/FLPA

© Jurgen & Christine Sohns/FLPA

Scrub hare (*Lepus saxatilis*) Sw: *sungura*. Weight: 2.7–4.5kg. This is the largest and most common African hare or rabbit. In some areas a short walk at dusk or drive after nightfall might reveal three or four scrub hares. They tend to freeze when disturbed.

Unstriped ground squirrel (*Xerus rutilus*) Weight: 1.4kg. An endearing terrestrial animal of arid savannah, the unstriped ground squirrel is grey to grey-brown with a prominent white eye-ring and silvery black tail. It spends much time on its hind legs, and has the characteristic squirrel mannerism of holding food in its forepaws. In Tanzania, it is most likely to be seen in the Serengeti.

Bush squirrel (*Paraxerus cepapi*) Sw: *kidiri*. Weight: 1kg. This is the typical squirrel of the eastern and southern savannah, rusty-brown in colour with a silvery-black back and white eye-rings. A great many other arboreal or semi-arboreal squirrels occur in the region, but most are found in denser forest and difficult to tell apart in the field.

NILE CROCODILE (*Crocodylus niloticus*) Size/weight: up to 6m and 1,000kg (in extreme cases). The order *Crocodilia* dates back at least 150 million years, and fossil forms that lived contemporaneously with dinosaurs are remarkably unchanged from their modern counterparts, of which the Nile crocodile regularly grows to lengths of up to 6m. Widespread throughout Africa, the Nile crocodile was once common in most large rivers and lakes, but it has been exterminated in many areas in the past century – hunted professionally for its skin as well as by vengeful local villagers. Contrary to popular legend, Nile crocodiles generally feed mostly on fish, at least where densities are sufficient. They will also prey on drinking or swimming mammals where the opportunity presents itself, dragging their victim under water until it drowns. They also frequently eat carrion, such as a hippo that has died of natural causes in the water. A large crocodile is capable of killing a lion or wildebeest, or an adult human for that matter, and in certain areas such as the Mara or Grumeti rivers in the Serengeti, large mammals do form their main prey. Today, large crocodiles are mostly confined to protected areas within Tanzania.

Rock python

Puff adder

SNAKES A wide variety of snakes are found in Tanzania, though they are typically very shy and unlikely to be seen unless actively sought. One of the most likely to be seen on safari is Africa's largest, the **rock python** (*Python sebae*), which has gold-on-black mottled skin and sometimes grows to lengths exceeding 5m. Non-venomous, pythons kill their prey by strangulation, wrapping their muscular bodies around it until it cannot breathe, then swallowing it whole and dozing off for a couple of months while it is digested. Pythons feed mainly on small antelopes, large rodents and similar animals. They are harmless to adult humans, but could conceivably kill a small child.

One of the most commonly encountered venomous snakes is the **puff adder** (*Bitis arietans*), a large, thickset resident of savannah and rocky habitats. Although it feeds mainly on rodents, it will strike when threatened, and it is rightly considered the most dangerous of African snakes, not because it is especially venomous or aggressive but because its notoriously sluggish disposition means it is more often disturbed than other snakes. The related **Gabon viper** (*Bitis gabonica*) is possibly the largest African viper, growing up to 2m long, very heavily built, and with a beautiful cryptic, geometric gold, black and brown skin pattern that blends perfectly into the rainforest litter it inhabits. Although highly venomous, it is more placid and less likely to be encountered than the puff adder.

Several cobra species (*Naja* spp), including some of the **spitting cobras**, are present in Tanzania, most with characteristic hoods that they raise when they're about to strike, though they are all very seldom seen. Another widespread family is the mambas, of which the **black mamba** (*Dendroaspis polylepis*) – which will only attack when cornered, despite an unfounded reputation for unprovoked aggression – is the largest venomous snake in Africa, measuring up to 3.5m long. Theoretically, the most toxic of Africa's snakes is said to be the **boomslang** (*Dispholidus typus*). This variably coloured and largely arboreal snake is back-fanged and very non-aggressive, so while it has been known to inflict a fatal bite on snake handlers, it is not really a threat in the wild.

Most snakes are in fact non-venomous and not even potentially harmful to any other living creature much bigger than a rat. One of the non-venomous snakes in the region is the **green tree snake** (*Dendrelaphis punctulata*) (sometimes mistaken for a boomslang, although the latter is never as green and more often brown), which feeds mostly on amphibians. The **mole snake** (*Pseudaspis cana*) is a common and widespread grey-brown savannah resident that grows up to 2m long, and feeds on moles and other rodents. The remarkable **egg-eating snake** (*Dasypeltis* spp) lives

Speckled green snake

exclusively on bird eggs, dislocating its jaws to swallow the egg whole, before eventually regurgitating the crushed shell in a neat little package. Many snakes will take eggs opportunistically, for which reason large-scale agitation among birds in a tree is often a good indication that a snake (or small bird of prey) is around.

Flat-headed rock agama

Nile monitor

LIZARDS All African lizards are harmless to humans, with the arguable exception of the **giant monitor lizards**, which could in theory inflict a nasty bite if cornered. Two species of monitor occur in East Africa, the water (*Varanus niloticus*) and the savannah (*Varanus exanthematicus*), the former growing up to 2.2m long and occasionally seen in the vicinity of termite mounds, the former slightly smaller but far more regularly observed by tourists, particularly around Lake Victoria. Their size alone might make it possible to fleetingly mistake a monitor for a small crocodile, but their more colourful yellow-dappled skin and smaller head precludes sustained confusion. Both species are predatory, feeding on anything from bird eggs to smaller reptiles and mammals, but will also eat carrion opportunistically.

Visitors to Tanzania will soon become familiar with the **common house gecko** (*Hemidactylus frenatus*), an endearing, bug-eyed, translucent white lizard, which reliably inhabits most houses as well as lodge rooms, scampering up walls and upside down on the ceiling in pursuit of pesky insects attracted to the lights. Also very common in some lodge grounds are various **agama** species, distinguished from other common lizards by their relatively large size of around 20–25cm, basking habits, and almost plastic-looking scaling – depending on the species, a combination of blue, purple, orange or red, with the flattened head generally a different colour from the torso. Another common family are the **skinks**: small, long-tailed lizards, most of which are quite dark and have a few thin black stripes running from head to tail. Tanzania is also home to around 20% of the world's chameleon species (see box, pages 204–5), a list that includes several very localised endemics, most associated with the Eastern Arc Mountains or other isolated forest habitats.

TORTOISES AND TERRAPINS These peculiar reptiles are unique in being protected by a prototypal suit of armour formed by their heavy exoskeleton. The most common of the terrestrial tortoises in the region is the **leopard tortoise** (*Stigmochelys pardalis*), named after its gold-and-black mottled shell, which can weigh up to 30kg, and has been known to live for more than 50 years in captivity. It is often seen motoring along in the slow lane of game reserve roads in northern Tanzania. Four species of terrapin – essentially the freshwater equivalent of turtles – are resident in East Africa, all somewhat flatter in shape than the tortoises, and generally with a plainer brown shell. They might be seen sunning on rocks close to water or peering out from roadside puddles. The largest is the **Nile soft-shelled terrapin** (*Trionyx triunguis*), which has a wide, flat shell and in rare instances might reach a length of almost 1m. In addition, five species of marine turtle have been recorded off Tanzania.

Leopard tortoise

Tanzania is one of the world's most bird-rich destinations. Indeed, the national checklist, which stood at below 1,000 species in 1980, now stands at more than 1,100 species, meaning that Tanzania now vies with Kenya as the African country with the second-most varied avifauna (after the Democratic Republic of Congo). Casual visitors will be stunned at the abundance and visibility of birds in the national parks: brilliantly coloured lilac-breasted rollers and superb starlings, numerous birds of prey, the giant ostrich – the list goes on. For more dedicated birdwatchers, Tanzania now stands second to South Africa among mainland African countries for its wealth of national endemics (species unique to the country). At present, up to 34 endemic species are recognised, including a couple of controversial splits, three species discovered and described in the 1990s, and four that still await formal description. Six of the national endemics are readily observed on the northern safari circuit, but a greater number are restricted to the Eastern Arc Mountains, together with about 20 eastern forest and woodland species whose core range lies within Tanzania. The forests of the Eastern Arc Mountains must therefore rank as the country's most important bird habitat, with the Amani Nature Reserve and Udzungwa Mountains National Park being among the most accessible sites for seeing some of the Eastern Arc specials. But virtually anywhere in Tanzania will offer rewarding birding: in many areas a reasonably competent novice to East African birds could hope to see up to 100 species in a day.

A full checklist of Tanzania's birds is downloadable at www.tanzaniabirding.com. Another superb resource is Tanzanian Birds & Butterflies (*www.tanzaniabirds.net*), which includes photographs of 982 species recorded in Tanzania, as well as detailed distribution maps based on data collected by the Tanzania Bird Atlas Project. A list of endemics and near endemics is included in *Appendix 3* (pages 396–8). Elsewhere, species of local interest are noted under the relevant site throughout the main body of this guide.

1 Endemic to northern Tanzania, the robust **rufous-tailed weaver** (*Histurgops ruficauda*) is an unusual weaver placed in its own genus. Associated with acacia woodland in the Serengeti, Ngorongoro Crater and surrounds, it is typically seen bobbing around noisily in small babbler-like parties. **2** A favourite with first-time safari goers, the aptly named **superb starling** (*Lamprotornis superbus*) is one of around 20 starling species recorded in Tanzania. It has a distinctive semi-upright stance, terrestrial habits and a strong pointed bill, and is often seen in at picnic sites and camps in the Serengeti. **3 Fischer's lovebird** (*Agapornis fischeri*) is a sociable and noisy small parrot with a parakeet-like bill whose upper mandible almost completely hides the lower one. Near-endemic to northern Tanzania, it nests in tree cavities and is most common in the Serengeti.

BUSH AND FOREST BIRDS The wooded habitats of Tanzania support a particularly varied and colourful avifauna. Broadly, they break up into two main habitat types. The more localised of these is closed canopy forest, which accounts for just 1% of Tanzania's surface area, but due to its patchiness tends to be an important centre of biodiversity – indeed, more than 20 of the bird species endemic to Tanzania are forest specialists. A far more widespread habitat, and one that forms the core of most safari routes, is open-canopied woodland and savannah, which tends to be dominated by acacia trees in the north and by Brachystegia woodland in the south, and is typically home to a wide variety of colourful weavers, waxbills, cuckoos, hornbills, bee-eaters, barbets, woodpeckers and rollers.

European visitors to Tanzania during the months of October to March may be surprised to encounter many familiar species that overwinter in East Africa. Probably the most conspicuous of these is the barn swallow, but a great many other species of warbler, shrike and wheatear are also present during these months, as are numerous migrant waders and birds of prey. Ironically, many of Europe's most glamorous and sought-after birds – among them the stunning Eurasian roller and Eurasian bee-eater – are more likely to be seen overwintering in East Africa than in most parts of Europe.

1 The exquisite **little bee-eater** (*Merops pusillusi*) is probably the most widespread member of a family of colourful birds that hawk bees and other insects from a conspicuous perch. **2 Von der Decken's hornbill** (*Tockus deckeni*) is a member of a family of characterful medium-to-large forest and woodland species named for their curved, heavy bills – in this case red and yellow in the male and black in the female. **3 Hartlaub's turaco** (*Tauraco hartlaubi*) is a sensationally colourful forest dweller most likely to be seen in Arusha National Park or on the Ngorongoro Crater rim. **4** Another firm safari favourite, the lovely **lilac-breasted roller** (*Coracias caudate*) might be seen perching conspicuously in any wooded savannah habitat. **5** The strikingly coloured **red-and-yellow barbet** (*Tricholaema erythrocephalus*), often seen in Tarangire National Park, performs a trilling clockwork-like duet on termite mounds. **6** Of all the region's many kingfisher species, the gemlike **malachite kingfisher** (*Alcedo cristata*), often observed perched motionless on waterside reeds and shrubs, most strongly resembles its European namesake. **7** The **African golden weaver** (*Ploceus subaureusi*) lacks the black mask typical of many males in the genus (see box, pages 316–17). **8** The **eastern double-collared sunbird** (*Cinnyris mediocris*) is a typically brightly coloured member of a bird family whose long curved beaks are used to draw nectar from flowers.

BIRDS OF PREY The raptorial Falconiformes, with their strong hooked bills, sharp talons, powerful wings and keen eyesight, are perhaps the most charismatic of avian orders – the feathered equivalent of the lions and other mammalian carnivores that stride across African savannah. Large, intelligent, dashing and boldly marked, these birds of prey have exerted a fascination over humankind since prehistoric times, and even today their appeal extends beyond hardcore birdwatchers to casual safari-goers. So it's pleasing to report that the Accipitridae – incorporating eagles, kites, hawks and Old World vultures – is the East Africa's most numerically diverse bird family, with 63 species recorded. In addition, there are 19 species of Falconidae, and a solitary representative of the monotypic family Sagittariidae. All of this makes Tanzania a mouth-watering destination for raptor enthusiasts, though occasionally frustrating when it comes to the identification of confusingly marked species.

1 Conspicuous along the shores of most rivers and lakes, the **African fish eagle** (*Hakliaeetus vocifer*) is a magnificent black-and-white raptor with a rich chestnut belly and yellow base to its large hooked bill. Its far-carrying banshee wail of a call, usually delivered as a duet with both birds throwing back their heads dramatically, is one of the most evocative sounds of the African bush. **2** Another unmistakable and widespread large eagle, the **bateleur** (*Terathopius ecaudatus*) is named for its unique tilting flight pattern, which is reminiscent of a tightrope walker wobbling along a suspended line, and is predominantly black, but offset by a striking bright red face mask, beak and legs. **3** Africa's largest raptor, the **lappet-faced vulture** (*Torgus tracheliotus*) is a massive bird, typically seen singly or in pairs on a carcass alongside some or all of the region's other five carrion-eating vulture species. Its habit of spreading open its heavy black wings like a cape reinforces its ghoulish presence. **4** One of the region's most conspicuous and handsome raptors, the medium–large **Auger buzzard** (*Buteo auger*) might have a black or white breast, but its short orange-red tail precludes confusion with any raptor other than the bateleur. **5** A nocturnal hunter, **Verreaux's eagle-owl** (*Bubo lacteus*), the largest of around 15 owl species resident in Tanzania, is often seen resting up in large trees by day, when black eyes distinguish it from other comparably sized species. **6** The largest and commonest of the region's all-brown raptors, the **tawny eagle** (*Aquila rapax*) has a 2m wingspan and a uniform plumage whose tone varies from dirty blond to buff to dark brown. **7** Associated with moist open savannah, the **dark (western) chanting goshawk** (*Melierax metabates*) has a distinctive upright perching stance and combination of grey back and finely barred underpart, pale rump and red legs. It is replaced by the similar but lighter pale (eastern) chanting goshawk (*M. poliopterus*) in drier habitats. **8** The **greater kestrel** (*Falco rupicolodes*), like other falcons and kestrel of the genus *Falco*, is a slim and cryptically marked small raptor often seen flying swiftly and directly in open country.

GROUND BIRDS The open grassland plains of the Serengeti are particularly rewarding for ground birds, a loosely defined term that embraces any species that spends most of its time foraging on the ground. These open-county specialists include the ostrich, the world's largest bird, whose immense bulk – up to 145kg – renders it incapable of flight. Many other large ground birds associated with the Serengeti and similar habitats are reluctant or clumsy flyers, a list headed by the Kori bustard, which weighs in at up to 19kg, making it the world's heaviest creature capable of taking flight. Smaller ground birds such as larks and pipits tend to be quite drab, as camouflage against predators in their open terrain.

1 Often seen scooting off towards the horizon on the open plains of the Serengeti, the **common ostrich** (*Struthio camelus*) might be the world's largest living bird, standing up to 2m tall, but in evolutionary terms it is a relatively petite relict of a once diverse order of hefty flightless birds known as ratites. Ostriches display strong sexual dimorphism, with the male being larger and very handsome with its striking black-and-white plumage, while the female is smaller, duller and scruffier. Ostrich eggs are the world's smallest in relation to the size of the adult bird, but still clock in at a whopping 1.5kg. **2** The **secretary bird** (*Sagittarius serpentarius*) is a bizarre and unmistakeable 1.5m-tall raptor with long skinny legs, a slender grey torso and long black wings and tail. It's often said that its name alludes to its flaccid black crest, which vaguely recalls the quills used by Victorian secretaries, but more likely that it's a corruption of the Arabic *saqr-et-tair* (hunting bird). Single birds and pairs stride purposefully though open grassland or savannah in search of their favoured prey of snakes, which are stamped to death in a flailing dance-like ritual. **3** The world's heaviest flying bird, the **kori bustard** (*Ardeotis kori*) is a widespread resident of grassland habitats and especially common in the Serengeti. **4** Typically seen marching through the savannah in small thuggish parties, the **southern ground hornbill** (*Bucorvus leadbeateri*) is a hefty and rather improbable turkey look-alike with a large casqued bill, conspicuous throat and eye wattles, and long fluttering eyelashes. A terrestrial hunter, it nests and roosts in trees. **5** The ubiquitous **helmeted guinea fowl** (*Numida meleagris*), named for its ivory crown, belongs to an endemic African family of large, gregarious fowls, all of which are spotted white-on-grey, and have bare blue heads. **6** With a range all but restricted to the Serengeti, the **grey-breasted spurfowl** (*Pternistis rufopictus*) is an endemic member of a widespread group of medium-to-small ground-dwelling fowls known as francolins and often seen calling conspicuously from a perch at dusk. **7** The most common and least water-dependent of Tanzania's storks is the **marabou** (*Leptoptilos crumeniferus*), a large and ungainly omnivore that can be distinguished by its scabrous bald head and inflatable flesh-coloured neck pouch, and is often attracted to carrion and rubbish dumps in both urban and natural environments. **8** The **yellow-throated longclaw** (*Macronyx croceus*) is the most common member of a group of colourful but inconspicuous long-tailed ground-dwellers affiliated to pipits and wagtails.

WATER BIRDS Tanzania's aquatic habitats embrace hundreds of kilometres of Indian Ocean frontage as well as vast freshwater marshes, tiny soda-crusted crater lakes, forest-fringed perennial rivers and a trio of expansive 'inland seas' in the form of lakes Victoria, Tanganyika and Nyasa-Malawi. These varied wetlands provide rich pickings for more than 100 species of non-passerine waterbirds, ranging from such widespread and familiar families as gulls, ducks and waders to engaging oddities such as pelicans, flamingos and spoonbills. Throughout Tanzania, waterbirds tend to be quite easy to observe and to identify, since most forage openly on the margins or in the shallows.

1 A unique bird with uncertain taxonomic affinities, the **hamerkop** (*Scopus umbretta*) is distinguished by the long flattened bill and angular crest that create the hammer-like appearance alluded to in its Afrikaans name (literally 'hammer head'). Its distinctive nest is a massive untidy construction built over several months using branches, sticks, mud, litter, natural debris and pretty much anything else it can lay its beak on. Abandoned hamerkop nests often acquire a veritable menagerie of squatters, including snakes, monitor lizards, owls and small mammals. **2** The tall and strikingly marked **grey crowned-crane** (*Balearica regulorum*) might be seen in moist wetlands throughout Tanzania. Listen out for its booing nasal call in the Ngorongoro Crater, where it is particularly common after the rains. **3** Herons and egrets are the most visible of East Africa's waterbird families, and the chestnut and purple-grey **goliath heron** (*Ardea goliath*) is the world's largest species, typically standing 1.5m tall. **4** The larger and more common of Tanzania's two pelican species, the larder-billed **great white pelican** (*Pelecanus onocrotalus*), weighing in at 15kg, is the region's bulkiest waterbird, often seen bobbing in flotillas of around ten individuals in the lakes of the Rift Valley and elsewhere. **5** Often seen in pink-tinged mixed flocks comprising many thousand birds, the **greater** and **lesser flamingo** (*Phoenicopterus ruber* and *P. minor*) are more-or-less resident on Lake Manyara and the saline lake at the centre of Ngorongoro Crater. They feed on algae and microscopic fauna sifted through filters contained within their unique down-turned bills. Their only known breeding site is remote Lake Natron in northern Tanzania. **6** Among the most common of 22 resident and migrant waterfowl species, the distinctive **white-faced whistling-duck** (*Dendrocygna viduata*) is often seen in large flocks alongside the closely affiliated but plainer rufous whistling-duck (*D. bicolor*). **7** Closely related to the ibises, spoonbills are large all-white birds with distinctive long spatulate bills, which they sweep partially submerged from side to side in search of small fish and invertebrates. The **African spoonbill** (*Platalea alba*), a common resident, can be distinguished from its European counterpart, a very scarce migrant, by its reddish (as opposed to black) face and legs. **8** Also known as the lily-trotter, the **African jacana** (*Actophilornis africanus*) is totally unmistakeable with its rich chestnut torso and wings, and exceptionally widely spread toes that allow it to walk on lily pads and other light floating vegetation.

3

Practical Information

WHEN TO VISIT

Tourist arrivals to Tanzania are highest during the northern hemisphere winter, but the country can be visited throughout the year, since every season has different advantages, depending strongly on which parts of the country you plan to include in your travel itinerary. A regional overview follows, but for those with the option, it is worth emphasising that there is much to be said for trying to avoid peak tourist seasons, as the parks and other main attractions will be less crowded.

NORTHERN SAFARI CIRCUIT The focal point of most northern circuit safaris is Serengeti National Park, and wildlife movement here is highly seasonal. The most accessible part of the Serengeti from Arusha, particularly for those on budget and mid-range road safaris, are the southeastern and south-central plains around Ndutu and Seronera, where wildlife activity peaks over the rainy seasons between early November and the end of May. The wildebeest migration disperses into the southern plains at this time of year, usually calving in February, and there is plenty of predator activity. It is also when the countryside is greenest, and it offers the best birdwatching, with resident species supplemented by a number of Palaearctic and intra-African migrants.

A few years back, the entire period between the Easter weekend and the end of September was regarded as low season in the Serengeti and elsewhere in northern Tanzania. However, a steady increase in tourist volumes, as well as the opening of several new camps in the far north and the western corridor, has resulted in more loosely defined tourist seasons. Indeed, many of the smaller camps and lodges in the western, central and northern Serengeti are actually busiest between June and October, since the migration is usually in the west/central Serengeti over June and July, and in the far north over August to October.

April and May are usually the wettest months in northern Tanzania, and thus the quietest time of the year in touristic terms. This has its advantages. For one, the lodges and camps that are open offer significantly cheaper low-season rates, which can greatly reduce the cost of a safari. And there is nothing wrong with the game viewing: plenty of wildlife can be seen in the south-central Serengeti over April and May, while the Ngorongoro Crater and Lake Manyara, which are incorporated into most northern safaris, are not so strongly seasonal in terms of wildlife movements, but they are far less crowded with 4x4s and more enjoyable to visit outside of peak tourist seasons.

Aside from the Serengeti, the most seasonal of the northern circuit parks is Tarangire, where animal concentrations generally peak between July and the start of the rains in November or early December.

ARUSHA

	Jan	Feb	Mar	Apr	May	Jun	Jul	Aug	Sep	Oct	Nov	Dec
Max (°C)	29	29	28	25	22	21	20	22	25	27	28	28
Min (°C)	10	12	12	14	11	10	10	9	9	10	10	10
Rain (mm)	50	85	180	350	205	20	10	15	15	20	105	100

MOSHI

	Jan	Feb	Mar	Apr	May	Jun	Jul	Aug	Sept	Oct	Nov	Dec
Max (°C)	36	35	34	30	29	29	28	30	31	32	34	34
Min (°C)	15	15	15	16	14	13	12	12	13	14	14	15
Rain (mm)	50	60	120	300	180	50	20	20	20	40	60	50

NGORONGORO CRATER RIM

	Jan	Feb	Mar	Apr	May	Jun	Jul	Aug	Sep	Oct	Nov	Dec
Max (°C)	23	23	22	21	20	19	19	20	21	22	22	22
Min (°C)	10	10	10	11	10	8	8	8	8	9	10	10
Rain (mm)	110	90	135	220	100	20	10	15	15	55	115	135

SERONERA (SERENGETI NP)

	Jan	Feb	Mar	Apr	May	Jun	Jul	Aug	Sep	Oct	Nov	Dec
Max (°C)	29	29	29	28	27	26	26	27	28	28	28	28
Min (°C)	26	16	16	16	15	15	14	15	15	16	16	16
Rain (mm)	80	100	135	160	90	35	15	30	60	70	115	105

ZANZIBAR TOWN

	Jan	Feb	Mar	Apr	May	Jun	Jul	Aug	Sep	Oct	Nov	Dec
Max (°C)	32	32	33	30	29	28	27	28	29	30	31	31
Min (°C)	25	25	26	26	25	24	23	23	23	25	25	26
Rain (mm)	50	65	140	310	290	45	25	25	35	60	180	135

MOUNT KILIMANJARO AND MERU Trekking conditions are best in the dry seasons, which run from January to early March and from August to October. There are several advantages to the period January to early March. The first is that it tends to be quieter in terms of tourists, an important consideration if you are following one of the more popular routes. The second is that it is probably the most beautiful time of year to climb, with the best chance of clear skies at higher altitudes. On the downside, it is also the coldest time of year on the mountain, though this does mean the snow cap tends be more extensive than in warmer months. The worst months for climbing in terms of weather are November and December.

ZANZIBAR AND THE COAST The coast can be visited throughout the year. However, the most pleasant time to be there is the long dry season, which runs from June to October. This is when temperatures are most comfortable (though still hot by European standards) and the humidity is lowest. There is also less chance of your holiday being disrupted by rain, and it is considerably safer than the wet season in terms of malaria and other mosquito-borne diseases. The wettest months of April and May are best avoided, while January to March, though drier, tend to be hot.

Tanzania is truly a country of highlights, most of which are centred on the north, and it also contains a wealth of off-the-beaten-track opportunities. The list below, broken down by category, only skims the surface:

BEST PUBLIC WILDLIFE DESTINATIONS

Serengeti National Park The linchpin of the popular northern safari circuit, this world-renowned park harbours large numbers of predators, as well as being the site of a legendary migration comprising million-strong herds of wildebeest and zebra. Overcrowding in this popular park is restricted to the southeast, so those with sufficient time and a suitable budget are advised to explore the more remote west and north.

Ngorongoro Crater Centrepiece of the Ngorongoro Conservation Area, the world's largest intact caldera is superb Big Five territory. Lion, buffalo and large tuskers are all common, and it's the best place in Tanzania to look for the endangered black rhinoceros.

Tarangire National Park Less celebrated than the Serengeti – and, as a consequence, less heavily touristed – Tarangire preserves a classic chunk of dry savannah studded with plentiful baobabs and home to prodigious elephant herds, along with plenty of other wildlife.

BEST EXCLUSIVE WILDLIFE CONCESSIONS

Klein's Camp Promising exclusive access to 100km² of hilly country bordering the northeast Serengeti, this long-established private reserve combines luxury and superb guiding with some of the best game viewing in Tanzania – it's particularly good for leopard and lion.

Grumeti Reserve North of the Serengeti National Park's Western Corridor lies an area of largely flat plains with the occasional hill. There are three very chic, high-quality lodges here: the grand, hilltop Sasakwa; the minimalist Faru Faru; and the old-Africa-style tented camp, Sabora Plains. Marketed by South Africa's top Singita team, these lodges command some of Tanzania's highest costs.

West Kilimanjaro Effectively the Tanzanian counterpart to Kenya's Amboseli National Park, but with little tourist traffic and no restrictions on walking, this game-controlled area is home to plenty of elephant alongside dry-country antelope such as gerenuk and oryx. It also lies right at the base of Kilimanjaro, offering fantastic views of the snow-capped icon along with several other distinctive northern Tanzanian mountains.

BEST HIKING AND WALKING

Mount Kilimanjaro National Park Encompassing the peaks and forested slopes of the continent's highest mountain, Kilimanjaro is climbed by thousands of tourists every year, not only to stand on the snow-capped pinnacle of Africa, but also to experience the other-worldly Afro-montane moorland habitat of the upper reaches.

West Usambara Mountains An affordable low-key alternative to Kilimanjaro, as well as being a good place to adapt to higher altitudes prior to a Kili climb,

Practical Information HIGHLIGHTS **3**

this beautiful mountain range southeast of Moshi offers unlimited opportunities for casual rambling.

Ol Doinyo Lengai Assuming it's not actually erupting when you visit, the affordable overnight ascent of Africa's most active volcano passes through some of the most dramatic rockscapes in the country.

BEST FOR BIRDS
Lake Manyara National Park All of the northern safari circuit offers good birding, but for first-time visitors to Africa this is the jewel in the region's avian crown, offering a good opportunity to tick off 100 species – from flamingos and storks to eagles and barbets – in a day.

Amani Nature Reserve This reserve in the Eastern Usambara Mountains, inland of Tanga, protects some of the most important montane forest in Tanzania along with a wealth of rare and endemic birds. There's inexpensive accommodation and a good range of walking trails – and it's easily accessible by public transport, too.

Rubondo Island Situated in the southeastern waters of the vast Lake Victoria, this forested island supports several species with a limited distribution elsewhere in Tanzania, with African grey parrots and other forest dwellers vying for attention with fish eagles, herons and other water-associated species.

BEST FOR CULTURE AND HISTORY
Zanzibar Stone Town Like a living embodiment of *One Thousand and One Nights*, this traditional quarter of Zanzibar is as notable for its lovely Arab-influenced architecture as it is the pervasive laid-back vibe associated with traditional Swahili culture. It's emphatically worth spending a night or two here before heading out to one of the idyllic beaches that surround the island.

Kondoa Rock Art Sites Probably the least publicised of Tanzania's several UNESCO World Heritage Sites, the fascinating and myriad painted shelters around Kondoa make for a great add-on to a northern Tanzania safari, offering a good opportunity to stretch the legs whilst exploring this enigmatic facet of the country's rich prehistory.

Cultural programmes Numerous official cultural programmes operate around northern Tanzania, allowing visitors to interact with traditional pastoralists, farmers and hunter-gatherers. These range from hunting with the Hadza at Lake Eyasi to taking a camelback trip with the Maasai of Mkuru.

ITINERARY PLANNING

Tanzania has a well-defined tourist circuit. It would be no exaggeration to say that as many as 90% of visitors divide their time in the country between the northern safari circuit and the island of Zanzibar. If this is what you plan on doing, then any suitably experienced tour operator or safari company will be able to put together a package to meet your requirements. A ten- to 14-day trip is ideal for the Zanzibar/safari combination. You might want to read the section *Organising a safari* on pages 76–9 before making contact with a tour operator. With Zanzibar, the main decision you need to make in advance is whether you want to be based at a hotel in the old

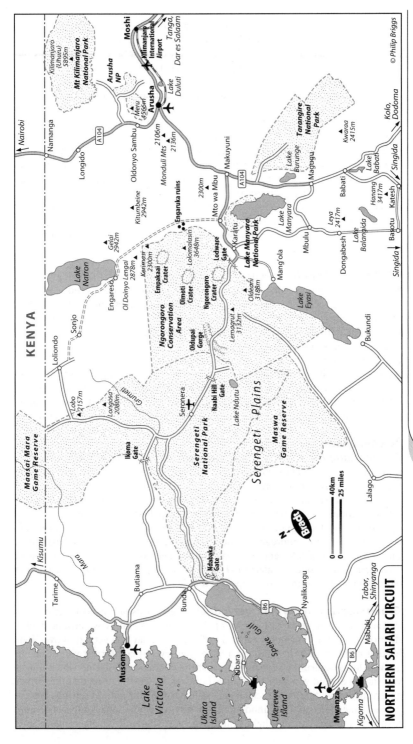

NORTHERN SAFARI CIRCUIT

© Philip Briggs

Stone Town, or out on one of the beaches, or a combination of the two. For a short trip to Tanzania, it is advisable to fly between Arusha (the springboard for safaris in northern Tanzania) and Zanzibar. If you are really tight for time, you'll get more out of your safari by flying between lodges. A fly-in safari will also be less tiring than the more normal drive-in safari.

After the northern safari circuit and Zanzibar, Tanzania's main tourist attraction is Kilimanjaro, which is normally climbed over five to seven days. A Kilimanjaro climb is one of those things that you either do or don't want to undertake: for a significant minority of travellers, climbing Kilimanjaro is the main reason for visiting Tanzania, but for the majority it is of little interest. If you want to do a Kili climb, it can be organised in advance through any number of tour operators and safari companies, and there is a lot to be said for arranging the climb through the same operator that organises your safari. As with budget safaris, it is generally possible to get cheaper prices on the spot. To combine a Kili climb with a few days on safari and a visit to Zanzibar you would need an absolute minimum of two weeks in the country, and even that would be very tight, allowing for no more than two nights on Zanzibar.

ORGANISING A SAFARI Several types of safari are on offer, with the major variables being accommodation type (budget camping, larger lodges such as those operated by the Sopa and Serena chains, or more exclusive lodges and tented camps), transportation (ie: whether you drive between the reserves using one vehicle throughout, or fly between reserves and go on game drives provided by the lodge or camp). There is some room for overlap between these types of accommodation and transport, and there are also a few more offbeat options. For instance, you might want to travel with a company that specialises in walking safaris, spend part or all of your time in exclusive private concessions bordering the parks (which typically offer extras such as guided game walks and night drives), or visit more far-flung areas such as Lake Eyasi (home to the Hadza hunter-gatherers) or Lake Natron.

Accommodation
Budget camping safaris These are generally designed to keep costs to a minimum, so they tend to make use of the cheapest camping options, often outside the national parks, and clients are normally expected to set up their own tents. Most backpackers and volunteers working in Tanzania go on budget camping safaris, although even with these there is a gap between the real shoestring operators (who'll skimp on everything) and those operators who offer a sensible compromise between affordability and adequate service. Given that high park fees, the introduction of VAT and an escalation in fuel costs have pushed the lowest realistic rate for a budget safari to US$200-plus per person per day, it really isn't worth going with a dodgy company to save a few dollars.

Group safaris staying at larger lodges These are usually fixed-itinerary trips that accommodate the largest volume of visitors, and generally costs around double the price of a budget camping safari. For the extra outlay you get a roof over your head at night, restaurant food and a far higher level of comfort. If you decide to go on a lodge safari, the probability is that the operator will decide which lodges you stay at. Should you have the choice, however, it's worth noting that the former government 'Wildlife Lodge' chain generally has the best natural settings but the poorest standards of accommodation and service, while Sopa Lodges are more luxurious and well run and slightly more expensive (but only the Ngorongoro Sopa

The combination of steep national park entrance and camping fees, and the expense of running 4x4 vehicles in northern Tanzania, places the northern safari circuit pretty much out of bounds for travellers on a very tight budget. It is possible, however, to see parts of the circuit relatively cheaply by using public transport and/or hiring vehicles locally.

The most affordable way of traversing the Serengeti National Park is on one of the buses and Land Rovers that run daily along the B144 between Mwanza and Arusha. This route passes through conservation areas for a total of about 250km, firstly the Serengeti's Western Corridor and Seronera Plains, then the plains of the western Ngorongoro Conservation Area and over the Ngorongoro Crater rim. You should get a good feel for the scenery and landscapes from the bus window, and between November and July you can see plenty of game, including large predators but of course the vehicle cannot be expected to stop for special sightings. The trip will entail paying park entrance fees of US$110 plus 18% VAT on top of the bus fare. In theory, it is possible to make advance arrangements for one of these buses to drop you off at Seronera, and pick you up at a later date but it's difficult to see any reason why anybody would want to do this.

A more satisfying option for travellers who specifically want to see the Serengeti, have time on their hands, and cannot afford a safari of several days' duration, is to approach the park from the western side. This cuts out the long drive and overnight stops coming from Arusha, and allows you to get within 1km of the entrance gate on public transport and to visit the park as a day or overnight trip rather than as part of a longer safari. The best place to set up something like this is Serengeti Stopover, a private campsite situated right next to the entrance gate to the Serengeti's Western Corridor and alongside the main road between the Lake Victoria ports of Mwanza and Musoma. The Western Corridor itself generally offers good game viewing, particularly when the migration passes through between May and July, and the game-rich Seronera Plains and campsite are only about 2 hours' drive from the western entrance gate.

On the eastern side of the northern safari circuit, affordable local buses run daily from Arusha to Karatu, stopping at Mto wa Mbu near the entrance of Lake Manyara National Park. Several lodges in Karatu and Mto wa Mbu rent out 4x4 vehicles for half- or full-day visits to Lake Manyara or Ngorongoro Crater. Worth noting, too, is that safari vehicles are found in abundance in Mto wa Mbu and Karatu, so there's every chance you could make cheaper private arrangements to hire a vehicle for a day. Were you to do something like this, you should be very clear about what the deal covers and how long you will spend in the game reserve – ambiguities at the negotiating stage often result in frayed tempers later in the day.

Hitching into any reserves in Tanzania is problematic; aside from being illegal there are numerous practical obstacles. And even if you were to catch a lift, you may well get stuck in the Serengeti or Ngorongoro and although you will see little game from a campsite or lodge, you will still have to pay park fees.

Practical Information   ITINERARY PLANNING

3

Lodge has a setting to compare with its Wildlife Lodge equivalent). The lodges in the Serena chain are more upmarket still, with modern facilities, good locations and attractive décor.

Safaris to small lodges or tented camps If you think sleeping under canvas and eating under the stars might be comparable in price to a lodge safari, think again. Smart tented camps allow for a far more holistic and integrated safari experience than one will ever have sleeping in 'hotels in the bush' designed to insulate travellers from the wilderness, especially after dark. So this third and most costly type of safari accommodation in Tanzania comprises a multiplying selection of smaller and more exclusive lodges and seasonal, mobile or semi-permanent tented camps. These are generally as luxurious as any of the large lodges and at their best they can provide food, service and (where game drives are included) guiding to a much higher standard. They are, however, usually unfenced, have few permanent structures and are designed to maximise the bush experience, so nervous first-time safari-goers might find them a little daunting!

The cost of a safari like this depends on your exact requirements, but it will usually be a lot more than a comparable lodge safari. Indeed, the best mobile and tented camps (as operated by the likes of &Beyond, Asilia and Nomad), although absolutely superlative, are generally more than double the price of larger chain lodges, so not within most safari-goers' means. Fortunately, there are also a small handful of tented or other more low-key camps that offer a bush atmosphere at rates comparable to the chain lodges – Tarangire Safari Lodge, Kirurumu Tented Camp and Ndutu Lodge stand out, as do the mobile camps operated by Wayo Africa, Wild Frontiers, Authentic Africa and Tanganyika Wilderness Safaris – and these are highly recommended to those seeking a bush experience at a relatively affordable price.

Getting around
Regular scheduled flights connect all the main reserves in northern Tanzania, and an increasingly high proportion of safari-goers choose to fly around rather than bump along the long, dusty roads that separate the parks. Flying around will be particularly attractive to those who have bad backs or who tire easily, but it is more expensive and does dilute the sense of magic attached to driving through the vast spaces that characterise this region. Fly-in safaris allow you to see far more wildlife in a shorter space of time, because you don't lose hours on the road. Now that the road from Arusha is surfaced as far as Ngorongoro Conservation Area, a popular compromise is to cover the closer parks (Manyara, Tarangire and the NCA) by road, fly on to one or two locations in the Serengeti ecosystem, then fly directly back to Arusha, or possibly to drive one-way, into the Serengeti, and then fly out at the end.

By private safari and car rental The most normal way of getting around northern Tanzania is on an **organised safari** by Land Cruiser, Land Rover or any other similarly hardy 4x4 with high clearance. It is standard procedure for safari companies to provide a driver/guide with a fair knowledge of local wildlife and road conditions, as well as some mechanical expertise. **Self-drive car hire**, although widely available in Zanzibar, isn't a particularly attractive or popular option in Tanzania; however, should you wish to drive independently, Roadtrip Tanzania (m *0682 075622;* e *info@ roadtriptanzania.com; www.roadtriptanzania.com; see ad, page 69*) provide RAV4 cars and Land Cruisers equipped with everything you need for a camping trip (*US$59–99/ day*). The website is a great source of information and the 24/7 road support they promise gives peace of mind to explore Tanzania on your own. Self-drivers should look at the electronic maps from www.tracks4africa.co.za – these can be downloaded on to some GPS receivers and most smartphones.

Group size One factor that all visitors should consider is the size of the group doing the safari. It is almost invariably cheaper to go on safari as part of a group, but it can also ruin things if the people in that group are not compatible. A group safari will be highly frustrating to those who have a special interest such as birding or serious wildlife photography. And, frankly, it is probably unfair to impose this sort of interest on other passengers, who will have little interest in identifying every raptor you drive past, or in waiting for 2 hours at a lion kill to get the perfect shot. Another consideration is that non-stretch Land Rovers can feel rather cramped with four people in the back, especially when the luggage is in the vehicle, and jostling for head room out of the roof can be a nightmare when four cameras are vying for the best position.

A small proportion of companies – generally the large package tour operators – use minibuses as opposed to conventional 4x4s. These have several disadvantages, notably that the larger group size (typically around eight people) creates more of a package tour atmosphere, and that it is difficult for a large group to take proper advantage of the pop-up roofs that are usually found on safari vehicles. In any event, bouncing around rutted roads in a Land Rover is an integral part of the safari experience – it just wouldn't be the same in a minibus.

Finally, there is the question of aesthetics. Without wishing to wax too lyrical, the thrill of being on safari doesn't derive merely from the animals you see. There is an altogether more elusive (some might say spiritual) quality attached to simply being in a place as wild and vast and wonderful as the Serengeti, one that is most easily absorbed in silence, whether you travel on your own or with somebody with whom you feel totally relaxed. It isn't the same when you have to make small talk to new acquaintances, crack the rote jokes about who should be put out of the vehicle to make the lion move, decide democratically when to move on, listen to the driver's educational monotones, and observe social niceties that seem at odds with the surrounding wilderness.

Activities In most national parks, activities are typically restricted to two daily game drives, one in the morning and one in the afternoon. This is due to park rulings that forbid walking except in special areas and circumstances. Whilst a diet of two daily game drives is undoubtedly the best way to see the most wildlife, it can become quite restrictive if you are used to incorporating a little more exercise into your daily routine. For this reason, there is a lot to be said for mixing up the national park visits with stays in bordering concessions where guided walks and/ or night drives are permitted (for instance Chem Chem or Manyara Ranch near Tarangire, or Klein's Camp in Loliondo), or other areas suited to walking (the Lake Eyasi and Natron hinterland, the lovely Empakaai Crater in the northern NCA, or the West Kilimanjaro region). For more dedicated walking safaris, Wayo Africa and Wild Frontiers are among the only operators licensed to take guided walking safaris through the national parks.

Tipping In all categories of safari, the price you are quoted should include the vehicle and driver/guide, fuel, accommodation or camping equipment and fees, meals and park entrance fees. You are expected to tip the driver and cook. Around US$10 per day per party seems to be par, but you should check this with the company. Drivers and cooks are poorly paid; if they have done a good job, be generous.

PLANNING YOUR ITINERARY Your itinerary will depend on how much time and money you have, and also the time of year. There are endless options, and most safari companies will put together the package you ask for. They know the ground well and can advise you on what is possible, but may tend to assume you will want to cover as many reserves as possible. This is not always the best approach.

Most budget safaris will take only five or six days to cover Ngorongoro, Serengeti, Manyara and Tarangire. A typical three-day trip takes in all these reserves except for the Serengeti. In the dry season (July to October) there is little game in the Serengeti and most safari companies will suggest you spend more time in Tarangire. The distances between these reserves are considerable and the roads are poor, so you will have a more relaxed trip if you visit fewer reserves. On a five-day safari, I would drop either the Serengeti or Tarangire. To visit all four reserves, six days is very rushed, seven or more would be better.

Three days isn't long enough to get a good feel for Tarangire, Manyara and Ngorongoro; four or even five days would be better. The combination of Ngorongoro and Tarangire would make an unhurried four-day safari. If you are limited to two days, you could either visit Tarangire on its own or do a combined trip to Manyara and Ngorongoro. If your budget is really limited, Tarangire can be visited as a day trip from Arusha; it is less than 2 hours' drive each way.

With all of the above, bear in mind that a fast driving itinerary will give you few chances to get away from the busier areas – as the busy areas are the ones which are most easily reached. For example, on a short one- or two-day trip to Tarangire, you're only ever likely to see the relatively busy north of the park; give yourself three nights and you can explore the park in much more detail, leave the crowds and reach the almost deserted southern half of the park. Similarly, if you pop into Manyara for a quick visit, then expect to be confined to the north side of the park, with plenty of other vehicles. Take a full day to see it, or stay inside the park and you can get much deeper in, and leave many of the crowds behind.

If your time is more limited than your budget, then a fly-in safari may be the answer. Then you can easily hop to the small lodges and safari camps deep within the parks, spending minimal time getting between them. Working like this, a trip of two nights in southern Tarangire, two nights at the Crater, and two in the northern Serengeti suddenly becomes viable.

Doing this area justice really requires both more time and more money. There's enough to see and do to warrant a safari of two weeks in duration, or even longer. You could easily spend three nights in Tarangire, three between Manyara and the Crater, and a further five or six in the Serengeti. On a two-week guided safari, you could also visit Lake Natron and Ol Doinyo Lengai, the Kondoa Rock Art Sites and/ or the Lake Eyasi area.

MISCELLANEOUS TIPS AND WARNINGS Malaria is present in most parts of the region, with the notable exception of the Ngorongoro Crater rim, and the normal precautions should be taken. Aside from malaria, there are no serious health risks attached to visiting this area.

Tsetse flies are seasonally abundant in well-wooded areas such as Tarangire and the Western Corridor of the Serengeti. Sleeping sickness is not a cause for serious concern, but the flies are sufficiently aggravating that it is worth applying insect repellent to your arms and legs before game drives (though this doesn't always deter tsetse flies) and avoiding the dark (in particular blue) clothing that tends to attract them.

Tarangire can be reached via a good tar road, and so too can Lake Manyara and the eastern entrance gate to Ngorongoro Conservation Area. By contrast, roads between the Ngorongoro Crater and Serengeti are very rough, for which reason safari-goers with serious back problems or a low tolerance for bumping around in the back of a vehicle might want to consider flying between the reserves. If one member of a safari party has a particular need to avoid being bumped around, they will be best off in the front passenger seat or the central row of seats – the seats above the rear axle tend to soak up the most punishment.

The combination of **dust and glare** may create problems for those with sensitive eyes. Sunglasses afford some protection against dust and glare, and if you anticipate problems of this sort, then don't forget to pack eye drops. Many people who wear contact lenses suffer in these dusty conditions, so it is a good idea to wear glasses on long drives, assuming that you have a pair.

Dust and heat can damage sensitive **camera equipment and film**. Keep your equipment in a sealed bag, and avoid exposing equipment to the sun when possible. Digital cameras are prone to collecting dust particles on the sensor which results in spots on the image. The dirt mostly enters the camera when changing lenses, so you should be careful when doing this. To some extent photos can be 'cleaned' up afterwards in Photoshop, but this is time-consuming. You can have your camera sensor professionally cleaned, or you can do this yourself with special brushes and swabs made for this purpose, but note that touching the sensor might cause damage and should only be done with the greatest care.

Many safari drivers earn a **commission** when their clients buy something from one of the many curio stalls in Mto wa Mbu and elsewhere in the region. There's nothing inherently wrong with this arrangement, but you might find that your safari driver is very keen to stop at a few stalls along the way. If this isn't what you want, then the onus is on you to make this clear the first time it happens – there's no need to be rude or confrontational, just explain gently that this isn't why you're on safari. Even if you do want to buy curios, don't fall into the obvious trap of assuming that you'll get a better deal buying locally. Many of the curios you see in places like Mto wa Mbu probably found their way there from outside, and they will generally be cheaper in Arusha than they will be at roadside stalls dealing exclusively with tourists.

Travellers on a budget camping safari who want to keep down their extra costs should be aware that drinks, although available at all game lodges, are very expensive. A beer at a lodge will typically cost around US$4–5, as opposed to US$1–2 in a shop or local bar, and prices of sodas are similarly inflated. Those travellers who don't want to spend the extra money should ask their driver where to buy drinks to bring back to the campsite – there are bars aimed at drivers near to all the budget safaris' campsites, and the prices are only slightly higher than in Arusha. It is definitely worth stocking up on **mineral water** in Arusha (at least one 1.5-litre bottle per person per day), since this will be a lot more expensive on the road.

Finally, and at risk of stating the obvious, it is both illegal and foolhardy to get out of your safari vehicle in the presence of any wild animal, and especially buffalo, elephant, hippo and lion.

TOURIST INFORMATION

The **Tanzania Tourist Board** (TTB) (*www.tanzaniatourism.com*) has improved greatly over recent years. The office in Arusha is reasonably helpful and well informed when it comes to tourist-class hotels and major tourist attractions, but it can't offer much help when it comes to more remote destinations. It is also a good source of information about the various cultural tourism programmes that have been established in northern Tanzania over the past few years. Its list of registered and blacklisted safari companies is a useful resource for travellers working through cheap safari companies.

TOUR OPERATORS

Northern Tanzania is featured by a vast spectrum of tour operators. At the lower-end of the price scale are companies that sell a handful of their own trips, and these are usually group trips with fixed itineraries and departure dates. If you're on a budget and are considering one of these trips, spend time comparing the companies who run them, as well as the actual itineraries, and see how past travellers have rated them.

At the higher-cost end of the market, many tour operators offer enticing trips to Tanzania, and some will be specialists with good knowledge of the country, backed by personal experience. Of those, a few will genuinely listen to what you want and do a good job of helping you choose the right places for your trip – offering a wide choice and unbiased advice. These companies are worth seeking out if you want the best trip possible.

Here we must, as authors, admit some personal interests in the tour-operating business. Chris runs Expert Africa (see below), which is one of the leading tailor-made operators for Tanzania that organises trips for travellers to Africa from all over the world. Philip acts as an adviser to Expert Africa, complementing the company's team and helping to develop its programmes with the benefit of his high country knowledge. Booking your tailor-made trip with Expert Africa (or, indeed, many other tour operators) will usually cost you the same as, or less than, if you contacted Tanzania's upmarket camps directly – plus you have the benefit of independent advice, full financial protection and experts to make the arrangements for you.

For a fair comparison, the following international tour operators specialise in Tanzania. Safari companies based in Tanzania are found under their different regions in *Part Two, The Guide*.

UK

Abercrombie & Kent ✆ 01242 547760; e info@ abercrombiekent.co.uk; www.abercrombiekent. co.uk. Worldwide individual & group holidays; upmarket selection & prices to match.
Africa Travel ✆ 020 7843 3500; e info@ africatravel.co.uk; www.africatravel.com. Substantial operator to all of Africa, with specialist sports travel & flight-only sections.
ARP Group ✆ 020 8423 0220; e alpha@alphauk. co.uk; www.arptravelgroup.com. Part of the same group as Ranger Safaris in Tanzania, which is all they sell.
Baobab – Alternative Roots to Travel ✆ 0121 314 6011; e info@baobabtravel.com; www.baobabtravel.com. Africa specialist with strong ethical credentials; focuses on ecotourism with some offbeat destinations.
Cazenove & Loyd Safaris ✆ 020 7384 2332; e info@cazloyd.com; www.cazloyd.com. Top-end,

tailor-made operator with worldwide options, including Tanzania.
Expert Africa ✆ 020 3405 6666 or (USA) +1 800 242 2434; e info@expertafrica.com; www.expertafrica.com; see ads, pages i & 266. Specialists to southern & East Africa & Seychelles, with a comprehensive website & an ethical ethos. Run by one of this book's authors (Chris) & advised on Tanzania by the other (Philip), it has probably the most complete & detailed choice of the best Tanzanian lodges, camps & destinations available anywhere. Safaris are flexible & start from about US$3,000/£2,000 pp for a week, including accommodation, meals & game activities, but excluding flights.
Explore Worldwide ✆ 01252 883931; e sales@ explore.co.uk; www.explore.co.uk. Market leader in small-group, escorted trips worldwide.
Footloose ✆ 01943 604030; www. footlooseadventure.co.uk. Tailor-made tours, safaris

& treks throughout Tanzania, including Zanzibar.

Gane & Marshall ✎01822 600600; e info@ganeandmarshall.com; www.ganeandmarshall.com; see ad, page 318. Long-established specialist to Africa with particularly strong ethics on Kilimanjaro climbs.

Hartley's Safaris ✎01673 861600; e info@hartleysgroup.com; www.hartleys-safaris.co.uk. Reliable safaris to southern & East Africa, as well as diving & island holidays in the region.

Imagine Africa ✎020 3468 0785; e info@imagineafrica.co.uk; www.imagineafrica.co.uk. Award-winning tour operator specialising in luxury travel & beach holidays in Africa.

Journeys by Design ✎01273 623790; e info@journeysbydesign.com; www.journeysbydesign.com. Stylish approach to safaris across southern & East Africa.

Journeys Discovering Africa ✎0800 088 5470; www.journeysdiscoveringafrica.com. High-end company specialising in tailored private & small group tours.

Rainbow Tours ✎020 7666 1250; e info@rainbowtours.co.uk; www.rainbowtours.co.uk. Africa & Latin America specialists, recently bought by a worldwide travel group: International Travel Connections Ltd.

Safari Consultants ✎01787 888590; e info@safari-consultants.com; www.safari-consultants.com; see ad, page 70. Long-established, knowledgeable tailor-made specialists to southern & East Africa, & the Indian Ocean islands.

Safari Drive ✎01488 71140; e info@safaridrive.com; www.safaridrive.com. Self-drive Land Rover safaris & expedition with their own fleet, & tailor-made safaris; they know the ground very well.

Steppes Travel ✎01258 601767; e enquiry@steppestravel.co.uk; www.steppestravel.co.uk. Worldwide tailor-made specialists with a long Africa history.

Tanzania Odyssey ✎020 8704 1216 or (USA) +1 866 356 4691; e info@tanzaniaodyssey.com; www.tanzaniaodyssey.com. The Tanzanian branch of African Odyssey, a company that offers tailor-made tours throughout Africa.

Tribes Travel ✎01473 890499; e enquiries@tribes.co.uk; www.tribes.co.uk; see ad, page 105. Consciously ethical range covering the globe, including some unique Tanzania offerings.

Wildlife Worldwide ✎01962 302086; e reservations@wildlifeworldwide.com; www.wildlifeworldwide.com. Tailor-made & small group trips worldwide.

World Odyssey ✎01905 731373; e info@world-odyssey.com; www.world-odyssey.com. Tailor-made trips across the globe.

US

Abercrombie & Kent ✎+1 888 611 4711; www.abercrombiekent.com. A leader in luxury adventure travel.

Africa Adventure Consultants ✎+1 866 778 1089; e info@adventuresinafrica.com; www.adventuresinafrica.com. Small Africa specialist with good ethics.

Big Five Tours & Expeditions ✎+1 800 244 3483; e info@bigfive.com; www.bigfive.com. Luxury operator to Asia, Africa & South America.

Exodus ✎+1 844 227 9087; www.exodustravels.com. Provides safaris, treks, expeditions & active vacations worldwide.

Expert Africa ✎+1 800 242 2434; e info@expertafrica.com; www.expertafrica.com; Californian office of the African specialists whose Tanzania programme is run & updated by author Chris McIntyre. See ads, pages i & 266.

Ker & Downey USA ✎+1 800 423 4236; e info@kerdowney.com; www.kerdowney.com. Long-established operator with Africa focus, now goes worldwide.

Micato Safaris ✎+1 800 642 2861; e inquiries@micato.com; www.micato.com. Smart, family-owned company, based in New York.

Naipenda Safaris ✎+1 888 404 4499; e jo@naipendasafaris.com; www.naipendasafaris.com. Small English- & French-speaking specialist operator to Tanzania, with bases in USA & Arusha.

Next Adventure ✎+1 800 562 7298; e safari@nextadventure.com; www.nextadventure.com. Small California-based operator with strong ties to Tanzania; also India & South America.

Thomson Safaris ✎+1 800 235 0289; e info@thomsonsafaris.com; www.thomsonsafaris.com. Long-established Tanzania specialist operating mostly set-departure small groups on fixed itineraries.

SOUTH AFRICA

Pulse Africa ✎+27 (0)11 325 2290; e info@pulseafrica.com; www.pulseafrica.com; see ad, page 318. Specialist operator featuring Egypt, Gabon & southern & East Africa, including Zanzibar.

Wild Frontiers ✆+27 (0)11 702 2035; e reservations@wildfrontiers.com; www. wildfrontiers.com. Experienced Johannesburg-based tour operator notable for its range of air tickets & set-departure group trips, including specialist ornithological safaris to East Africa. It also has its own Arusha office & runs several good-value tented camps in northern Tanzania.

Classic Safari Company ✆(Australia) +61 (0)29 327 0666; e info@classicsafaricompany.com.au; www.classicsafaricompany.com.au. Reliable old-school tour operator now organising tailor-made trips across Africa, India & Latin America.
Expert Africa ✆(New Zealand) +64 (0)4 976 7585 or (Australia) +1 800 995 397; e info@ expertafrica.com; www.expertafrica.com. Antipodean office of African specialists whose Tanzania programme is run & updated by author Chris McIntyre. See ads, pages i & 266.

RED TAPE

Check well in advance that you have a valid **passport** and that it won't expire within six months of the date on which you intend to leave Tanzania. Should your passport be lost or stolen, it will generally be easier to get a replacement if you have a photocopy of the important pages.

If you want to drive or hire a vehicle while you're in the country, either bring your normal driving licence or organise an **international driving licence** through the AA. You may sometimes be asked at the border or international airport for an **international health certificate** showing you've had a yellow fever shot.

For security reasons, it's advisable to keep a record of all your important information. You can do this by detailing it on one sheet of paper, photocopying it, and distributing a few copies in your luggage, your money-belt, and among relatives or friends at home. Or alternatively, you can email yourself and a few close friends or family the relevant information. The sort of things you want to include are your travel insurance policy details and 24-hour emergency contact number, passport number, details of relatives or friends to be contacted in an emergency, bank and credit card details, camera and lens serial numbers, etc. See also page 88.

For up-to-the-minute advice, also check www.gov.uk/foreign-travel-advice.

VISAS Visas are required by most visitors to Tanzania, including UK and US passport holders, and cost US$30–60, depending on your nationality. Visas can be obtained on arrival at any international airport, or at any border post. This is a straightforward procedure: no photographs or other documents are required, but the visa must be paid for in hard currency. The visa is normally valid for three months after arriving in the country, and it allows for multiple crossings into Uganda and Kenya during that period. Note, however, that the regional East African travel visa that can be issued by Kenya, Uganda and Rwanda, and that allows freedom of movement between these three countries, does not include Tanzania. For current information about visa requirements, visit www.tanzaniatourism.com.

EMBASSIES AND DIPLOMATIC MISSIONS Most embassies and high commissions are based in the former capital Dar es Salaam, as opposed to in Arusha (the main safari centre) or Dodoma (the current national capital). In 2016, it was widely thought that the new president John Magufuli intended to encourage most embassies to relocate to Dodoma, but this kind of rumour has been in circulation for years, so whether it will ever happen is an open question. Most embassies and high commissions are open mornings only and closed at weekends. Typical hours are 09.00 to 12.30, but this varies considerably. A full list of embassies and other diplomatic missions in Tanzania is posted at www.embassypages.com/tanzania.

GETTING THERE AND AWAY

BY AIR There are two international airports on the Tanzanian mainland. **Julius Nyerere International Airport** in Dar es Salaam (airport code DAR) is the traditional point of entry for international airlines, and it is generally convenient for business travellers but less so for tourists; many visitors who arrive in Dar transfer directly on to a flight to elsewhere in the country. The more useful point of entry for most tourists is **Kilimanjaro International Airport** (often abbreviated to KIA although its official airport code is JRO), which lies midway between Moshi and Arusha, and is now used by several international airlines.

Budget travellers looking for flights to East Africa may well find it cheapest to use an airline that takes an indirect route. London is a good place to pick up a cheap ticket; many continental travellers buy their tickets there. It is generally cheaper to fly to Nairobi than to Dar es Salaam, and getting from Nairobi to Arusha by shuttle bus is cheap, simple and quick. Several airlines also operate daily flights between Nairobi and Kilimanjaro International Airport.

Airlines Major international airlines that fly to Dar es Salaam and/or Kilimanjaro include the following:

✈ **EgyptAir** www.egyptair.com
✈ **Emirates** www.emirates.com
✈ **Ethiopian Airlines** www.flyethiopian.com
✈ **Fastjet** www.fastjet.com
✈ **Kenya Airways** www.kenya-airways.com
✈ **KLM** www.klm.com

✈ **Oman Air** www.omanair.com
✈ **Qatar** www.qatarairways.com
✈ **Rwandair** www.rwandair.com
✈ **South African Airways** www.flysaa.com
✈ **Swiss** www.swiss.com
✈ **Turkish Airlines** www.turkishairlines.com

Flight specialists
From the UK
Flight Centre ☏0800 587 0058; www.flightcentre.co.uk. An independent flight provider with over 450 outlets worldwide. They also have offices in Australia, New Zealand, South Africa & Canada.
STA Travel ☏0333 321 0099; e enquiries@statravel.co.uk; www.statravel.co.uk. STA has 10 branches in London & 50 or so around the country & at different university sites. STA also has several branches & associate organisations around the world.
Trailfinders ☏020 7368 1200; www.trailfinders.com. Has several offices in the UK. With origins in the discount flight market, Trailfinders now provides a one-stop travel service including visa & passport service, travel clinic & foreign exchange.
Travel Bag ☏0871 402 1644; www.travelbag.co.uk. Provides tailor-made flight schedules & holidays for destinations throughout the world.
WEXAS ☏020 7590 0610; www.wexas.com.

More of a club than a travel agent. Membership is inexpensive, but for frequent fliers the benefits are many.

From the USA
Airtech ☏+1 212 219 7000; www.airtech.com. Standby seat broker that also deals in consolidator fares, courier flights & a host of other travel-related services.
Council on International Educational Exchange ☏+1 207 553 4000; e contact@ciee.org; www.ciee.org. Although the Council focuses on work-exchange trips, it also has a large travel department.
Bridge the World ☏+1 0800 988 6884; www.bridgetheworld.com. Has several branches around the country.
Worldtek Travel ☏+1 203 772 0470; e info@worldtek.com; www.worldtek.com. Operates a network of rapidly growing travel agencies.

From Canada

Flight Centre ☎+1 877 967 5302; www.flightcentre.ca. Has a network of branches around the country.

Travel CUTS ☎+1 800 667 2887; e support@travelcuts.com; www.travelcuts.com. A student-based travel organisation with several offices throughout Canada.

From Australasia

Flight Centre (Australia): ☎+61 133 133; www.flightcentre.com.au; (New Zealand): ☎+64 0800 243 544; www.flightcentre.co.nz. A good place to start for cheap air fares.

STA Travel ☎+61 134 782; www.statravel.com.au. A student travel specialist with a network of branches around Australia.

From South Africa

Flight Centre ☎+27 0877 405 000; www.flightcentre.co.za. Part of the international chain with a number of branches around the country.

Student Flights ☎+27 0877 405 033; www.studentflights.co.za. This outfit is linked to the Flight Centre network.

Web-based flight sites

www.expedia.com Worldwide with a number of local websites.

www.lastminute.com Made its name selling last-minute trips.

www.opodo.com Pan-European family of flight sales sites.

www.travelocity.com Another global travel company.

OVERLAND The viability of the established overland routes between Europe and East Africa depends on the current political situation. In recent years, it has often been possible to reach East Africa via Egypt, Sudan and Ethiopia. However, it's not easy to predict the local political situation in advance, so do some online research and talk to several companies operating in the area before setting off.

A route via the Sahara and West Africa used to be favoured by several overland truck companies but unfortunately it has been impassable since the mid 1990s. At first this was due to banditry, then a major bridge collapsed in what was then Zaire, and then there was the civil war in the Democratic Republic of Congo. This route has always been tough going for independent travellers, whether or not they have a vehicle, and in the present climate of instability it should not be considered.

The most popular overland route in Africa these days connects Kenya to South Africa via Tanzania and a combination of Mozambique, Malawi, Zambia, Zimbabwe, Botswana and Namibia. It is a good route for self-drivers, can be covered with ease using public transport, but is also serviced by a proliferation of overland truck companies – recommendations include **Acacia Expeditions** (*www.acacia-africa.com*), **Dragoman** (*www.dragoman.co.uk*) and **Exodus** (*www.exodus.co.uk*).

Border crossings Tanzania borders eight countries, but the only overland port of entry used with any regularity by fly-in safari-goers is the Namanga border between Nairobi and Arusha. A number of shuttle companies such as Riverside (*www.riverside-shuttle.com*) and Impala (*www.theclassictours.com/portfolio/impala-shuttle*) run 4-hour minibus transfers between Arusha, Moshi and Nairobi twice daily. You can also travel between Nairobi and Arusha more cheaply (and more masochistically) in stages, catching a minibus between Nairobi and Namanga (these leave Nairobi from Ronald Ngala Road), crossing the border on foot, and then catching a shared taxi to Arusha. Expect this to take around 6 hours.

Provided that your papers are in order, Namanga is a very straightforward border crossing. There is a bank where you can change money during normal banking hours but at other times you'll have to change money with private individuals – don't change more than you need, as there are several con artists about.

SAFETY

Crime exists in Tanzania as it does practically everywhere in the world. There has been a marked increase in crime in Tanzania over recent years, and tourists are inevitably at risk because they are far richer than most locals, and are conspicuous in their dress, behaviour and (with obvious exceptions) skin colour. For all that, Tanzania remains a lower crime risk than many countries, and the social taboo on theft is such that even a petty criminal is likely to be beaten badly should they be caught in the act. With a bit of care, you would have to be unlucky to suffer from more serious crime while you are in Tanzania. Indeed, a far more serious concern is reckless and drunk driving, particularly on public transport along major roads. Generally buses are regarded to be safer than light vehicles such as minibuses, though this cannot be quantified statistically. Safari drivers are generally a lot more sedate and safe behind the wheel than bus and minibus drivers. Self-drivers should take a far more defensive attitude to driving than they would at home, and be alert to the road-hog mentality of many local drivers.

MUGGING There is nowhere in Tanzania where mugging is as commonplace as it is in, say, Nairobi or Johannesburg, but there are certainly several parts of the country where walking around alone at night would place you at some risk of being mugged. Mugging is generally an urban problem, with the main areas of risk being Arusha and Zanzibar Town. Even in these places, the risk is often localised, so ask advice at your hotel, since the staff there will generally know of any recent incidents in the immediate vicinity. The best way to ensure that any potential mugging remains an unpleasant incident rather than a complete disaster is to carry as little as possible on your person. If you are mugged in Tanzania, the personal threat is minimal provided that you promptly hand over what is asked for.

CASUAL THEFT The bulk of crime in Tanzania consists of casual theft such as bag-snatching or pickpocketing. This sort of thing is not particularly aimed at tourists (and as a consequence it is not limited to tourist areas), but tourists will be considered fair game. The key to not being pickpocketed is not having anything of value in your pockets; the key to avoiding having things snatched is to avoid having valuables in a place where they could easily be snatched. Most of the following points will be obvious to experienced travellers, but they are worth making:

- Many casual thieves operate in bus stations and markets. Keep a close watch on your belongings in these places, and avoid having loose valuables in your pocket or daypack.
- Keep all your valuables – passport, money, etc – in a money-belt. One you can hide under your clothes has obvious advantages over one of the currently fashionable codpieces that are worn externally.
- Never carry spending money in your money-belt. A normal wallet is fine provided it contains only a moderate sum of money. Better still is a wallet you can hang around your neck. If I plan to visit a risky area such as a busy market, I sometimes wear shorts under my trousers and keep my cash in the pockets of the shorts. In my opinion, it is difficult for somebody to stick a hand in the front pocket of a shirt unobserved, for which reason this is normally my favourite pocket for keeping ready cash.

- Distribute your money throughout your luggage. I always keep the bulk of my foreign currency in my money-belt, but I like to keep some cash hidden in various parts of my pack and daypack.
- Many people prefer to carry their money-belt on their person at all times, but it is probably safer to leave it locked away in a bag or safe in your hotel room. It's not impossible for a locked hotel room to be broken into, but it is far less common than pickpocketing, mugging or bag-snatching. Circumstances do, however, play a part – in a large city, valuables are best locked away somewhere, whereas in a game lodge the risk of theft from a room has to be greater than that of theft from your person.
- If you have jewellery that is of high personal or financial value, leave it at home.
- If you are robbed, think twice before you chase the thief, especially if the stolen items are of no great value. An identified thief is likely to be descended on by a mob and quite possibly beaten to death.

DOCUMENTATION The best insurance against complete disaster is to keep things well documented. If you carry a photocopy of the main page of your passport, you will be issued a new one more promptly. In addition, email yourself and a few close friends or family a chart with full details of your passport, flights, bank, credit card, travel insurance policy, travellers cheques (if you have them) and camera and other electronic equipment (including serial numbers). See also page 84.

You will have to report promptly to the police the theft of any item against which you wish to claim insurance.

SECURITY Tanzania is a very secure country, with a proud record of internal stability since independence. The bombing of the US embassies in Dar es Salaam and Nairobi resulted in large-scale cancellations of US tours to Tanzania in late 1998, despite a mass of evidence that would provide any rational human with greater cause to give a wide berth to US embassies than to cancel a holiday in East Africa. Aside from this, those parts of Tanzania regularly visited by tourists have a good safety record, although occasional armed robberies might occur anywhere, and Zanzibar has a recent record of sporadic political instability.

WOMEN TRAVELLERS Women travellers in Tanzania have little to fear on a gender-specific level. Nevertheless, it would be prudent to pay some attention to how you dress in more conservative parts of the country, particularly along more remote parts of the Islamic coast, where people are unused to tourists, and skimpy clothing (shorts or skirts that reveal the knees, or shirts with bare shoulders) might cause offence. On safari, in larger towns, and in other areas where tourists are commonplace, you can dress as you like within reason. Women travellers should also be alert to the reality that, under certain circumstances, revealing clothes might be perceived to be provocative or to make an unintended declaration of availability.

More mundanely, tampons are not readily available in smaller towns, although you can easily locate them in Arusha, and in game lodge and hotel gift shops. When travelling in out-of-the-way places, carry enough tampons to see you through to the next time you'll be in a large city, bearing in mind that travelling in the tropics can sometimes cause heavier or more regular periods than normal. Sanitary pads are available in most towns of any size.

On the beaches in Zanzibar, 'beach boys' can be persistent in declaring their affection, but stick to your guns and they will eventually get the message and leave you alone or switch out of lover mode into normal conversation.

There are two governing principles with regard to packing for Tanzania. The first is to bring everything that you could possibly need and that mightn't be readily available when you need it. The second is to travel as light as possible. Somewhat contradictory directives, so the key is to find the right balance, something that probably depends on personal experience and taste as much as anything. Worth stressing is that most genuine necessities are surprisingly easy to get hold of in the main centres in Tanzania, and that most of the ingenious gadgets you can buy in camping shops are unlikely to amount to much more than deadweight on the road. If it came to it, you could easily travel in Tanzania with little more than a change of clothes, a few basic toiletries and a medical kit.

CARRYING YOUR LUGGAGE Make sure that your suitcase is tough and durable, and that it seals well, so that its contents will survive bumpy, dusty drives to the game reserves. A lock is a good idea, not only for flights but also for when you leave your case in a hotel room – rare incidents of theft from upmarket hotels in Africa tend to be opportunistic and a locked suitcase is unlikely to be tampered with. A daypack will be useful when on safari, and you should be able to pack your luggage in such a manner that any breakable goods can be carried separately in the body of the vehicle and on your lap when necessary – anything like an iPod, laptop, tablet or camera will suffer heavily from vibrations on rutted roads. If you are likely to use public transport, then a backpack is the most practical way to carry your luggage.

CAMPING EQUIPMENT On a budget safari or organised Kilimanjaro climb, camping equipment will be provided by the company you travel with. Taken together with the limited opportunities for camping outside of the safari circuit, this means that for most travellers a tent will be deadweight in Tanzania. An all-weather sleeping bag is required on Mount Meru or Kilimanjaro, and you may want to bring your own sleeping bag for any camping safari.

CLOTHES Assuming that you have the space, you might want to carry one change of shirt and underwear for every day you will spend on safari. At budget to mid-range lodges, organising laundry along the way is costly and tiresome, and dusty conditions practically enforce a daily change of clothes. It's a good idea to keep one or two shirts for evening use only. By contrast, many more upmarket camps – particular those catering to a predominantly fly-in clientele – now offer free laundry to visitors staying two or more nights.

When you select your clothes, remember that jeans are heavy to carry, hot to wear, and slow to dry. Far better to bring lightweight quick-dry travel trousers and, if you intend spending a while in montane regions, thermal underwear and waterproof trousers, which will provide extra cover on wet or chilly nights. Skirts are best made of a light natural fabric such as cotton. T-shirts are lighter and less bulky than proper shirts, although the top pocket of a shirt (particularly if it buttons up) is a good place to carry spending money in markets and bus stations, since it's easier to keep an eye on than trouser pockets. One sweater or sweatshirt will be adequate in most parts of the country, although you will need serious alpine gear for Kilimanjaro and to a lesser degree Mount Meru.

Socks and underwear should be made from natural fabrics. Bear in mind that re-using sweaty undergarments will encourage fungal infections such as athlete's foot, as well as prickly heat in the groin region. As for footwear, genuine hiking boots are worth considering only if you're a serious off-road hiker, since they are very heavy, whether on your feet or in your pack. A good pair of walking shoes, preferably made of leather and with good ankle support, is a good compromise. It's also useful to carry sandals, flip-flops or other light shoes.

Another factor in deciding what clothes to bring is the sensibilities of Tanzania's large Islamic population. Women can wear shorts at most beach resorts, in game reserves and cities where locals are used to tourists, but in smaller coastal settlements it would be better to wear a skirt that covers your knees and a modest shirt that doesn't expose shoulders or cleavage.

Men, too, should be conscious of what they wear. Shorts are acceptable, but few Tanzanian men wear them and trousers are considered more respectable in an urban setting. Walking around in a public place without a shirt is unacceptable.

OTHER USEFUL ITEMS Your **toilet bag** should at the very minimum include soap (secured in a plastic bag or soap holder unless you enjoy a soapy toothbrush!), shampoo, toothbrush and toothpaste. This sort of stuff is easy to replace as you go along, so there's no need to bring family-sized packs. Men will probably want a **razor**. Nobody should forget to bring a **towel**, or to keep handy a roll of **toilet paper**, which, although widely available at shops and kiosks, cannot always be relied upon to be present where it's most urgently needed.

Other essentials include a **torch**, a **penknife** and a compact **alarm clock** for those early-morning starts. You should carry a small **medical kit** (page 108) and **mosquito nets**. If you wear **contact lenses**, bring all the fluids you need, since they are not available in Tanzania. You might also want to bring a pair of **glasses** to wear on long bus rides and on safari – many lens wearers suffer badly in dusty conditions. In general, since many people find the intense sun and dry climate irritates their eyes, you might consider reverting to glasses.

Binoculars are essential if you want to get a good look at birds, or to watch distant mammals in game reserves. For most purposes, lightweight 7x21 compact binoculars will be fine, although some might prefer traditional 7x35 binoculars for their larger field of vision. Serious birdwatchers will find a 10x30 or 10x50 magnification more useful, and should definitely carry a good field guide.

MONEY AND BANKING

The unit of currency is the Tanzanian shilling (pronounced *shillingi*), which is in theory divided into 100 cents. The Tanzanian shilling comes in Tsh10,000, 5,000, 1,000, 500 and 200 denomination bills. It is often very difficult to find change for larger denomination bills, so try always to have a fair spread of notes available. The bulky small denomination coins are worth considerably less than their weight in whatever leaden metal it is that's used to mint them! The rate of exchange has deteriorated against all hard currencies over the last two decades. Between 1999 and 2017, the exchange rate against the US dollar has slid from Tsh670 to around Tsh2,200, a drop of around 10% annually. It is reasonable to expect a similar trend will persist during the lifespan of this edition. For rates of exchange, see box, page 2.

Most upmarket hotels and safari companies in Tanzania quote rates in US dollars. Some will also demand payment in this or another prominent hard currency, although some hotels and lodges actually prefer payment in local currency. The situation with national parks and other conservation areas is variable, but if you expect to pay fees directly rather than through an operator, then you'll need a Visa or MasterCard (or failing that, to get a Tanapa smartcard and load it with US dollars cash at a bank) – see box, page 92. These exceptions noted, most things in Tanzania are best paid for in local currency, including restaurant bills, goods bought at a market or shop, mid-range and budget accommodation, public transport and most other casual purchases. Indeed, most service providers geared towards the local economy will have no facility for accepting any currency other than the Tanzanian shilling.

Note that most prices in this book are quoted in US dollars rather than Tanzanian shillings. This is because of the local currency's propensity for devaluation against hard currencies, which means that even where prices are quoted locally in shillings, a US dollar price is more likely to hold steady over the book's lifespan. However, in the few instances where a hotel quotes its rates in euros or sterling, we have followed suit.

CASH, TRAVELLERS' CHEQUES AND CREDIT CARDS Traditionally, there are three ways of carrying money in Africa: hard currency cash, travellers' cheques or a credit card. Over recent years, **travellers' cheques** have been rendered all but obsolete as credit cards have become more widely accepted in East Africa. In any case, they are now difficult to exchange in Tanzania, so are best avoided altogether.

Far more convenient are **credit or debit cards**, which can be used to draw local currency at 24-hour ATMs in most towns of any size and at both main international airports, as well as for paying bills at upmarket hotels, and for paying national park fees. Depending on the bank, a transaction limit of Tsh400,000 (around US$180) is imposed, but it is possible to do several transactions in a row, to a maximum daily withdrawal limit of Tsh1,200,000–2,000,000 (around US$500–900). It is important to note that the only widely accepted cards are Visa, MasterCard, Maestro and Cirrus, most or all of which are now accepted by most or all ATMs associated with the NCB, NMB, CRDB, Exim Bank, Barclays, Stanbic and Standard Chartered. Other cards will be of little or no use. Note, too, that ATM facilities are not available in any national parks, or in some smaller towns and beach resorts. Budget travellers can safely assume that hotels and other facilities within their reach cannot process card payments. It's advisable to take along more than one card (ie: a credit and a debit) as banks have an annoying habit of freezing your card at inopportune moments without telling you. And just in case that happens, include an overseas number for your bank's fraud department with your emergency contacts so that you can call and get any freeze lifted as soon as possible.

It is still a good idea to carry some of your funds in hard currency **cash**, ideally US dollars, although euros and pounds sterling are also widely accepted. Note that US$100 and US$50 bills usually attract a significantly better exchange rate than smaller denominations, and that US dollar bills printed before 2006 will be refused by almost all outlets that accept or exchange foreign currency.

Carry your hard currency and credit cards, as well as your passport and other important documentation, in a money-belt that can be hidden beneath your clothing. Your money-belt should be made of cotton or another natural fabric, and everything inside the belt should be wrapped in plastic to protect it against sweat.

FOREIGN EXCHANGE Foreign currencies can be changed into Tanzanian shillings at any bank or bureau de change (known locally as forex bureaux). Most banks are open from around 09.00 to 12.30 on weekdays and in many larger towns they stay open until 15.00 or later. They open from 09.00 to at least 11.30 on Saturdays. Most private forex bureaux stay open until 16.00 or later. You can change money at any time of day at Julius Nyerere International Airport (Dar es Salaam) or Kilimanjaro International

3

Airport (between Arusha and Moshi). Most private forex bureaux deal in cash only.

Generally, private forex bureaux offer a better rate of exchange than banks, although this is not as much the case as it was a few years ago, and some forex bureaux actually give notably lower rates than the banks. It's worth shopping around before a major transaction. The private bureaux are almost always far quicker for cash transactions than the banks, which might be a more important consideration than a minor discrepancy in the rate they offer. Before you change a large sum of money, check the bank or forex bureau has enough high denomination banknotes, or you'll need a briefcase to carry your local currency.

The legalisation of private forex bureaux has killed off the black market that previously thrived in Tanzania. Private individuals may give you a slightly better rate than the banks, but the official rate is so favourable it seems unfair to exploit this. In Dar es Salaam or Arusha you will be offered exceptionally good rates on the street, but if you are stupid or greedy enough to accept these, you can expect to be ripped off. There are plenty of forged US$100 bills floating around Tanzania, and you can assume that anyone who suggests a deal involving a US$100 bill is trying to unload a forgery.

GETTING AROUND

BY AIR Several private airlines run scheduled flights around Tanzania, most prominently Fastjet, Regional Air Services, Precision Air, Coastal Aviation, Auric Air and Zanair. Between them, these carriers offer reliable services to most parts of the country that regularly attract tourists, including Dar es Salaam, Zanzibar, Pemba, Mafia, Kilimanjaro, Arusha, Serengeti, Ngorongoro, Lake Manyara, Mwanza, Rubondo Island, Kigoma and most of the southern parks. There are also regular flights between Kilimanjaro and the Kenyan cities of Mombasa and Nairobi. Several of the airlines now offer a straightforward online booking service. Contact details are as follows:

✈ **Auric Air** www.auricair.com
✈ **Coastal Aviation** www.coastal.co.tz
✈ **Fastjet** www.fastjet.com/tz/en
✈ **Precision Air** www.precisionairtz.com

✈ **Regional Air Services**
www.regionaltanzania.com
✈ **Safari Airlink** www.safariaviation.info
✈ **Zanair** www.zanair.com

BY PUBLIC TRANSPORT Good express coach services, typically travelling at faster than 60km/h, connect Arusha and Moshi to Dar es Salaam and Nairobi (Kenya). **Dar** and **Kilimanjaro Express** are particularly recommended, approaching (although far from attaining) Greyhound-type standards, and they operate several buses daily between Dar es Salaam and Arusha. Express coaches also connect Arusha to Moshi, Lushoto, Tanga, Mwanza and Dar es Salaam.

For long trips on major routes, ensure that you use an 'express bus', which should travel directly between towns, stopping only at a few prescribed places, rather than stopping wherever and whenever a potential passenger is sighted or an existing passenger wants to disembark. Be warned that as far as most touts are concerned, any bus that will give them commission is an express bus, so you are likely to be pressured into getting on to the bus they want you to get on. The best way to counter this is to go to the bus station on the day before you want to travel, and make your enquiries and bookings in advance, when you will be put under less pressure and won't have to worry about keeping an eye on your luggage.

The alternative to buses on most routes is a *dalla-dalla* – a generic name that seems to encompass practically any light public transport. On the whole, dalla-dallas tend to be overcrowded by comparison with buses, and they are more likely to try to overcharge tourists, while the manic driving style results in regular fatal accidents.

When you check bus times, be conscious of the difference between Western time and Swahili time. Many Tanzanians will translate the Swahili time to English without making the 6-hour conversion – in other words, you might be told that a bus leaves at 11.00 when it actually leaves at 05.00. The best way to get around this area of potential misunderstanding is to confirm the time you are quoted in Swahili – for instance ask '*saa moja?*' if you are told a bus leaves at 13.00. See pages 389–90 for more details.

BY PRIVATE SAFARI AND CAR RENTAL The most normal way of getting around northern Tanzania is on an **organised safari** by Land Cruiser, Land Rover or any other similarly hardy 4x4 with high clearance. It is standard procedure for safari companies to provide a driver/guide with a fair knowledge of local wildlife and road conditions, as well as some mechanical expertise. **Self-drive car hire** isn't a particularly attractive or popular option in northern Tanzania (although see page 78 for one option), but it is widely available in Zanzibar.

ACCOMMODATION

The number of hotels in major urban tourist centres such as Zanzibar Town, Arusha and Moshi is quite remarkable. So, too, is the variety in standard and price, which embraces hundreds of simple local guesthouses charging a couple of US dollars a night, as well as fantastic exclusive beach resorts and lodges charging in the ballpark of US$2,000 for a room – and everything in between.

All accommodation listings in this guidebook are placed in one of six categories: exclusive, upmarket, moderate, budget, shoestring, and camping. The purpose of this categorisation is twofold: to break up long hotel listings that span a wide price range, and to help readers isolate the range of hotels that will best suit their budget and taste. The application of categories is not meant to be rigid. Aside from an inevitable element of subjectivity, hotels are categorised on their feel as much as their rates (the prices are quoted anyway), and this is often influenced by the standard of other accommodation options in the same place – a budget option in some safari destinations might cost more than an upmarket lodge in an urban setting!

Before going into more detail about the different accommodation categories, it's worth noting a few potentially misleading quirks in local hotel-speak. In Swahili, the word *hoteli* refers to a restaurant while what we call a hotel is generally called a lodging, guesthouse or *gesti* – so if you ask a Tanzanian to show you a hotel you might well be taken to an eatery. Another local quirk is that most Tanzanian hotels in all ranges refer to a room with an en-suite shower and toilet as being self-contained. Finally, at most hotels in the moderate category or below, a single room will as often as not be one with a three-quarter or double bed, while a double room will be what we call a twin, with two single or double beds. 'B&B' refers to bed and breakfast, 'HB' to half board, 'FB' to full board.

For quick reference, a price-band symbol is appended to all hotel and other accommodation listings. This is usually based on the establishment's cheapest or standard high-season rate for a double unit. Obviously these price bands are very broad, so do also refer to the detailed rates that are given for all but a handful of lodges that only advertise rates upon application. Price bands are as follows:

$	under US$15	$$$$$	US$200–500
$$	US$15–40	$$$$$$	US$500–1,000
$$$	US$40–75	$$$$$$$	US$1,000+
$$$$	US$75–200		

EXCLUSIVE This category does not generally embrace conventional international-style hotels, but rather small and atmospheric tented camps, game lodges and beach resorts catering to the most exclusive end of the market. Lodges in this category typically (but not invariably) contain significantly fewer than 20 accommodation units built and decorated in a style that complements the surrounding environment. The management will generally place a high priority on personalised service and quality food and wine, with the main idea being that guests are exposed to a holistic 24-hour bush or beach experience, rather than just a hotel room and restaurant in a bush/beach location. In several instances, lodges that fall into the exclusive category might be less conventionally luxurious, in terms of air conditioning and the like, than their competitors in the upmarket category. It is the bush experience and not the range of facilities that lends lodges in this category a quality of exclusivity. Rack rates are typically upwards of US$1,000 all-inclusive for a double room, but many cost twice as much as that (with substantial discounts for operators). This is the category to look at if you want authentic, atmospheric bush or beach accommodation and have few financial restrictions.

UPMARKET This category includes most hotels, lodges and resorts that cater almost entirely to the international tourist or business travel market. Hotels in this range would typically be accorded a two- to four-star ranking internationally, and they offer smart accommodation with en-suite facilities, mosquito netting, air conditioning or fans depending on the local climate, and satellite television in cities and some beach resorts. Hotels in this bracket might charge anything from under US$100 to upwards of US$600 for a double room, depending on quality and location, but they are generally at the higher end of that range in national parks and other safari destinations. As a rule, upmarket hotels in areas that see few foreign visitors are far cheaper than equivalent hotels in or around urban tourist centres such as Arusha, which are in turn cheaper than beach hotels and lodges in national parks and game reserves. Room rates for city and beach hotels invariably include breakfast, while at game lodges they will also normally include lunch and dinner. Most package tours use accommodation in this range.

MODERATE In Tanzania, as in many African countries, there is often a wide gap in price and standard between the cheapest hotels geared primarily towards tourists and the best hotels geared primarily towards local travellers and budget travellers. For this reason, the moderate bracket is rather more nebulous than other accommodation categories, essentially consisting of hotels which, for one or another reason, couldn't really be classified as upmarket, but equally are too expensive or of too high quality to be considered budget lodgings. Many places listed in this range are superior local hotels that will suffice in lieu of any genuinely upmarket accommodation in a town that sees relatively few tourists. The category also embraces decent lodges or hotels in recognised tourist areas that charge considerably lower rates than their upmarket competitors, but are clearly a notch or two above the budget category. Hotels in this range normally offer comfortable accommodation in self-contained rooms with hot water, fan and possibly satellite television, and they will have decent restaurants and employ a high proportion of English-speaking staff. Prices for moderate city and beach hotels are generally in the US$50–150 range, more in some game reserves. This is the category to look at if you are travelling privately on a limited or low budget and expect a reasonably high but not luxurious standard of accommodation.

BUDGET Hotels in this category are aimed largely at the local market and definitely don't approach international standards, but are still reasonably clean and comfortable, and a definite cut above the basic guesthouses that proliferate in most towns. Hotels in this bracket will more often than not have a decent restaurant attached, English-speaking staff, and comfortable rooms with en-suite facilities, running cold or possibly hot water, fans (but not air conditioning) and good mosquito netting. The hotels in this category typically charge up to US$50 for a self-contained double room, and may charge as little as US$15–20 in relatively out-of-the-way places. This is the category to look at if you are on a limited budget, but want to avoid total squalor!

SHOESTRING This category is aimed at travellers who want the cheapest possible accommodation irrespective of quality. In most Tanzanian towns, this will amount to a choice of dozens of small private guesthouses, which are almost exclusively used by locals, are remarkably uniform in design, and generally charge below US$15 for an uncluttered room, often a lot less. The typical guesthouse consists of around ten cell-like rooms forming three walls around a central courtyard, with a reception area or restaurant at the front. Toilets are more often than not long-drops. Washing facilities often amount to nothing more than a lockable room and a bucket of water, although an increasing number of guesthouses do have proper showers, and a few have hot water. There are several cheap Church-run guesthouses and hostels in Tanzania, and these are normally also included under the shoestring listings.

CAMPING There are surprisingly few campsites in Tanzania, and those that do exist tend to be in national parks, where camping costs US$30 per person. In Moshi and Arusha, several private sites cater to backpackers and overland trucks. If you ask at moderate hotels in out-of-the-way places, you may sometimes be allowed to camp in their grounds for a small fee.

EATING AND DRINKING

FOOD Most tourists will eat 90% of their meals at game lodges or hotels that cater specifically to tourists and whose kitchens serve Western-style food, ranging in standard from adequate to excellent. Game lodges tend to offer a daily set menu with a limited selection, so it is advisable to have your tour operator specify in advance if you are a vegetarian or have other specific dietary requirements. First-time visitors to Africa might take note that most game lodges in and around the national parks have isolated locations, and driving within the parks is neither permitted nor advisable after dark, so that there is no realistic alternative to eating at your lodge. You will rarely be disappointed.

Most game lodges offer the option of a packaged breakfast and/or lunch box, so that their guests can eat on the trot rather than having to base their game-viewing hours around set meal times. The standard of the packed lunches is rather variable (and in some cases pretty awful) but if your first priority is to see wildlife, then taking a breakfast box in particular allows you to be out during the prime game-viewing hours immediately after sunrise. Packed meals must be ordered the night before you need them. It is best to ask your driver-guide to make this sort of arrangement, rather than doing it yourself.

When you are staying in towns such as Arusha and Moshi, there is a fair selection of eating-out options. Indian eateries are particularly numerous in most towns, thanks to the high resident Indian population, and good continental restaurants and pizzerias are also well represented. Seafood is excellent on the coast. Options tend to be more limited in smaller towns such as Lushoto, and very basic in villages off the main tourist trail. A selection of the better restaurants in each town is listed in the main part of the guide.

As for the local cuisine, it tends to consist of a bland stew eaten with one of four staples: rice, chapati, *ugali* or *batoke*. Ugali is a stiff maize porridge eaten throughout sub-Saharan Africa. Batoke or *matoke* is cooked plantain, served boiled or in a mushy heap. In the Lake Victoria region, batoke replaces ugali as the staple food. The most common stews are chicken, beef, goat and beans, and the meat is often rather tough. In coastal towns and around the great lakes, whole fried fish is a welcome change. The distinctive Swahili cuisine of the coast makes generous use of coconut milk and is far more spiced than other Tanzanian food.

Mandaazi, the local equivalent of doughnuts, are tasty when freshly cooked. They are served at hotelis and sold at markets. You can eat cheaply at stalls around markets and bus stations. Goat kebabs, fried chicken, grilled groundnuts and potato chips are often freshly cooked and sold in these places. A very popular and filling (though not exactly healthy) street dish throughout Tanzania is *chipsi mayai*, which essentially consists of potato chips cooked in an omelette-like mix of eggs (mayai).

KiSwahili names for various foods are given on pages 390–1.

DRINK The most widely drunk beverage is *chai*, a sweet tea where all ingredients are boiled together in a pot. Along the coast chai is often flavoured with spices such as ginger. In some places chai is served *ya rangi* or black; in others *maziwa* or milky. Sodas such as Coke, Pepsi, Sprite and Fanta are widely available, and normally cost less than US$0.50 in outlets geared towards locals, and up to five times that price in tourist-oriented lodges. In large towns you can often get fresh fruit juice. On the coast and in some parts of the interior, the most refreshing, healthy and inexpensive drink is coconut water, sold by street vendors who will decapitate the young coconut of your choice to create a natural cup, from which the juice can be sipped. Tap water in Tanzania is often dodgy, and most travellers try to stick to mineral water, which comes in 1.5-litre bottles that cost a few hundred shillings in supermarkets in Arusha but are very overpriced at game lodges – it is advisable to stock up with a dozen bottles or so before your safari leaves Arusha.

TRADITIONAL MBEGE BANANA BEER   *Emma Thomson*

This party brew is prepared for many different Chagga ceremonies, but it is always drunk from a dried squash plant that has been hollowed out to form an enormous chalice, with the village landlord's clan name engraved upon it. Below is a rough recipe, as the measurements are only approximate.

INGREDIENTS
1kg mashed banana
1 litre water
1kg finger millet

METHOD Boil bananas in water until they turn red, and then cover for three days.

Meanwhile, wash the finger millet, cover and leave in a wet, warm and dark place for three to four days until the millet begins to sprout. Then grind the millet into flour.

From this, make porridge by mixing two parts flour to one part water. Next add ten parts of the boiled banana to one part porridge, mix and cover until the next day.

Let the celebrations begin. (The longer you leave it, the stronger the brew.)

The two main alcoholic drinks are beer and *konyagi*, a spirit made from sugarcane. It tastes a bit strange on its own, but it mixes well and is very cheap. The local Safari lager used to be appalling, but since the national brewery was taken over by South African Breweries a few years ago there has been a dramatic improvement not only in the quality of Safari, but also in the selection of other brands available. Around ten different lager beers are now available, of which Tusker, Castle, Kilimanjaro and Serengeti seem to be the most popular. All beers come in 500ml bottles and cost anything from US$1 at a local bar to US$5 at the most upmarket hotels, although some lodges also serve smaller 330ml cans. A variety of imported spirits are available in larger towns. A varied selection of wines, usually South African in origin, is available at most mid-range and upmarket lodges and hotels, and they are generally quite reasonably priced by international standards.

PUBLIC HOLIDAYS

Tourists visiting Tanzania should take note of public holidays, since all banks, forex bureaux and government offices will be closed. In addition to Good Friday, Easter Monday, Eid-al-Fitr, Islamic New Year and the Prophet's Birthday, which fall on different dates every year, the following public holidays are taken in Tanzania:

1 January	New Year's Day
12 January	Zanzibar Revolution Day
7 April	Karume Day (anniversary of the assassination of Vice President Abeid Amani Karume in 1972)
26 April	Union Day (anniversary of the union between Tanganyika and Zanzibar)
1 May	International Workers' Day

7 July	Saba Saba (Peasants') Day
8 August	Nane Nane (Farmers') Day
14 October	Nyerere Memorial Day
9 December	Independence Day
25 December	Christmas Day
26 December	Boxing Day

SHOPPING

Until a few years ago it was difficult to buy anything much in Tanzania. One of my most vivid memories of Dar es Salaam in 1986 was walking into a general store where a lone shelf of teaspoons was the only stock. Things have improved greatly since then. In most large towns a fair range of imported goods is available, although prices are often inflated. If you have any very specific needs – unusual medications, for instance – bring them with you. Toilet roll, soap, toothpaste, pens, batteries and locally produced food are widely available. Shopping hours are normally 08.30 to 16.30, with a lunch break between 13.00 and 14.00, but *dukas*, the stalls you see around markets or lining roads, are cheaper than proper shops and stay open for longer hours.

CURIOS A variety of items specifically aimed at tourists is available: Makonde carvings, Tingatinga paintings (see box, page 136), batiks, musical instruments, wooden spoons and various soapstone and malachite knick-knacks. Arusha is the best place to shop for curios, as prices are competitive and the quality is good. Prices in shops are fixed, but you may be able to negotiate a discount. At curio stalls, haggling is necessary. Unless you are good at this, and know the going rate for the thing you want to buy, then expect to pay more than you would in a shop. The colourful *vitenge* (the singular of this is *kitenge*) worn by most Tanzanian women can be picked up cheaply at any market in the country.

MEDIA AND COMMUNICATIONS

NEWSPAPERS The English-language *Daily News* (*www.dailynews.co.tz*), *Citizen* (*www.thecitizen.co.tz*) and *Guardian* (*www.guardian.co.tz*), available in all major towns, carry a fair bit of syndicated international news, and the local news can also make for interesting reading. The Kenyan *Daily Nation* (*www.nation.co.ke*), available in Arusha and a few other towns, is slightly better. The excellent *East African* (*www.theeastafrican.co.ke*) is a weekly newspaper published in Kenya but distributed throughout the three countries to which it dedicates roughly equal coverage, ie: Kenya, Tanzania and Uganda. Stalls and vendors around the Clock Tower in Arusha sometimes sell *Time* and *Newsweek*, as well as a variety of European, British and American papers.

TELEPHONES
Phone calls If you want to make an international phone call or send a fax, a TCC Extelcomms centre can be found in most large towns. Calls are cheap by international standards, and some Extelcomms centres will receive as well as send faxes. The costlier but more convenient alternative is to phone directly from your lodge or hotel. If you are carrying a mobile phone that receives international calls, the satellite network is pretty good in and around towns but rather less so in more remote parts of the game reserves.

Mobile phones If you bring a mobile phone (commonly referred to as 'cell phone' in Tanzania), it's emphatically worth the minor investment in a Tanzanian SIM card (which costs less than US$1 and gives you a local number), airtime cards (available in a wide selection of units from Tsh500 to Tsh50,000), and a data package allowing you cheap and widespread internet access. International text messages are very cheap (US$1 will buy you around a dozen text messages to anywhere in the world) and international calls work out at around US$1 for 3–4 minutes. For internet access and emails, a 3GB data package, valid for 30 days, costs a wallet-friendly US$15. By contrast, you'll rack up a hefty bill if you use your home phone number for calls and/or messages, since in most instances these are charged at international rates out of your home country, even when you phone home. The most useful providers are Airtel and Vodacom, whose SIM and airtime cards can be bought at specialist Airtel or Vodacom outlets (there are several in Zanzibar Town, Arusha and Moshi) or at numerous other small shops displaying the ubiquitous Vodacom and Airtel stickers. Some travellers bring an old, spare mobile phone to use with their Tanzanian SIM card, to have the best of both worlds.

Network reception is increasingly widespread, even in the national parks. Many mobile numbers serve as fixed lines because the land lines are so bad in Tanzania – indeed, there are now more than 100 mobile phones in the country for every landline! Legally, you have to register a new SIM or the number may be deactivated after a few days. If you buy the SIM card direct from a Vodacom or Airtel shop you can register it on the spot, provided you bring along your passport. Mobile money is getting bigger in East Africa, including for paying for flights. It's probably of marginal interest to tourists at this stage, but could potentially evolve into the tourist mainstream over the next few years.

INTERNET AND EMAIL The post-millennial spread of internet use in Africa has been remarkable, and the existence of email represents a real communications revolution on a continent where fixed telephone lines tend to be unreliable and expensive. Internet and email have caught on particularly quickly in Tanzania, and internet cafés are prolific and affordable in most major urban tourist centres. The servers are usually quite fast, although not comparable to international broadband, and rates are very affordable. Email and internet access is patchier and more erratic in most game reserves and national parks. The easiest and most reliable way to stay online on a more-or-less ongoing basis to inset a local SIM card (see above) in your phone and load it up with data. Failing that, an increasing number of game lodges or camps now offer free Wi-Fi to their clients, though some still charge high rates to discourage abuse of the facility.

CULTURAL ETIQUETTE

Tanzania has perhaps the most egalitarian and tolerant mood of any African country that I've visited. As a generalisation, Tanzanians tend to treat visitors with a dignified reserve, something that many Westerners mistake for a stand-offish attitude, but in my opinion is more indicative of a respect both for our culture and their own. Granted, dignified probably won't be the adjective that leaps to mind if your first interaction with Tanzanians comes from the pestilence of touts that hang around bus stations in Arusha or Moshi, or somewhere similar. But then in most poor countries, you'll find that people who make a living on the fringe of the tourist industry tend to be pushy and occasionally confrontational in their dealings – from their perspective, they probably have to be in order to make a living. But I do think that anybody who spends time travelling in Tanzania will recognise the behaviour of touts to be wholly unrepresentative of what is essentially a conservative, unhurried and undemonstrative society.

On the whole, you would have to do something pretty outrageous to commit a serious faux pas in Tanzania. But, like any country, Tanzania does have its rules of etiquette, and while allowances will always be made for tourists, there is some value in ensuring that they are not made too frequently.

GENERAL CONDUCT Perhaps the most important single point of etiquette to be grasped by visitors to Tanzania is the social importance of formal greetings. Tanzanians tend to greet each other elaborately, and if you want to make a good impression on somebody who speaks English, whether they be a waiter or a shop assistant (and especially if they work in a government department), you would do well to follow suit. When you need to ask somebody directions, it is rude to blunder straight into interrogative mode without first exchanging greetings. With Tanzanians who don't speak English, the greeting '*Jambo*' delivered with a smile and a nod of the head will be adequate.

Whenever I visit Tanzania after travelling elsewhere in Africa, I am struck afresh by how readily people greet passing strangers, particularly in rural areas. In Tanzania, this greeting doesn't normally take the form of a shrieked '*Mzungu*' (or whatever local term is used for a white person), or a 'Give me money', something that you become accustomed to in some African countries. On the contrary, in Tanzania adults will normally greet tourists with a cheerful '*Jambo*', and children with a subdued '*Shikamu*' (a greeting reserved for elders). I find this to be a very charming quality in Tanzanian society, one that is worth reinforcing by learning a few simple Swahili greetings (pages 388–9).

Among Tanzanians, it is considered poor taste to display certain emotions publicly. Affection is one such emotion: it is frowned upon for members of the opposite sex to hold hands publicly, and kissing or embracing would be seriously offensive. Oddly, it is quite normal for friends of the same sex to walk around hand in hand. Male travellers who get into a long discussion with a male Tanzanian shouldn't be surprised if that person clasps them by the hand and retains a firm grip on their hand for several minutes. This is a warm gesture, one particularly appropriate when the person wants to make a point with which you might disagree. On the subject of intra-gender relations, homosexuality is as good as taboo in Tanzania, to the extent that it would require some pretty overt behaviour for it to occur to anybody to take offence.

It is also considered bad form to show anger publicly. It is difficult to know where to draw the line here though because many touts positively invite an aggressive response, and I doubt that many people who travel independently in Tanzania will get by without the occasional display of impatience. Frankly, I doubt that many bystanders would take umbrage if you responded to a pushy tout with a display of anger, if only because the tout's behaviour itself goes against the grain of Tanzanian society. By contrast, losing your temper will almost certainly be counterproductive when dealing with obtuse officials, dopey waiters and hotel employees, or unco-operative safari drivers.

MUSLIM CUSTOMS Visitors should be aware of the strong Muslim element in Tanzania, particularly along the coast and in Zanzibar. In Muslim society, it is insulting to use your left hand to pass or receive something or when shaking

EATING THE NEWS   *Emma Thomson*

In the same way that it is rude not to greet a Tanzanian with the standard 'Hujambo' or 'Mambo', no Maasai will encounter another without going through the amusing paces of a ritual known as 'eating the news'. It is basically a quick catch-up on the health of the family, state of the livestock, etc. The aim is to race through these formalities as fast as possible so you can continue with the rest of the conversation. Bizarrely, even if you are on your deathbed, you must reply that all is well to maintain the front of warrior strength integral to Maasai psychology. Give it a go and they will be bowled over!

Man:	*Yeyio …*	Mother …
Woman:	*Eeu …*	Yes …
Man:	*Takwenya!*	I greet you!
Woman:	*Iko! Apaayia …*	Hello! Warrior …
Man:	*Ooe …*	Yes …
Woman:	*Supai!*	I greet you!
Man:	*Epa!*	Hello!
Woman:	*Ayia, koree indae?*	OK, how are you?
Man:	*Kitii …*	We are around …
Woman:	*Ee*	Uh-huh
Man:	*Kira sedan*	We are fine
Woman:	*Ee*	Uh-huh
Man:	*Kira biot*	We are healthy
Woman:	*Ee*	Uh-huh
Man:	*Supat inkera*	The children are well
Woman:	*Ee*	Uh-huh
Man:	*Biot inkishu*	The cattle are healthy
Woman:	*Ee*	Uh-huh
Man:	*Metii endoki torono*	There are no problems
Woman:	*Ayia*	OK
Woman:	*Kira siyook …*	As for us …
Man:	*Ee*	Uh-huh
Woman:	*Mekimweyaa*	We are not sick
Man:	*Ee*	Uh-huh
Woman:	*Biot inkera*	The children are healthy
Man:	*Ee*	Uh-huh
Woman:	*Supat indare*	The goats are well
Man:	*Ee*	Uh-huh
Woman:	*Ayia*	OK
Man:	*Ayia, enda serian*	OK, that's good news

hands. If you eat with your fingers, it is also customary to use the right hand only. Even those of us who are naturally right-handed will occasionally need to remind ourselves of this (it may happen, for instance, that you are carrying something in your right hand and so hand money to a shopkeeper with your left). For left-handed travellers, it will require a constant effort. In traditional Muslim societies it is offensive for women to expose their knees or shoulders, a custom that ought to be taken on board by female travellers, especially on parts of the coast where tourists remain a relative novelty.

A surprisingly frequent cause of friction on safaris is the somewhat entrepreneurial Maasai attitude to being photographed by tourists. It's an issue that frequently leads visitors to conclude that the Maasai are 'too commercialised', a misguided allegation that reflects Western misconceptions and prejudices about Africa far more than it does any aspect of modern Maasai culture.

The root cause of this misunderstanding is a Western tendency to distinguish between 'authentic' traditional practices and more cosmopolitan influences, rather than recognising both as equally valid components in the ever-evolving hybrid that is modern African culture. To give one clearly identifiable example, you'll find that most Africans are devout Christians or Muslims, yet many also simultaneously adhere to an apparently conflicting traditional belief system. On the streets of Arusha, suited businessmen yapping into mobile phones and trendy safari guides brush past traditional Maasai street hawkers, a co-existence of modernity and traditionalism that seems contradictory to outsiders but is unremarkable to the country's inhabitants. What's more, the same slick businessmen or casually dressed safari guides might well visit traditional healers on occasion, or return home for tribal ceremonies dressed in traditional attire, to all outward purposes indistinguishable from less 'Westernised' relatives who always dress that way.

The point is that the Maasai, like us, are living in the 21st century, and a variety of external factors – among them, population growth, the gazetting of traditional grazing land as national parks, exposure to other Tanzanian cultures and exotic religions, the creation of a cash economy – have combined to ensure that their culture is not a static museum piece, but a dynamic, modern entity.

Another point of confusion is the only direct exposure to Maasai culture experienced by most visitors takes place in 'cultural villages' where tourists wander around as they please and photograph whomever they like after paying a fixed fee. There is nothing wrong with these villages, and much that is commendable about them, but they should be approached with realistic expectations – essentially, as cottage industries whose inhabitants derive a substantial portion of their living from tourist visits. And most such villages are long-standing Maasai settlements whose inhabitants live a largely traditional lifestyle. Indeed, it is we, the tourists, who are the distorting factor in their behaviour.

TIPPING AND GUIDES The question of when to tip and when not to tip can be difficult in a foreign country. In Tanzania, it is customary to tip your guide at the end of a safari and/or a Kilimanjaro climb, as well as any cooks and porters who accompany you. A figure of roughly US$10 per recipient per day is the benchmark, although it is advisable to check this with your safari company in advance. I see no reason why you shouldn't give a bigger or smaller tip based on the quality of service. Bear in mind, however, that most guides, cooks and porters receive nominal salaries, which means that they are largely dependent on tips for their income. It would be mean not to leave a reasonable tip in any but the most exceptional of circumstances.

In some African countries, it is difficult to travel anywhere without being latched on to by a self-appointed guide, who will often expect a tip over and above any agreed fee. This sort of thing is comparatively unusual in Tanzania, but if you do take on a freelance guide, then it is advisable to clarify in advance that whatever price you agree is final and inclusive of a tip. By contrast, any guide who is given to you by a

Make no mistake, were you to wander off into a Maasai boma that doesn't routinely deal with tourists, the odds are that its inhabitants would simply refuse to be photographed no matter what payment you offered. What's more, you might well find a spear dangling from the end of your lens if you don't respect their wishes. So concluding that the Maasai are 'too commercialised' on the basis of an inherently contrived form of interaction is as daft as walking into a London shop and concluding that the English are 'too commercialised' because the assistant expects you to pay for the items you select.

There is a deeper irony to this cultural misunderstanding. Here we have well-off visitors from media-obsessed, materialistic Europe or North America fiddling with their Blackberries and video cameras, straightening their custom-bought safari outfits, and planning the diet they'll go on back home to compensate for the endless lodge buffets. They are confronted by a culture as resilient, non-materialistic and ascetic as that of the Maasai, and they accuse it with a straight face of being 'commercialised'. This genuinely concerns me: are we so culture bound, so riddled with romantic expectations about how the Maasai should behave, that any slight deviation from these preconceptions prevents us from seeing things for what they are?

So let's start again. The Maasai are proud and dramatically attired pastoralists who adhere almost entirely to the traditions of their forefathers. They fascinate us, but being the bunch of gadget-obsessed wazungu we are, our response is not to absorb their presence or to try to communicate with them, but to run around thrusting cameras in their faces. And this, I would imagine, irritates the hell out of those Maasai who happen to live along main tourist circuits, so they decide not to let tourists photograph them except for a fee or in the context of an organised tourist village. In theory, everybody should be happy. In practice, we somehow construe this reasonable attempt by relatively poor people to make a bit of honest money as rampant commercialism. OK, I recognise this is a bit simplistic, but we create the demand, the Maasai satisfy it, and if we pay to do so, that's just good capitalism, something the West has always been keen to encourage in Africa. If you don't like it, save space on your memory card and buy a postcard – in all honesty, you'll probably get a lot more from meeting these charismatic people if you leave your camera behind and enjoy the moment!

company should most definitely be tipped, as tips will probably be their main source of income. In Zanzibar and Arusha, a freelance guide may insist upon helping you find a hotel room, in which case they will be given a commission by the hotel, so there is no reason for you to provide an additional tip. In any case, from the guide's point of view, finding you a room is merely the first step in trying to hook you for a safari or a spice tour, or something else that will earn a larger commission.

It is not customary to tip for service in local bars and hotelis, although you may sometimes want to leave a tip (in fact, given the difficulty of finding change in Tanzania, you may practically be forced into doing this in some circumstances). A tip of 5% would be very acceptable and 10% generous. Generally any restaurant that caters primarily to tourists and to wealthy Tanzanian residents will automatically add a service charge to the bill. Since the government claims the lion's share of any formal service charge, it would still be reasonable to reward good service with a genuine tip.

TAKING PHOTOS It is unacceptable to photograph local people in Tanzania without permission, and many people will refuse to pose or will ask for a donation. In such circumstances, don't try to sneak photographs as you might get yourself into trouble. Even the most willing subject will often pose stiffly when a camera is pointed at them; relax them by making a joke, and take a few shots in quick succession to improve the odds of capturing a natural pose.

BARGAINING Tourists to Tanzania will sometimes need to bargain over prices, but generally this need exists only in reasonably predictable circumstances, for instance when chartering a private taxi, organising a guide, agreeing a price for a safari or mountain trek, or buying curios and to a lesser extent other market produce. Prices in hotels, restaurants and shops are generally fixed, and overcharging in such places is too unusual for it to be worth challenging a price unless it is blatantly ridiculous.

You may well be overcharged at some point in Tanzania, but it is important to keep this in perspective. After a couple of bad experiences, some travellers start to haggle with everybody from hotel owners to old women selling fruit by the side of the road, often accompanying their negotiations with aggressive accusations of dishonesty. Unfortunately, it is sometimes necessary to fall back on aggressive posturing in order to determine a fair price, but such behaviour is also very unfair on those people who are forthright and honest in their dealings with tourists. It's a question of finding the right balance, or better still looking for other ways of dealing with the problem.

The main instance where bargaining is essential is when buying curios. What should be understood, however, is that the fact a curio seller is open to negotiation does not mean that you were initially being overcharged or ripped off. Curio sellers will generally quote a price knowing full well that you are going to bargain it down (they'd probably be startled if you didn't) and it is not necessary to respond aggressively or in an accusatory manner. It is impossible to say by how much you should bargain the initial price down. Some people say that you should offer half the asking price and be prepared to settle at around two-thirds, but my experience is that curio sellers are far more whimsical than such advice allows for. The sensible approach, if you want to get a feel for prices, is to ask the price of similar items at a few different stalls before you actually contemplate buying anything.

In fruit and vegetable markets and stalls, bargaining is the norm, even between locals, and the healthiest approach to this sort of haggling is to view it as an enjoyable part of the African experience. There will normally be an accepted price band for any particular commodity. To find out what it is, listen to what other people pay and try a few stalls. A ludicrously inflated price will always drop the moment you walk away. When buying fruit and vegetables, a good way to feel out the situation is to ask for a bulk discount or a few extra items thrown in. And bear in mind that when somebody is reluctant to bargain, it may be because they asked a fair price in the first place.

A final point to consider on the subject of overcharging and bargaining is that it is the fact of being overcharged that annoys; the amount itself is generally of little consequence in the wider context of a trip to Tanzania. Without for a moment wanting to suggest that travellers should routinely allow themselves to be overcharged, I do feel there are occasions when we should pause to look at the bigger picture. If you find yourself quibbling over a pittance with an old lady selling a few piles of fruit by the roadside, you might perhaps bear in mind that the notion of a fixed price is a very Western one. When somebody is desperate enough for money, or afraid that their perishable goods might not last another day, it may well be possible to push them down to a lower price than they would normally accept. In such circumstances, I see nothing wrong with erring on the side of generosity.

SEND US YOUR SNAPS!

We'd love to follow your adventures using our *Northern Tanzania* guide – why not send us your photos and stories via Twitter (*@BradtGuides*) and Instagram (*@bradtguides*) using the hashtag #northerntanzania. Alternatively, you can upload your photos directly to the gallery on the northern Tanzania destination page via our website (*www.bradtguides.com*).

4

Health

With Dr Felicity Nicholson

Tanzania, like most parts of Africa, is home to several tropical diseases unfamiliar to people living in more temperate and sanitary climates. However, with adequate preparation, and a sensible attitude to malaria prevention, the chances of serious mishap are small. To put this in perspective, your greatest concern after malaria should not be the combined exotica of venomous snakes, stampeding wildlife, gun-happy soldiers or the Ebola virus, but something altogether more mundane: a road accident.

Private clinics, hospitals and pharmacies can be found in most large towns, and doctors generally speak good English. Consultation fees and laboratory tests are inexpensive when compared with most Western countries, so if you do fall sick, don't allow financial considerations to dissuade you from seeking medical help. Commonly required medicines such as broad-spectrum antibiotics, painkillers, asthma inhalers and various antimalarial treatments are widely available. If you are on any short-term medication prior to departure, or you have specific needs relating to a less common medical condition (for instance if you are allergic to bee stings or nuts), then bring necessary treatment with you.

PREPARATIONS

Sensible preparation will go a long way to ensuring your trip goes smoothly. Particularly for first-time visitors to Africa, this includes a visit to a travel clinic to discuss matters such as vaccinations and malaria prevention. A full list of travel clinic websites worldwide is available at www.itsm.org, and other useful websites for prospective travellers include www.nathnac.org/ds/map_world.aspx and www.netdoctor.co.uk/travel. The Bradt website now carries a health section online (*www.bradtguides.com/africahealth*) to help travellers prepare for their African trip, elaborating on most points raised below, but the following summary points are worth emphasising:

- Don't travel without comprehensive medical **travel insurance** that will fly you home in an emergency.
- Make sure all your **immunisations** are up to date. Tanzania is not considered a risk for yellow fever but a yellow-fever certificate is required if you are coming from a yellow fever endemic zone or are transiting for more than 12 hours in an airport in a yellow fever endemic zone. It's also reckless to travel in the tropics without being up to date on tetanus, polio and diphtheria (now given as an all-in-one vaccine, Revaxis), typhoid and hepatitis A. Immunisation against hepatitis B, rabies and tuberculosis may also be recommended.
- The biggest health threat is **malaria**. There is no vaccine against this mosquito-borne disease, but a variety of preventative drugs is available, including

mefloquine, Malarone and the antibiotic doxycycline. The start and stop times of the malaria tablets vary and can be as little as two days before and seven days after (Malarone) to two to three weeks before and four weeks after (mefloquine). The most suitable choice of drug varies depending on the individual and the country they are visiting, so visit your GP or a travel clinic for medical advice. If you will be spending a long time in Africa, and expect to visit remote areas, be aware that no preventative drug is 100% effective, so carry a cure too. It is also worth noting that no homeopathic prophylactic for malaria exists, nor can any traveller acquire effective resistance to malaria. Those who don't make use of preventative drugs risk their life in a manner that is both foolish and unnecessary.

- Though advised for everyone, a **pre-exposure rabies vaccination**, involving three doses taken over a minimum of 21 days, is particularly important if you intend to have contact with animals, or are likely to be 24 hours away from medical help.

- Anybody travelling away from major centres should carry a **personal first-aid kit**. Contents might include a good drying antiseptic (eg: iodine or potassium permanganate), Band-Aids, suncream, insect repellent, aspirin or paracetamol, antifungal cream (eg: Canesten), ciprofloxacin or norfloxacin (for severe diarrhoea), antibiotic eye drops, tweezers, condoms or femidoms, a digital thermometer and a needle-and-syringe kit with accompanying letter from a healthcare professional.

- Bring any **drugs or devices relating to known medical conditions** with you. That applies both to those who are on medication prior to departure, and those who are, for instance, allergic to bee stings, or are prone to attacks of asthma. You should also bring a copy of the prescription with you and ensure that medication is clearly labelled with your name.

- Prolonged immobility on long-haul flights can result in **deep-vein thrombosis (DVT)**, which can be dangerous if the clot travels to the lungs to cause pulmonary embolus. The risk increases with age, and is higher in obese or pregnant travellers, heavy smokers, those taller than 6ft/1.8m or shorter than 5ft/1.5m, and anybody with a history of clots, recent major operation or varicose veins surgery, cancer, a stroke or heart disease. If any of these criteria apply, consult a doctor before you travel.

COMMON MEDICAL PROBLEMS

MALARIA This potentially fatal disease is widespread in tropical Africa. Within Tanzania, it is possible to catch malaria almost anywhere below the 2,000m contour, a category that incorporates all parts of the country except the upper slopes of high mountains such as Kilimanjaro and Meru. In mid-altitude locations, malaria is largely but not entirely seasonal, with the highest risk occurring during the rainy season. Moist and low-lying areas such as the coast are high risk throughout the year, but the risk is greatest during the rainy season. As such, all travellers to Tanzania should assume that they will be exposed to malaria and take suitable preventative drugs and other precautions throughout their trip.

Since no malaria prophylactic is 100% effective, it makes sense to take all reasonable precautions against being bitten by the nocturnal *Anopheles* mosquitoes that transmit the disease (see box, page 112). Malaria usually manifests within two weeks of transmission, but it can take months, which means that short-stay visitors are most likely to experience symptoms after they return home. These typically include a rapid rise in temperature (over 38°C), and any combination of a headache, flu-like aches and pains, a general sense of disorientation, and possibly even nausea and diarrhoea. The earlier malaria is detected, the better it usually responds to treatment. So if you display possible symptoms anything from seven days after being in a malaria area, *get to a doctor or clinic immediately.* A simple test is usually adequate to determine whether you have malaria. However, you need three negative tests to be sure that you don't have malaria so it may be necessary to stay around for further tests. And while experts differ on the question of self-diagnosis and self-treatment, the reality is that if you think you have malaria and are not within easy reach of a doctor, it would be wisest to start treatment.

TRAVELLERS' DIARRHOEA Many visitors to unfamiliar destinations suffer a dose of travellers' diarrhoea, usually as a result of imbibing contaminated food or water. Rule one in avoiding diarrhoea and other sanitation-related diseases is arguably to wash your hands regularly, particularly before snacks and meals, and after handling money. As for what food you can safely eat, a useful maxim is: PEEL IT, BOIL IT, COOK IT OR FORGET IT. This means that fruit you have washed and peeled yourself should be safe, as should hot cooked foods. However, raw foods, cold cooked foods, salads, fruit salads prepared by others, ice cream and ice are all risky. It is rarer to get sick from drinking contaminated water but it happens, so stick to bottled water, which is widely available.

If you suffer a bout of diarrhoea, it is dehydration that makes you feel awful, so drink lots of water and other clear fluids. These can be infused with sachets of oral rehydration salts, though any dilute mixture of sugar and salt in water will do you good, for instance a bottled soda with a pinch of salt. If diarrhoea persists beyond a couple of days, it is possible it is a symptom of a more serious sanitation-related illness (typhoid, cholera, hepatitis, dysentery, worms, etc), so get to a doctor. If the diarrhoea is greasy and bulky, and is accompanied by sulphurous (eggy) burps, one likely cause is giardia, which is best treated with tinidazole (four x 500mg in one dose, repeated seven days later if symptoms persist).

BILHARZIA Also known as schistosomiasis, bilharzia is an unpleasant parasitic disease transmitted by freshwater snails most often associated with reedy shores where there is lots of water weed. It cannot be caught in hotel swimming pools, but should be assumed to be present in any freshwater river, pond, lake or similar habitat, probably even those advertised as 'bilharzia free'. The riskiest shores will be within 200m of villages or other places where infected people use water, wash clothes, etc. Ideally, however, you should avoid swimming in any fresh water other than an artificial pool. If you do swim, you'll reduce the risk by applying DEET insect repellent first, staying in the water for under 10 minutes, and drying off vigorously with a towel. Bilharzia is often asymptomatic in its early stages, but some people experience an intense immune reaction, including fever, cough, abdominal pain and an itching rash, around four to six weeks after infection. Later symptoms vary but often include a general feeling of tiredness and lethargy. Bilharzia is difficult to diagnose, but it can be tested for at specialist travel clinics, ideally at least six weeks after likely exposure. Fortunately, it is easy to treat at present.

RABIES This deadly disease can be carried by any mammal and is usually transmitted to humans via a bite or scratch. Beware village dogs and habituated monkeys, but assume that *any* mammal that bites or scratches you (or even licks you over intact skin) might be rabid. First, scrub the wound with soap under a running tap, or while pouring water from a jug, then pour on a strong iodine or

LONG-HAUL FLIGHTS, CLOTS AND DVT   *Dr Felicity Nicholson*

Any prolonged immobility, including travel by land or air, can result in deep-vein thrombosis (DVT) with the risk of embolus to the lungs. Certain factors can increase the risk and these include:

- History of DVT or pulmonary embolism
- Recent surgery to pelvic region or legs
- Cancer
- Stroke
- Heart disease
- Inherited tendency to clot (thrombophilia)
- Obesity
- Pregnancy
- Hormone therapy
- Older age
- Being over 6ft or under 5ft

A deep-vein thrombosis causes painful swelling and redness of the calf or sometimes the thigh. It is only dangerous if a clot travels to the lungs (pulmonary embolus). Symptoms of a pulmonary embolus (PE) – which commonly start three to ten days after a long flight – include chest pain, shortness of breath, and sometimes coughing up small amounts of blood. Anyone who thinks that they might have a DVT needs to see a doctor immediately.

PREVENTION OF DVT
- Wear loose comfortable clothing
- Do anti-DVT exercises and move around when possible
- Drink plenty of fluids during the flight
- Avoid taking sleeping pills unless you are able to lie flat
- Avoid excessive tea, coffee and alcohol
- Consider wearing flight socks or support stockings (*www.leghealthwarehouse.com*)

If you think you are at increased risk of a clot, ask your doctor if it is safe to travel.

---

alcohol solution, which will guard against infections and might reduce the risk of the rabies virus entering the body. Whether or not you underwent pre-exposure vaccination, it is vital to obtain post-exposure prophylaxis as soon as possible after the incident. However, the treatment needed is much simpler and will be available in Tanzania if you have had the vaccine prior to exposure whereas that is not usually the case of you have not had the vaccine before. Death from rabies is probably one of the worst ways to go, and once you show symptoms it is too late to do anything – the mortality rate is 100%.

TETANUS Tetanus is caught through deep dirty wounds, including animal bites, so ensure that such wounds are thoroughly cleaned. Immunisation protects for ten years, provided you don't have an overwhelming number of tetanus bacteria on board. If you haven't had a tetanus shot in ten years, or you are unsure, get a booster immediately.

HIV/AIDS Rates of HIV/AIDS infection are high in most parts of Africa, and other sexually transmitted diseases are rife. Condoms (or femidoms) greatly reduce the risk of transmission.

TICK BITES Ticks in Africa are not the rampant disease transmitters that they are in the Americas, but they may spread tickbite fever along with a few dangerous rarities. They should ideally be removed complete as soon as possible to reduce the chance of infection. The best way to do this is to grasp the tick with your finger nails as close to your body as possible, and pull it away steadily and firmly at right angles to your skin (do not jerk or twist it). If possible douse the wound with alcohol (any spirit will do) or iodine. If you are travelling with small children, remember to check their heads, and particularly behind the ears, for ticks. Spreading redness around the bite and/or fever and/or aching joints after a tick bite imply that you have an infection that requires antibiotic treatment, so seek advice.

SKIN INFECTIONS Any mosquito bite or small nick is an opportunity for a skin infection in warm humid climates, so clean and cover the slightest wound in a good drying antiseptic such as dilute iodine, potassium permanganate or crystal (or gentian) violet. Prickly heat, most likely to be contracted at the humid coast, is a fine pimply rash that can be alleviated by cool showers, dabbing (not rubbing) dry and talc, and sleeping naked under a fan or in an air-conditioned room. Fungal infections also get a hold easily in hot moist climates, so wear 100% cotton socks and underwear and shower frequently.

EYE PROBLEMS Bacterial conjunctivitis (pink eye) is a common infection in Africa, particularly for contact-lens wearers. Symptoms are sore, gritty eyelids that often stick closed in the morning. They will need treatment with antibiotic drops or ointment. Lesser eye irritation should settle with bathing in salt water and keeping the eyes shaded. If an insect flies into your eye, extract it with great care, ensuring you do not crush or damage it, otherwise you may get a nastily inflamed eye from toxins secreted by the creature.

SUNSTROKE AND DEHYDRATION Overexposure to the sun can lead to short-term sunburn or sunstroke, and increases the long-term risk of skin cancer. Wear a T-shirt and waterproof sunscreen when swimming. When visiting outdoor historical sites or walking in the direct sun, cover up with long, loose clothes, wear a hat, and use sunscreen. The glare and the dust can be hard on the eyes, so bring UV-protecting sunglasses. A less direct effect of the tropical heat is dehydration, so drink more fluids than you would at home.

UNUSUAL MEDICAL PROBLEMS

SNAKE AND OTHER BITES All manner of venomous snakes occur in Tanzania, but they are unlikely to be encountered since they generally slither away when they sense the seismic vibrations made by a walking person. You should be most alert to snakes on rocky slopes and cliffs, particularly where you risk putting your hand on a ledge that you can't see. Rocky areas are the favoured habitat of the puff adder, which is not an especially venomous snake but is potentially lethal and unusual in that it won't always move off in response to human footsteps. Wearing good boots when walking in the bush will protect against the 50% of snake bites that occur below the ankle, and long trousers will help deflect bites higher up on the leg,

The *Anopheles* mosquitoes that spread malaria are active at dusk and after dark. Most bites can thus be avoided by covering up at night. This means donning a long-sleeved shirt, trousers and socks from around 30 minutes before dusk until you retire to bed, and applying a DEET-based insect repellent to any exposed flesh. It is best to sleep under a net, or in an air-conditioned room, though burning a mosquito coil and/or sleeping under a fan will also reduce (though not entirely eliminate) bites. Travel clinics usually sell a good range of nets and repellents, as well as Permethrin treatment kits, which will render even the tattiest net a lot more protective, and helps prevent mosquitoes from biting through a net when you roll against it. These measures will also do much to reduce exposure to other nocturnal biters. Bear in mind, too, that most flying insects are attracted to light: leaving a lamp standing near a tent opening or a light on in a poorly screened hotel room will greatly increase the insect presence in your sleeping quarters.

It is also advisable to think about avoiding bites when walking in the countryside by day, especially in wetland habitats, which often teem with diurnal mosquitoes. Wear a long loose shirt and trousers, preferably 100% cotton, as well as proper walking or hiking shoes with heavy socks (the ankle is particularly vulnerable to bites), and apply a DEET-based insect repellent to any exposed skin.

reducing the quantity of venom injected. Lethal snake bites are a rarity – in South Africa, which boasts almost as many venomous snakes as Tanzania, more people are killed by lightning – but in the unlikely event you are bitten, it's worth knowing that a free snakebite clinic operates out of the Meserani Snake Park 25km from Arusha (page 146).

OTHER INSECT-BORNE DISEASES Although malaria is the insect-borne disease that attracts the most attention in Africa, and rightly so, there are others, most too uncommon to be a significant concern to short-stay travellers. These include dengue fever and other arboviruses (spread by diurnal mosquitoes), sleeping sickness (tsetse flies), and river blindness (blackflies). Bearing this in mind, however, it is clearly sensible, and makes for a more pleasant trip, to avoid insect bites as far as possible (see box, above). Two nasty (though ultimately relatively harmless) flesh-eating insects associated with tropical Africa are *tumbu* or *putsi* flies, which lay eggs, often on drying laundry, that hatch and bury themselves under the skin when they come into contact with humans, and jiggers, which latch on to bare feet and set up home, usually at the side of a toenail, where they cause a painful boil-like swelling. Drying laundry indoors and wearing shoes are the best way to deter this pair of flesh-eaters. Symptoms and treatment of all these afflictions are described in greater detail on Bradt's website (*www.bradtguides.com/africahealth*).

OTHER SAFETY CONCERNS

WILD ANIMALS The dangers associated with Africa's wild animals have frequently been overstated since the days of the so-called Great White Hunters – who, after all, rather intensified the risk by shooting at animals that are most likely to turn nasty when wounded – and others trying to glamorise their chosen way of life. Contrary to the fanciful notions conjured up by images of rampaging elephants, man-eating lions and psychotic snakes, wild animals generally fear us more than we fear them, and their normal response to human proximity is to flee. That said, many travel guides have responded to the exaggerated ideas of the dangers associated with wild animals by being overly reassuring. The likelihood of a tourist being attacked by an animal is indeed very low, but it can happen and there have been a number of fatalities caused by such incidents in recent years, particularly in southern Africa.

The need for caution is greatest near water, particularly around dusk and dawn, when hippos are out grazing. Hippos are responsible for more human fatalities than any other large mammal, not because they are aggressive but because they tend to panic when something comes between them and the safety of the water. If you happen to be that something, then you're unlikely to live to tell the tale. Never consciously walk between a hippo and water, and never walk along riverbanks or through reed beds, especially in overcast weather or at dusk or dawn, unless you are certain that no hippos are present.

Watch out, too, for crocodiles. Only a very large crocodile is likely to attack a person, and then only in the water or right on the shore. Near towns and other settlements, you can be fairly sure that any such crocodile will have been consigned to its maker by its potential human prey, so the risk is greatest away from human habitation.

There are areas where hikers might still stumble across an elephant or a buffalo, the most dangerous of Africa's terrestrial herbivores. Elephants almost invariably mock charge and indulge in some hair-raising trumpeting before they attack in earnest. Provided that you back off at the first sign of unease, they are unlikely to take any further notice of you. If you see them before they see you, give them a wide berth, bearing in mind they are most likely to attack if surprised at close proximity. If an animal charges you, the safest course of action is to head for the nearest tree and climb it. Black rhinos are prone to charging without apparent provocation, but they're too rare in Tanzania to be a cause for concern. Elephants are the only animals to pose a potential danger to a vehicle, and much the same advice applies – if an elephant evidently doesn't want you to pass, then back off and wait until it has crossed the road or moved further away before you try again. In general, it's a good idea to leave your engine running when you are close to an elephant, and you should avoid letting yourself be boxed in between an elephant and another vehicle.

There are campsites in Tanzania where vervet monkeys and baboons have become pests. Feeding these animals is highly irresponsible, since it encourages them to scavenge and may eventually lead to them being shot. Vervet monkeys are too small to progress much beyond being a nuisance, but baboons are very dangerous and have often killed children and maimed adults with their teeth. Do not tease or underestimate them. If primates are hanging around a campsite and you wander off leaving fruit in your tent, don't expect the tent to be standing when you return. Chimpanzees are also potentially dangerous but are unlikely to be encountered except on a guided forest walk when there is little risk as long as you obey your guide's instructions at all times.

The dangers associated with large predators are often exaggerated. Most predators stay clear of humans and are only likely to kill accidentally or in self-defence. Lions are arguably the exception, but it is unusual for a lion to attack a human without cause. Should you encounter one on foot, the important thing is not to run since this is likely to trigger the instinct to give chase. Of the other cats, cheetahs represent no threat and leopards generally attack only when they are cornered. Hyenas are often associated with human settlements, and are potentially very dangerous but in practice aren't aggressive towards people and will most likely slink off into the shadows when disturbed. A slight but real danger when sleeping in the bush without a tent is that a passing hyena or lion might investigate a hairy object sticking out of a sleeping bag, and you might be decapitated through predatory curiosity. In areas where large predators are still reasonably common, sleeping in a sealed tent practically guarantees your safety – but don't sleep with your head sticking out and don't at any point put meat in the tent.

When all is said and done, the most dangerous animal in Africa, exponentially a greater threat than everything mentioned above, is the *Anopheles* mosquito, which carries the malaria parasite. Humans – particularly when behind a steering wheel – run them a close second!

CAR ACCIDENTS Dangerous driving is probably the biggest threat to life and limb in most parts of Africa. On a self-drive visit, drive defensively, being especially wary of stray livestock, gaping pot-holes, and imbecilic or bullying overtaking manoeuvres. Many vehicles lack headlights and most local drivers are reluctant headlight-users, so avoid driving at night and pull over in heavy storms. On a chauffeured tour, don't be afraid to tell the driver to slow or calm down if you think he is too fast or reckless.

Part Two

THE GUIDE

5

Arusha and Around

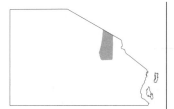

Set at a temperate altitude of 1,350m in the fertile southern foothills of Mount Meru, bustling Arusha, the third-largest city in Tanzania, is the most popular and convenient springboard from which to explore the country's legendary northern safari circuit. Less than 100km from the Kenyan border as the crow flies, this self-styled 'safari capital' is also an important gateway to Tanzania, not only for travellers driving across the border from Nairobi, but also for the growing number of tourists who arrive at nearby Kilimanjaro International Airport.

First impressions are that practically everything in Arusha revolves around the safari industry, a perception that is largely reinforced by more prolonged exposure. In the old town centre and back roads north of the stadium, it can feel like every second person you pass has something to sell, be it a safari, a batik or last week's edition of a foreign newspaper, while the roads are cluttered with 4x4s adorned with one or other safari company logo. And yet Arusha's rare economic vitality is buoyed by several other factors, among them its fertile surrounds, the tanzanite mining boom, and its role as capital of the East African Community.

Arusha is an attractively green town, with a northern skyline – weather permitting – dominated by the imposing hulk of Africa's fifth-highest mountain, the 4,566m Mount Meru. Situated in the mountain's rain-shadow, it also makes for a climatically temperate – and, during the rainy season, often downright soggy – introduction to tropical Africa. For first-time visitors to Africa, the town centre is an agreeable introduction to urban Africa. It's neither as intimidating nor as sprawling as Nairobi or Dar es Salaam, and there are plenty of trendy bars, restaurants and cafés catering to expatriates, tourists and wealthier locals.

In most other respects, however, Arusha remains something of an African everytown, where low-rise, colonial-era buildings rub shoulders with an ever-increasing number of more modern structures. Indeed, it could be argued that the wealth generated by the safari industry serves to accentuate both the vast economic gulf between the haves and have-nots, and the spectrum of cultural influences that play havoc with visitors seeking to pigeonhole the 'Real Africa'. Which is it, then: the colourfully dressed Maasai and Arusha women who sell traditional beadwork on the pavement, the suited businessmen who scurry in and out of the International Conference Centre, or the swaggering, sunglass-shrouded wide-boys who scurry about offering cheap safaris, change money, marijuana …?

Paradoxically, while Arusha's status as northern Tanzania's safari capital is not in dispute, only a small proportion of fly-in safari-goers actually spend a night in town. This is because many people fly or drive straight into the parks and for those who do stop over in Arusha, the top accommodation options mostly lie out of town, along the main road to Moshi and Kilimanjaro International Airport, or in the vicinity of Arusha National Park, as covered in *Chapter 6*. These out-of-town lodges tend to be more overtly African in character than their functional urban counterparts. Weather permitting, most of them also offer sterling views to Mount Meru and the more distant snow-capped peak of Kilimanjaro.

HISTORY

Little is known about the Arusha area prior to the 17th century, when the Bantu-speaking Meru people – migrants from the west with strong linguistic and cultural affinities to the Chagga of Kilimanjaro – settled and farmed the fertile and well-watered northern foothills of Mount Meru. In 1830 or thereabouts, the southern slopes of the mountain verging on the Maasai Steppes were settled by the Arusha, a Maasai subgroup who lost their cattle and territory in one of the internecine battles characteristic of this turbulent period in Maasailand. The Arusha people speak the same Maa language as the plains Maasai and share a similar social structure based around initiated age-sets, but when they settled in the Mount Meru area they forsook their pastoralist roots, turning instead to agriculture as a primary source of subsistence.

The Arusha economy was boosted by the trade in agricultural produce – in particular tobacco – with the closely affiliated Maasai of the plains. The Arusha also became known as reliable providers of food and other provisions for the Arab slave caravans that headed inland from the Pangani and Tanga area towards modern-day Kenya and Lake Victoria. Invigorated by this regular trade, the Arusha had, by 1880, cleared the forested slopes of Mount Meru to an altitude of around 1,600m to make way for cultivation. As their territory expanded, however, the Arusha people increasingly came into contact with their northern neighbours, the Meru, resulting in several territorial skirmishes and frequent cattle raids between the two tribes.

In 1881, prompted by the need to defend their combined territories against the Maasai and other potential attackers, the incumbent warrior age-sets of the Arusha and Meru united to form a formidable military force. Since they were settled on the well-watered slopes of Mount Meru, and their subsistence was not primarily dependent on livestock, the Arusha and Meru people were less affected than the plains pastoralists by the devastating series of droughts and rinderpest epidemics of the 1880s and early 1890s. As a result, the combined army, known as the Talala – the Expansionists – was able to exert considerable influence over neighbouring Maasai and Chagga territories.

The Talala staunchly resisted German attempts to settle in their territory, killing the first missionaries to arrive there and repelling an initial punitive attack by the colonial army. In October 1896, however, the Arusha and Meru were soundly defeated by a military expedition out of Moshi led by Karl Johannes and consisting of 100 German troopers supported by some 5,000 Chagga warriors. In the aftermath of this defeat, the Germans drove home the point by razing hundreds of Arusha and Meru smallholdings, killing the men, confiscating the cattle and repatriating women of Chagga origin to the Kilimanjaro area.

In 1889, the Germans established a permanent settlement – modern-day Arusha town – on the border of Arusha and Maasai territories, and used forced Arusha and Maasai labour to construct the boma that can still be seen on the north end of Boma Road. Relations between the colonisers and their unwilling subjects remained tense, to say the least. During the construction of the fort, a minor dispute led to some 300 labourers being massacred while marching peacefully along present-day Boma Road, and several local chiefs from outlying areas were arbitrarily arrested and taken to Moshi to be hanged in the street.

Following the construction of the boma, Arusha quickly developed into a significant trading and administrative centre, with about two-dozen Indian and

Arab shops clustered along what is today Boma Road. John Boyes, who visited Arusha in 1903, somewhat fancifully compared the boma to 'an Aladdin's Palace transported from some fairyland and dropped down in the heart of the tropics'. The town, he wrote, was 'a real oasis in the wilderness' and 'spotlessly clean', while 'the streets [were] laid out with fine sidewalks, separated by the road from a stream of clear water flowing down a cemented gully'.

At the outbreak of World War I, the small German garrison town was of some significance as a local agricultural and trade centre, but it remained something of a backwater in comparison to Moshi, which lay a week's ox-wagon trek distant at the railhead of the Tanga line. Much of the area around Arusha was, however, settled by German farmers, who had forcibly displaced the original Arusha and Meru smallholders. In 1916, British troops captured Arusha and expelled the German farmers, resulting in some resettlement by indigenous farmers, but the German farmland was eventually reallocated to British and Greek settlers. The British also set aside large tracts of land around Arusha for sisal plantations, which meant that by 1920, less than 20% of the land around Mount Meru was available to local farmers, most of it on dry foothills unsuited to cultivating the local staple of bananas.

Arusha grew steadily between the wars. The settler economy was boosted by the introduction of coffee, sisal and other export crops, and trade links were improved with the construction of road links to Moshi and Nairobi and the opening of the railway line to Moshi and the coast in 1929. Yet the land issues continued to simmer, eventually coming to a head after World War II, with the eviction of thousands of Meru farmers from north of Mount Meru to make way for a peanut production project overseen by 13 white farmers. The peanut project, aside from being a dismal and costly failure, resulted in the pivotal Meru Land Case, which not only caused great embarrassment to the UN Trusteeship Council, but also proved to be an important catalyst to the politicisation of the anti-colonial movement in Tanganyika.

Prior to independence, Arusha remained a relatively small town whose primary role was to service the surrounding agricultural lands. The official census of 1952 placed the urban population at fewer than 8,000 people, of which more than half were of Asian or European stock. All that changed in the post-independence era, when the town attracted, and continues to attract, large numbers of domestic migrants from surrounding rural areas and beyond. Indeed, by 1978 Arusha had become the ninth-largest town in Tanzania, supporting a population of 55,000. It was accorded city status in 2006, and recently overtook Dodoma as the country's third-largest settlement, with a population of around 450,000.

Arusha's recent growth can be attributed to a number of factors, not least the town's location in the foothills of Mount Meru, whose drizzly sub-montane microclimate nurtures the rich volcanic soil to agricultural profligacy. There is also its proximity to the Mererani Hills, the only known source of the increasingly popular gemstone tanzanite. A more ephemeral economic boost was provided by the presence of UN and other NGO personnel linked to the United Nations Security Council's Rwandan War Crimes Tribunal, which operated out of the Arusha International Conference Centre from 1995 until its eventual completion in December 2015. Arusha has also served as the main administrative base of the East African Community, a regionally significant international organisation comprising Tanzania, Kenya, Uganda, Burundi and Rwanda, since it was revived in 2000. The key to Arusha's modern economic growth, however, has undoubtedly been its role as the main urban pivot servicing a lucrative tourist industry focused on the likes of the Serengeti National Park, Ngorongoro Crater and lofty Mount Kilimanjaro.

BY AIR The main local point of entry is **Kilimanjaro International Airport** (often abbreviated to KIA, though the official airport code is JRO), which lies roughly two-thirds along the 80km asphalt road that runs eastward from Arusha to Moshi. Several international carriers now fly to KIA, among them Ethiopian Airlines, Air Kenya, Rwandair Express, KLM, Air France, SAS and Turkish Airlines, so that it is no longer necessary to travel to northern Tanzania via Nairobi or Dar es Salaam. Most new arrivals will be collected by their hotel or safari company, but charter taxis are also available at the airport, at a fixed price of US$60. Travellers with problematic flight times might think about booking into KIA Lodge (page 153), which lies just 1km from the airport.

If you are flying to Arusha from within Tanzania, check your ticket carefully as most domestic flights now leave from and arrive at the smaller **Arusha Airport** (airport code ARK), which lies about 5km out of town along the Serengeti road. Daily flights connect this airport to all major airstrips on the northern Tanzania safari circuit, including Manyara, Ngorongoro, Seronera, Grumeti and Lobo, as well as to Dar es Salaam and Zanzibar. There are also regular scheduled flights to the likes of Mwanza, Rubondo Island, Mafia Island and the reserves of the southern safari circuit.

Most tourists flying around Tanzania will have made their flight arrangements in advance through a tour operator, and this is certainly the recommended way of going about things, but it is generally possible to buy tickets from Arusha to major destinations such as Dar es Salaam and Zanzibar at short notice.

Airlines The offices of the main airlines are mostly dotted along Boma Road in the old town centre. **Ethiopian Airlines** [125 C4] (📞 *027 250 4231; www. ethiopianairlines.com*) is immediately south of the New Safari Hotel, and **Precision Air** (📞 *027 254 5489; www.precisionairtz.com*) is only a door or two further south. For domestic airlines, **Air Excel** (📞 *027 297 0248; www.airexcelonline.com*) has a desk at Arusha Airport and **Fastjet** at the Corridor Springs hotel [123 E6] (m *0784 108900; www.fastjet.com/tz*). The **Regional Air** office is out of town near the Arusha Coffee Lodge so it's best to call them (m *0753 500300*). **KLM** no longer has an office in Arusha, but you can contact the Dar es Salaam office (📞 *022 213 9790; e reservations.daressalaam@klm.com*) for assistance.

BY ROAD There are two main **bus stations** in Arusha. The old central station at the south end of Colonel Middleton Road [131 E4/5], facing the stadium, is the terminus of all minibuses and other dalla-dallas, as well as most buses to relatively local destinations such as Moshi, Namanga and Babati. The newer Makao Mapya bus station [130 D2], often referred to as Dar Express after the best-known operator there, consists of a row of perhaps two-dozen coach company offices off Stadium Road about 300m west of the old bus station.

The old bus station can be somewhat chaotic and intimidating, thanks to the high density of 'flycatchers' and touts who to try to latch on to fresh arrivals (or to get in the middle of negotiations with travellers buying a ticket out of town). These guys can be annoyingly persistent, but they pose no serious threat, though it is definitely advisable to make it clear you don't want their services. By contrast, Makao Mapya is very orderly and quiet, and you can usually buy tickets at any of the offices there without hassle. For long hauls it is always advisable to buy a ticket the day before you want to travel.

SAFETY

Arusha can be a daunting prospect on first contact, particularly if you arrive by bus. Competition between budget safari companies is fierce, and 'flycatchers' – the street touts who solicit custom for these companies – know that their best tactic is to hook travellers who don't have a pre-booked safari when they arrive. As a consequence, when you arrive in Arusha by bus you're likely to spend your first few minutes dodging the attention of a dozen yelling touts, all of whom will claim to be able to offer you the cheapest safari and room in town. In most cases, the touts probably will show you to a decent room, but, unfortunately, by allowing them to get involved like this, you will open the door to your sense of obligation being exploited later in your stay.

Fortunately, once you've run the bus station gauntlet, things do calm down somewhat, though the flock of flycatchers, newspaper vendors and curio sellers who hang around the old town centre can be a nuisance. Unlike in some other parts of Africa, however, it is unusual for such an exchange to descend into something truly unpleasant: most touts here seem capable of taking a good-humoured 'No' for an answer, especially one spoken in Swahili, and they will usually back down at any show of genuine irritation. As for the dodgy money-changers that sometimes hang around with the touts, don't let the offer of a superior rate sucker you in – changing money on the street in Arusha as elsewhere in Tanzania is a definite no-no!

Such annoyances aside, Arusha is not an especially threatening city, though it is certainly not unheard of for tourists to be mugged after dark. The usual common sense rules apply: avoid walking around singly or in pairs at night, especially on unlit roads and in parks, and avoid carrying valuables on your person or taking out significantly more money than you need for the evening. After dark, the dodgiest part of town for muggings is probably the area east of the Themi River, in particular the quiet, unlit roads between the Arusha Hotel, Impala Hotel and Mount Meru Hotel. On the whole, Arusha is very safe by day, but do be wary of bag-snatchers and pickpockets in the central market area.

The best **coach service** for Dar es Salaam and other destinations along the B1 is the Dar Express (m *0754 946155*), and buses depart every 30 minutes between 05.30 and 08.30, as well as at 10.00 and 14.30. Tickets cost US$18–20 depending on the type of coach, and the trip takes about 12 hours. Cheaper bus services between Arusha and Dar es Salaam are plentiful, but aren't really worth bothering with, as they are less comfortable and tend to stop at every town, taking around 15 hours to cover the same distance.

The quickest and most efficient road transport between Arusha and Nairobi are the **minibus shuttles** run by various operators. Among the most reliable of these is the Riverside Shuttle (m *0754 474968*), which costs US$25 for non-residents (it is, however, often possible to negotiate to pay the resident rate, equivalent to US$16) and which leaves from a parking area in front of the Picasso Café on Simeon Road [123 G6], although you can usually arrange to be picked up elsewhere. Departures in either direction are at 08.00 and 14.00 daily, and the trip takes 4–5 hours. In Nairobi, passengers are dropped and collected at the Parkside Hotel or at Jomo Kenyatta Airport, and the contact number is m +254 (0)722 826368 or (0)725 999121. Another recommended service is the Impala Shuttle, which costs the same and leaves at the same times from the car park of the

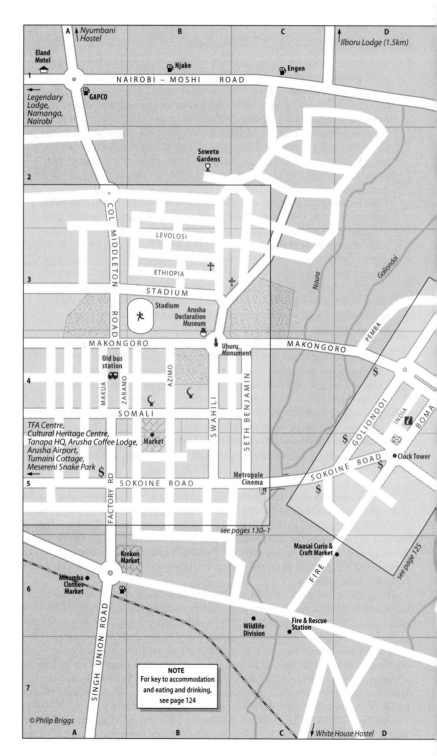

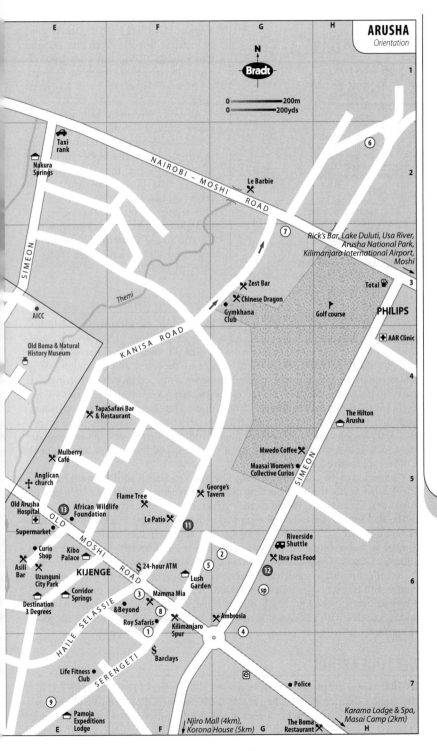

ARUSHA
Orientation

Bradt

N

0 ——————— 200m
0 ——————— 200yds

E   F   G   H

Taxi rank

Nakura Springs

NAIROBI – MOSHI ROAD

Le Barbie

Rick's Bar, Lake Duluti, Usa River,
Arusha National Park,
Kilimanjaro International Airport,
Moshi

SIMEON

Themi

Zest Bar
Chinese Dragon
Gymkhana Club

Golf course

PHILIPS

Total

AICC

AAR Clinic

Old Boma & Natural
History Museum

KANISA ROAD

TapaSafari Bar
& Restaurant

The Hilton
Arusha

Mulberry
Café

Mwedo Coffee

Anglican
church

Maasai Women's
Collective Curios

SIMEON

Old Arusha
Hospital

African Wildlife
Foundation

Flame Tree

George's
Tavern

Le Patio

Supermarket

Riverside
Shuttle

Curio
Shop

Kibo
Palace

24-hour ATM

Ibra Fast Food

Asili
Bar

Uzunguni
City Park

KIJENGE

Lush
Garden

Corridor
Springs

Mamma Mia

Destination
3 Degrees

&Beyond

Roy Safaris

Ambrosia

Kilimanjaro
Spur

HAILE SELASSIE

OLD MOSHI ROAD

SERENGETI

Life Fitness
Club

Barclays

Police

Pamoja
Expeditions
Lodge

Njiro Mall (4km),
Korona House (5km)

The Boma
Restaurant

Karama Lodge & Spa,
Masai Camp (2km)

123

Impala Hotel [123 G6]. Tickets can be bought directly from the Impala Hotel (page 128), and the drop-off points in Nairobi are the Silver Springs or Parkside Hotel, or Jomo Kenyatta Airport.

A steady stream of minibuses and buses connect Moshi and Arusha. I would avoid using minibuses along this route due to the higher incidence of accidents, but they are generally quicker than buses. This trip usually takes between 1 and 2 hours. There are also regular buses to other relatively local destinations such as Mto wa Mbu, Karatu, Mbulu, Babati and Kondoa; the best company servicing these routes is Mtei (**m** *0755 717117*).

ORIENTATION

Unlike Dar es Salaam or Zanzibar's labyrinthine Stone Town, Arusha is not a difficult town to familiarise yourself with. Its most significant geographical features are the Naura and Goliondoi rivers, which run parallel to each other through the town centre, cutting it into two distinct parts. To the east of the rivers lies the **'old' town** centre, a relatively smart area whose main north–south thoroughfares – Boma, India and Goliondoi roads – are lined with upmarket hotels, tourist-friendly restaurants, safari companies, curio shops, banks, bookshops and tourist offices. Major landmarks in this part of town include the Clock Tower, the Old Boma (now a museum) and the Arusha International Conference Centre (AICC).

Connected to the old town centre by Sokoine Road in the south and Makongoro Road in the north, the more bustling **modern town** centre consists of a tight grid of roads west of the rivers centred on the market and the old central bus station south of the stadium. This area is well equipped with small budget hotels and affordable restaurants, but it boasts few facilities that approach international standards. Similar in feel, though more residential and less commercially orientated, is the suburb of Kaloleni immediately north of the stadium.

Another important suburb is **Kijenge**, which lies to the southeast of the old town centre, and is reached by following Sokoine Road across a bridge over the Themi River to become the Old Moshi Road. Kijenge has a spacious, leafy character and it is dotted with half-a-dozen relatively upmarket hotels and numerous good restaurants, as well as an increasing number of safari company offices.

GETTING AROUND

BY TAXI There are plenty of taxis in Arusha. Good places to pick them up include the market and bus station, the rank at the junction of Goliondoi Road and Joel Maeda [125 B5], and the open area at the north end of Boma and India roads [125 B3]. A taxi ride within the town centre should cost roughly US$4–6, though

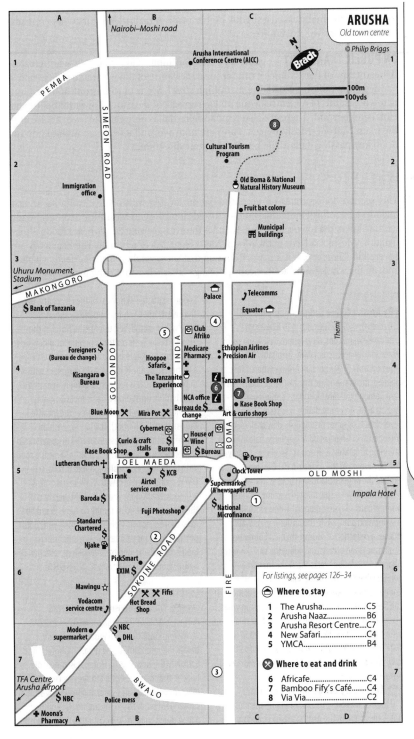

0 — 100m
0 — 100yds

Nairobi–Moshi road

Arusha International
Conference Centre (AICC)

8

Cultural Tourism
Program

Old Boma & National
Natural History Museum

Fruit bat colony

Municipal
buildings

Immigration
office

PEMBA

SIMEON ROAD

Uhuru Monument,
Stadium

MAKONGORO

Bank of Tanzania

Palace

Telecomms

Equator

Club
Afriko

4

5

INDIA

Medicare
Pharmacy

Ethiopian Airlines
Precision Air

Foreigners
(Bureau de change)

Hoopoe
Safaris

The Tanzanite
Experience

Tanzania Tourist Board

6

NCA office

7 Kase Book Shop

Kisangara
Bureau

Blue Moon   Mira Pot

Bureau de
change

Art & curio shops

Cybernet

Curio & craft
stalls

House of
Wine

Bureau

Kase Book Shop

Oryx

Lutheran Church

JOEL MAEDA

BOMA

Clock Tower

OLD MOSHI

Taxi rank

Airtel
service centre

KCB

Supermarket
(& newspaper stall)

Impala Hotel

Baroda

Standard
Chartered

Njake

Fuji Photoshop

2

1

National
Microfinance

PickSmart

EXIM

SOKOINE ROAD

FIRE

Mawingu

Vodacom
service centre

Fifis

Hot Bread
Shop

Modern
supermarket

NBC

DHL

TFA Centre,
Arusha Airport

BWALO

3

NBC

Police mess

Moona's
Pharmacy

tourists are normally asked a slightly higher price. A taxi ride to somewhere outside the town centre will cost more.

ON PUBLIC TRANSPORT A good network of minibus dalla-dallas services Arusha. A steady flow of these vehicles runs around the centre of town, though they are now banned from Sokoine Road, the main high street. Some of these continue west out of town past the TFA Centre, while others run east of the Clock Tower to the Impala Hotel and beyond. There are also regular dalla-dallas between the town centre and the main Nairobi–Moshi bypass. Fares are nominal, and it's easy enough to hop on or off any passing dalla-dalla heading in your direction.

WHERE TO STAY

This section concentrates on accommodation located within the city limits. It also includes a handful of individual hotels situated along the Old Moshi and Serengeti roads within 5km of the town centre, but excludes the ever-growing assortment of lodges that flank the Moshi road east of the Mount Meru Hotel. All hotels in the latter category are covered in *Chapter 6*, but it is worth noting that most would make a perfectly viable – and, on the whole, more aesthetically pleasing – alternative to staying in the town itself.

EXCLUSIVE

Arusha Coffee Lodge [map, page 148] (30 rooms) % 027 2500 630; m 0782 600047; e info@elewana.com, reservations@elewana.com; www.elewanacollection.com. Justifiably billed as 'the first truly 5-star hotel in Arusha' when it first opened, the immaculate Arusha Coffee Lodge still ranks among the most luxurious options in the Arusha area. Accommodation is in standalone split-level chalets or suites distinguished by their elegant Victorian décor, hardwood floors, huge balconies & stunning fireplaces, & in-room percolators to provide the true aroma of the coffee estate. Designed around the original plantation houses, the excellent restaurant serves a spit-roasted lunchtime grill & a sumptuous à la carte dinner. Facilities include a swimming pool, while the onsite Traders Walk houses a collection of African-themed boutiques & gourmet food outlets, including the well-known Shanga Foundation Workshop & the friendly & comfortable Kahawa Coffee Shop. Arusha Coffee Lodge is situated about 5km out of the city alongside the Serengeti road, close to Arusha Airport, on what is reputedly the largest coffee estate in Tanzania, with a good view of Mount Meru. *US$413/550 en-suite sgl/dbl, or US$578/770 sgl/dbl suite, all B&B, with discounted low-season rates available Mar–May & Nov–mid Dec.* **$$$$$**

Legendary Lodge [map, page 148] (10 rooms) m 0685 701725. Arguably the plushest hotel anywhere in the Arusha area, Legendary

Lodge is situated 3km west of the city centre on the Selari Coffee Estate, founded by the same family that established the Arusha Hotel in the 1980s. The lodge is centred upon the original early 20th-century estate house – which now serves as a common lounge & dining area complete with period décor – & is set in lush gardens teeming with birdlife (including what is most probably the most westerly breeding pair of the localised brown-throated barbet). The vast open-plan semi-detached cottages, decorated in understated contemporary classic style, consist of a sitting room with leather sofas, fireplace, minibar & flatscreen DSTV, a king-sized bed with walk-in netting, & a spacious bathroom with tub & shower. Two of the rooms are set up as family cottages & provide even more space, as well as everything you could possibly need for your family stay. The superb food is complemented by an excellent selection of house wines. *US$550pp all-inc.* **$$$$$**

UPMARKET

✳ **The Arusha Hotel** [125 C5] (86 rooms) \ 027 250 7777/8870; m 0754 250777; e reservations@thearushahotel.com or info@thearushahotel.com; www.thearushahotel.com. Formerly the New Arusha Hotel, this stately old hotel is the smartest option in the city centre following a change of ownership in 2004 & several subsequent renovations, including the addition of a new guest wing in 2016. Situated right opposite the Clock Tower, it stands in large wooded grounds that run down towards the Themi River, & the décor has an Edwardian feel, befitting its status as the oldest hostelry in Arusha. The spacious rooms & suites all come with DSTV, netting, in-room internet access, a smoke detector, electronic safes & tea-/coffee-making facilities. AC & non-smoking rooms are available. Facilities include 24hr room service, a business centre, a craft shop, 24hr Wi-Fi internet access, a heated swimming pool, 3 bars, 2 restaurants & an airport shuttle service. *US$230/260 sgl/dbl executive rooms B&B, or US$330/360 suite.* **$$$$$**

✱ 🏠 **Karama Lodge & Spa** [map, page 148] (26 rooms) m 0754 475188; e info@karama-lodge.com; www.karama-lodge.com. Aptly named after the Swahili word for 'blessing', this fabulous eco-lodge possesses a genuine bush atmosphere, despite lying only 3km from central Arusha along the Old Moshi Rd. Perched on the small but densely wooded Suye Hill, part of which is protected in a forest reserve, the wooded grounds harbour a wide range of brachystegia-associated birds (brown-throated barbet prominent among them) as well as small nocturnal mammals such as bushbaby, genet & civet. Accommodation is in stilted wood-&-makuti units with Zanzibar-style beds draped in netting, with en-suite shower & toilet, & private balcony facing Kilimanjaro. They also offer a family house ideal for travelling with children. The restaurant serves tasty snacks & meals, & offers views to Kilimanjaro & Meru on a clear day. The highly rated spa offers massage, sauna, yoga & other treatments. Overall, it's a highly recommended & affordable alternative to the bland upmarket city hotels that characterise central Arusha, though the sloping grounds would make it a poor choice for elderly travellers & those with disabilities. *US$106/142 sgl/dbl B&B, with resident & low-season discounts.* **$$$$**

🏠 **The Eight Boutique Hotel** [123 G6] (5 rooms) 🌑027 254 3055; m 0758 777333; e reservation@theeight.co.tz or info@theeight.co.tz; www.theeight.co.tz. This stylish boutique hotel on leafy Vijana Rd is under new management as of 2016 & comprises just 5 individually decorated rooms, most with parquet floor, tasteful ethnically influenced décor, flatscreen DSTV, AC & spacious modern bathrooms. The ground-floor restaurant offers some excellent fine dining &

is known for its relaxing family-friendly Sun brunches. *US$120 dbl or US$160 suite.* **$$$$**

🏠 **The African Tulip** [123 F6] (29 rooms) 🌑027 254 3004/5; e info@theafricantulip.com; www.theafricantulip.com. Owned & managed by Roy Safaris (page 140), their office is next door, this chic service-oriented boutique hotel is set in a green suburban garden with a swimming pool. The 22 deluxe rooms & 7 suites are large & attractively decorated with Zanzibar-style wooden furnishing, & have good facilities including a safe, minibar, Wi-Fi, satellite TV & large en-suite bathroom with a choice of a tub or shower. There's a well-stocked gift shop on the ground floor, along with the aptly named Zanzibar Bar & promising Baobab Restaurant. *US$191.50/233 sgl/dbl B&B or US$313/506 sgl/dbl suite.* **$$$$$**

🏠 **Mount Meru Hotel** [123 G3] (178 rooms) 🌑027 297 0256; e info@mountmeruhotel.co.tz; www.mountmeruhotel.com. Formerly The Arusha Hotel & recently reopened following privatisation & several years of renovations, this veteran 7-storey landmark stands in large green grounds bordering the golf course immediately northeast of the city centre. Geared more towards business travellers than tourists, it nevertheless offers some of the most comfortable accommodation & best facilities – 3 restaurants, a large swimming pool with children's area, a business centre, forex bureau & several onsite shops – within the city limits. Several types of en-suite room are available, all spacious & contemporary in feel, including family rooms, suites & 2 rooms designed for disabled access. All rooms are well equipped with minibar, free Wi-Fi, DSTV & pay-per-view movie channel, safe, AC, & tea-/coffee-making facilities. *US$195/235 standard sgl/dbl B&B, US$245/280/400 executive sgl/dbl/trpl B&B, suites from US$450/490 sgl/dbl.* **$$$$$**

🏠 **Gold Crest Hotel** [123 F6] (40 rooms) 🌑027 254 5302; e reservations@goldcresthotel.com; www.goldcresthotel.com/arusha. Previously the East African All-Suite, this slick hotel on the Old Moshi Rd doesn't exactly evoke a safari atmosphere, but the accommodation is to a very high standard, consisting of large suites with varied facilities, including flatscreen DSTV, king-sized bed, safe, kitchen with stove & fridge, large bathroom with combination tub/shower, AC, & extensive leather furnishing that creates a slightly cluttered effect. The restaurant serves an

Symbolic of Arusha's growing significance in the 1920s was the opening of the New Arusha Hotel in lushly wooded grounds formerly occupied by the small town's only hostelry, the small boarding house operated by the Bloom family since the late 1890s. A 1929 government brochure eulogised the newly opened establishment as having 'hot and cold water in all bedrooms, modern sanitation, teak dancing floor, electric light and really excellent food, as well as golf, tennis, big game and bird shooting'. Less complimentary was the description included in Evelyn Waugh's amusingly acerbic travelogue *A Tourist in Africa* in 1960: it 'seeks to attract by the claim to be exactly midway between Cape Town and Cairo … I did not see any African or Indian customers. Dogs howled and scuffled under the window at night. Can I say anything pleasant about this hotel? Yes, it stands in a cool place in a well-kept garden and it stocks some potable South African wines in good conditions.' The New Arusha continued its slide, hosting the likes of John Wayne along the way, until finally it closed for overdue renovations a few years back. It reopened in 2004 as the Arusha Hotel, the smartest establishment in the city centre.

imaginative selection of contemporary dishes & there's a swimming pool & cigar bar. Good value. *US$120/140 sgl/dbl loft suite, US$160/180 sgl/dbl executive suite or US$380/410 sbl/dbl presidential suite with 2 bedrooms.* **$$$$**

MODERATE

L'Oasis Lodge [123 H2] (29 rooms) 027 250 7089; m 0757 557802; e info@loasistanzania. com; www.loasistanzania.com. Set in large green grounds about 500m north of the Moshi road, along a side road signposted opposite the prominent Mount Meru Hotel, this pleasantly rustic lodge is one of the best-value options in its range. A variety of comfortable en-suite rooms are available, including some attractive stilted bungalows, while other facilities include a large bar alongside the swimming pool, & the wonderful Lounge at Oasis, whose funky but earthy décor is complemented by a cosmopolitan menu of light snacks, salads, wraps & full meals. *US$81/111 sgl/dbl B&B, or US$113/174 FB, with low-season discounts available.* **$$$$**

Outpost Lodge [123 E7] (28 rooms) 37A Serengeti St; 027 254 8405; m 0754 318523; e reservations@outpost-lodge.com or outposttanzania@gmail.com; www.outpost-lodge. com. The welcoming & homely Outpost, set in a suburban garden on Kijenge's Serengeti Rd, has proved to be consistently popular with travellers seeking its combination of affordability & comfort since it opened in 1990. Following extensive

renovations in early 2012, the lodge offers a range of rooms in the main house & the garden bungalows, including sgls, dbls, trpls, & even a dorm room. All come with en-suite bathrooms, netting & DSTV. Outpost is also well equipped to care for travellers with disabilities, & has 1 dedicated, wheelchair-friendly room. Cheap & tasty lunches & dinners are available. *US$61.25/81 sgl/dbl.* **$$$$**

Impala Hotel [123 G6] (177 rooms) 027 254 3082/7; m 0754 678678/008448; e impala@ impalahotel.com; www.impalahotel.com. The constantly expanding Impala Hotel, situated in Kijenge about 10mins' walk from the city centre, is justifiably rated by many tour operators as the best-value hotel in the immediate vicinity of Arusha, & it's certainly one of the largest, busiest, smoothest running & most reasonably priced, despite being somewhat deficient in character. Facilities include 4 restaurants of which the Indian is strongly recommended, while the others specialise in more ordinary Italian, Chinese & continental cuisine. Other facilities include an internet café, a forex bureau offering good rates, a swimming pool, a gift shop, an inexpensive shuttle service to Nairobi as well as to Kilimanjaro International Airport, & an in-house safari operator. The newer rooms are comfortable & attractively decorated (the old ones are rather less so), & all have free Wi-Fi, satellite TV, hot showers & a fridge. *US$90/110/155 sgl/dbl/trpl B&B, US$150 executive dbl, US$230 dbl suite.* **$$$$**

🏠 **Tumaini Cottage** [122 A5] (10 rooms) m 0784 588698/0754 588698; e info@ tumainicottage.com; www.tumainicottage.com. This friendly family-run lodge close to the African Cultural Heritage Centre has a relaxed atmosphere, a quiet out-of-town location, & good facilities including free internet & a restaurant serving African & international cuisine. *US$65/80 en-suite sgl/dbl B&B, or US$160 for a family cottage.* **$$$$**

🏠 **New Safari Hotel** [125 C4] (48 rooms) 📞 027 254 59420; e reservation@newsafarihotel. com; www.newsafarihotel.com. This long-serving but recently renovated hotel on Boma Rd, once popular with the hunting fraternity, now seems more geared towards business travellers, with its convenient – though potentially noisy – central location a few mins from the AICC & a number of government offices & restaurants. Facilities include a ground-floor internet café & a good restaurant. The large, tiled en-suite rooms with DS TV have a modern feel, & seem fair value. *US$100/125 sgl/ dbl B&B, or US$200/220 suite.* **$$$$**

BUDGET

✳️ 🏠 **Hotel Le Jacaranda** [123 F6] (23 rooms) 📞 027 254 4624; m 0784 986116; e jacaranda@tz2000.com; jacaranda.chez.com. Situated in the garden suburbs immediately east of the city centre, this converted colonial-era homestead ranks among the most characterful hotels in Arusha, & it's also exceptionally good value, set in pretty overgrown grounds with a mini-golf course & shady & highly rated restaurant/bar area. The individually styled en-suite rooms all have a 4-poster bed with netting & hot water. *US$35/60/80 sgl/dbl/trpl, with low-season discounts available.* **$$$**

🏠 **Olduvai Inn** [123 F6] (15 rooms) 📞 027 254 3044; m 0753 341578; e manager@olduvai-inn. com; www.olduvai-inn.com. Set in large gardens on the junction of Serengeti & Old Moshi roads, this is a great little guesthouse offering clean & reasonably priced en-suite accommodation with nets, TV & hot shower. There's internet access onsite & plenty of choice of restaurants within a few hundred metres. *US$35/45/55 sgl/dbl/trpl B&B.* **$$$**

🏠 **Korona House** [123 F7] m 0687 666808; e room@koronahouse.com; www.koronahouse. com. Situated almost at the end of Njiro road (5km south of Impala Hotel) in the quiet suburbs, right on the edge of development, this smart B&B

consists of 2 separate buildings with thoughtfully equipped & decorated rooms & a pool. A restaurant serves good main courses for around US$5–6 & a 4-course meal for US$15. It also offers easy access to dusty fields & countryside that are safe for hiking. *US$45/65/80 sgl/dbl/trpl, or US$50/70/100 sgl/dbl/trpl in the annex. All rates B&B.* **$$$**

🏠 **White House Hostel** [122 C7] (7 rooms) m 0714 285823; e whitehouseoftanzania@ gmail.com; www.whitehouseoftanzania-arusha-hostel.com. Somewhat buried in the estate south of the fire station & across the old railway line (taxi US$2–3, phone for directions), this neat, backpacker-style hostel has 7 rooms with shared bathroom surrounding a central decorated courtyard with free Wi-Fi. Good value for money. *US$18–20pp FB.* **$$**

🏠 **Natron Palace Hotel** [131 F4] (30 rooms) m 0767 785276; e info@natronpalacehotel. com; www.natronpalacehotel.com. This modern 9-storey hotel overlooking the central bus station may somewhat lack character, but it has a useful location for early starts or late arrivals, & the comfortable en-suite rooms with DSTV, AC, minibar & private balcony are excellent value. *US$45 standard dbl.* **$$$**

🏠 **Arusha Bimel Hotel** [131 H5] (20 rooms) 📞 027 254 8523; m 0784/0785 959088; e bimelhotel@gmail.com. A few blocks east of the market & central bus station, this 4-storey hotel is one of the best budget deals in central Arusha, thanks largely to the switched-on & helpful owner-manager. The clean en-suite rooms have netting, a TV & telephone, & facilities include laundry, internet & a massage room. *US$20/30pp sgl/dbl B&B.* **$$**

🏠 **Golden Rose Hotel** [131 F2] (22 rooms) 📞 027 250 7959; m 0754 588507; e goldenrose@ habari.co.tz; goldenrosehotel.tripod.com/ goldenrosehotel. This well-known landmark on the western side of the city is close to both bus stations & is the most central departure point for the Riverside shuttle to/from Nairobi. The small but comfortable en-suite rooms come with TV, fan, net & balcony, & though a little timeworn & gloomy are pretty good value following a recent drop in price. *US$40/50 sgl/dbl B&B, with a 35% discount to residents.* **$$$**

🏠 **Spices & Herbs** [123 G6] (14 rooms) m 0754 313162/0768 356191; e auzum_spices@ hotmail.com. One of Arusha's most interesting

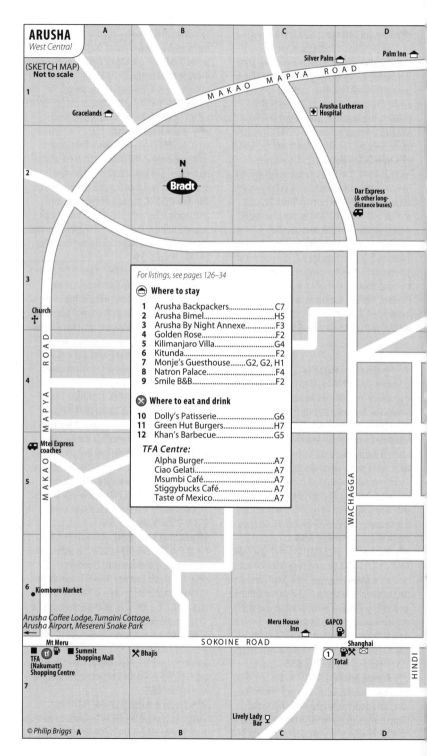

ARUSHA
West Central

(SKETCH MAP)
Not to scale

Silver Palm
Palm Inn

MAKAO MAPYA ROAD

Gracelands

Arusha Lutheran Hospital

N

Bradt

Dar Express (& other long-distance buses)

Church

MAKAO MAPYA ROAD

Mtei Express coaches

WACHAGGA

Kiomboro Market

Arusha Coffee Lodge, Tumaini Cottage,
Arusha Airport, Mesereni Snake Park

Meru House Inn
GAPCO

Mt Meru
SOKOINE ROAD
Shanghai

TFA (Nakumatt) Shopping Centre
Summit Shopping Mall
Bhajis
Total
HINDI

Lively Lady Bar

For listings, see pages 126–34

⬮ **Where to stay**

1	Arusha Backpackers	C7
2	Arusha Bimel	H5
3	Arusha By Night Annexe	F3
4	Golden Rose	F2
5	Kilimanjaro Villa	G4
6	Kitunda	F2
7	Monje's Guesthouse	G2, G2, H1
8	Natron Palace	F4
9	Smile B&B	F2

✖ **Where to eat and drink**

10	Dolly's Patisserie	G6
11	Green Hut Burgers	H7
12	Khan's Barbecue	G5

TFA Centre:

Alpha Burger	A7
Ciao Gelati	A7
Msumbi Café	A7
Stiggybucks Café	A7
Taste of Mexico	A7

© Philip Briggs

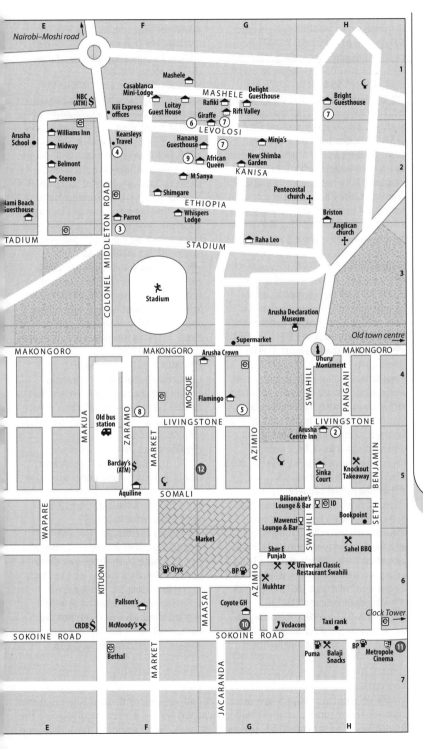

Nairobi–Moshi road

E F G H

1

Mashele

Casablanca
Mini-Lodge
NBC
(ATM)
Kili Express
offices

MASHELE

Delight
Guesthouse

Bright
Guesthouse

Loitay
Guest House

Rafiki

Rift Valley

Williams Inn

Arusha
School

Midway

Belmont

Stereo

Kearsleys
Travel

Giraffe

LEVOLOSI

Hanang
Guesthouse

African
Queen

Minja's

New Shimba
Garden

KANISA

M Sanya

iami Beach
Guesthouse

Shimgare

ETHIOPIA

Pentecostal
church

Parrot

Whispers
Lodge

Briston

Anglican
church

TADIUM

STADIUM

Raha Leo

2

Stadium

STADIUM

3

Arusha Declaration
Museum

Old town centre

Supermarket

MAKONGORO

MAKONGORO

Arusha Crown

Uhuru
Monument

MAKONGORO

4

Old bus
station

Flamingo

LIVINGSTONE

Arusha
Centre Inn

LIVINGSTONE

Barclay's
(ATM)

Sinka
Court

Knockout
Takeaway

Aquiline

SOMALI

Billionaire's
Lounge & Bar

Mawenzi
Lounge & Bar

Bookpoint

5

Market

Sahel BBQ

Sher E
Punjab

Universal Classic
Restaurant Swahili

Oryx

BP

Mukhtar

Pallson's

Coyote GH

Taxi rank

Clock Tower

CRDB

McMoody's

Vodacom

SOKOINE ROAD

SOKOINE ROAD

6

Bethal

Puma

Balaji
Snacks

BP

Metropole
Cinema

7

E F G H

131

restaurants serving good Ethiopian food, Spices & Herbs offers accommodation in small but clean en-suite rooms within easy walking distance of the Riverside Shuttle. *US$45/55 sgl/dbl B&B, or US$ 65/85 sgl/dbl FB.* **$$$**

🏠 **Arusha Naaz Hotel** [125 B6] (21 rooms) ✆027 250 2087; m 0755 785276; e reservations@ arushanaaz.net; www.arushanaaz.net. Situated on Sokoine Rd close to the Clock Tower, this clean, convenient & secure hotel has long been a favourite with budget travellers. There is a good, inexpensive Indian restaurant on the ground floor. Unfortunately, the cramped en-suite rooms with net, fan, hot water & DSTV seem overpriced for what they are. *US$40/60/75 sgl/dbl/trpl with discount resident rate available.* **$$$**

SHOESTRING & CAMPING

🏠 **Smile B&B** [131 F2] (9 rooms) m 0786 395254. This good-value guesthouse, set in the backstreets behind the stadium, has clean twin rooms with fan, writing desk, tea-/coffee-making facilities & en-suite hot shower. *US$12/14 sgl/dbl.* **$**

🏠 **Arusha Backpackers Hotel** [130 C7] (29 rooms) m 0773 377795/0715 377795; e reservations@arushabackpackers.co.tz; www. arushabackpackers.co.tz. On Sokoine Rd & within easy walking distance of the central bus station, this safe & reliable set-up is a favourite rendezvous for budget-conscious travellers. The small but clean rooms have a desk & fan, & the use of communal hot showers & toilets. *US$12/22 sgl/dbl B&B, or US$9/10 for a dorm bed.* **$$**

🏠 **Arusha By Night Annexe** [131 F3] (22 rooms) m 0755 260975. This stalwart hotel close to the stadium & central bus station has unquestionably seen better days, but the one-price-for-all-comers policy means that the faded but spacious rooms with twin or dbl bed, TV, fan, writing desk & en-suite hot shower feel like one of the best deals in this range. *US$12/13 sgl/dbl.* **$**

🏠 **Kitunda Guesthouse** [131 F2] (24 rooms) m 0766 515957; e kghouset@gmail. com. Among the best of the innumerable little guesthouses scattered around the backstreets

behind the stadium, this has a neat little restaurant serving simple b/fasts, & clean tiled rooms with a writing desk, net, TV & hot shower. *US$10 en-suite sgl/dbl B&B.* **$**

🏕 **Masai Camp** [map, page 148] m 0713 172099/0787 479983; e info@tropicaltrails.com. Situated about 2km out of the city along the Old Moshi Rd, Masai Camp is one of the best campsites in Tanzania, & it also offers simple accommodation in huts. Facilities include an ablution block with hot water, a pool table, volleyball & a lively 24hr bar, & an excellent safari company called Tropical Trails is onsite. The restaurant is well known for its pizzas. If you're without transport, you can get a taxi here for around US$3. *US$10pp dorm, US$18/25/35 sgl/dbl/ trpl non en-suite rooms, US$40/50 sgl/dbl en suite, camping US$10pp, all bed only.* **$$**

🏠 **Nyumbani Hostel** [123 A1] (4 rooms) m 0758 463228/0686 490500; e info@nyumbani-hostel.com; www.nyumbani-hostel.com. Set in a maze of narrow streets north of the Eland Hotel, & owned by Tini & Tizia, this is literally *nyumbani* (our house). Free pickup from town or you can get a taxi for $4. *US$17pp HB.* **$$**

🏠 **YMCA** [125 B4] ✆027 254 4032; e ymcatanzania@hotmail.com. This Arusha institution is looking pretty rundown these days, but it has a conveniently central location on India Rd, decent food, & feels like relatively good value. *US$10/13 sgl/dbl.* **$**

🏠 **Kilimanjaro Villa** [131 G4] (8 rooms) m 0767 355999. A long-standing backpacker standby situated close to the market & central bus station, the Kilimanjaro Villa is nothing special but it's friendly, clean & reasonably priced. *US$7/10 sgl/dbl using common showers.* **$**

🏠 **Monje's Guesthouse** [131 G2 & H1] m 0782 999011/0769 206303; e info@monjestz. com; www.monjestz.com. Long-serving favourites among the myriad guesthouses in the back roads north of the stadium, this quiet, family-run business now operates 4 guesthouses within a block or 2 of each other. All 4 places have clean rooms, friendly staff & hot showers! A touch overpriced. *US$18/25 en-suite sgl/dbl.* **$$**

✗ WHERE TO EAT AND DRINK

Plenty of good restaurants are dotted around Arusha, with many international cuisines represented and most budgets catered for by a number of places. The following is an alphabetical selection of some long-standing favourites and interesting recent additions, but new places open and close frequently, so don't be afraid to try restaurants that aren't listed.

Eateries in the **old town centre** mostly cater to local business people and office workers at lunch, but generally stay open in the evening long enough for an early dinner. There are also decent restaurants at most central hotels, the pick being the à la carte eatery at The Arusha Hotel (pages 126–7), which also has a very pleasant bar.

The selection of restaurants listed in the **market area** section, below, are mainly limited to indifferent local eateries, but it does host two unpretentious but exceptional Indian restaurants, both open in the evenings.

There are several good places to eat in the **TFA (Nakumatt) Shopping Centre** [130 A7], most tending to be at the higher end of the price spectrum.

The leafy suburb of **Kijenge** is the main centre of Arusha's dining scene, boasting a cosmopolitan selection of mostly quite upmarket restaurants concentrated within a few minutes' walk of each other.

OLD TOWN CENTRE

✕ Africafe [125 C4] Boma Rd; m 0782 515634/0684 746892; e info@africafetanzania.com; www.africafetanzania.com; ⏱ 07.30–21.00 Mon–Sat, 08.00–21.00 Sun. This clean, modern restaurant serves good fresh coffee & juices, tasty muffins & other freshly baked goods, as well as a long list of cooked b/fasts, burgers, salads, sandwiches & other meals. It is a popular spot for lunch, with most mains in the US$7–10 range.

✕ Bamboo Fify's Café [125 C4] Boma Rd; ☎027 250 6451; m 0754 317801; e bamboocafe2000@yahoo.com; ⏱ 07.00–20.00 daily. This homely restaurant serves decent coffee, fruit juices, sandwiches, pancakes & snacks, & full meals for around US$5–7. The lunch of the day is usually a bargain.

✕ Green Hut Burgers [131 H7] Sokoine Rd. Excellent & inexpensive burgers & other greasy fast-food staples & light meals. No alcohol.

✕ Via Via Restaurant [125 C2] Boma Rd; m 0753 492400; www.viaviacafe.com/en/arusha; ⏱ 09.30–22.00 daily, closing later Thu & Sat. This Belgian-owned garden restaurant-cum-bar tucked away behind the Old Boma has a relaxing suburban atmosphere & the most eclectic selection of music in Arusha. There is a lunchtime buffet for US$8pp, & it also hosts occasional film evenings, live music & cultural events involving artistes from all of Africa.

MARKET AREA

✕ Dolly's Patisserie [131 G6] Sokoine Rd; ☎027 254 4013; ⏱ 09.00–18.00 Mon–Sat. This highly rated bakery sells fresh bread & cakes, along with tasty pastries & sandwiches to take away.

✕ Khan's Barbecue [131 G5] Mosque St; m 0754 652747; ⏱ 18.00–21.00. This singular eatery near the market is a motor spares shop by day & street BBQ in the evening. A mixed grill including beef, chicken & mutton kebabs, with a huge selection of salads, naan bread & the like, costs around US$5. No alcohol.

TFA CENTRE [130 A7]

For freshly made Italian ice cream, head to **Ciao Gelati**.

✕ Alpha Burger m 0688 813954. Excellent burgers (*US$5–6*) & good-value sushi (*US$5–10 for 8 pcs*). It's also a fish & meat supplier.

✕ Msumbi Café m 0754 789603; ⏱ 08.00–19.00 daily. Excellent freshly brewed coffee, a varied selection of teas, & b/fasts & light lunches in the US$2–4 range are all on offer at this clean & modern-looking patisserie.

✕ Stiggybucks Café m 0754 375535; ⏱ 09.00–17.00 Mon–Sat. This great owner-managed coffee shop has indoor & outdoor seating, & it serves a tempting selection of cakes, bagels, salads, sandwiches & light lunches, mostly for under US$5.

✕ Taste of Mexico m 0719 707217; www.tasteofmexico.co.tz; ⏱ 10.00–22.00 daily. Fine Mexcan food & ice-cold beer, all dishes reasonably priced in the US$5–10 range.

KIJENGE

✕ Blue Heron Coffee & Bookshop [123 F5] Haile Selassie Rd; m 0783 885833; e theheron@ars.bol.co.tz; ⏱ 09.00–16.00 Mon–Thu, 09.00–22.00 Fri, 10.00–16.00 Sat. Combining classic colonial architecture with contemporary décor, this stylish coffee shop is a great spot for a relaxed open-air lunch, with seating on the veranda & in the green garden. Wholesome pasta dishes, salads & filled paninis cost around US$6–10, & there is also a selection of cheaper dishes & excellent coffee.

✗ Impala Hotel [123 G6] Old Moshi Rd; ☏027 254 3082/7; www.impalahotel.com. The Indian restaurant in this large hotel is justifiably rated as one of the best in Arusha – & there are 3 other (lesser) specialist restaurants to choose from if Indian isn't your thing.

✗ Picasso Café [123 G6] Simeon Rd; m 0683 608636; ⊕ 09.00–23.00 Mon–Sat, 09.00–17.00 Sun. This stylish café – which feels like it's been transplanted from Italy or France despite its peculiar location in a large car park – serves a sumptuous selection of cakes & pastries, as well as an imaginative menu of filled crepes & salads for US$6–8. There are more substantial mains for around US$10, & the whole menu is complemented by good coffee & a great wine list.

✗ Pizza Point [123 E5] m 0754 294359; ⊕ 08.00–22.00 daily. One of the more affordable options in this part of the city, this pleasant & unpretentious garden restaurant serves pizzas for around US$4–6, along with a selection of standard meat dishes for under US$4.

✗ Spices & Herbs [123 G6] Simeon Rd; m 0768 356191; ⊕ lunch & dinner daily. The best Ethiopian restaurant in Arusha lies close to the Impala Hotel & serves distinctive Ethiopian staples such as *kai wat* (a spicy meat or vegetarian stew) served with *injera* (flat round sour bread). There's occasional live music, & an internet café onsite. Vegetarian dishes under US$5, other mains close to US$10.

OUT OF THE CITY

✗ Traders Walk [map, page 148] m 0783 509279; ⊕ 10.00–14.30 daily. In the grounds of the Arusha Coffee Lodge (page 126), this houses a coffee shop (Kahawa) & an African restaurant (Jikoni), the Shanga Workshop (page 137), plus a jewellers & a gift shop. The lodge's restaurant is also open to the public.

ENTERTAINMENT AND NIGHTLIFE

BARS AND NIGHTSPOTS There are several decent bars in the same area as the cluster of guesthouses behind the Golden Rose Hotel. The best place to drink in this part of the city is **Soweto Gardens** [122 B2], a relaxed but atmospheric garden bar that often hosts live bands over the weekends. Another good spot for live Tanzanian music is **Via Via** (page 133). Further out of the city, **Masai Camp** (page 132) on the Old Moshi Road is usually lively at night over weekends.

CINEMA The best cinema is the **Arusha Cinemax** [123 F7] (m *0732 102221/0755 102221; www.zoomtanzania.com/century-cinemax-arusha;* ⊕ *13.00 Tue–Sun*) in the out-of-town Njiro Mall, where the three screens show a varied selection of reasonably current Hollywood and Bollywood fare. Seats start at under US$5.

SHOPPING

BOOKS The best bookshop by far is the branch of **A Novel Idea** next to the Barclays Bank in the TFA Centre [130 A7] (☏ *027 254 7333; anovelidea.co.tz;* ⊕ *09.00–17.30 Mon–Fri*). This stocks a very good range of contemporary and classic novels, current bestsellers, guidebooks, field guides, and books about Tanzania. More central and also pretty good are the two branches of **Kase Book Shop** (☏ *027 250 2640;* ⊕ *09.00–17.00 Mon–Sat*), one of which lies on Boma Road next to Bamboo Fify's Café [125 C4], and the other on Joel Maeda Road more or less opposite the Kenya Commercial Bank [125 B5]. Both stock a good range of books about Tanzania and a more limited selection of contemporary bestsellers and novels. A few vendors usually hang around the Clock Tower selling maps and national park booklets at highly inflated prices, and most of the upmarket hotels also sell a limited selection

MAKONDE CARVINGS

The Makonde of the Tanzania–Mozambique border area are the finest traditional sculptors in East Africa. According to oral tradition the males of this matrilineal society have been practising this craft to woo their women for at least 300 years. Legend has it that the first person on earth, not yet male or female, living alone in the foothills of the Makonde Plateau, carved a piece of wood into the shape of a human figure. The carver left his creation outside his home overnight, and awoke to find it had been transformed into a living woman. Twice the woman conceived, but both times the child died after three days. Each time, the pair moved higher on to the plateau, believing this would bring them luck. The third child lived, and became the first true Makonde. The mother is regarded to be the spiritual ancestor of all the Makonde, and the legend is sometimes said to be a parable for the difficulty of creation.

In their purest form, the intricate, stylised carvings of the Makonde relate to this ancestral cult of womanhood, and are carried only by men, as a good-luck charm. Traditional carvings almost always depict a female figure, sometimes surrounded by children, and the style was practically unknown outside of Tanzania until a carving workshop was established at Mwenge in suburban Dar es Salaam during the 1950s. Subsequently, like any dynamic art form, Makonde sculpture has been responsive to external influences and subject to changes in fashion, with new styles of carvings becoming increasingly abstract and incorporating wider moral and social themes.

The most rustic of the new styles is the Binadamu sculpture, which depicts traditional scenes such as old men smoking pipes or women fetching water in a relatively naturalistic manner. Altogether more eerie and evocative is the Shetani style, in which grotesquely stylised human forms, sometimes with animal-like features, represent the impish and sometimes evil spirits for which the style is named. Many Makonde and other East Africans leave offerings for Shetani sculptures, believing them to be possessed by ancestral spirits. Most elaborate of all are the naturalistic Ujamaa sculptures, which depict many interlocking figures and relate to the collective social policy of Ujamaa fostered by the late President Nyerere. Also known as People Poles or Trees of Life, these statues sometimes incorporate several generations of the carver's family, rising in circular tiers to be up to 2m high. A newer style called Mawingu – the Swahili word for clouds – combines human figures with abstract shapes to represent intellectual or philosophical themes. Today, the finest examples of the genre fetch prices in excess of US$5,000 from international collectors.

The Makonde traditionally shape their creations exclusively from *Dalbergia melanoxylon*, a hardwood tree known locally as *mpingo* and in English as African blackwood or (misleadingly) African ebony. The carver – always male – will first saw a block of wood to the required size, then create a rough outline by hacking away excess wood with an instrument called an adze. The carving is all done freehand, with hammers, chisels and rasps used to carve the fine detail, before the final sculpture is sanded and brushed for smoothness. A large Ujamaa sculpture can take several months to complete, with some of the carving – appropriately – being undertaken communally. Traditionally, the craft was more or less hereditary, with sons being apprenticed to their fathers from a young age, and different families tending to work specific subjects related to their own traditions.

of reading matter in their curio shops. To buy or exchange secondhand novels, there are a couple of stalls dotted around the city, one in the alley connecting Boma and India roads and several along Sokoine Road west of the market.

CRAFTS AND CURIOS Arusha is one of the best places in East Africa to buy Makonde carvings, Tingatinga paintings, batiks, Maasai jewellery and other souvenirs. The curio shops are far cheaper than those in Dar es Salaam and their quality and variety are excellent. Most of the curio shops are clustered between the Clock Tower and India Road, though be warned that the outdoor stalls can be full of hassle.

Three places stand out. The **Cultural Heritage Centre** (☏ *027 250 7496;* m *0741 510429; www.culturalheritage.co.tz;* ⊕ *09.00–17.00 Mon–Sat, 09.00–14.00 Sun*), about 3km out of the city on the main road towards the Serengeti, diagonally

---

TINGATINGA PAINTINGS

The brightly coloured paintings of fabulous creatures you might notice at craft stalls in Arusha and elsewhere in the region are Tingatinga paintings, a school of painting that is unique to Tanzania and named after its founder Edward Tingatinga. The style arose in Dar es Salaam in the early 1960s, when Tingatinga fused the vibrant and popular work of Congolese immigrants with art traditions indigenous to his Makua homeland in the Mozambique border area (a region well known to aficionados of African art as the home of Makonde carving). When Tingatinga died in 1972, the accidental victim of a police shoot-out, his commercial success had already spawned a host of imitators, and shortly after that a Tingatinga art co-operative was formed with government backing.

In the early days, Tingatinga and his followers produced fairly simple paintings featuring a large, bold and often rather surreal two-dimensional image of one or another African creature on a monotone background. But as the paintings took off commercially, a greater variety of colours came into play, and a trend developed towards the more complex canvases you see today. Modern Tingatinga paintings typically depict a menagerie of stylised and imaginary birds, fish and mammals against a backdrop of natural features such as Kilimanjaro or an abstract panel of dots and whorls. An offshoot style, reputedly initiated by Tingatinga himself, can be seen in the larger, even more detailed canvases that depict a sequence of village or city scenes so busy you could look at them for an hour and still see something fresh.

Tingatinga painters have no pretensions to producing high art. On the contrary, the style has been commercially driven since its inception: even the largest canvases are produced over a matter of days and most painters work limited variations around favourite subjects. It would be missing the point altogether to talk of Tingatinga as traditional African art. With its bold, bright images – tending towards the anthropomorphic, often subtly humorous, always accessible and evocative – Tingatinga might more appropriately be tagged Africa's answer to Pop Art.

Labels aside, souvenir hunters will find Tingatinga paintings to be a lively, original and surprisingly affordable alternative to the identikit wooden animal carvings that are sold throughout East Africa (and, one suspects, left to gather dust in cupboards all over Europe). Take home a Tingatinga panel, and you'll have a quirky but enduring memento of your African trip, something to hang on your wall and derive pleasure from for years to come.

opposite the Tanzania National Parks' headquarters, stocks the most vast collection of Tanzanian and other African crafts, ranging from towering carvings to colourful batiks and jewellery, and a useful selection of books about Tanzania. It's where the likes of King Harald of Norway and former South African and US presidents Thabo Mbeki and Bill Clinton did their curio shopping in Arusha, and an onsite branch of DHL can arrange shipping to anywhere in the world. It can be visited on the way back from a safari, or as a short taxi trip from Arusha.

Also on the Serengeti Road, at Traders Walk in the Arusha Coffee Lodge (page 126), **Shanga** (e *info@shanga.org; www.shanga.org*), named for the Swahili word meaning 'bead', is an eco-friendly handicraft workshop founded in 2007 and now providing employment to more than 40 craftsmen with disabilities. It sells a variety of high-quality handmade items combining colourful local beadwork and fabrics with recycled materials such as glass and aluminium.

Altogether different in atmosphere is **Maasai Craft & Curio Market** on Fire Road about 200m south of the Clock Tower [122 D5]. Here, some 50-plus stalls sell Maasai beadwork, Tingatinga and other local paintings, batiks, jewellery and pretty much any other ethno-artefact you might be interested in. Prices are lower than the Cultural Heritage Centre, and very negotiable, but the downside is that there is a bit more hassle, though generally of a friendly rather than intimidating nature.

SHOPPING MALLS AND SUPERMARKETS The biggest and best shopping mall, situated at the west end of Sokoine Road, is the **TFA Centre** [130 A7], also often referred to as the Nakumatt Centre after the eponymous supermarket. This is the largest shop there (\ *027 254 4516; www.nakumatt.co.ke;* ⊕ *09.00–21.00 Mon–Fri, 09.00–17.00 Sat, 09.00–13.00 Sun*), a warehouse-sized representative of the major Kenyan chain that stocks a huge range of imported and local goods (including South African wines at a third of the price charged by the hotels) as well as fresh meat, bread and vegetables, making it an excellent place to stock up with whatever goodies you need before you head out on safari. Also in the TFA Centre are half-a-dozen upmarket restaurants and coffee shops (page 133), Tanzania's first gourmet chocolate producer, Chocolate Mamas (m *0789 380807;* e *jaki@ chocolatemamastz.com*), which sells locally made fair-trade chocolate, as well as several safari outfitters and a good selection of other clothing and craft shops, hairdressers, banks with ATMs, internet cafés, etc. The more out-of-town **Njiro Mall** [123 F7], 4km south of the Impala Hotel, also boasts several eateries, and Arusha's best cinema (page 134), as well as the excellent Village Supermarket, but the selection of shops is limited.

OTHER PRACTICALITIES

BANKS, ATMS AND FOREIGN EXCHANGE Various private and bank-related bureaux de change are dotted all around Arusha, and it is worth shopping around to find the best rate for US dollars cash – US$100 and US$50 notes get a much better rate than the smaller bills. Many bureaux de change won't accept less widely used international currencies or travellers' cheques, but the **National Bank of Commerce** on Sokoine Road [125 A7] will, as will the bureau de change at the Impala Hotel [123 G6]. Whatever else you do, don't change money on the streets of Arusha, as you are sure to be ripped off. If you are desperate for local currency outside banking hours, **Foreigners Bureau de Change** on Goliondoi Road [125 A4] is open seven days a week from 07.00 to 18.30, and later than that you will probably have to ask a safari company or hotel to help you out with a small transaction.

5

There are now numerous 24-hour ATMs where local currency can be drawn against a Visa or MasterCard. These include the ATMs at the **Standard Chartered Bank** on Goliondoi Road [125 A6], the **Barclays Bank** on Serengeti Road [123 F7], various ATMs operated by the MBC, NMB and Exim Bank, and the ATMs in the **Njiro Mall** [123 F7] and **TFA Centre** [130 A7]. Most ATMs impose a transaction limit of Tsh400,000 (slightly less than US$200) but you can usually do several transactions in a row.

MEDIA AND COMMUNICATIONS

Internet and email There are numerous internet cafés dotted all over Arusha, generally asking less than US$1 per hour. One of the best is the **Telecom-run internet café** on the first floor of the post office building on Boma Road [125 C5]. Also good are the **Cybernet Centre** on India Road [125 B5] and the **Hot Bread Shop** on the east end of Sokoine Road [125 B6]. Many hotels also offer internet access, often for free to hotel residents.

Newspapers A selection of local newspapers is available on the day of publication, as is the *Nation,* a Kenyan paper which is generally stronger on international news. You won't need to look for these newspapers, because the vendors who sell them will find you quickly enough. The excellent weekly *East African* is available at several newspaper kiosks. The American weeklies *Time* and *Newsweek* are widely available in Arusha.

Post and telephone The main **post office** is on Boma Road facing the Clock Tower [125 C5]. The **telecommunications centre** further along Boma Road [125 C3] is a good place to make international phone calls and send faxes. If you want to buy a local SIM card for your mobile phone, the best and cheapest place to do so is the **Vodacom service centre** at the junction of Sokoine and Goliondoi roads [125 A6] – it should cost around Tsh300, though you'll need to buy some pay-as-you-go airtime (*Tsh500–50,000*) to activate it.

MEDICAL The **Arusha Lutheran Medical Centre** (ALMC) off Colonel Middleton Road [130 C1] (m *0736 502376; www.almc.habari.co.tz*) is generally regarded to be the best in Arusha. For other recommendations, consult your hotel reception or safari company.

SWIMMING The swimming pools at the **Ilboru Lodge** [122 D1] and **Impala Hotel** [123 G6] are open to non-residents for a small daily fee.

TOURIST INFORMATION

The **Tanzania Tourist Board** (TTB) office on Boma Road [125 C4] (✆ *027 250 3840;* e *ttbarusha@cybernet.co.tz; www.tanzaniatourism.com;* ⏰ *08.00–16.00 Mon–Fri, 08.30–13.00 Sat*) is refreshingly helpful and well informed. It stocks a useful colour road map of Tanzania as well as a great street plan of Arusha, both given free of charge to tourists (though this doesn't stop the book vendors out on the street from trying to sell the same maps at silly prices). If you want to check out a safari company, the TTB office keeps a regularly updated list of all registered safari and trekking companies, as well as those that are blacklisted.

The TTB has been actively involved in the development of cultural tourism programmes in Ng'iresi, Mulala, Mkuru, Longido, Mto wa Mbu, Usambara, North Pare and South Pare, as well as several projects further afield. The Arusha office stocks informative pamphlets about these programmes, and can help out with information on prices and access. Details are also available at the **Cultural Tourism Programme** office in the Old Boma [125 C2] (✆ *027 250 0025;* e *culturaltourism@ habari.co.tz; www.tanzaniaculturaltourism.com*).

The head office of **Tanzania National Parks** (Tanapa) is located in the Mwalimu J K Nyerere Conservation Centre about 3km out of town along the Serengeti road (✆ *027 250 3471;* e *info@tanzaniaparks.go.tz; www.tanzaniaparks.go.tz*), roughly opposite the Cultural Heritage Centre.

The **Ngorongoro Conservation Authority** (NCA) has a helpful information office on Boma Road [125 C4] (✆ *027 253 7006; www.ngorongorocrater.org*) close to the tourist board office. In addition to some worthwhile displays on the conservation area, it sells a good range of books and booklets about the northern circuit.

The **Wildlife Division** (WD) office (✆ *027 254 8750*) is on River Road [122 C6] and houses the CITES office among other conservation and wildlife departments. The WD is responsible for issuing permits to visit Wildlife Management Areas (WMAs), which are community-managed conservation areas. There are currently 38 WMAs across Tanzania, and they may be included in your safari plans by your operator, or you may decide to head into one of these little-visited areas yourself. If you plan to visit one of the WMAs, your fees can be paid by a tour operator registered on the WD online system, or directly to the Wildlife Division. The latter course of action entails popping into the WD office to check the fee, depositing the appropriate amount into their bank account, then returning with your bank slip to fill in a form at the CITES office, and handing them in together. They will then print your permit ready to go.

SAFARI OPERATORS

The list given here is not definitive, but it provides a good cross-section of the sort of services that are on offer and, except where otherwise noted, it sticks to companies that have maintained high standards over the years. The listed companies generally specialise in northern circuit safaris, but most can also set up Kilimanjaro and Meru climbs, fly-in safaris on the southern safari circuit, and excursions to Zanzibar.

Africa Dream Safaris m 0752 225554 or (US toll-free) +1 877 572 3274; e safari@ africadreamsafaris.com; www.africadreamsafaris. com; see ad, inside front cover. An award-winning outfit specialising in upmarket customised safaris for serious wildlife enthusiasts & photographers, using intimate tented camps & knowledgeable driver/guides who place strong emphasis on early-morning & full-day game drives, avoiding circuits that suffer from overcrowding.

Awaken to Africa m 0754 387061, (US) +1 732 271 8269 or (toll-free) +1 888 271 8269;

e info@awakentoafrica.com; www. awakentoafrica.com; see ad, page 69. Managed by its enthusiastic & hands-on Tanzanian–US owners, this small new company specialises in tailor-made upmarket safaris using exclusive intimate camps. It has plenty of experience with, & is highly recommended to, dedicated photographers.

Bush2Beach Safaris m 0734 503700/ 0754 096006; e info@bush2beach.com; www. bush2beach.com. With over 16 years of designing custom-made private wildlife safaris, B2B are a specialised tour operator that offers good value for money for safaris, mountain climbs & beach holidays.

Fair Travel Tanzania m 0786 025886/8;
e res@fairtraveltanzania.com; www.fairtravel.
com; see ad, page 191. This admirable company
is, as its name suggests, strongly committed to
ecologically sound travel that pays fair wages
to drivers & other staff, channels all profit into
community projects, & still offers competitive
rates to its clients (for further details, see the
informative website).
A recommended mid-range option.

Hoopoe Safaris [125 B4] 027 250 7011;
e information@hoopoe.com; www.hoopoe.
com. This long-serving & highly regarded
owner-managed safari company specialises in
personalised luxury camping & lodge safaris.
It owns tented camps outside Lake Manyara &
Tarangire national parks, & is also a good contact
for trekking & walking safaris in Natron, the
Ngorongoro Highlands, & the game-rich Maasai
Plains to the east of the Serengeti.

Kearsleys Travel [131 F2] 022 213 7713;
e sales@kearsleys.com; www.kearsleys.com.
Established in 1948, this is the oldest safari
company in Tanzania, with dynamic management
& staff, & well-maintained vehicles. Though it
has traditionally focused on the more 'difficult'
southern safari circuit, Kearsleys now has an office
in Arusha (next to the Golden Rose Hotel) & is also
a thoroughly reliable choice for safaris along the
northern circuit.

Ker & Downey Tanzania 027 250 8917;
e info@legendaryadventure.com; www.
keranddowneytanzania.com. This established
operator specialises in ultra-exclusive photographic
safaris centred on its private concessions bordering
the Ngorongoro Conservation Area & Lake Natron,
as well as a mobile camp following the migration
through the Serengeti.

Leopard Tours 027 250 8441; e leopardtours@
leopardtours.co.za; www.leopard-tours.com.
This large-scale operator specialises in mid-range
safaris concentrating on the larger lodges & more
established game-viewing areas, & offers a highly
reliable service to those who want to stick firmly to
the beaten track.

Nature Discovery m 0732 971859; e info@
naturediscovery.com; www.naturediscovery.com.
This eco-friendly operator is widely praised for
its high-quality, top-end Kilimanjaro climbs, & it
also arranges standard northern circuit safaris as

well as trekking expeditions in the Ngorongoro
Highlands & elsewhere.

Roy Safaris [123 F6] 027 250 2115;
e roysafaris@intafrica.com; www.roysafaris.com.
This dynamic & efficient owner-managed company
is recommended for reliable but reasonably
priced budget & mid-range camping, semi-luxury
camping safaris & lodge safaris.

Safari Infinity m 0688 285354/0684 864483;
e info@safari-infinity.com; www.safari-infinity.
com. This highly regarded Arusha-based venture
operates reliable tailor-made upmarket safaris
throughout the northern safari circuit.

Safari Makers m 0732 979195/0754 300817;
e safarimakers@habari.co.tz; www.safarimakers.
com. Owner-managed by a dynamic hands-on
American–Tanzanian couple, Safari Makers runs
competitively priced camping & lodge safaris,
as well as arranging visits to various cultural
programmes in communities outside Arusha,
making it a recommended first contact at the
budget to mid-range level.

Summits Africa m 0784 522090; e info@
summits-africa.com; www.summits-africa.com.
As its name suggests, this small adventure-
orientated company specialises in Kilimanjaro &
Mount Meru climbs, often using the less well-
known routes, but it is also a great contact for
visits to Lake Natron & Ol Doinyo Lengai, as well
as putting together more conventional tailor-
made safaris.

Tanzania Adventure m 0786 019944;
e info@tanzania-adventure.com; www.tanzania-
adventure.com. This joint German–Tanzanian
company offers a wide selection of safaris, including
an extensive walking programme in the Ngorongoro
Highlands & Serengeti border areas. It is especially
recommended to German-speakers.

Tropical Trails 027 250 0358; e info@
tropicaltrails.com; www.tropicaltrails.com. Based
at Masai Camp (page 132), this eco-friendly
budget-oriented company arranges standard
lodge-based & camping safaris, walking excursions
on the fringes of the main national parks, & Kili
climbs along the less usual routes.

TrueAfrica (South Africa) +27 (0)21 418 0500;
e info@trueafrica.com; www.trueafrica.com.
Strongly affiliated to the excellent Asilia chain of
exclusive tented camps, this company specialises
in tailor-made upmarket safaris at some of the
country's top camps & lodges.

Wayo Africa m 0784 203000; e info@wayoafrica.com; www.wayoafrica.com. This environmentally minded operator can arrange safaris for most tastes & budgets, but its main speciality is walking safaris in wilderness areas within the Serengeti National Park, as well as bush camps set in more remote parts in the other parks. The standard of guiding can be exceptional, & it is highly recommended to active travellers seeking a genuine wilderness experience at reasonable rates.

Wild Frontiers ☏ 027 702 2035; m (South Africa) +27 (0)72 927 7529; e reservations@wildfrontiers.com; www.wildfrontiers.com. Based in South Africa but with its own ground operation in Arusha, this well-established & flexible company offers a varied range of motorised, walking & combination safaris using standard lodges or its own excellent tented camps. Recommended to those seeking a relatively unpackaged safari at a reasonable price.

Wild Things Safaris ☏ 022 261 7166; m 0773 503502; e enquiries@wildthingssafaris.com; www.wildthingssafaris.com; see ad, page 292. Operating all over the country & highly experienced in both northern & southern circuits, Wild Things offers high-quality, well-priced tailor-made safaris to anywhere you want to go. They are also a great source of information for adventures to less-visited & more remote destinations.

&Beyond [123 F6] ☏ (South Africa) +27 (0)11 809 4447; e safaris@andbeyond.com; www.andbeyond.com. Formerly known as CCAfrica, &Beyond operates some of the most sumptuous lodges in northern Tanzania, notable for their fine attention to detail, informal & personalised service, well-trained guides & rangers, & general air of exclusivity. It arranges fly-in, drive-in (or mixed) safaris throughout northern Tanzania, as well as mobile safaris using seasonal camps in the 'Under Canvas' brand.

WHAT TO SEE AND DO

MUSEUMS   Arusha is better known as a base for safaris and other excursions than as a sightseeing destination in its own right. However, a trio of museums dot the centre of town, none of which could be described as a 'must see', but all worth a passing look if you're in the area. Further afield, Arusha National Park, described in *Chapter 6*, makes for a great half- or even full-day excursion out of town.

National Natural History Museum   [125 C2] (*Boma Rd*; ◼ *NNHMArusha*; ⊕ *09.00–18.00 daily; entrance US$5 non-resident adult, US$2 foreign student*) Housed in the old German Boma, this might more accurately be renamed the Archaeological or Palaeontological Museum. The limited displays – you can walk around the museum in a minute – include a selection of animal and hominid fossils unearthed at Oldupai and Laetoli in the Ngorongoro Conservation Area, as well as life-size models of *Australopithecus* hunter-gatherers at play.

Arusha Declaration Museum   [131 G4] (*Uhuru Monument Circle*; ⊕ *08.30–17.30; entrance US$5*) Dedicated primarily to 20th-century developments in Tanzania, this has some interesting displays on the colonial and post-independence Nyerere era. It also contains a few decent ethnographic displays, but seems overpriced for what it is.

The Tanzanite Experience   [125 B4] (*3rd Floor, Blue Plaza Bldg, India Rd*; m *0767 600990*; e *info@tanzaniteexperience.com; www.tanzaniteexperience.com*; ⊕ *08.30–17.30 Mon–Fri, 09.00–15.00 Sat; free entrance*) Operated by TanzaniteOne, the world's largest tanzanite mining company, this modern museum provides a fascinating overview of the discovery and extraction of this exquisite blue gem, which occurs in Tanzania only. Imaginative multi-media displays and enthusiastic staff are complemented by many examples of rough and cut tanzanite (and other striking local rocks). There is also the chance to purchase certified gemstones direct from source, along with tanzanite and diamond jewellery.

CULTURAL TOURS A number of cultural tourism programmes have been implemented around Arusha with the assistance of the Dutch agency SNV. Any one of these programmes makes for an excellent half- or full-day trip out of Arusha, offering tourists the opportunity to experience something of rural Africa away from the slick lodges and main safari circuit. You can ask your safari company to tag a visit to one of the cultural programmes on to your main safari, or can arrange a standalone day trip once you arrive in Arusha. Several of the programmes also offer the opportunity to spend a night in a village, although it should be stressed that accommodation of this sort is not up to accepted tourist-class standards. Of the various programmes, the one at Longido can be easily visited on public transport, but the rest are only realistically visited in a private vehicle. The TTB office on Boma Road and the Cultural Tourism Office in the Old Boma (page 139) stock useful pamphlets about all the cultural programmes, and can advise you about current costs and accessibility.

Mkuru Camel Safari (m *0784 472475;* e *info@mkurucamelsafari.com; www. mkurucamelsafari.com*) The most successful of the cultural tourism programmes around Arusha is based at Mkuru at the northern base of Mount Meru. It's a very well-organised set-up, offering a selection of facilities and activities that seems to increase with every passing year, although these days it's pitched more at the mid-range market than budget travellers. The main attraction here is organised camelback trips, which range in duration from day outings and overnight trips into the wildlife-rich plains towards Longido to a week-long trek to Ol Doinyo Lengai and Lake Natron, for around US$140 per person per day. In addition to camel rides, it offers a variety of day walks – a bird walk on the plain, a hike to the top of Ol Doinyo Landare, cultural visits to local healers and women's craft groups – for around US$30 per person. All activities are slightly cheaper as group sizes increase.

Activities run out of the down-to-earth and reasonably priced Mkuru Camel Camp (US$45pp FB), 55km from Arusha, which is situated near the pyramidal Ol Doinyo Landare (literally 'Mountain of Goats') and Ngare Nanyuki (on the northern border of Arusha National Park) and it offers great views of Kilimanjaro and Meru. This solar-powered camp has comfortable accommodation in furnished standing tents, simple ground tents with beds, sleeping bags, sheets and towels – or you can pitch your own tent.

Longido (m *0787/0767 855185;* e *touryman1@yahoo.com; www. tanzaniaculturaltourism.com*) This cultural tourism project run out of the overgrown village of Longido is one of the most accessible in the region for independent travellers, and it is an excellent place to visit for those who want to spend time among the Maasai. The original programme co-ordinator was a local Maasai who studied abroad as a sociologist before he was paralysed in a serious accident, and his successor can tell you anything you want to know about Maasai culture. Three different walking modules are on offer to tourists. On all modules, you can expect to see a variety of birds (including several colourful finches and barbets), and there is a fair amount of large game left in the area, notably gerenuk, lesser kudu, giraffe, Thomson's gazelle and black-backed jackal. It is worth trying to be in Longido on Wednesday, when a hectic cattle market is held on the outskirts of the village.

The first module is a half-day bird walk (*US$40pp*) through the Maasai Plains, which also includes a visit to a rural Maasai boma, and a meal cooked by the local women's group. Then there is a full-day tour (*US$60pp*) that follows the same route as the bird walk, before climbing to the top of the 2,637m Longido Mountain, an ascent of roughly 400m, offering views to Mount Meru and Kilimanjaro on a clear day, as well as over the Maasai Plains to Kenya. The two-day module (*US$105pp*) follows the same route as the full-day walk, but involves camping out overnight in the green Kimokouwa Valley, before visiting a dense rainforest that still harbours a number of buffalo as well as the usual birds and monkeys. The project can also organise a guide (*US$10*), cook (*US$20*) and tent with sleeping bag and mattress (*US$10/day*).

Longido straddles the main Namanga road roughly 100km from Arusha, so any of the regular minibuses and taxis that run between Arusha and Namanga can drop you there – these usually leave Arusha from the north end of the bus station opposite the stadium. The tourist project maintains a neat and inexpensive guesthouse about 100m from the main road (*US$7–20pp*), or you can arrange to pitch a tent at a Maasai boma for a small fee (*US$10*). A limited selection of cheap Tanzanian fare is available from one or two small restaurants that lie along the main road, and a couple of local bars (with pool table) serve cold beers and soft drinks.

Ng'iresi village
(m *0754 320966*; e *lotisareyo@yahoo.com or nfo@arusha-ngiresi. com; www.arusha-ngiresi.com*) Set on the slopes of Mount Meru some 7km from Arusha town, this cultural tourism programme based in the traditional Wa-Arusha village of Ng'iresi offers many insights into the local culture and agricultural practices. There are also some lovely walks in the surrounding Mount Meru foothills, an area characterised by fast-flowing streams, waterfalls and remnant forest patches. From Ng'iresi, it is possible to walk to Lekimana Hill, from where there are good views over the Maasai Steppes and on a clear day to Kilimanjaro. Another walk takes you to Kivesi Hill, an extinct volcano whose forested slopes support a variety of birds and small mammals.

Three different 'modules' are available at Ng'iresi, all inclusive of meals prepared by the Juhudi Women's Group and guided activities (*US$23pp*). There is no public transport to Ng'iresi, so you must either set up a visit through a safari company or make arrangements with a private vehicle.

Mulala village
(m *0756 477294/0784 378951*; e *agapetourism@yahoo.com; www. tanzaniaculturaltourism.com*) This is another cultural tourism programme situated in a village on the footslopes of Mount Meru. Mulala lies at an altitude of 1,450m, some 30km from Arusha, in a fertile agricultural area, which produces coffee, bananas and other fruit and vegetables. Several short walks can be undertaken in the surrounding hills, including one to the forested Marisha River, home to a variety of birds and primates, and to Mazungu Lake, where it is said that a mzungu was once lured to his death by a demon. Another local place of interest is Mama Anna's dairy, which supplies cheese to several upmarket hotels in Arusha. The tourist programme here is run in conjunction with the Agape Women's Group, which provides most of the guides as well as snacks and camping facilities. The tour costs US$25 per person for a half-day or US$30 per person for a full-day with lunch.

Monduli Juu
(m *0786 799688/0787 756299*; e *mpoyoni@yahoo.com or olejackson@ yahoo.com; www.tanzaniaculturaltourism.com*) The settlement of Monduli Juu (Upper Monduli) is situated some 50km west of Arusha in the Monduli Hills, a forested range that rises from the Rift Valley floor to an altitude of 2,660m, offering some superb views to other larger mountains such as Kilimanjaro, Meru and Ol Doinyo Lengai. Monduli Juu consists of a cluster of four Maasai villages, namely Emairete, Enguiki, Eluwai and Mfereji, the first of which is set alongside

In 1962, local legend tells, a Maasai cattle herder called Ali Juyawatu was walking through the Mererani Hills after a bush fire, and noticed some unusual blue crystals lying on the ground. Ali picked up the beautiful stones and took them to the nearby town of Arusha, from where they somehow made their way to the New York gemstone dealer Tiffany & Co, which had never seen anything like them before. In 1967, Tiffany launched the newly discovered gem on the market, naming it tanzanite in honour of its country of origin.

Tanzanite is by any standards a remarkable stone. A copper brown variety of zoisite, it is rather dull in its natural condition, but responds to gentle heating, transforming into a richly saturated dark-blue gem, with purple and violet undertones that have been compared among other things to the eyes of Elizabeth Taylor! Tanzanite comes only from Tanzania's Mererani Hills – rumours of a second deposit in Usangi, 75km from Arusha, have yet to be confirmed – and it is a thousand times rarer than diamonds. Despite its upstart status in the jewellery world, tanzanite has rocketed in popularity since its discovery. By 1997, 30 years after its launch, it had become the second most popular gemstone in the North American market, second to sapphires and ahead of rubies and emeralds, generating an annual trade worth US$300 million in the USA alone.

Remarkable, too, is the degree of controversy that the tanzanite trade has attracted in recent years. In the late 1990s, the Tanzanian government, comparing international tanzanite trade figures against their documented exports, realised that as much as 90% of the tanzanite sold in the USA was being smuggled out of Tanzania, resulting in a huge loss of potential government revenue in taxes and royalties. The ease with which the stones were being smuggled was clearly linked to the unregulated nature of the workings at Mererani, which consisted of more than 300 small claims operating in what has been described by more than one observer as a Wild West atmosphere. For the small claim holders, rather than distributing the stones they collected through legitimate sources, it was more profitable – and considerably more straightforward – to sell them for cash to illicit cross-border traders.

The lack of regulations at Mererani, or at least the lack of a body to enforce what regulations do exist, is also largely to blame for a series of tragedies that has dogged the workings in recent years. The greatest single catastrophe occurred during the El Niño rains of 1998, when one of the shafts at Block D flooded and at least 100 miners drowned. But it has been estimated that a similar number of miners died underground subsequent to this mass tragedy, as a result of suffocation, inept dynamite blasting, or periodic outbreaks of violent fighting over disputed claims. Aside from such incidents, it has long been rumoured that miners who are down on their luck will kidnap and sacrifice children from neighbouring villages, in the hope it will bring them good fortune and prosperity.

a spectacular crater that betrays the mountains' volcanic origins and is still held sacred by locals.

The cultural programme at Monduli Juu offers several programmes, ranging from a few hours to several days in duration. For nature lovers, a recommended option is the hike to Monduli Peak, passing through patches of montane forest that support a large variety of monkeys, antelope, birds and butterflies as well as

In 1999, the Tanzanian government put out to tender a lease on Block C, the largest of the four mining blocks, accounting for about 75% of the known tanzanite deposit. The rights were acquired by a South African company – with a 25% Tanzanian stake – called African Gem Resources (AFGEM), which reputedly pumped US$20 million into establishing the mine with the intention of going online in early 2000. This goal proved to be highly optimistic, as local miners and stakeholders, understandably hostile to the corporate intrusion on their turf, not to mention the threat it posed to the illicit tanzanite trade, attempted to disrupt the new project and persuade AFGEM to withdraw.

The long-simmering tensions erupted in April 2001, when a bomb was set off in the new mining plant, killing nobody, but causing large-scale material damage nonetheless. Later in the same month, AFGEM security guards opened fire on a group of 300 irate miners who had invaded the plant, killing one trespasser and causing serious injury to nine. When the Minister for Energy and Minerals visited the scene a few days later, the trespassers claimed to have been protesting against AFGEM's alleged complicity in the alleged death of 20 miners who were buried alive. AFGEM refuted the claims as pure fabrication, part of a smear campaign designed to discredit them and protect the illicit tanzanite trade. The result of the official investigation into the incident has yet to be released.

The tanzanite plot took a new and wholly unexpected twist in late December 2001, when press reports linked four of the men convicted on charges relating to the 1998 US embassy bombings in Nairobi and Dar es Salaam with the illicit tanzanite trade. Amid wild speculation that the underground tanzanite trade was funding Osama bin Laden and his al-Qaeda organisation, three major US jewellery dealers announced a total boycott on the purchase or sale of the gem. Among them, ironically, was the retailer that had first placed it in the spotlight back in 1967. Tiffany & Co publicly conceded a lack of hard evidence supporting the bin Laden link, but announced that it 'troubled' them regardless. By the end of January 2002, the price of tanzanite dropped to a third of its 2001 level.

The Tanzanian government elected to suspend operations at Mererani until the claims were investigated. At a Tucson trade fair in February 2002, the American Gem Trade Association and the Tanzanian Minister of Energy and Minerals signed a protocol that placed significant new controls on local access to the tanzanite mines. After the protocol was signed, the US State Department praised Tanzania for having 'done everything in its power to assist us in the war against terrorism' and declared it had 'seen no evidence that … any terrorist group is currently using tanzanite sales to finance its efforts or launder money'. Sales of the gem have since boomed, and many specialist stores line the streets of Arusha, while a new museum called the Tanzanite Experience (page 141) has raised the gem's profile. Prices remain volatile, ranging from US$650 to more than US$1,000 per carat, depending on the size and quality of the individual gemstone.

relict populations of elephant and buffalo – an armed ranger is mandatory. Other attractions include visits to a traditional healer, Naramatu bead factory and general cultural programmes including a Maasai boma visit and a meat market.

Two-way transport from Monduli to the village costs US$110, while tours cost US$35 for a half day or US$90 for a full day per person with lunch. A three-day, two-night itinerary can be crafted for visitors costing US$160 per person. A few local families in Monduli Juu offer camping sites. Meals – traditional or Western, as you like – can be prepared with a bit of notice.

MESERANI SNAKE PARK (**m** *0754 445911/440800*; **e** *meseranisnakepark@gmail.com*; *www.meseranisnakepark.com*; ☉ *07.30–18.00 daily; entrance US$15pp*) Situated 25km out of Arusha along the main Serengeti Road, this long-serving establishment combines a snake park (home to more than 40 species including the deadly venomous black mamba and red spitting cobra) with a Maasai Cultural Museum. It also operates a free snakebite clinic. Other facilities include a popular campsite (*US$8pp*) and a characterful bar and restaurant serving burgers, toasted sandwiches and the like in the US$2–3 range.

6

Arusha National Park and the Moshi Highway

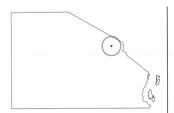

Many safari itineraries treat Arusha town as little more than an overnight staging post *en route* to the Serengeti National Park and the other world-famous reserves of northwest Tanzania. However, the surrounding area is well worth exploring in its own right. Several of the region's most attractive hotels flank the asphalt road that runs east from Arusha to Moshi via Lake Duluti, Usa River and Kilimanjaro International Airport, and the area to the north of the Moshi Highway is protected within two relatively little-visited wildlife sanctuaries in the form of Arusha National Park and the more loosely defined West Kilimanjaro region. Arusha National Park in particular is an underrated conservation area that amply repays whatever time and effort you choose to invest in it – be it a quick afternoon game drive, a couple of nights at one of the lodges on its periphery, or the altogether more challenging ascent of the mighty Mount Meru. Also of interest is Lake Duluti, a pretty forest-fringed crater lake that can be explored by boat, or along a 5km walking trail that circumnavigates its shores.

THE MOSHI HIGHWAY

The most important – or at least the busiest – trunk road in northern Tanzania is the 80km tract of asphalt that connects Arusha to Moshi via Kilimanjaro International Airport, the main air gateway to the region. Though it currently comprises one (often congested) lane running in either direction, the road is in the process of being upgraded to a dual carriageway, the first stage in a US$225 million project to revive road links between Arusha and Mombasa via the Holili–Taveta border southeast of Mount Kilimanjaro. With the exception of nearby Lake Duluti and Arusha National Park, the highway boasts no tourist attractions of note. It's an attractive area, however – lush, fertile and bisected by numerous forest-fringed streams that rise on Mount Meru – and many tourists prefer to stay here instead of in Arusha or Moshi town, thanks to a proliferation of mid-range to upmarket accommodation, mostly set in large grounds offering views towards Mount Meru and Kilimanjaro.

TOWARDS LAKE DULUTI The road running immediately east from Arusha towards Lake Duluti provides access to some of the most popular lodges in the Arusha area, including Moivaro, Machweo and Onsea House, and Kigongoni Lodge.

Where to stay *Map, page 148*
Exclusive
☀ 🏠 **Machweo & Onsea House** (9 & 4 rooms, with 2 more under construction at the latter) **m** 0784 833207; **e** info@onseahouse. com; www.onseahouse.com, www.machweo. com. These attractive & intimate boutique hotels,

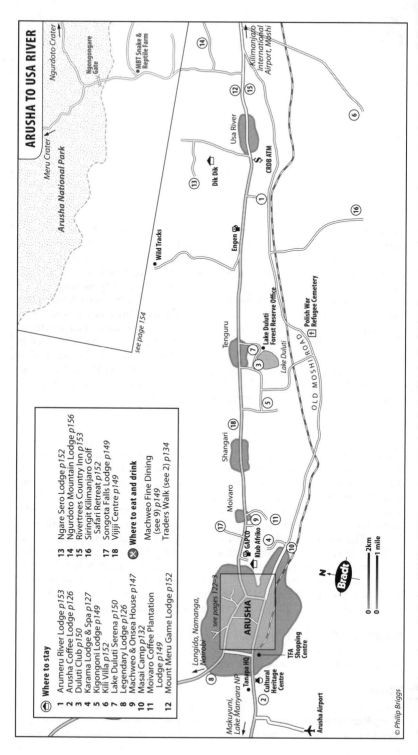

ARUSHA TO USA RIVER

Where to stay
1 Arumeru River Lodge *p153*
2 Arusha Coffee Lodge *p126*
3 Duluti Club *p150*
4 Karama Lodge & Spa *p127*
5 Kigongoni Lodge *p149*
6 Kili Villa *p152*
7 Lake Duluti Serena *p150*
8 Legendary Lodge *p126*
9 Machweo & Onsea House *p147*
10 Masai Camp *p132*
11 Moivaro Coffee Plantation
   Lodge *p149*
12 Mount Meru Game Lodge *p152*
13 Ngare Sero Lodge *p152*
14 Ngurdoto Mountain Lodge *p156*
15 Rivertrees Country Inn *p153*
16 Siringit Kilimanjaro Golf
   Safari Retreat *p152*
17 Songota Falls Lodge *p149*
18 Vijiji Centre *p149*

Where to eat and drink
   Machweo Fine Dining
   (see 9) *p149*
   Traders Walk (see 2) *p134*

© Philip Briggs

under the same Belgian owner-manager, are situated alongside each other on the slopes of Namasi Hill less than 10mins' drive from central Arusha on the south side of the Moshi road. The older & smaller Onsea House consists of 4 rooms with funky but understated African décor, 2 of which can be rented out as a separate house, while the offshoot Machweo offers the choice of 3 honeymoon suites or 6 semi-detached cottage suites decorated in simple classic contemporary style. All rooms have a minibar, walk-in netting, safe & flatscreen DSTV. There are 2 swimming pools on the combined property, as well as a highly rated wellness centre & spa, a games room with pool table, & a walking trail on the forested bird-rich hill behind the property. The complex is also home to arguably the top restaurant in Arusha, managed by the same Michelin-trained Belgian chef since it opened in 2006, serving innovative European cuisine with an African twist (see below). All rooms are the same price, but M3, with a private terrace offering the best view on the property, is the most covetable. *US$310/375 sgl/dbl B&B & US$410/575 FB high season, with low- & green-season discounts.* **$$$$$$**

Upmarket

✱ 🏠 **Moivaro Coffee Plantation Lodge** (41 rooms) 📞 027 250 3243; 📱 0754 324193; 📧 marketing@moivaro.com; www.moivaro. com. This elegantly rustic lodge, set on a well-wooded 16ha coffee estate 7km from central Arusha & 1.5km from the Moshi road, offers accommodation in recently revamped makuti-roofed bungalows with ethnic-style décor, en-suite tub & shower, & a secluded private balcony shaded by mature indigenous trees inhabited by forest birds & monkeys. The country-style main building opens out to a wide terrace facing Mount Meru, & flowering lawns centred on a large freeform swimming pool. Facilities include walking & jogging paths, Wi-Fi & a massage room. *US$206/273 sgl/dbl B&B, or US$251/363 sgl/dbl FB. Substantial discounts Mar–Jun & Sep–mid Dec.* **$$$$$**

🏠 **Kigongoni Lodge** (20 rooms) 📞 027 255 3087; 📱 0732 978876; 📧 manager@kigongoni.

net; www.kigongoni.net. Set on a forested hilltop in a 70ha coffee plantation about 10km from Arusha along the Moshi road, this well-run lodge consists of 20 large, airy & organic en-suite chalets, all of which come with a private balcony, 2 dbl beds with netting, hot shower & bath, & log fire. The countrified atmosphere of the accommodation is complemented by superb food & a good wine list, while other attractions include a swimming pool & plenty of monkeys & birds in the grounds. A significant portion of the profits is used to support Sibusiso, a home for Tanzanian children with disabilities, situated on the same coffee estate. *Rates on application.* **$$$$$**

Moderate

✱ 🏠 **Vijiji Center** (12 rooms) 📱 0754 322664; 📧 vijijicenter@yahoo.com; www.vijijicenter.com. Set in green & brightly painted 2-acre gardens in Sokolandizi village on the north side of the Moshi road, this attractive & friendly new lodge – established in 2013 to help the Vijiji Foundation fund nearby Moivaro Primary School – arguably ranks as the best-value mid-range option anywhere in the greater Arusha area. The en-suite makuti-roofed cottages come with king-sized or twin bed, fitted nets, hot shower & private veranda, while facilities include Wi-Fi, swimming pool, an open-sided restaurant serving mostly organic & free-range fare, & an onsite operator offering cultural day trips & longer safaris. *US$70/90 sgl/dbl B&B.* **$$$$**

🏠 **Songota Falls Lodge** (5 rooms) 📱 0754 095576; 📧 info@songotafallslodge.com; www.songotafallslodge.com. Situated along a rough 1.5km dirt road that runs northward from the Moshi road, Songota Falls Lodge consists of a few unfussy but clean en-suite bungalows overlooking the large green valley below the Songota Waterfall – to which guided walks are offered when underfoot conditions are reasonably dry. It's a refreshingly unpretentious set-up, owned & managed by a friendly Tanzanian woman with years of experience in the hotel trade. *US$62/70/100 sgl/dbl/trpl B&B, or US$77/100/145FB.* **$$$$**

✗ Where to eat and drink *Map, page 148*

✗ **Machweo Fine Dining** 📱 0787 112498; www.machweo.com; ⏰ lunch & dinner daily.

Widely regarded as offering the top fine-dining experience in Tanzania, this Belgian restaurant serves a different set menu every night, usually comprising 3 *amuse-bouches*, as well as soup, starter, main & dessert, optionally accompanied by wines selected to match the dishes. Bookings are mandatory for those not staying at the hotel. US$50 for 4 courses & wine.

TENGERU AND LAKE DULUTI Straddling the Moshi Highway some 10km east of Arusha, the small market town of Tengeru is best known to tourists as the site of pretty forest-fringed Lake Duluti, set within an extinct volcanic crater whose formation was linked to that of Mount Meru. It is also the site of a busy market that peaks in activity on Wednesdays and Saturdays. The original village of Tengeru stood about 3km further south, between Lake Duluti and the Old Moshi Road. During World War II, it housed a Polish refugee camp and cattle farm that was taken over by the Ministry of Agriculture in 1952, to be developed as an agricultural research and training institute that is active to this day.

Getting there and away Tengeru lies about 10km east of Arusha, a drive that can take up to 30 minutes in heavy traffic. Once at Tengeru, it's about 2km south to Lake Duluti. The turn-off to Duluti Club is signposted to the right as you enter Tengeru, and entrance to the Lake Duluti Forest Reserve, on foot only, is via a manned entrance gate that lies along the same rough road about 500m east of the Duluti Club. The turn-off from the main road to the Serena is another 200m or so towards Moshi. On public transport, any vehicle heading from Arusha towards Moshi can drop you at Tengeru, from where you can either walk the 2km to the lake, or charter a *boda-boda* (motorcycle taxi).

Where to stay and eat *Map, page 148*

Upmarket

Lake Duluti Serena Hotel (42 rooms) 027 255 3313–5; e reservations@serenahotels. com; www.serenahotels.com. With expansive green lawns offering fabulous views across the canopy to the gorgeous Lake Duluti as well as more distant Mount Meru & Kilimanjaro, the former Mountain Village Lodge is easily one of the most attractive upmarket hotels in the greater Arusha area. The main building is a converted thatched farmhouse dating to the colonial era, & accommodation is in comfortable self-contained chalets with makuti roofs, flatscreen DSTV, walk-in nets & private balconies. High standards of service, meals & décor match the atmospheric setting, & amenities include a swimming pool, Wi-Fi & onsite office of Wayo Tours offering day trips to Lake Duluti & Arusha National Park. *US$265/365 sgl/dbl B&B, US$35pp FB supplement, low-season discounts.* **$$$$**

Camping

Å Duluti Club m 0754 373977. The lovely & surprisingly little-used campsite at the Duluti Club is slightly rundown, but there's an ablution block with hot showers & the lakeshore setting is fabulous. Facilities include a cafeteria serving basic & reasonably priced meals & chilled drinks. *US$10pp.* **$**

What to see and do

Lake Duluti Situated immediately south of Tengeru, this lovely crater lake fed by subterranean springs has an extent of around 60ha and is claimed to be several hundred metres deep. Although much of the surrounding area is cultivated and settled, the steep crater walls support a fringing gallery of riparian forest, while the lake itself is lined with beds of papyrus. On clear days, good views of Mount Meru and Kilimanjaro can be had from the lakeshore. The relatively developed northern lakeshore is open to the public, but the southern, eastern and western shores are now protected in the small **Lake Duluti Forest Reserve** (*entrance US$12pp*), which can be explored over a couple of hours along a 5km circular walking trail. The forest comprises more than 50 tree species, while wildlife includes blue monkey, vervet monkey, monitor lizard and forest birds such as Hartlaub's turaco, crowned and silvery-cheeked hornbills, Narina trogon, brown-breasted and white-eared barbets, African broadbill, little greenbul, black-throated wattle-eye, paradise flycatcher, white-starred robin and black-breasted apalis. Services of a guide are included in the entrance fee, but a tip will be expected. Canoe trips on Duluti are operated out of the nearby Serena Hotel by Wayo Africa (*US$35pp; see page 150*). The Tengeru Cultural Tourism Programme (see below) also offer canoeing trips for US$40 per person, as well as guided hikes around the forest reserve for US$35 per person.

Polish War Refugee Cemetery   During World War II, Tengeru was selected as the site of a refugee camp whose 5,000 inhabitants were deported to Siberian work camps following the German and Russian invasion of Poland in 1939, then released in 1942 in the wake of Russia's decision to side with the Allies. Around 18,000 of these Polish refugees were shipped to Mombasa to start a new life in Britain's East African colonies, where Tengeru became the largest of half-a-dozen refugee camps established in what was then Tanganyika. By 1944, the camp at Tengeru was a well-organised agricultural settlement comprising about ten schools, a few hospitals, several Orthodox and Catholic churches, and one synagogue catering to the small Jewish community. The refugees were permitted to go back to Europe after the war ended, but many had little reason to return, and decided to stay on in Tengeru. A well-signposted and well-tended Polish War Cemetery housed within a magnolia-shaded compound in the former refugee camp (now a Livestock Training Institute) contains 143 Christian and five Jewish graves, most of which date to the 1940s, when many freshly arrived refugees succumbed to malaria or influenza. Others are more recent. Indeed, the last surviving member of the refugee community, Edward Wojtowicz, who stayed on in Tengeru for the rest of his days, was buried there in March 2015 following his death at the age of 85. The cemetery lies about 3km south of modern Tengeru close to the Old Moshi Road; a boda-boda from Tengeru market will cost around US$1.

Coffee walks   A company called **Wild Tracks** (m *0784 420342/416317;* e *info@wild-tracks.com; www.wild-tracks.com/coffee-tour.html*) runs informative coffee walks on a local organic and fair-trade farm in the village of Nkoaranga, which lies on the fertile Mount Meru footslopes 25km east of Arusha. Tours incorporate a visit to the oldest Lutheran church on Mount Meru, a visit to a primary or secondary school and to small subsistence farms (*shambas*) where local people grow various vegetables and fruits. The farms visited are all part of the organic Aranga co-operative and you'll be shown the entire process from planting saplings to picking the beans, and roasting and grinding them. A traditional buffet lunch is included in the price of US$35 per person, as is a bag of fresh Tanzanian coffee and pickup from your hotel.

Based in the village, the **Tengeru Cultural Tourism Programme** (m *0756 981602;* e *tengeru_culture_tourism@yahoo.com; www.tengeruculturaltourism.org*) arranges interesting banana and coffee tours leading through valleys, rivers and waterfalls to a local market. Visitors are also welcome to take part in community works, or to offer a helping hand to orphans and primary schools in the area. The full-day tour with an overnight stay costs US$50 per person. Market tours on Wednesdays and Saturdays cost US$25 per person, and it can also arrange trips to Lake Duluti.

USA RIVER   The small and rather amorphous village of Usa River flanks the Moshi road about 20km east of Arusha near the turn-off to Arusha National Park. It is of interest to tourists primarily for a cluster of upmarket hotels, several of which rank as among the most attractive in the Arusha area, as well as being conveniently located for day safaris into the national park. If you're staying in the area, there are several good boutiques and adequate eateries in and around the Usa Mall, which also has an internet café and banking facilities.

Where to stay and eat *Map, page 148*

Exclusive

Kili Villa (15 rooms) m 0715 524800; e info@kilivilla.com; www.kilivilla.com. Set on a private golf & wildlife estate south of the Moshi road, this plush new lodge is currently the most exclusive in the vicinity of Usa River, & particularly well suited to golf & horseriding enthusiasts. The 15 rooms are split across 4 villas, each with its own swimming pool, making it feel more like a homestay than a lodge. The attractive décor combines ethnic & colonial influences, & all rooms have 4-poster beds. The bush setting – restored incredibly, from a former sisal estate – is home to resident wildlife such as zebra, around 10 species of antelope, & a vast array of birds. *From US$225/350 sgl/dbl B&B or US$275/450 FB. Villas start at US$960 B&B for 4 people.* **$$$$$**

Siringit Kilimanjaro Golf Safari Retreat (6 rooms) m 0732 971771; e reservations@intimate-places.com; www. siringit.com. This luxurious, modern villa is booked on an exclusive basis, & is best for small groups & families. Siringit feels like a stylish country estate & is located 20km west of Kilimanjaro Airport, by the 5th fairway of Kili Golf (Tanzania's 1st 18-hole championship course). The lavish en-suite bedrooms are professionally decorated in a minimalist, afro-chic style. The villa has a large pool & a chef who prepares top-quality meals. Activities that can be arranged from Siringit include golf, horseriding, bicycle riding, polo & bird walks. *US$450/600 sgl/dbl B&B with low-season discounts.* **$$$$$$**

Upmarket

✱ **Ngare Sero Lodge** (15 rooms) m 0732 978931/0764 305435; e reservations@ngare-sero-lodge.com; www.ngare-sero-lodge.com. One of the most attractive places to stay anywhere near Arusha, particularly for those who enjoy outdoor pursuits, is this small, family-owned & -managed country-style lodge set on a forested 25ha estate dating to the German colonial era. As implicit in the name Ngare Sero (Maasai for 'dappled water'), the estate is fed by several streams that

rise on the higher slopes of Mount Meru, & flow into a crystal-clear reservoir below the lodge. The forest & lake support an incredibly varied selection of birds & butterflies, including resident pairs of grey crowned crane and African fish eagle, making it a popular base for birdwatching tours. Semi-habituated troops of blue monkey & black-&-white colobus are often seen frolicking through the grounds. A superb range of activities & facilities includes horseback excursions, coffee farm tours, boat rides on the lake, cultural visits to a nearby village, a swimming pool, internet access & massages in an old watchtower that presumably dates to World War I. The garden rooms, although set out in a rather tight row opposite the main building, are spacious & attractively decorated with Zanzibar-style king-sized or twin beds & tiled en-suite bathrooms with combined tub/shower. Meals are made using organic ingredients from the estate & other locally sourced produce, & are taken in the original century-old farmhouse, which is furnished & decorated in period style. *US$150 B&B or US$200pp FB garden room, US$270pp FB suite. Substantial low-season discounts.* **$$$$$**

✱ **Mount Meru Game Lodge** (14 rooms) m 0689 706760; e info@mtmerugamelodge.com; www.mtmerugamelodge.com. Situated 1km east of Usa River & immediately before the turn-off to Arusha National Park, this long-serving & highly recommended lodge was established in 1959 & it retains something of an *Out of Africa* ambience, one further enhanced by extensive refurbishments undertaken in early 2016 by a dynamic new management team. The main stone building & semi-detached wooden cabins are stylishly decorated in classic contemporary Edwardian safari style. All rooms come with twin or king-sized 4-poster bed, walk-in net, fan & organic wood & cane furnishing. A large open enclosure in front of rooms 1 & 2 is stocked with zebras & various antelope, while the swamps attract saddle-billed & yellow-billed storks & blue monkeys make mischief on the lawn, nicely setting the tone for your safari. *Good value at US$130pp B&B or US$155 FB.* **$$$$**

Rivertrees Country Inn (24 rooms)
027 255 3894; m 0732 971667/0713 339873;
e info@rivertrees.com; www.rivertrees.com.
Situated 300m from the main Moshi road
facing the Mount Meru Game Lodge, this highly
regarded lodge is set in magnificently shady
green gardens on an old family estate offering
great views of Mount Meru & Kilimanjaro, &
bounded by a forest-fringed stretch of the Usa
River. Centred on a rambling old farmhouse,
the inn offers comfortable accommodation in
spacious en-suite rooms with large wooden
4-poster beds, as well as a more exclusive river
cottage & a stunning river house with 2 dbl
bedrooms. Facilities include free internet access,
a swimming pool & a highly rated restaurant
serving hearty country food, while activities on
offer include massage services, village tours,
mountain biking & bird walks. *US$188/249/329*

*standard sgl/dbl/trpl B&B, with low-season
discounts, plus US$56pp FB.* **$$$$$**

Arumeru River Lodge (29 rooms)
m 0732 979908; e info@arumerulodge.com;
www.arumerulodge.com. This reasonably priced
owner-managed lodge, set on a lushly vegetated
6ha plot bounded by 2 rivers, is centred upon a
stunning open-sided thatch restaurant & reception
area that overlooks a heated swimming pool, &
serves top-notch continental cuisine. Some of the
rooms face the river & associated swampland,
which is home to 3 monkey species & a wide
variety of birds. The tiled semi-detached standard
rooms have a pleasing airy organic feel, & come
with king-sized bed & en-suite hot shower, & there
are 6 newer junior suites with more contemporary
décor & a larger bathroom. *US$200/290 sgl/dbl
B&B, or US$255/400 FB, Jan–Mar & Jun–Dec,
low-season discounts available.* **$$$$$**

KILIMANJARO INTERNATIONAL AIRPORT The only international airport serving
northern Tanzania, KIA, as it is often referred to locally, lies in almost total
isolation roughly midway between Arusha and Moshi, making it a reasonably
convenient point of access for both towns but absolutely ideal for neither.
Most visitors arrange for their safari operator or hotel to meet them, or take a
taxi. Another option for a one-night stay in the area is to book into **KIA Lodge**
(*20 rooms;* 027 255 3243; e *reservations@kialodge.com; www.kialodge.com;
US$206/273 sgl/dbl B&B, US$251/363 sgl/dbl FB, substantial discounts Mar–Jun &
Sep–mid Dec;* **$$$$$**). Under the same management as Moivaro Coffee Plantation
Lodge, and similar in feel and quality, this is recommended to visitors with unusual
or inconvenient flight times, as it lies just 1km from the airport and the staff are
used to monitoring flight arrivals and departures for guests. It's an attractive set-up,
with a good makuti restaurant and hilltop swimming pool, plenty of birdlife in the
surrounding acacia scrub, and great views towards Kilimanjaro (the mountain, that
is), but the noise from overhead flights makes it less than ideal for an extended stay.

ARUSHA NATIONAL PARK

The most accessible wildlife destination in northern Tanzania, Arusha National Park
lies a mere 45 minutes' drive from the eponymous town, and it's even closer to the
many lodges in the vicinity of Tengeru and Usa River, making it an easy target for a
half- or full-day trip at the start of a safari. Despite this, the park remains somewhat
neglected by the safari industry, largely because it offers limited possibilities to
see the so-called Big Five. This one perceived failing aside, however, it is a quite
extraordinary conservation area. Established in 1960 and recently extended from
137km² to 542km², it is dominated by Mount Meru, which rises on the western
boundary to an altitude of 4,566m, making it Africa's fifth-highest massif and a
popular goal for dedicated hikers. For non-hikers, a cluster of attractive lakes can
be explored by road or on organised canoe trips, with stirring views of Kilimanjaro
looming large on the eastern skyline, while the spectacular forest-swathed Ngurdoto
Crater is an intact caldera reminiscent of a smaller version of Ngorongoro.

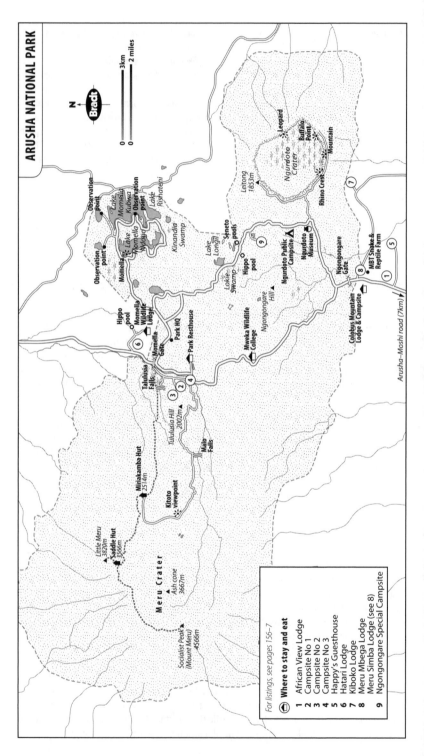

ARUSHA NATIONAL PARK

For listings, see pages 156–7

Where to stay and eat

1 African View Lodge
2 Campsite No 1
3 Campsite No 2
4 Campsite No 3
5 Happy's Guesthouse
6 Hatari Lodge
7 Kiboko Lodge
8 Meru Mbega Lodge (see 8)
  Meru Simba Lodge (see 8)
9 Ngongongare Special Campsite

Arusha–Moshi road (7km)

Meru Crater

Socialist Peak
(Mount Meru)
4566m

Ash cone
3667m

Little Meru
3820m
Saddle Hut
3566m

Miriakamba Hut
2514m

Kitoto
viewpoint

Maio
Falls

Tululusia Hill
2002m

Talulusia
Falls

Park Resthouse

Park HQ

Momella
Gate

Momella Wildlife
Lodge

Hippo
pool

Observation
point

Observation
point

Lake
Momella Kubwa

Lake
Tshomella
Ndogo

Lake
Rishatehi

Observation
point

Kinandia
Swamp

Lake
Longil

Seneto
pools

Hippo
pool

Lokie
Swamp

Mweka Wildlife
College

Ngongongare
Hill

Ngurdoto Public
Campsite

Ngurdoto
Museum

Ngongongare
Gate

Colobus Mountain
Lodge & Campsite

MBT Snake &
Reptile Farm

Leitong
1853m

Ngurdoto
Crater

Leopard

Buffalo
Point

Mountain

Rhino Crest

N

Bradt

0   3km
0   2 miles

FLORA AND FAUNA Despite its relatively small size, Arusha National Park incorporates a diversity of habitats reflecting its wide altitudinal variations. Lower-lying areas support a cover of moist savannah, but the slopes of Mount Meru and Ngurdoto are swathed in evergreen montane rainforest, giving way to alpine moorland at higher altitudes. The forest around Ngurdoto is one of the best places in Tanzania to see forest primates such as black-and-white colobus and blue monkey. Elsewhere, other common mammals include hippo, giraffe, zebra, buffalo and a waterbuck population intermediate to the Defassa and common races. Look out, too, for pairs of Kirk's dik-dik, an attractively marked small antelope that seems to be less skittish here than it is elsewhere in the country. Around 200 elephants are more-or-less resident in the park, but they tend to stick to the forest zone of Mount Meru, so sightings are relatively infrequent except along the road towards Meru Crater. The only large predators are leopard and spotted hyena. More than 400 bird species have been recorded, including a wide variety of aquatic and forest specialists.

FEES AND FURTHER INFORMATION A detailed booklet, *Arusha National Park*, containing information on every aspect of the park's ecology and wildlife, is widely available in Arusha, as is Giovanni Tombazzi's excellent map, which has useful details of the ascent of Mount Meru on the flip. Independent visitors should note that all fees – including the park entrance fee of US$45 plus 18% VAT per person per 24 hours, as well as camping or guide fees as applicable – must be paid with a Visa or MasterCard, or one of the Tanapa cards that can be issued at any Exim Bank. No other cards are accepted, nor is cash (see box, page 92). As is the case with other national parks, Arusha has officially operated a single-entry policy since late 2015, meaning that visitors who exit the park – even if just to lunch at a lodge outside the boundary – are required to pay a second set of fees if they want to re-enter. In practice, if you ask nicely, the rangers will often allow you to enter twice provided it is within the same 24-hour period, but this cannot be relied upon.

GETTING THERE AND AWAY Most visitors explore Arusha National Park on an organised half- or full-day safari, which can be arranged through any operator in Arusha town. Prior to 2015, it was possible to pitch up at the park gate and arrange a Mount Meru climb on the spot, but climbs – which require a minimum of three days – must now be arranged through a registered safari operator. Hikes to Meru Crater can still be arranged at the gate for US$20 per person, but a private vehicle is still required to reach the trailhead at Kitoto.

Self-drivers coming from Arusha must follow the Moshi Highway east to Usa River, then take the turn-off signposted left for Arusha National Park. After about 8km, this road enters the park boundary, where park entrance fees are paid at Ngongongare Gate. The road reaches Hatari and Momella lodges after another 15km or so, immediately outside the northern national park boundary. This road is in fair condition and can normally be driven in an ordinary saloon car, though a 4x4 may be necessary after rain.

Technically, it is possible to reach Arusha National Park on public transport. From Arusha, catch a bus or dalla-dalla along the Moshi road as far as the Usa River turn-off, from where 4x4 vehicles serve as dalla-dallas to the village of Ngare Nanyuki about 3km past the park's northern boundary, passing through Ngongongare Gate on the way. In practice, it is practically impossible to explore beyond the gates without private transport.

WHERE TO STAY AND EAT *See map, page 154, unless otherwise stated*

In addition to the lodges listed below, there are a number of scenically located national park **campsites** (*US30pp*; **$$$**), all with drop toilets and firewood. Three sites (Nos 1, 2 and 3) lie at the foot of Tululusia Hill, 2km from Momella Gate, while another (Ngongongare) is situated in the forest near Ngurdoto Gate. Note, however, that you may not walk between the campsites and the entrance gates without an armed ranger.

Exclusive

＊ Hatari Lodge (8 rooms) m 0752 553456; e marlies@theafricanembassy.com; www. hatarilodge.de. This characterful owner-managed lodge, situated in a patch of moist yellow-fever woodland just outside the Momella Gate, is named after the 1961 film *Hatari!* (danger), & stands on a property formerly owned by Hardy Kruger, one of the film's co-stars. Accommodation is in large en-suite dbl chalets with king-sized beds & tall makuti ceilings, while the individualistic décor is an imaginative, colourful blend of a classic African bush feel & a more 'retro' look dating back to the era of the film. The common areas – littered with *Hatari!* memorabilia – overlook a swampy area inhabited by buffalo, waterbuck, crowned crane & various other water birds. The food is excellent, the service is highly personalised, & there are also stirring views across to nearby Kilimanjaro & Meru. Activities on offer include game drives & walks, canoeing on the Momella Lakes & birdwatching excursions. *Rates on application.* **$$$$$$$**

Upmarket

Ngurdoto Mountain Lodge [map, page 148] (237 rooms) ☏ 027 294 2217; e ngurdoto@ thengurdotomountainlodge.com; www. thengurdotomountainlodge.com. Situated on a 70ha coffee plantation alongside the road between Usa River & Arusha National Park, this large tourist village has exceptional facilities, including a 9-hole golf course, a gym, a 600-seat conference centre, a large swimming pool, 24hr internet access, 2 restaurants & 2 bars. Given the hotel's size, the rooms – all en suite with king-sized bed, fireplace & balcony – possess a surprising amount of character, making use of wrought iron & wood to create a contemporary ethnic look. It's also very competitively priced, especially in the high season. *US$110/150 sgl/dbl standard rooms B&B, cottages US$140/180, executive rooms US$170/210. Additional meals US$15pp.* **$$$$**

Meru Simba Lodge (8 rooms) m 0788 273278; e meru-simba-lodge@baobabvillage. com; www.meru-simba-lodge.com. Under the same management as the more established Meru Mbega Lodge (page 157), & right next door to it, this consists of a row of comfortable & spacious en-suite cottages with private balconies facing the park boundary – which means that quite a bit of game comes past seasonally. Good value. *US$95/140 sgl/dbl B&B, or US$135/270 FB.* **$$$$**

Moderate

African View Lodge (20 rooms) m 0784 419232; e info@africanview.co.tz; www. african-view.com. This friendly new lodge, owned & managed by a hands-on German/English couple with years of hospitality experience in the area, lies alongside the road from Usa River, about 1.5km south of where it enters the national park. The en-suite rooms, dotted around a large swimming pool surrounded by lounger chairs, are modern, comfortable & reasonably priced. The owners are active mountain guides with plenty of experience setting up Kilimanjaro & Meru climbs. *US$100/140 sgl/dbl B&B, or US$125/190 FB.* **$$$$**

Kiboko Lodge (21 rooms) m 0767 185948; e kibokolodge@watotofoundation. nl; www.kibokolodge.nl; see ad, page 160. This attractively rustic lodge, which overlooks a swampy area bordering Arusha National Park, is named for the solitary hippo (*'kiboko'*) that spends much of its time in the area (but sometimes retreats into the national park when it suffers too much harassment from locals). It offers great views of Mount Meru & excellent birding, with several species of weaver and bishop breeding seasonally in the swamp. Profits help fund the Watoto Foundation, a Dutch NGO dedicated to rehabilitating & educating former street children, & most of the staff are graduates of the school. Accommodation is in comfortable en-suite chalets reached via a wooden boardwalk over the swamp. Great value. *US$75pp FB.* **$$$$**

Meru Mbega Lodge (12 rooms)
m 0732 978230/0788 273278; e mbegalodge@
mt-meru.com; www.mt-meru.com. Part of
a chain of affordable lodges run by Mbega,
this unpretentious family-friendly set-up has
comfortable en-suite accommodation with
netted beds in dbl-storey buildings that offer
views over a small pond towards Mount Meru.
An attractive makuti structure serves as the bar
& restaurant. It's a good place to arrange Meru
climbs. *US$90/110 sgl/dbl B&B, or US$120/170
FB.* **$$$$**

Budget

Happy's Guesthouse (3 rooms) m 0683
616650; e happytimoth@gmail.com. Set in a
suburban garden about 1km along a rough track
heading east from the road between Usa River
& Arusha National Park, this friendly family-run
guesthouse has a real homestay feel. The pleasant
tiled bungalows have DSTV, fridge & en-suite hot
shower, & meals are taken with the German–
Tanzanian family, who speak excellent English.
US$40pp dinner & B&B. **$$$**

EXPLORING ARUSHA NATIONAL PARK

Ngurdoto Crater Coming from Arusha, a good first goal is this fully intact
3km-wide, 400m-deep volcanic caldera, which has often been described as a mini
Ngorongoro. Tourists are not normally permitted to descend into the crater, but the
views from the forest-fringed rim over the lush crater floor are fantastic. A large herd
of buffalo is resident on the crater floor, and with binoculars it is normally possible to
pick out other mammals, such as warthog, baboon and various antelope. Look out,
too, for augur buzzard, Verreaux's eagle and other cliff-associated raptors soaring
above the crater. The forest around the crater rim harbours many troops of black-
and-white colobus and blue monkey, as well as a good variety of birds including
several types of hornbill and the gorgeous Hartlaub's turaco and cinnamon-chested
bee-eater. If the view from the top isn't sufficient, hikes to the floor cost US$30 per
person and take around 3 hours return, but should ideally be booked at Ngongongare
Gate a few days in advance.

Momella Lakes Underground streams feed this group of shallow alkaline lakes,
which lie to the north of Ngurdoto, and each has a different mineral content and
is slightly different in colour. In the late evening and early morning, it is often
possible to stand at one of the viewpoints over the lakes and see Kilimanjaro on
the eastern horizon and Mount Meru to the west. This is the best part of the park
for large mammals such as buffalo and hippo, while a wide variety of water birds
can be seen, including various herons, ducks (including the otherwise uncommon
maccoa), waders, flamingos, pelicans and little grebe. A very tranquil way to enjoy
the birdlife and scenery is the canoe safaris offered by Wayo Africa (*US$35pp; see
page 141*).

Meru Crater drive and hike Best undertaken with a reasonably early start and a
packed lunch, this half- to full-day outing will be a highlight of any visit to Arusha
National Park, though an armed ranger (*US$20pp*) must be collected at one of the
entrance gates if you want to hike into the crater or drive further up the mountain
than Kitoto. The first leg, about an hour's drive to Kitoto, climbs through a beautiful
stretch of primary forest with lots of tall trees, ferns and epiphytes, a good place
to look for elephant, black-and-white colobus monkeys, the raucous and very
beautiful Hartlaub's turaco, and Harvey's red duiker (a small antelope associated
with montane forests of the East African interior). At one point the road passes
through the famous **Fig Tree Arch**, a natural formation at the base of an immense
strangler fig large enough for a Land Cruiser to pass under (provided no heads are
sticking out of the roof, take note).

From the car park at Kitoto, which lies at 2,500m, the guided hike through the crater takes at least 2 to 3 hours. The hike is not too demanding in terms of climbing, since the eastern wall of the crater has collapsed, but the scenery is truly spectacular, set below the 1,500m-high cliff that forms the western wall and peak of Mount Meru. Wildlife is scarce at this altitude, but you may well see klipspringers on the cliffs, as well as cliff-nesting raptors such as Verreaux's eagle, augur buzzard, and the scarce and eagerly sought lammergeyer (bearded vulture).

Mount Meru Arusha National Park's tallest landmark and most publicised attraction is Mount Meru, an active stratovolcano whose upper slopes and peak lie within its boundaries. The Arusha and Meru people deify Mount Meru as a rain god, but it is unlikely that any local person actually reached the peak prior to Fritz Jaeger's pioneering ascent in 1904. Mount Meru, like nearby Kilimanjaro, is a product of the same volcanic activity that formed the Great Rift Valley 15 to 20 million years ago, and it attained a height similar to that of its loftier neighbour until 250,000 years ago, when a massive eruption tore out its eastern wall. The most recent major eruption on Meru took place around 7,800 years ago, when the current ash cone was formed. A less cataclysmic lava flow was documented as recently as 1879, and while there is no particular reason to suppose anything dramatic will happen in the foreseeable future, a recurrence is possible at any time, with potentially devastating results for people living in the vicinity.

Often overlooked by tourists because it is 'only' the fifth-highest mountain in Africa, Meru is no substitute for Kilimanjaro for achievement-orientated travellers. On the other hand, those who climb both mountains invariably enjoy Meru more. Also going in its favour, Meru is less crowded than Kilimanjaro, considerably less expensive and – although steeper and almost as cold – less likely to engender the health problems associated with Kilimanjaro's greater altitude. Meru is just as interesting as Kilimanjaro from a biological point of view and, because comparatively few people climb it, you are more likely to see forest animals and plains game on the lower slopes.

Meru can technically be climbed in two days, but three days is normal, allowing time to explore Meru Crater and to look at wildlife and plants, and the official park rules recommend four days. As of 2015, it is no longer permitted to make arrangements with park officials at the gate, since all climbs must be arranged through a registered safari company in Arusha (see pages 139–41 for options). The going rate for a budget four-day hike is around US$550–900 per person, a large chunk of which is swallowed up by national park fees (entrance costs US$45 per person per 24 hours, while hut fees are US$30 per night, guide and porter fees are US$15 per day, the rescue fee is US$20 per person per climb, and 18% VAT is also levied). Meru is very cold at night, and you will need to bring clothing adequate for alpine conditions. In the rainy season, mountain boots are necessary. At other times, good walking shoes will probably be adequate. The best time to climb is from December to February, but June to August is also good. Accommodation is in simple bunkhouses at Miriakamba Hut and Saddle Hut. These might be fully booked during peak seasons, in which case the only alternative is camping.

Day 1: Momella Gate (1,500m) to Miriakamba Hut (2,514m) This relatively gentle 3-hour ascent passes through well-developed woodland where there is a good chance of seeing large animals such as giraffe. At an altitude of about 2,000m you enter the forest zone. If you leave Momella early, there will be ample time to explore Meru Crater in the afternoon. The 1,500m cliff rising to Meru

Peak overlooks the crater. The 3,667m-high ash cone in the crater is an hour from Miriakamba Hut, and can be climbed.

Day 2: Miriakamba Hut (2,514m) to Saddle Hut (3,566m) A bit steeper than the previous day's walk, this is another 3-hour hike, initially passing through forest, where there is a good chance of seeing black-and-white colobus. At about 3,000m, you enter a moorland zone similar to that on Kilimanjaro. It is not unusual to see Kilimanjaro peeking above the clouds from Saddle Hut. If you feel energetic, you can climb Little Meru (3,820m) in the afternoon. It takes about an hour each way from Saddle Hut.

Day 3: Saddle Hut (3,566m) to the summit (4,566m) and back You will need to rise very early to ascend the 4,566m peak, probably at around 02.00. This ascent follows a very narrow ridge above the inner crater and takes 4–5 hours. It is then a 2–3-hour walk back down to Saddle Hut.

Day 4: Saddle Hut (3,566m) to Momella Gate (1,500m) The last day retraces the route taken on the first two days, but in reverse, and usually takes about 4 hours.

MBT Snake and Reptile Farm Signposted a short distance from the entrance to Arusha National Park, this long-serving private park, though looking a little rundown on last inspection, is home to Nile crocodile, various chameleon species and other lizards, and a fearsome collection of snakes, including spitting cobras, mambas, puff adders, Gabon viper, water snakes and some hefty pythons. It lies outside the national park so no park fees are payable but an entrance ticket inclusive of guided tour costs around US$4.

WEST KILIMANJARO

Also sometimes referred to as South Amboseli, this vaguely defined area is essentially the wedge of dry savannah country that divides the northwestern base of Kilimanjaro from the legendary Amboseli National Park in neighbouring Kenya. Some 2–3 hours' drive northeast of Arusha, it consists of several blocks of Maasai community land that recently amalgamated to form the 1,800km² **Enduimet Wildlife Management Area** (*EWMA; www.enduimet.org*), where local pastoralists live alongside the wildlife that ranges through this cross-border ecosystem. A major attraction here is the superb close-up view of Kilimanjaro, but the vast horizon is studded with several other notable peaks, including Mount Meru, Longido Mountain and Namanga Mountain (on the Kenyan side of the eponymous border crossing to Nairobi). The area also retains a genuine wilderness feel, since only two small permanent tented camps are situated within it.

Despite being surrounded by dramatic peaks, much of West Kilimanjaro is composed of very flat land where the fine volcanic soil once formed the bed of Lake Amboseli (then twice as big as present-day Lake Manyara) before it started to dry up some 10,000 to 15,000 years ago. As the lake dried it left calcareous deposits that were later mined by the Germans in order to make the famous meerschaum tobacco pipes. The abandoned pits left behind by the open-cast mines are now an important part of the ecosystem, since they trap rainwater thereby providing drinking water for the Maasai cattle as well as the wildlife at the driest times of the year.

Ecologically, the EWMA supports a near-pristine cover of lightly wooded acacia savannah where Maasai herdsmen co-exist with a remarkable variety of wildlife, including wildebeest, zebra, eland, impala, Grant's gazelle, hartebeest and yellow baboon, as well as one of the few Tanzanian populations of the remarkable stretch-necked gerenuk. Predator densities are low, but cheetah and lion are still present and quite often observed. The area also forms part of a migration corridor used by the local elephant population – noted for its even temperament and the immense tusks of the bulls – to cross between the Kenyan part of the Amboseli ecosystem and the forested slopes of Kilimanjaro. Many impressive bulls are resident throughout the year, but numbers peak in June and July, after the rains, when the smaller family groups merge to form 100-strong herds. This also is when mating takes place, and irascible bulls follow the family herds accompanied by a fanfare of trumpeting.

GETTING THERE AND AWAY West Kilimanjaro is about 2 hours' drive from Arusha. Realistically it can only be visited by prior arrangement on an organised safari using one of the lodges listed below.

WHERE TO STAY AND EAT

Shu'mata Camp (5 tents) \027 255 3456; e marlies@theafricanembassy.com; www. shumatacamp.com. Under the same dynamic owner-management as Hatari Lodge (page 156), this small but luxurious camp sprawls across the eponymous hill, whose Maasai name translates as something close to 'heaven'. The camp has a lovely situation, offering panoramic views over the plains capped by Kilimanjaro to the southeast & Longido & Namanga to the northwest, marred only by the fierce winds that often blow in from the direction of Kilimanjaro. The large & stylish standing tents all have 2 dbl beds, a writing desk, colourful drapes & matting, a curvaceous adobe-style en-suite hot shower, & a private balcony. The camp has a flexible attitude to activities, which include game drives (night & day), guided walks (highly recommended) & visits to a local Maasai boma. Game densities don't quite compare with the national parks & animals tend to be a little more skittish than across the border in Kenya, but there is plenty of wildlife around & the sense of isolation & immersion in this wonderful tract of bush more than compensates. *Rates on application.* **$$$$$$**

Kambi ya Tembo (14 tents) m 0736 502471/0785 069944; e reservations@ tanganyikawildernesscamps.com; www. tanganyikawildernesscamps.com. Literally translating as 'Camp of Elephants', this aptly named lodge lies in the Sinya Concession bordering Amboseli National Park. Accommodation is in comfortable standing tents with twin or king-sized beds protected by walk-in nets, en-suite hot shower, & private balconies facing Kilimanjaro or the Amboseli Plains. In addition to game drives, activities include hikes on the Kilimanjaro foothills & Maasai village visits. *US$360/490 sgl/dbl FB, with huge discounts Mar–Jun & Nov.* **$$$$$**

7

Moshi and the Kilimanjaro Foothills

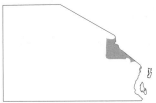

Situated at the heart of a major coffee-growing region about 80km east of Arusha, the smaller but not insubstantial town of Moshi – population around 200,000 – is a likeable if intrinsically unremarkable commercial centre salvaged from anonymity by its spectacular location.

At dusk or dawn, when the great white-helmeted dome of Kilimanjaro is most likely to emerge from its customary blanket of cloud, Moshi can boast a backdrop as imposing and dramatic as any in Africa. And yet, the teasing proximity of that iconic snow-capped silhouette notwithstanding, Moshi is not the cool, breezy highland settlement you might expect it to be. Indeed, situated at an altitude of 810m, it is generally far hotter than Arusha, and not as drizzly, with a hint of stickiness in the air that recalls the coast.

Stirring views of Kilimanjaro aside, there is little to do or see in Moshi that you couldn't do or see in pretty much any similarly sized African market town. But it's a pleasant enough place to explore on foot, with an interesting central market area, and it comes across as far less tourist-oriented than Arusha, despite the inevitable attention paid to any visiting mazungu by a coterie of (mostly very affable) flycatchers offering relatively cheap 'n' dodgy Kilimanjaro climbs.

In terms of facilities, Moshi boasts an immense selection of decent budget to mid-range hotels, as well as several commendable and affordable restaurants. An ever-increasing selection of smarter hotels is concentrated in the attractively leafy and somewhat misleadingly named suburb of Shantytown, a short walk north of the town centre and the Arusha Highway. There are also plenty of more upmarket options in the villages of Marangu and Machame on the Kilimanjaro footslopes, and the area can be explored from the lodges that run along the main road between Arusha and Usa River (pages 172–3).

HISTORY

Prior to the arrival of the Germans, Moshi was the capital of the area ruled by Rindi, who came to power in about 1860 and, largely through his diplomatic skills, became one of the most important chiefs in the area. By allying with the Maasai, Rindi extracted high taxes from passing caravans. He made a favourable impression on John Kirk, the British consul in Zanzibar, and signed a treaty with Carl Peters in 1885. When the first German colonial forces arrived at Kilimanjaro in 1891, Rindi assured them he ruled the whole area. At his insistence, they quelled his major rival, Sina of Kibosha. A German military camp called Neu-Moschi was established at the site in 1893.

Moshi is the Swahili word for smoke, but exactly when and why the town acquired that name is something of a mystery. Some sources suggest that it is

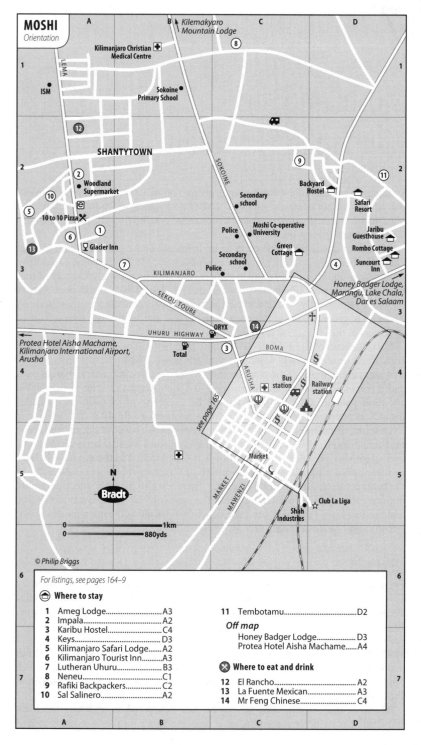

MOSHI
Orientation

Kilemakyaro
Mountain Lodge

Kilimanjaro Christian
Medical Centre

ISM

Sokoine
Primary School

SHANTYTOWN

Woodland
Supermarket

10 to 10 Pizza

Glacier Inn

KILIMANJARO

SEKOU TOURE

UHURU HIGHWAY

ORYX

Total

Protea Hotel Aisha Machame,
Kilimanjaro International Airport,
Arusha

SOKOINE

Secondary
school

Police

Moshi Co-operative
University

Secondary
school

Police

Green
Cottage

Backyard
Hostel

Safari
Resort

Jaribu
Guesthouse

Rombo Cottage

Suncourt
Inn

Honey Badger Lodge,
Marangu, Lake Chala,
Dar es Salaam

BOMA

ARUSHA

Bus
station

Railway
station

Market

MARKET

MAWENZI

Shah
Industries

Club La Liga

Bradt

N

0 _____ 1km
0 _____ 880yds

© Philip Briggs

For listings, see pages 164–9

🏠 **Where to stay**

1	Ameg Lodge	A3
2	Impala	A2
3	Karibu Hostel	C4
4	Keys	D3
5	Kilimanjaro Safari Lodge	A2
6	Kilimanjaro Tourist Inn	A3
7	Lutheran Uhuru	B3
8	Neneu	C1
9	Rafiki Backpackers	C2
10	Sal Salinero	A2

| 11 | Tembotamu | D2 |

Off map

Honey Badger Lodge | D3
Protea Hotel Aisha Machame | A4

❌ **Where to eat and drink**

12	El Rancho	A2
13	La Fuente Mexican	A3
14	Mr Feng Chinese	C4

because Moshi served as the terminus for the steam railway line from Tanga after 1912, but this seems unlikely given that the name pre-dates the arrival of the railway by many years. Equally improbable is the suggestion that the reference to smoke is due to the town lying at the base of a volcano, since Kilimanjaro hadn't displayed any significant activity for thousands of years when its present-day Bantu-speaking inhabitants arrived there. Moshi was accorded full municipal status in 1988 and it seems likely to be upgraded to be a city during the lifespan of this edition. Within Tanzania, Moshi is known for having the highest adult literacy rate of any of the country's 129 districts.

GETTING THERE AND AWAY

BY AIR **Kilimanjaro International Airport**, often referred to locally as KIA, though the international code is JRO (*www.kilimanjaroairport.co.tz*), lies about 40km from Moshi town centre off the Arusha road. Several international carriers operate flights there, among them Ethiopian Airlines, Air Kenya, Rwandair Express, KLM, Air France, SAS and Turkish Airlines. It is also an important hub for domestic flights to the likes of Dar es Salaam and Zanzibar operated by Precision Air, Fastjet and other private airlines. A potential source of confusion for travellers booking their own flights is that flights to the Serengeti and other national parks on the northern safari circuit don't leave from KIA, but from **Arusha Airport** on the outskirts of Arusha.

Most tourists flying into KIA are met by their hotel or safari company. However, there are plenty of **taxis** waiting to meet all flights, and these usually charge around US$30 for a transfer to Moshi.

BY ROAD The town centre runs southward from the main surfaced road to Dar es Salaam some 80km east of Arusha. The driving time from Arusha in a **private vehicle** is about 60–90 minutes, and from Dar es Salaam at least 7 hours. It is possible to drive from Nairobi (Kenya) to Moshi via Namanga and Arusha in about 5 hours.

Express coaches between Dar es Salaam and Moshi take roughly 7 hours, with a 20-minute lunch break in Korogwe or Mombo. The best service is **Dar Express** [165 A3] (m *0787 870766*), which leaves at 11.00 daily from Boma Road opposite the Aroma Coffee House, and costs around US$18 per person. Alternatively, numerous cheaper and inferior bus services leave from the chaotic main bus station [165 C4], mostly in the morning.

There are also plenty of direct buses between Moshi and Tanga, which can drop you off at Same, Mombo, Muheza and other junction towns *en route*. In addition, a steady flow of **buses** and **dalla-dallas** connects Arusha to Moshi, charging around US$3.50 and taking up to 2 hours, as well as to Marangu. There is no need to book ahead for these routes as vehicles will leave when they fill up, but be warned that there is a high incidence of accidents, particularly with minibuses.

Most **shuttle bus** services between Nairobi and Arusha continue on to Moshi, or start there, a total journey time of 6 to 7 hours. The **Impala Shuttle** (℘ *027 275 1786*; m *0754 293119*), based in an office on Kibo Road next to Chrisburgers [165 C2], runs two services daily, leaving at 06.30 and 11.30, while the **Riverside Shuttle** (℘ *027 275 0093*) on Boma Road opposite Stanbic Bank [165 C2] operates one service daily, leaving at 11.30. Note that timings may change to fit in with departure and arrival times for Arusha.

7

BY TRAIN All passenger trains to and from Moshi were suspended indefinitely in the 1990s and services are unlikely to resume.

 ## WHERE TO STAY

In addition to the two out-of-town options listed below (both excellent in their differing ways), there is plenty of accommodation in and around Marangu, the main starting point for Kilimanjaro hikes (pages 172–3).

MOSHI CENTRE
Upmarket
🏠 **Ameg Lodge** [162 A2] (20 rooms)
📞027 275 0175/0185; **m** 0754 058268; **e** info@ ameglodge.com; www.ameglodge.com. This modern lodge, set in a 2ha plot in the leafy northern suburbs of Shantytown, is probably now the smartest hotel within the city limits, & certainly the best-value option in the mid to upper price range. The large, airy en-suite rooms are unusually stylish, combining an ethnic feel with a contemporary touch, & they all come with DSTV, fan & private balcony. Other facilities include the well-developed green gardens, a swimming pool with views of Kilimanjaro, a gym, free 24hr Wi-Fi, & a good restaurant serving Indian & continental cuisine. *US$82/106 standard sgl/dbl B&B, US$135/159 dbl suite with AC.* **$$$$**

🏠 **Keys Hotel** [162 D3] (30 rooms) 📞027 275 2250; **m** 0757 117784; **e** info@keys-hotel-tours.com; www.keys-hotel-tours.com. In attractive suburban grounds about 1km from the Clock Tower, the Keys Hotel has offered good value for several years, & it remains one of the most popular hotels within its price range. Visitors have the choice of a room in the dbl-storey main building or a makuti-roofed cottage in the gardens behind it. All rooms are en suite & have hot water, satellite TV & nets. There is a swimming pool & a decent restaurant serving typical Tanzania hotel fare. Keys is also one of the more reliable places to organise climbs of Kilimanjaro, & while rates are a little higher than at some other places, they do include 1 night's HB accommodation at the hotel on either side of the climb. *US$78/91 sgl/dbl self-contained rooms B&B, heavily discounted for Tanzanian residents; camping at Keys Lodge US$7pp. Rooms* **$$$$**, *camping* **$**

🏠 **Sal Salinero Hotel** [162 A2] (27 rooms)
📞027 275 2240; **m** 0732 972864; **e** info@ salsalinerohotel.com; www.salsalinerohotel.com. Set in compact palm-shaded gardens, this slightly pretentious hotel in Shantytown has large rooms with terracotta tiled floors, king-sized beds, wooden

ceilings, huge changing rooms & excellent facilities, including satellite TV, tea-/coffee-making facilities & a large en-suite bathroom with separate tub & shower. Unfortunately, the otherwise high quality of the accommodation is let down by the imposing décor. The gloomy public areas are similarly schizoid, with classy finishes set alongside some decidedly tacky touches. Far nicer are the restaurant & bar, with outdoor seating in a green garden. *US$110/171 sgl/dbl standard rooms B&B, suites US$246.* **$$$$**

🏠 **Impala Hotel** [162 A2] (11 rooms) 📞027 274 3082; **e** impala@impalahotel.com; www. impalahotel.com. Related to its namesake in Arusha (page 128), but smaller & plusher, the Impala Hotel lies on Lema Rd in the leafy suburbia of Shantytown about 2km from the town centre. The large wood-panelled rooms with fan, hot bath & satellite TV are fair value, although standards vary a bit so ask to see a couple. Facilities include

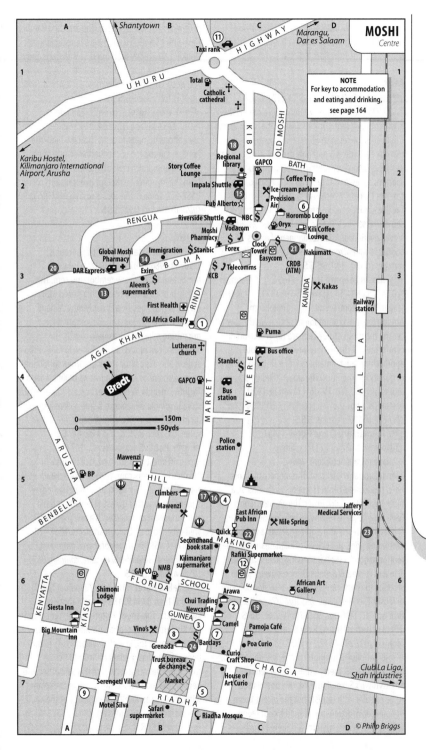

MOSHI
Centre

Shantytown

HIGHWAY

Marangu,
Dar es Salaam

NOTE
For key to accommodation
and eating and drinking,
see page 164

Taxi rank

(11)

UHURU

Total

Catholic
cathedral

Karibu Hostel,
Kilimanjaro International
Airport, Arusha

KIBO

OLD MOSHI

BATH

(18)

Regional
library

GAPCO

Coffee Tree

Story Coffee
Lounge

Ice-cream parlour

Impala Shuttle

(15)

Precision
Air

(6)

Pub Alberto

Horombo Lodge

RENGUA

Riverside Shuttle

NBC

Oryx

Kili Coffee
Lounge

Moshi
Pharmacy

Vodacom

Global Moshi
Pharmacy

Immigration

Stanbic

Forex

Clock
Tower

Easycom

Nakumatt

(20)

(14)

BOMA

Telecomms

(21)

DAR Express

Exim

KCB

CRDB
(ATM)

KAUNDA

(13)

Aleem's
supermarket

Kakas

AGA KHAN

First Health

Old Africa Gallery

(1)

Railway
station

Puma

Lutheran
church

Bus office

Stanbic

GAPCO

MARKET

Bus
station

GHALLA

NYERERE

ARUSHA

Police
station

BENBELLA

Mawenzi

BP

HILL

Climbers

(17)(16)(4)

Mawenzi

East African
Pub Inn

Nile Spring

Jaffery
Medical Services

Quick

MAKINGA

(22)

Secondhand
book stall

(23)

Kilimanjaro
supermarket

Rafiki Supermarket

(12)

KENYATTA

Shimoni
Lodge

GAPCO

NMB

FLORIDA

SCHOOL

African Art
Gallery

KIASU

Siesta Inn

Arawa

Chui Trading
Newcastle

(2)

Big Mountain
Inn

GUINEA

(3)

Camel

(19)

Vino's

Pamoja Café

(8)

(7)

Grenada

Barclays

(24)

Poa Curio

Curio
Craft Shop

CHAGGA

Club La Liga,
Shah Industries

Serengeti Villa

Trust bureau
de change

(9)

Market

House of
Art Curio

Motel Silva

RIADHA

Safari
supermarket

Riadha Mosque

© Philip Briggs

N
Bradt

0   150m
0   150yds

a swimming pool, internet café & forex bureau, & a good restaurant specialising in Indian dishes. *US$90/100 dbl/twin B&B.* **$$$$**

Moderate

🏠 **Bristol Cottages** [165 B3] (17 rooms) 📞027 275 5083; e info@bristolcottages.com; www.bristolcottages.com. Located close to the bus station, this neat lodge set in small, secure & peaceful manicured gardens is probably the pick in this range, as well as being very central. Accommodation is in spacious suites & cottages with AC & hot shower, satellite TV, nets, 2 beds & attractive modern décor. Facilities include secure parking, internet, email & secretarial services. The clean open-sided restaurant serves a variety of Asian & continental dishes. *US$60/90 sgl/dbl rooms in new wing B&B, suites & cottages US$70–140.* **$$$$**

🏠 **Moshi Leopard Hotel** [165 B7] (47 rooms) 📞027 275 0884/5134; m 0756 983311; e info@leopardhotel.com; www.leopardhotel.com. Among the most commodious options in the town centre, the multi-storey Leopard Hotel is clean, comfortable & thoroughly adequate without approaching the Kilimanjaro Crane Hotel in terms of quality or amenities. The smart, tiled en-suite rooms have AC, fan, TV, dbl or twin bed with netting, & a hot shower. Free Wi-Fi. *US$60/70 sgl/dbl B&B, US$90 dbl suite.* **$$$**

🏠 **Kilimanjaro Crane Hotel** [165 C2] (30 rooms) 📞027 275 1114; e info@kilimanjarocranehotel.com; www.kilimanjarocranehotel.com. This modern high-rise hotel has a useful central location on Kaunda St, a block east of the Clock Tower. The en-suite rooms have large beds, DSTV, private balcony, netting, fan & hot bath. There's also a green garden, a welcome swimming pool, great views of Kilimanjaro from the rooftop, a good restaurant serving pizzas, Chinese & Indian cuisine, & a ground-floor souvenir shop stocking the most comprehensive selection of books in Moshi. Excellent value. *US$50/60/75 sgl/dbl/trpl B&B with AC, TV, fridge, US$110 dbl suite.* **$$$**

🏠 **Lutheran Uhuru Hotel** [162 B3] (72 rooms) 📞027 275 4512; m 0753 037216; e reservations@uhuruhotel.org; www.uhuruhotel.org. Set in vast & pretty suburban gardens on Shantytown's Sekou Toure Rd, this hostel used to be popular with tourists but the recent boom in hotel construction in & around Moshi seems to have reduced its custom, & it feels a touch

overpriced for non-residents. The attached Bamboo Restaurant serves decent meals, but smoking & drinking are strictly prohibited. The hostel is about 3km out of town. *US$45/55 en-suite sgl/dbl with fan, or US$50/60 sgl/dbl with AC & TV. About 50% cheaper for residents.* **$$$**

🏠 **Q-Wine Hotel** [165 A7] (23 rooms) 📞027 275 4382; m 0753 645844; e info@qwinehotelkilimanjaro.com. This new high-rise hotel, set at the top of the Riadha Rd hill, offers superb panoramic views of Moshi & Kilimanjaro from the top-floor restaurant, where mains cost US$8–12. *Comfortable rooms cost US$40/60/70/90 sgl/dbl/twin/trpl B&B.* **$$$**

Budget

✳ 🏠 **Tembotamu** [162 D2] (4 rooms) m 0754 498690/0757 983007; e info@tembotamu.com; www.tembotamu.com. This highly praised & very reasonably priced B&B is owned & managed by a friendly New Zealand couple who also have a good reputation for organising reliable Kilimanjaro climbs. The spacious clean rooms are decorated in funky ethnic style, & there is a large tropical garden surrounded by local shambas & offering views of Kilimanjaro. Facilities include free internet access, a safe, vehicle storage, dinner by request, & free pickup & drop-off in Moshi town on arrival & departure. Great value. *US$20pp B&B, or US$35pp HB.* **$$**

✳ 🏠 **Rafiki Backpackers** [162 C2] (up to 60 guests) m 0714 422500; e info@rafikibackpackeers.com; www.rafikibackpackers.com. A new & funky backpacker hotel split over 2 premises & sporting a list of awards. It has a small museum attached with a few rooms of well-labelled local Chagga artefacts. *US$8–12 dorm bed, US$18/30 sgl/dbl shared bathroom, US$25/34/45 sgl/dbl/trpl en suite, camping US$5 (US$6 hired tent).* **$$**

🏠 **Zebra Hotel** [165 C6] (72 rooms) 📞027 275 0611; m 0754 951865; e zebrahotels@kilinet.co.tz. This smart 7-storey hotel, set behind the Kindoroko, is exceptional value for money, partly because the lack of elevator access to the upper storeys has made it difficult to market in the moderate category, where it would otherwise belong. The rooms are clean & spacious, & come with AC, fan, satellite TV & en-suite hot shower. A ground-floor restaurant is attached. *US$35/40 en-suite sgl/dbl B&B. A 40% discount for residents.* **$$**

🏠 **Kilimanjaro Tourist Inn** [162 A3] (8 rooms) ☎027 275 3262; e kkkmarealle@yahoo.com. This converted colonial house set in a large suburban garden on Lema Rd has a friendly, homely atmosphere that will appeal to travellers who avoid more institutionalised hotels. It's good value too, & all rooms come with net, fan & en-suite shower. *US$25/40 sgl/dbl, camping US$5, dinner US$7.* **$$**

🏠 **Kindoroko Hotel** [165 C7] (38 rooms) m 0715 377795/0753 377795; e reservations@kindorokohotels.com; www.kindorokohotels.com. For some years the smartest of the cluster of popular budget hotels situated on & around Nyerere Rd a couple of blocks south of the bus station, the 4-storey Kindoroko has maintained high standards & reasonable prices. The small but very clean rooms come with hot shower, fan, netting & DSTV. Facilities include a lively courtyard bar, popular with both travellers & locals, a restaurant serving adequate meals, an onsite internet café & a massage centre. The hotel also arranges reliable Kilimanjaro climbs. *US$20/30/45 sgl/dbl/family B&B.* **$$**

🏠 **Neneu Hotel** [162 C1] (11 rooms) ☎027 2751185; m 0753 076426; e newneneulodge@gmail.com. Situated up the KCMC road in the quiet back streets, the new Neneu has a pleasant & well-designed green courtyard surrounded by rooms. Free internet, fridge, AC. *US$25/37 sgl/dbl.* **$$**

Shoestring

✳ 🏠 **Karibu Hostel** [162 C4] (6 rooms) m 0764 892056/0776 349087; e borntolearn.ngo@gmail.com; www.karibuhostel.com. Aimed at volunteers & backpackers, this pleasant & sociable hostel comprises a converted private house set in large secure gardens shaded by mango & banana trees on the Arusha Rd, about 10mins' walk from the town centre. There is a large terrace & a living room with TV & a selection of DVDs. All proceeds are used to fund the NGO Born To Learn (see website for details). Meals are available on request. *Dbl rooms US$12 & dorms US$10pp B&B, dinner US$3. Discounts for long-term volunteers.* **$**

🏠 **Buffalo Hotel** [165 C6] (35 rooms) m 0756 765903; e buffalocompanyltd@yahoo.com. This clean & perennially popular budget hotel is spacious with brightly tiled rooms with en-suite hot showers. The attached restaurant serves tasty

& inexpensive Indian & Chinese meals. *US$12/16 sgl/dbl with fan, or US$23 exec dbl with AC, US$33 suite.* **$$**

🏠 **Kilimanjaro Backpackers Hotel** [165 B7] (16 rooms) m 0713 377795; e reservations@kilimanjarobackpackers.com; www.kilimanjarobackpackers.com. Situated 1 block south of the affiliated Kindoroko, the former Hotel Da Costa is perhaps the most popular cheapie in Moshi, offering accommodation in clean but no-frills tiled rooms & dormitories with net, fan & access to a common shower with a 24hr hot-water supply. Fair value. *US$12/20/30 sgl/dbl/trpl B&B, or US$10 per dorm bed. Lunch & dinner an additional US$4pp each.* **$$**

🏠 **Hill Street Accommodation** [165 C5] (10 rooms) ☎027 275 3919; m 0754 461469; e azim_omer@hotmail.com or azimomar61@gmail.com. This friendly hotel on Hill St has a convenient location close to the bus station & several good eateries. All the rooms have tiled floors & en-suite hot showers, but no fan or netting. *US$10/12/16 en-suite sgl/dbl/trpl.* **$**

🏠 **Kilimanjaro Safari Lodge** [162 A2] ☎027 275 2857; e kilisafarislodge@yahoo.com; kilimanjarosafarislodge.yolasite.com. A neat lodge at the cheaper end of the market for Shantytown. *Rooms at US$20/25/30 sgl/dbl/trpl.* **$$**

🏠 **YMCA Hostel** [165 C1] (47 rooms) ☎027 275 1754; e ymcatanzania@gmail.com. On the opposite side of town to the above hotels, the YMCA is a perennial favourite with budget travellers, offering clean & secure accommodation in green grounds with a large swimming pool. *US$17/19 small sgl/dbl B&B using communal showers.* **$$**

🏠 **Haria Hotel** [165 B6] (8 rooms) m 0763 056613/0785 580901. Formerly a downmarket annexe to the Kindoroko Hotel, this remains one of the best-value cheapies in Moshi, offering secure accommodation in large, clean rooms with tiled floors & nets. *US$25 for a room using common showers, or US$35 for an en-suite twin with hot shower, dorm beds US$10pp.* **$$**

OUT OF TOWN
Upmarket

🏠 **Protea Hotel Aisha Machame** [162 A4] (30 rooms) ☎027 275 6941/8; e proteaaishareservations@satconet.com. Situated along the surfaced Machame road about

12km from Moshi & 27km from KIA, this smart rural hotel, managed by the South African Protea Hotels group, is easily the most upmarket option in the vicinity of Moshi. The motel-style en-suite rooms aren't exactly bursting with character but the property itself is lovely, with a large thatched dining room & bar area facing a patch of indigenous forest on the footslopes of the great mountain. The hotel specialises in Kilimanjaro climbs & has good equipment, but it also offers a variety of excursions to more sedentary guests, ranging from local cultural tours & horseback trips to day visits to Lake Chala, Arusha National Park & a short walk to the 30m-high Makoa Waterfall & bat-infested Matangalima Cave. The swimming pool is solar heated. *US$130/160 sgl/dbl B&B, camping US$12pp. Standing tents* **$$$$**, *camping* **$**

Moderate & camping

🏠 **Honey Badger Lodge** [162 D4] (11 rooms) m 0767 551190; e info@ honeybadgerlodge.com; www. honeybadgerlodge.com. Situated 6km out of town along the Dar es Salaam road, this is a friendly, owner-managed lodge that combines a rustic feel & an eco-friendly ethos with comfortable accommodation, good food & excellent facilities. It is a thoroughly refreshing low-key alternative to the budget hotels in town. It started life as a converted house & campsite set within a fenced green family compound, but has since been expanded with the addition of a wonderful swimming pool area dotted with sunbeds & thatched gazebos, very comfortable en-suite rooms with hot showers, dormitories for large groups. Traditional drumming performances & lessons can be arranged, along with traditional Chagga *ngoma* (drum) performances with songs, & acting depicting stories about marriage, harvesting time & initiation rites. Can also arrange day hikes on the Kilimanjaro foothills, as well as full Kilimanjaro climbs with experienced guides. All proceeds are channelled into the adjacent Second Chance Education Centre, which is run by the owner's mother & which provides secondary schooling to children who have slipped through the cracks of the normal education system. *US$25pp dorm bed, US$50/70/90 en-suite sgl/dbl/trpl low season, US$60/90/110 en-suite sgl/dbl/trpl high season. All rates are B&B. A 3-course dinner costs US$15–20.* **$$$–$$$$**

✗ WHERE TO EAT AND DRINK

Many of the places listed under *Where to stay* on pages 164–8 have restaurants. Otherwise, the majority of standalone restaurants are in the town centre, but there are also several smarter options in the suburb of Shantytown to the north. The Shantytown restaurants are not accessible by public transport, so travellers staying more centrally will need to walk there and back (probably not a clever idea after dark) or arrange to be collected by taxi.

✗ **Abbasali Hot Bread Shop** [165 B3] 📞027 275 3099; ⏰ 08.00–20.00 Mon–Fri, 08.00–16.00 Sat. This bakery on Boma Rd sells the best bread in town, along with fresh pies, muffins & pastries.

✗ **Fresh Garden Restaurant** [165 C3] ⏰ 07.00–18.30 daily. Located opposite the Clock Tower & close to the bus station, this is a convenient spot for a quick alfresco cold drink or greasy local meal. Meals & 'bitings' are in the US$2–4 range.

✗ **Chrisburgers** [165 C2] m 0754 499118; ⏰ 24hrs but closed 22.00 Mon to 07.00 Tue. Cheap snacks such as hamburgers, samosas & excellent fruit juice, opposite the Clock Tower.

✗ **The Coffee Shop** [165 C5] 📞027 275 2707; e coffee-shop-moshi@yahoo.com; ⏰ 08.00– 20.00 Mon–Fri, 08.00–18.00 Sat. Tucked away on Hill St between the bus station & the market, this Church-run institution offers an irresistible selection of homemade cakes, burgers, quiches, sandwiches, pies, snacks & light lunches, mostly at around US$2–3, Chinese dishes US$4–5, served indoors or in a tranquil courtyard garden. It's also a good spot for b/fast.

✗ **Deli Chez Restaurant** [165 B5] 📞027 275 1144; m 0784 786241; ⏰ 09.30–21.30 Wed– Mon. This deli on the corner of Hill & Market streets serves a great selection of Indian dishes, as well as a more limited selection of Chinese meals & fast food, & a sumptuous selection of milkshakes, sundaes & other desserts. No alcohol.

✕ Fify's Café [165 C2] **m** 0755 837740; ⏰ 24hrs. At the north end of the town centre, behind the library, this new restaurant chain (with another 2 cafés in Arusha) serves a selection of European dishes. Mains in the US$5–10 range.

✕ El Rancho [162 A2] ☎ 027 275 5115; ⏰ 12.30–23.00 Tue–Sun. Top-notch Indian restaurant & bar in a converted old house & green garden close to the Impala Hotel in Shantytown. A broad selection of vegetarian mains is available for around US$5, while meat dishes are slightly more expensive. Highly recommended.

✕ Indo-Italiano Restaurant [165 C6] ☎ 027 275 2195; ⏰ 10.00–22.00 daily. This popular restaurant has a convenient location opposite the Buffalo Hotel & it serves a wide range of Indian & Italian dishes – tandoori grills & pizzas particularly recommended – in the US$6–7 range. Meals can be served indoors or on the wide veranda.

✕ Jay's Kitchen [165 A3] **m** 0744 722527; ⏰ 10.00-22.00 daily except Tue. A new restaurant at the top of the Boma road hill after Dar Express Bus office. Korean dishes for around US$6. For keen chefs, the recipes for each dish are included in the menu.

✕ La Fuente Mexican [162 A3] **m** 0784 369005; **e** lafuentemoshi@gmail.com; ⏰ 09.00–21.00 Tue–Sat. A new Mexican restaurant in Shantytown, serving all the usual Mexican dishes for around US$4–6.

✕ Milan's Restaurant [165 C6] **m** 0754 269802; **e** ehitentpandya@gmail.com; ⏰ 11.00–21.30 daily. As the name doesn't suggest, this low-key but thoroughly commendable eatery specialises in Indian vegetarian food, with around 40 dishes to choose from, but it also serves a limited Chinese selection & pizzas. Catering mostly to a local clientele, the décor is decidedly no-frills but the food is excellent value at around US$3–4 for a main. It also serves affordable *lassis*, fruit juices & milkshakes, but no alcohol.

✕ Mr Feng Chinese Restaurant [162 C4] **m** 0768 565656; ⏰ 06.00–22.00 weekdays, 11.00–22.00 Sat & Sun. This new Chinese has dishes in the US$7–8 range. It also has 2 rooms for US$20 & US$40 B&B respectively.

✕ Sikh Club [165 D6] ☎ 027 275 2473; ⏰ 10.30–15.00 & 18.00–23.00 Tue–Sun. This long-serving Indian eatery on Ghalla St (near the old railway station) is as short on pretensions as it is long on value & it serves a great selection of tasty meat & vegetarian curries & tandoori grills, mostly for under US$5.

☕ Aroma Coffee House [165 A3] ☎ 027 275 1347; **e** asiakimaryo@gmail.com; www.aromacoffee.co.tz; ⏰ 07.00–20.00 daily. This cosy café on Boma Rd serves delicious Kilimanjaro coffee, light snacks, pastries & fresh juice. It also has a swimming pool for Tsh10,000.

☕ Kilijava Coffee [165 C3] ⏰ 08.30–20.30 daily. Found outside the Nakumatt Supermarket, this terrace café serves good coffee & fruit juice, plus a selection of sandwiches, snacks & salads for around US$2.

☕ Tanzania Coffee Lounge [165 B7] **m** 0754 610892; ⏰ 08.00–20.00 Mon–Sat, 10.00–17.00 Sun. Arguably the tastiest caffeine fix in Moshi, with filter, espresso, latte & cappuccino all available at around US$1, this trendy little place on Chagga Rd also serves great fruit juice, waffles, cakes & pastries, & the tasty lunchtime salads will satisfy those desperate for some fresh greens. Meals cost around US$3–6. There's a high-speed internet café at the back.

NIGHTLIFE

☆ Club La Liga [162 D5] **m** 0767 770022/0715 750076; ⏰ 18.00–late Tue–Sun; entrance US$5 Fri & Sat, but only US$2 for men & free for women on other nights. Moshi's premier nightclub lies about 500m from the town centre, among a row of old warehouses that can be reached by following Chagga Rd eastward across the railway tracks, to where it becomes Viwanda Rd. It usually has live music on Thu, while DJs play a selection of *bongo flava* (Tanzanian hip-hop) & other dance music on other nights.

☆ Pub Alberto [165 C2] ⏰ 18.00–04.00 Tue–Sun. Brightly decorated nightclub next to Chrisburgers. Good place for a last round.

♀ East African Pub Inn [165 C5] Nyerere Rd, 2 blocks north of the Kindoroko Hotel. This lively,

2-storey bar has a wooden roof, TV & loud music, with cheap 'n' cheerful drink prices aimed at a predominantly local clientele. **♀ Glacier Inn** [162 A3] **m** 0762 881834. Set in large jacaranda-shaded gardens on the corner of Lema & Kilimanjaro Rd, this is a great spot for a few outdoor drinks in suburban Shantytown. It also serves local food in the US$4–7 range. A satellite TV ensures its popularity during major international sporting events.

SHOPPING

BOOKS A good **secondhand bookstall** can be found on Nyerere Road [165 C6], between the bus station and the Newcastle Hotel. For new books, particularly material relating specifically to Tanzania, the bookshop on the ground floor of the **Kilimanjaro Crane Hotel** (page 166) is the best stocked in town.

CRAFTS AND SOUVENIRS Although Moshi doesn't boast quite the proliferation of curio stalls and shops associated with Arusha, there are still plenty around, and prices tend to be a bit lower, as does the pushiness factor. The main concentration of craft shops in the town centre lies along Chagga Road close to the main cluster of budget hotels, and there's no better starting point here than the vast and hassle-free **I Curio Craft Shop** [165 C7], which stocks a good selection of books and postcards alongside the usual carvings, paintings and other local crafts. The smaller **House of Art Curio** is opposite. Follow Chagga Road east across the railway tracks towards Club La Liga to visit **Shah Industries** [162 C6] (\ *027 275 2414;* **e** *info@shahleather.com; www.shahleather.com*), an excellent craft workshop specialising in leatherwork and staffed mainly by Tanzanians with disabilities. Another superior outlet is the **Old Africa Gallery** [165 B4] (**m** *0784 182208;* ⊕ *09.00–18.00 Mon–Sat, 11.00–16.00 Sun*), which sells some worthwhile West African masks and Makonde sculptures along with a fairly typical selection of Tanzanian paintings, carvings and beadwork.

SUPERMARKETS The best supermarket by far, the **Nakumatt** [165 C3] (\ *027 275 4501;* ⊕ *08.30–22.00 Mon–Sat, 10.00–21.30 Sun*) is part of a well-known Kenyan chain, and in addition to a wide range of local and imported manufactured products, it sells a good selection of baked goods, fresh vegetables and fruit, and frozen meat. Elsewhere, **Aleem's supermarket** on Boma Road [165 B3] stocks a good range of imported goods and foods. There are also several good supermarkets on Nyerere Road between the bus station and the central market.

OTHER PRACTICALITIES

BANKS, ATMS AND FOREIGN EXCHANGE The **National Bank of Commerce** opposite the Clock Tower [165 C2] changes cash at the usual rate of commission, but there are usually long queues. Several forex bureaux are dotted around town, but while exchange rates are fairly good, you will generally get better in Arusha or Dar es Salaam.

There are now many **24-hour ATMs** where up to Tsh400,000 cash can be withdrawn with major certain brand credit or debit cards (most accept some or all of MasterCard, Cirrus, Visa and Maestro, but not Diners Club or American Express). These include the CRDB [165 C3], National Bank of Commerce [165 C2], Barclays Bank [165 B7], Exim Bank [165 B3] and Stanbic [165 B3].

MEDICAL The best place to head to in the case of a medical emergency is the **Kilimanjaro Christian Medical Centre (KCMC)** in Shantytown [162 B2] (\ *027 275 4377; www.kcmc.ac.tz*), about 5km north of the town centre. More central options include the **First Health Hospital** on Rindi Road [165 B3] (✆ *027 275 4051*), and **Jaffery Medical Services** [165 D5] (✆ *027 275 1843; ⏱ 08.30–17.00 Mon–Fri, until 13.00 Sat*) on Ghala Street.

IMMIGRATION Situated in Kibo House on Boma Road a few doors west of the Stanbic Bank, the immigration office in Moshi [165 B3] can process visa extensions on the spot during office hours (⏱ *08.00–15.00 Mon–Fri*).

INTERNET AND EMAIL A few internet cafés are dotted around town. Most charge around Tsh500 per 30 minutes – the more expensive cafés generally provide a faster service – and stay open from around 08.00 to 20.00 daily, though some close on Sundays. **Easycom** in Twiga House on the main traffic circle [165 C3] and **Tanzania Coffee Lounge** on Chagga Road [165 B7] are both recommended. Several restaurants/cafés such as Fify's (page 169) have Raha Wi-Fi spots (free registration).

SWIMMING Use of the swimming pool at the **YMCA** [165 C1] is free to hostel residents, but visitors must pay a daily entrance fee of Tsh3,000. The **Keys Hotel** [162 D3] charges a similar price to casual swimmers, but the pool is smaller and it is further out of town. You could also try the pool at the **Kilimanjaro Crane Hotel** [165 C2]. Another option, especially for those with time to kill and private transport, is the wonderful swimming pool at **Honey Badger Lodge**, 6km along the Dar es Salaam road. Non-residents pay US$10 for a full three-course meal with use of the pool, or US$7 for pool usage only. The newly opened Aroma Coffee House [165 A3] charges Tsh10,000.

TOURIST INFORMATION AND TOUR OPERATORS

There's no tourist information office in Moshi; the closest is in Arusha (pages 138–9). Most of the tour operators in town can provide local travel information, but this will not necessarily be impartial. A useful resource is the website www.kiliweb.com.

The companies listed below all specialise foremost in Kilimanjaro climbs, but most also arrange safaris and Zanzibar stays.

Honey Badger m 0767 551190; e info@ honeybadgerlodge.com; www.honeybadgerlodge. com.Based out of the lodge of the same name, this small ethically minded operator is recommended both for its prices & socially conscious attitude to the treatment of porters & guides.

Keys Hotel ✆027 275 2250/1870; e info@ keys-hotel-tours.com; www.keys-hotel-tours. com. Excellent & experienced operator based at one of the town's best hotels (page 164), & very reasonably priced.

Pristine Trails Adventures & Safaris ✆027 275 4463; e info@pristinetrails.com; www. pristinetrails.com; see ad, page 70. Moshi-based

company that operate trips to Mount Kilimanjaro & Zanzibar.

Snowcap Tanzania Tours ✆027 275 4826; m 0759 114527; e info@snowcap.co.tz; www. snowcap.co.tz; see ad, page 176. Another very experienced but reasonably priced operator known for its ethical treatment of porters & guides.

Shah Tours m 0787 141052; e info@shah-tours. com; www.shah-tours.com; see ad, page 175

Zara Tours m 0754 451000; e zara@zaratours. com; www.zaratours.com. Situated on Rindi Lane diagonally opposite the Stanbic Bank, Zara Tours has been one of the most prominent & reliable budget/mid-range climb operators for decades.

AROUND MOSHI

The most popular tourist destination in the vicinity of Moshi is of course Mount Kilimanjaro, the upper slopes and ascent of which are detailed in *Chapter 8*. Other lesser attractions in the region include the villages of Marangu and Machame; Chagga ecotourism projects in the Kilimanjaro foothills and a spectacular crater lake called Chala on the Kenyan border. The closest safari destination is Mkomazi National Park, covered in *Chapter 9*.

MARANGU The village of Marangu, whose name derives from the local Chagga word meaning 'spring water', is situated on the lower slopes of Kilimanjaro about 40km from Moshi and 5km south of the main entrance gate to Mount Kilimanjaro National Park. Unlike lower-lying Moshi, Marangu has an appropriately alpine feel, surrounded as it is by lush vegetation and bisected by a babbling mountain stream, and it remains a popular springboard for Kilimanjaro ascents using the Marangu Route. For those who lack the time, inclination or money to climb Kilimanjaro, Marangu is a pleasant place to spend a night or a few days exploring the lower slopes of the great mountain, with several attractive waterfalls situated within easy striking distance.

Getting there and away The 40km drive from Moshi shouldn't take much longer than 30 minutes in a **private vehicle**. To get there, first head out along the Dar es Salaam road, bearing left after 23km as if heading towards Taveta, then turning left again after another 4km at the junction village of Himo. **Buses** and **dalla-dallas** between Moshi and Marangu leave in either direction when they are full, normally at least once an hour, and generally take 45–60 minutes.

Where to stay and eat

Upmarket
Marangu Hotel (26 rooms) m 0717 408615; e info@maranguhotel.com; www. maranguhotel.com; see ad, page 175. Unquestionably the top accommodation in the area, this stalwart family-run hotel, situated along the Moshi road 5km before Marangu, has an unpretentiously rustic feel, all ivy-draped walls & neat hedges that might have been transported straight from the English countryside. It also has a long-standing reputation for organising reliable Kilimanjaro climbs, whether you're looking at the standard all-inclusive package or the 'hard way' package aimed at budget travellers. Accommodation is in self-contained rooms, but camping is also available (page 173). *US$85–120 sgl, US$150–200 dbl FB (low/high season).* **$$$$**

Capricorn Hotel (50 rooms) 027 275 1309; m 0755 005062; e info@thecapricornhotels. com. Straggling over a steep hillside some 2km from Marangu along the road towards Kilimanjaro National Park's Marangu Entrance Gate, this is one of the newer hotels in the Marangu area but the en-suite rooms with satellite TV & minibar are rather variable in quality & the older ones are starting to look very frayed at the edges. Situated within the forest zone, the lushly wooded 2.5ha garden is teeming with birds. The restaurant has a mediocre reputation, but Kilimanjaro climbs arranged through the hotel are as reliable as it gets. *US$70 B&B, US$80pp HB, US$90pp FB.* **$$$$**

Moderate
Nakara Hotel (18 rooms) 027 275 6599; m 0754 277300; e info@nakarahotels.com; www. nakarahotels.com. This smart but soulless high-rise lies about 3km past Marangu & around 2km before the eponymous entrance gate to Mount Kilimanjaro National Park. The self-contained twin rooms are small & rather lacking in character but are well maintained. Unfortunately, the rather cramped grounds lack the greenery & interest of other options in this price range, & on last inspection the staff was spectacularly inefficient. *US$60pp B&B.* **$$$**

Kibo Hotel (35 rooms) 027 275 1309; m 0754 038747; e kibohotel@outlook.com. The venerable Kibo Hotel stands in attractive flowering gardens roughly 1km from the village centre towards the park entrance gate. Formerly on a par with the Marangu Hotel, the Kibo has emphatically seen better days – incredibly, lest it escape your attention, former US president Jimmy Carter stayed here in 1988 – but it has retained a winning air of faded dignity epitomised by the liberal wood panelling & creaky old verandas. If nothing else, following a recent change of management & sensible cut in rates, the large, self-contained rooms are good value. Facilities include a swimming pool, internet access, gift shop & a decent restaurant bursting with character, & the hotel makes a great base for casual rambling in the Kilimanjaro foothills. It has been arranging reliable Kilimanjaro climbs for decades. *US$45/55/65 sgl/dbl/trpl B&B, US$15/20 for lunch/dinner, camping US$10pp per night.* **$$$**

🏠 **Babylon Lodge** (21 rooms) ☏ 027 275 6355; **m** 0762 016016/0757 997799; **e** info@babylonlodge.com; www.babylonlodge.com. Situated 500m from Marangu Post Office along the Mwika road, this former budget hotel has undergone a series of facelifts over the past decade. The en-suite rooms with combination tub/shower & attractive ethnic décor are immaculately kept, but a touch on the cramped side. Overall, it's one of the best-value lodges in the Marangu area, especially when it comes to cleanliness & quality of service. *US$50/70/80 sgl/dbl/trpl B&B, another US$15pp for lunch or dinner.* **$$$–$$$$**

Budget & camping
It is also possible to camp at the Kibo Hotel.

🏠 **Coffee Tree Campsite** (3 rooms) ☏ 027 275 6604; **m** 0715 544022; **e** kilimanjaro@iwayafrica.com. Situated alongside the Nakara Hotel, this neatly laid-out site is a good place to arrange budget Kilimanjaro climbs, & while the simple rooms aren't great value, you won't find cheaper in Marangu. The camping seems a bit dear too, & even allowing for the above-average facilities (fridge, bar, BBQ, sauna & hot shower) the campsite at the Marangu or Kibo hotels seem infinitely better value. Tents & gas stoves are available for hire, various cultural tours can be arranged & there are onsite email & internet facilities. If you don't fancy self-catering, you could eat at the adjacent Nakara Hotel. *US$12pp for a simple room, US$8pp camping.* **$**

⛺ **Marangu Hotel** ☏ 027 275 6594; **e** info@maranguhotel.com; www.maranguhotel.com. The large green campsite behind the main hotel buildings has a hot shower & is probably the best value for campers in the Marangu area. *US$10pp.* **$**

Excursions from Marangu

Kinukamori Waterfall (**m** *0754 317113; entrance US$7*) The most central tourist attraction in Marangu is the Kinukamori – 'Little Moon' – Waterfall. Situated about 20 minutes' walk from the town centre, from where it is signposted, this approximately 15m-high waterfall lies in a small park maintained by the district council as an ecotourism project in collaboration with two nearby villages. It's pretty enough without being an essential side trip, though the wooded banks of the Unna River above the waterfall harbour a variety of forest birds, and regularly attract troops of black-and-white colobus in the rainy season. A legend associated with Kinukamori relates to an unmarried girl called Makinuka, who discovered she was pregnant, a crime punishable by death in strict Chagga society, and decided to take her own life by jumping over the waterfall. When Makinuka arrived at the waterfall and looked over the edge, she changed her mind and turned to go home to plead for mercy. As she did so, however, she came face to face with a leopard and ran back screaming in fear, forgetting about the gorge behind her, to plunge to an accidental death. A statue of Makinuka and her nemesis stands above the waterfall. The waterfall can be visited independently, or by arrangement with your hotel as part of a longer sightseeing tour.

Kilasia Waterfall Clearly signposted to the left of the dirt road connecting the Kibo Hotel and Kilimanjaro Mountain Resort lies the rather spectacular Kilasia Waterfall, the centrepiece of a new ecotourism community that charges US$5 per person for a guided nature walk. Approximately 30m high, the waterfall tumbles into the base of a sheer-sided gorge before running through a set of violent rapids into a lovely pool that's said to be safe for swimming. The waterfall is at its most powerful during the rains, but it flows solidly throughout the year – the name Kilasia derives from a Chagga word meaning 'without end', reputedly a reference to its reliable flow. The path to the base

Several cultural tourism projects operate in the Kilimanjaro foothills in association with local communities. In addition to offering insights into Chagga culture and the opportunity to limber up the limbs before a full-on ascent of Kilimanjaro, these cultural tours allow non-climbers to get a good look at the scenic Kilimanjaro foothills, with a chance of catching a glimpse of the snow-capped peak itself. In addition to the local telephone contacts given below, full details of the programmes can be obtained through the central website infojep.com/culturaltours.

MACHAME CULTURAL TOURISM PROGRAMME (✆ *027 275 7033*) This programme is based at the village of Kyalia, close to the Machame Gate of Kilimanjaro National Park. A good day tour for those with a strong interest in scenery is the 5-hour Sieny-Ngira Trail, which passes through the lush montane forest to a group of large sacred caves, a natural rock bridge over the Marire and Namwi rivers, and a nearby waterfall. For those with a greater interest in culture, the 5-hour Nronga Tour, which visits a milk purification and processing co-operative run by women, is best done on Monday, market day in Kyalia village. Of similar duration, the Nkuu Tour focuses instead on agriculture, in particular coffee production. Longer excursions include the two-day Ng'uni Hike and three-day Lyamungo Tour. In a private vehicle, Kyalia can be reached by following the Arusha road out of Moshi for 12km, then following the turn-off signposted for Machame Gate and driving for another 14km. The road to Kyalia is surfaced in its entirety, and regular dalla-dallas run to Kyalia from the junction on the Moshi–Arusha road.

MARANGU CULTURAL TOURISM PROGRAMME Geared primarily towards travellers staying in Marangu prior to a Kilimanjaro climb, this programme offers a variety of half-day trips taking in various natural and cultural sites on the surrounding slopes. Popular goals include any of three waterfalls, as well as the first coffee tree planted in Tanzania more than a century ago, and a traditional conical Chagga homestead. Few prospective climbers will be unmoved by the grave of the legendary Yohanu Lauwo, who guided Hans Meyer to the summit of Kilimanjaro back in 1889, continued working as a guide into his seventies, and reputedly lived to the remarkable age of 124! Other walks lead to nearby Mamba and Makundi, known for their traditional Chagga blacksmiths and woodcarvers, and for the Laka Caves, where women and children were hidden during the frequent 19th-century clashes with the Maasai of the surrounding plains. Guided tours can be arranged through any of the hotels in and around Marangu.

of the falls, though no more than 500m long, is very steep and potentially dangerous when wet. The rocky gorge below the waterfall is lined with ferns and evergreen trees, and a troop of blue monkeys often passes through in the early morning and late afternoon. For further details, contact the community project manager.

LAKE CHALA Straddling the Kenyan border some 30km east of Moshi as the crow flies, this roughly circular crater lake, a full 3km wide yet invisible until you virtually topple over the rim, is one of northern Tanzania's true off-the-beaten-track scenic gems. The brilliant turquoise water, hemmed in by sheer cliffs draped in tropical greenery, is an arresting sight at any time, and utterly fantastic when Kilimanjaro emerges from the clouds to the immediate west. Not for the faint-hearted, a very steep footpath leads from the rim to the edge of the lake, its translucent waters plunging near-vertically to an undetermined depth from the rocky shore. Abundant birdlife aside, wildlife is in short supply, though Chala, in common with many other African crater lakes, is said locally to harbour its due quota of mysterious and malignant Nessie-like beasties. A more demonstrable cause for concern should you be nurturing any thoughts of dipping a toe in the water, however, is the presence of crocodiles, one of which killed a British volunteer off the Kenyan shore in March 2002.

Getting there and away For the time being, the only practical way to reach Chala is as an **organised day or overnight trip** out of Moshi, or in a **private 4x4 vehicle**. If you're driving, follow the Dar es Salaam road out of Moshi for 25km until you reach the junction at Himo, where a left turn leads to the Kenyan border at Taveta. About 7km along the Taveta road, turn left on to the rough road signposted for Kilimanjaro Mountain Lodge, which you must follow for about 40 minutes to reach the lake.

Where to stay and eat
🏠 **Lake Chala Safari Camp** (10 units) **m** 0753 249118/0784 249118; **e** lakechala@ gmail.com; www.lakechalasafaricamp.com. The only functional accommodation in the vicinity of Chala, this place opened on the crater rim in early 2010, initially as a campsite, bar & restaurant but upmarket standing tents are now available. *US$135/250 sgl/dbl.* **$$$$–$$$$$**

FOR INFORMATION PLEASE
VISIT OUR WEBSITE
WWW.SNOWCAP.CO.TZ

8

Mount Kilimanjaro National Park

Reaching an altitude of 5,895m (19,340ft), Kilimanjaro is the highest mountain in Africa, and on the rare occasions when it is not veiled in clouds, its distinctive silhouette and snow-capped peak form one of the most breathtaking sights on the continent. There are, of course, higher peaks on other continents, but Kilimanjaro is effectively the world's largest single mountain, a free-standing entity that towers an incredible 5km above the surrounding plains. It is also the highest mountain anywhere that can be ascended by somebody without specialised mountaineering experience or equipment.

Kilimanjaro straddles the border with Kenya, but the peaks all fall within Tanzania and can only be climbed from within the country. There are several places on the lower slopes from where the mountain can be ascended, but most people use the Marangu Route (which begins at the eponymous village) because it is the cheapest option and has the best facilities. The less heavily trampled Machame Route, starting from the village of the same name, has grown in popularity in recent years. A number of more obscure routes can be used, though they are generally only available through specialist trekking companies. Most prospective climbers arrange their ascent of 'Kili' – as it is popularly called – well in advance, through an overseas tour operator or online with a local operator, but you can also shop around on the spot using specialist trekking companies based in Moshi, Marangu or even Arusha. Kilimanjaro can be climbed at any time of year, but the hike is more difficult in the rainy months, especially between March and May.

GEOLOGY

In geological terms, Kilimanjaro is a relatively young mountain. Like most other large mountains near the Rift Valley, it was formed by volcanic activity, first erupting about one million years ago. The 3,962m-high Shira Peak collapsed around half a million years ago, but the 5,895m-high Uhuru Peak on Mount Kibo (the higher of Kilimanjaro's two main peaks) and 5,149m-high Mawenzi Peak continued to grow until more recently. Shira Plateau formed 360,000 years ago, when the caldera was filled by lava from Kibo after a particularly violent eruption. Kibo is now dormant, and nobody knows when it last displayed any serious volcanic activity. The Kilimanjaro National Park, gazetted in 1977, protects the entire Tanzanian part of the mountain above the 2,700m contour, an area of 756km².

HISTORY

Blessed by fertile volcanic soil and reliable rainfall, Kilimanjaro has probably always been a magnet for human settlement. Ancient stone tools of indeterminate age have

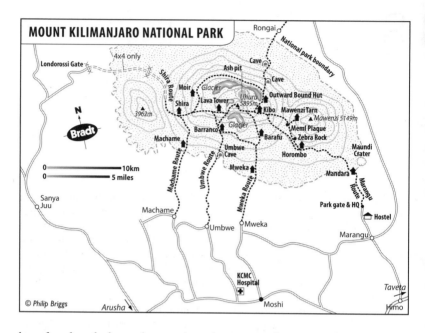

been found on the lower slopes, as have the remains of pottery artefacts thought to be at least 2,000 years old. Archaeological evidence suggests that, between 1,000 and 1,500 years ago, Kilimanjaro was the centre of an Iron Age culture spreading out to the coastal belt between Pangani and Mombasa. Before that, it's anybody's guess really, but references in Ptolemy's *Geography* and the *Periplus of the Erythraean Sea* suggest that the mountain was known to the early coastal traders, and might even have served as the terminus of a trade route starting at modern-day Pangani and following the eponymous river inland. Kilimanjaro is also alluded to in an account written by a 12th-century Chinese trader, and by 16th-century Spanish geographer Fernandes de Encisco.

These ancient allusions fired the curiosity of 19th-century geographers, who outdid each other in publishing wild speculations about the African interior. In 1848, locals told Johan Rebmann, a German missionary working in the Taita Hills, about a very large silver-capped mountain known to the Maasai as Ol Doinyo Naibor – White Mountain – and reputedly protected by evil spirits that froze anybody who tried to ascend it. When Rebmann visited the mountain, he immediately recognised the spirit-infested silver cap to be snow, but this observation, first published in 1849, was derided by European experts, who thought it ludicrous to claim there was snow so near the Equator. Only in 1861, when an experienced geologist, Von der Decken, saw and surveyed Kilimanjaro, was its existence and that of its snow-capped peaks accepted internationally. Oral tradition suggests that no local person had successfully climbed Kilimanjaro – or at least returned to tell the tale – before Hans Meyer and Ludwig Purtscheller reached the summit in 1889.

Kilimanjaro is home to the Chagga people, a group of Bantu-speaking agriculturists whose ancestors are said to have arrived in the area in the 15th century. This dating is contradicted by a Chagga legend describing an eruption of Kilimanjaro, which doesn't tally with the geological evidence for the past 500 years, so it's probable that the story was handed down by earlier inhabitants. The Chagga have no tradition of central leadership, and an estimated 100 small chieftaincies existed in the region in the mid 19th century. Today, the Chagga have a reputation for industriousness and are generally relatively well educated; for that reason you'll find that a high proportion of salaried workers and safari guides come from the Kilimanjaro region.

VEGETATION AND BIOLOGY

There are five vegetation zones on Kilimanjaro: the cultivated lower slopes; the forest; heath and moorland; alpine; and the barren arctic summit zone. Vegetation is sparse higher up due to lower temperatures and rainfall.

The **lower slopes** of the mountain were probably once forested, but are now mainly cultivated. The volcanic soils make them highly fertile and they support a dense human population. The most biologically interesting aspect of the lower slopes is the abundance of wild flowers, seen between Marangu and the park entrance gate.

The **montane forest zone** of the southern slopes lies between the altitudes of 1,800m and 3,000m. Receiving up to 2,000mm of rainfall annually, this zone displays a high biological diversity, and still supports a fair amount of wildlife. The most frequently seen mammals are the black-and-white colobus and blue monkeys, while typical forest antelope include three duiker species and the beautifully marked bushbuck. Leopard, bushpig and porcupine are fairly common but seldom encountered by hikers, while eland, buffalo and elephant are present in small numbers. The forest is home to many varieties of butterfly, including four endemic species. The forests of Kilimanjaro are less rich in birds (particularly endemics) than the more ancient forests of the Eastern Arc Mountains, but some 40 species peculiar to Afro-montane forest have been recorded. Most forest birds are quite difficult to observe, but trekkers should at least hear the raucous silvery-cheeked hornbill and beautiful Hartlaub's turaco.

The semi-alpine **moorland zone**, which lies between 3,000m and 4,000m, is characterised by heath-like vegetation and abundant wild flowers. As you climb into the moorland, two distinctive plants become common. These are *Lobelia deckenii*, which grows to 3m high, and the groundsel *Senecio kilimanjarin*, which grows up to 5m high and can be distinguished by a spike of yellow flowers. The moorland zone supports a low density of mammals, but pairs of klipspringer are quite common on rocky outcrops and several other species are recorded from time to time. Hill chat and scarlet-tufted malachite sunbird are two birds whose range is restricted to the moorland of large East African mountains. Other localised birds are lammergeyer and alpine swift. Because it is so open, the views from the moorland are stunning.

8

WHAT'S IN A NAME?

Nobody is sure about the meaning of the name Kilimanjaro, or even whether it is Swahili, Maasai or Chagga in origin. That the term 'kilima' is Swahili for little mountain (a joke?) is not in doubt. But 'njaro' could derive from the Chagga word for caravan (the mountain was an important landmark on the northern caravan route), or from the Maasai word 'ngare' meaning water (it is the source of most of the region's rivers), or the name of a Swahili demon of cold. Another unrelated version of the name's origin is that it's a bastardisation of the phrase 'kilemakyaro' (impossible journey), the initial Chagga response to European queries about trekking to the peak!

The **alpine zone** between 4,000m and 5,000m is classified as a semi-desert because it receives an annual rainfall of less than 250mm. The ground often freezes at night, but ground temperatures may soar to above 30°C by day. Few plants survive in these conditions; only 55 species are present, many of them lichens and grasses. Six species of moss are endemic to the higher reaches of Kilimanjaro. Large mammals have been recorded at this altitude, most commonly eland, but none is resident.

Approaching the summit, the **arctic zone** starts at an altitude of around 5,000m. This area receives virtually no rainfall, and supports little permanent life other than the odd lichen. Two remarkable records concern a frozen leopard discovered here in 1926, and a family of hunting dogs seen in 1962. The most notable natural features at the summit are the inner and outer craters of Kibo, surrounding a 120m-deep ash pit, and the Great Northern Glacier, which has retreated markedly since Hans Meyer and Ludwig Purtscheller first saw it in 1889. Indeed, since that historic ascent, it is thought that Kilimanjaro's distinctive snow cap has retreated by more than 80%, probably as a result of global warming, and some experts predict that it will vanish completely by 2020.

CLIMBING KILIMANJARO

As Africa's highest peak and most identifiable landmark, Kilimanjaro offers an irresistible challenge to many tourists. Dozens of visitors to Tanzania set off for Uhuru Peak every day, ranging from teenagers to pensioners, and those who make it generally regard the achievement to be the highlight of their time in the country. A major part of Kilimanjaro's attraction is that any reasonably fit person stands a fair chance of reaching the top. The ascent requires no special climbing skills or experience; on the contrary, it basically amounts to a long uphill slog over four (or more) days, followed by a more rapid descent.

The relative ease of climbing Kilimanjaro should not lull travellers into thinking of the ascent as some sort of prolonged Sunday stroll. It is a seriously tough hike, with potentially fatal penalties for those who are inadequately prepared or who belittle the health risks attached to being at an altitude of above 4,000m. It should also be recognised that there is no such thing as a cheap Kilimanjaro climb (see box, page 185). A five-day Marangu climb generally costs at least US$1,200 per person,

A ROYAL VISIT

An unsubstantiated legend holds that Emperor Menelik I of Ethiopia, the illegitimate son of King Solomon and the Queen of Sheba, visited Kilimanjaro about 3,000 years ago while returning from a successful military campaign in East Africa. The emperor camped on the saddle for a night, and then ascended Kibo, where he suddenly fell ill and died, possibly from exposure and/or altitude-related causes. Menelik's slaves buried the imperial corpse in the snowy crater, where the story says it remains to this day, together with a royal cache of jewels, religious scrolls and other treasures. An extension of this legend prophesies that a descendant of Menelik I will one day ascend Kibo, find the frozen body and claim the seal ring of Solomon worn by it, thereby endowing himself with the wisdom of Solomon and heroic spirit of Menelik. Pure apocrypha, as far as I can ascertain, is the story that the ancient Ethiopian emperor's 19th-century successor and namesake Menelik II once climbed Kilimanjaro in an unsuccessful bid to fulfil this centuries-old prophecy.

The names of Kilimanjaro's two main peaks, Kibo and Mawenzi, derive from local Chagga words respectively meaning 'cold' and 'jagged'. According to Chagga legend, the peaks are sisters and both were once as smoothly shaped as the perfect dome of Kibo is today. But the younger sister Mawenzi was habitually too lazy to collect her own firewood and kept borrowing from Kibo until one day the elder sister instructed her to go out and gather her own. When Mawenzi refused, the enraged Kibo reached into her woodpile, grabbed the largest log there, and started beating her over the head, resulting in the jagged shape of the younger sister today.

depending to some extent on group size, while six-day climbs start at around US$1,400. People using high-quality operators and/or more obscure routes should expect to pay considerably more.

MARANGU ROUTE Starting at the Marangu Gate some 5km from the village of the same name, the so-called 'tourist route' is the most popular way to the top of Kilimanjaro, largely because it is less arduous than most of the alternatives, as well as having better facilities and being cheaper to climb. Marangu is also probably the safest route, due to the volume of other climbers and good rescue facilities relative to more obscure routes, and it offers a better chance of seeing some wildlife. It is the only route where you can sleep in proper huts throughout, with bathing water and bottled drinks normally available, too. The main drawback of the Marangu Route is that it is heavily trampled by comparison with other routes, for which reason many people complain that it can feel overcrowded.

Day 1: Marangu to Mandara Hut (*12km; 4hrs*) On an organised climb you will be dropped at the park entrance gate a few kilometres past Marangu. There is a high chance of rain in the afternoon, so it is wise to set off on this 4-hour hike as early in the day as you can. Foot traffic is heavy along this stretch, which means that although you pass through thick forest, the shy animals that inhabit the forest are not likely to be seen. If your guide will go that way, use the parallel trail, which meets the main trail halfway between the gate and the hut. Mandara Hut (2,700m) is an attractive collection of buildings with room for 200 people.

Day 2: Mandara Hut to Horombo Hut (*15km; 6hrs*) You continue through forest for a short time before reaching the heather and moorland zone, from where there are good views of the peaks and Moshi. The walk takes up to 6 hours. Horombo Hut (3,720m) sleeps up to 120 people. It is in a valley and surrounded by giant lobelia and groundsel. If you do a six-day hike, you will spend a day at Horombo to acclimatise.

Day 3: Horombo Hut to Kibo Hut (*15km; 6–7hrs*) The vegetation thins out as you enter the desert-like alpine zone, and when you cross the saddle Kibo Peak comes into view. This 6–7-hour walk should be done slowly: many people start to feel the effects of altitude. Kibo Hut (4,703m) is a stone construction that sleeps up to 120 people. Water must be carried from a stream above Horombo. You may find it difficult to sleep at this altitude, and as you will have to rise at around 01.00 the next morning, many people feel it is better not to bother trying.

Days 4 and 5: Kibo Hut to the summit to Marangu (*5km; 6hrs*) The best time to climb is during the night, as it is marginally easier to climb the scree slope to Gillman's Point on the crater rim when it is frozen. This ascent typically takes about 6 hours, so you need to get going between midnight and 01.00 to stand a chance of reaching the summit in time to catch the sunrise. From Gillman's Point it is a further 2-hour round trip along the crater's edge to Uhuru Peak, the highest point in Africa. From the summit, it's a roughly 7-hour descent with a break at Kibo Hut to Horombo Hut, where you will spend your last night on the mountain. The final day's descent from Horombo to Marangu generally takes 7–8 hours, so you should arrive in Marangu in the mid afternoon.

OTHER ROUTES Although the majority of trekkers stick to the Marangu Route, which is both the easiest and quickest ascent route up Kilimanjaro, with the best overnight facilities, an increasing proportion opt for one of five relatively off-the-beaten-track alternatives. While the merits and demerits of avoiding the Marangu Route are hotly debated, there is no doubt about two things: firstly that you'll see relatively few other tourists on the more obscure routes; and secondly that you'll pay considerably more for this privilege. Aesthetic and financial considerations aside, an unambiguous logistical disadvantage of the less-used routes is that, with the exception of Rongai, they are tougher going (though only the Umbwe is markedly so). Also, huts, where they exist, are virtually derelict, which enforces camping.

Machame Route In recent years, the Machame Route has grown greatly in popularity. It is widely regarded to be the most scenic viable ascent route, with great views across to Mount Meru, and as a whole it is relatively gradual, requiring at least six days for the full ascent and descent. Short sections are steeper and slightly more difficult than any part of the Marangu Route, but this is compensated for by the longer period for acclimatisation.

The route is named after the village of Machame, from where it is a 2-hour walk to the park gate (1,950m). Most companies will provide transport as far as the gate (at least when the road is passable), and then it's a 6–8-hour trek through thick forest to Machame Hut, which lies on the edge of the moorland zone at 2,890m. The Machame Hut is now a ruin, so camping is necessary, but water is available. The second day of this trail consists of a 9km, 4–6-hour hike through the moorland zone of Shira Plateau to Shira Hut (3,840m), which is near a stream. Once again, this hut has fallen into disuse, so the options are camping or sleeping in a nearby cave.

From Shira, a number of options exist: you could spend your third night at Lava Tower Hut (4,630m), 4 hours from Shira, but the ascent to the summit from here is tricky and only advisable if you are experienced and have good equipment. A less arduous option is to spend your third night at Barranco Campsite (3,950m), a tough 12km, 6-hour hike from Shira, then to go on to Barafu Hut (4,600m) on the fourth day, a walk of approximately 7 hours. From Barafu, it is normal to begin the steep 7–8-hour clamber to Stella Point (5,735m) at midnight, so that you arrive at sunrise, with the option of continuing on to Uhuru Peak, a 2-hour round trip, before hiking back down to Mweka Hut via Barafu in the afternoon. This day can involve up to 16 hours of walking altogether. After spending your fifth night at Mweka Hut (3,100m), you will descend the mountain on the sixth day via the Mweka Route, a 4–6-hour walk.

The huts along this route are practically unusable, but any reliable operator will provide you with camping equipment and employ enough porters to carry the camp and set it up.

PORTER TREATMENT GUIDELINES

These guidelines are produced by the Kilimanjaro Porters Assistance Project (KPAP) (*Hill St, behind the Coffee Shop, Moshi;* m *0754 817615;* e *info@kiliporters.org; www.kiliporters.org*), an initiative of the International Mountain Explorers Connection, a non-profit organisation based in the United States.

Visit the website for further information, including a list of local and international operators that it regards to be committed to responsible treatment of porters. You can also drop into the office in Moshi to attend a 'Porter Briefing', obtain a free Swahili–English language card, purchase discounted maps, arrange for off-the-beaten-path trips and homestays that directly support the local people, report any instances of porter abuse, or make a donation of clothing, money or volunteer help.

1 Ensure your porters are adequately clothed with suitable footwear, socks, waterproof jackets and trousers, gloves, hats, sunglasses, etc. Clothing for loan is available at the KPAP office in Moshi.
2 Fair wages should be paid. Kilimanjaro National Park now recommends US$10 per day. Ask your company how much your porters are paid (and whether it includes food) to encourage fair treatment from operators and guides.
3 Porters should eat at least two meals a day and have access to water.
4 Check the weight of the loads. The recommended maximum of 25kg includes the porter's personal gear (assumed to be 5kg), so the load for the company should not exceed 20kg. If additional porters need to be hired make sure that the tour company is paying each porter their full wage when you return.
5 Count the number of porters every day: you are paying and tipping for them. Porters should not be sent down early as they will not receive their tips, and the other porters are then overloaded.
6 Make sure your porters are provided with proper shelter. Where no shelter is available, porters need proper sleeping accommodation that includes tents and sleeping bags. Sleeping in the mess tent means that the porters have to wait outside for climbers to finish their meals.
7 Ensure that each porter receives the intended tip. If you give tips to one individual you run the risk that they may not distribute the proper amount to the crew.
8 Take care of sick or injured porters. Porters deserve the same standard of treatment, care and rescue as their clients. Sick or injured porters need to be sent down with someone who speaks their language and understands the problem. If available, porters should also be provided with insurance.
9 Get to know your porters. Some porters speak English and will appreciate any effort to speak with them. Free Swahili-language cards are available at the KPAP office in Moshi. The word *pole* (which translates loosely as 'sorry') shows respect for porters after a long day carrying your bags. *Asante* means 'thank you'.
10 After your climb, report any instances of abuse or neglect by email or by visiting the office.

Mweka Route This is the steepest and fastest route to the summit. There are two huts along it – Mweka (3,100m) and Barafu (4,600m), each sleeping up to 16 people – though neither is reportedly habitable at the time of writing. There is water at Mweka but not at Barafu. This route starts at the Mweka Wildlife College, 12km from Moshi. From there it takes about 8 hours to get to Mweka Hut, then a further 8 hours to Barafu, from where it replicates the Machame Route. The Mweka Route is not recommended for ascending the mountain, since it is too short for proper acclimatisation, but is often used as a descent route by people climbing the Machame or Shira routes.

Shira Route Although this route could technically be covered in five days by driving to the high-altitude trailhead, this would allow you very little time to acclimatise, and greatly decrease the odds of reaching the summit. A minimum of six days is recommended, but better seven so that you can spend a full day at Shira Hut to acclimatise. The route starts at Londorossi Gate on the western side of the mountain, from where a 19km track leads to the trailhead at around 3,500m. It is possible to motor to the trailhead in a 4x4, but for reasons already mentioned it would be advisable to walk, with an overnight stop to camp outside Simba Cave, which lies in an area of moorland where elephants and buffalo are regularly encountered. From the trailhead, it's a straightforward 4km to the campsite at the disused Shira Hut. If you opt to spend two nights at Shira in order to acclimatise, there are some worthwhile day walks in the vicinity. From Shira Hut, the route is identical to the Machame Route, and it is normal to return along the Mweka Route.

Rongai Route The only route ascending Kilimanjaro from the northeast, the Rongai Route starts close to the Kenyan border and was closed for several years due to border sensitivity. In terms of gradients, it is probably less physically demanding than the Marangu Route, and the scenery, with views over the Tsavo Plains, is regarded to be as beautiful. The Rongai Route can be covered over five days, with equally good if not better conditions for acclimatisation than the Marangu Route, though as with Marangu the odds of reaching the summit improve if you opt for an additional day.

The route starts at the village of Nale Moru (2,000m) near the Kenyan border, from where a footpath leads through cultivated fields and plantation forest before entering the montane forest zone, where black-and-white colobus monkeys are frequently encountered. The first campsite is reached after 3–5 hours, and lies at about 2,700m on the frontier of the forest and moorland zones. On the five-day hike, the second day involves a gentle 5–6-hour ascent, through an area of moorland where elephants are sometimes seen, to Third Cave Campsite (3,500m). On the third day, it's a 4–5-hour walk to School Campsite (4,750m) at the base of Kibo, with the option of camping here or else continuing to the nearby Kibo Hut, which is more crowded but more commodious. The ascent from here is identical to the Marangu Route. A six-day variation on the above route involves spending the second night at Kikelewa Caves (*3,600m, 6–7hr walk*), a night at Mawenzi Tarn near the synonymous peak (*4,330m, 4hr walk*), then crossing the saddle between Mawenzi and Kibo to rejoin the five-day route at School Campsite.

Umbwe Route This short, steep route, possibly the most scenic of the lot, is not recommended as an ascent route as it is very steep in parts and involves one short stretch of genuine rock climbing. It is occasionally used as a descent route, and can be tied in with almost any of the ascent routes, though many operators understandably prefer not to take the risk, or charge a premium for using it. Umbwe

Route descends from Barranco Hut, and comes out at the village of Umbwe. It is possible to sleep in two caves on the lower slopes along this route.

ARRANGING A CLIMB The only sensible way to go about climbing Kilimanjaro is through a reliable specialised operator. Readers who pre-book a climb through a known tour operator in their own country can be reasonably confident that they will be going with a reputable ground operator in Tanzania. Readers who want to make their arrangements online or after they arrive in Tanzania will find an almost infinite number of trekking companies operating out of Moshi, Arusha and to a lesser extent Marangu, and they should be able to negotiate a far better price by cutting out the middleman, but should also be circumspect about dealing with any company that lacks a verifiable pedigree. A list of respected operators is included in the box on page 189, and while such a list can never be close to comprehensive, it is reasonable to assume that anybody who can offer you a significantly cheaper package than the more budget-friendly companies on this list is not to be trusted.

Kilimanjaro climbs do not come cheaply (see box, below). Five-day Marangu climbs with a reliable operator start at an all-inclusive price of around US$1,200–1,400 per person for two people. You may be able to negotiate the price down slightly, especially for a larger group, but when you are paying this sort of money, it strikes me as sensible to shop around for quality of service rather than a fractional saving. A reputable operator will provide good food, experienced guides and porters, and reliable equipment – all of which go a long way to ensuring not only that you reach the top, but also that you come back down alive. You can assume that the cost of any package with a reputable operator will include a registered guide, two porters per person, park fees, food, and transport to and from the gate. It is, however, advisable to check exactly what you are paying for, and (especially for larger parties) to ensure that one porter is also registered

COSTING A CLIMB

The reason why climbing Kilimanjaro is so expensive boils down to the prescribed park fees charged by Tanapa. For the 2016–17 season, the daily entrance fee is US$70 per person, then there's a hut fee of US$60 or camping fee of US$50 per person per night, as well as a one-off rescue fee of US$20 per person per climb, plus 18% VAT. This creates a fixed cost of US$670–700 per person for a five-day hike up Marangu, plus an additional US$140 per person per extra day, before any actual services are provided. On top of this, there are set fees of US$20 per guide and US$15 per cook per party per day, and US$10 per porter per day, which would for example add another US$187.50 per person (plus VAT) for two people taking a five-day hike with two porters each, or US$112.50 per person (plus VAT) for four people taking a six-day hike with one porter each. Or to put it another way, an operator charging US$1,200 per person for two people to climb via the Marangu Route will be forking out at least US$800 in fees and other fixed costs, even before budgeting for transportation, food, equipment, etc, as well as the general running costs attached to operating any business.

It is worth noting that hikers should set aside around 10% of the cost of their climb to tipping guides, cooks and porters at the end of the trip. Usual tipping guidelines per day per party are around US$10–20 per guide, US$8–15 per cook, and US$5–10 per porter.

as a guide, so that if somebody has to turn back, the rest of the group can still continue their climb. It might also be worth pointing out the potential risk attached to forming an impromptu group with strangers merely to cut 5% or so off the price. If you hike on your own or with people you know well, you can dictate your own pace and there is less danger of personality clashes developing mid climb.

The standard duration of a climb on the Marangu Route is five days. Many people with repeated experience of Kilimanjaro recommend adding a sixth day to acclimatise at Horombo Hut. The majority opinion among operators and mountain experts is that this will improve the odds of reaching the summit by as much as 20%. However, other operators say that that the extra day makes little difference except that it adds a similar figure to the cost of the climb. No meaningful statistics are available to support one view or the other, but we would certainly recommend those can who afford it to take an extra day or two over the ascent.

In this context, it is worth noting that the exhaustion felt by almost all hikers as they approach the peak is not merely a function of altitude. On the Marangu Route, for instance, most people hike for 6–8 hours on day three, and then after a minimal dose of sleep (if any at all), rise at around midnight to start the final 5–6-hour ascent to the peak. In other words, when they reach the peak, they will usually have been walking for up to 14 of the last 20-odd hours, without any significant sleep – something that would tire out most people even if they weren't facing an altitudinal increase of around 2,000m! On that basis alone, an extra night along the way would have some value in pure recuperative terms. And certainly, my firm impression is that travellers who spend six days on the mountain enjoy the climb far more than those who take five days, whether or not they reach the peak.

Of the less popular routes up Kilimanjaro, the one most frequently used by tourists, the Machame Route, requires a minimum of six days. Most operators will charge at least US$1,500–1,600 per person for this route, because it requires far more outlay on their part. The huts along the Machame Route are in such poor condition that tents and camping equipment must be provided, along with a coterie of porters to carry and set up the makeshift camp. The same problem exists on all routes except Marangu, so that any off-the-beaten-track climb will be considerably more costly than the standard one. Should you decide to use a route other than Marangu, it is critical that you work through an operator with experience of that route.

Do not attempt to climb Kilimanjaro unless you are reasonably fit, or if you have heart or lung problems (although asthma sufferers should be all right). Bear in mind, however, that very fit people are more prone to altitude sickness because they ascend too fast.

Above 3,000m you may not feel hungry, but you should try to eat. Carbohydrates and fruit are recommended, whereas rich or fatty foods are harder to digest. You should drink plenty of liquids, at least three litres of water daily, and will need enough water bottles to carry this. Dehydration is one of the most common reasons for failing to complete the climb. If you dress in layers, you can take off clothes before you sweat too much, thereby reducing water loss.

Few people climb Kilimanjaro without feeling some of the symptoms of altitude sickness: headaches, nausea, fatigue, breathlessness, sleeplessness and swelling of the hands and feet. You can reduce these by allowing yourself time to acclimatise by taking an extra day over the ascent, eating and drinking properly, and trying not to push yourself. If you walk slowly and steadily, you will tire less quickly than if you try to rush each day's walk. Acetazolamide (Diamox) helps speed acclimatisation and many people find it useful; take 250mg twice a day for five days, starting two or three days before reaching 3,500m. However, the side effects from this drug may resemble altitude sickness and therefore it is advisable to try the medication for a couple of days about two weeks before the trip to see if it suits you.

Should symptoms become severe, and especially if they are clearly getting worse, then descend immediately. Even going down 500m is enough to start recovery. Sleeping high with significant symptoms is dangerous; if in doubt descend to sleep low.

Pulmonary and cerebral oedemas are altitude-related problems that can be rapidly fatal if you do not descend. Symptoms of the former include shortness of breath when at rest, coughing up frothy spit or even blood, and undue breathlessness compared with accompanying friends. Symptoms of high-altitude cerebral oedema are headaches, poor co-ordination, staggering like a drunk, disorientation, poor judgement and even hallucinations. The danger is that the sufferer usually doesn't realise how sick he/she is and may argue against descending. The only treatment for altitude sickness is descent.

Altitude-related illness is also a potential problem on Mount Meru, and similar precautions should be taken. Other mountains in Tanzania are not high enough for it to be a cause for concern.

Hypothermia is a lowering of body temperature usually caused by a combination of cold and wet. Mild cases usually manifest themselves as uncontrollable shivering. Put on dry, warm clothes and get into a sleeping bag; this will normally raise your body temperature sufficiently. Severe hypothermia is potentially fatal: symptoms include disorientation, lethargy, mental confusion (including an inappropriate feeling of well-being and warmth!) and coma. In severe cases the rescue team should be summoned.

A US$20 rescue fee is paid by all climbers upon entering the national park. The rescue team ordinarily covers the Marangu Route only; if you use another route their services must be organised in advance.

The dubious alternative to using a reputable company is to take your chances with a small operator or private individual who approaches you on the street. These people will offer climbs for around US$100 cheaper than an established operator, but the risks are greater and because they generally have no office there is little accountability on their side. A crucial point when comparing this situation with the similar one that surrounds arranging a safari out of Arusha is that you're not merely talking about losing a day through breakdown or a similar inconvenience. With Kilimanjaro, you could literally die on the mountain. I've heard several stories of climbers being supplied with inadequate equipment and food, even of travellers being abandoned by their guide mid climb. The very least you can do, if you make arrangements of this sort, is to verify that your guide is registered; he should have a small wallet-like document to prove it, though even this can be faked.

OTHER PREPARATIONS Two climatic factors must be considered when preparing to climb Kilimanjaro. The obvious one is the cold. Bring plenty of warm clothes, a windproof jacket, a pair of gloves, a balaclava, a warm sleeping bag and an insulation mat. During the rainy season, a waterproof jacket and trousers will come in useful. A less obvious factor is the sun, which is fierce at high altitudes. Bring sunglasses, sunscreen and a hat.

Other essentials are water bottles, and solid shoes or preferably boots that have already been worn in. Most of these items can be hired in Moshi or at the park gate,

RECORD KILIMANJARO CLIMBS

First recorded ascent: Hans Meyer and Ludwig Purtscheller, 1889
Fastest ascent: Killan Jornet (Spain) in 5 hours 23 minutes, 2010
Fastest ascent and descent: Karl Egloff (Switzerland–Ecuador) in 6 hours 56 minutes, 2015
Fastest ascent by a woman: Anne-Marie Flammersfeld (Germany) in 8 hours 32 minutes, 2015
Youngest to summit: Keats Boyd (USA), seven years old, 2008
Oldest person to summit: Angela Vorobeva (Russia), 86 years and 267 days, 2015
Oldest man to summit: Robert Wheeler (USA), 82 years and 201 days, 2014

Almost any international agent selling safaris to Tanzania can also arrange a Kilimanjaro climb through a reliable local operator. However, travellers who want to book their climb direct through a local operator, whether they do it online or after arriving in Tanzania, will soon realise that there are a daunting number of options, ranging from costly quality operators with vast experience of the mountain through to small local operators offering cut-throat prices and similar services – and pretty much every gradation in between. It is impossible for a guidebook of this sort to attempt to assess every last operator in such a busy and competitive market, but the following companies can all be recommended as reputable and reliable.

MOSHI It is difficult to walk far in some parts of Moshi without having a local guide or self-styled tour operator trying to persuade you to arrange a climb. These guys may offer marginally cheaper rates than established operators, but they are notoriously unreliable. Our advice is to ignore anybody who approaches you on the street in favour of a proper travel agency, of which Honey Badger, Keys Hotel, Snowcap Tanzania Tours and Zara Tours stand out (page 171).

MARANGU The family-run **Marangu Hotel** has been taking people up Kilimanjaro for decades, and they have an impeccable reputation. The standard packages aren't the cheapest available, but they are pretty good value, and the standard of service and equipment is very high. The self-catering 'hard-way' climbs organised by the Marangu Hotel are probably the cheapest reliable deals you'll find anywhere in Tanzania. Also reliable are the **Kibo Hotel** and **Babylon Lodge** (pages 172–3).

ARUSHA Most safari companies in Arusha arrange Kilimanjaro climbs, but will generally work through a ground operator in Moshi or Marangu, which means that they have to charge slightly higher rates. Any of the Arusha-based safari companies listed in that section (pages 139–41) can be recommended, and short-stay visitors who are already going on safari with one of these companies will probably find that the ease and efficiency of arranging a Kilimanjaro climb through them outweighs the minor additional expenditure.

There are a few companies that arrange their own Kili climbs out of Arusha. **Summits Africa** and **Hoopoe Safaris** both have a long track record of organising ascents along the lesser-known routes, and are well worth contacting if you're prepared to pay a premium for top guides and equipment. So too is **Nature Discovery**, a highly regarded company that specialises in the more obscure routes up the mountain, and routinely sets up camp in the crater of Kibo, allowing you to explore the peaks area and ash cone at relative leisure. **Tropical Trails**, based at Masai Camp on the outskirts of Arusha, has an excellent reputation for Kili climbs. **Roy Safaris** also arranges its own trekking and climbing on Kilimanjaro, Mount Meru and elsewhere. **Fair Travel** takes the novel approach of paying guides, cooks and porters around double the going rate rather than forcing them to be dependent on tips.

Mount Kilimanjaro National Park   CLIMBING KILIMANJARO

8

or from the company you arrange to climb with. We've heard varying reports about the condition of locally hired items, but standards seem to be far higher than they were only a few years back.

A good medical kit is essential, especially if you are climbing with a cheap company. You'll go through plenty of plasters if you acquire a few blisters (assume that you will), and can also expect to want headache tablets.

You might want to buy biscuits, chocolate, sweets, glucose powder and other energy-rich snacks to take with you up the mountain. No companies supply this sort of thing, and although they are sometimes available at the huts, you'll pay through the nose for them.

MAPS AND FURTHER READING Trekkers are not permitted on the mountain without a registered guide, and all sensible trekkers will make arrangements through a reliable operator, which means that there is no real need for detailed route descriptions once you're on the mountain. Nevertheless, many trekkers will benefit from the detailed practical advice and overview of route possibilities provided in a few specialist Kilimanjaro guidebooks. The pick of these is undoubtedly the 368-page *Kilimanjaro: The Trekking Guide to Africa's Highest Mountain* by Henry Stedman (Trailblazer Guides, 4th edition 2014), which can be bought locally or ordered in advance through online bookshops such as abebooks.com, amazon. co.uk and amazon.com. Also recommended is *Kilimanjaro: A Complete Trekker's Guide* by Alexander Stewart (Cicerone Press, 2004).

More concerned with the overall geology and natural history of Kilimanjaro, making it a more useful companion to trekkers on organised hikes, *Kilimanjaro: Africa's Beacon* is one of a series of informative pocket-sized guides published by the Zimbabwe-based African Publishing Group in association with Tanapa. It is

ABBOTT'S DUIKER

An antelope occasionally encountered by hikers on Kilimanjaro is Abbott's duiker (*Cephalophus spadix*), a montane forest species known as *minde* in Swahili. Formerly quite widespread in suitable East African habitats, it is today endemic only to eastern Tanzania due to environmental loss and poaching elsewhere in its natural range. After Ader's duiker, a lowland species of the East African coastal belt, Abbott's is the most threatened of African duikers, categorised as Endangered in the IUCN Red Data list for 2016, but based on present trends it is likely to decline to a status of Critically Endangered in the foreseeable future. Abbott's duiker is today confined to five forested montane 'islands' in eastern Tanzania, namely Kilimanjaro, Usambara, Udzungwa, Uluguru and Rungwe. It is a notoriously secretive creature (the first photograph of one was taken in 2003) and the total population is unknown, but a 1998 estimate of 2,500 based on limited data is not implausible, and more recent estimates place the total at only 1,500. Either way, Udzungwa probably harbours the most substantial and secure single population, followed by Kilimanjaro. Should you be lucky enough to stumble across this rare antelope, it has a glossy, unmarked off-black torso, a paler head and a distinctive red forehead tuft. Its size alone should, however, be diagnostic: the shoulder height of up to 75cm is the third largest of any duiker species, and far exceeds that of other more diminutive duikers that occur in Tanzania.

widely available in Arusha and Moshi for around US$8. Its predecessor, the 60-page national park handbook *Kilimanjaro National Park*, is arguably more informative but less attractively put together, and is still widely available in Arusha and Moshi.

Giovanni Tombazzi's *New Map of Kilimanjaro National Park*, sold in Arusha and Moshi, is arguably the best available map and certainly the most visually attractive. Current climbing tips are printed on the back, along with a close-scale map of the final ascent to Kibo, and day-by-day contour 'graphs' for the more popular routes.

Before you leave home – or as a memento when you get back – try to get hold of *Kilimanjaro* by John Reader (Elm Tree Books, London, 1982), which is long out of print but available cheaply secondhand through the likes of Amazon. Although it is superficially a coffee-table book, it offers a well-written and absorbing overview of the mountain's history and various ecosystems, far more so than any more recent book of its type. The photographs are good, too.

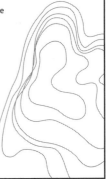

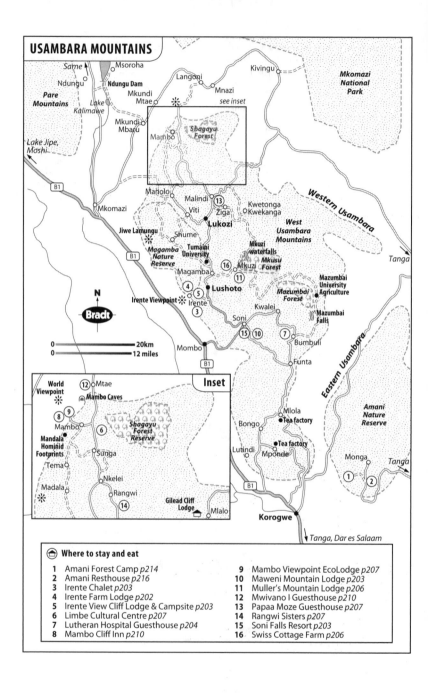

USAMBARA MOUNTAINS

Same
Msoroha
Ndungu
Ndungu Dam
Langoni
Kivingu
Mkundi
Mtae
Mnazi
Mkundi
Mbaru
Mambo
Shagayu Forest
see inset

Pare Mountains
Lake Kalimawe

Lake Jipe, Moshi

B1
Mkomazi

Manolo
Malindi
(13)
Kwetonga
Kwekanga
Viti
Ziga
Lukozi
West Usambara Mountains

Jiwe Lamungu
Shume
Mkuzi waterfalls
Western Usambara

Tanga

Magamba Nature Reserve
Tumaini University
Magamba
(16)
Mkuzi
Mkusu Forest
(11)
Lushoto
(4)
(5)
Mazumbai Forest
Mazumbai University Agriculture

Irente Viewpoint
Irente
(3)
Kwalei
Mazumbai Falls

Soni
(15)(10)
(7)
Bumbuli

N

Bradt

0 ———— 20km
0 ———— 12 miles

Mombo
B1
Funta

Inset

World Viewpoint
(12) Mtae
Mambo Caves
(8)(9)
Mambo
(6)
Shagayu Forest Reserve
Mandala Hominid Footprints
Sunga
Tema
Nkelei
Madala
Rangwi
(14)
Gilead Cliff Lodge
Mlalo

Mlola
Tea factory
Bongo
Tea factory
Lutindi
Mponde
Monga
(1)(2)
Tanga

B1
Korogwe

Tanga, Dar es Salaam

⌂ Where to stay and eat

1 Amani Forest Camp *p214*
2 Amani Resthouse *p216*
3 Irente Chalet *p203*
4 Irente Farm Lodge *p202*
5 Irente View Cliff Lodge & Campsite *p203*
6 Limbe Cultural Centre *p207*
7 Lutheran Hospital Guesthouse *p204*
8 Mambo Cliff Inn *p210*

9 Mambo Viewpoint EcoLodge *p207*
10 Maweni Mountain Lodge *p203*
11 Muller's Mountain Lodge *p206*
12 Mwivano I Guesthouse *p210*
13 Papaa Moze Guesthouse *p207*
14 Rangwi Sisters *p207*
15 Soni Falls Resort *p203*
16 Swiss Cottage Farm *p206*

9

Usambara and the Northeast

Tourism to northern Tanzania is largely confined to the national parks and other conservation areas that run west from Moshi and Arusha towards Lake Victoria. However, the little-visited northeast also boasts some more low-key but worthwhile attractions. Foremost among these is the Usambara Mountains, a single geological entity split into discrete eastern and western components by a deeply incised river valley. Known for its rich biodiversity (see box, pages 208–9), these mountains offer some great hiking opportunities, with the Western Usambara, centred on the attractive town of Lushoto, being better for cultural interaction and scenery, while the Amani Nature Reserve in the Eastern Usambara is more alluring for forest wildlife and endemic birds. Points of interest *en route* to the Usambara include the bird-rich Lake Jipe and underrated Mkomazi National Park, both of which abut the border with Kenya.

LAKE JIPE

Shallow, narrow and enclosed by dense beds of tall papyrus, Lake Jipe runs for 10km along a natural sump on the Kenyan border east of Kilimanjaro (its main source of its water) and Mkomazi National Park. It's an atmospheric body of water, overlooked by the Pare Mountains to the south, Chala crater rising from the flat plain to the east, and – when the clouds clear – Kilimanjaro to the the northeast. With part of the northern shore being protected within Kenya's unfenced Tsavo West National Park, the lake hinterland also hosts a fair bit of wildlife. Gazelle and other antelope are likely to be seen in the arid country approaching the lake, and cheetah and lion are occasionally observed darting across the road. The lake itself is teeming with hippopotami and crocodiles, and the papyrus beds harbour several localised birds such as lesser jacana, African water rail, pygmy goose and black egret. Elephant regularly come to drink and bathe along the northern shore, especially during the dry season. Look out, too, for the lovely impala lily – this shrub-sized succulent, known for its bright pink-and-white flowers, is common in the dry acacia plains approaching the lake.

GETTING THERE AND AWAY Kifaru, the junction town for Lake Jipe, straddles the B1 some 40km south of Moshi. From there, drive east for 15km along the reasonable dirt road towards Kiwakuku, then turn left on to a track that arrives at Makuyuni and the lakeshore after another 2km. In a **private vehicle**, the drive from Kifaru takes 30–45 minutes, depending on road conditions, making it more than feasible to visit Jipe as a day trip from Moshi, or *en route* from there to Mkomazi or Lushoto. One **bus** daily runs between Kifaru and Kiwakuku via Makuyuni junction, leaving from Kiwakuku before sunrise and starting the return trip from Kifaru in the early afternoon. Once at Makuyuni, it's straightforward enough to arrange to be poled on to the lake in a local **dugout canoe**, whether you want to fish, watch birds, look for hippo, or just enjoy the lovely scenery and hope for glimpses of big game on the nearby Kenyan shore. Expect to pay around US$5–10 for a short excursion or US$15 for a full day on the lake. The best time to head out is in the early morning or late afternoon, when it's not too hot, game is more active and Kilimanjaro is most likely to be visible.

WHERE TO STAY AND EAT There is no accommodation on the Tanzanian shore, but it is permitted to pitch a tent in Makuyuni for a nominal fee. Aside from fish, no food is available locally, and you'll need to bring drinking water too. Mosquitoes (and occasionally lake flies) are prolific, so cover up at dusk. Away from the lake, a few basic guesthouses can be found in Kifaru.

MKOMAZI NATIONAL PARK

Gazetted as a game reserve in 1951 and upgraded to national park status in 2008, Mkomazi is effectively a southern extension of Kenya's vast Tsavo National Park, covering an area of 3,234km² to the east of Kilimanjaro and immediately north of the Pare Mountains. Together with Tsavo, it forms part of one of East Africa's most important savannah ecosystems, characterised by the semi-arid climatic conditions of the Sahel Arc, and housing a great many dry-country species rare or absent elsewhere in Tanzania. Prior to becoming a national park, Mkomazi was practically undeveloped for tourism. It had also been subject to considerable pressure as the human population around its peripheries grew in number. As a result, wildlife is thinly distributed and can still be rather skittish, though this is gradually changing. Yet while Mkomazi doesn't offer game viewing to compare with other reserves in northern Tanzania, this is compensated for by the impressive birdlife, the wild scenery – mountains rise in all directions, with Kilimanjaro often visible to the northwest at dawn and dusk – and the near-certainty of not seeing another tourist.

FLORA AND FAUNA Mkomazi supports a cover of wooded savannah set on predominantly red soils similar to those associated with the Tsavo East and West national parks in neighbouring Kenya. It is classified as part of the Somali-Maasai biome and the dominant flora comprises grasses and trees of the Acacia and Commiphora families. More than 1,300 plant species have been identified in the park but none is endemic to it, and the overall impression is of a rather uniform cover of dense scrubby woodland.

In 1992, the Tanzanian government invited the Royal Geographical Society (RGS) to undertake a detailed ecological study of Mkomazi. Although mammal populations were very low, it was determined that most large mammal species present in Tsavo are either resident in Mkomazi or regularly migrate there from Kenya, including lion, cheetah, elephant, giraffe, buffalo, zebra, impala and Tanzania's most significant gerenuk population. African wild dogs were reintroduced into Mkomazi in the 1990s, as was a herd of black rhinos from South Africa, but neither is likely to be seen on an ordinary safari.

Mkomazi is listed as an Important Bird Area, with more than 400 species recorded, including several northern dry-country endemics that were newly added to the Tanzania list by the RGS – for instance three-streaked tchagra, Shelley's starling, Somali long-billed crombec, yellow-vented eremomela and the extremely localised Friedmann's lark. It is the only place in Tanzania where the lovely vulturine guineafowl, notable for its bright cobalt chest, is likely to be seen. Other conspicuous large ground birds include common ostrich, secretary bird, southern ground hornbill and various francolins and bustards. The birdlife is particularly visible and impressive in the rainy season, when weavers, whydahs and widows enter their breeding plumage, and resident species are joined by migrants such as the prolific European roller.

FEES AND FURTHER INFORMATION An entrance fee of US$30 per 24 hours plus 18% VAT is levied on foreign visitors. As with most other national parks, this is valid for a single entry, which means that anyone using Same as a base for a safari to Mkomazi would need to pay a second entrance fee were they to enter the park twice, even if it falls within the same 24-hour period. The nearby Mambo View Lodge maintains an informative website about the park: www.mkomazi.info.

GETTING THERE AND AWAY Little visited it may be, but Mkomazi is among the most accessible of Tanzania's national parks. The gateway town is Same, a small but busy trading centre that straddles the main Dar es Salaam Highway about 105km southeast of Moshi. The drive from Moshi to Same shouldn't take longer than 90 minutes in a **private vehicle**, and any **public transport** heading from Moshi to places further south can drop you off there. In Same, 4x4s and other vehicles are usually available for hire at a negotiable rate for the good 5km dirt road that runs to the Zange Entrance Gate, where you need to pay the entrance fee. Although several more easterly entrance gates exist, they may not have facilities to accept entrance fees, which makes it difficult to explore the eastern two-thirds of the national park at the time of writing. Mkomazi is best avoided in the rainy season, due to the poor roads.

Although Mkomazi is not often included on northern Tanzania safari itineraries, **Kanyambo Safaris** (m *0783 330046;* e *kanyambo.safaris@gmail.com; www.kanyambosafaris.com*) is a specialist operator that runs general photographic and birding safaris to Mkomazi out of its base at Mambo View Lodge in the northern Usambara Mountains (only a couple of hours away by road).

WHERE TO STAY AND EAT
Upmarket
Babu's Camp (5 tents) 027 254 8840; e anasasafaris@gmail.com; www.anasasafari.com. This exclusive tented camp, currently situated 13km inside the park coming from Zange Entrance Gate, but scheduled to relocate to the more scenic & remote Vitewari Viewing Point in 2017, is spaciously laid out within a grove of gigantic baobabs & acacias. The spacious walk-in tents all have their own balcony & a private open-roof shower & toilet out the back, offering fabulous views of the sparkling African night sky. Both the present & future locations are usefully based for game drives to the circuit focused on Dindera Dam. The birdlife around camp can be fabulous, & African wild dogs & other predators occasionally pass through. US$314/568 sgl/dbl FB. **$$$$$**

Mkomazi Maore Camp (up to 4 units) m 0786 019965; e info@authentictanzania.com; www.authentictanzaniasafaris.com. This simple old-style mobile camp is set up by request for a minimum of 3 nights at one of several locations on the Kenya/Tsavo border east of the main road circuit. Aimed mainly at walking enthusiasts, it hosts 1 party at a time, & while game volumes are low, the thrill of encountering wildlife on foot is amplified by the improbability of seeing any other tourists in this remote corner of the country's least-visited national park. *Rates depend on group size & duration of stay, ranging from US$495pp/pn for 2 people staying 3 nights to US$275pp/pn for 6+ people staying 5+ nights. Meals, drinks & activities are included, but park fees are extra.* **$$$$$**

Budget

🏠 **Elephant Motel** (20 rooms) ☎027 275 8193; **m** 0754 839545; **e** manager@ elephantmotel.com; www.elephantmotel.com. The smartest accommodation in the vicinity of Same is this motel set in large green grounds about 1.5km south of the town centre along the B1 to Dar es Salaam. It offers clean en-suite rooms with netting, TV & hot running water. Good Indian, Tanzanian & Western meals in the restaurant or garden are in the US$6–8 range. *US$40/45 standard sgl/dbl, or US$60/85 exec sgl/dbl, all rates B&B. If it's not too busy, the residents' rate – about*

50% cheaper – is likely to be offered to walk-in clients upon request. **$$–$$$**

Shoestring

🏠 **Amani Lutheran Centre** (12 rooms) ☎027 275 8107; **m** 0784 894140. Situated on the main tar road through Same, about 200m uphill from the bus station, this clean & long-serving hostel consists of around a dozen rooms enclosing a small green courtyard. It's a friendly set-up with an internet café, canteen & safe parking. *US$12/15 en-suite dbl/twin B&B.* **$**

WHAT TO SEE AND DO The best game-viewing circuit in the park is the 3–4-hour loop that runs south from Zange Entrance Gate to Dindera Dam, then northeast via Vitewari Viewing Point (the new site for Babu's Camp) and Norbanda Dam. This takes you through a mixture of open grassland and thicker woodland where you should see plenty of topi, giraffe, common zebra, dik-dik and gazelles, and might also encounter eland, impala and lesser kudu. The thicker bush further east, though somewhat less accessible, is the main population centre for the dry-country antelope such as fringe-eared oryx, lesser kudu and gerenuk.

LUSHOTO AND THE WESTERN USAMBARA

Set at an elevation of 1,400m (4,550ft), Lushoto is the principal town of the Western Usambara, the most densely populated and cultivated mountain range in northern Tanzania. The town peaked in significance during German colonial times, which may account for the slightly anachronistic aura that pervades it today. Many buildings on the main street date to the early 20th century, when Lushoto – then known as Wilhelmstal – provided weekend relief for German settlers farming the dry, dusty Maasai Steppes below. But if the main street of Lushoto dimly recalls an alpine village, the side roads are unambiguously African in architecture and spirit. So, too, is the vibrant market – busiest on Sunday and Thursday – where colourfully dressed Shambaa women sell fresh fruit and other agricultural produce grown on the surrounding slopes.

The vegetation around Lushoto is similarly dichotomous. Broad-leafed papaya and banana trees subvert neat rows of exotic pines and eucalyptus, which in turn are interspersed by patches of lush indigenous forest alive with the raucous squawking of silvery-cheeked hornbills and the banter of monkeys. These scenic highlands form superb walking country, riddled with small footpaths and winding roads, and studded with spectacular viewpoints over the low-lying plains below.

Less than an hour's drive from the main road between Moshi and Dar es Salaam, Lushoto has developed into the focal point of a travel scene that feels delightfully down-to-earth in comparison with the hype, hustle and extravagant prices associated with the likes of Arusha and Zanzibar. Indeed, a plethora of guides, community tourism projects and affordable guesthouses aimed at independent travellers makes it an ideal diversion for anybody interested in experiencing everyday Tanzanian culture away from the beach resorts and game reserves.

HISTORY The Shambaa of the Western Usambara are Bantu-speaking agriculturalists whose modern population totals around 200,000. Their origin is

PORTRAIT OF A LION KING

Richard Burton's account of his 1857 visit to the Lion King of Shambaai, published in Volume 83 of *Blackwood's Edinburgh Magazine* in 1858, is probably the most revealing description of pre-colonial Shambaai ever printed. Some edited extracts follow:

Kimweri half rose from his cot as we entered, and motioned us to sit upon dwarf stools before him. He was an old, old man, emaciated by sickness. His head was shaved, his face beardless, and wrinkled like grandam's; his eyes were red, his jaws disfurnished, and his hands and feet were stained with leprous spots. The royal dress was a Surat cap, much the worse for wear, and a loinwrap as tattered. He was covered with a double cotton cloth, and he rested upon a Persian rug, apparently coeval with himself. The hut appeared that of a simple cultivator, but it was redolent of dignitaries, some fanning the Sultan, others chatting, and all holding long-stemmed pipes with small ebony bowls.

Kimweri, I was told, is the fourth of a dynasty ... originally from Nguru, a hilly region south of the river ... Kimweri, in youth a warrior of fame, ranked in the triumvirate of mountain kings above Bana Rongua of Chagga, and Bana Kizunga of the Wakuafy. In age he has lost ground [and] asserts kinghood but in one point: he has 300 wives, each surrounded by slaves, and portioned with a hut and a plantation. His little family amounts to between 80 and 90 sons, some of whom have Islamised, whilst their sire remains a 'pragmatical pagan'. The Lion [King]'s person is sacred; even a runaway slave saves life by touching royalty. Presently [Kimweri] will die, be wrapped up in matting, and placed sitting-wise under his deserted hut, a stick denoting the spot. Dogs will be slaughtered for the funeral-feast, and [Kimweri's son] Muigni Khatib will rule in his stead, and put to death all who dare, during the two months of mourning, to travel upon the king's highway.

Kimweri rules ... by selling his subjects – men, women, and children, young and old, gentle and simple, individually, or, when need lays down the law, by families and by villages ... Confiscation and sale are indigenous and frequent. None hold property without this despot's permission ... In a land where beads are small change, and sheeting and 'domestics' form the higher specie, revenue is thus collected. Cattle-breeders offer the first fruits of flocks and herds; elephant-hunters every second tusk; and traders a portion of their merchandise. Cultivators are rated annually at ten measures of grain ... The lion's share is reserved for the royal family; the crumbs are distributed to the councillors and [royal bodyguards].

Fuga, a heap of some 3000 souls, [is] defenceless, and composed of ... circular abodes [made with] frameworks of concentric wattles, wrapped with plantain-leaves ... fastened to little uprights, and plastered internally with mud ... The [people] ... file their teeth to points, and brand a circular beauty-spot in the mid-forehead; their heads are shaven, their feet bare, and, except talismans round the neck, wrists, and ankles, their only wear is a sheet over the shoulders, and a rag or hide round the loins. A knife is stuck in the waist-cord, and men walk abroad with pipe, bow, and quiverless arrows. The women are adorned with charm-bags; and collars of white beads – now in fashion throughout this region – from three to four pounds weight, encumber the shoulders of a 'distinguished person'. Their body-dress is the African sheet bound tightly under the arms, and falling to the ankles ...

9

difficult to ascertain. Some clans claim they have always lived in the mountains, others that they moved there during times of drought, or in response to the 18th-century Maasai invasion of the plains. Quite possibly, these divergent accounts simply reflect divergent clan histories, since the ancestral Shambaa had a reputation for welcoming refugees, and the loosely structured political system that characterised the region until about 300 years ago would have encouraged the peaceful assimilation of newcomers. The notion that Shambaa identity was initially forged by physical proximity (rather than cultural affiliation or centralised leadership) is reinforced when you realise that their name derives from the geographical term used to describe the more moist upper reaches of the mountains, ie: Shambaai ('where the banana trees thrive').

Prior to the 18th century, the social structure of Shambaai was similar to the ntemi chieftaincies of western Tanzania. Each clan lived in a clearly defined territory with its own petty leadership of elders. A regional council of elders had the authority to settle disputes between different clans, and to approve marriages that would help cement inter-clan unity. According to tradition, the move towards centralised power – probably a response to the threat posed by the Maasai – was led by an outsider called Mbegha, the first Simba Mwene (Lion King) of Shambaai.

That Mbegha is a genuine historical figure is not in doubt, and the oral traditions of neighbouring tribes support the local story that he moved to the mountains from the plains below and became king after resolving a major crisis in Shambaai. Quite how Mbegha achieved his leonine coup is open to question. One – rather implausible – local tradition has it that, as a hunter of renown, Mbegha was called upon by a delegation of elders to rid the mountains of the bushpigs that were destroying all their crops, and was so effective in his campaign that he was appointed ruler of all Shambaai.

Mbegha went on to forge regional unity by taking a wife from each major clan and placing their firstborn son in charge of it. The Shambaa invested Mbegha and the Kilindi dynasty of Lion Kings that succeeded him with supernatural powers, believing among other things that they were able to control the elements. The dynasty consolidated power under the rule of Mbegha's grandson Kinyashi, who adopted a militaristic policy with the aim of forging the most important state between the coast and the great lake region. This ambition was realised by Kinyashi's son and successor, Kimweri, the greatest Simba Mwene of them all. Towards the end of his reign, Kimweri was held in sufficient esteem outside his kingdom that the explorer Richard Burton undertook the trek inland from Pangani to visit the Shambaa capital of Fuga (now more often called Vuga), close to modern-day Bumbuli (see box, page 197).

Kimweri's death, a few years after Burton's visit, was the catalyst for the first major rift in Shambaa. Vuga was too deep in the mountains to have attracted regular contact with the Kilimanjaro-bound caravans. Not so the Shambaa town of Mazinde, on what is now the main Moshi–Dar es Salaam road, whose chief Semboja exerted considerable influence over passing traders and was able to stockpile sufficient arms to overthrow Kimweri's successor at Vuga. This event split the Shambaa into several different splinter groups, and although Semboja retained nominal leadership of Shambaa, he controlled a far smaller area than Kimweri had before him.

Shambaa unity was further divided under German rule. Although the people of the Usambara played a leading role in the Abushiri Uprising of 1888–89, their resistance crumbled after Semboja's son and successor Mputa was hanged by the Germans in 1898. The Kilindi dynasty has, however, retained a strong symbolic role in modern Shambaa culture. Mputa's grandson Kimweri Mputa Magogo, who took the throne in 1947 and died in September 2000, was one of the most respected traditional leaders in Tanzania prior to the title being abolished in 1962 following independence.

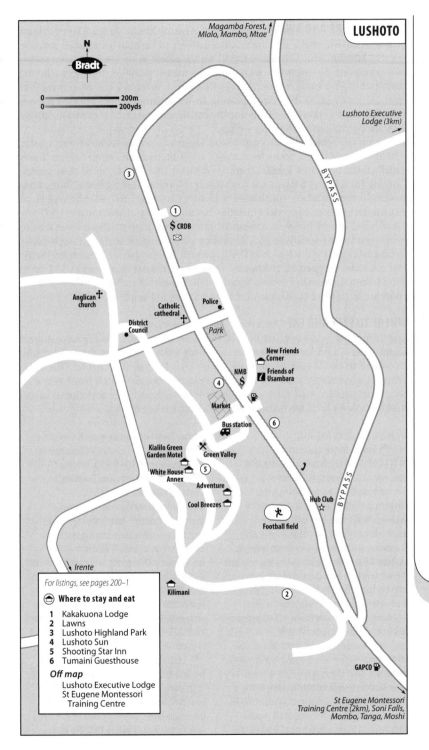

LUSHOTO

Magamba Forest,
Mlalo, Mambo, Mtae

Lushoto Executive
Lodge (3km)

N

Bradt

0 ———— 200m
0 ———— 200yds

BYPASS

③

① $ CRDB
✉

Anglican ✝
church

Catholic
cathedral ✝   Police ●

District
Council ●

Park

New Friends
Corner

NMB   Friends of
$ ℹ Usambara

④

Market

Bus station 🚌   ⑥

Kialilo Green
Garden Motel   ✕
          Green Valley

White House
Annex   ⑤

Adventure

Cool Breezes   Hub Club ☆

Football field 🏃

BYPASS

Irente

Kilimani

②

GAPCO ⛽

St Eugene Montessori
Training Centre (2km), Soni Falls,
Mombo, Tanga, Moshi

For listings, see pages 200–1

◉ Where to stay and eat

1 Kakakuona Lodge
2 Lawns
3 Lushoto Highland Park
4 Lushoto Sun
5 Shooting Star Inn
6 Tumaini Guesthouse

Off map
Lushoto Executive Lodge
St Eugene Montessori
    Training Centre

GETTING THERE AND AWAY Coming from Arusha, Moshi, Tanga, Dar es Salaam or almost anywhere else in Tanzania, the gateway to Lushoto is the small junction town of **Mombo**, which straddles the B1 on the plains below the Usambara massif (and shouldn't be confused with similarly named Mambo, higher up in the mountains). Mombo is connected to Lushoto by a surfaced 33km road that offers splendid views in all directions, passing *en route* through Soni with its famous waterfall; the trip takes 40–60 minutes by car, depending on how cowed the driver is by the precipitously steep drop-offs.

In a **private vehicle**, the driving time to Lushoto is about 4 hours from Arusha, 3 hours from Moshi, 2 hours from Tanga and 4 hours from Dar es Salaam. **Buses** usually take about 50% longer. There are direct daily buses along all these routes. Coming from Dar es Salaam, the best of several options leaving from Ubungo bus station are the Burudani and Shambalai Luxury Coaches (*US$7.50–10; 5hrs*). From Arusha, recommended services include Chakito, Fasiha and Mwambaro (*US$7.50–10; 6hrs*), all of which leave at around 06.00 and arrive at noon. Other buses tend to be slow and stop regularly to pick up or drop off passengers, so it is generally better to take an express service such as Dar Express or Kilimanjaro Express along the B1 and ask to be dropped off at Mombo, from where regular **minibuses** (*US$2; up to 60mins*) run through to Lushoto. Several of the buses that arrive at Lushoto at noon continue on to Mate or Mlalo and sites in-between in the afternoon.

WHERE TO STAY AND EAT   *Map, page 199*
The listings below are restricted to places within a 3km radius of Lushoto. A great many other – and for the most part arguably better – options are to be found elsewhere in the Western Usambara, as covered later in this chapter. The town centre is surprisingly short on standalone eateries, but the hotels listed below all serve adequate to good food, while street food such as beans and rice or chipsi mayai is sold by local women around the market in the evening.

Moderate & camping

✳ 🏠 **Lawns Hotel** (22 rooms) m 0759 914144/0715 019321; e contact@lawnshotel. com; www.lawnshotel.com. Centred on a c1900 German homestead, the venerable Lawns Hotel has been owned by the same Greek family for decades, though management duties were assumed by a dynamic new generation in 2016. The most characterful accommodation option in Lushoto, it is set in large gardens on a low hill above the town centre & has a cheerful bar decorated with banknotes & plates from around the world & all sorts of other quirky paraphernalia. The freshly renovated en-suite rooms retain a period feel & come with piping-hot showers, while the restaurant, housed in a colonial-era cinema, now serves a new Mediterranean-style menu dominated by Italian & Greek dishes in the US$5–8 range. Other facilities include satellite TV, table tennis, a pool table, a sauna, a children's playground, Wi-Fi & a book-swap library. The campsite is popular with overland trucks, so it can be a lively place for

a drink. Rooms are variable in size & standard, & prices reflect this. *US$35–80 dbl B&B, camping US$10pp. Rooms* **$$$–$$$$**, *camping* **$**

🏠 **St Eugene Montessori Training Centre** (14 rooms) m 0784 523710; e steugenes_hostel@yahoo.com or info@ usambara-st-eugene.com; www.usambara-st-eugene.com. This modern training centre run by the Usambara Sisters is 2km from Lushoto town centre at Ubiri on the Soni road. It is known locally for producing good jam, cheese, & banana wine. Within the landscaped grounds stands a comfortable & well-maintained hostel & a good restaurant. All rooms are en suite with hot water & TV. *US$25/45/54/60 sgl/dbl/trpl/suite B&B. Lunch or dinner an additional US$7pp.* **$$$**

🏠 **Lushoto Executive Lodge** (18 rooms) m 0784 360624; e info@lushotoexecutivelodge. co.tz; www.lushotoexecutivelodge.co.tz. Set in large forested gardens 3km out of town, this potentially lovely lodge is centred on a former German homestead built in 1902. The spacious en-suite deluxe & executive rooms & standing tents, though a bit down-at-heel, are reasonably priced for what they are, & come with hot shower & DSTV. *From US$45–65 dbl B&B.* **$$$**

⌂ **Lushoto Highland Park Hotel** (21 rooms) m 0789 428911;e lushotohighlandhotel@gmail.com. About 100m north of the main post office, this multi-storey hotel is probably the smartest option in the town centre but it's decidedly lacking in character. The rooms are small but clean & tidy, & come with TV, en-suite hot shower, & in some cases a balcony. A decent restaurant with garden seating serves mains in the US$4–5 range. *US$35/40 sgl/dbl B&B.* **$$$**

Budget

✳ ⌂ **Tumaini Guesthouse** (21 rooms) ☏ 027 266 0094; e tumaini@elct.org. This perennially popular Church-run 2-storey guesthouse on the main road may be too institutional for some tastes, but otherwise it's arguably the best choice in this range – clean, secure, friendly & very central, with the bonus of a pleasant green courtyard with seating. All rooms have nets, showers are hot, there's a good internet café next door. The popular ground-floor restaurant serves pizzas, pasta, seafood & curry dishes for US$3–4; you can eat indoors, on the street-facing balcony, or in the courtyard gardens,

but no alcohol is served. *US$7 sgl using common showers, US$17 en-suite dbl, US$23 suite.* **$$**

⌂ **Kakakuona Lodge** (10 rooms, 16 more under construction) m 0754 106969; e kakakuonainfo@yahoo.com; ⨍ kakakuonalodgetz. This rather smart lodge at the north end of the town centre has comfortable, modern en-suite accommodation with tiled floors, pine furniture, TV & hot shower. The excellent balcony restaurant overlooks a tree-fringed stream & serves a great range of Western & Indian dishes in the US$2–3 bracket, though be warned that meat dishes take at least an hour to prepare. It is one of the few eateries in Lushoto to serve alcohol. Good value. *US$15/17 sgl/dbl.* **$$**

Shoestring

⌂ **Shooting Star Inn** (10 rooms) ☏ 027 264 0192; m 0782 734440. The pick of a dozen or more simple lodges scattered along the hillside above the bus station, this 2-storey hotel has clean & pleasant dbl rooms with nets, DSTV & en-suite hot shower. Very good value. *US$10 dbl.* **$**

⌂ **Lushoto Sun Hotel** (15 rooms) m 0652 120870/0719 990128. This established travellers' favourite has a usefully central location & welcoming atmosphere. The rooms are a little tired but seem good value. An adequate local restaurant is attached. *US$7.50 en-suite dbl with hot shower, or US$5 using common shower.* **$**

OTHER PRACTICALITIES

Foreign exchange The **CRDB** ATM next to the post office takes foreign cards, at least when the system is up. Foreign exchange services are available at the **National Microfinance Bank**, but the ATM there doesn't accept foreign cards. The internet café at **Tumaini Guesthouse** can exchange small amounts of hard currency cash.

Internet Your best option is the internet café in Tumaini Guesthouse, but a few other cafés are scattered around town. The services here are all quite slow and unreliable.

TOURIST INFORMATION AND TOUR OPERATORS The best source of tourist information in Lushoto, and to arrange a guided trip elsewhere in the mountains, is the TTB-endorsed tourist office run by the **Friends of Usambara** (☏ *027 266 0132; m 0787 094725; e info@usambaratravels.com; www.usambaratravels.com; ⨁ 06.00– 19.00 daily*). Prominently signposted opposite the park, this organisation stocks plenty of useful brochures, and the staff – most of whom double as guides – can arrange any walk or activity around Lushoto. They are also willing to dispense advice without being pushy about paid services. The fee structure is rather complex, but most guided day trips work out at around US$15–20 per person, while the daily rate for overnight excursions is about double that. The office also arranges bicycle, tent, sleeping bag and roll-mat hire. All profits go towards the development of community projects.

Several other semi-official and private operators are dotted around Lushoto, distinguishing themselves from the Friends of Usambara mainly by having more of a hard-sell approach. You can expect to hear quite a bit of backbiting between the various tourist agencies, all of which regard the other as lacking professionalism, but this seems to be so much hot air – though do be circumspect about taking on any guide who doesn't operate out of a proper office.

Another excellent source of travel information is Mambo Viewpoint EcoLodge's website (*www.usambaramountains.com*), which covers the entire Usambara and includes contact details for several guesthouses. For those heading through to Mambo, about 60km north of Lushoto, visit the EcoLodge's own website (pages 207–10) for details of organised biking and hiking from Mombo (the junction town on the B1) to Mambo via Lushoto.

AROUND LUSHOTO A number of day and overnight trips can be undertaken in the Western Usambara, whether independently or with a guide provided by the Friends of Usambara tourist office in Lushoto. Popular day trips from Lushoto include Soni Falls, Irente Viewpoint and Magamba Forest. Worthwhile destinations further afield include Bumbuli and Mlalo. More remote still is the wonderfully scenic far north of the range, around the villages of Mambo and Mtae, an area covered under the separate heading *Northern Usambara Escarpment* (pages 206–11), along with the route there from Lushoto.

Irente About 7km from Lushoto by road, Irente Viewpoint is the most popular day trip in the Usambara. It lies at the western edge of the Usambara massif and offers a fantastic, vast view across the Maasai Steppes, 1,000m below. A village development fee equivalent to US$1 is charged to visit it. A second viewpoint at Yoghoi, about 1km further south, offers a very similar panorama encompassing the viewpoint at Irente. Either of the two viewpoints can be visited as a round trip from Lushoto, or you can loop between the two on foot. A popular option is to combine the walk with a picnic at Irente Farm Lodge (see contact details below), which can provide a delicious home-cooked lunch of rye bread, homemade cheese, organic vegetables, fruit juice and other farm produce between 10.00 and 14.00 Monday to Saturday for around US$6 per person, but do call in advance to make arrangements. The farm shop at Irente (⊕ *08.00–16.00 daily*) also sells an array of local produce such as cheese for consumption off the premises. The birding here can be rewarding, with more than 80 species recorded in the area.

Getting there and away The road to Irente and Yoghoi leads eastward out of Lushoto from the Catholic Church. Once you're on it, there's no serious likelihood of getting lost. After about 3km, it passes through the village of Yoghoi and a large junction – keep going straight for Irente, or turn left for Yoghoi. By road, it's 4km from here to either viewpoint. There's no direct road between the viewpoints, but there is a clear footpath. It's perfectly possible to head out here alone, but most travellers arrange an official guide through the tourist office. The round trip takes around 3 hours.

🏠 ***Where to stay and eat*** *Map, page 192*

❋ 🏠 **Irente Farm Lodge** (10 rooms) m 0788 503002/0783 685888; e info@irentefarmlodge.com; www.irentefarmlodge.com. This popular backpackers' retreat is set within the 6ha Irente Biodiversity Reserve, which has been replanted with indigenous trees in the hope of recreating the original forest cover, & is located within a 200ha working farm that started life as a German experimental coffee estate in 1896 & has been owned by the ELCT (Lutheran) Church since 1963. The farm doubles as an orphanage & school for the blind, funded partially by profits from the excellent home produce sold in its shop, as well as proceeds from the various accommodation options on the property. These include 3 dbl or trpl *bandas*, a recently constructed backpackers' lodge comprising 5 twin rooms with shared bathrooms, & a 6-bed self-catering lodge with 2 bedrooms, a kitchen with gas stove & fridge, a sitting & dining room & a private bathroom with hot shower. There is also a campsite. Tasty home-cooked meals are served in the characterful main house & cost US$6–12. The farm is clearly signposted about 1.5km before you reach Irente Viewpoint. *US$17pp B&B room with shared showers, US$110 self-catering cottage sleeping 6, US$32–65 en-suite dbl inc b/fast & dinner.* **$$**

🏠 **Irente View Cliff Lodge & Campsite** (25 rooms) m 0787 866877; e info@irenteview. com; www.irenteview.com. Smarter than anything

available in Lushoto itself, this undersubscribed modern-looking lodge boasts an impressive thatched roof, a decent restaurant & a stunning clifftop location. The en-suite rooms are also quite comfortable, & come with DSTV & balcony, but are let down slightly by poor-quality fittings. A clifftop campsite with hot shower is attached. Good value. *US$50/65 standard sgl/dbl, US$60/80 superior sgl/dbl, US$120 dbl suite. All rooms B&B. Camping US$5pp in your own tent or US$10pp in theirs. Rooms* **$$$**, *camping* **$**

🏠 **Irente Chalet** (3 rooms) m 0787 925324; e irente.chalet@gmail.com; www.irentechalet. com. Situated in a plantation forest close to the escarpment only 1km from Irente View Cliff Lodge, this lovely self-catering house sleeps up to 5 people in 3 bedrooms, & also has a lounge, equipped kitchen & shared bathroom with hot water. *US$100 for the whole house.* **$$**

Soni Falls

Straddling the surfaced road that connects Mombo to Lushoto, the small town of Soni is of interest primarily for the attractive but less than spectacular Soni Falls. This waterfall is visible from the main road to Lushoto, but to see it properly you need to stop in the town, from where a short, steep path leads to the rocky base. The quickest and best path to the waterfall, attracting a nominal fee, starts in the grounds of what was formerly the Soni Falls Hotel (established in 1930) but what is now the Soni Education Centre.

Getting there and away The drive between Lushoto and Soni takes no more than 30 minutes in either direction, using one of the regular **minibuses** that run back and forth to Mombo. If you visit Soni as a day trip, there is no reason to take a guide along. The Friends of Usambara tourist office in Lushoto organises a **half-day tour** out of Soni, taking in Kwa Mongo peak, known for its colourful butterflies, as well as the 300-year-old grave of the Shambaa King Mbegha and the so-called Magila 'Growing Rock' (whose base is exposed further every year as a result of soil erosion).

🏠 ***Where to stay and eat*** *Map, page 192*

✳ 🏠 **Soni Falls Resort** (3 rooms) m 0784 384603; e merymockray@yahoo.com. One of the most attractive lodges in the Usambara region, this Bavarian-style dbl-storey building originally dates to the German colonial era. Lovingly renovated & restored, it is set in well-wooded hilltop grounds, signposted to the right as you enter the village of Soni coming from Mombo. *US$22 dbl, US$35 family room sleeping 4. All rates B&B but other meals prepared by arrangement for around US$4pp.* **$$**

🏠 **Maweni Mountain Lodge** (17 rooms) ☎027 264 0427; m 0784 297371; e info@ maweni.com; www.maweni.com. This rustic farm retreat lies 2km from Soni along a side road signposted from the Mombo–Lushoto road near the junction with the Bumbuli road. Set in pretty gardens below a tall granite cliff, the main building consists of a 1920 farmhouse, & there's a more modern but dingier annexe & standing tents, too. *From US$65 dbl B&B or US$80/105 sgl/dbl FB.* **$$$**

Bumbuli

Locally renowned for its old Lutheran Mission and associated hospital, Bumbuli lies 23km from Soni near the eastern rim of the Western Usambara, where King Mbegha reputedly entered the mountains some 300 years ago. A small waterfall can be found on the outskirts of the town, close to the Soni road, and the

Saturday market is very colourful. The town lies in the shadow of Mazumbai Peak, whose upper slopes, covered in high montane forest, protect a variety of indigenous plants and rare birds. Bumbuli can be visited independently, but the Friends of Usambara tourist office in Lushoto also offers overnight hikes to the town and Mazumbai Forest, inclusive of guide, public transport and accommodation.

Getting there and away The 23km road between Soni and Bumbuli takes 45 minutes to cover in a **private vehicle**, passing through Mbelai, Kiboani and Kwahangara on the way. Using **public transport**, there are several direct buses daily between Bumbuli and Korogwe, Mombo and Lushoto. All these buses pass through Soni, so if no direct bus is about to leave, you could always catch one of the more frequent minibuses along the Mombo–Lushoto road, and hop off at Soni to board the next Bumbuli-bound vehicle.

 Where to stay and eat *Map, page 192*

Lutheran Hospital Guesthouse (8 rooms) Set in the mission grounds a 10min walk uphill from the town centre, this atmospheric restored colonial building has neat rooms with common hot shower & bath, as well as a lounge & self-catering kitchen. Cheap meals are also available. *US$10pp.* **$**

In Tanzania, you're most likely to come across a chameleon by chance when it is crossing a road, in which case it should be easy to take a closer look at it, since most chameleons move painfully slowly and deliberately. Chameleons are also often seen on night game drives, when their ghostly nocturnal colouring shows up clearly under a spotlight – as well as making it pretty clear why these strange creatures are regarded with both fear and awe in many local African cultures. More actively, you could ask your guide if they know where to find a chameleon – a few individuals will be resident in most lodge grounds.

The **flap-necked chameleon** (*Chamaeleo delepis*) is probably the most regularly observed species in savannah and woodland habitats in East Africa. Often observed crossing roads, the flap-necked chameleon is generally around 15cm long and bright green in colour with few distinctive markings, but individuals might be up to 30cm in length and will turn tan or brown under the right conditions. Another closely related and widespread savannah and woodland species is the similarly sized **graceful chameleon** (*Chamaeleo gracilis*), which is generally yellow-green in colour and often has a white horizontal stripe along its flanks.

Characteristic of East African montane forests, **three-horned chameleons** form a closely allied species cluster of some taxonomic uncertainty. Typically darker than the savannah chameleons and around 20cm in length, the males of all taxa within this cluster are distinguished by a trio of long nasal horns that project forward from their face. The most widespread three-horned chameleon in Tanzania is **Johnston's chameleon** (*Chamaeleo johnstoni*), while the most localised is the **Ngosi three-horned chameleon** (*Chamaeleo fuelleborni*), confined to the forested slopes of Ngosi Volcano in the Poroto Mountains. Perhaps the most alluring of East Africa's chameleons is the **giant chameleon** (*Chamaeleo melleri*), a bulky dark-green creature with yellow stripes and a small solitary horn, mainly associated with the Eastern Arc forests, where it feeds on small reptiles (including snakes) as well as insects.

Magamba Nature Reserve Situated 15km from Lushoto, the most accessible indigenous forest in the Western Usambara covers the slopes of 2,230m Mount Magamba, the highest peak in the range. It is of great interest to birdwatchers, with the track to the old sawmill in particular offering a good chance of seeing Usambara weaver and Usambara akalat (both endemic to Western Usambara forests) and the localised red-capped forest warbler. A variety of mammals also live in this forest, although only black-and-white colobus and blue monkey are likely to be encountered by the casual visitor. It is also a stronghold for the endemic Western Usambara two-horned chameleon.

Guided day walks can be arranged through the tourist office in Lushoto, but it is possible to visit Magamba independently and explore it along a few self-guided trails. Either way, an entrance fee of US$10 is now levied. The most popular goal for day walks in the Magamba Forest is a small but pretty waterfall on the forest-fringed Mkuzu River about 2km from Migambo village. To reach this waterfall, take the right fork as you enter Migambo on the Magamba road. Follow this road downhill for about 20 minutes, passing a group of rocks in the river where local people wash their clothes, until you reach a bridge across the river. To your right, immediately before crossing the river, a footpath to the left follows the riverbank for about 10 minutes to the waterfall.

Getting there and away Any vehicle heading north from Lushoto to Mtae, Mlalo or Mlola can drop you at the Magamba junction, 7km from Lushoto. The road heading to the right of this junction leads through the heart of the forest, following the course of the lushly vegetated Mkusu River for 7km to Migambo village. You could walk the length of this road in about 90 minutes in either direction, and it is also covered by a bus that runs daily between Lushoto and Mlola.

 Where to stay and eat *Map, page 192*

Muller's Mountain Lodge
(16 rooms) \027 264 0204; m 0782 315666; e mullersmountainlodge@yahoo.com or info@mullersmountainlodge.co.tz; www. mullersmountainlodge.co.tz. This family-run 1930s farm cottage, set in flowering gardens within the Magamba Forest, is arguably the most attractive place to stay anywhere in the Western Usambara, & an excellent base for birdwatchers. Home-cooked meals are available in the small restaurant or the gardens. Several day trails lead from the lodge; maps & directions can be supplied. It lies about 6km past Magamba junction on the Migambo road. A free transfer to/from Lushoto is offered to parties of 2 or

more. *From US$45/60 B&B en-suite sgl/dbl, camping US$10pp. Rooms* **$$$**, *camping* **$**

Swiss Cottage Farm (3 chalets) \027 264 0155; m 0715 700813; e info@swiss-farm-cottage.co.tz; www.swiss-farm-cottage.co.tz. This is another peaceful rustic retreat set on a working farm in the Magamba Forest area, & offering home-cooked lunch & dinners using organic farm produce. Coming from Magamba junction, the 1.5km turn-off to Swiss Farm Cottage lies to the left about 5km along the Migambo road, & 500m before the turn-off to Muller's. *US$50/65 sgl/dbl B&B.* **$$$**

Mlalo
This bizarre town sprawls over a large valley some 50km from Lushoto along a road that forks from the Mtae road at Malindi, 30km from Lushoto. Mlalo has an insular, almost otherworldly feel, epitomised by the unusual style of many of the buildings: two-storey mud houses whose intricately carved wooden balconies show German or Swahili influences.

Three buses run daily between Lushoto and Mlalo, leaving Lushoto in the early afternoon and Mlalo at around 07.00. The trip takes around 2 hours. Once there, accommodation options are limited to a few very basic guesthouses such as the **Afilex** and **Mlalo Motel**, both charging comfortably under US$5 for a room.

NORTHERN USAMBARA ESCARPMENT
Though it traditionally sees less tourism than Lushoto, in part because it is more difficult to access, the most scenic part of the Western Usambara is undoubtedly the far north, where the high escarpment offers scintillating views across the expansive dry plains below to Lake Kalimawe, the Pare Mountains, Mkomazi National Park and Kilimanjaro, 250km distant but still a striking sight on a clear morning. For many years, the only possible travel base in the area was the small but idyllically sited village of Mtae, which boasts a few small and undistinguished guesthouses, but is otherwise largely undeveloped for tourism. These days, however, tourist activity is focused on the superb Mambo Viewpoint EcoLodge, which lies on the escarpment at Mambo village, about 5km from Mtae, and offers an exciting range of guided and unguided hikes as well as vehicle-based activities organised through its in-house tour operator. Highlights include Mtae itself (surely one of the most scenically located villages anywhere in Africa), as well as a variety of day walks along the escarpment and on the nearby forested slopes of Shagayu Mountain, as well as day or overnight camping trips to Lake Kalimawe and Mkomazi National Park.

Getting there and away Mtae and Mambo lie about 65km north of Lushoto by road, a 2-hour drive. If you are **driving** yourself, take the main road running north out of Lushoto, turn left at the junction shortly after the Lushoto Highland Park Hotel, then left again after 7km when you reach the junction for Magamba Forest. When you reach Lukozi, the main road to Mtae and Mambo branches left in the small town centre, but if you are thinking of overnighting at Papaa Moze or the Rangwi Sisters (see below), then you need to keep going straight through town along a rough road that reconnects with the main road after about 20km at Nkelei. About 3km further on lies Sunga, from where it is about 10km without further diversions to Mtae, or a similar distance to Mambo, turning left at a signposted junction about 3km before Mtae. Using **public transport**, a few local buses connect Lushoto to Mtae and Mambo, usually leaving between noon and 14.00, and charging around US$3 per person.

Coming from Arusha or Moshi in a **4x4** or on a **motorbike**, a scenic short-cut entails following the B1 towards Dar es Salaam for about an hour past Same to the village of Mkomazi (not to be confused with the eponymous national park), where a dirt road to the left is signposted for Mambo Viewpoint. Follow this road towards Mnazi, then after about an hour, turn right at Langoni (where there is another signpost for Mambo Viewpoint) and follow a clear diversion through a riverbed towards the base of the mountains, from where a steep but very striking scenic pass leads up the slopes to Mtae. This road should not be attempted after heavy rain, and a 4x4 is required in all conditions.

For **independent travellers**, it is also possible to do the trip between Mombo/Lushoto and Mtae/Mambo in stages, stopping *en route* at small montane settlements such as Lukozi (which hosts a big Monday market), Malindi, Rangwi and Sunga. You could easily hike this yourself, or hop along using whatever public transport or lifts come your way, overnighting at some of the lodges listed below under the heading *En route from Lushoto*. Alternatively, Mambo Viewpoint EcoLodge has set out a few overnight hiking and mountain biking routes from Mombo or Lushoto, details of which are on their website.

Where to stay and eat *Map, page 192*

En route *from Lushoto*

🏠 **Rangwi Sisters** m 0784 716529. Situated about 12km north of Lukozi, close to the junction village of Nkelei, this long-serving guesthouse, set on a Catholic Mission, offers the most comfortable accommodation *en route* from Lushoto to Mtae, & it also serves good home cooking. *US$16/20 en-suite sgl/dbl FB.* **$$**

🏠 **Papaa Moze Guesthouse** (8 rooms) m 0784 599019; e lucasshem@yahoo.com. This friendly owner-managed guesthouse is set in a small but leafy garden in the village of Malindi, about 4km north of Lukozi. It has a campsite, restaurant, bar & shop, along with clean & cosy en-suite rooms with hot shower. *US$14 dbl.* **$**

🏠 **Limbe Cultural Centre** (4 rooms) m 0786 887661. Situated on a smallholding on the right side of the main road 6km before Mtae & 3km past the village of Sunga, this rundown but friendly family-managed guesthouse has basic but clean rooms, & it can also serve meals upon request. *US$3/4 sgl/dbl.* **$**

Mambo & Mtae

🏠 **Mambo Viewpoint EcoLodge** (5 cottages & 3 luxury tents) m 0785 272150; e info@mamboviewpoint.org; www.mamboviewpoint.org. Founded & managed by an environmentally & socially committed Dutch couple, this exemplarily eco-friendly lodge has a spectacular setting at an altitude of 1,900m on a stretch of escarpment offering stunning views to the Pare Mountains, the expansive plains of Mkomazi National Park & distant Kilimanjaro. It lies on the outskirts of Mambo, a village of 5,000, & is deeply committed to providing employment to locals & creating other grassroots economic opportunities through tourism. Accommodation is in a range of attractive individually styled cottages & en-suite luxury tents, & camping is also permitted. It also offers a range of overnight hiking & biking trips to/from other villages in & around the mountains, ranging from 1 to 6 nights in duration. The excellent website contains more details of these activities. Other attractions

Dr Jon Lovett coined the phrase 'Eastern Arc' in the mid 1980s to describe a string of 13 physically isolated East African mountain ranges that share a very similar geomorphology and ecology. All but one of these crystalline ranges lies within Tanzania, forming a rough crescent that runs from Pare and Usambara in the north to Udzungwa and Mahenge in the south. Following a fault line that runs east of the more geologically recent Rift Valley, these are the oldest mountains in East Africa, having formed at least 100 million years ago, making them 50 times older than Kilimanjaro.

For the past 30 million years, the Eastern Arc has supported a cover of montane forest, one that flourished even during the drier and colder climatic conditions that have periodically affected the globe, thanks to a continuous westerly wind that blew in moisture from the Indian Ocean. It was during one such dry phase, ten million years ago, that these became isolated from the lowland rainforest of western and central Africa. More recently, each of the individual forested ranges became a discrete geographical entity, transforming the Eastern Arc into an archipelago of forested islands jutting out from an ocean of low-lying savannah. And as with true islands, these isolated ancient forests became veritable evolutionary hotspots.

The Eastern Arc Mountains host an assemblage of endemic races, species and genera with few peers anywhere in the world. In the two Usambara ranges alone, more than 2,850 plant species have been identified, a list that includes 680 types of tree, a greater tally than that of North America and Europe combined. At least 16 plant genera and 75 vertebrate species are endemic to the Eastern Arc forests. Their invertebrate wealth can be gauged by the fact that 265 invertebrate species are thus far known from just one of the 13 different ranges – an average of 20 endemics per range. Little wonder that the Eastern Arc is classified among the world's 20 top biodiversity hotspots, and is frequently referred to as the Galápagos of Africa.

Eastern Arc endemics fall into two broad categories: old endemics are modern relics of an ancient evolutionary lineage, while new endemics represent very recently evolved lineages. A clear example of a 'living fossil' falling into the former category are the giant elephant shrews of the suborder Rhynchocyonidae, whose four extant species are almost identical in structure to more widespread 20-million-year-old ancestral fossils. In many cases, these older, more stable endemics are affiliated to extant West African species from which they have become isolated: Abbott's duiker (see box, page 190) and the endemic monkey species of Udzungwa are cases in point.

The origins of new endemics are more variable. Some, such as the African violets, probably evolved from an ancestral stock blown across the ocean from Madagascar in a freak cyclone. Others, including many birds and flying insects, are local variants on similar species found in neighbouring savannah habitats or in other forests in East Africa. The origin of several other Eastern Arc endemics is open to conjecture: four of the endemic birds show sufficient affiliations to Asian species to suggest they may have arrived there at a time when moister coastal vegetation formed a passage around the Arabian Peninsula.

The forests of the Eastern Arc vary greatly in extent, biodiversity and the degree to which they have been studied and accorded official protection. A 1998 assessment by Newmark indicates that the Udzungwa range retains almost 2,000km² of natural forest, of which 20% has a closed canopy, while the forest cover on Kenya's Taita Hills is reduced to a mere 6km². The most significant forests in terms of biodiversity are probably Udzungwa, East Usambara and Uluguru. However, ranges such as Nguru and Rubeho remain little studied compared with the Usambara and Udzungwa, so they may host more endemics than is widely recognised.

The Eastern Arc forests are of great interest to birdwatchers as the core of the so-called Tanzania–Malawi Mountains Endemic Bird Area (EBA). This EBA includes roughly 30 forest pockets scattered across Malawi, Mozambique and Kenya, but these outlying forests cover a combined 500km^2 as compared with 7,200km^2 of qualifying forest in Tanzania. Of the 37 range-restricted bird species endemic to this EBA, all but five occur in Tanzania, and roughly half are confined to the country. In terms of avian diversity, the Udzungwa Mountains lead the pack with 23 regional endemics present, including several species found nowhere else or shared only with the inaccessible Rubeho Mountains. For first-time visitors, however, Amani Nature Reserve has the edge over Udzungwa in terms of ease of access to prime birding areas.

Distribution patterns of several range-restricted bird species within the EBA illuminate the mountains' pseudo-island ecology, with several species widespread on one particular range being absent from other apparently suitable ones. The Usambara akalat, for instance, is confined to the Western Usambara, while Loveridge's sunbird and the Uluguru bush-shrike are unique to the Uluguru. The most remarkable distribution pattern belongs to the long-billed tailorbird, a forest-fringe species confined to two ranges set an incredible 2,000km apart – the Eastern Usambara in northern Tanzania and Mount Namuli in central Mozambique. Stranger still is the case of the Udzungwa partridge: this evolutionary relic, discovered in 1991 and known only from Udzungwa and Rubeho, has stronger genetic affiliations to Asian hill partridges than to any other African bird.

The Eastern Arc has suffered extensive forest loss and fragmentation in the past century, primarily due to unprecedented land use pressure – the population of the Western Usambara, for instance, increased twentyfold in the 20th century. Of the 12 Eastern Arc ranges within Tanzania, only one – the inaccessible Rubeho massif – has retained more than half of its original forest cover, while five have lost between 75% and 90% of their forest in the last two centuries. Fortunately, none of Tanzania's Eastern Arc forests has yet approached the crisis point reached in Kenya's Taita Hills, where a mere 2% of the original forest remains.

Given that many Eastern Arc species are highly localised and that animal movement between forest patches is inhibited by fragmentation, it seems likely that 30% of Eastern Arc endemics have become extinct in the last century, or might well do so in the immediate future. True, the salvation of a few rare earthworm taxa might be dismissed as bunny-hugging esoterica, but the preservation of the Eastern Arc forests as water catchment areas is an issue of clear humanistic concern. Most of the extant Eastern Arc forests are now protected as forest reserves. The proclamation of a large part of the Udzungwa Mountains as a national park in 1992 is a further step in the right direction. Even more encouraging is the more recent creation of Amani Nature Reserve as part of a broader effort to introduce sustainable conservation and ecotourism with the involvement of local communities in the Eastern Usambara.

Anybody wishing to come to grips with the fascinating phenomenon of 'island' ecology in the Eastern Arc Mountains (and elsewhere on the African mainland) is pointed to Jonathon Kingdon's superb book *Island Africa*.

include the delicious home-cooked food, which is eaten communally, free Wi-Fi, & the opportunity to participate as a volunteer in local community projects. The grounds protect some interesting wildlife: the striking West Usambara 2-horned chameleon (*Kinyongia multituberculata*) is common (ask the staff to locate one for you) & the rare Taita falcon nests on the cliffs below. *US$50/65 sgl/dbl B&B luxury tent, rooms from US$70/90 sgl/dbl B&B, camping US$8/10 sgl/ dbl in your own tent, or US$15/20 in a hired tent. Lunch & dinner US$10 & US$15pp respectively. Rooms* **$$$**, *camping* **$**

🏠 **Mambo Cliff Inn** (5 rooms) **m** 0785 272150; **e** ndegec@gmail.com. Only 500m

from Mambo Viewpoint & owned by its local manager, this clifftop lodge provides a relatively affordable alternative to its smarter neighbour. Accommodation is in neat little en-suite rooms with a balcony & a view, & a restaurant or bar is under construction. It is also possible to eat at Mambo Viewpoint & to participate in activities offered there. *US$25/35 sgl/dbl.* **$$**

🏠 **Mwivano I Guesthouse** The best of a few very basic local lodgings in Mtae, this guesthouse has a friendly owner, rooms with access to a communal cold shower, & an attached restaurant serving tasty, filling meals for next to nothing. *US$3 dbl.* **$**

What to see and do

Mtae This small but sprawling village has perhaps the most spectacular location in the Western Usambara. Boasting several fine examples of traditional Shambaa mud houses, it runs for about 2km along what is in effect a dry peninsula, jutting out to the north of the range, and with a drop of several hundred metres on either side offering breathtaking views. The name Mtae translates as 'Place of Counting', a reference to its strategic importance to the Shambaa people during the 19th-century Maasai wars, when it was the site of several battles won by the Shambaa, who were able to see and count any raiding Maasai war party from afar.

The striking Lutheran church that stands in the middle of the town was built in the late 19th century on a site where, formerly, the most powerful ancestral spirits were believed to reside. The story is that the local chief showed this site to the missionaries, expecting them to flee in fear. Instead, the missionaries were unmoved, and the chief – concluding that they must be in touch with more powerful spirits – granted them permission to build a church there.

Mambo Several day hikes run from Mambo Viewpoint (page 207) to sites on the nearby escarpment. The hike to the **Mambo Caves**, on the cliffs below the ecolodge, entails a 400m ascent and descent over 4km and takes around 3 hours, with a good chance of spotting cliff-nesting raptors, including the rare Taita falcon.

Another very scenic hike of similar length leads to the so-called **Mandala Hominid Footprints**, which some local sources reckon were imprinted in volcanic ash by early hominid inhabitants of the area perhaps a million years ago – an unlikely claim, given that the bedrock here is very ancient and non-volcanic in origin, and the impressions look a lot more like a function of weathering than they do footprints. Mambo Viewpoint can also arrange a cultural day tour encompassing a visit to a local healer, lunch with a local family, and meetings with local farmers.

Shagayu Forest Reserve The second-largest indigenous forest in the Western Usambara, Shagayu extends over some 60km² along the slopes of the eponymous mountain, which rises to an altitude of 2,228m a few kilometres east of Mtae and Mambo. The forest here is thought to be in more pristine condition than the larger Magamba Forest Reserve, and it harbours a rich and varied forest birdlife, including the colourful Hartlaub's turaco, eagerly sought bar-tailed trogon, and Eastern Arc endemics such as Usambara akalat, Usambara double-collared sunbird, white-chested alethe and Usambara weaver. Visits to the forest can be arranged inexpensively through Mambo Viewpoint (page 207). These include dedicated birding walks with knowledgeable guides, while non-birders can follow the scenic route to the **Kideghe Waterfall**, set deep in the forest, or undertake an overnight camping trip to the peak.

AMANI NATURE RESERVE AND THE EASTERN USAMBARA

The Eastern Usambara is one of the smallest of the Eastern Arc ranges, as well as one of the lowest, barely exceeding 1,500m in elevation. It also ranks among the Eastern Arc's most ecologically important components, since it supports extensive tracts of evergreen forest sustained by the annual rainfall of up to 2,000mm. In places, the indigenous vegetation has been replaced by tea plantations, and there has also been more recent encroachment by subsistence farmers, but at least 500km² of reasonably undisturbed forest remains. In common with the other montane forests of eastern Tanzania, the Eastern Usambara is cited as a biodiversity hotspot, characterised by a high level of endemism (see box, pages 208–9). It is also a vital catchment area, providing fresh water to some 200,000 people, and the East Usambara Catchment Management Project (EUCAMP), funded by Finnish aid, has implemented a community-based conservation plan to protect the catchment forests.

The main tourist focus in the Eastern Usambara is the quirky little village of Amani, which was settled in 1902 by German scientists, who established the 3km² Amani Botanical Garden (reputedly the second-largest such entity in the world) as an agricultural research station and arboretum specialising in long-term botanical trials for exotic plant species. Lying at an elevation of roughly 900m, Amani remains a biological and medical research station of note, and the old village – dominated by buildings that date to the German and British colonial eras – has the genteel but rather ramshackle appearance of a European country village transplanted to the African jungle. The development of ecotourism has been a high priority since 1997, when the Amani Nature Reserve, protecting 84km² of relatively undisturbed forest, was amalgamated from various pre-existing forest reserves, as well as the Amani Botanical Garden and a further 10km² of forest managed by local tea estates. Today, Amani ranks among the most underrated reserves anywhere in northern Tanzania, offering the combination of excellent walking, beautiful forest scenery and a wealth of animal life.

FLORA AND FAUNA The Eastern Usambara supports some 220km² of lowland forest and 280km² of submontane forest, both of which are protected within the Amani Nature Reserve. The most common of several near-endemic tree species found around the old botanical garden is *Allanblackia stuhlmannii*, which can be distinguished by its foot-long fruits, whose kernels produce a hard white fat used as soap or for cooking. As might be expected, many exotic trees planted by the Germans also flourish around the botanical gardens, but mostly these have not penetrated through to the forest interior. Smaller plants found in the forest around Amani include various endemic wild coffee species, and the well-known African violets of the genus *Saintpaulia* (see box, page 213).

In the early colonial era, elephants, buffalo and leopards still roamed the forests of the Eastern Usambara. Large mammals are relatively poorly represented today, the most conspicuous exception being Angola colobus and blue monkey, both of which are common and draw attention to themselves with their regular vocalisations, as does the smaller but very pretty Tanganyika mountain squirrel. At night, various bushbabies and the eastern tree hyrax are more often heard than seen, while 16 species of bats flit through the forest. Other range-restricted mammals associated with Amani Nature Reserve include the impressive Zanj elephant shrew and rather less striking lesser pouched rat. More than 100 forest-associated bird species have been recorded in the reserve, several of them endemic or near-endemic (see box, page 214).

Amani Nature Reserve is particularly impressive when it comes to less glamorous wildlife. A long list of reptiles includes at least 25 snake and seven chameleon species. Particularly impressive are the Usambara three-horned chameleon (*Trioceros deremensis*), a near-endemic that can grow to 35cm in length, and the Eastern Usambara two-horned chameleon (*Kinyongia matschiei*), an endemic subspecies that occasionally attains a length of 40cm. These and several other smaller species might be encountered on a guided 'chameleon walk' out of Amani Forest Camp (pages 214–16).

Amani's checklist of 34 amphibian species includes eight endemics, most notably the spectacular Usambara blue-bellied frog (*Hoplophryne rogersi*), which is sometimes seen in leaf litter in Amani Forest Camp. Amani supports a rare wealth of invertebrates, and although these are relatively poorly documented, those families that have been studied show a high level of endemism – of the 40 millipede species recorded at Amani, for instance, around three-quarters are known only from the Eastern Usambara. Among the more conspicuous insects, *Hypolimnas antevorta* is a large black, blue and white butterfly endemic to the Eastern Usambara, while the Amani flatwing (*Amanipodagrion gilliesi*), placed in a monotypic genus and endemic to fast-flowing streams that run downhill from Amani to Sigi, is a critically endangered damselfly whose unusually long slender abdomen ends in a conspicuous white tip.

FEES AND FURTHER INFORMATION Sigi Visitors Centre, also known as Zigi or Kisiwani (m *0784 587805/0716 535038;* e *anaminaturereserve@yahoo.com;* ☉ *07.00–18.00 daily*), lies some 7km before Amani on the main road coming from Muheza. Here, a rehabilitated German stationmaster's house doubles as an entrance gate, ticket office and information centre, while an adjoining resthouse offers visitors a lower-elevation site from which to explore the forest. Guided hikes can also be arranged at the conservation office next to the Amani Resthouse, but this is closed on Sunday.

A one-off entrance fee of US$10 per person is valid for the full duration of your stay. Other fees include a daily vehicle entrance fee equivalent to around US$5 (or US$25 if the vehicle is foreign-registered), and an additional charge of US$15 per person per day for the services of a guide.

GETTING THERE AND AWAY The springboard for visits to Amani is the small town of **Muheza**, 40km west of Tanga on the main surfaced road to Moshi. There is plenty of **local transport** between Tanga and Muheza, and the trip takes less than 2 hours. Alternatively, any **bus** heading to Tanga from Arusha, Lushoto, Moshi or Dar es Salaam can drop you there. Muheza is at its liveliest on the local market days of Thursday and Sunday, and there are numerous small guesthouses should you need to spend a night. From Muheza, the road to Amani is clearly signposted, and the drive should take about 90 minutes, passing through the entrance gate at Sigi after an hour. Driving times will depend on the condition of the road, in particular the spectacular but steep 7km stretch between Sigi and Amani. It is rumoured that some or all of this road will be surfaced in the near future, a development that would reduce the driving time to less than an hour.

Three buses daily run between Muheza and Sigi, leaving Muheza between noon and the mid afternoon, and arriving about 2 hours later. One bus continues from Sigi up the steep road to Amani, usually arriving there in the later afternoon (but sometimes after dark), then carries on for another 8km to the Konkoro Tea Estate, passing the turn-off 3.5km from Amani Forest Camp *en route*. The return bus from Konkoro Tea Estate to Muheza leaves at around 05.30–06.00, and passes through Amani at about 06.30 and Sigi 30 minutes later.

THE GENUS *SAINTPAULIA*

Of the 3,500 species of vascular plants recorded in the Usambara Mountains, more than 25% are thought to be endemic or near-endemic. Without doubt the most familiar of these unique taxa is a small flowering plant first collected in the Eastern Usambara in 1892 by the District Commissioner of Tanga, Baron Walter von Saint Paul Illaire. Subsequently described as *Saintpaulia ionantha* in honour of its discoverer, the African violet (as it is more commonly known) was made commercially available in 1927, when ten different blue-flowered strains were put on the market. It is today one of the world's most popular perennial pot plants, with thousands of cultivated strains generating a global trade worth tens of millions of US dollars, and yet few enthusiasts realise that the wild flower is threatened within its natural range.

Although they vary greatly in shape and colour, most cultivated strains of African violet are hybrids of the original seeds collected by Baron Saint Paul, which belonged to two highly malleable races, *S. i. ionantha* and *S. i. grotei*. The specific taxonomy of the genus *Saintpaulia* is controversial: at one time more than 20 species were recognised but a 2006 study has reduced that number to six. The genus is unique to the Eastern Arc Mountains, and its main strongholds are the Eastern Usambara and Nguru Mountains.

Not affiliated to the true violets, *Saintpaulia* is a relatively recently evolved genus whose ancestral stock was most likely blown across from Madagascar in a cyclone (a flowering plant in the genus *Streptocarpus* has been cited as the probable ancestor). The wild *Saintpaulia* has probably never enjoyed a wide distribution or a high level of habitat tolerance. In the wild, as in the home, most species require continuous shade and humidity in order to flourish and because it depends on surface rather than underground moisture, *Saintpaulia* has an unusually shallow root system. It typically grows in moist cracks in porous rocks close to streams running through closed-canopy forest – though some specimens do lead an epiphytic existence on cycad trunks or the shady branches of palms.

The main threat to the wild *Saintpaulia* is the logging of tall trees, which creates breaks in the closed canopy. Researchers in the Eastern Usambara have come across dead or dying plants at several established *Saintpaulia* sites where the canopy has been broken due to logging. One of the many positive effects of the gazetting of Amani Nature Reserve in 1997 is that it should help secure the future of the genus – or at least those species that are resident within the reserve. Local guides will be able to show you the wild flowers on several of the established walking and driving trails.

Eastern Usambara takes second place to the Udzungwa as the most important avian site in the Eastern Arc Mountains, but it is still one of the most significant birding sites anywhere in East Africa. Amani in particular has several logistical advantages over the best birdwatching sites in the Udzungwa, namely relative ease of access, proximity to the established tourist circuit of northern Tanzania, and a superior tourist infrastructure and quality of guides. The Eastern Usambara's avifauna has received far more scientific attention than that of the other Eastern Arc ranges, dating from 1926 to 1948 when Amani was the home of the doyen of Tanzania ornithology, Reginald Moreau, credited with discovering and describing several new species including the long-billed tailorbird. This extensive study is reflected in a checklist of 340 bird species, including 12 that are globally threatened and 19 that are either endemic to the Eastern Arc Mountains or to the East African coastal biome.

The temptation on first arriving at Amani might be to rush off along one of the trails into the forest interior. In fact some of the most productive general birdwatching is to be had in the gardens and forest fringe around Amani village, slow exploration of which is likely to yield up to 50 forest-associated species including half-a-dozen genuine rarities. One of the more conspicuous and vocal residents around the resthouses is the green-headed oriole, a colourful bird that is restricted to a handful of montane forests between Tanzania and Mozambique. The flowering gardens are a good site for three of the four range-restricted sunbirds associated with the Eastern Usambara (ie: Amani, banded green and Uluguru violet-backed sunbird). The rare long-billed tailorbird has been discovered breeding at two sites in Amani village.

Having explored the resthouse area, the guided Turaco and Mbamole Hill trails are recommended for sighting further montane forest specials. Noteworthy birds resident in the forest around Amani include the Usambara eagle owl, southern banded snake eagle, silvery-cheeked hornbill, half-collared kingfisher, African green ibis, Fischer's turaco, African broadbill, East Coast akalat, white-chested alethe, Kenrick's and Waller's starlings, and several forest flycatchers. It is also worth noting that several of the more interesting Usambara specials are lowland forest species, more likely to be seen in and around Sigi than at Amani. Among the birds to look out for on the trails around Sigi are eastern green tinkerbird, African cuckoo-hawk, square-tailed drongo, bar-tailed trogon and chestnut-fronted helmet-shrike.

More straightforwardly, a trickle of dalla-dallas runs back and forth between Muheza and Amani throughout the day, charging around US$2 per person, while a boda-boda will cost US$5–15 one-way (depending on whether you continue to Amani Forest Camp), and a taxi around US$30–40.

WHERE TO STAY AND EAT

Amani Forest Camp [map, page 192] (9 rooms) m 0782 656526; e reservations@amaniforestcamp.com; www.amaniforestcamp.com. Situated outside the nature reserve about 7km from Amani village & 3.5km off the road to Konkoro Tea Estate, this environmentally responsible camp, formerly known as Emau Hill, offers the choice of comfortable en-suite stone or tented cottages, simple standing tents using common showers, or spaces to pitch your own

GALAGO DIVERSITY IN TANZANIA

The Prosimian galago family is the modern representative of the most ancient of Africa's extant primate lineages, more closely related to the lemurs of Madagascar than to any other mainland monkeys or apes. With their wide round eyes and agile bodies, they are also – as their alternative name of bushbaby suggests – uniquely endearing creatures, bound to warm the heart of even the least anthropomorphic of observers. And no natural history lover could fail to feel some excitement at the revolution in the taxonomy of the galago family that has taken place over recent years, largely due to research undertaken in the forests of Tanzania by the Nocturnal Primate Research Group (*www.nprg.org*) of Oxford Brookes University.

In 1975, only six species of galago were recognised by specialists. Today, it is thought there may be as many as 40 species, a quarter of which are confirmed or likely to occur in Tanzania, including three national endemics. The reasons behind this explosion of knowledge probably lie in the animals' nocturnal habits, which makes casual identification tricky, particularly in relatively inaccessible forested habitats. Previously biologists based their definition of galago species largely on superficial visual similarities. It has been recently recognised, however, that the distinctive vocal repertoires of different populations, as well as differences in the penile structure, provide a more accurate indicator of whether two populations would or indeed could interbreed given the opportunity – in other words, whether they should be regarded as discrete species.

By comparing the calls, penile structures and DNA of dwarf galago populations around Tanzania, the Nocturnal Primate Research Group has discovered several previously undescribed species since the early 1990s. These are Grant's galago (*Galago granti*; coastal woodland south of the Rufiji River); Matundu galago (*G. udzungwensis*; Udzungwa Mountains); Zanzibar galago (*G. zanzibaricus*; Zanzibar); Uluguru galago (*G. orinus*; Uluguru and Usambara Mountains); and Rondo galago (*G. rondoensis*). The last of these species was initially thought to be confined to the Rondo Plateau inland of Lindi but has been recently discovered living in the Pugu Hills, right outside the country's largest city. Nevertheless, it is regarded as Critically Endangered by the International Union for Conservation of Nature and has been listed by them as one of the 'World's 25 Most Endangered Primates'. It is not so much possible as certain that further galago species await discovery: in East Africa alone populations that require further study are found in southeast Tanzania, in the isolated forests of Mount Marsabit in northern Kenya, and in the mountains along the northern shores of Lake Nyasa-Malawi.

Simon Bearder of the Nocturnal Primate Research Group argues convincingly that the implications of these fresh discoveries in galago taxonomy might extend to other 'difficult' groups of closely related animals. He points out that our most important sense is vision, which makes it easiest for us to separate species that rely primarily on vision to recognise or attract partners. It becomes more difficult for us to separate animals that attract their mates primarily by sound and scent, more so if they use senses we do not possess such as ultrasound or electric impulses. 'Such "cryptic" species', Bearder writes, 'are no less valid than any other, but we are easily misled into thinking of them as being much more similar than would be the case if we had their kind of sensitivity. The easiest way for us to distinguish between free-living species is to concentrate on those aspects of the communication system that the animals themselves use to attract partners.'

tent. Surrounded by natural & plantation forest, the gardens are regularly visited by both monkey species associated with Amani, while a short unguided trail below the site is a good place to look for African violets in season. In addition, more than 130 bird species have been recorded in the immediate vicinity, including the lovely Fischer's turaco & green-headed oriole, & all the key endemics (a reasonably reliable site for long-billed tailorbird is only 3km away). The camp operates a good network of trails outside the reserve: these can be walked unguided for free, or a guide can be supplied for US$10pp. The camp can also arrange expert bird guides to accompany serious twitchers (around US$25 per half-day), while early-evening chameleon walks often yield up to 4 species of these fascinating reptiles, including the giant two-horned & three-horned varieties. *US$112/172 en-suite sgl/dbl B&B (add US$32pp for FB), US$14pp in* *standing tent or camping US$7pp (add US$42pp for FB).* **$$–$$$$**

🏠 **Amani Resthouse** [map, page 192] (18 rooms) m 0784 587805/0716 535038; e amaninaturereserve@yahoo.com. This comfortable no-frills resthouse, situated next to the conservation office in Amani, has adequate en-suite rooms & a canteen serving meals for around US$3, & the usual selection of drinks. *US$10–15pp, depending on room size, bed only US$10pp.* **$**

🏠 **Sigi Resthouse** (8 rooms) m 0784 587805/0716 535038; e amaninaturereserve@yahoo.com. The resthouse at Sigi is similar in standard to the one at Amani, but has a more modern feel. The clean en-suite twin rooms have fitted nets, writing desk & hot shower. A canteen serves meals for around US$3 & the usual selection of drinks. *US$7.50pp bed only.* **$**

WHAT TO SEE AND DO Nine walking trails have been demarcated in the reserve, ranging in length from 3km to 12km, and leaflets with trail descriptions are available to visitors at the entrance gate. The directions in the leaflets are reportedly not 100% accurate, so it might be worth hiking with a trained guide, who will also help you to spot birds and monkeys. It is worth consulting with the guides about the trail most suited to your specific interest.

The 10km **Konkoro Trail**, which can be covered on foot or in a vehicle, is good for African violets, and it cuts through several different forest types, as well as passing a viewpoint and terminating in an overnight campsite in the heart of the forest. The shorter **Turaco** and **Mbamole Hill** trails are recommended first options for birdwatchers. In addition to the prescribed walking trails, there is much to be seen along the roads and paths that lie within the research centre and botanical garden. Wandering around the forest-fringed village, you are likely to encounter a wide variety of birds, as well as Angola colobus and blue monkey – and you might even catch a glimpse of the bizarre and outsized Zanj elephant shrew.

NORTHERN TANZANIA ONLINE

For additional online content, articles, photos and more on northern Tanzania, why not visit www.bradtguides.com/northerntanzania.

10

Tarangire and the Central Rift Valley

The semi-arid Central Rift Valley south of Arusha has two main points of touristic interest. The better known and busier of these is Tarangire National Park, a world-class wildlife-viewing destination best renowned for its daunting concentrations of baobab trees and elephants, supplemented by influxes of migrant grazers during the dry season (July to November), when it is appended to most northern safari itineraries and also forms a worthwhile goal for a short self-standing safari out of Arusha. Although most tourists confine their exploration of the area to Tarangire and surrounds, another important (albeit relatively obscure) attraction is the Kondoa Rock Art, an alfresco collection of 150-plus prehistoric artworks inscribed as a UNESCO World Heritage Site in 2006. Other geographic landmarks include pretty Lake Babati and the volcanic Mount Hanang, and the area is also notable for its traditional pastoralist inhabitants, most famously the Maasai, whose traditional grazing grounds enclose Tarangire National Park, but also the Barabaig and other sub-groups of the Datoga who live further southwest.

TARANGIRE NATIONAL PARK

The 2,850km² Tarangire National Park lies at the core of a 20,000km² semi-arid ecosystem that also incorporates several more-or-less contiguous Wildlife Management Areas (WMAs) created since 2006 in consultation with local communities. These are the Randileni WMA to the north, the Levolosi WMA to the northwest, the Burunge WMA running west towards Lake Manyara, and the vast but undeveloped 5,372km² Makame WMA extending southwards across the Maasai Steppes. Inherently drier than the Serengeti, and less well publicised, Tarangire National Park is nevertheless a highly rewarding wildlife destination, especially during the latter half of the year, when it's a recommended inclusion on any safari itinerary of a week or longer. The park is best known for its year-round proliferation of elephants, but predators are also well represented, the birdlife is consistently rewarding, and large herds of migrant grazers are drawn to the perennial water of the Tarangire River when other sources dry up.

FLORA AND FAUNA The Tarangire ecosystem tends to be more densely vegetated than the Serengeti, supporting a tangle of semi-arid acacia and mixed woodland. Its dominant geographic feature, bisecting the national park, is the Tarangire River, which is flanked by dense patches of elephant grass and a sporadic ribbon of riparian woodland dotted with the occasional palm tree. A striking feature of the park's flora is the abundance of massive bulbous baobab trees that line the slopes away from the river. It is an important stronghold for elephants, with a count of almost 2,500 individuals in a census undertaken in 2009, and more recent studies suggest that

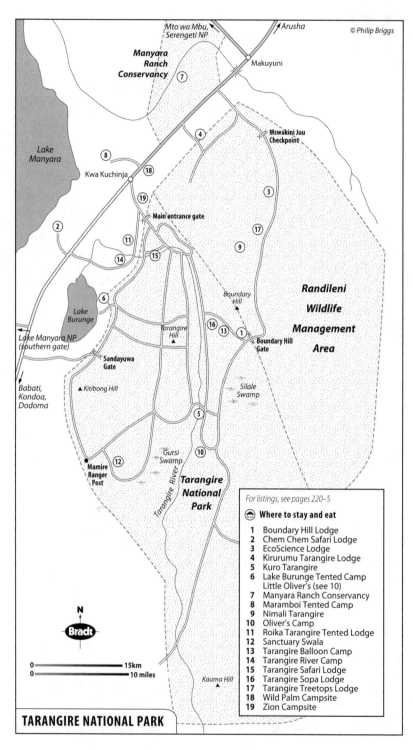

For listings, see pages 220–5

🏠 **Where to stay and eat**

1 Boundary Hill Lodge
2 Chem Chem Safari Lodge
3 EcoScience Lodge
4 Kirurumu Tarangire Lodge
5 Kuro Tarangire
6 Lake Burunge Tented Camp
  Little Oliver's (see 10)
7 Manyara Ranch Conservancy
8 Maramboi Tented Camp
9 Nimali Tarangire
10 Oliver's Camp
11 Roika Tarangire Tented Lodge
12 Sanctuary Swala
13 Tarangire Balloon Camp
14 Tarangire River Camp
15 Tarangire Safari Lodge
16 Tarangire Sopa Lodge
17 Tarangire Treetops Lodge
18 Wild Palm Campsite
19 Zion Campsite

TARANGIRE NATIONAL PARK

along with the Serengeti, it is one if the few places in Tanzania where numbers are on the increase. The elephants of Tarangire have been less keen to cross outside the park boundaries in recent seasons, presumably as a result of an increased risk of poaching. It is difficult to put reliable figures on other wildlife populations associated with Tarangire, as the most recent census was completed around 30 years ago, but there is no reason to suppose that the numbers recorded then – including 25,000 wildebeest, 30,000 zebra, 6,000 buffalo, 2,700 giraffe, 5,500 eland, 30,000 impala and 2,000 warthog – have significantly changed.

As with Serengeti-Ngorongoro, the greater Tarangire ecosystem is characterised by a great deal of seasonal migratory movement. During the dry season, between July and November, elephant numbers can be little short of phenomenal, and large herds of zebra, wildebeest, antelope and other game are attracted to the near-perennial waters of the Tarangire River. This isn't to say, that Tarangire is without merit at other times of the year. True, a lot of wildlife disperses outside the park during the wetter months – wildebeest and zebra northwest to the Rift Valley floor between Manyara and Natron, other species southward across the Maasai Steppes – but the park is also greener and more scenic during the rains, and the birdlife can be astounding. Also, contrary to expectations, lions seem to be easier to locate in the wet season, possibly because the tall grass makes them more inclined to walk and hunt along roads, and to rest up on them at night.

FEES AND FURTHER INFORMATION The park entrance fee of US$45 per person per 24 hours plus 18% VAT can be paid by Visa, MasterCard or with a Tanapa smartcard (issued at any Exim Bank). No other cards are accepted, nor is cash – for more details, see box, page 92. In common with most other national parks, Tarangire now operates a single-entrance rule, which means that visitors based at a lodge outside the park are required to pay another set of fees every time they enter, even if it is within the 24-hour period for which they have already theoretically paid. As a result, operators who place their clients at lodges outside the national park tend to push towards doing one long post-breakfast game drive daily, staying out in the midday heat, rather than the more conventional, productive and enjoyable regime of two daily game drives incorporating peak viewing hours (ie: early morning and late afternoon).

Those staying at lodges set within any of the bordering WMAs require a permit bought in advance from the Wildlife Division in Arusha (page 139); most lodges will arrange this on behalf of their clients and incorporate it into the room price.

A detailed booklet, *Tarangire National Park*, is widely available in Arusha and some of the park's lodges.

GETTING THERE AND AWAY Most people tag a visit to Tarangire on to a longer safari, but if time or money is limited, a one- or two-day standalone safari would be a viable option, since the park is less than 2 hours' drive south of Arusha. In principle, any public transport running along the Babati road could drop you at the junctions mentioned below, but there is no realistic way of exploring the park itself without private transport.

There are three main access points, the most useful of which depends on which lodge or camp you are booked into.

The main entrance gate lies about 7km east of the main Arusha–Dodoma road. Coming from Arusha, the road is surfaced as far as the clearly signposted turn-off at Kwa Kuchinja, a small village situated about 100km south of Arusha and 25km past Makuyuni (the junction for Manyara and the Serengeti). This is the best approach for most lodges and camps set within the park, as well as those set along the northwestern boundary close to the main gate.

Coming from Arusha, the three lodges set in the Randileni WMA (Tarangire Treetops, Nimali and EcoScience) are all best reached by following the Arusha–Dodoma road for about 5km past Makuyuni junction, then turning left on to a signposted dirt road that reaches the Mswakini Juu checkpoint (where your pre-bought permit for the WMA must be shown) after 20 minutes and the lodges after another 30–45 minutes. Access to the national park from these lodges is via the westerly Boundary Hill Gate.

The recently opened Sandayuwa Gate lies about 8km east of the Arusha–Dodoma road along a side road signposted about 35km south of the turn-off for the main gate. The camps situated around Lake Burunge lie just outside this gate, which also provides the easiest access for the more southerly camps within the park.

🏠 WHERE TO STAY AND EAT *Map, page 218*

Tarangire is now serviced by the best part of 20 lodges and camps. All else being equal, we would give preference to those properties situated within the national park, as they generally have the best locations for wildlife viewing, and – especially following the recent introduction of the single-entry ruling – are more conducive to a regime of two game drives daily.

Lodges inside Tarangire As well as the lodges below, there are a couple of campsites within Tarangire for those on camping safaris. These are strong on bush atmosphere but short on facilities, and rather costly at the customary US$30 per person.

Exclusive

✳ 🏠 **Sanctuary Swala** (12 tents) ☎027 250 9817 or (UK) +44 (0)20 7190 7728; e reservations.tanzania@sanctuaryretreats.com; www.sanctuaryretreats.com; ⊕ closed Apr & May. Situated in the southern half of the park, this classic luxury tented camp stands in a grove of tall acacia trees overlooking the remote Gurusi Swamp, where it is wonderfully isolated from any other lodge or the more popular game-viewing circuits. The camp itself is something of a magnet for wildlife: the swala (antelope) after which it is named are much in evidence, especially a resident herd of impala, accompanied by a noisy entourage of vervet monkeys, guineafowl & various plovers, buffalo-weavers & starlings. The small waterhole in front of the camp attracts elephants in Jul & Aug, while a near-resident lion pride & the occasional leopard passes through with surprising regularity. The food is excellent, especially the bush dinners held in a grove of baobabs about 5mins' drive from camp, & the quality of tented accommodation is in line with the best lodges of this type in southern Africa. *US$1,045/1,380 FB sgl/dbl inc drinks & guided activities. Substantial discount Jan–Mar & Nov–mid Dec.* $$$$$$

✳ 🏠 **Oliver's Camp** (10 rooms) ☏(South Africa) +27 (0)21 418 0468; m 0736 500515/ 0784 111331; www.asiliaafrica.com; ⊕ closed Apr–mid May. This excellent bush camp, overlooking the floodplain of the Minyonyo Pools & close to Silale Swamp, also lies within the park boundaries, but far enough from the busy northern section that activities can usually be undertaken without seeing other tourists. One of the few camps to undertake walking safaris within the national park, it offers 2-night stays incorporated into more wide-ranging safaris, as well as extended walking-oriented stays of 3 days or more, usually spending 1 or more nights at a mobile fly-camp. The lodge itself is unpretentious & comfortable rather than opulently luxurious, the guides are unusually personable & knowledgeable, & a superb library of natural history books underscores the emphasis on substance over style – strongly recommended to anybody seeking a genuinely holistic bush experience. *US$1,290/1,840 sgl/dbl Sep & Oct & 20 Dec–5 Jan, US$1,390/1,980 sgl/dbl Jul & Aug inc all meals, drinks & activities, dropping to between US$400 & US$700pp in other months.* $$$$$$$

🏠 **Little Oliver's** (5 rooms) 📞 (South Africa) +27 (0)21 418 0468; **m** 0736 500515/0784 111331; www.asiliaafrica.com; 🕐 closed Apr–mid May. Tucked just around the corner from Oliver's Camp is its smaller & younger sibling. The 2 camps are almost identical in décor, amenities & activities, but being half the size, Little Oliver's offers guests a more personal, intimate experience. It's worth taking advantage of the fly-camping, night drives & guided walks that are offered here, as these activities are seldom available in northern Tanzania. *Rates same as Oliver's Camp.* $$$$$$$

🏠 **Kuro Tarangire** (6 tents) **m** 0787 595908; **e** info@nomad-tanzania.com; www.nomad-tanzania.com; 🕐 closed late Mar–late May. Opened in 2014, this exclusive new addition to the excellent Nomad portfolio is spread across an acacia grove on the west bank of the Tarangire River about 18km south of the Sopa, making it sufficiently far south of the main game-viewing circuit to retain some distance from the crowds, but close enough to ensure top-notch game viewing, particularly in the dry season. Spacious safari tents come with verandas, solar lighting, en-suite bucket showers & flush eco-toilets. An open-sided thatched lounge & dining room furnished with hides & colourful local fabrics serves superb food. *US$1,200/1,710 FB sgl/dbl inc drinks & activities, discounted Jun & Nov.* $$$$$$$

Upmarket

✴ 🏠 **Tarangire Safari Lodge** (35 tents & 5 bungalows) 📞 027 254 4752; **m** 0784 202777; **e** bookings@tarangiresafarilodge.com or tarangiresafarilodge@gmail.com; www.tarangiresafarilodge.com. This unpretentious owner-managed lodge is the oldest in the park, & one of the most characterful, boasting a sublime location on a tall bluff overlooking the Tarangire River. Game viewing from the veranda can be stupendous, with large herds of elephants, hippo, giraffe, etc, coming down to the river to drink. The grounds are also highly attractive to birders, both for the habituated hornbills, buffalo-weavers & starlings that parade around the common areas, & for the host of more secretive small

birds resident in the acacia scrub. The compact & well-maintained standing tents are comfortable rather than luxurious, but all come with en-suite hot showers & toilets, & private balconies. The meals are to an unusually high standard for buffets, with different lunchtime themes. It is also ideally located for game drives, only minutes from the rewarding grassland area known as Little Serengeti. Facilities include a swimming pool, the new Patuuvu Spa that offers massages accompanied by sensational views over a stretch of river behind the main lodge, & a well-stocked book & gift shop. Arguably the best-value lodge on the northern circuit; highly recommended. *US$270/440 sgl/dbl FB.* $$$$$

🏠 **Tarangire Sopa Lodge** (75 rooms) **m** 0784 250630/1; **e** info@sopalodges.com; www.sopalodges.com. Set in the heart of the national park, the Tarangire Sopa is the largest, most conventionally luxurious & least 'bush' of the lodges around Tarangire. The facilities & accommodation match the customary high standards of this chain, with smart self-contained suites & excellent food. The indifferent location, alongside a small & normally dry watercourse below a baobab-studded slope, is compensated for by the superb game viewing – the roads between here & Tarangire Safari Lodge are far & away the most rewarding in the park. *US$385/680 sgl/dbl FB, with substantial low-season discounts.* $$$$$

🏠 **Tarangire Balloon Camp** (10 rooms) **m** 0682 513163; **e** tarangire@madahotels.com; www.madahotels.com. Situated in the east of the park, this isolated bush camp has a lovely – albeit rather tsetse-ridden – location on a slope close to Boundary Hill Gate, a fabulous swimming pool set in the rocks, & spacious en-suite standing tents with 4-poster beds, walk-in nets & private balcony, but it's undermined by a décor style that doesn't quite gel with the bush setting. It is well placed for game drives & is the base of Adventures Aloft, the only company that offers balloon safaris in Tarangire (page 226). *US$330/650 sgl/dbl FB.* $$$$$

Lodges west of the national park The lodge and camps below all lie outside one of the two western park entrance gates and most are set within the Burunge or Levolosi WMAs, which extends westward across from Tarangire National Park to the eastern shore of Lake Manyara. Managed in consultation with local Maasai

10

communities, these WMAs form part of the historically important wildlife corridor between Tarangire and Lake Manyara national parks, whose respective northern and southeastern tips lie only 20km apart but are separated by ranchland and the surfaced Arusha–Dodoma Highway. Of particular note are Manyara Ranch and Chem Chem, a pair of exclusive private camps set in private concessions that are not only playing an important role in reopening the migration route between the two parks, but also offer visitors the opportunity to combine guided walks and drives within the concession with day trips to Tarangire. The other lodges listed below mostly stand very close to one of the national park entrance gates and would be well positioned for undertaking two game drives daily were it not for the single-entry ruling.

Exclusive

✳ 🏠 Chem Chem Safari Lodge

(8 rooms) m 0689 119349/0683 637909; e reservations@chemchemsafari.com; www.chemchemsafari.com; ⏰ closed Apr–mid May. This classy owner-managed lodge lies on a 40km² concession running between the southeast shore of Lake Manyara & the main road west of the Burunge area of Tarangire. Accommodation is in ultra-spacious & earthily stylish cottages with canvas walls & roofs, each with king-sized bed, walk-in nets, large bathroom with indoor tub & outdoor shower, & 2 private balconies. Long stilted wooden walkways link the cottages to the open-sided sitting & dining area, which overlooks a grassy floodplain, a line of borassus palms marking the distant shore of Manyara, & the tall escarpment above the lake. The unfenced concession forms part of the important wildlife corridor connecting Tarangire to Lake Manyara, & plains wildlife – in particular, giraffe, zebra, various antelope – is prolific. The main activity within the concession is guided walking safaris, which offer an opportunity to get close to plenty of wildlife. Walking is also the best way to experience the superb birdlife associated both with the tangled acacia scrub & the open floodplain of Manyara, a good site for coursers, pratincoles, storks, flamingos, avocets & other wading birds. The lodge is also a useful springboard for day trips into Tarangire National Park, & to the little-visited southern end of Lake Manyara National Park, making it a great base for newly arrived safari-goers to settle in for a few days before heading further west to the Serengeti, etc. The smaller (& pricier) 'Little Chem Chem' recently opened on the same property. US$1,575/2,010 sgl/dbl full game package. Seasonal discounts Mar, mid May–mid Jun & Nov. $$$$$$

🏠 Manyara Ranch Conservancy (8 tents)

📞 027 254 5284; m 0683 918888; e reservations@manyararanch.com; www.manyararanch.com; ⏰ closed Apr & May. Established as a cattle ranch during the colonial era, the 120km² Manyara Ranch was taken over by the African Wildlife Foundation in 2000, & it now doubles as a commercial ranch & part of an important wildlife corridor connecting the Natron/Manyara region to Tarangire National Park. The emphasis here is strongly on game walks, which offer a good opportunity for close encounters with the likes of elephant, giraffe, wildebeest & zebra, as well as more localised antelope such as fringe-eared oryx, eland & lesser kudu. Night drives are also offered, with a chance of sighting lion, spotted hyena & bat-eared fox. Birdlife is varied too, thanks to the wide variety of habitats ranging from open grassland to lush riparian forest. It is also a good base for day trips to Tarangire & Lake Manyara national parks, both of which lie a 30–45min drive way. Accommodation comprises a wonderfully rustic & intimate tented camp space out in a shady acacia grove alive with birds & overlooking a floodplain that frequently attracts wildlife. The large screened tents are in the classic safari style, with hardwood floor, king-sized bed, en-suite bathroom with hot shower, private balcony with camp chairs, & a great night chorus. Like Chem Chem, it's a great place to spend a few days at the start of a safari. US$840/1,380 sgl/dbl FB inc drinks, or US$990/1,680 sgl/dbl FB full game package. Low-season discounts offered. $$$$$$$

Upmarket

✳ 🏠 Maramboi Tented Camp (40 rooms)

m 0736 502471/0785 069944; e reservations@tanganyikawildernesscamps.com; www.tanganyikawildernesscamps.com. Like the two more exclusive camps listed above, Maramboi is set within a private concession overlooking the eastern floodplain of Lake Manyara on the west side of the Arusha–Dodoma road. Accommodation is in spacious tents set on a wooden platform & equipped with walk-in nets, electricity, ceiling fans, en-suite hot showers & private balconies looking towards the lake & Rift Escarpment. Unless your budget stretches to Chem Chem or Manyara Ranch, we'd rate this attractive, well-managed & realistically priced camp as the best option outside the park, not least because morning game drives into Tarangire can be supplemented with Maasai-guided afternoon nature walks on the property, which supports plenty of giraffe, zebra & other plains wildlife as well as a preponderance of birds. *US$285/430 sgl/dbl FB, with low-season discounts Mar–Jun & Nov.* $$$$$

🏠 **Kirurumu Tarangire Lodge** (10 tents) ☎ 027 250 7011/7541; e info@kirurumu.net; www.kirurumu.net. Set on the national park boundary less than 30mins' drive from the main park gate, the former Tamarind Camp offers accommodation in spacious en-suite tents set apart in a patch of dense bush often frequented by elephant & other large mammals. Raised on solid stone bases & suspended under thatch, the tents are fairly minimalistic in style & simple in design, but come with king-sized or twin bed, electricity & a modern tiled bathroom with hot running shower. It also offers Maasai-guided nature walks & village visits. Very good value. *US$230/364 sgl/dbl FB. Low-season discounts. Full game package inc game drives, drinks & transfers to nearest airstrip available at an extra cost.* $$$$$

🏠 **Lake Burunge Tented Camp** (30 tents) m 0736 502471/0785 069944; e reservations@ tanganyikawildernesscamps.com; www. tanganyikawildernesscamps.com. Overlooking the seasonal Lake Burunge, this lodge lies in the eponymous WMA around 10mins' drive outside the park boundary, some distance south of the main Tarangire tourist circuit, in an area of dense bush known for its populations of dry-country antelope such as lesser kudu & gerenuk. Accommodation is in spacious & attractively rustic en-suite twin & dbl tents built on stilted platforms & shaded by makuti roofs. The camp is well positioned for game drives, & it also offers guided nature walks, along with canoe trips when the lake holds water. Underutilised & very good value. *US$220/314 sgl/ dbl FB, with low-season discounts Mar–Jun & Nov.* $$$$$

🏠 **Tarangire River Camp** (20 tents) m 0737 206420; e tarangirecamp@mbalimbali.com; www. mbalimbali.com; 🕐 closed Apr. Situated 3.5km outside the main gate as the crow flies (but more like 15km by road) this tented camp lies within a 250km² concession, set aside for conservation by the Maasai community of Minjingu, along the northwest boundary of the national park. The camp is set below a massive old baobab on a cliff overlooking the (normally dry) Minjingu River, a tributary of the Tarangire that you'll need to be ferried across during the rainy season, & wildlife can be quite prolific in the vicinity seasonally, even though it is not in the park. The lodge is centred on a vast stilted thatch & timber structure composed of a main lounge, a small library, & a dining & cocktail area, offering sweeping views across the riverbed to the Maasai Steppes. The large en-suite tents have private balcony, 2 x ¾ beds & 24hr solar power. *US$355/610 sgl/dbl FB, dropping to US$255/410 Mar & May.* $$$$$

Moderate
🏠 **Roika Tarangire Tented Lodge** (21 tents) ☎ 027 250 9994; m 0754 001444/0787 003444; e reservation@tarangireroikatentedlodge.com; www.tarangireroikatentedlodge.com. Situated in a stand of tangled acacia scrub about 5km from the park entrance gate *en route* to Tarangire River Lodge, Roika Tarangire offers accommodation in large en-suite standing tents set on stilted wooden platforms. Shaded by makuti roofs, the tents are very comfortable, with 2 dbl beds each, & decorated simply in safari style, though the rustic mood is undermined somewhat by the tackily sculpted animal-shaped baths. The main building is thatched with open sides & overlooks a large swimming pool. Good value. *US$145pp FB.* $$$$

Camping
⚔ **Wild Palm Campsite** m 0758 438799. Set in Maasai land west of the park but outside any WMA (so no additional fees are levied), this pleasant camp is shaded by indigenous trees (no palms, though) & facilities include a toilet, shower & bar but no restaurant. *US$5pp.* $

⚔ **Zion Campsite** m 0765 870079. This small & very basic private camp is used by many budget camping safaris. To get there, turn off the Arusha–Dodoma road as if heading towards the main entrance gate to Tarangire. The campsite is immediately to the left after about 2km. There's a bar but no restaurant. *US$10pp.* **$**

Lodges east of the national park

The concession lodges and camps below all lie outside the eastern park boundary within the thick bush of the Randileni WMA, which attracts fair volumes of wildlife during the dry season. Access to Tarangire is via the Boundary Hill Gate, which lies about an hour's drive through tsetse-infested bush from all the lodges except nearby Boundary Hill Lodge, which makes them relatively inconvenient for game drives within the national park. On the plus side, because they lie outside the national park, game walks and night drives are permitted and can be very rewarding.

Exclusive

⌂ **Tarangire Treetops Lodge** (20 rooms) \027 254 0630/9; e info@elewana.com; www. elewana.com; ⊕ closed Apr & May. Situated within the TCA to the northeast of the national park, this architecturally innovative lodge consists of 20 spacious & luxurious stilted en-suite treehouses sitting up in the canopy, where they offer great birding opportunities, soundtracked by a lively night chorus led by bushbabies. The treehouses boast a floor area of 65m², as well as canvas sides, a wooden floor & deck, & an open-plan layout. The organic feel is complemented by the uncluttered minimalist décor, & they are so atmospheric & comfortable it almost seems a shame to leave them to go on a game drive! Because the lodge lies on private land, the usual diurnal game drives can be supplemented by other activities such as game walks, birding walks along a nearby watercourse, night drives & mountain-biking excursions. The quality of game viewing in the immediate vicinity varies seasonally. Ideal for honeymooners, this lodge is also a wonderful place to recover from jetlag at the start of a safari, or to stretch your legs at the end of one. A portion of the room rate funds community projects. *US$1,118/1,490 sgl/dbl FB, inc most drinks, laundry & transfer to/from Kuro airstrip. Seasonal discounts available Jan–Mar, Nov & early Dec. Full game package inc game drives an additional US$150pp.* **$$$$$$$**

⌂ **Nimali Tarangire** (6 tents) m 0758 311750; e reservations@nimaliafrica.com; www. nimaliafrica.com. This fabulous new camp is strung along a normally dry riverbed lined with riverine trees & teeming with birds, only a few kilometres east of the national park boundary as the crow

flies. Accommodation is in hybrid tent/cottages with canvas-&-netting sides, slate tile floors, modern bathroom with excellent water pressure & quality fittings, & private stilted balconies spaced widely along the river to ensure privacy. Meals are taken in a raised dining area overlooking a waterhole that's regularly visited by elephants, & amenities include Wi-Fi & a swimming pool. Game drives into the park can be supplemented with night drives on the concession & sundowners on a nearby hill, as well as guided game walks. *US$975/1,300 sgl/dbl FB inc drinks. Low-season discounts available. Add US$100pp for full game package.* **$$$$$$$**

⌂ **EcoScience Lodge** (8 units) m 0629 677877; e lodge@ecoscience.co.tz; www. ecoscience.co.tz. This sumptuous new property, owned by an enthusiastic Dutch volcanologist & his wife, is divided into 2 camps: one a conventional lodge aimed at tourists, the other a science centre offering medium-term stays to scientists & researchers. The central building is a fabulous domed construction – a kind of futuristic version of a local African hut – tastefully decorated in local & imported antique furniture. The circular lodge rooms have a similar aesthetic of minimalist luxury & come with king-sized bed, large dressing room, en-suite showers & private balcony, while standing tents in the science camp are equally comfortable but more conventionally laid out & decorated. The food is excellent & wildlife is seasonally plentiful, but the USP is the opportunity to interact with visiting scientists or explore the science centre dedicated to the volcanology of East Africa. *US$580pp FB lodge room or US$650/870 FB scientist tent. Low-season discounts Apr & May. Email directly for ongoing special rates.* **$$$$$$**

Upmarket

🏠 **Boundary Hill Lodge** (8 rooms)
m 0787 293727; e info@tanzanianhorizons.com;
www.tanzanianhorizons.com. Set on a hilltop a
short way outside the Boundary Hill Gate, this
new lodge is the first in Tanzania to have a local
community shareholding, with the Maasai village
of Lokisale owning 50%. The 8 spacious suites, set
among the rocky cliffs, are individually designed
& lavishly decorated, & have private sitting areas
& wide balconies offering spectacular views over
the Silale & Gosuwa swamps, where elephant
& buffalo are resident. En-suite facilities include
cast-iron baths. In addition to daytime game
drives into the national park, the lodge offers
guided game walks with the local Maasai & night
drives. The concession lies on a migration route
& is particularly busy with wildlife Nov–Mar.
US$350/400 sgl/dbl FB. **$$$$$**

WHAT TO SEE AND DO

Game drives Most people spend only one full day in Tarangire and thus
concentrate on the game-viewing roads along its well-developed northern circuit,
which follows the river between the Tarangire Safari Lodge and Tarangire Sopa
Lodge, and incorporates several small loops down to the riverbank. This is
unambiguously the best game-viewing area, especially in the dry season, when
wildebeest, zebra, buffalo, giraffe, impala, gazelle and warthog congregate along the
river, the only source of water for many kilometres.

Tarangire is justifiably famous for the prolific elephant herds that congregate
along the river during the dry season. In peak times, it is no exaggeration to say
that you might see 500 elephants over the course of a day here. Tarangire's elephants
used to be a lot more skittish than their counterparts in Manyara and Ngorongoro,
but they are generally very relaxed these days.

The full range of large predators is present on the main tourist road circuit too,
but the dense vegetation can make it relatively difficult to pick up the likes of lion
and leopard, even though they are quite common. Two localised antelope that
occur in Tarangire are the fringe-eared oryx and gerenuk, although neither is seen
with great regularity. A good place to look for lion and oryx are the Little Serengeti
plains close to Tarangire Safari Lodge. Of the smaller mammals, the colonial dwarf
mongoose is characteristic of the park, and is often seen on the termite hills where
it breeds.

For those with sufficient time to explore beyond the main tourist circuit, the
Lake Burunge area offers the best chance of seeing bushbuck and lesser kudu, while
the Kitibong Hill area is home to large herds of buffalo, and Lamarkau Swamp
supports hippo and numerous water birds during the wet season. Further south,
cheetahs favour the southern plains, while Mkungero Pools is a good place to look
for buffalo, waterbuck and gerenuk.

Birding Tarangire is a great park for birdwatching, with around 500 species
recorded to date. A good starting point is the grounds of Tarangire Safari Lodge,
where some of the more common acacia birds – hornbills, swallows, starlings,
weavers and the like – are very habituated and approachable. Characteristic acacia
birds are yellow-necked spurfowl, orange-bellied parrot, barefaced go-away bird,
red-fronted barbet and silverbird. A personal favourite is the red-and-yellow
barbet, with its quaintly comical clockwork duet, typically performed on termite
mounds. A wide range of resident raptors includes bateleur, fish eagle and palmnut
vulture, while the river supports saddle-billed and yellow-billed storks and several
other water birds.

Tarangire's location at the western limit of the Somali-Maasai biome means it
harbours several dry-country bird species at the extremity of their range, among

10

them vulturine guineafowl, Donaldson-Smith's nightjar, pink-breasted lark, northern pied babbler and mouse-coloured penduline tit. It is also the easiest place to observe a pair of bird species endemic to the dry heartland of central Tanzania: the lovely yellow-collared lovebird, and the somewhat drabber ashy starling, both of which are common locally.

Balloon trips Hot-air balloon trips over Tarangire are now offered by Adventures Aloft (m *0682 513163*), which is based out of Tarangire Balloon Camp (page 221) and sets off at around 06.30 daily, though pre-dawn transfers can be arranged from most other lodges in the vicinity. The trip costs US$450 per person for a minimum group size of four and maximum of 12. The trip lasts for up to 1 hour, and includes a champagne bush breakfast.

BABATI

Set below the prominent Mount Kwaraha, the bustling and fast-growing market town of Babati straddles the Arusha–Dodoma road some 70km south of Kwa Kuchinja (the junction for the main gate to Tarangire National Park) and 95km north of Kondoa. For those using public transport, the junction town is a useful springboard for climbing Mount Hanang, which overlooks the Singida Road near the small town of Katesh 75km to the west, or continuing southward to the Kondoa Rock Art Sites around Kolo. Further justification for stopping over here is the eponymous Lake Babati, which lies on the town's southern outskirts and hosts large numbers of birds and hippos, and – if you are in the area at the right time – the impressive all-day livestock and general market held about 5km along the Kondoa Road on the 17th and 26th of every month.

GETTING THERE AND AWAY Babati lies 170km south of Arusha on a good surfaced road. It shouldn't take longer than 2½ hours to cover the full distance in a **private vehicle**. **Buses** in either direction leave throughout the day, taking 3–4 hours, and tickets cost around US$5. The best service is Mtei Express Coaches; hourly buses from Arusha to Babati leave from their own station on Makao Mapya Road hourly between 06.00 and 16.00. There are also several buses daily to Katesh in the west, as well as to Kondoa via Kolo in the south.

 WHERE TO STAY *Map, page 227*
Moderate
🏠 **Ango Tree Guesthouse** (8 rooms) m 0756 589659. Set in the east side of the Arusha–Dodoma road 2km north of Babati in a village called Maisaka, this pleasant new guesthouse lies in pretty green gardens & offers a wide variety of smart en-suite rooms, all with twin or dbl bed, fitted net, AC, flatscreen DSTV, tea-/coffee-making facilities & hot shower. The décor leaves a little to be desired, but it is streets ahead of anything else in the vicinity, & a good restaurant serves mains for around US$7 & 4-course menus for US$10. *From US$45/65 dbl/twin.* **$$$**

Budget
🏠 **Winners Hotel** (12 rooms) m 0754 670453; e winnerhotel2012@gmail.com. Situated a block east of the main road close to the bus station, this smart little hotel is evidently aimed at local business travellers. The clean tiled rooms all have nets, DSTV & en-suite hot shower, & the attached restaurant serves a varied menu of meat, fish & chicken dishes, as well as pizzas, sandwiches & salads, in the US$3–5 range. *US$17/22 sgl/dbl.* **$$**

Shoestring
🏠 **Kahembe's Modern Guesthouse** (8 rooms) m 0784 397477; e kahembeculture@yahoo.com; www.kahembeculturalsafaris.com.

This pleasant guesthouse is less than 500m from the bus station, next door to the office of the affiliated Kahembe Trekking (see below). A restaurant serving continental dishes is attached. All rooms use common showers. *US$10/12/15 sgl/dbl/twin inc a good b/fast.* **$**

🏠 **Royal Beach Hotel** m 0758 244491. Boasting an idyllic situation on a small peninsula that juts out into Lake Babati, this is a great spot for an inexpensive lakeshore drink or meal, but the en-suite cottages with net & hot shower are now offputtingly musty & rundown, & the campsite also looks a little insecure. *US$15 dbl chalet, US$7.50pp to camp.* **$**

✖ WHERE TO EAT AND DRINK *Map, opposite*

Aside from the good restaurant at the **Winners Hotel**, the **Ango Restaurant**, on the east side of the main road opposite the bus station, is a decent local eatery, with a pleasant outdoor sitting area and great lunchtime buffets for US$3.50.

TOURIST INFORMATION AND OPERATORS

Kahembe Trekking m 0748 397477; e kahembeculture@yahoo.com; www. kahembeculturalsafaris.com. This commendable Babati institution started life in the mid 1990s as a private ecotourism concern, & has since been formalised into an official cultural tourism project. An excellent point of contact for travellers who want to explore this little-known part of Tanzania in an organised manner, it arranges informative overnight trips which – though not luxurious by any standard – offer an unforgettable glimpse into African traditions without making you pay through the nose. The most popular trips are the 3- & 2-day Mount Hanang climbs out of Babati. Other possibilities range from a 3-day Barabaig walking safari, to 7- & 8-day walking itineraries that visit several local bomas as well as incorporating walks on the game-rich verges of Lake Manyara & Tarangire national parks. Day trips on Lake Babati & to local villages can also be arranged, & special requests & interests can be catered for with

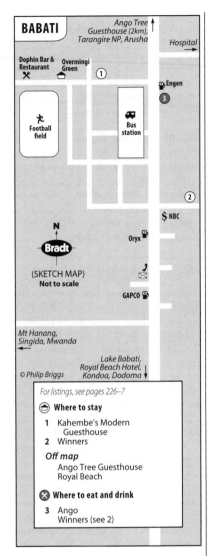

BABATI

Ango Tree Guesthouse (2km), Tarangire NP, Arusha

Hospital

Dophin Bar & Restaurant

Overmingi Green

①

Engen

③

Football field

Bus station

②

$ NBC

N

Oryx

Bradt

(SKETCH MAP)
Not to scale

GAPCO

Mt Hanang, Singida, Mwanda

Lake Babati, Royal Beach Hotel, Kondoa, Dodoma

© Philip Briggs

For listings, see pages 226–7

🛏 **Where to stay**
1 Kahembe's Modern Guesthouse
2 Winners
Off map
Ango Tree Guesthouse
Royal Beach

✖ **Where to eat and drink**
3 Ango
Winners (see 2)

advance notice. Check the website or email for more details.

Babati Guides m 0688 522450; e erineuss@yahoo.com. Informally based at the lakeshore Royal Beach Hotel, this friendly small operator offers 3hr boat trips on Lake Babati for around US$12pp.

WHAT TO SEE AND DO

Lake Babati Measuring almost 10km from north to south, but nowhere more than 2km wide, serpentine Lake Babati lies immediately south of the eponymous town, and is easily reached by walking along the Kondoa road for about 10 minutes.

The papyrus-fringed stretch of shore alongside the road supports a good selection of water birds – egrets, waders and storks – while flotillas of pelican sail pompously across the open water. The lake is also known for its large numbers of hippo, which sometimes venture close to town by night, but are unlikely to be seen by day unless you take a boat out on to the water. Boat trips can be arranged with either of the operators mentioned above, or by chatting to local fishermen in the vicinity of the Royal Beach Hotel (page 227), which is an attractive spot for a lakeside drink.

Mount Kwaraha Rising to a peak of 2,415m about 5km east of Babati, this prominent mountain has a rather volcanic appearance, but is in fact a granite inselberg. Its upper slopes are protected in the Ufoime Forest Reserve and give rise to around two-dozen springs that flow westward into Lake Babati. The mist forest above the 1,800m contour is still home to small numbers of elephant and buffalo, as well as a profusion of birds and monkeys. Inexpensive guided day or (better) overnight hikes, inclusive of the US$10 per person forestry permit, can be arranged through Kahembe Trekking.

MOUNT HANANG

Tanzania's fourth-highest mountain after Kilimanjaro, Meru and Lolmalasin (in the Crater Highlands), volcanic Mount Hanang is a product of the same geological upheavals that sculpted the Great Rift, and it is the only one of these mountains to actually rise from the valley floor. The dormant caldera towers to an elevation of 3,418m above the low-lying plains, and is visible from hundreds of kilometres away on a clear day. Not surprisingly, this imposing free-standing mountain is revered by the Barabaig who inhabit its lower slopes, and it features prominently in their myths. Hanang supports its own distinct microclimate and forms an important local watershed. Most of the rain falls on the northern and eastern slopes, where extensive forests still support elusive populations of bushbuck, duiker and various monkeys, as well as a wide range of forest birds.

Seldom visited by tourists, Hanang lies outside the national park system and forms a very affordable alternative montane hike to Kilimanjaro or Meru. The slopes support the usual range of montane forest and grassland habitats, and offer excellent views over a stretch of the Rift Valley studded with smaller volcanic cones and shallow lakes. The attractions of the Hanang area are not restricted to the mountain. On the contrary, the primal scenery of the surrounding plains is enhanced by the colourful presence of traditional pastoralists such as the Barabaig, people who have consciously retained their traditional way of life. Several substantial lakes also lie in the vicinity of Katesh, including the shallow and highly saline Lake Balangida, which is set at the base of the Rift Valley scarp immediately north of Mount Hanang.

GETTING THERE AND AWAY Most aspirant hikers place themselves in the experienced hands of Kahembe Trekking (page 227), who will take care of all aspects of the climb including transport from Babati. The springboard for independent climbs is Katesh, which lies at the mountain's southern base 75km southwest of Babati. In a **private vehicle**, the drive from Arusha to Katesh will take less than 5 hours, and from Babati about 90 minutes. For those dependent on **public transport**, buses run between Babati and Singida via Katesh throughout the day, taking 2–3 hours in either direction between Babati and Katesh. Several buses travel between Arusha and Singida via Katesh; the thrice-daily service operated by Mtei Express Coaches is recommended.

WHERE TO STAY AND EAT If you need to overnight in Katesh, the **Summit Hotel** (m *0787 242424;* **$**) near the municipal offices charges around US$10 for a good en-suite single/double. The **Pick 'n Pay Guest House** (m *0784 467001;* **$**) opposite the bus station is marginally scruffier and cheaper. **Mama Kabwogi's Hoteli** has long been the pick of a few unexceptional eateries.

WHAT TO SEE AND DO
Climbing Mount Hanang
Several ascent routes exist, but only two are suited to first-time climbers. The marginally easier Jorodom (or Katesh) Route starts at the eponymous village on the southern slopes 2km from Katesh, offering the best choice for those making their own arrangements. The Giting Route starts on the wetter eastern slopes 10km out of town, and is more densely forested, but also more slippery underfoot during the rains.

Hanang can be climbed as a full-day round trip out of Katesh, but this reduces the hike to something of an endurance test, with little opportunity to enjoy the scenery. What's more, while a very fit hiker could complete the full ascent and descent in 12 hours, others may struggle. An overnight climb is therefore recommended. There are several good places to pitch a tent, or you can sleep in the caves on the Giting Route (checking in advance that your guide knows their location). Either way, the upper slopes of Hanang get very chilly at night, so you'll need a good sleeping bag or thick blanket, and enough warm clothes.

The most straightforward option is to arrange a climb with Kahembe Trekking in Babati (page 227). This costs around US$125–150 per person, inclusive of lodging in Katesh either side of the climb, forest reserve fees, food, porters, and an experienced English-speaking guide. You could lower the cost slightly by arranging your own climb, but you would still need to pay for your own accommodation, as well as the forest reserve fee of US$10 per person, the village fee of US$2 per person, guide and porter fees (around US$5–10 per day), and your own food. If you decide to do this, visit the Forestry Office (in Katesh's municipal offices near the Summit Hotel) to sort out fees and find out about a reliable guide (ideally one who speaks English). Porters can also usually be arranged here. No permanent water source exists on the mountain, so bring all the drinking water you'll require. This is an *absolute* daily minimum of four litres per climber, more during the hot, dry season. Bottled mineral water is available in Katesh, but not in Giting or Jorodom.

Climbers intending to use the **Jorodom Route** will need to walk the 2km from Katesh to Jorodom village. From Jorodom, the hike to a good campsite on the lower ridge takes about 6 hours. The upper ridge looks deceptively close at this point, but is in fact at least 4 hours distant. It is thus advisable to camp at the top of the lower ridge, then tackle the final ascent and full descent the next day.

To get to the trailhead for the **Giting Route**, follow the Babati road out of Katesh for 5km to Nangwa, then turn left on to a side road and continue for another 4km to the village of Giting. The Hanang Forestry Department has an office here where you can arrange a guide and porters at the same rate charged in Katesh or Jorodom. There's no accommodation in Giting, but you can camp in the Forestry Department compound.

Mount Hanang road loop
A loop of rough road near Katesh circles around the north side of Mount Hanang, making for an interesting half-day drive for motorised travellers who don't particularly want to climb the mountain. The scenery along this road is lovely, passing through cultivated montane meadows and lower-lying acacia scrub, with the mountain looming to the south and Lake Balangida and the Rift Valley Escarpment about 5km to the north. A diversion to the lake and its

THE BARABAIG

The Barabaig are the most populous of a dozen closely related tribes, collectively known as the Datoga or Tatoga. At around 100,000, the Datoga are one of Tanzania's smaller ethno-linguistic groupings, but their territory, centred on Mount Hanang, extends into large semi-arid tracts within Arusha, Dodoma and Singida.

Superficially similar to, and frequently confused with, their Maasai neighbours by outsiders, the Barabaig are dedicated cattle-herders, speaking a Nilotic tongue, who have steadfastly resisted external pressure to forsake their semi-nomadic pastoralist ways. Unlike the Maasai, however, the Barabaig are representatives of the earliest-known Nilotic migration into East Africa from southwest Ethiopia. Their forebears probably settled in western Kenya during the middle of the first millennium AD, splitting into two groups. One – the Kalenjin – stayed put. The other, the proto-Datoga, migrated south of Lake Natron 500 to 1,000 years ago to the highlands of Ngorongoro and Mbulu, and Rift Valley plains south towards Dodoma.

Datoga territory was greatest before 1600, thereafter being eroded by migrations of various Bantu-speaking peoples into northern and central Tanzania. The most significant incursion came in the early 19th century, with the arrival of the Maasai. Oral traditions indicate that several fierce territorial battles were fought between the two pastoralist groups, resulting in the Maasai taking over the Crater Highlands and Serengeti Plains, and the Datoga retreating to their modern homeland near Mount Hanang. The Lerai Forest in Ngorongoro Crater is said to mark the grave of a Datoga leader who fell in battle in about 1840, and the site is still visited by Datoga elders from the Lake Eyasi area. The Maasai call the Barabaig the 'Mangati' (feared enemies), and the Barabaig territory around Mount Hanang is sometimes referred to as the Mangati Plains.

The Barabaig used to move around the plains according to the feeding and watering requirements of their herds. They tend a variety of livestock, including goats, donkeys and chickens, but their culture and economy revolve around cattle, which are perceived to be a measure of wealth and prestige, and every part and product of the animal, including the dung, is ingested, or worn or used in rituals. In recent years, agriculture has played an increasingly significant support role in the subsistence of the Barabaig, which together with increased population pressures has more or less put paid to the nomadic lifestyle.

Barabaig territory receives an average annual rainfall of less than 500mm, which means that water is often in short supply. Although the area is dotted with numerous lakes, most are brackish and unsuitable to drink from. Barabaig women often walk kilometres every day to collect gourds of drinking water, much of which comes from boreholes dug with foreign aid. The cattle cannot drink from the lakes directly when water levels are low and salinity is high, but the Barabaig get around this by digging wells on the lakes' edges and allowing the water to filter through the soil. Even so, the herders won't let their cattle drink from these wells on successive days for fear that it will make them ill.

Barabaig social structure is not dissimilar to that of the Maasai, although it lacks the rigid division into hierarchical age-sets pivotal to Maasai and other East African pastoralist societies. The Barabaig do not recognise one centralised leader, but are divided into several hereditary clans, each answering to a chosen elder who sits on a tribal council. The central unit of society is the family homestead or *gheida*, dwelt in by one man, his wives and their unwed offspring. This consists of a tall outer protective wall, built of thorny acacia branches and shaped like a figure of eight, with one outer gate entered through a narrow passage. Within this wall stand several small rectangular houses – low, thick-roofed constructions of wooden poles plastered with mud – and the all-important cattle stockade. Different huts are reserved for young men, young women, wives and elders. A number of gheida may be grouped together to create an informal community, and decisions are made communally rather than by a chief.

Patrilineal polygamy is actively encouraged. Elders accumulate four or more wives, up to three of which might share one hut, but marriage within any given clan is regarded to be incestuous. The concept of divorce is not recognised, but a woman may separate from her husband and return to her parents' home under some circumstances. The Barabaig openly regard extramarital sex to be normal, even desirable, although a great many taboos and conventions dictate just who may have intercourse with whom, and where they can perform the act. Traditionally, should a married woman bear a child whose biological father is other than her husband, the child remains the property of the husband – even when husband and wife are separated.

The appearance of the Barabaig is striking. The women wear heavy ochre-dyed goatskin or cowhide dresses, tasselled below the waist, and decorated with colourful yellow and orange beads. They adorn themselves with brass bracelets and neck-coils, tattoo circular patterns around their eyes, and some practise facial scarification. Men are less ornate, with a dyed cotton cloth draped over the shoulders and another around the waist. Traditionally, young men would prove themselves by killing a person (other than a Datoga) or an elephant, lion or buffalo, which might be used as the base of a ceremonial headdress along with the pelts of other animals they had killed.

The Barabaig are monotheists who believe in a universal creator whom they call Aseeta. The sun – to which they give the same name – is the all-seeing eye of Aseeta, who lives far away and has little involvement in their lives. Barabaig legend has it that they are descended from Aseeta's brother Salohog, whose eldest son Gumbandaing was the first true Datoga. Traditionally, most Barabaig elders can trace their lineage back over tens of generations to this founding father, and ancestral worship plays a greater role in their spiritual life than direct worship of God. Oddly, given the arid nature of their homeland, the Barabaig have a reputation as powerful rainmakers. It is said that only 1% of the Barabaig have abandoned their traditional beliefs in favour of exotic religions – a scenario which, judging by the number of internet sites devoted to the state of the Barabaig's souls, has spun quite a few evangelical types into a giddy froth.

The above statistic is indicative of the Barabaig's stubborn adherence to a traditional way of life. In the colonial era, the Barabaig refused to be co-opted into the migrant labour system, on the not unreasonable basis that they could sell one good bullock for more than the typical labourer would earn in a year. Other Tanzanians tend to view the Barabaig as embarrassingly primitive and ignorant – when the Nyerere government outlawed the wearing of traditional togas in favour of Westernised clothing, the Barabaig resolutely ignored them. Even today, few have much formal education or speak a word of English – it would, for that matter, be pretty unusual to meet a Barabaig who could hold a sustained conversation in Swahili.

The Barabaig are enthusiastic beekeepers, and their unique wine Gesuda is made from honey, together with a rare local root that is gathered on the upper slopes of Mount Hanang and said to lend the drink a medicinal property. Gesuda is fermented in huge gourds, the size of a half keg, and it takes a week to reach perfection, during which period entry to the room in which it is being made is restricted to the brewers.

Reserved for special occasions, the drinking of Gesuda is governed by a complex and rigid set of rules and procedures. The wine is traditionally drunk from hollowed cow horns, and since the drinking rules revolve around age and rank, the most important people are served using the biggest horns. The man who supplies the honey for any given batch of Gesuda will monitor the drinking, and you need his invitation – or to be a member of his family – to join a drinking party. A close friend or brother of the host will be designated wine pourer, in charge of keeping the guests' horns filled, and of refusing to refill the horn of any man who is obnoxious or drinking irresponsibly. Any outsider who is offered the drink should regard it to be a great honour.

hinterland offers good birding and the opportunity to seek out some little-known rock paintings, as well as exposure to rustic Barabaig and Iraqw villages.

Leave Katesh along the Babati road, and after 5km you'll reach Nangwa, a small settlement noted locally for its Catholic church with impressive stained-glass windows. A left turn at Nangwa leads you on to the loop road and, after about 4km, the semi-urban sprawl of Giting, also the trailhead for the Hanang ascent route of that name. From Giting, you'll probably need to ask somebody to point you in the right direction for Barjomet, which lies another 5–6km along the loop. The cultivated highlands between Giting and Barjomet buffer the forest zone of Hanang, and once you reach Barjomet, a small crater, clearly visible from the road, hosts a seasonal lake where local villagers bring cattle and sheep to drink. Moving on from Barjomet, the road deteriorates and becomes little more than a rough track as it descends into a hot valley, densely covered in acacia woodland. After about 5km and 10km respectively, it passes through the small traditional villages of Gendabi and Dawar, with fine views of Lake Balangida to the north. About 2km past Dawar, the loop road emerges on the main road between Katesh (to the left) and Basotu (to the right).

A worthwhile **side trip** from this loop, best undertaken in the company of a local guide and about 5km long in either direction, leads from Giting to Gidawira and the shore of Lake Balangida. This shallow body of water, far too saline to drink, is set in the sweltering depression that divides Hanang from the Rift Valley scarp, and it frequently harbours substantial concentrations of flamingos. In recent years, Balangida has often been reduced to a puddle, or has dried up entirely, during the dry season. When this happens, the extensive white flats are exposed, and the local Barabaig can be seen extracting coarse salt by the bucket load. Also of interest are some faded rock paintings, depicting both animals and people, which can be reached by scrambling up a rock face close to Gidawira. This is a hot walk, with no potable water to be found along the way, so do bring some bottled water with you.

Lake Basotu The little-known but very accessible Lake Basotu lies about 40km northwest of Katesh, and is reached via a scenic road that ascends the Rift Valley scarp north of Mount Hanang and Lake Balangida before passing through grassy highlands populated by Barabaig and Bulu pastoralists. Lake Basotu is a lovely, atmospheric spot, fringed by stands of papyrus and tall yellow fever trees, with Hanang towering on the eastern horizon. Large numbers of hippo are resident in the shallows, and troops of vervet monkey commandeer the wooded shore. The birdlife is fabulous, too, particularly on the far eastern shore, where a ghostly forest of waterlogged trunks supports a seasonal breeding colony of reed cormorant, pink-backed pelican and black-headed, grey and squacco heron.

The aforementioned heronry can be explored on foot at the point where the road from Katesh first skirts the eastern shore of the lake. This is also a favourite watering spot for traditionally attired Barabaig, Bulu and Maasai, who march their cattle here from many kilometres away. Directly opposite this stretch of shore, only 50m from the road but invisible until you stand on the wooded rim, is a small green crater lake with waters too saline to support any fish. The cattle herders who congregate here don't see many tourists and, based on our experience, are likely to be more than willing to show you the lake – ask for it by the Barabaig name of Gida Monyot (Salt Lake). Assuming you have a fair grasp of Swahili, you might also want to enquire about the folklore surrounding the lake. It is said that the local Barabaig used to throw their dead into it, because it is so deep, and also that when a woman had sexual intercourse outside of marriage she would undress and wade into the lake up to her shoulders to cleanse herself of wrongdoing.

After reaching the eastern part of Lake Basotu, the road from Katesh continues roughly parallel to the shore for about 3km before reaching the town of Basotu, which sprawls across a pretty peninsula on the southern shore of the lake. Today a sleepy and unexpectedly traditionalist small fishing town, though somewhat more bustling on Monday, the main market day, Basotu was the scene of the decisive battle in the German campaign to coerce the resistant Barabaig into their colony before World War I. The German garrisons at Singida and Mbulu marched into Barabaig territory, converging on Basotu, where after a short battle they hanged 12 leading elders and the most revered of the Barabaig medicine men, leaving the bodies dangling from the scaffold to discourage future resistance.

Whether in a private vehicle or on public transport, it is perfectly feasible to visit Basotu as a self-standing day trip out of Katesh. The drive takes about 60–90 minutes, following the Singida road for a few kilometres out of Katesh and then turning right at the first major intersection. A bus service runs between Katesh and Haidom (about 50km past Basotu) daily except for Sundays. This leaves from Katesh in the early morning, passes through Basotu 2 or 3 hours later, then passes through again in the early to mid afternoon on the return trip, allowing you a good 4 or 5 hours to explore the area. Should you choose to overnight in Basotu, there's at least one guesthouse, and a couple of no-frills restaurants serve fresh fish from the lake.

KONDOA ROCK ART SITES

Inscribed as a UNESCO World Heritage Site in 2006, the prehistoric rock art that adorns the Maasai Escarpment south of Tarangire is the most intriguing outdoor gallery of its sort in East Africa, and among the most ancient and stylistically varied anywhere on the continent. Although it extends over an area of 2,350km^2, the best-known panels are centred around the blink-and-you'll-miss-it village of Kolo, which straddles the Arusha–Dodoma road between Kondoa and Babati.

The rock art around Kolo and Kondoa is the most prolific in equatorial Africa. This is partly due to the lay of the land. Like the equally rich uKhahlamba-Drakensberg region in South Africa, Kondoa is endowed with numerous granite outcrops tailor-made for painting. The major rock art panels here are generally sited within small caves or beneath overhangs aligned to an east–west axis, a propensity that might reflect the preferences of the artists, or might have provided the most favourable conditions for preservation against the elements. The age of the paintings is tentatively placed at between 200 and 4,000 years, but their intent is a matter of speculation (see box, pages 240–1).

The pigments for the paintings were made with leaf extracts (yellow and green), powdered ochre and manganese (red and black) and possibly bird excrement (white), bound together by animal fat. Subjects and styles vary greatly. The most widely depicted animals are giraffe (26%) and eland (14%), which may have held mystical significance to the artists, or might simply have been their favoured prey. A large number of panels also contain human figures, generally highly stylised and often apparently engaged in ritual dances or ceremonies. At some sites, particularly those of the relatively recent and unformed 'late white' style, readily identifiable subjects are vastly outnumbered by abstract or geometric figures, the significance of which can only be guessed at. A common feature of the more elaborate panels is the jumbled superimposition of images, which is now widely thought to be a deliberate ploy to associate two or more significant images with each other.

The proposal to enshrine the Kondoa Rock Art as a UNESCO World Heritage Site stated that 'in terms of conservation, most of the sites are stable and relatively well preserved although there are a variety of problems including salt encrustation, erosion, water damage, and fading caused by sunlight'. Exposure to the elements notwithstanding, the rock art has been left undisturbed by locals in the past because it is regarded as sacred or taboo. In 1931, a government employee, A T Culwick, documented an example of one such taboo, so deeply ingrained that its source had evidently been forgotten. When Culwick needed to climb Ilongero Hill near Singida on official business, the chief of the village at the base warned him off, saying that the hill was inhabited by a demon. Culwick eventually persuaded the reluctant chief and entourage to accompany him on the ascent, where he discovered a large shelter covered with ancient rock art. The fear displayed by the villagers before climbing, combined with their startled reaction to the rock panel, left Culwick in no doubt that they had never suspected the existence of the paintings.

The erosion of traditional beliefs in recent years places the art at greater threat of local interference. Already, a few sites are partially defaced by graffiti or scratching, while other paintings are deteriorating as a result of unofficial guides splashing water on them to bring out the colours, or through repeated exposure to flash photography, which damages sensitive organic pigments. More bizarrely, a local legend that the Germans buried a hoard of gold near one of the rock art sites during World War I has resulted in fortune-seekers manually excavating and dynamiting close to several rock sites. Under such circumstances, UNESCO's inscription of the rock art as a World Heritage Site is welcome indeed, although more formal protection is overdue.

GETTING THERE AND AWAY The first port of call for any visit to the rock art sites is Kolo, a small junction village situated about 25km north of Kondoa and 80km south of Babati. The road in either direction is in poor condition for most of the way, but roadworks were underway at the time of writing (2016) and it should be surfaced in its entirety within a couple of years. For now, you should allow about 4 hours from Arusha, 3 hours from Tarangire National Park, and 2 hours from Babati, but you can probably cut an hour from that once the road is ready.

Although very few people do so, it is perfectly feasible to tag the Kondoa Rock Art Sites on to a standard northern circuit safari. One possibility is to visit as a day

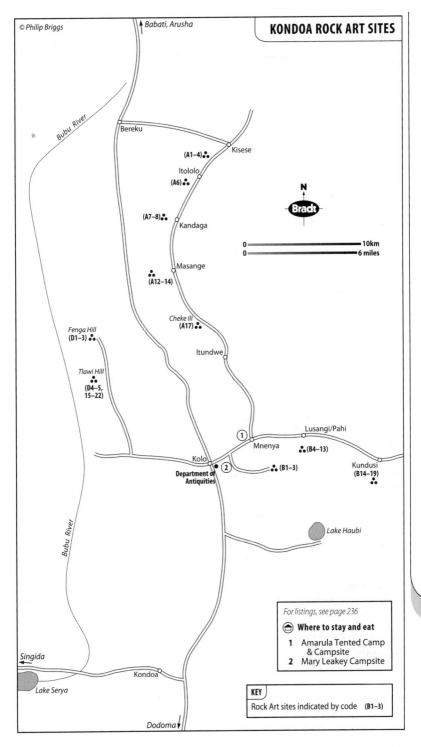

© Philip Briggs

KONDOA ROCK ART SITES

↑ Babati, Arusha

Bubu River

Bereku

(A1–4) • • Kisese

Itololo
(A6) • •

N
Bradt

(A7–8) • • Kandaga

0 ——————— 10km
0 ——————— 6 miles

Masange

• •
(A12–14)

Cheke III
(A17) • •

Fenga Hill
(D1–3) • •

Itundwe

Tlawi Hill
• •
(D4–5,
15–22)

Lusangi/Pahi

①
Mnenya   • • (B4–13)

Kolo ②   • • (B1–3)
**Department of
Antiquities**

Kundusi
(B14–19)
• •

Bubu River

Lake Haubi

Singida →

Kondoa

Lake Serya

Dodoma ↓

For listings, see page 236

⊖ **Where to stay and eat**

1   Amarula Tented Camp
    & Campsite
2   Mary Leakey Campsite

KEY

Rock Art sites indicated by code   (B1–3)

Tarangire and the Central Rift Valley   KONDOA ROCK ART SITES

10

trip out of Tarangire National Park, a slightly pressured but by no means impossible foray, with the advantage to comfort-conscious travellers of allowing them to make use of one of the commodious lodges in and around Tarangire.

Details on reaching the individual sites are provided above, but be aware that while distances between sites are relatively short, roads are very rough (4x4 only) and visiting most sites will entail some walking, often on steep slopes. For this reason, even motorised travellers will find it unrealistic to visit more than one cluster in the space of one morning or afternoon, and a full three days would be required to explore the lot.

For more adventurous or budget-conscious travellers, the best plan would be to **bus** to Kolo (US$1 from Kondoa or US$3 from Babati) and camp there. Once at Kolo, the guides can arrange a boda-boda to take you to the Mungomi wa Kolo complex for around US$8–10. The fare to more remote sites is negotiable.

WHERE TO STAY The closest proper hotels are situated in **Kondoa** town. The pick of these is the Annex Climax Hotel (☏ 026 236 0389; m 0656 085819/0782 734100; $), which stands close to the bus station and charges US$10 for an en-suite room with net, fan and running water. Other older and lesser options include the New Planet Hotel (☏ 026 236 1957; m 0784 669322; $) and the Sunset Beach Hotel (m 0784 948858; $), both of which charge around US$10 for a no-frills en-suite room.

Accommodation options close to **Kolo** are very limited. The attractive Mary Leakey Campsite (*map, page 235; $*), run by the Department of Antiquities in Kolo, stands on the banks of the seasonal Kolo River about 3km east of Kolo town in the direction of Mungomi wa Kolo and Mnenya. It charges US$7 per person to pitch a tent and another US$5 if you need to hire one. A more attractive option, situated about 5km east of Kolo along the Pahi Road, is the Amarula Tented Camp & Campsite (*map, page 235; m 0654 290933; $$*), which charges US$15 per person to pitch a tent, or US$20 per person to sleep in a standing tent. Water and toilet facilities are available at both campsites, but food and other drinks must be brought from Kolo.

There are a few very basic local guesthouses in **Pahi** and **Masange**, both of which lie below the Maasai Escarpment within walking distance of several good rock art sites.

TOURIST INFORMATION AND OPERATORS First port of call in Kolo is the **Department of Antiquities** (m 0785 070442/0769 222113; e kolokondoarockarts@ gmail.com; ⏰ 07.00–18.00 daily) office, where you must pay an entrance fee equivalent to US$13, and collect a mandatory guide, which costs US$15 per party for every complex you visit. The fee also includes entry to the office's small museum, whose displays include photographs and reproductions of some of the main paintings, and shamanic and other ancient artefacts – some up to 7,000 years old – uncovered at the excavated sites.

Kahembe Trekking in Babati (page 227) and **Kondoa Irangi Cultural Tourism Programme** (m 0784 948858; e info@tanzaniaculturaltours.com; www. tanzaniaculturaltours.com) both arrange tours aimed at budget travellers.

MAJOR ROCK ART SITES

Mungomi wa Kolo
Most visitors with limited time are taken to the region's recognised showpiece, a cluster of ten sites scattered across the craggy upper slopes of Ichoi Hill about 10km from Kolo by road. Prosaically labelled B1–3, more evocatively known as Mungomi wa Kolo (The Dancers of Kolo), the three finest panels here provide a good overview of the region's rock art, and – aside from the last, very steep, foot ascent to the actual panels – it is easily reached in a 4x4 vehicle.

To get there from Kolo, you need to follow the Mnenya road west for about 4km, crossing the normally dry Kolo River on the way, before turning right on to a rough 4x4 track that reaches the base of the hill after about 6km.

Probably the most intriguing of the panels is **B2**, which lies in a tall overhang right at the top of the hill. This panel includes more than 150 figures, including several fine, but very faded, paintings of animals (giraffe, leopard, zebra and rhino), as well as some abstract designs and numerous humanoid forms. Richard Leakey regarded this site as representing a particularly wide variety of superimposed styles and periods, and it must surely have been worked over hundreds if not thousands of years. One striking scene, which Mary Leakey dubbed 'The Abduction', depicts five rather ant-like humanoid forms with stick bodies, spindly limbs and distended heads. The two figures on the right have elongated heads, while the two on the left have round heads, as does the central figure, which also appears to have breasts and whose arms are being held by the flanking figures. Leakey interpreted the painting as a depiction of an attempted abduction, with the central female figure being tugged at by two masked people on the right, while friends or family try to hold on to her from the left. Of course, a scene such as this is open to numerous interpretations, and it could as easily depict a ritual dance as an abduction. And why stop there? I recently stumbled across a web page that makes an oddly compelling case for this haunting scene, and other paintings in Kondoa, providing evidence of extraterrestrial visits to Kondoa region in the distant past. If this sort of speculation tickles you, the long-snouted figures to the right, according to this interpretation, are alien abductors, while a separate scene to the right shows another alien standing in a hot-air balloon!

Panel **B1**, also in an overhang, is even larger and more elaborate, though most of the paintings have been partially obliterated by termite activity. Prominent among several animal portraits are those of elephants and various antelope. The most striking scene consists of three reposed humanoid figures with what appear to be wild, frizzy hairstyles (some form of headdress?) and hands clutching a vertical bar. A small cave in front of the panel is used for ceremonial purposes by local rainmakers, and sacrifices are still sometimes left outside the shelter. Finally, near the base of the mountain, the most accessible of the three main panels, **B3**, depicts the animated humanoids that gave rise to the local name, along with a few faded animal figures, including a cheetah and buffalo.

Pahi, Lusangi and Kinyasi Panels B4–13 all lie close to the base of the escarpment near the twin villages of Lusangi and Pahi, about 12km from Kolo. To reach them from Kolo, follow the same road you would to get to Mungomi wa Kolo, but instead of turning right after crossing the river, keep straight on the main road, passing through Mnenya until you reach Lusangi. This site is normally accessible in any vehicle, though a 4x4 may be useful after rain. Lusangi can be reached by dalla-dalla from Kolo, and there is a guesthouse about 1km away in Pahi. A 1km *piste* leads from the main road to the base of the escarpment, from where a flat 100m footpath leads to three shelters about 20m apart.

The art at Lusangi is not as impressive as that at Mungomi wa Kolo, but it is probably a more suitable goal for those unwilling or unable to climb steep footpaths. Several figures do stand out, however, the most notable being a 70cm-high outlined giraffe superimposed on a very old painting of a rhino. Below this, a red and yellow figure of an eland-like antelope with a disproportionately small head is regarded by archaeologists as one of the very oldest paintings known in Kondoa region. Only a couple of clear humanoid figures are found at these sites, and several of the panels are dominated by bold, childlike patterns in the 'late white' style and are often superimposed over older and more finely executed portraits. From Pahi it is possible to drive another 12km to Kinyasi, where sites B14–19 are situated in a valley below the 1,000m-high Kome Mountain. The most interesting of these sites is a 1m² panel of small, finely executed antelope, which also includes one of the few known examples of a painting depicting a homestead.

Mnenya to Kisese Sites A1–18 all lie along the stretch of the Maasai Escarpment that runs immediately east of the reasonable dirt road connecting Mnenya to Kisese. This road itself runs roughly parallel to, and about 10km east of, the Great North Road, and is connected to it by a roughly 8km road between Kolo and Mnenya in the south and about a 15km road between Bereku and Kisese in the north. Ideally, travellers driving southwards from Babati or Arusha along the Great North Road would explore sites A1–18 by turning on to the Kisese road at Bereku, then following the Mnenya road south and returning to the Great North Road at Kolo. Unfortunately, however, it is mandatory to pass through Kolo first to pay fees and collect a guide, which will enforce quite a bit of backtracking for southbound travellers (but makes no real difference to travellers driving north from Kondoa). There isn't much public transport on the Mnenya–Kisese road, but a few dalla-dallas run along it daily, and there is basic accommodation in Masange.

Running northwards from Mnenya, the direction in which regulations practically force you to travel, the first major site is **A17** or Cheke III, which lies about 5km along the Kisese road. This extensive, intricate panel contains at least 330 figures, is rich in superimposition, and is studded with various animals as well as surreal humanoids with circular heads and pincer legs and a couple of unusually robust human figures seemingly draped in robes. The shelter is dominated by the so-called Dance of the Elephant, a red painting of a solitary elephant surrounded by perhaps a dozen people – who might as easily be worshipping or hunting the elephant as dancing around it. Getting to Cheke III involves following a 2km track west of the main road, followed by a short but steep ascent to the actual panel.

About 5km further along the road, you arrive at Masange village, from where a roughly 1km-long side road leads to the base of the escarpment, and another 5–10 minutes' climb brings you to sites **A12–14**. The most compelling panel in this cluster is A13, another elaborately decorated overhang with numerous superimposed paintings, but A14 is of interest for its solitary painting of ten faded human figures in a row. Most of the sites between Masange and Kisese lie some distance from the main road, but site **A9** or Kandaga III, 6km past Masange, consisting of a series of geometric representations in the 'late white' style first described in 1931 by Julian Huxley, is particularly recommended to serious enthusiasts. The excellent and well-preserved site dubbed Kisese II or **A4** lies another 8km past Kandaga on a tall rock no more than 10 minutes' walk from the road.

Bubu River Sites Unlike the other rock art sites within the proposed reserve, this cluster lies to the west of the Great North Road, overlooking the Bubu River about 12km from Kolo. Short of walking there and back from Kolo, this is the one cluster that cannot easily be reached without private transport, ideally a 4x4. It is, nevertheless, perhaps the best cluster of them all, with several panels in close proximity and in a particularly good state of preservation.

Of the three panels D1–3 situated on Fenga Hill, the most worthwhile is **D3**, sometimes referred to as the Trapped Elephants. Covered in a jumble of superimposed red features, including several slim humanoid figures with distended heads and headdresses, this panel is named for the central painting of two elephants surrounded by a stencilled oblong line. Some experts believe that this depicts an elephant trap, a theory supported by three fronds below the elephants that might well represent branches used to camouflage a pit. Others believe that it might have a more mystical purpose, placing the elephants in a kind of magic circle. A trickle of circles dripping from the left base of the picture could be blood, or the elephants' spoor.

About 3km south of Fenga Hill, the immediate vicinity around Twali Hill hosts at least ten panels, numbered D4–5 and D15–22. A dedicated enthusiast could easily devote half a day to this cluster of very different sites. Panel **D19** is notable for an almost life-size and unusually naturalistic attempt to paint a human figure in a crouched or seated position, and it also contains some finely executed paintings of animals, including a buffalo head and a giraffe leaning forward. Directly opposite this panel, site **D20** depicts several seated human figures, while 500m further away site **D22** is also known as the Red Lion for the striking painting of a lion, with a stencilled black outline and red fill, that dominates the shelter.

Five minutes' walk along the same ridge towards the Bubu River brings you to a pair of shelters called **D17** or The Hunter, for a rare action painting of a hunter

BACKGROUND TO THE ROCK ART OF KONDOA DISTRICT

Outside attention was first drawn to the rock art of Kondoa District in the 1920s, although it would be several decades before the full extent of its riches was grasped. In 1923, District Commissioner Bagshawe visited and described the two main shelters at Mungomi wa Kolo, and six years later several of the sites on and around Twali Hill were visited by Dr T Nash. In the early 1930s, the eminent archaeologists Louis and Mary Leakey explored a handful of new sites, notably Cheke III, on which was based Louis Leakey's formative attempt at stylistic categorisation and relative chronology, published in his 1936 book *Stone Age Africa*.

By the late 1940s, enthusiasts and archaeologists had located 75 sites in the Kondoa region, and their discoveries led to the publication in 1950 of a unique special edition of *Tanganyika Notes and Records* dedicated solely to the rock art. The first intensive survey of the region was undertaken in 1951 by Mary Leakey, who boosted the tally of known panels for A sector alone from 17 panels to 186, of which one-third were sufficiently well preserved to be studied. Leakey traced and redrew 1,600 figures and scenes, an undertaking that formed the basis of her 1983 book *Africa's Vanishing Art: The Rock Paintings of Tanzania*. Leakey said of her time in the Kondoa region, 'No amounts of stone and bone could yield the kinds of information that the paintings gave so freely … here were scenes of life, of men and women hunting, dancing, singing and playing music'. Bizarrely, the only major excavations to have taken place since then were undertaken by Ray Inskeep in 1956.

The two works mentioned above are out of print, but Mary Leakey's book is freely available through online vendors such as AbeBooks and Amazon. Also worth the small asking price, however, is the National Museums of Tanzania's Occasional Paper No 5 *The Rock Art of Kondoa and Singida*, written by Fidelis Masao and available at the National Museum in Dar es Salaam. A newer book with detailed coverage of the Kondoa Rock Art placed within a broader African context, is *African Rock Art: Paintings and Engravings on Stone* by David Coulson and Alec Campbell, published by Harry N Abrams in 2000.

10

There is a strangely eerie sensation attached to emerging from a remote and nondescript tract of bush to be confronted by an isolated panel of primitive paintings executed by an artist or artists unknown, hundreds or maybe thousands of years before the time of Christ. Faded as many of the panels are, and lacking the perspective to which modern eyes are accustomed, you can still hardly fail to be impressed by the fine detail of many of the animal portraits, or to wonder at the surrealistic distortion of form that characterises the human figures. And, almost invariably, first exposure to these charismatic works of ancient art prompts three questions: how old are they, who were the artists and what was their intent?

When, who and why? The simple answers are that nobody really knows. The broadest time frame, induced from the absence of any representations of extinct species in the rock galleries of Kondoa, places the paintings at less than 20,000 years old. The absence of a plausible tradition of attribution among the existing inhabitants of the area – a Gogo claim that the paintings were the work of the Portuguese can safely be discounted – makes it unlikely that even the most modern paintings are less than 200 years old. Furthermore, experts have noted a clear progression from the simplest early styles to more complex, expressive works of art, and a subsequent regression to the clumsy graffiti-like finger painting of the 'late white' phase, indicating that the paintings were created over a substantial period of time.

Early attempts at dating the Kondoa Rock Art concentrated on categorising it chronologically based on the sequence of superimposition of different styles on busy panels. The results were inconclusive, even contradictory, probably because the superimposition of images was an integral part of the art, so that a foreground image might be roughly contemporaneous with an image underneath it. It is also difficult to know the extent to which regional style, or even individual style, might be of greater significance than chronological variation. The most useful clue to the age of the paintings is the stratified organic debris deposited alongside red ochre 'pencils' at several sites. Carbon dating of a handful of sites where such deposits have been found suggests that the earliest-surviving paintings might be up to 7,000 years old, but that the artists were most active about 3,000 years ago. The crude 'late white' paintings, on the other hand, are widely agreed to be hundreds rather than thousands of years old, and there is evidence to suggest that some underwent ritual restoration by local people who held them sacred into historical times.

The identity of the artists is another imponderable. In the first half of the 20th century, the rock art of southern Africa was solely attributed to 'Bushmen' hunter-gatherers, a people whose click-based Khoisan tongue is unrelated to Bantu and who are of vastly different ethnic stock from any Bantu-speakers. True, the Bushmen are the only people who practised the craft in historical times, but much of the rock art of southern Africa (like that of eastern Africa) dates back thousands of years. Coincidentally, two of East Africa's few remaining click-tongued hunter-gatherers, the Sandawe and the Hadzabe, both live in close proximity to the main concentration of Tanzanian rock art, but neither has a tradition relating to the paintings.

Given that the archaeological record indicates east-southern Africa was populated entirely by hunter-gatherers when the paintings were probably executed, furthermore that a succession of human migrations has subsequently passed through the region, postulating an ancestral link between the artists of Kondoa and modern hunter-gatherers would be tenuous in the extreme.

If anything, the probable chronology of the rock art points in the opposite direction. Assuming that creative activity peaked some 3,000 years ago, it preceded the single most important known migration into East Africa: the mass invasion of the Bantu-speakers who today comprise the vast majority of Tanzania's population. Most probable, then, that a Bantu- or perhaps Nilotic-speaking group, or another group forced to migrate locally as a ripple effect of the Bantu invasion, moved into the Kondoa region and conquered or assimilated the culture responsible for the rock art, resulting in the gradual stylistic regression noted by archaeologists. All that can be said about the artists with reasonable certainty is that they were hunter-gatherers whose culture, were it not for the painted testament left behind on the granite faces of Kondoa, would have vanished without trace.

The most haunting of the questions surrounding the rock art of Kondoa is the intent of its creators. In determining the answer to this, one obstacle is that nobody knows just how representative the surviving legacy might be. Most extant rock art in Kondoa is located in caves or overhangs, but the small number of faded paintings that survive on more open sites must be a random subset of similarly exposed panels that have been wiped clean by the elements. We have no record, either, of whether the artists dabbled on canvases less durable than rock, but unless one assumes that posterity was a conscious goal, it seems wholly presumptuous to think otherwise. The long and short of it, then, is that the extant galleries might indeed represent a sufficiently complete record to form a reliable basis for any hypothesis, but they might just as easily represent a fraction of a percentage of the art executed at the time. Furthermore, there is no way of telling whether rocks were painted only in specific circumstances – it is conceivable that the rock art would maker greater sense viewed in conjunction with other types of painting that have not survived.

Two broad schools of thought surround the interpretation of Africa's ancient rock art. The first has it that the paintings were essentially recreational, documentary and/or expressive in intent – art for art's sake, if you like – while the second regards them to be mystical works of ritual significance. It is quite possible that the truth of the matter lies between these poles of opinion. A striking feature of the rock art of Kondoa is the almost uniform discrepancy in the styles used to depict human and non-human subjects. Animals are sometimes painted in stencil form, sometimes filled with bold white or red paint, but – allowing for varying degrees of artistic competence – the presentation is always naturalistic. The people, by contrast, are almost invariably heavily stylised in form, with elongated stick-like bodies and disproportionately round heads topped by a forest of unkempt hair. Some such paintings are so downright bizarre that they might be more reasonably described as humanoid than human (a phenomenon that has not gone unnoticed by UFO theorists searching for prehistoric evidence of extraterrestrial visits; see page 237).

The discrepancy between the naturalistic style favoured for animals and highly stylised presentation of humans has attracted numerous theoretical explanations. Most crumble under detailed examination of the evidence, but all incline towards supporting the mystical or ritualistic school of interpretation. Ultimately, however, for every tentative answer we can provide, these enigmatic ancient works pose a dozen more questions. It is an integral part of their charisma that we can speculate to our heart's content, but will never know the whole truth.

To maintain the balance of power between the sexes, the Rangi people of Kondoa have devised an ingenious plan. From sunrise to sunset the men are in charge, but come sunset the rule of power shifts to the women, allowing them to reign supreme until daybreak.

This female empowerment was established following the legend of the cat, told to me by a village member one starry night near Kelema:

The cat was looking for a hero. While walking through the jungle one day he befriended a cheetah. 'This cheetah is surely the strongest and fastest animal in the forest – he will be my hero,' exclaimed the cat.

The next day, while walking with the cat through the undergrowth, the cheetah encountered a lion. They fought until the cheetah fell to the ground dead. 'The lion then must be the strongest and fiercest animal in the forest – he will be my new hero,' decided the cat.

The following day the two felines encountered an elephant foraging in the trees. Startled, the elephant charged, killing the lion. Bemused, the cat approached the elephant: 'You truly are the king of the jungle – will you be my hero?'

One day the elephant and cat were surprised by a man hunting. In fear the man killed the elephant and after cutting the meat from the body he turned for home. The cat decided to follow this beast that could defeat an animal without even touching it.

On arriving home the man approached his wife who took the elephant meat from him and set to work in the kitchen. The cat gasped: 'This woman surely must be the queen of all beasts – an animal that can take from another without fighting! She will forever be my hero.' From that day on, the cat is always to be found in the kitchen admiring its heroine.

---

killing a large antelope – presumably an eland – with his bow and arrow. Several other interesting human figures are found on these twin shelters. Another 10–20 minutes' walk downhill towards the river stand two large rock faces, **D4 and D5**, respectively known as The Rhino and The Prancing Giraffe. The former is named for the 60cm-long portrait of a rhino with a rather narrow head, and it also depicts what appears to be a herd of antelope fleeing from human pursuers. The nominated painting at site D5 is a strikingly lifelike depiction of a giraffe with its front legs raised as if cantering or rearing, but no less interesting is a tall pair of very detailed, shaggy-headed human figures sometimes referred to as The Dancers.

DODOMA

Situated at an elevation of 1,135m on the windswept, drought-prone plains of the central plateau, Dodoma is the principal town of the Gogo people. It was an important stopover on the 19th-century caravan route between the coast and Lake Tanganyika, and it became a regional administration centre after Germany built a railway station there in 1910. As the country's most central town, it was chosen as the designate capital of Tanzania in 1974, a role that was formalised in 1996 when parliament relocated there (though most government offices stayed in Dar es Salaam and are still there today).

The name Dodoma is derived from the Gogo word *idodomya*, which means 'place of sinking'. The most widely accepted explanation for this name is that it was coined by a group of villagers who came down to a stream to collect water, to find an elephant stuck irretrievably in the muddy bank. Another version of events is that a local clan stole some cattle from a neighbouring settlement, slaughtered and ate the stolen beasts, then placed their dismembered tails in a patch of swamp. When a search party arrived, the thieves claimed that the lost animals had sunk in the mud. Whether or not anybody actually believed this unlikely story goes unrecorded!

Since becoming the capital, Dodoma has experienced a high influx of people from surrounding rural areas, but it remains unremittingly small-town in atmosphere and of no specific interest to tourists (unless perhaps there are those who collect capital cities as others collect passport stamps). Dodoma is also the focal point of Tanzania's low-key viniculture industry, founded by an Italian priest in 1957, though the product is as readily available in Arusha and other tourist centres.

GETTING THERE AND AWAY Dodoma lies about 420km south of Arusha via Babati, Kolo and Kondoa. The last 250km of this road is currently unsurfaced and much of it is in poor condition, so allow up to 8 hours in a private vehicle. Buses along this road are notoriously slow and unreliable, but this is likely to change once the road is fully surfaced, which should happen during the lifespan of this edition.

Dodoma lies 450km inland of Dar es Salaam. This road is surfaced in its entirety and shouldn't take longer than 6 hours to cover in a **private vehicle**. It is also serviced by a steady stream of **buses**, which generally leave before midday and take around 7 hours, stopping briefly in Morogoro.

All **trains** on the central railway from Dar es Salaam to Tabora and Kigoma stop at Dodoma, often for several hours.

WHERE TO STAY AND EAT

New Dodoma Hotel (96 rooms) ☎026 232 1641; e info@newdodomahotel.com; www. newdodomahotel.com. The top place to stay, conveniently located opposite the railway station, this stalwart hotel has a gym, swimming pool, health club, internet café, hair salon & 2 good restaurants serving Indian, Chinese & continental dishes, & comfortable en-suite rooms with AC & DSTV. *Starting at US$50/70 standard sgl/dbl.* **$$$**

Christian Council of Tanzania (CCT) Hostel m 0756 090816/0713 475741; e director@cct-centre.org; cct-tz.org. There's no shortage of cheap guesthouses dotted around the town centre, but the pick remains this long-serving hostel, which is only 300m from the railway station. *US$10 s/c sgl/dbl.* **$**

SEND US YOUR SNAPS!

We'd love to follow your adventures using our *Northern Tanzania* guide – why not send us your photos and stories via Twitter (*@BradtGuides*) and Instagram (*@bradtguides*) using the hashtag #northerntanzania. Alternatively, you can upload your photos directly to the gallery on the northern Tanzania destination page via our website (*www.bradtguides.com*).

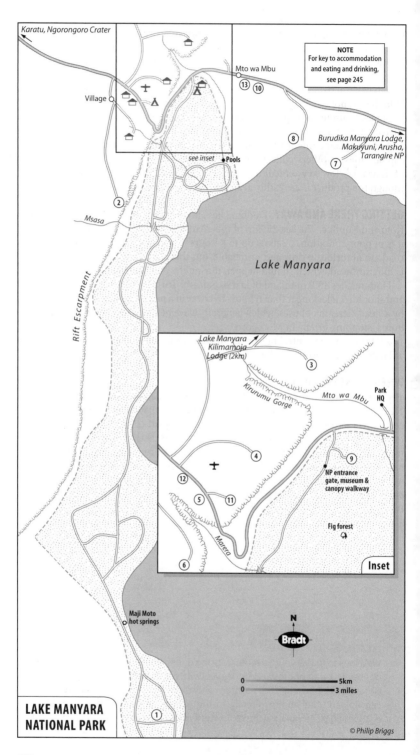

Karatu, Ngorongoro Crater

Mto wa Mbu

⑬ ⑩

NOTE
For key to accommodation
and eating and drinking,
see page 245

Village

⑧

Burudika Manyara Lodge,
Makuyuni, Arusha,
Tarangire NP

⑦

see inset • Pools

②

Msasa

Lake Manyara

Rift Escarpment

Lake Manyara
Kilimamoja
Lodge (2km)

③

Kirurumu Gorge

Mto wa Mbu

Park
HQ

④

⑨

⑫

NP entrance
gate, museum &
canopy walkway

⑤ ⑪

Fig forest

Marera

⑥

Inset

Maji Moto
hot springs

N

Bradt

0 ————— 5km
0 ————— 3 miles

**LAKE MANYARA
NATIONAL PARK**

①

© Philip Briggs

11

Lake Manyara and the Northern Rift Valley

The dramatic stretch of the Rift Valley separating Arusha from the Ngorongoro Highlands supports a chain of shallow mineral-rich lakes of which the largest three – Eyasi, Natron and Manyara – all attain a length of 50km or greater when full. The most accessible and popular of these scenic landmarks is Lake Manyara, which lies only 2 hours' drive from Arusha town (along the same asphalt road that continues to Ngorongoro and the Serengeti), and whose northwestern shores are protected in an ecologically varied national park famed for its dense elephant population, tree-climbing lions and prodigious birdlife. The other two lakes are considerably more remote but still form worthwhile off-the-beaten-track deviations from a standard northern safari itinerary. Lake Eyasi, to the south of Manyara, is of interest primarily for the Hadza hunter-gatherers and Datoga pastoralists who inhabit its dry hinterland. To the north of Manyara, the inhospitable Lake Natron – which nudges up to the border with Kenya along a little-used back route to the northern Serengeti – is renowned as the site of Ol Doinyo Lengai, a majestic (and climbable) active volcano whose Maasai name translates as 'God's Mountain'.

LAKE MANYARA NATIONAL PARK

A popular first port of call on any northern Tanzanian safari, Lake Manyara National Park is named after its dominant geographic feature, a shallow, alkaline lake set at the base of the tall wooded cliffs of the western Rift Valley Escarpment. This scenic sanctuary protects the lake's northwestern shore, along with a diversity of terrestrial habitats that seems truly remarkable considering that water comprised up to two-thirds of the park's surface area of 330km² (prior to the recent incorporation of

LAKE MANYARA NATIONAL PARK
For listings, see pages 247–51

🍽 Where to stay and eat

1 &Beyond Lake Manyara Tree Lodge
2 Escarpment Luxury Lodge
  Kiboko Bush Camp (see 8)
3 Kirurumu Manyara Lodge
4 Lake Manyara Serena Safari Lodge
5 Lake Manyara View Lodge
6 Lake Manyara Wildlife Lodge
7 Manyara Wildlife Safari Camp
  Migunga Campsite (see 8)

8 Migunga Forest Camp
9 National park bandas & campsite
10 Njake Jambo Lodge & Campsite
11 Panorama Safari Camp
12 Sunbird Garden Guesthouse
13 Twiga Campsite & Lodge

Off map
  Burudika Manyara Lodge
  Lake Manyara Kilimamoja Lodge

the largely inaccessible 250km² Marang Forest Reserve). Lake Manyara National Park has long been touted as the best place in Tanzania to see tree-climbing lions, an accolade that now more accurately belongs to the Serengeti, but more reliable highlights include the large habituated baboon troops, often accompanied by blue monkeys, that inhabit the groundwater forest close to the entrance gate, and a hippo pool that also offers some great aquatic birdwatching. Only one (very exclusive) permanent lodge stands within the park boundaries, but several decent upmarket lodges run along the escarpment overlooking the lake, while a selection of cheaper lodgings and campsites is centred on the village of Mto wa Mbu near the entrance gate. Although Manyara and its well-defined game-viewing circuit kick off a high proportion of safaris through northern Tanzania, it gets mixed feedback: some find it rather low-key and boring compared with the Serengeti and Ngorongoro, while others relish the opportunity to see several species that are less common or shyer elsewhere in the region. Certainly, those with strong time or budgetary restrictions might want to consider passing over Manyara in favour of spending more time in other reserves.

FAUNA AND FLORA The accessible terrestrial portion of Lake Manyara National Park is dominated by open grassland on the lake floodplain and denser acacia woodland towards the rocky escarpment that runs along its western boundary. An important feature of the park is the dense groundwater forest, dominated by shady *ficus* trees, that extends for about 5km south of the entrance gate. There is also some impressive forest in the far south, while a 250km² tract of escarpment forest overlooking the lake was annexed to the park as a result of the incorporation of the former Marang Forest Reserve in 2012.

This habitat diversity is reflected in Manyara's varied mammalian fauna. Among the more commonly seen large mammals are buffalo, giraffe, hippo, olive baboon, blue monkey and various antelope, all of which are likely to be sighted in the course of any game drive. Large predators include a dense but skittish leopard population, while the lions of Manyara are renowned for their conspicuous tree-climbing ways (see box, pages 252–3) – and might still be seen in arboreal action from time to time, though these days this behaviour is actually more likely to be seen in parts of the Serengeti.

The elephants of Manyara were immortalised by Iain Douglas-Hamilton, author of *Amongst the Elephants*, in the 1970s, and while the population suffered a slight decline in the 1980s due to poaching, this was not as severe as in many larger parks in southern Tanzania. By the 1990s, the Manyara population had recovered fully, and its elephants were generally well endowed on the tusk front, and very relaxed around vehicles, making for great viewing. Sadly, this situation has changed in recent years following a fresh spate of poaching; indeed, on recent research trips, we were struck by how skittish and bad-tempered Manyara's elephants have become, and how few large tuskers we observed.

Manyara, despite its small size, is a great birding reserve, with around 400 species recorded. As Duncan Butchart, writing in the &Beyond *Ecological Journal*, has noted, 'If a first-time birdwatcher to Africa had the time to visit only a single reserve in Tanzania, then Manyara must surely be it.' It's perfectly feasible for a casual birder to see 100 species here in a day, ranging from a variety of colourful bee-eaters, barbets, kingfishers and rollers to the gigantic ground hornbill and white-backed pelican. Substantial flocks of flamingo are also present when the water level is suitable. In rainy years, the trees around the entrance gate often support large and pungent breeding colonies of the handsome yellow-billed stork and pink-backed pelican between February and June.

A remarkable 51 diurnal raptor species are known from the park, of which 28 are resident or regular. Two unusual species worth looking out for are crowned eagle, which is commonly observed in the forests close to the entrance gate, and African hawk-eagle, which often rests up on rocks and stumps immediately south of the hot springs. Also common is the African fish eagle and superficially similar palmnut vulture, the latter often associated with doum palms. In addition, six species of owl are regularly recorded.

The recent annexation of Marang Forest Reserve has not only expanded Lake Manyara National Park's area by almost 80%, but it also helped secure an ancient elephant migration corridor connecting the lake to the highlands to its west. Marang, though relatively unexplored, hosts a selection of highland forest birds similar to those associated with the Crater Highlands, so in time it will greatly increase the already impressive bird checklist for this small national park.

FEES AND FURTHER INFORMATION Several locally published booklets, providing detailed coverage of the park's flora and fauna, can be bought from street vendors and shops in Arusha and elsewhere on the northern safari circuit. The park entrance fee of US$45 per person per 24 hours plus 18% VAT can be paid by MasterCard, Visa or Tanapa smartcard only. No other cards are accepted, and neither is cash. For more details, see box, page 92.

Lake Manyara National Park now operates to a one-entry rule, which means that visitors who are staying outside the park and want to do a morning and afternoon game drive within the same 24-hour period will need to pay two sets of entrance fees. If you have the choice, we would recommend a morning game drive, as the park tends to be quieter then, and wildlife is more conspicuous.

GETTING THERE AND AWAY The main entrance gate, used by at least 99% of visitors to Lake Manyara, lies at the northern end of the park on the outskirts of the small town of Mto wa Mbu. The 120km drive from Arusha follows the Babati road as far as the junction village of Makuyuni, where you need to turn right for Mto wa Mbu. The road is surfaced in its entirety and the drive usually takes less than 2 hours.

A second and very little-used entrance gate lies in the far south of the park, close to Lake Manyara Tree Lodge. To get there from outside the park, follow the surfaced Babati road south past Makuyuni for 54km, then turn right on to an unsurfaced road that leads to the gate after another 35km or so.

WHERE TO STAY AND EAT *Map, page 244*
The only permanent accommodation set within the park boundaries is &Beyond Lake Manyara Tree Lodge, which functions almost as a private concession in the far south, a long way from the busy northern circuit near Mto wa Mbu. Also situated within the park are a number of special campsites favoured as sites for temporary camps by operators that want to offer clients a true bush experience. Otherwise, national park bandas and campsites aside, all the accommodation servicing Manyara lies outside the park, either on the Rift Valley Escarpment overlooking the lake, or in and around Mto wa Mbu. Listed under Tarangire as they are closer to that park (page 222), the exclusive Chem Chem and Manyara Ranch both lie in the wildlife corridor connecting Tarangire and Lake Manyara national parks and make a feasible base for day trips to Manyara.

Within the park
Exclusive
✳ 🏠 **&Beyond Lake Manyara Tree Lodge** (10 rooms) ➚(South Africa) +27 (0)11

809 4300; e safaris@andbeyond.com; www. andbeyond.com/lake-manyara-tree-lodge; 🕐 closed Apr. Offering the ultimate Manyara

experience, Tree Lodge is a small & very exclusive property operated by &Beyond deep in a mahogany forest about 20mins' drive south of the hot springs at Maji Moto & 45km south of the main entrance gate. Accommodation is in 10 treehouse-like hardwood suites with banana leaf roofs, large en-suite bathrooms with indoor tub & outdoor shower, & private decks offering intimate views into the forest. The surrounding forest supports a wealth of birds & monkeys, & is frequently visited by large tuskers, while bushbabies call throughout the night. Important features of the lodge are the exceptional standard of guiding & the feeling of having this beautiful park pretty much to yourself, as very few day trippers make it this far south & those that do tend to be there around midday rather than during prime game-viewing hours. Night drives, village visits & exclusive lakeshore sundowners are also offered, while facilities include a swimming pool, the usual superb

&Beyond food, & personal butler service. *US$2,680 FB dbl inc all drinks & activities. Substantial discounts in Mar, May, Oct, Nov & early Dec, or for long stays.* **$$$$$$$**

Budget & camping

❋ 🏠 **National park bandas & campsite**
☏ 027 250 3471/4082; e info@tanzaniaparks.com; www.tanzaniaparks.go.tz. Situated in a lovely forest glade immediately outside the national park entrance gate, this is easily the most inherently attractive place to stay in this price category, & comparatively good value, too. Clean self-contained brick bandas have hot water but no net – the latter a serious omission in the swampy vicinity, so bring a good insect spray. Facilities include a kitchen & dining area, & an elevated treehouse looking into the forest canopy. *US$30pp banda accommodation for non-residents, camping US$30pp (both plus 18% VAT).* **$$**

Mto wa Mbu and the Rift Valley floor
The small town of Mto wa Mbu is the funnel through which almost all tourist traffic to Lake Manyara National Park must pass. Pronounced like its one word 'mtowambu', the name literally means 'River of Mosquitoes', and if you do spend the night here, then you'll be in no doubt as to why. Several decent budget lodges are scattered around the one-street town, while the likes of Manyara Wildlife Safari Camp, Burudika Camp and Migunga Forest Camp provide more rustic and upmarket accommodation on the nearby Rift Valley floor.

Upmarket

🏠 **Manyara Wildlife Safari Camp**
(10 tents & 16 cottages) m 0712 332211; e info@wildlifecamp.co.tz; www.wildlifecamp.co.tz. Set in lovely wooded grounds on the northeast lake floodplain 4km from Mto wa Mbu & only 10mins' drive from the park entrance gate, this agreeable new camp offers excellent views across the lake to the escarpment from its thatched dining area & swimming pool. Standing tents are set on stilted wooden platforms below a cool thatch roof & come with rough wooden furniture, including 1 dbl & 1 ¾ bed, & a modern tiled bathroom at the back. The 2-storey cottages have a more solid feel & similar furnishing but lack the view. Nothing special but well located, comfortable & good value. *US$275/350 sgl/dbl FB, low-season discounts available.* **$$$$$**

Moderate

❋ 🏠 **Burudika Manyara Lodge** (6 cottages)
m 0758 394481; e info@burudikalodges.com;

www.burudikalodges.com. Opened in 2015, this unpretentious lakeside property, set in a Wildlife Management Area populated by a fair amount of wildlife & plenty of birds, is undoubtedly the best-value option in the vicinity of Manyara. The spacious makuti-roofed cottages are widely spaced across the property & come with dbl or twin bed with walk-in net, private lake-facing balcony & en-suite hot shower, while the dining area & bar are centred on a spectacular old baobab tree. Activities with a knowledgeable local guide include canoeing on the lake (*US$35pp*), biking (*US$20pp*) and nature walks focusing on birds or trees (*US$25pp*). *US$177/330 sgl/dbl FB, with significant seasonal discounts.* **$$$$–$$$$$**

🏠 **Migunga Forest Camp** (19 tents) ☏ 027 250 6315; m 0754 324193; e reservations@moivaro.com; www.moivaro.com. This well-established but little-known Moivaro camp has a winning location in a yellow-fever forest about 2km by road from Mto wa Mbu, & within walking distance of the lake when water levels are high.

Accommodation is in comfortable dbl standing tents with en-suite hot showers. Though a little frayed at the edges, it's an excellent compromise between price & comfort, with the added bonus of a real bush feel. Reedbuck, bushbuck & buffalo sometimes pass through, vervet monkey & banded mongoose are resident, bushbabies are often heard at night, & 70-odd acacia-associated bird species have been recorded in camp. *US$246/348 sgl/dbl FB late Dec, Jan, Feb, Jul, Aug, dropping to US$201/288 Jun, Sep, Oct & US$156/203 other months.* **$$$$$**

Budget & camping
🏠 **Kiboko Bush Camp** (8 tents) **m** 0757 922884; **e** oscarphabian@gmail.com. Situated a few hundred metres away from Migunga, but with a more nondescript setting, this unpretentious & rather understaffed camp provides adequate accommodation in en-suite standing tents set on a stilted wooden platform with a small private veranda. The best value in this range value. *US$30pp room only or US$60pp FB.* **$$–$$$**
🏠 **Njake Jambo Lodge & Campsite** (16 rooms) ☎027 250 1329; **e** info@njake.com; www. njake.com. Set in the heart of Mto wa Mbu, this quality budget lodge offers accommodation in 4 dbl-storey blocks each containing 4 smart en-suite rooms with 2 4-poster beds with netting, satellite TV, fridge, phone & tiled bathroom with hot shower. The large green gardens also host

a restaurant, bar & large swimming pool area, as well as a shady campsite. It lacks the bush atmosphere of many other lodges around Manyara, & would seem overpriced almost anywhere else, but seems like fair value in context. *US$90/120 sgl/dbl B&B, or US$120/160 FB, camping US$10pp in your own tent or US$20pp in theirs. Rooms* **$$$$**, *camping* **$$**
🏠 **Twiga Campsite & Lodge** (34 rooms) ☎027 253 9101; **m** 0758 510000; **e** twigacampsite@yahoo.com; www. twigalodgecampsite.com. Long-serving Twiga Lodge lies in neatly cropped gardens, centred upon a good restaurant & large clean swimming pool, in the heart of Mto wa Mbu. The spacious campsite is justifiably popular with budget safari operators, but given the characterless setting, the en-suite rooms with hot water & net seem overpriced for what they are. *US$100/120 FB ordinary sgl/dbl, US$130/150 en-suite exec sgl/dbl with DSTV, fan, desk & fridge, camping US$10pp. Rooms* **$$$$**, *camping* **$**
▲ **Migunga Campsite** ☎027 250 6315; **m** 0754 324193; **e** reservations@moivaro. com; www.moivaro.com. Situated alongside the eponymous tented camp & under the same management (page 248), this campsite boasts a stunning setting amid the yellow-fever trees, & facilities include hot showers – highly recommended. *US$8pp.* **$**

Escarpment lodges
The lodges below all stand on the cultivated escarpment overlooking Lake Manyara and most offer fabulous views over the national park or its surrounds.

Exclusive
✳ 🏠 **Escarpment Luxury Lodge** (16 rooms) **m** 0767 804856; **e** info@escarpmentlodge.co.tz; www.escarpmentlodge.co.tz. Probably the most stylish & exclusive of the lodges on the escarpment above Manyara, this has received plenty of praise from operators & safari-goers since it opened in 2011. A swimming pool set in lush bush offers stunning views over the national park, & the funky but organic interiors create a contemporary African feel. The state-of-the-art suites are large & very comfortable, & come with wooden floor, fan, AC, internet access, king-sized bed with walk-in netting, large bathroom with indoor tub & outdoor shower, & private deck with a view. In addition to

game drives in the park, activities on offer include cycling, bird walks & village visits. *US$788/1,050 FB sgl/dbl inc drinks & guide walks, with substantial discounts Mar–May, Nov & early Dec.* **$$$$$$$**

Upmarket
✳ 🏠 **Kirurumu Manyara Lodge** (30 tents) ☎027 250 7011; **e** info@kirirumu.net; www. kirurumu.net. This long-serving & perennially popular tented lodge is perched on the Rift Escarpment to the north of the Serena, from where it offers a grand view across the plains of the Rift Valley to the north of Lake Manyara. The unpretentious rustic atmosphere contrasts strongly with other more built-up lodges on the

11

Rift Escarpment, & it will be far more attractive to people who want a real bush experience. There's plenty of small wildlife around: bush squirrels, foot-long yellow-speckled plated lizards & abundant birds by day, while hedgehogs & bushbabies come past by night. The food is adequate & the service friendly & efficient. Accommodation is in comfortable & secluded en-suite dbl tents, all with a private veranda – higher numbered rooms generally have the best views! *US$263/418 sgl/dbl B&B, or US$293/487 FB in high season, dropping to a fabulously competitive US$116pp FB low season.* **$$$$$**

🏠 **Lake Manyara Kilimamoja Lodge** (49 rooms) e reservations@lakemanyaralodgetz. com; www.lakemanyaralodgetz.com. Opened in Jun 2015, this swanky new lodge perched on the escarpment past Kirurumu boasts massive gardens (guests are transported to their chalet in a golf cart) & an impressive array of facilities includes a spa, gym, cinema & large swimming pool. The thatched chalets are also very impressive, coming as they do with king-sized bed, walk-in net, stone fireplace, old-style bathtub, outdoor & indoor shower & much else besides. At the price, it would be the clear pick in this category were it not for the décor, which veers towards the ostentatious, aiming for an Edwardian safari look – plenty of mock zebra-stripe & leopard-spot fabrics – but rather overshooting the mark. Still, if unabashed luxury is what you're after, this place has it in spades, at very realistic rates. *US$510/680 sgl/ dbl FB, with substantial discounts Mar–May, Nov & early Dec.* **$$$$$**

🏠 **Lake Manyara Serena Safari Lodge** (67 rooms) ☎027 254 5555; e lakemanyara@ serena.co.tz; www.serenahotels.com. This smart & popular upmarket lodge is situated on the edge of the escarpment overlooking the lake & its environs. Like other lodges in the Serena chain, it is a very appealing set-up, run through by a small wooded stream that attracts a wide range of birds including chattering flocks of breeding weavers. Accommodation is in attractively furnished ethnic-looking *rondawels* (round African-style huts) with private balconies. The buffet food is generally very good. *US$410/660 sgl/dbl FB. Substantial discounts Mar–May, Nov & early Dec.* **$$$$$**

🏠 **Lake Manyara Wildlife Lodge** (100 rooms) ☎027 254 4595; e res@hotelsandlodges-tanzania.com; www.hotelsandlodges-tanzania.

com. The oldest & most spectacularly located property lining the escarpment above Lake Manyara, this former government lodge underwent an ambitious facelift a few years back & the redecorated common areas – complete with antique African & Asian statues & furniture – are now in line with other similarly priced lodges on the northern safari circuit. The en-suite rooms are smallish & retain a few old-fashioned touches, but come with tub/shower, private balcony, safe & tea-/coffee-making facilities. The attractively wooded grounds are centred upon a large swimming pool & offer an utterly peerless view over Manyara's groundwater forest & lake, with the Rift Valley hills fading to the horizon. With binoculars, you should be able to pick out elephant, giraffe & buffalo on the Rift Valley floor; closer to home, there is good birding within the lodge grounds. The most consistent complaint is the variable quality of the buffet meals. *A touch overpriced at US$375/500 sgl/dbl FB.* **$$$$$$**

Budget

🏠 **Lake Manyara View Lodge** (26 rooms) m 0712 501392; e info@njake.com; www.njake. com. Set on the escarpment alongside the main asphalt road to Karatu, this unsophisticated lodge offers stunning views over Lake Manyara & the Rift Valley floor, but its enormous potential is totally undermined by the lack of a convincing management presence & general aura of operating with all lights dimmed. Facilities include a clean swimming pool & bleakly cavernous dining area. Having said that, there's nothing wrong much with the rooms, all of which come with dbl bed, walk-in net, writing table, en-suite hot shower & private balcony (some with lake view), & the once lofty rates have been dropped to reflect its second-rate feel, making it decent budget value. *US$73/145 sgl/dbl FB.* **$$$$**

Shoestring & camping

🏠 **Sunbird Garden Guesthouse** (9 rooms) m 0754 754421. Aimed mainly at safari drivers, this agreeable local guesthouse flanking the main road to Karatu just above the escarpment has acceptable en-suite tiled dbl rooms with fitted net, TV & cold shower. A bar & restaurant are attached. *Great value at US$5 dbl.* **$**

🏠 **Panorama Safari Camp** m 0763 075130. Boasting a prime location on the escarpment overlooking the lake, this campsite set only 500m from the main asphalt road towards Karatu forms an attractively located alternative to the more mundane cheapies in town. There's a clean shower & toilet block with running hot water, & other facilities include a bar & restaurant. *US$15pp in a tiny 'igloo' or US$10pp for a large standing tent with bedding & towel provided.* $

OTHER PRACTICALITIES Mto wa Mbu, less than 1km from the main park entrance, is a well-equipped town with a busy market, several supermarkets, and as of early 2016, a CRDB Bank with an ATM outside.

EXPLORING LAKE MANYARA

Game drives For logistical reasons, most safari operators visit the national park in the afternoon, but there's much to be said for doing a morning game drive instead (or in addition), starting as soon as possible after the entrance gate opens at 06.30. Manyara is wonderfully and unexpectedly peaceful at this time, and you'll probably see fewer other vehicles over 2 or 3 hours than you would in 5 minutes in the late afternoon. By being the first car through the gate, you also stand a chance of disturbing one of the park's plentiful but skittish leopards before it vanishes into the thickets for the day.

Unless you are staying overnight in the park, all game drives start at the entrance gate, which lies on the northern boundary near Mto wa Mbu. From here, the main road winds for several kilometres through a cool, lush, mature groundwater forest dominated by large ficus trees and a tangle of green epiphytes. With appropriate jungle noises supplied by outsized silvery-cheeked hornbills, this is one part of the northern safari circuit that might conjure up images of Tarzan swinging into view. It's a good place to see olive baboons (Manyara supports a density of 2,500 baboons in 100km²), which plonk themselves down alongside the road, often in the company of the smaller and more beautiful blue monkey, which is also common in the forest. The shy bushbuck might also be encountered here, but otherwise the main point of faunal interest is the diversity of birds and butterflies.

The road emerges from the forest on to the northern floodplain, where a series of small pools on the Mto wa Mbu River supports a wide variety of birds, notably giant kingfisher and African and painted snipe. This is a lovely spot, too, with the Rift Valley Escarpment rising to the west, and the sparsely vegetated floodplain of Lake Manyara stretching to the south. Giraffes are common in this area, many of them so dark in colour that they appear to be almost melanistic. As of 2014, the nearby hippo pool is overlooked by a stilted viewing platform from where you'll usually see around a dozen soaking, yawning hippos. The final stretch of road to the hippo pool is flanked by a marshy area that offers excellent aquatic birdwatching and good photography opportunities. In addition to larger birds such as yellow-billed stork and pink-backed pelican, the reed beds are a nesting site for a variety of passerines (including yellow bishop, thick-billed weaver and Jackson's golden-backed weaver), while the shallows support waders such as glossy ibis, common snipe, black crake, collared pratincole and various lapwings and sandpipers.

For large mammals, the best road runs inland of the lake to the Maji Moto (literally 'Hot Water') springs in the south. The tangled acacia woodland here – quite dry for most of the year, but spectacularly lush after the rains – offers views across the floodplain, where you should see large herds of zebra and wildebeest, and the occasional warthog, impala, Kirk's dik-dik and giraffe. The acacia woodland is the place to look out for the famous tree-climbing lions of Manyara (see box, pages 252–3), although on an afternoon game drive the safari driver grapevine is bound to ensure that you know about any arboreal lions long before you encounter

11

them. As you head further south, several large seasonal waterfalls tumble over the escarpment, most visibly during the rainy season. The marshy area around the hot springs reliably harbours waterbuck and plenty of buffalo, while several pairs of klipspringer are resident on the rocky escarpment base towards the southern end of the park.

If you arrive in Mto wa Mbu without a vehicle, Wayo Africa (page 141) charges US$200 per group for a full-day game drive, inclusive of vehicle, driver-guide, fuel and the driver and vehicle entrance fee, but exclusive of personal park entrance fees.

Cultural tours The small town of Mto wa Mbu, which lies outside the main northern entrance gate to Lake Manyara National Park, is said locally to be the only place in the country where representatives of all 120 Tanzanian tribes are resident. It is also the starting point for a clutch of inexpensive walking tours established as part of a cultural tourism programme with the assistance of SNV (Stichting Nederlandse Vrijwilligers [Foundation of Netherlands Volunteers]). One of the most interesting of these walks is the papyrus lake tour, which takes you to the Miwaleni Waterfall,

THE TREE-CLIMBING LIONS OF MANYARA

Lake Manyara National Park is famous for its tree-climbing lions, which habitually rest up in the branches for most of the day, to the excitement of those lucky tourists who chance upon them. But while the tree-climbing phenomenon is well documented, the explanation behind it remains largely a matter of conjecture.

In the 1960s, Stephen Makacha undertook research into lion behaviour at Manyara to compare with similar studies being conducted by George Schaller in the Serengeti. In Schaller's book, *The Serengeti Lion: A Study of Predator–Prey Relations*, he noted that:

The lions in the Lake Manyara National Park climbed trees far more often than those in the Serengeti. They were resting in trees on two-thirds of the occasions on which we encountered them during the day. The reason why Manyara lions rest in trees so often is unknown. Fosbrooke noted that lions in the Ngorongoro Crater ascended trees during an epidemic of biting flies, but this is an unusual situation ... and the vegetation in the various parks is in many respects so similar that no correlation between it and tree climbing is evident. The Manyara lions sometimes escaped from buffalo and elephant by climbing trees, but there would seem to be no reason for lions to remain in them all day because of the remote chance that they might have to climb one. I think that the behaviour represents a habit, one that may have been initiated by for example, a prolonged fly epidemic, and has since been transmitted culturally.

Schaller's suggestion that the lions were climbing trees to avoid flies made the most sense to me, but I had also heard that the lions climbed to enjoy the cool breezes that came off the lake, and to keep a lookout for prey and threats. So I decided to make notes whenever I saw the lions in order to explore these theories. For every sighting, I noted whether flies were present on the ground or in the trees; the temperature and breeze conditions; whether buffalo or elephant were in the vicinity; how high up the tree the lions were and the view it afforded; and the species of tree.

In the 1960s, Iain Douglas-Hamilton noted that on 80% of the occasions when tree-climbing lions were observed, they were in one of just 17 individual trees. These favoured trees were so well known to park guides at the time that they were given particular names and – to protect them from debarking and destruction by elephants – wrapped in coils of wire mesh. My observations indicated a similar pattern. Lions were found to be resting in trees as well as to a papyrus lake where Rangi people collect basket- and mat-weaving material, and to the homesteads of Sandawe hunter-gatherers. Other tours take you to Balaa Hill, which boasts excellent views over the village and lake, and to Chagga farms and Maasai bomas.

The tourism programme is run out of the Red Banana Café in the centre of Mto wa Mbu. This is where you must pay your fees, arrange a guide and (if you like) rent a bicycle, as well as pay the mandatory village development fee. For more details, visit the website mtoculturalprogramme.tripod.com or contact the guides (✆ *027 253 9303*; m *0748 606654*; e *mtoculturalprogramme@hotmail.com*).

Less formally, at least half-a-dozen Maasai *manyattas* (settlements) signposted along the road between Makuyuni and Mto wa Mbu welcome tourist visits. The going rate is US$20–30 per vehicle irrespective of the group size.

Other activities An exciting aspect of Lake Manyara is a varied selection of mild adventure activities operated exclusively by Wayo Africa. The most popular is **mountain biking** down the Rift Valley Escarpment, with a variety of different

on about half of the times they were sighted, and although six different tree species were used, three – *Acacia tortilis*, *Kigelia africana* and *Balanites aegyptiaca* – accounted for 90% of sightings. Specific trees were usually favoured, and the lions often moved a considerable distance to reach them.

In most cases the lions were seen to be resting during the heat of the day, and they would usually come down at dusk. Only 5% of sightings coincided with hot weather and breezy conditions, and at most sightings there was no significant breeze, so it seems unlikely that the lions climb to escape the heat. Although buffalo have been documented killing lions at Manyara, there was never any sign of the lions taking to trees to avoid harassment. Most of the time the lions were found to be resting approximately 5–6m above the ground, which afforded them a better view of their surroundings, but since the trees were normally in densely vegetated areas, it would have been difficult for them to observe any potential prey or threat.

My conclusions were similar to those of Makacha and Schaller. Although lions that I found resting on the ground were apparently not greatly concerned by biting flies, lions observed in trees were surrounded by flies in only 10% of cases, when flies were present on the ground below them about 60% of the time. Because the lions generally rested above 5m and flies were seldom encountered at this height, it seems likely that the behaviour was originally initiated during a fly epidemic, and it has since been passed on culturally. I observed the cubs of the Maji pride begin their attempts to climb up to the adults when they were about seven or eight months old. It seemed definitely to be a case of 'lion see, lion do', as there was no apparent reason as to why they should have climbed. Once they had mastered climbing, they too spent a lot of time playing and climbing up and down the trees. More thorough research would be required to fully understand the reasons for this unusual and fascinating behaviour.

Edited from *Notes on Tree-climbing Lions of Manyara* by Kevin Pretorius, a former manager of Lake Manyara Tree Lodge, as originally published in the &Beyond Ecological Journal, volume 2:79–81 (2000). Interestingly, since it was written, tree climbing has become less frequent among the lions of Manyara, and more frequent in the Serengeti, particularly during the rains, evidently confirming the behaviour is essentially cultural and habitual.

itineraries available. Also offered is an **afternoon walk** through the groundwater forest in the Kirurumu Gorge outside the national park entrance, and a **village walk** with a local guide through agricultural areas around Mto wa Mbu with a local lunch on a banana plantation. Most of these activities cost US$40 per person. No experience is required, and all equipment is supplied.

Wayo Africa is the only company to offer **night drives** in Lake Manyara National Park. These cost US$55–77 per person, depending on group size, though this excludes the national park entrance fee of US$45 per person and the night drive fee of US$50 per person (both plus 18% VAT).

THE LAST HUNTER-GATHERERS

The Hadza (or Hadzabe) of the Lake Eyasi hinterland, which lies to the east of Karatu, represent a unique – and increasingly fragile – link between modern East Africa and the most ancient of the region's human lifestyles and languages. Numbering at most 1,000 individuals, the Hadza are Tanzania's only remaining tribe of true hunter-gatherers, and their Hadzame language is one of only two in the country to be classified in the Khoisan family, a group of click-based tongues that also includes the San (Bushmen) of southern Africa.

The Hadza live in nomadic family bands, typically numbering about 20 adults and a coterie of children. Their rudimentary encampments of light grass shelters are erected in the space of a couple of hours, and might be used as a base for anything from ten days to one month before the inhabitants move on. These movements, though often rather whimsical, might be influenced by changes in the weather or local game distribution, and a band will also often relocate close to a fresh kill that is sufficiently large to sustain them for several days. The Hadza are fairly indiscriminate about what meat they eat – anything from mice to giraffe are fair game, and we once saw a family roasting a feral cat, fur and all, on their campfire – but baboons are regarded to be the ultimate delicacy and reptiles are generally avoided. Hunting with poisoned arrows and honey gathering are generally male activities, while women and children collect roots, seeds, tubers and fruit – vegetarian fodder actually accounts for about 80% of the food intake.

The Hadza have a reputation for living for the present and they care little for conserving food resources, probably because their lifestyle inherently places very little stress on the environment. This philosophy is epitomised in a popular game of chance, which Hadza men will often play – and gamble valuable possessions on – to while away a quiet afternoon. A large master disc is made from baobab bark, and each participant makes a smaller personal disc, with all discs possessing distinct rough and smooth faces. The discs are stacked and thrown in the air, an action that is repeated until only one of the small discs lands with the same face up as the large disc, deciding the winner.

Many Hadza people still dress in the traditional attire of animal skins – women favour impala hide, men the furry coat of a small predator or baboon – which are often decorated with shells and beads. Hadza social groupings are neither permanent nor strongly hierarchical: individuals and couples are free to move between bands, and there is no concept of territorial possession. In order to be eligible for marriage, a Hadza man must kill five baboons to prove his worth. Once married, a couple might stay together for several decades or a lifetime, but there is no taboo against separation and either partner can terminate the union at any time by physically abandoning the other partner.

Also recently opened by Wayo Africa is Tanzania's first **canopy walkway**. Situated close to the main gate, this 500m walkway crosses a series of nine suspended bridges with thick netting on the sides to reach an 18m-high viewing deck offering a monkey's-eye view into the canopy. The walk takes about an hour and costs US$35 per person, though an additional fee of US$15 plus 18% VAT is levied by Tanapa.

An upcoming addition to Wayo Africa's Manyara menu is **overnight hiking expeditions** into the little-known Marang Forest, which lies on the escarpment above the lake and was recently incorporated into the national park. Expect to pay US$350–400 per person per day including all park fees.

The Hadza might reasonably be regarded as a sociological and anthropological equivalent of a living fossil, since they are one of the very few remaining adherents to the hunter-gatherer lifestyle that sustained the entire human population of the planet for 98% of its history. In both the colonial and post-independence eras, the Hadza have resolutely refused to allow the government to coerce them into following a more settled agricultural or pastoral way of life. The last concerted attempt to modernise Hadza society took place in the 1960s, under the Nyerere government, when a settlement of brick houses with piped water, schools and a clinic was constructed for them alongside an agricultural scheme. Within ten years, the model settlement had been all but abandoned as the Hadza returned to their preferred lifestyle of hunting and gathering. The government, admirably, has since tacitly accepted the right of the Hadza to lead the life of their choice; a large tract of communal land fringing Lake Eyasi has been set aside for their use and they remain the only people in Tanzania automatically exempt from taxes!

Classified as part of the Khoisan language group on account of its click-based sounds, the Hadza tongue has no close modern affiliates, but is thought to be an isolated relic of a linguistic family that possibly dominated eastern and southern Africa until perhaps 3,000 years ago. As Bantu-speaking agriculturists and pastoralists swept into the region from the northwest, however, the Khoisan-speaking hunter-gatherer communities were killed or assimilated into Bantu-speaking communities or forced to retreat into arid and montane territories ill-suited to herding and cultivation. This slow but steady marginalising process has continued into historical times: it has been estimated that of around 100 documented Khoisan languages only 30 are still in use today, and that the total Khoisan-speaking population of Africa now stands at fewer than 200,000.

That most Khoisan languages, if not already extinct, are headed that way, takes on an added poignancy if, as a minority of linguists suggested throughout the 20th century, the unique click sounds are a preserved element of the very earliest human language. In order to investigate this possibility, the anthropological geneticists Alec Knight and Joanna Mountain analysed the chromosome content of samples taken from the geographically diverse San and Hadza, and concluded that they 'are as genetically distant from one another as two populations could be'. Discounting the somewhat improbable scenario that the clicking noises of the Hadza and San languages arose independently, this wide genetic gulf would imply a very ancient common linguistic root indeed. Several linguists dispute Knight and Mountain's conclusion, but if it is correct, then Hadzame, along with Africa's other dying Khoisan languages, might represent one last fading echo of the first human voices to have carried across the African savannah.

11

Advance bookings for these activities can be made through any safari operator or by contacting **Wayo Africa** (m *0784 203000/0783 141119*; e *info@wayoafrica.com; www.wayoafrica.com*). Alternatively, just pop into their well-signposted Mto wa Mbu office (🕐 *08.30–17.30 daily*), which stands on the south side of the main road a couple of doors up from Njake Jambo Lodge & Campsite.

LAKE EYASI AND THE YAEDA VALLEY

Connected to the outside world by just one rough road running southwest from the small town of Karatu, Lake Eyasi verges on the remote southern border of the Ngorongoro Conservation Area, and lies at the base of the 800m Eyasi Escarpment, part of the western Rift Valley wall. In years of plentiful rain, this shallow soda lake can extend for 80km from north to south, but in drier periods it sometimes dries out altogether to form an expansive white crust. Most of the time, it falls somewhere between the two extremes: an eerily bleak and windswept body of water surrounded by a muddy white soda crust and tangled dry acacia scrub. In the middle of the day, it can have a rather desolate appearance but it is very beautiful in the softer light of early morning and late afternoon, especially when the sun sets dramatically behind the tall escarpment that hems it in.

Also known as the Yaeda Valley (after the eponymous river), the Eyasi area was very sparsely inhabited in prehistoric times, since it was unsuited to cultivation, and tsetse flies made it unattractive to livestock farmers. Back then, the region's only semi-permanent inhabitants were the Hadza, hunter-gatherers who still inhabit the area today, and practise a largely traditional lifestyle (see box, pages 254–5), despite several more recent human influxes, most significantly the Datoga, a pastoralist people with many cultural affinities to the Maasai (see box, pages 274–5). In addition, thanks to an irrigation scheme dating to the colonial era, the Yaeda Valley is now the most important onion-growing area in East Africa, and the main supplier to both Nairobi and Arusha. Eyasi is also an important source of fish for Arusha. Indeed, during the wet season, when the water is highest, the shores often hold temporary encampments populated by fishermen from all over northern Tanzania.

Lake Eyasi supports large seasonal concentrations of water birds, including hundreds of thousands of flamingos at some times of year. Otherwise, little wildlife is resident, and most of what is around – a list that includes lesser kudu, Kirk's dik-dik and olive baboon – tends to be rather shy. Overall, Lake Eyasi is less of interest for its wildlife than the opportunities for cultural interaction. Guided visits to Datoga homesteads and Hadza encampments are easily arranged through the tourist office in Mang'ola (also known as Ghorofani), an overgrown village that qualifies as the most important settlement in the area, and it is also possible to go hunting with the Hadza or visit an onion farm.

GETTING THERE AND AWAY The gateway town to the Yaeda Valley is Karatu, which lies in the Ngorongoro Highlands along the surfaced road connecting Lake Manyara National Park to the Ngorongoro Conservation Area (page 267). Mang'ola lies about an hour's drive on dirt from Karatu, and can be reached by following the Ngorongoro road out of town for about 5km, then taking a left turn towards the lake. Once at Mang'ola, it's easy enough to locate the guides and arrange a visit to a Hadza encampment. Most visitors stay in the area overnight, but it could be visited as a full- or half-day trip out of Karatu. The recent growth in the onion farming industry means that Mang'ola is now reasonably accessible by **public transport**:

a few 4x4s run back and forth to Karatu daily (*US$2.50; 1½hrs*) and there are also two daily buses from Arusha (*US$5; 5hrs*), leaving at around 05.00.

WHERE TO STAY AND EAT
Upmarket

🏠 **Kisima Ngeda** (7 tents) 📞 027 254 8840; e anasasafaris@gmail.com; www.anasasafari. com. Recently incorporated into the Anasa chain, this remote tented camp is set in a shady grove of doum palms near the eastern shore of Lake Eyasi, with magnificent views across to the kilometre-tall western Rift Valley Escarpment, the Ngorongoro Highlands & the Oldeani Mountains. It makes an excellent base for visiting a Hadza encampment or exploring the arid lake hinterland. The accommodation is comfortable but simple rather than luxurious, & the structures around the en-suite tents are made entirely from organic local materials. The excellent food includes fresh tilapia from the lake. *US$389/540 sgl/dbl FB.* **$$$$$$**

that serves adequate meals & a limited selection of alcoholic & other drinks. Nothing fancy, but it's good value & the staff can arrange Hadza hunts & other activities around Mang'ola. *US$246/348 sgl/dbl FB late Dec, Jan, Feb, Jul, Aug, dropping to US$201/288 Jun, Sep, Oct & US$156/203 other months.* **$$$$$**

🏠 **Lake Eyasi Safari Lodge** (14 rooms) 📞 027 253 4083; m 0683 707770; e reservations@ lakeeyasi.com; www.lakeeyasi.com. This new lodge, set on an acacia-studded slope offering a fabulous view over the lake, features the only swimming pool in the Eyasi area & offers accommodation in stone cottages with twin or dbl bed, fitted nets, private balcony & en-suite hot shower. *US$185/325 sgl/dbl FB.* **$$$$$**

Moderate

🏠 **Tindiga Tented Camp** (10 tents) 📞 027 250 6315; m 0754 324193; e reservations@moivaro. com; www.moivaro.com. Set on a bushy slope about 10mins' drive from Mang'ola & the tourist office, this comfortable & welcoming camp consists of large no-frills standing tents with twin beds, nets, en-suite hot shower, & a dining room bar

Camping

🏕 **Lake Eyasi Bush Camp** m 0753 178241/0756 712801; e eyasibushcamp@yahoo. com. Situated a few hundred metres from Tindiga, this spacious & little-used campsite has a pleasant location in a glade of acacias, & facilities include a small ablution block with old showers & a cooking area. *US$15pp.* **$$**

TOURIST INFORMATION The centre of tourist activity is the **Lake Eyasi Cultural Tourism Programme** (*LECTP*; m *0753 808601/0764 295280;* e *eyasiculturaltourismprogramme@yahoo.com; www.tanzaniaculturaltourism.com/ dumbe.htm*), which was founded in 2011 to regulate tourism in the area. It operates a tourist office at the road barrier where you enter Mang'ola coming from Karatu. You'll need to stop here to pay the mandatory entrance fee of US$20 per vehicle, and it is also where all activities and guides must be arranged.

WHAT TO SEE AND DO All cultural activities in the area must be arranged through the tourist office operated by the Lake Eyasi Cultural Tourism Programme. This offers a number of guided activities, including Hadza hunts and visits, Datoga village excursions, and visits to a Datoga blacksmith (who makes copper and tin jewellery from recycled car parts, broken padlocks and other junk). All activities cost US$20 for a party of up to ten, plus a guide fee of US$30 per party covering all activities undertaken.

The definite must-do here is a visit to a Hadza encampment. The people struck us as being very warm and unaffected, and going on an actual hunt is a primal and exciting experience – though do be warned that a temporary conversion to vegetarianism might be in order should you come back with a baboon or another large mammal and be offered the greatest delicacy, which is the raw liver. It might be expected that regular exposure to tourists could erode the traditional lifestyle of certain Hadza bands, but we have seen no sign of this over repeated visits, perhaps because the Hadza have chosen their nomadic lifestyle despite the attempts by successive governments to settle them.

NORTH OF MANYARA

The vast majority of Serengeti safaris head directly west from Manyara along the asphalt road that climbs the Rift Valley Escarpment into the Ngorongoro Highlands, and then return to Arusha exactly the same way. An offbeat alternative to this well-trodden route, one that will transform your safari itinerary into a genuine loop, is the spine-jarring 250km road that connects Mto wa Mbu to the northern Serengeti via the parched stretch of the Rift Valley abutting the border with Kenya. This is not, it should be stressed, a route that should instil any great enthusiasm in anybody who nurses a dodgy back or chronic agoraphobia, or who has limited tolerance for simple travel conditions. But equally this half-forgotten corner of northern Tanzania also possesses some genuinely alluring off-the-beaten-track landmarks in the form of the ruined city of Engaruka, the brooding Lake Natron, and above all perhaps the fiery volcanic majesty of Ol Doinyo Lengai.

Technically, it is possible to travel between Mto wa Mbu and the northern Serengeti via Natron in one (very long) day, but this would rather defeat the point of the exercise. More realistic is to split the drive over two days, stopping for a night at the lakeshore village of Engaresero, or two nights if you intend to climb Ol Doinyo Lengai or undertake any other exploration of the region. It is common practice to tag this area on to the end of a safari, but there is a strong case for slotting it in between the Tarangire/Manyara and Ngorongoro/Serengeti legs of your itinerary, if for no other reason than it will break up the vehicle-bound regime of game drives with a decent leg-stretch – whether you opt for a gentle stroll around the Engaruka ruins or the southern shore of Natron, the slightly more demanding hike to the Engaresero Waterfall in the escarpment west of Natron, or the decidedly challenging nocturnal ascent of Ol Doinyo Lengai.

ENGARUKA RUINS Situated below the Rift Valley Escarpment about 65km north of Manyara, Engaruka is the Maasai name for the extensive ruins of a mysterious terraced city and irrigation system constructed at least 500 years ago by a late Iron Age culture in the eastern foothills of Mount Empakaai. Nobody knows for sure who built the city: some say it was the Mbulu, who inhabited the area immediately before the Maasai arrived there; others that it was built by Datoga settlers from the north. Locally, the city is said to have been home to forebears of the Sukuma, whose greeting 'Mwanga lukwa' was later bastardised to Engaruka by the Maasai – more likely, however, is that the name of this well-watered spot has roots in the Maasai word 'ngare' (water).

The discovery of the ruins by outsiders is generally credited to Dr Fischer, who followed the base of the Rift Valley through Maasailand in 1883, and wrote how: 'peculiar masses of stone became suddenly apparent, rising from the plain to heights up to ten feet. Partly they looked like mouldering tree trunks, partly like the tumbled down walls of ancient castles.' An older reference to Engaruka can be found on the so-called Slug Map drawn up by the missionaries Krapf and Erhardt in 1855. The first person to excavate the site was Hans Reck in the early 20th century, followed by the legendary Louis Leakey, who reckoned it consisted of seven large villages containing roughly 1,000 homes apiece and thought the total population must have exceeded 30,000.

The ruined villages overlook a complex stone-block irrigation system that extends over some 25km² and is fed by the perennial Engaruka River. This highly specialised and integrated agricultural community was abandoned in the 18th century, probably due to a combination of changes in the local hydrology and the immigration of more militaristic pastoralist tribes from the north. Yet Engaruka is unique only in scale, since a number of smaller deserted sites in the vicinity form part of the same cultural and agricultural complex, and radiocarbon dating suggests it might be older than has been assumed in the past – possibly as old as the 4th century AD, which would make it a likely precursor to the great centralised empires that thrived in pre-colonial Uganda and Rwanda.

Guided tours of the ruins can be arranged easily through the **Engaruka Cultural Tourism Office** (m *0787 228653/0754 507939;* e *engaruka@yahoo.com; www. tanzaniaculturaltourism.com/engaruka.htm*), which is based at Engaruka Ruins Campsite (see below). An entrance fee equivalent to around US$5 is payable here, while your guides will expect to be paid around US$5–10 per party. Without a local guide, it's debatable whether the ruins would convey anything much to the average tourist. However, the floor plan of the main village is still quite clear, and a few of the circular stone houses remain more or less intact to around waist level, their floors strewn with shards of broken earthenware. Substantial sections of the irrigation canal are still in place, as are some old burial mounds that might or might not be related to the war with the Maasai that caused the village to be abandoned.

Getting there and away The feeder road to the ruins runs westward from Engaruka Chini, a junction village situated on the dirt road between Mto wa Mbu and Engaresero. The junction lies about 50km from Mto wa Mbu along a good stretch of dirt road that can be covered in under an hour, and 40km from Engaresero along a much more erratic road that takes more like 1½ hours. From Engaruka Chini, the feeder road continues through a semi-urban sprawl for about 5km before reaching Engaruka Juu, site of the Jerusalem Campsite, from where it is a 10-minute walk to the nearest ruined village.

Using **public transport**, at least one bus connects Arusha to Engaruka via Mto wa Mbu daily, charging around US$5 for a journey in either direction. It leaves Engaruka Chini from the station next to the Engaruka Ruins Campsite at 06.00, passes through Mto wa Mbu about 2 hours later, and usually arrives in Arusha by noon before turning around again to make the return trip. However, it tends to be very slow and crowded, so there is much to be said for bussing directly to Mto wa Mbu and then picking up local transport, which is most prolific on Monday and Wednesday, respectively the main market days in Engaruka Juu and Engaruka Chini.

Where to stay and eat In addition to the campsites below, a very basic and seemingly anonymous **guesthouse** with four rooms stands 20m from the Engaruka toll gate in Engaruka Chini. Rooms cost US$2.50.

⚊ Engaruka Ruins Campsite m 0676 511219; e engaruka@yahoo.com. Set in compact green grounds next to the bus station, this friendly campsite has the best facilities in town, including hot running water, electricity, flush toilets, simple standing tents (at no extra charge), a bar & a restaurant. It also houses the Engaruka Cultural Tourism Office, which arranges guided tours of the ruins, as well as visits to local Maasai bomas, traditional dancing displays & ascents of Ol Doinyo Lengai. *US$10pp.* **$**

⚊ Jerusalem Campsite Set alongside the Lutheran Church in a pretty grove close to the ruins, this site has no facilities other than toilets, making it more suitable for groups than for independent travellers. *US$5pp.* **$**

11

LAKE NATRON There are but a handful of places where the Rift Valley evokes its geologically violent origins with graphic immediacy. Ethiopia's Danakil Desert is one such spot; the volcanic Virunga Range in the Albertine Rift is another. And so, too, is the most northerly landmark in the Tanzanian Rift Valley, the low-lying Lake Natron, a shallow sliver of exceptionally alkaline water that extends southward from the Kenyan border near Mount Shompole for 58km. The Natron skyline is dominated by the textbook volcanic silhouette of Ol Doinyo Lengai, which rises more than 2km above the surrounding Rift Valley floor to an altitude of 2,960m, its harsh black contours softened by an icing of white ash that glistens brightly below the sun, as if in parody of Kilimanjaro's snows. Then there is the lake itself, a thrillingly primordial phenomenon whose caustic waters are enclosed by a crust of sodden grey volcanic ash and desiccated salt, punctuated by isolated patches of steamy, reed-lined swamp where the hot springs that sustain the lake bubble to the surface.

Thought to be about 1.5 million years old, Natron is a product of the same tectonic activity that formed the Ngorongoro Highlands and Mount Gelai, the latter being a 2,941m-high extinct volcano that rises from the eastern lakeshore. Nowhere more than 50cm deep, it has changed shape significantly since that time, largely as a result of volcanic activity associated with the creation of Ol Doinyo Lengai to its immediate south. It lies at an altitude of 610m in an unusually arid stretch of the rift floor, receiving an average of 400mm of rainfall annually, and it would have probably dried out centuries ago were it not also fed by the freshwater Ewaso Ngiro River, which has its catchment in the central Kenyan Highlands, and the hot springs that rise below its floor. The alkaline level has also increased drastically over the millennia, partially because of the high salinity of ash and lava deposits from Lengai, partially because the lake's only known outlet is evaporation. Today, depending on recent rainfall, the viscous water has an average pH of 9–11, making it almost as caustic as ammonia when the level is very low, and it can reach a temperature of up to 60°C in extreme circumstances.

Fauna The area around Lake Natron supports a thin population of large mammals typical of the Rift Valley. Zebra and giraffe are quite common in the vicinity of Engaresero, and other wildlife includes wildebeest, zebra, fringe-eared oryx, Grant's and Thomson's gazelle, and even the odd lion and cheetah. Natron's hyper-salinity makes it incapable of sustaining any but the most specialised life forms. The only resident vertebrates are a few species of small fish, notably the endemic white-lipped tilapia (*Oreochromis alcalica*) that congregate near hot-spring inlets where the water temperature is around 36–40°C. The microbiology of the lake is dominated by halophytic (salt-loving) organisms such as spirulina, a form of blue-green algae whose red pigments make the salt-encrusted flats in the centre of the lake look bright red when seen from the air. Natron is also the only known breeding ground for East Africa's 2.5 million lesser flamingos, which usually congregate there between August and October, feeding on the abundant algae (whose pigments are responsible for the birds' trademark pink hue). The breeding ground's inhospitality to potential predators makes it an ideal flamingo nursery, but it also makes it difficult for human visitors to access – situated in the centre of the lake, it was discovered as recently as the 1950s and it can only be seen from the air today. In addition to the flamingos, Natron attracts up to 100,000 migrant water birds during the European winter.

Getting there and away The centre of tourist activity on Natron is the small lakeshore village of Engaresero (also spelled Ngare Sero), bisected by the wooded

Mikuyu River from whence derives its Maasai name ('black water', 'clear water', 'dappled water' or 'forest of water', depending on who does the translating). Engaresero lies about 90km north of Mto wa Mbu along an erratic road that usually takes about 2½ hours to cover in its entirety, though this might improve as and when proper bridges are built across the larger watercourses north of Engaruka. Coming to/from the northern Serengeti, Engaresero is about 160km from Klein's Gate, a drive that takes 5–6 hours without stops, and involves a spectacular ascent/descent of the Rift Escarpment to the west of the lake.

The only **public transport** to Engaresero are the Coastline and Loliondo buses that run daily between Arusha and Loliondo town. These leave Arusha from opposite the Namanga bus station at 06.00 daily, and take around 4–5 hours to get to Engaresero. The fare from Arusha is around US$10 but in the opposite direction you'll need to get your lodge or camp to reserve you a seat from Loliondo and to pay the full fare of US$15.

Be warned that a trio of roadblocks on the road between Mto wa Mbu and Natron has been established by the Engaruka, Longido and Ngorongoro district councils. Each currently levies a toll fee of US$10–15 per person to all non-Tanzanian passengers, whether they travel by bus on a private vehicle, payable in US dollars or local currency. The legitimacy of these barriers is questionable, but you are highly unlikely to talk your way past them. Do at least ensure you obtain a receipt for any payment, if only to make sure the money doesn't go straight into the pocket of the person at the gate. And if you'll be returning the way you came, hold on to the receipt, as – at least in theory – the fee should cover the trip in both directions.

A more ambitious approach to Lake Natron would be **on foot**, via one of several overnight trekking routes that lead there from Empakaai Crater and elsewhere in the Ngorongoro Conservation Area. For more details, see the box on page 287, or contact Lake Natron Camp (see below), which specialises in setting up this kind of trip.

Where to stay

Upmarket

✳ 🏠 **Lake Natron Camp** (11 tents) m 0784 522090; e info@lake-natron-camp.com; www. lake-natron-camp.com. Set around a spring-fed oasis in a 315ha Maasai concession on the soda flats that hem in the southern lakeshore, this old-style eco-friendly bush camp doesn't offer the sort of under-canvas luxury you associate with Tanzania's top tented camps, but it will appeal greatly to those seeking an isolated wilderness experience in arguably the most spectacular stretch of the Tanzanian Rift Valley. Accommodation consists of spacious net-shaded safari tents containing an outdoor sitting area, queen-sized beds (with walk-in nets), en-suite compost toilets & hot showers. The net-shaded dining area, bar & lounge is surprisingly cool during the heat of the day, & while there is no swimming pool, it is great fun to swim in the clear & rather soapy spring-fed stream that runs in front of the sleeping tents, though be warned that the

white-lipped tilapia here enjoy nibbling gently on dead skin, a sensation that can be disconcerting at first, but is actually quite enjoyable, like a natural pedicure, once you get used to it. The camp offers superb views of Mounts Lengai & Gelai, wonderful star-studded night skies, a good chance of sighting zebras & other ungulates, & access to some of the oldest hominid footprints yet discovered (page 263), as well as to a section of the lakeshore rich in flamingos & other birds. It also arranges a range of activities further afield, including Natron climbs. *US$350pp FB inc drinks & WMA fees.* **$$$$$**

Moderate

🏠 **Natron Tented Camp** (9 rooms) 📞027 250 6315; m 0754 324193; e reservations@moivaro.com; www.moivaro.com. Established in 1989, this low-key camp is in wooded grounds on the southern outskirts of Engaresero. It has a spectacular position some 4km from the southern lakeshore, & offers great views across the floodplain to Mount Gelai. Though it has a somewhat no-frills feel compared with most tented camps & lodges in Tanzania, this is in keeping with the austere surrounds, & it does have a welcoming swimming pool & pleasant restaurant & bar area. Accommodation is in en-suite tents or chalets with twin or dbl beds, netting & hot water. Inexpensive organised guided climbs of nearby Ol Doinyo Lengai are offered, too. *US$256/373 sgl/dbl FB Jan, Feb, Jul, Aug & late Dec, US$216/318 Mar, Jun & Sep–early Dec, low-season discount Apr & May.* **$$$$$**

🏠 **Lengai Safari Lodge** (10 rooms) m 0754 823563; e lengailodge@gmail.com; www.lengaisafarilodge.com. Perched on a slope a few hundred metres from the start of the waterfall trail, this out-of-town lodge offers great views towards Lengai & a swimming pool is under construction. The simple octagonal huts have nets, en-suite showers & private balconies, & there's a 2-storey restaurant decorated with Tingatinga-style paintings. *Overpriced at US$132pp FB Jun–Sep, but better value the rest of the year at US$85/168 sgl/dbl FB.* **$$$$$**

🏠 **Natron River Camp** (8 tents) m 0680 941778; e info@wildlandssafaris.com; www.wildlandssafaris.com. Situated alongside the Mikuyu River, on the southern edge of Engaresero, this pleasant but overpriced little camp lies in tree-shaded grounds with a plunge pool, makuti-shaded dining room/bar & great views towards Lengai. Accommodation is in neat standing tents with dbl beds, nets & en-suite hot showers. *US$300 dbl FB.* **$$$$$**

Budget & camping
✶ 🏠 **Maasai Giraffe Eco-Resort** (3 cottages) m 0762 922221/0776 300425; e info@maasaigiraffe.com; www.maasaigiraffe. com. The pick of the budget options scattered around Natron, this friendly new resort stands in large wooded out-of-town grounds at the junction of the main road from Mto wa Mbu & the feeder road to Lake Natron Camp. The simple but comfortable thatched cottages have nets, en-suite shower & private balcony, & facilities include a pleasant restaurant/bar & Wi-Fi. A range of guided activities is offered, & it's only 45mins on foot to the southern lakeshore & hominid footprints. *US$50 dbl or twin bed; camping costs US$10pp in your own tent or US$20pp if you borrow one of theirs. Add US$28pp FB.* **$$–$$$**

🛆 **World View Campsite** m 0786 466133. This shady campsite opposite Lengai Safari Lodge caters mainly to groups & is probably a bit remote for most independent travellers. *US$10pp.* **$**

🛆 **Mikuyu Riverside Campsite** m 0759 334810. This no-frills campsite is set in large shady grounds alongside Natron River Camp. Facilities include a bar, but campers unequipped for self-catering will need to eat at one of the handful of small local eateries running along the main road through Engaresero. *US$10pp.* **$**

✗ **Where to eat and drink** If you are not eating at your camp, a few simple bars and restaurants serving local staples, along with nyama choma and chips, line the short main road through Engaresero. Cold beers and other bottled drinks are served at several places; rather unexpectedly, a few shops even stock imported wine.

What to see and do The activities described below can be arranged indirectly through the various camps and campsites in the area, or directly through the **Engaresero Eramatac Community Development Initiative** (*EECDI;* \ *027 205 0025;* e *engareserotourism@gmail.com or culturaltourism@habari.co.tz*), which maintains an out-of-town office alongside the main road to Mto wa Mbu more-or-less opposite the feeder road to Lake Natron Camp. Here, all visitors are required to pay a community tourist fee of US$20, which is currently good for your entire visit and includes access to all the sites listed below (except Ol Doinyo Lengai), as well as the services of a mandatory guide, who will expect a tip.

Southern lakeshore To reach the southern lakeshore from Engaresero, you need to drive for around 5km to an unofficial parking spot about 1km from the water's edge, then walk for about 10 minutes across salt-encrusted flats to a series of pockmarked black volcanic protrusions that serve as vantage points over the water. It's a lovely spot with Lengai looming in the background, and it hosts a profusion of water birds, most visibly large flocks of the pink-tinged lesser flamingo but also various pelicans, egrets, herons and waders. Wildebeest and zebra are also often seen in the area. If your driver doesn't know the way to the lakeshore – it's a rather obscure track – then ask for a local guide at one of the campsites. Whatever else you do, don't let the driver take the vehicle beyond the tracks left behind by his predecessors, or you run a serious risk of getting stuck in the treacherously narrow saline crust that surrounds the lake.

Engaresero human footprints One of the most important sites of its type in the world, this set of 58 human footprints is embedded in a layer of tuff-like compressed ash close to the southern shore of Natron. Although much older hominid fossil footprints have been discovered elsewhere in East Africa, these might well be the earliest-known ones associated with *Homo sapiens*. The prints were discovered by a Maasai herder in 1998 but only investigated properly by scientists about ten years later. It is thought that they were made by a party of 18 adults and children as they traipsed through a field of muddy ash when Lengai erupted around 120,000 years ago. The footprints are remarkably clear (although they can be obscured below a layer of fine dust) and their presence here only goes to underscore the prehistoric feel of this vast volcanic stretch of the Rift Valley. The site lies on the concession operated by Lake Natron Camp, about 10 minutes' walk from the camp itself, but is open to day visitors provided they are accompanied by a guide from the EECDI. Try to visit in the early morning or the very late afternoon, as shoes must be taken off before you enter the fenced-off site, and walking barefoot on the sun-baked black rocks is all but impossible during the heat of the day.

Engaresero Waterfall The Engaresero River forms a series of pretty waterfalls as it descends from the Nguruman Escarpment west of Lake Natron, a kilometre or two south of the village of Engaresero. The lowest two falls can be reached by driving out to Waterfall Campsite, and then following the river upstream on foot for 45–60 minutes through the gorge it has carved into the escarpment wall. If you are not already sufficiently doused by the time you reach the second waterfall, there's a chilly natural swimming pool below it. There is no clear footpath through the gorge: you will need to wade across the river several times (potentially dangerous after heavy rain) and can also expect to do a fair bit of clambering along ledges and rocks. This walk can only be recommended to reasonably fit and agile travellers, and it's advisable to take somebody who knows the way to help you navigate a couple of tricky stretches – a guide can be arranged at any of the camps listed on pages 261–2, or through the EECDI.

Ol Doinyo Lengai Estimated to be around 350,000–400,000 years old, Ol Doinyo Lengai – the Maasai 'Mountain of God' – is one of the youngest volcanoes in East Africa and possibly the most active. Its crater is known to have experienced almost continuous low-key activity since 1883, when Dr Fischer, the first European to pass through this part of Maasailand, observed smoke rising from the summit and was told secondhand that the mountain regularly emitted rumbling noises. At least a dozen minor or major eruptions have occurred since then. An interesting feature of Lengai is that it is the only active volcano known to emit carbonate lava, a form of molten rock that contains almost no silicon, is about 50% cooler than other forms of lava at around 500°C, and is also exceptionally fluid, with a viscosity comparable to water.

The most impressive eruption of Ol Doinyo Lengai in recorded history occurred in the latter part of 1966, when ash fall was reported as far away as Seronera, more than 100km to the west, as well as at Loliondo and Shombole, both some 70km further north. It is believed that the otherwise inexplicable death of large numbers of game around Empakaai Crater in that year was a result of an ash fall that coated the grass up to 2cm deep, though it is unclear whether the animals starved to death or they succumbed to a toxin within the ash. The effect on Maasai livestock was also devastating according to Tepilit Ole Saitoti, who recalled the incident as follows in his excellent book *Worlds of a Maasai Warrior*:

In the year 1966, God, who my people believe dwells in this holy mountain, unleashed Her fury unsparingly. The mountain thunder shook the earth, and the volcanic flame, which came from deep down in the earth's crust, was like a continuous flash of lightning. During days when the eruption was most powerful, clouds of smoke and steam appeared. Many cattle died and still more would die. Poisonous volcanic ash spewed all over the land as far as a hundred miles away, completely covering the pastures and the leaves of trees. Cattle swallowed ash each time they tried to graze and were weakened. They could not wake up without human assistance. We had to carry long wooden staffs to put under the fallen animals to lift them up. There must have been more than enough reason for God to have unleashed Her anger on us, and all we could do was pray for mercy. My pastoral people stubbornly braved the gusting warm winds as they approached the flaming mountain to pray. Women and men dressed in their best walked in stately lines towards God, singing. The mountain was unappeased and cattle died in the thousands. Just before the people started dying too, my father decided to move; as he put it: 'We must move while we still have children, or else we will all lose them'.

During an eruption in 2004, plumes in the crater could be seen from as far away as Engaresero and many local Maasai herdsmen moved their livestock out of the area. The mountain once again experienced a high level of volcanic activity between July 2007 and June 2008. On 18 July 2007, tremors emanating from the mountain measured 6.0 on the Richter scale and were felt as far away as Nairobi city. Ol Doinyo Lengai erupted spectacularly on 4 September 2007, emanating an ashen steamy plume almost 20km downwind and sending fresh lava flows along the north and west flanks. Activity continued intermittently into mid 2008, with further eruptions occurring in March, April and August. Lengai has been relatively quiet since then, but the crater formed by the 2007–08 eruptions is gradually filling with lava, so another eruption might occur at any time.

Climbing Ol Doinyo Lengai The ascent of Lengai is a popular hike with adventurous travellers, and it forms an excellent budget alternative to climbing Kilimanjaro, at least when the volcano is sufficiently placid. The ascent passes through some magnificently arid scenery and offers spectacular views back towards the Rift Valley, before leading to the bleakly visceral lunar landscape of the crater, studded with ash cones, lava pools, steam vents and other evidence of volcanic activity. Suitable only for reasonably fit and agile travellers, the normal northern ascent route to the top of Lengai is very steep, climbing in altitude from around 800m to around 2,900m, while the descent on loose scree can be very tough on knees and ankles. The climb normally takes 5–6 hours along slopes practically bereft of shade, for which reason many locals recommend leaving late at night (around 23.00–midnight) to avoid the intense heat and to reach the crater rim in time for sunrise. If you ascend by day an 05.00 start is advised, and precautions should be taken against dehydration and sunstroke. Either way, the descent takes about 2 hours.

Most adventure safari operators in Arusha offer guided Lengai climbs (pages 139–41), but it is also possible to arrange a one-day climb locally, either at the EECDI or at one of the camps dotted around Engaresero village. The mountain lies outside any conservation area so no park fees are charged, but a fixed fee of US$100 for one person, US$70 per person for two, or US$60 per person for larger parties is levied by the EECDI. This includes the services of an experienced guide, who will need to be tipped.

All hikers should be aware that the cones on the crater floor can easily collapse under pressure and they often cover deadly lava lakes. Under no circumstances should you climb on a cone, or walk inside a partially collapsed cone. It is inadvisable (and may be forbidden) to climb the mountain during periods of high activity.

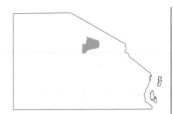

12

Ngorongoro and the Crater Highlands

Immediately west of Lake Manyara, the main road towards the Serengeti switchbacks up a spectacular stretch of the Rift Valley Escarpment to reach the fertile slopes of the volcanically formed Crater Highlands, which rise to a maximum altitude of 3,648m and are pockmarked with dormant and extinct calderas, most famously the wondrous Ngorongoro Crater. Much of the Crater Highlands are protected within the Ngorongoro Conservation Area (NCA), a vast biosphere reserve where the iconic Maasai people live alongside a bewildering diversity of wildlife, from the lions and elephants that strut fearlessly across the floor of Ngorongoro Crater to the secretive forest birds that flit through its jungle-swathed rim. Coming from Arusha or Lake Manyara, the gateway to the Ngorongoro, only 8km before the main Lodware Entrance Gate, is Karatu, a small but rapidly expanding agricultural town whose immediate environs support an ever-growing number of hotels, lodges and campsites designed to supplement the relatively limited options situated within the NCA itself.

KARATU AND SURROUNDS

Set at an altitude of 1,500m along the main road to Ngorongoro, unassuming Karatu outstrips Mto wa Mbu as the largest settlement between Arusha and the Serengeti, supporting a population estimated at around 20,000. As its local nickname of 'Safari Junction' suggests, the town is a minor route focus, situated close to the junction for Lake Eyasi (pages 256–8) and another road leading via Mbulu to Mount Hanang (pages 228–33). Most tourists hurtle through Karatu *en route* to more glamorous

---

OLOIBONI   *Emma Thomson*

The *oloiboni* acts as a spiritual psychiatrist within Maasai communities, using stones to divine past, present and future events. Members of the homestead are able to consult him about family or mental and physical health problems, the answers to which come to the oloiboni in dreams. A reading involves the patient sitting cross-legged before him, spitting on the stones to infuse them with his/her spirit, and waiting for the results.

The skills are only passed on through the patrilineal line, and even then sons are not permitted to practise their powers of mediation until their twentieth birthday.

Intriguingly, two oloibonis are forbidden to meet each other, so if a neighbouring spiritual leader appears to be stealing business or enjoying good trade, villagers will claim that their oloiboni will send lions to attack the offending culprit.

MODERN-DAY MAASAI *Emma Thomson*

The future of the Maasai seems an uncertain one. The Tanzanian government regards them as primitive and criticises them for 'holding the country back'. They are banned from wearing their distinctive *rubega/shuka* (robes) on public transport and in order to attend primary or secondary school the children are forced to remove their elaborate bead jewellery, and dress in Western-style clothes, while boys must shave off their long hair. All this follows a scheme launched by the government in the 1960s named the 'official national ideology of development', whose unspoken aims were to integrate the Maasai forcibly into mainstream society and settle them so the government could implement taxation.

Originally transhumant pastoralists, alternating the movement of their cattle between established wet- and dry-season pastures, the Maasai have now lost these latter areas to commercial farmers and wildlife conservation. Increasingly unpredictable rains leave grass and cattle dehydrated, and freak outbreaks of rinderpest and east coast fever (brought by explorers in the early 19th century) combine to often wipe out herds all together.

Squeezed into this bottleneck of depleted herds and land, the Maasai have had to overcome one of their greatest taboos – the ban on 'breaking the ground' and destroying grass, believed to have been sent by the Creator as sacred food for the cattle – in order to grow crops. Skills were acquired from nearby neighbours, the Chagga and Meru, and the latest studies show that now 40–45% of Maasai in East Africa trade meat for beans and maize, with only 50% living purely on the traditional diet of milk, blood and meat.

Unfortunately, when farming fails as a result of nutrient-poor soil, members of the family come back into the towns in search of paid work to supplement the unavoidable financial needs of providing for their families in the modern world. Men often find employment as nightwatchmen, while the women may have to resort to petty trading, beer brewing and, increasingly, prostitution.

However, the Maasai are both resourceful and resilient and the developing tourist industry brings new opportunities. Gemma EnoLengila, co-founder of the NGO Serian UK, stresses that 'the real challenge lies in creating sustainable projects that are developed in partnership with (traditional) communities, in a way that empowers rather than oppresses them'.

locations further west, but it does boast a fair selection of tourist facilities, including several mid-range and budget lodgings, a few restaurants, and some filling stations, internet cafés, adequately stocked supermarkets and banks with ATMs (including a branch of the CRDB that serves as the closest place to the NCA where entrance fees can be paid; see box, page 92). The fertile slopes running from Karatu north and west towards the forested NCA border also host at least a dozen tourist lodges that are routinely used as bases for game drives into Ngorongoro Crater.

GETTING THERE AND AWAY Karatu lies about 30km from Mto wa Mbu along a good surfaced road that can be covered in 30 minutes. Coming directly from Arusha, the 140km drive takes about 2 hours. There is plenty of **public transport**: minibus-taxis depart from Arusha throughout the day and cost around US$3, while the best of several slightly cheaper bus services is probably Dar Express, which leaves Arusha from the new bus terminus a few hundred metres west of the central bus station.

Maasai jewellery beads are composed of nine main colours. It's a common misconception that the colours are blended to create complex messages. In fact, while the colours carry meaning, the combinations are randomly selected, mainly for beauty. It's often possible to tell the age of some necklaces according to the fashionable arrangement of colours that vary from year to year. Tendons extracted from the meat consumed originally served as string to hold these intricate designs together but these have now been replaced with shredded plastic bags.

The meanings for each colour vary from area to area but in general they mean the following:

black	God/rain	orange	rainbow
blue	water	red	warrior/blood/bravery
dark blue	God in the sky	white	milk/peace
gold	ground water	yellow	sun
green	life/spring	(rainy season)	

If you arrive in Karatu without transport, Ngorongoro Camp & Lodge [270 G4] (📞 025 253 4287) behind the Kisamo Filling Station rents out 4x4s carrying up to eight people for day trips to Manyara/Ngorongoro for US$160/180 inclusive of fuel and driver but exclusive of park fees.

WHERE TO STAY The choice of accommodation in and around Karatu is enormous. It includes several upmarket lodges dotted around the slopes west of town, some of which actually border the NCA, along with a number of more moderate options within the town itself. In all cases, the lodges' *raison d'être* is as a base for day trips to the popular Ngorongoro Crater, and to supplement the limited accommodation within the NCA. In most cases, the lodges around Karatu are inherently better value than their counterparts within the NCA, and they tend to have greater room availability in high seasons. The negative is that they lack the spectacular views and sense of immediacy associated with sleeping on the crater rim, while entrance gate opening times preclude their guests from getting the early start required to make the best of the crater.

In & around town
Upmarket
✳ 🏠 **Acacia Farm Lodge** [270 D3] (28 cottages) 📞027 253 4654; m 0767 465557/0784 465556; e info@karatuacacialodge.com; www. karatuacacialodge.com. Opened in 2014, this exceptional new all-suite lodge lies about 2km from Karatu on a wooded hill offering views towards Ngorongoro. High standards of hospitality are complemented by stylish contemporary African décor, while amenities include a large swimming pool, children's pool, spa, gym, Wi-Fi throughout, coffee bar, restaurant serving organic vegetables grown in the gardens, & a range of children's activities. It can also arrange bird walks,

coffee-farm visits & waterfall hikes. Decorated in understated shades of grey & blue, the extra-spacious cottages have a king-sized bed with walk-in netting, wide private balcony & sitting room with flatscreen DSTV, minibar & tea/coffee facilities. *US$435/580 sgl/dbl FB.* **$$$$$**

Moderate
✳ 🏠 **Eileen's Trees Inn** [270 F4] (20 rooms) m 0783 379526/0685 758296; e info@eileenstrees. com; www.eileenstrees.com. This service-oriented owner-managed lodge, set back 500m from the main road, is easily the most appealing option in Karatu town. It sprawls across quiet leafy grounds that feature an inviting swimming pool & a plantation-style stilted

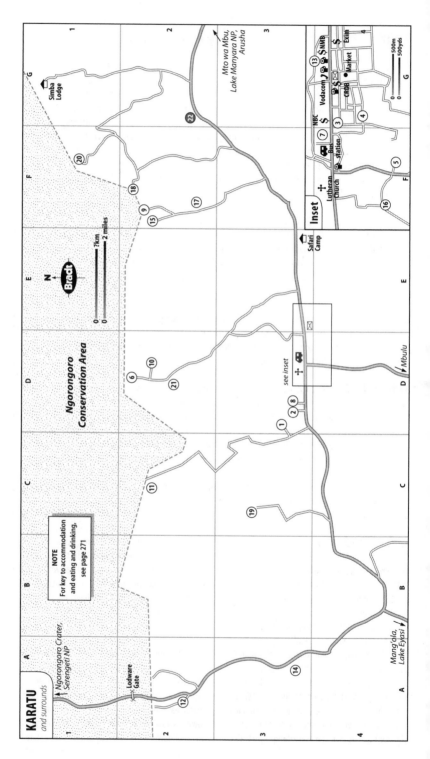

KARATU
and surrounds

Ngorongoro Crater,
Serengeti NP

NOTE
For key to accommodation
and eating and drinking,
see page 271

Ngorongoro
Conservation Area

0   2km
0   2 miles

Lodware
Gate

Mang'ola,
Lake Eyasi

Simba
Lodge

Mto wa Mbu,
Lake Manyara NP,
Arusha

Safari
Camp

see inset

Mbulu

Inset

Lutheran
Church

Bus
station

NBC

Vodacom

Market

CRDB

NMB

Exim

0   500m
0   500yds

restaurant/bar with wooden floor, upstairs dining room, & makuti roof. The large uncluttered rooms are stylishly decorated & come with queen-sized or 2 ¾ 4-poster beds, fitted nets, en-suite bathroom with terracotta tiles & hot shower, & private balcony. All rooms are the same price but newer ones are larger & slightly smarter. Excellent value. *US$100/150/180 sgl/dbl/trpl FB, substantial discounts Apr–Jun, cheaper resident rates.* **$$$$**

🏠 **Karatu Country Lodge** [270 D3] (24 rooms) \027 253 4622; m 0789 582982; e info@ countrylodgekaratu.com; www.countrylodgekaratu. com. Situated 1km out of town alongside the better-known Bougainvillea Lodge, this new & dynamically managed lodge is set around a large shady garden centred on a swimming pool with lots of seating & lounger beds. The comfortable, spacious & earthily decorated rooms come with 4-poster bed, fitted net, banana-leaf ceiling, wood furniture, fireplace, fridge, balcony, en-suite hot shower & dressing room. Good value. *US$122/214 sgl/dbl FB.* **$$$$$**

🏠 **Bougainvillea Lodge** [270 D3] (32 rooms) \027 253 4083; e bougainvillea@habari.co.tz; www.bougainvillealodge.net. Set in large well-developed flowering gardens just 1km outside Karatu & only 200m from the main road towards NCA, this unpretentious lodge offers an attractive compromise between quality & cost. The neat &

comfortably decorated tiled cottages are set in a circle around the swimming pool area, & come with 4-poster twin or king-sized beds with fitted netting, a fan, a fireplace, a sitting area with cane furniture & a private balcony facing the pool. The lodge serves good meals & facilities include a massage spa & gift shop specialising in local Iraqw beadwork. Decent value. *US$125/230 sgl/dbl FB.* **$$$$$**

🏠 **Octagon Lodge** [270 F4] (15 rooms) m 0787 858485/0784 650324; e sales@ octagonlodge.com or octagonlodgetz@gmail. com; www.octagonlodge.com; see ad, page 290. Set in compact green gardens in the backstreets of Karatu close to Eileen's, this is another modest & reasonably priced set-up offering en-suite accommodation in airy wooden cottages with queen-sized or twin beds, walk-in nets, colourful but earthy décor & private balcony. Buffet-style meals are served & the characterful 'Irish Bar' actually has more of an African feel with its thatched roof. One of the longest-serving lodges on Karatu, it remains more than adequate, but these days there are better options in a similar price range. *US$95/170/245 sgl/dbl/trpl FB, low-season discounts offered.* **$$$$**

Budget

🏠 **Crater Rim View Inn** [270 G4] (14 rooms) m 0755 656502. Plugging the rather wide gaps between local guesthouses &, well, everything else, this neat little lodge lies in pleasant green gardens 300m from the main road. It's nothing flash, & arguably quite overpriced, but the clean rooms with 4-poster bed, net, DSTV & en-suite hot shower look comfortable enough, & a decent restaurant is attached. *US$80/139 sgl/dbl FB.* **$$$$**

Shoestring

🏠 **CBA Guesthouse** [270 G4] (10 rooms) m 0757 491755. The pick of several local guesthouses in central Karatu, this new place has clean tiled en-suite rooms with TV & net. If it's full, the Remas Guesthouse opposite or Land Guesthouse next door look almost as good. *US$5/7 sgl/dbl.* **$**

🏠 **Giraffe Executive Inn** [270 F4] (15 rooms) Possibly the only hotel in the world with electronic card-type room keys but no telephone contact details, this cheerlessly managed lodge opposite the bus station has decent rooms with DSTV, fitted net & en-suite hot shower. *US$12 dbl.* **$**

Camping

🏠 **Ngorongoro Camp & Lodge** [270 G4] (32 rooms) 📞 025 253 4287. The en-suite rooms at this well-established but utterly characterless complex in Karatu are very overpriced for what you get, but it still has a good campsite, heated swimming pool & restaurant serving a good range of tasty Indian & continental dishes. *US$90/140 sgl/dbl B&B, camping US$10pp. Rooms* **$$$$**, *camping* **$**

Towards Ngorongoro Conservation Area
Exclusive

☀ 🏠 **Gibb's Farm** [270 D2] (22 rooms) 📞 027 253 4397; **e** reservations@gibbsfarm.net; www.gibbsfarm.net. This long-serving hotel, set on a family-run farm on the eastern border of the NCA, was transformed into one of Tanzania's most sumptuously exclusive boutique lodges by radical renovations in 2008. Situated 6km from Karatu along a rough dirt road, it lies on an active coffee estate bordering an extensive patch of indigenous forest on the Ngorongoro footslopes. The main building, a converted 1920s farmhouse, retains a strong period feel with its red polished cement floor, tall bay windows, hearty home-style 4-course meals, & leather & wood furnishing, & its colonial ambience is far removed from the relative uniformity that characterises so many upmarket lodges in northern Tanzania. The exquisite guest cottages combine a more contemporary feel with farmhouse rusticity, & are seriously spacious, with 2 dbl beds in each bedroom, varnished wood floors, comfy armchairs, lovely views from the balcony, & the choice of indoor or outdoor shower. Activities include bird walks with the resident naturalist, cultural & farm excursions, a 2hr hike to a waterfall & cave made by elephants on the forested slopes of the crater, & a massage room & spa (traditional Maasai treatments from a Maasai elder). There is no TV or swimming pool. *US$630/900 sgl/dbl FB Jan & Feb, Jun–Aug & late Dec, seasonal discounts available during other months.* **$$$$$$**

🏠 **The Manor at Ngorongoro** [270 C2] (20 rooms) 📞 027 254 0630; **m** 0784 250630; **e** info@elewana.com; www.elewana.com. Boasting a magnificent hilltop setting on a coffee estate running along the forested border of the NCA, this handsome lodge with whitewashed exteriors, tall gables, slate tiled roofs & neatly tended gardens is architecturally reminiscent of the Cape Dutch style associated with the wine estates of South Africa. Though purpose built, the main building, comprising several dining & sitting areas, recalls a 19th-century manor house, with hardwood floors, muted period décor & furnishings, & a wide shaded balcony. Accommodation is in semi-detached cottages, each containing 2 large split-level open-plan suites with king-size or twin beds, a comfortable sitting area, fireplace, large windows, & a en-suite bathroom with old-fashioned tub & shower. Excellent service & top-quality food makes this perhaps the most sumptuous in the Ngorongoro area. *US$1,118/1,490 sgl/dbl FB inc most drinks, & laundry, seasonal discounts available Jan–Jun, Nov & early Dec. Full game package inc game drives an additional US$100pp.* **$$$$$$$**

Upmarket

☀ 🏠 **Rhotia Valley Tented Lodge** [270 F1] (16 tents) **m** 0784 446579; **e** rhotiavalley@gmail.com; www.rhotiavalley.com. This low-key hilltop lodge abuts the NCA, but lies 30–45mins' drive away from the Lodware Entrance Gate along a 5km feeder road clearly signposted about 6km out of Karatu along the road back to Mto wa Mbu. A significant portion of the proceeds go to support the affiliated Rhotia Valley Children's Home, a Dutch-run NGO that accommodates around 50 orphaned or otherwise homeless schoolchildren on the opposite slope. Accommodation is in small but cosy en-suite standing tents with balconies facing the forest slopes of Ngorongoro. The restaurant bar & lounge are housed in a wonderful open-sided thatched construction whose stylish but down-to-earth décor has a European-countryside-meets-classic-safari feel. The home-cooked meals, made largely from organic ingredients grown in the sprawling vegetable & herb garden, are a real treat. Several nature trails run through the scenic property, which also has a swimming pool & is occasionally passed through by elephants & other wildlife from the NCA. Visits to the orphanage are encouraged and usually take place at around 17.30. *US$270/420 sgl/dbl FB, with discounts Mar–Jun, Sep–Nov & early Dec.* **$$$$$**

☀ 🏠 **Plantation Lodge** [270 C3] (24 rooms) **m** 0784 260799; **e** reservation@plantation-lodge.com; www.plantation-lodge.com. This popular German-owned lodge is set in flowering 10ha grounds only 2km north of the main road & 15mins' drive from Lodware Entrance Gate. It has a classic whitewash & thatch exterior, complemented by the stylish décor of the spacious self-contained rooms, making for a refreshingly individualistic contrast to the chain lodges that characterise the northern circuit, while also forming a good base for day trips to Ngorongoro Crater. All food is grown onsite or sourced from local suppliers. Amenities include a swimming pool, Wi-Fi & spa offering massage & other treatments. *US$370/580 sgl/dbl FB, suites from US$750 dbl FB inc drinks.* **$$$$$$**

🏠 **Kitela Lodge** [270 D2] (20 rooms) **m** 0767 333223/0784 207727; **e** reservations@ tanganyikawildernesscamps.com; www. tanganyikawildernesscamps.com. The most intimate & upmarket of Tanganyika Wilderness Camps' trio of properties around Karatu, Kitela lies on a coffee estate bordering the NCA & offering good views to the forested foothills of the Crater Highlands. The massive cottages, decorated in understated colonial style, incorporate a king-sized bed & walk-in net, writing desk, private balcony, & a spacious bathroom with tub, shower & 2 sinks. *US$430/575 sgl/dbl FB, substantial discounts Mar–Jun & Nov.* **$$$$$$**

🏠 **Ngorongoro Farm House** [270 A3] (50 rooms) **m** 0767 333223/0784 207727; **e** reservations@tanganyikawildernesscamps.com; www.tanganyikawildernesscamps.com. Situated on a large coffee farm about halfway between Karatu & the NCA, this stylish lodge offers luxurious en-suite accommodation in 3 separate camps of large semi-detached thatched cottages with views across to the forested slopes of Ngorongoro. There's a very pleasant swimming pool area & the restaurant serves good country-style cooking. In terms of location, it doesn't quite match up to the lodges on the crater rim. Guided nature walks, mountain biking & other leg-stretching activities are on offer, too. *US$250/370 sgl/dbl standard room, or US$430/575 suite. All rates FB. Substantial discounts Mar–Jun & Nov.* **$$$$$$**

🏠 **Neptune Ngorongoro Luxury Lodge** [270 A2] (20 rooms) **m** 0736 502496; **e** info.ngorongoro@neptunehotels.com; www. neptunehotels.com. Opened in Jun 2012 under the name Exploreans, this plush all-suite lodge literally borders the NCA & lies only 2km by road from the Lodware Entrance Gate. Accommodation is in spacious, airy & uncluttered standalone

cottages with makuti-thatch roof, wooden floor, lounge with fireplace & stylish hardwood furniture, large bedroom with king-sized or twin ¾ beds in a walk-in net, spacious private balcony with forest view, Wi-Fi, safe, minibar & en-suite bathroom with tub or shower. Facilities include a good à la carte restaurant, a large swimming pool with a great view, & a spa. Service is superb, too. *From US$648/865 sgl/dbl all inc, dropping to US$346/463 low season.* **$$$$$$**

Moderate

✳ 🏠 **Tloma Lodge** [270 D2] (34 rooms) **m** 0767 333223/0784 207727; **e** reservations@ tanganyikawildernesscamps.com; www. tanganyikawildernesscamps.com. Situated about 1km from Gibb's Farm & sharing a similarly lovely view over the forested Ngorongoro footslopes, this attractive & very competitively priced lodge is set in spacious grounds that lead down to a wooden deck enclosing a large swimming pool. Accommodation is in large, cosy earth-coloured cottages with colonial-style green corrugated-iron roofs, screed floors, wood ceilings, fireplaces, 4-poster king-sized or twin beds, & a large bathroom with shower. The food is excellent, & facilities include birdwatching tours, massage, village walks, internet, coffee plantation demonstrations & day tours to Ngorongoro Crater. *US$210/285 standard sgl/dbl FB. Substantial discounts Mar–Jun & Nov.* **$$$$$**

🏠 **Olea Africana Safari Lodge** [270 F2] (10 rooms) **m** 0768 046571/0788 418658; **e** info@ oleaafricana.com; www.oleaafricana.com. Named for the stately African olive tree in the centre of the large green garden, this small & rather stylish owner-managed lodge offers accommodation in huge cottages with banana-leaf ceiling, screed floor, dbl bed with fitted net, fireplace, sitting area, en-suite bathroom with stone floor, tub & shower, & a large private balcony. The restaurant/bar has a farmhouse feel, surrounded by a wide balcony, & amenities include a swimming pool & Wi-Fi. Unpretentious & good value. *US$125/200 sgl/dbl FB.* **$$$$$**

🏠 **Pembeni Rhotia** [270 F2] (15 tents) ☎ 027 275 5705; **e** travel@pembeniafrica. com; www.pembeniafrica.com. This new lodge on the NCA border north of Karatu consists of comfortable standing tents set on hardwood platforms in 2 neat & compact rows, giving

12

THE MAASAI

The northern safari circuit is the homeland of the Nilotic-speaking Maasai, whose reputation as fearsome warriors ensured that the 19th-century slave caravans studiously avoided their territory, which was one of the last parts of East Africa ventured into by Europeans. The Maasai today remain the most familiar of African people to outsiders, a reputation that rests as much on their continued adherence to a traditional lifestyle as on past exploits. Instantly identifiable, Maasai men drape themselves in toga-like red blankets, carry long wooden poles, and often dye their hair with red ochre and style it in a manner that has been compared to a Roman helmet. And while the women dress similarly to many other Tanzanian women, their extensive use of beaded jewellery is highly distinctive, too.

The Maasai are often regarded to be the archetypal East African pastoralists, but are in fact relatively recent arrivals to the area. Their language Maa (Maasai literally means 'Maa-speakers') is affiliated to those languages spoken by the Nuer of southwest Ethiopia and the Bari of southern Sudan, and oral traditions suggest that the proto-Maasai started to migrate southward from the lower Nile area in the 15th century. They arrived in their present territory in the 17th or 18th century, forcefully displacing earlier inhabitants such as the Datoga and Chagga, who respectively migrated south to the Hanang area and east to the Kilimanjaro foothills. The Maasai territory reached its greatest extent in the mid 19th century, when it covered most of the Rift Valley from Marsabit (Kenya) south to Dodoma. Over the 1880s/90s, the Maasai were hit by a series of disasters linked to the arrival of Europeans – rinderpest and smallpox epidemics exacerbated by a severe drought and a bloody secession dispute – and much of their former territory was recolonised by tribes whom they had displaced a century earlier. During the colonial era, a further 50% of their land was lost to game reserves and settler farms. These territorial incursions notwithstanding, the Maasai today have one of the most extensive territories of any Tanzanian tribe, ranging across the vast Maasai Steppes to the Ngorongoro Highlands and Serengeti Plains.

The Maasai are monotheists whose belief in a single deity with a dualistic nature – the benevolent Engai Narok (Black God) and vengeful Engai Nanyokie (Red God) – has some overtones of the Judaic faith. They believe that Engai, who resides in the volcano Ol Doinyo Lengai, made them the rightful owners of all the cattle in the world, a view that has occasionally made life difficult for neighbouring herders. Traditionally, this arrogance does not merely extend to cattle: agriculturist and fish-eating peoples are scorned, while Europeans' uptight style of clothing earned them the Maasai name Iloredaa Enjekat – Fart Smotherers! Today, the Maasai co-exist peacefully with their non-Maasai compatriots, but while their tolerance for their neighbours' idiosyncrasies has increased in recent decades, they show little interest in changing their own lifestyle.

The Maasai measure a man's wealth in terms of cattle and children rather than money – a herd of about 50 cattle is respectable, the more children the better, and

it a rather barracks-like feel. The tents all contain king-sized or twin 4-poster beds with wrought-iron fitted nets, & en-suite hot shower & private balcony – with units 8–15 offering uninterrupted views to the forested slopes of Ngorongoro, but lower numbers having their

views disrupted by the tent in front. No better than ordinary. *US$150pp FB, dropping to US$120 out of season.* **$$$$**

🏠 **Ngorongoro Forest Tented Camp**
[270 F2] (10 rooms) ☏ 027 250 8089; **m** 0789 607118; **e** info@ngorongoroforestlodge.com;

a man who has plenty of one but not the other is regarded as poor. Traditionally, the Maasai will not hunt or eat vegetable matter or fish, but feed almost exclusively off their cattle. The main diet is a blend of cow's milk and blood, the latter drained – it is said painlessly – from a strategic nick in the animal's jugular vein. Because the cows are more valuable to them alive than dead, they are generally slaughtered only on special occasions. Meat and milk are never eaten on the same day, because it is insulting to the cattle to feed off the living and the dead at the same time. Despite the apparent hardship of their chosen lifestyle, many Maasai are wealthy by any standards. On one safari, our driver pointed out a not unusually large herd of cattle that would fetch the market equivalent of three new Land Rovers.

The central unit of Maasai society is the age-set. Every 15 years or so, a new and individually named generation of warriors or Ilmoran will be initiated, consisting of all the young men who have reached puberty and are not part of a previous age-set – most boys aged between 12 and 25. Every boy must undergo the Emorata (circumcision ceremony) before he is accepted as a warrior. If he cries out during the 5-minute operation, which is performed without any anaesthetic, the post-circumcision ceremony will be cancelled, the parents spat on for raising a coward, and the initiate taunted by his peers for several years before he is forgiven. When a new generation of warriors is initiated, the existing Ilmoran graduate to become junior elders, who are responsible for all political and legislative decisions until they in turn graduate to become senior elders. All political decisions are made democratically, and the role of the chief elder or Laibon is essentially that of a spiritual and moral leader.

Maasai girls are permitted to marry as soon as they have been initiated, but warriors must wait until their age-set has graduated to elder status, which will be 15 years later, when a fresh warrior age-set has been initiated. This arrangement ties in with the polygamous nature of Maasai society: in days past, most elders would typically have acquired between three and ten wives by the time they reached old age. Marriages are generally arranged, sometimes even before the female party is born, as a man may 'book' the next daughter produced by a friend to be his son's wife. Marriage is evidently viewed as a straightforward, child-producing business arrangement: it is normal for married men and women to have sleeping partners other than their spouse, provided that those partners are of an appropriate age-set. Should a woman become pregnant by another lover, the prestige attached to having many children outweighs any minor concerns about infidelity, and the husband will still bring up the child as his own. By contrast, although sex before marriage is condoned, an unmarried girl who falls pregnant brings disgrace on her family, and in former times would have been fed to the hyenas.

For further details about Maasai society and beliefs, get hold of the coffee-table book *Maasai*, by the photographer Carol Beckwith and Maasai historian Tepilit Ole Saitoti (Harry N Abrams, New York, reprinted 1993).

12

www.ngorongoroforestlodge.com. The self-proclaimed 'lodge that defines a new dimension of luxury' might more realistically be described as the epitome of mid-range mediocrity. The standing tents, protected by a thatch shelter & connected by a stilted wooden walkway, are comfortable enough – twin or dbl beds with walk-in net, en-suite hot shower & private balcony offering forest views – without being especially memorable, & it all seems a little frayed at the seams & short on management presence. OK at the price. *US$150/200 sgl/dbl FB.* **$$$$**

Budget & camping

🏠 **Karatu Forest Tented Camp** [270 F2]
(5 tents) 📞027 275 0248; **m** 0736 502488.
Carved into a forest glade bordering right on
the NCA, this no-frills camp offers the choice
of a simple standing tent set under a makuti
roof & with a rustic shower & toilet at the
back, or pitching your own tent. It feels more
like a mobile camp than a lodge, the setting is
fabulous, & it seems great value at the price.
US$100 dbl or twin FB, US$10pp in own tent. Tents
$$$$, *camping* **$**

🍴 **WHERE TO EAT AND DRINK** The selection of bespoke eateries in Karatu itself is
rather limited, but several small establishments serve the usual local staples, and
there are more cosmopolitan restaurants at Eileen's Trees Inn, Crater View Inn and
Ngorongoro Camp & Lodge.

🍴 **Coffee Corner** [270 G2] **m** 0788 165441;
🕐 08.00–18.00 daily. Under the same
management as Rhotia Valley Tented Lodge, this
roadside eatery about 5km east of Karatu is the
ideal place to break for lunch *en route* from Mto
wa Mbu or Arusha. It serves burgers, chicken
skewers, pasta, salads & soups in the US$5–7
range, as well as a good selection of smoothies,
coffee & juices. Further assets include a friendly
welcome, clean toilets & lovely view from
the balcony.

NGORONGORO CONSERVATION AREA

Inscribed as a UNESCO World Heritage Site and listed as an International Biosphere
Reserve, the Ngorongoro Conservation Area (NCA) extends over 8,292km² to the
southeast of the Serengeti National Park, with which it shares a border of roughly
80km. Its dominant feature is the geological marvel known as the Ngorongoro
Crater – the world's largest intact volcanic caldera, and a shoo-in contender for any
global shortlist of natural wonders thanks to its gobsmacking scenic beauty and
the wildlife that teems across its verdant 260km² floor. The rest of the NCA can be
divided into two distinct parts. The eastern Crater Highlands comprise a sprawling
volcanic massif studded with craggy peaks and gaping craters, while the lower-lying
western plains are essentially a continuation of the Serengeti ecosystem, supporting
a cover of short grass that attracts immense concentrations of grazers during the
rainy season.

Coming from the direction of Arusha, the road ascent of Ngorongoro Crater is
a sensational scene setter, switchbacking through densely forested slopes to Heroes
Point, where most visitors will catch their first breathtaking view from the rim to
the crater floor 600m below. Even at this distance, it is often possible to pick out
hundred- or even thousand-strong ant-like formations foraging across the crater
floor – herds of wildebeest, zebra and buffalo – and with binoculars you might
also pick out some of the elephants that haunt the fringes of Lerai Forest. The
drive along the crater rim to your lodge will be equally riveting: patches of forest
interspersed with sweeping views back across to a patchwork of farmland around
Karatu, and the possibility of encountering buffalo, zebra, bushbuck, elephant and
even the occasional leopard.

The Ngorongoro Crater is the main focal point of tourist activity in the NCA
but those who have the time can explore any number of less-publicised natural
features further afield. Oldupai Gorge, for instance, is the site of some of Africa's
most important hominid fossil finds, and can easily be visited *en route* from the
crater rim to the Serengeti. Other highlights include the Empakaai Crater and (to
a lesser extent) Olmoti Crater in the northern NCA, while the crater rim is highly
rewarding for montane forest birds.

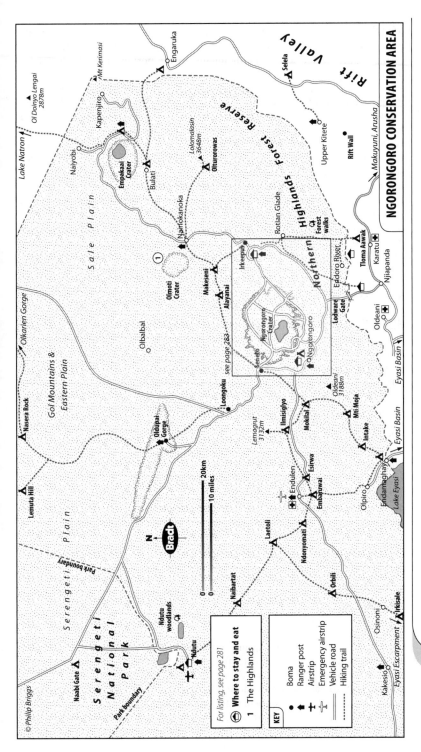

NGORONGORO CONSERVATION AREA

NGORONGORO CONSERVATION AREA

For listing, see page 281

Where to stay and eat
1 The Highlands

KEY
- Boma
- Ranger post
- Airstrip
- Emergency airstrip
- Vehicle road
- Hiking trail

© Philip Briggs

12

GEOLOGY With an altitudinal span of 1,230m to 3,648m, the NCA is among the most geologically spectacular reserves in Africa, comprising flat short-grass plains in the southwest and low rocky mountains in the northwest, while the west is dominated by the so-called Crater Highlands, a tall breezy plateau studded with standalone mountains. The mountains of the NCA date from two periods. The Gol Range, to the north of the main road to the Serengeti, is an exposed granite block that formed some 500 million years ago. Somewhat less antiquated, at least in geological terms, the Crater Highlands and associated free-standing mountains of the eastern NCA are volcanic in origin, their formation linked to the same fracturing process that created the Rift Valley 15–20 million years ago. Most of the Crater Highlands stand above the 2,000m contour, with the 3,648m-high Lolmalasin being the third-highest mountain in Tanzania after Kilimanjaro and Meru.

Ngorongoro Crater itself is the relic of an immense shield volcano that attained a similar height to that of Kilimanjaro before it imploded violently some two to three million years ago. It is regarded to be the sixth-biggest volcanic caldera anywhere in the world, and the largest to possess an unbroken wall. Eight smaller craters in the NCA, most notably Olmoti and Empakaai, are the product of similar eruptions. The Crater Highlands are no longer volcanically active, but the free-standing Ol Doinyo Lengai immediately northeast of the main highland block is among the world's most active volcanoes, having last erupted between 2007 and 2008.

HISTORY Based on fossil evidence unearthed at Oldupai Gorge in the western NCA, it is known that various species of hominid have occupied this area for at least three million years. It was the domain of hunter-gatherers until a few thousand years ago, when pastoralists moved in. The fate of these early pastoralists is unknown, because a succession of immigrants replaced them: the ancestors of the Cushitic-speaking Mbulu some 2,000 years ago and those of the Nilotic-speaking Datoga about 300 years ago. A century later the militaristic Maasai drove both of these groups out of what is now the NCA: the Datoga to the Eyasi Basin and the Mbulu to the highlands near Manyara. Most place names in the area are Maasai, and although several explanations for the name Ngorongoro are floating around, the most credible is that it is named after a type of Maasai bowl.

Europeans settled in the NCA around the turn of the 20th century. Two German brothers farmed on the crater floor until the outbreak of World War I. One of their old farmhouses is still used by researchers, and a few sisal plants dating to this time can be seen in the northeast of the crater. Tourism began in the 1930s when the original Ngorongoro Crater Lodge was built on the crater rim. The NCA formed part of the original Serengeti National Park as gazetted in 1951, but Maasai protests at being denied access to such a huge tract of their grazing land led to it being split off from the national park in 1959 and downgraded to a multi-use conservation area. The NCA was inscribed as a UNESCO World Heritage Site in 1979, and two years later it was declared an International Biosphere Reserve, together with the neighbouring Serengeti.

FEES The entrance fee to NCA, currently US$60 per person per 24 hours for non-residents, is payable by all who enter the conservation area, even those in transit to or from Serengeti National Park. A vehicle fee of Tsh20,000 (around US$10) per 24 hours is also payable for all Tanzanian-registered vehicles (as well as privately registered vehicles from elsewhere in East Africa) with a tare weight up to 2,000kg. Foreign-registered vehicles with a similar tare weight pay US$40 per 24 hours. In addition, a Crater Service Fee (CSF) of US$250 per vehicle is charged for each and every descent into the Ngorongoro Crater itself. At one point, the authorities threatened to impose a 6-hour limit on each crater visit, a ruling that has never been implemented, but is sometimes quoted by budget operators as a pretext to restrict game drives to 6 hours and save on fuel costs. All fees attract 18% VAT.

Visitors on organised safaris will almost invariably find that the NCA fees are included in the price, and won't have to concern themselves with the logistics of payment. However, self-drive or other independent travellers, who will need to deal with it themselves, should be prepared for several complications. Primary among these is that neither credit cards nor cash are accepted at any entrance gate to the NCA. Instead, fees must be paid in advance (with US dollars cash or a Visa or MasterCard) at a branch of Barclays Bank (represented in Arusha and Mwanza) or the CRDB (in both these towns as well as Karatu). The bank will then issue a receipt for presentation at the entrance gate, where the sum paid is loaded on to a temporary NCA smartcard. This smartcard is then swiped through a machine upon entering or exiting the conservation area (at Lodware Gate in the east or Naabi Hill Gate in the west) until the funds are depleted, after which it will be reclaimed by the NCA authorities.

This byzantine system enforces independent visitors to calculate their exact fee requirements in advance, eliminating any possibility of spontaneous plan changes once past Karatu. It is vital to get the sums right, as entry will be refused unless sufficient funds are loaded, but unused money is not refunded. So, in addition to individual and vehicle entrance fees and the CSF mentioned previously, you will need to add on any camping fees (*US$30pp per night*) as well as guide fees (*US$20 per party for any walking safaris, inc a visit to Empakaai Crater*).

Furthermore, if the plan is to enter the NCA from the east, cross the Serengeti at Naabi Hill, and then travel back through the NCA on your return leg to Arusha, you must allow for this second transit in your calculations (otherwise you risk being turned away at Naabi Hill Gate and having to drive all the way back to Mwanza). And it is imperative that you swipe your NCA smartcard when you exit the conservation area, otherwise the system will continue to deduct fees while you are in the Serengeti, depleting your funds before you return.

Another potential complication is that the CRDB and Barclays only operate during normal banking hours (⏰ *08.00–15.00 Mon–Fri, 09.00–noon Sat*), which means that fees cannot be paid in the late afternoon or on Sundays or public holidays. Also, be aware that the CSF can be processed against your smartcard only at Lodware Gate during opening hours (⏰ *06.00–18.00*) or at the administrative headquarters near Ngorongoro Crater Lodge during office hours (⏰ *08.00–16.00*). If you try to descend into the crater without a permit issued at one of the above offices, you will be turned back at the entry barrier. And if you plan on an early-morning start, it's best to sort out your CSF the afternoon before you want to enter the crater.

FURTHER INFORMATION The official NCA website (*www.ngorongorocrater.org*) is a useful source of up-to-date information. Also worthwhile, the 84-page booklet *Ngorongoro Conservation Area*, similar in style to the national park booklets, is readily available in Arusha and has good information on the crater and Oldupai Gorge. For a more detailed overview of the NCA, Veronica Roodt's excellent *Tourist Travel & Field Guide to the Ngorongoro Conservation Area* is widely available at hotel gift shops and craft shops in Arusha and elsewhere in northern Tanzania.

GETTING THERE AND AWAY The road from Arusha to Lodware Entrance Gate, the only access point along the eastern border of the NCA, runs via Makuyuni, Mto wa

Mbu and Karatu. It can comfortably be covered in less than 3 hours, with another 30–60 minutes required to get from Lodware Gate to any of the lodges on the crater rim. All roads within the NCA are unsurfaced, and a decent **4x4** is required to reach the crater floor. Most tourists visit Ngorongoro as part of a longer safari, but those with time or budgetary restrictions could think about visiting the crater as a self-contained one-night safari out of Arusha.

 WHERE TO STAY AND EAT *Map, page 283, unless otherwise stated*

No accommodation or camping facilities exist within Ngorongoro Crater, but a handful of upmarket lodges and camps are perched on the rim, most offering superb views to the crater floor, as does the public campsite there. If you stay on the crater rim, be warned that it gets very cold at night, and is often blanketed in mist in the early morning, so you will need a jumper or two, and possibly a windbreaker if you are camping. Ngorongoro Crater is also often visited as a day trip from one of the lodges in and around Karatu, covered earlier in this chapter, but this does mean you'll miss out on the stirring view over the crater at dusk, and the possibility of a dawn game drive on the crater floor. The anomalous Ndutu Lodge, though set inside the western border of the NCA, is not a realistic base from which to explore Ngorongoro Crater, so it is covered in the chapter on the Serengeti, to which it has closer ecological affiliations.

Exclusive

✳ 🏠 **Lemala Ngorongoro** (12 tents) m 0788 071035/0682 913045; e res@ lemalacamp.com; www.lemalacamp.com; ☺ closed Apr & May. This semi-permanent luxury tented camp is situated in a wonderful stand of lichen-stained flat-topped red-thorn acacias on the crater rim immediately inside the Lemala Gate (the start of the same ascent & descent road used by Ngorongoro Sopa Lodge). The views from the camp are great, it has an outdoor atmosphere lacking from most other camps on the rim, & it also has a prime location for early-morning game drives into the crater itself. The tents are very spacious & decorated in classic safari style, with a wooden floor & canvas top, & all have twin or king-sized beds, solar-powered lighting & hot water. Best suited to outdoorsy types (the crater rim under canvas can be quite chilly at night), it must rank as the 1st choice at Ngorongoro for anybody seeking to experience the crater in a real bush atmosphere. *US$900/1,340 sgl/dbl FB. Low-season discounts Mar, Nov & early Dec.* **$$$$$$$**

✳ 🏠 **Lion's Paw Camp** (8 tents) m 0752 225552/0767 000053; e info@ karibucampcollection.com; www. karibucampcollection.com. Situated close to Lemala & similar in general feel, this intimate old-style tented camp is recommended to dedicated outdoors types & serious photographers seeking

a bush experience & prime access to the crater floor, which is only 15mins' drive away. Set in a red-thorn acacia forest on the crater rim, the well-spaced tents all have a small front porch, 4-poster queen or twin bed with fitted net, small desk, 24hr charging points, bucket shower & toilet. There's a campfire at night & good food. *US$839/1,188 sgl/ dbl FB all-year round.* **$$$$$$$**

✳ 🏠 **&Beyond Ngorongoro Crater Lodge** (40 rooms) 🌂 (South Africa) +27 (0)11 809 4300; e safaris@andbeyond.com; www. andbeyond.com/ngorongoro-crater-lodge. This unique top-of-the-range lodge, which started life in 1934 as a private hunting lodge with a commanding view over the crater, was converted to a hotel shortly after independence in 1961. Acquired & rebuilt from scratch by &Beyond in 1995, it is a truly fantastic & architecturally innovative creation that largely lives up to its billing as 'the finest safari lodge in Africa'. Each individual suite consists of 2 adjoining round structures that resemble oversized Maasai huts, but are distorted in an almost Dadaist style. The large interiors combine elements of Baroque, classical, African & colonial décor to create an effect as ostentatious as it is eclectic. As might be expected of such a trend-flaunting lodge, it does divide opinion (the defiantly non-'bush' atmosphere often irks safari purists, though to be fair a traditional tented camp would be a seriously chilly prospect at this sort of altitude) but it is difficult to fault in terms of ambition & originality. For all its architectural flourishes the lodge literally never loses sight of its spectacular location – it is designed in such a way that the crater is almost constantly in sight, & even the baths & the toilets have a view. Likewise, the in-house guides are immensely experienced & knowledgeable both about the crater & wildlife in general. The food is world class, too – from the sumptuous packed b/fasts taken on early-morning drives into the crater to the mouth-watering homemade chocolate in the room – as is the butler service & overall ambience. *US$1,670pp, dropping to US$1,040 Mar–May & Oct–mid Dec, inc all meals, most drinks & game drives. No sgl supplement.* **$$$$$$$**

The Highlands [map, page 277] (8 rooms) (South Africa) +27 (0)21 418 0468; **m** 0736

500515; www.asiliaafrica.com. The latest addition to the superb Asilia portfolio is a blissfully isolated luxury tented camp set on the forested southwest wall of Olmoti Crater about 45mins' drive from the same ascent/descent road for Ngorongoro Crater used by the Sopa Lodge. Accommodation is in unique domed tented structures set on wooden platforms designed to combine a contemporary bush feel with the degree of natural incubation suited to this relatively chilly climate. *Rates on application.* **$$$$$$$**

Upmarket

✳ **Ngorongoro Sopa Lodge** (96 rooms) 027 250 0630–9; **e** info@sopalodges.com; www.sopalodges.com. Situated on the forested eastern edge of the crater rim some 20km distant from the headquarters & main cluster of lodges,

---

THE RHINOS OF NGORONGORO

Ngorongoro Crater has always been noted for its density of black rhinos. Back in 1892, Dr Oscar Baumann, the first European to visit the area, remarked on the large numbers of rhino, particularly around Lerai Forest – and he shot seven of the unfortunate beasts to prove his point. More recently, the biologist John Goddard estimated the resident population at greater than 100 in 1964. By 1992, poaching had reduced the crater's rhino population to no more than ten individuals, although this number had increased to 18 by 1998, including a mother and calf relocated from South Africa's Addo National Park to boost the local genetic pool. Sadly, five of these rhinos died soon after, one taken by a lion and the remainder thought to be victims of a tick-borne disease linked to the low rainfall of 2000/01. Since then, numbers have gradually recovered: the population resident in the crater stood at around 20 individuals in 2008 and various sources place the current population as between 30 and 45. The crater's rhinos all have a tracking device implanted in their horns, to discourage poachers and to enable the rangers to monitor movements.

Despite the overall decline in numbers since the 1960s, Ngorongoro is today the only accessible part of the northern safari circuit where these endangered animals are seen with any regularity. For many visitors to the crater, therefore, rhino sightings are a very high priority, and fortunately the chances are pretty good. In the wet season, the rhinos are often seen in the vicinity of the Ngoitokitok Springs and the Sopa road. For most of the year, however, they range between the Lerai Forest by night and Lake Magadi by day.

The crater's rhinos display a couple of local quirks. The black rhino (unlike its 'white' cousin) is normally a diurnal browser, which makes it rather odd to see them spending most of the day in open grassland, but the story is that they mostly feed by night while they are in the forest. Baumann noted that the crater's rhinos were unusually pale in colour, a phenomenon that is still observed today and is due to their predilection for bathing and rolling in the saline lake and fringing salt flats.

12

this attractive modern hotel is similar in standard to its rivals listed below. However, it has the huge advantage of being the only lodge (as opposed to tented camp) situated close to the combined descent & ascent road from the northwest rim, which greatly reduces the driving time either side of game drives, & is particularly useful for photographers wanting an early morning start. Accommodation is in vast semi-detached suites, each with 2 dbl beds, a heater, a large bathroom, a fridge, & a wide bay window facing the crater & Ol Mokarot Mountain. There is a swimming pool in front of the bar, & the food & service are excellent. One thing that stands out about this lodge is the large, forested grounds, a good place to look for characteristic montane forest birds, with sunbirds (tacazze, golden-winged & eastern double-collared) well represented & a variety of weavers, seedeaters & robins present. *US$385/680/867 sgl/dbl/trpl FB Jan & Feb, Jun–Oct & late Dec, low-season discounts available during other months.* $$$$$$

🏠 **Ngorongoro Serena Safari Lodge** (75 rooms) ☎ 027 254 5555; e reservations@serena.co.tz; www.serenahotels.com. Meeting the usual high Serena standards, this is the pick of the more conventional lodges on the crater rim in terms of facilities, & it receives consistent praise from tourists & from within the safari industry. It lies on the western crater rim along the road towards Seronera, several kilometres past the park headquarters & Crater Lodge. It is the closest of the lodges to the main descent road into the crater, a decided advantage for those who want to get to the crater floor as early as possible. The setting is a secluded wooded valley rustling with birdlife & offering a good view over the crater. The facilities, food & service are all of a high standard, & rooms are centrally heated. *US$520/870 sgl/dbl FB. Low-season discounts Mar–May, Nov & early Dec.* $$$$$$

🏠 **Ngorongoro Wildlife Lodge** (72 rooms) ☎ 027 254 4595; e res@hotelsandlodges-tanzania.com; www.hotelsandlodges-tanzania.com. Situated roughly 2km away from &Beyond Ngorongoro Crater Lodge, this former government hotel is one of the oldest on the crater rim & it shows its antiquity in the rather monolithic architecture. Despite a minor facelift following privatisation a few years back, the décor, service & food remain a little substandard. This is compensated for by the finest location of all the crater rim lodges, directly above the yellow fevers of Lerai Forest. Rooms are comfortably functional, with piping-hot baths & windows facing the crater. The grounds support a fair range of forest birds. *US$405/610 FB, low-season discounts Mar–May & Nov.* $$$$$$

Moderate
✳ 🏠 **Rhino Lodge** (24 rooms) m 0785 500005; e rhino@ngorongoro.cc; www.ngorongoro.cc. Formerly the home of the first conservator of NCA & later managed as a guesthouse by the NCA, this modest low-rise lodge is now managed under lease by the Dar es Salaam-based operator Coastal Aviation (page 92). It is far & away the most affordable lodge on the crater rim, & though it lacks a direct crater view, the surrounding mist-swathed forest has a charm of its own, & the location is very convenient for game drives. Accommodation is in simple but comfortable ground-floor rooms with twin or dbl beds & en-suite hot shower, & rates include good buffet meals in the cosy dining room, which comes complete with log fire. Superb value. *US$160/290 sgl/dbl FB.* $$$$$

Camping
🏕 **Simba Campsite** Situated about 2km from the park headquarters, this is the only place where you can pitch a tent on the crater rim, & it's hardly great value given that facilities are limited to basic latrines, cold showers & a rubbish pit. Still, the wonderful view makes it a preferable option to camping in Karatu, assuming you place a greater priority on the experience than creature comforts. The village near the headquarters has a few basic bars & shops, & there is nothing preventing you from dropping into nearby Ngorongoro Wildlife Lodge for a drink or snack. *US$30pp.* $$

WHAT TO SEE AND DO
Ngorongoro Crater floor The opportunity of spending a day on the crater floor is simply not to be missed. There are few places where you can see so reliably such large concentrations of wildlife all year round, and your game viewing (and photography) will only be enhanced by the striking backdrop of the 600m-high crater wall. The crater is also excellent Big Five territory: lion, elephant and buffalo

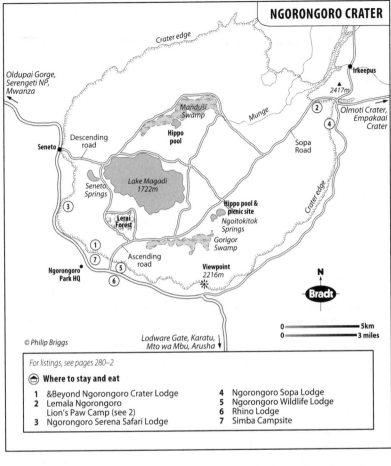

Oldupai Gorge,
Serengeti NP,
Mwanza

Crater edge

Irkeepus

2417m

Mandusi
Swamp

Munge

Olmoti Crater,
Empakaai
Crater

Descending
road

Hippo
pool

Sopa
Road

Seneto

Seneto
Springs

Lake Magadi
1722m

Crater edge

Hippo pool &
picnic site

Ngoitokitok
Springs

Lerai
Forest

Gorigor
Swamp

Ascending
road

Viewpoint
2216m

Ngorongoro
Park HQ

N

Bradt

0 ———— 5km
0 ———— 3 miles

© Philip Briggs

Lodware Gate, Karatu,
Mto wa Mbu, Arusha

For listings, see pages 280–2

Where to stay and eat

1 &Beyond Ngorongoro Crater Lodge
2 Lemala Ngorongoro
  Lion's Paw Camp (see 2)
3 Ngorongoro Serena Safari Lodge

4 Ngorongoro Sopa Lodge
5 Ngorongoro Wildlife Lodge
6 Rhino Lodge
7 Simba Campsite

are all but guaranteed, rhino are regularly seen, and a leopard is chanced upon from time to time. The official road down to the crater descends from Malanja Depression to the western shore of Lake Magadi, while the official road up starts near Lerai Forest and reaches the rim on the stretch of road between Wildlife and Crater lodges. There is a third road into the crater, which starts near the Sopa Lodge, and this can be used either to ascend or to descend.

There are several notable physical features within the crater. **Lerai Forest** consists almost entirely of yellow fever trees, large acacias noted for their jaundiced bark (it was once thought that this tree, which is often associated with marsh and lake fringes, the breeding ground for mosquitoes, was the cause of yellow fever and malaria). To the north of this forest, **Lake Magadi** is a shallow soda lake that varies greatly in extent depending on the season. Standing close to the lakeshore is a cluster of **burial cairns** that show some similarities with the tombs at the Engaruka Ruins further east, and are presumably a relic of the Datoga occupation of the crater prior to the arrival of the Maasai. To the south and east of this, the **Gorigor Swamp** also varies in extent seasonally, but it generally supports some water. There is a permanent hippo pool at the **Ngoitokitok Springs** at the eastern end of the swamp. The northern half of the crater is generally drier, though it is bisected by the **Munge**

River, which is lined by thickets and forms a seasonally substantial area of swamp to the immediate north of Lake Magadi.

The open grassland that covers most of the crater floor supports large concentrations of wildebeest and zebra (the population of these species is estimated at 10,000 and 5,000 respectively), and smaller numbers of buffalo, tsessebe, and Thomson's and Grant's gazelle. The vicinity of Lerai Forest is the best area in which to see waterbuck, bushbuck and eland. The forest and adjoining Gorigor Swamp are the main haunt of the crater's elephant population, which typically stands at around 70.

NOT A ZOO

You won't spend long in northern Tanzania before you hear somebody complain that Ngorongoro Crater is 'like a zoo'. It's a common allegation, but one as facile as it is nonsensical. The defining quality of a typical zoo is surely its total artificiality: the captive inmates have been placed there by people largely for entertainment, a high proportion are exotic to the zoo's location, they are invariably confined within enclosures of some sort (with different species, particularly predator and prey, normally kept apart), and most are fed manually like pets.

Ngorongoro Crater could scarcely be more different from a typical zoo. The wildlife you see in the crater is neither caged nor artificially fed. Indeed, with the exception of a few reintroduced black rhinos, it is all 100% indigenous and free to come and go as it pleases, forming part of the same cohesive ecosystem that includes the Serengeti and Maasai Mara.

The only respect in which the crater is faintly zoo-like is that the wildlife mostly seems very relaxed. But that doesn't mean it is tame, merely habituated to vehicles (in the same way that the mountain gorillas of Rwanda or the chimps at Mahale are habituated to pedestrian visits). This creates superb opportunities to observe wildlife interaction and behaviour at close quarters – trust me, an infinitely more satisfying experience than travelling through a reserve where the wildlife is so skittish that most sightings amount to little more than a rump disappearing into the bush.

Perhaps the notion of Ngorongoro as a glorified zoo stems from something else entirely. Namely, the high volume of tourist traffic, a factor that does tend to dilute the crater's wilderness character and has some potential for environmental damage, but is of questionable impact on the animals. In fact, the wildlife of Ngorongoro is clearly less affected by the presence of vehicles than, say, the elephants and giraffes in the Selous, which regularly display clear signs of distress at the approach of a vehicle.

So, no, Ngorongoro Crater is not a zoo. It's nothing like one. But the high tourist volume within its confines can jar against our sense of aesthetics – especially when game spotting entails looking for a group of vehicles clustered together in the distance rather than looking for an actual animal! Personally, I feel that the scenery and abundance of animals more than makes up for the mild congestion, but if crowds put you off then there are other places to visit in Tanzania. Instead of adding to the tourist traffic and then moaning about it, why not give the crater a miss? Or better still, make the effort to be in the crater first thing in the morning when, for a brief hour or so before the post-breakfast crowds descend, it really does live up to every expectation of untrammelled beauty.

All the elephants resident in the crater are old males (although females and families sometimes pass through the area), and you stand a good chance of seeing big tuskers of the sort that have been poached away elsewhere in East Africa. Two curious absentees from the crater floor are impala and giraffe, both of which are common in the surrounding plains. Some researchers attribute the absence of giraffe to a lack of suitable browsing fodder, others to their presumed inability to descend the steep crater walls. Quite why there are no impala in the crater is a mystery.

The crater floor reputedly supports the densest concentration of predators in Africa. The resident lion population has fluctuated greatly ever since records were maintained, partly as a result of migration in and out of the crater, but primarily because of the vulnerability of the concentrated and rather closed population to epidemics. Over the course of 1962, the lion population dropped from an estimated 90 to about 15 due to an outbreak of disease spread by biting flies, but it had recovered to about 70 within a decade. In recent years, the pattern of fluctuation saw the population estimated at 80 in 1995, 35 in 1998, and 55 divided into four main prides and a few nomadic males in 2000. The crater's lions might be encountered just about anywhere, and are generally very relaxed around vehicles. The most populous large predator is the spotted hyena, the population of which is estimated at around 400. You won't spend long in the crater without seeing a hyena: they often rest up on the eastern shore of Lake Magadi during the day, sometimes trying – and mostly failing – to sneak up on the flamingos in the hope of a quick snack.

In the 1990s, no cheetahs were resident within the crater, surprising given that the open grassland is textbook cheetah habitat but probably due to the high density of competing predators. However, two different female cheetahs colonised the crater floor in 2000, and a small population has been present – and regularly sighted – ever since. Leopards are resident, particularly in swampy areas, but they are not often seen. Other common predators are the golden and black-backed jackals, with the former being more frequently encountered due to its relatively diurnal habits.

The crater floor offers some great birding. Lake Magadi normally harbours large flocks of flamingo, giving its edges a pinkish tinge when seen from a distance. The pools at the **Mandusi Swamp** can be excellent for water birds, with all manner of waders, storks, ducks and herons present. The grassland is a good place to see a number of striking ground birds. One very common resident is the kori bustard, reputedly the world's heaviest flying bird, and spectacular if you catch it during a mating dance. Ostrich are also common, along with the gorgeously garish crowned crane, and (in the rainy season) huge flocks of migrant storks. Less prominent, but common, and of great interest to more dedicated birders, is the lovely rosy-throated longclaw. Two of the most striking and visible birds of prey are the augur buzzard, sometimes seen here in its unusual melanistic form, and the foppish long-crested eagle. The localised Egyptian vulture – whose ability to crack open ostrich eggs by holding a stone in its beak makes it the only bird that arguably uses tools – is sometimes seen in the vicinity of Mungu Stream.

There are a few hippo pools in the crater, but the one most often visited is Ngoitokitok Springs, a popular picnic spot where lunch is enlivened by a flock of black kites that have become adept at swooping down on tourists and snatching the food from their hands.

The authorities rigidly forbid tourists from entering the crater before 07.00, and they must be out of the crater before 18.00. This is a frustrating ruling for photographers, since it means that you miss out on the best light of the day, and it has encouraged a situation where most safari drivers suggest that their clients take breakfast before going on a game drive, and carry a picnic lunch. This programme is difficult to avoid on a group safari, but for those on a private safari it is well worth getting down to the crater as early as permitted. Photography aside, this is the one time of the day when you might have the crater to yourself, the one time, in other words, when you can really experience the Ngorongoro Crater of television documentary land. Note that it is forbidden to descend to the floor after 16.00, and that a 'crater service fee' of US$200 per vehicle is payable every time you enter the crater.

Empakaai and Olmoti craters

The NCA also protects two major craters other than Ngorongoro, both relics of the volcanic activity that shaped the Crater Highlands over the past ten million years or so. These are the Empakaai and Olmoti craters, and while both are dwarfed in size and reputation by the peerless Ngorongoro, they are also well worth a visit, offering a welcome opportunity to break the typical safari regime of twice-daily game drives with a stiff steep walk in lovely mountain scenery. Furthermore, the view from the rim of Empakaai has to rank among the most spectacular in East Africa.

The more alluring of the two craters is **Empakaai**, which is around 540m deep and has a diameter of almost 8km. The crater floor, enclosed by sheer forested cliffs, supports a sparkling soda lake that covers about half of its area and has a depth of around 60m. The emerald lake's shallows are frequently tinged pink with thousands of flamingos, and a variety of other aquatic birds are common, too. As for mammals, elephant and leopard are still present in the area, but bushbuck, buffalo and blue monkey are more likely to be seen, especially on the crater rim.

The drive from Ngorongoro to Empakaai takes around 90 minutes, leaving from the crater rim close to the Sopa Lodge. A 4x4 is required, and if you want to hike to the crater floor you need to stop *en route* at Nainokanoka village to pick up a mandatory armed ranger for US$20. Past Nainokanoka, the road descends to the grassy bowl of the Embulbul Depression, which dips to a low point of 2,325m at the bases of the 3,260m Mount Losirua and 3,648m Lolmalasin (the highest point in the Crater Highlands, and third-highest peak in Tanzania). The road then climbs Empakaai's outer slopes, passing through alpine moorland and lush Afro-montane forest, before reaching the rim and its fantastic views over the crater to Ol Doinyo Lengai and, on very clear days, Kilimanjaro and Lake Natron.

A road circles part of the forested rim, which reaches an elevation of 3,200m in the east. An excellent footpath to the crater floor was constructed in 2008 – a steep but wonderful walk that takes around 45 minutes each way, longer if you're looking out for the (plentiful) forest birds – which definitely requires decent walking shoes. There is a campsite with rustic ablution facilities on the crater rim a few metres from the start of the footpath, but no other accommodation in the area.

If that walk hasn't sapped your energy, the smaller and less dramatic **Olmoti Crater**, a sunken caldera situated close to Nainokanoka, is worth a stop on the way back to Ngorongoro. A motorable track leads from Nainokanoka to a ranger post further west, from where the crater rim can only be reached on foot, following a footpath through montane forest that takes about 30 minutes up and 20 minutes back down. From the ranger post it is a half-hour walk to the rim. This is a shallow crater, covered in grass and bisected by a river valley, and it offers good grazing for Maasai cattle and also sometimes supports a few antelope. From the viewpoint at the rim, you're bound to see pairs of augur buzzard cartwheeling high in the sky, and might also catch a glimpse of the mighty cliff-loving Verreaux's eagle. On a clear day, the viewpoint also offers glimpses of the distant southern wall of Ngorongoro Crater, and you can follow a short footpath to the seasonal Munge Waterfall, where the eponymous river leaves the crater.

Because the NCA lies outside the national park system, it is permissible to walk and hike along a number of trails covering most main points of interest (but not the crater floor) in the company of an authorised guide. Indeed, you could theoretically spend a fortnight exploring the NCA along a trail network that connects Lake Eyasi in the south to Lake Natron in the north, as well as running west across the plains towards Laetoli and Lake Ndutu and northwest to Oldupai Gorge. Other possible targets for hikers include the Olmoti and Empakaai craters, Mount Lolmalasin (the third-highest in Tanzania), and the remote Gol Mountains. At least five different one-day hiking trails from the crater rim can be arranged at the headquarters at short notice, though it's best to make contact in advance to make sure an armed ranger is available (this can be done through the NCA Information Centre on Boma Road in Arusha; see page 138 for contact details).

Trekking expert Akë Lindstrom notes: 'More ambitiously, multi-day treks from one to six days all the way from Lake Eyasi to Lake Natron via the Crater Highlands are possible. For those with limited time, a superlative option would be to start at Empakaai Crater in the east and trek down to the base of Ol Doinyo Lengai over two days, then transfer by vehicle to the Lake Natron area. Lightweight camps supported by donkeys are the norm as it is very remote and the views are quite simply stunning. A number of tour operators offer this route and there are options of both public and private campsites on this sector.' For more details, contact Akë via Lake Natron Camp (page 261).

A useful colour map and brochure showing all hiking routes in the NCA is downloadable from www.ngorongorocrater.org/downloads/pdf/Walking_Safaris.pdf.

Oldupai Gorge It's difficult to believe today perhaps, but for much of the past two million years the seasonally parched plains around Oldupai – the Maasai name for the sisal plant, often but incorrectly transcribed as Olduvai – were submerged beneath a lake that formed an important watering hole for local animals and our hominid ancestors. This was a fluctuating body of water, at times expansive, at other times drying up altogether, creating a high level of stratification accentuated by sporadic deposits of fine ash from the volcanoes that surrounded it. Then, tens of thousands of years ago, volcanic activity associated with the rifting process caused the land to tilt, and a new lake formed to the east. The river that flowed out of this new lake gradually incised a gorge through the former lakebed, exposing layers of stratification up to 100m deep. Oldupai Gorge thus cuts through a chronological sequence of rock beds preserving a practically continuous archaeological and fossil record of life on the plains over the past two million years.

The significance of Oldupai Gorge was first recognised by the German entomologist Professor Katwinkle, who stumbled across it in 1911 while searching for insect specimens. Two years later, Katwinkle led an archaeological expedition to the gorge, and unearthed a number of animal fossils before the excavations were abandoned at the outbreak of World War I. In 1931, the palaeontologist Louis Leakey visited the long-abandoned diggings and realised that the site provided ideal conditions for following the hominid fossil record back to its beginnings. Leakey found ample evidence demonstrating that ancient hominids had occupied the site, but lacking for financial backing, his investigations went slowly and frustratingly refused to yield any truly ancient fossilised hominid remains.

Tanzania's wealth of invertebrate life, though largely overlooked by visitors, is perhaps most easily appreciated in the form of butterflies and moths of the order Lepidoptera. Almost 1,000 butterfly species have been recorded in the country, compared with roughly 650 in the whole of North America, and a mere 56 in the British Isles. Several forests in Tanzania harbour 300 or more butterfly species, and one might easily see a greater selection in the course of a day than one could in a lifetime of exploring the English countryside. Indeed, I've often sat at one roadside pool in an East African forest and watched ten to 20 clearly different species converge there over the space of 20 minutes.

The Lepidoptera are placed in the class Insecta, which includes ants, beetles and locusts among others. All insects are distinguished from other invertebrates, such as arachnids (spiders) and crustaceans, by their combination of six legs, a pair of frontal antennae, and a body divided into a distinct head, thorax and abdomen. Insects are the only winged invertebrates, though some primitive orders have never evolved wings, and other more recently evolved orders have discarded them. Most flying insects have two pairs of wings, one of which, as in the case of flies, might have been modified beyond immediate recognition. The butterflies and moths of the order Lepidoptera have two sets of wings and are distinguished from all other insect orders by the tiny ridged wing scales that create their characteristic bright colours.

The most spectacular of all butterflies are the **swallowtails** of the family Papilionidae, of which roughly 100 species have been identified in Africa. Named for the streamers that trail from the base of their wings, swallowtails are typically large and colourful, and relatively easy to observe when they feed on mammal dung deposited on forest trails and roads. Sadly, this last generalisation doesn't apply to the African giant swallowtail (*Papilio antimachus*), a powerful flier that tends to stick at canopy level and seldom alights on the ground. With a wingspan known to exceed 20cm, this black, orange and green gem is the largest butterfly on the continent, and possibly the world.

The Pieridae is a family of medium-sized butterflies, generally smaller than the swallowtails and with wider wings, of which almost 100 species are present in Tanzania, several as seasonal intra-African migrants. Most species are predominantly white in colour, with some yellow, orange, black or even red and blue markings on the wings. One widespread member of this family is the

The pay-off for the long years of searching came in 1959 when Mary Leakey – Louis's wife, and a more than accomplished archaeologist in her own right – discovered a heavy fossilised cranium whose jawbone displayed unambiguous human affinities but was also clearly unlike any other fossil documented at the time. Nicknamed 'nutcracker man' in reference to its bulk, the cranium proved to belong to a robust Australopithecine that lived and died on the ancient lakeshore around 1.75 million years earlier (palaeontological taxonomy being a somewhat fluid science, the Leakeys named their discovery *Zinjanthropus boisei*, but it was later designated as *Australopithecus boisei*, and is now usually known as *Paranthropus boisei*). And while 'nutcracker man' would later be superseded by more ancient fossils unearthed elsewhere in East Africa, it was nevertheless a critical landmark in the history of palaeontology: the first conclusive evidence that hominid evolution stretched back over more than a million years and had been enacted on the plains of East Africa.

oddly named **angled grass yellow** (*Eurema desjardinsii*), which has yellow wings marked by a broad black band, and is likely to be seen in any savannah or forest fringe habitat. The orange and lemon *Eronia leda* also has yellow wings, but with an orange upper tip, and it occurs in open grassland and savannah countrywide.

The most diverse of African butterfly families is the Lycaenidae, which accounts for almost one-third of the continental tally of around 1,500 recorded species. Known also as **gossamer wings**, this varied family consists mostly of small- to medium-sized butterflies, with a wingspan of 1–5cm, dull underwings, and brilliant violet blue, copper or rufous-orange upper wings. The larvae of many Lycaenidae species have a symbiotic relationship with ants – they secrete a fluid that is milked by the ants and are thus permitted to shelter in their nests. A striking member of this family is *Hypolycaena hatita*, a small bluish butterfly with long tail streamers, often seen on forest paths throughout Tanzania.

Another well-represented family in Tanzania is the Nymphalidae, a diversely coloured group of small to large butterflies, generally associated with forest edges or interiors. The Nymphalidae are also known as brush-footed butterflies, because their forelegs have evolved into non-functional brush-like structures. One of the more distinctive species is the **African blue tiger** (*Tirumala petiverana*), a large black butterfly with about two-dozen blue-white wing spots, often observed on forest paths, near puddles or feeding from animal droppings. Another large member of this family is the **African queen** (*Danaus chrysippus*), which has a slow, deliberate flight pattern, orange or brown wings, and is as common in forest edge habitats as it is in cultivated fields or suburbia.

The family Charaxidae, regarded by some authorities to be a subfamily of the Nymphalidae, is represented by roughly 200 African species. Typically large, robust, strong fliers with one or two short tails on each wing, the butterflies in this family vary greatly in coloration, and several species appear to be scarce and localised since they inhabit forest canopies and are seldom seen. Rather less spectacular are the 200–300 **grass-skipper** species of the family Hersperiidae, most of which are small and rather drably coloured, though some are more attractively marked in black, white and/or yellow. The grass-skippers are thought to form the evolutionary link between butterflies and the generally more nocturnal moths, represented in Tanzania by several families of which the most impressive are the boldly patterned **giant silk moths** of the family Saturniidae.

This important breakthrough shot the Leakeys' work to international prominence, and with proper funding at their disposal, a series of exciting new discoveries followed, including the first fossilised remains of *Homo habilis*, a direct ancestor of modern man that would have dwelt on the lakeshore contemporaneously with its Australopithecine cousin. After Louis's death in 1972, Mary Leakey continued working in the area until she retired in 1984. In 1976, at the nearby site of Laetoli, she discovered footprints created more than three million years ago by a party of early hominids that had walked through a bed of freshly deposited volcanic ash – still the most ancient hominid footprints ever found.

Today, the original diggings may only be explored with a guide, and – since all fossils are removed upon discovery – they are probably of greater immediate geological than archaeological interest. Not so the excellent **site museum**, however, which displays replicas of some of the more interesting hominid fossils unearthed at the site as well as the Laetoli footprints. Also on display are genuine fossils of some of the extinct animals that used to roam the plains: pygmy and short-necked giraffes, giant swine, river elephant, various equines and a bizarre antelope with long de-curved horns.

Oldupai Gorge lies within the conservation area about 3km north of the main road between Ngorongoro Crater and the Serengeti, and is a popular and worthwhile place to stop for a picnic lunch. Outside the museum, evolutionary diversity is represented by the variety of colourful – and very alive – dry-country birds that hop around the picnic area: red-and-yellow barbet, slaty-coloured boubou, rufous chatterer, speckle-fronted weaver and purple grenadier are practically guaranteed. There is no charge to stop at the site for a picnic, but in order to enter the museum or explore the diggings, you need to pay the entrance fee, which was recently hiked up to Tsh27,000 (equivalent to US$16).

ADVENTURES 'MONEY CAN'T BUY'

Tanzania is proud to boast 16 National Parks that have vast potential as tourist destinations. While visiting the parks, you will be privileged to enjoy unique, incomparable and exceptional wildlife viewing and other experiences including:

- Game viewing (day and night)
- Bush meals
- Picnicking
- Wilderness walks
- Bird watching
- Sports fishing
- Mountain trekking

- Chimpanzee tracking and habituation experience
- Canoeing and boating
- Balloon safaris
- Horseriding
- Cycling
- Paragliding

For more information visit: www.tanzaniaparks.go.tz,
Email: info@tanzaniaparks.go.tz/dg@tanzaniaparks.go.tz,
Facebook: tanzanianational parks, Instagram:tanzaniaparks

13

Serengeti National Park

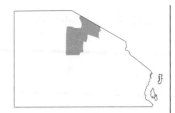

Tanzania's oldest, largest and most famous national park, the 14,763km² Serengeti is the centrepiece of a twice-larger ecosystem that also incorporates the Ngorongoro Conservation Area, several smaller Tanzanian wildlife reserves, and the Maasai Mara in neighbouring Kenya. Home to unusually dense populations of lions and other predators, the Serengeti is probably the leading contender for the accolade of Africa's finest game-viewing destination, renowned above all for the annual migration of millions of wildebeest and other ungulates across its vast plains. And while sceptics might fear that such a heavily hyped icon is unlikely to match expectations, our experience over more than a dozen safaris is that the Serengeti seldom disappoints: the variety and volume of its wildlife truly is second to none, as is the liberating sense of space attached to exploring its immense plains.

HISTORY

Much of the area now protected within Serengeti National Park was formerly inhabited by the Maasai (see box, page 268), who grazed their cattle on the eastern plains, but had a more sporadic presence in the west due to the seasonal profusion of tsetse flies, which carry the parasite responsible for nagama (a disease that can be fatal to cows). The Maasai are actually relatively recent arrivals to the region, having migrated there from the north in the 17th century, when they forcefully displaced their Datoga predecessors. The name Serengeti derives from the Maa word 'serengit', meaning 'Endless Plain', and it most properly refers to the short-grass plains of the southeast rather than the whole park. The notorious inhospitality of the Maasai meant that the Serengeti remained little known to outsiders until after World War I, when the first European hunters moved in to bag its plentiful wildlife.

The original Serengeti National Park, as it was gazetted in 1951, also incorporated what is now the Ngorongoro Conservation Area (NCA). However, when the newly gazetted park's Maasai residents realised they were threatened with forceful eviction from the entire area, they staged widespread protests. Eventually a compromise was reached wherein the NCA was split off from the national park and the Maasai were allowed to live and graze their cattle there but not within the national park. The Serengeti became world famous partly as a result of the pioneering work of the German zoologist Professor Bernhard Grzimek (pronounced 'Jimek'), who served as president of the Frankfurt Zoological Society (FZS) for 40 years prior to his death in 1987. Grzimek was the author and director of the book and Academy Award-winning film *Serengeti Shall Not Die*, both of which were released to public acclaim in 1959. Tragically, Bernhard's son Michael died in an aeroplane crash over the Serengeti aged just 24, and is buried at Heroes Point on the Ngorongoro Crater rim. The FZS still plays an important role in conservation and research today.

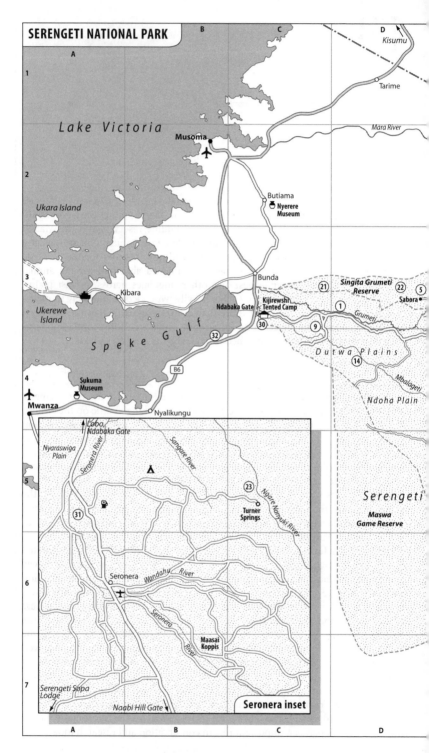

SERENGETI NATIONAL PARK

Kisumu

Tarime

Lake Victoria

Musoma

Mara River

Butiama
Nyerere
Museum

Ukara Island

Bunda

Singita Grumeti
Reserve

㉑ ㉒ ⑤

Sabora

Kibara

Ndabaka Gate

Kijirewshi
Tented Camp

① Grumeti

Ukerewe
Island

㉚ ⑨

Speke Gulf

㉜

Dutwa Plains

⑭

B6

Mbalageti

Sukuma
Museum

Ndoha Plain

Mwanza

Nyalikungu

Serengeti

Lobo
Ndabaka Gate

Seronera River

Sangare River

Maswa
Game Reserve

Nyaraswiga
Plain

㉓

Ngare Nanyoki River

Turner
Springs

㉛

Seronera

Wandahu River

Seronera River

Maasai
Koppis

Serengeti Sopa
Lodge

Naabi Hill Gate

Seronera inset

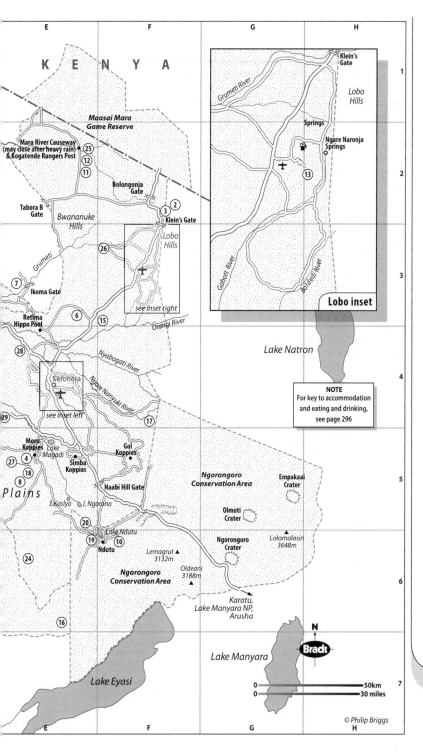

see inset right

Lobo inset

see inset left

NOTE
For key to accommodation
and eating and drinking,
see page 296

Lake Natron

KENYA

Maasai Mara
Game Reserve

Mara River Causeway
(may close after heavy rain)
& Kogatende Rangers Post

Bolongonja
Gate

Tabora B
Gate

Bwananuke
Hills

Klein's Gate

Lobo
Hills

Ikoma Gate

Retima
Hippo Pool

Orangi River

Nyabogati River

Seronera

Ngare Nanyuki River

Moru
Koppies

Lake
Magadi

Simba
Koppies

Gol
Koppies

Plains

Naabi Hill Gate

Ngorongoro
Conservation Area

Empakaai
Crater

L Kaslya

L Ngorono

Olmoti
Crater

Lake Ndutu

Ndutu

Lemagrut ▲
3132m

Ngorongoro
Crater

Lolomalasin
3648m

Oldeani
3188m ▲

Ngorongoro
Conservation Area

Karatu,
Lake Manyara NP,
Arusha

Lake Eyasi

Lake Manyara

N

Bradt

0   50km
0   30 miles

© Philip Briggs

Klein's
Gate

Lobo
Hills

Grumeti River

Springs

Ngare Naronja
Springs

Gabott River

Bologedi River

Grumeti

FLORA

Much of the Serengeti comprises flat plains whose fertile soil is essentially volcanic soil deposited by Ngorongoro and other calderas in the Crater Highlands to the east. The main vegetation type is open grassland, with the two most common species being *Sporobolus ioclados* and *Digitaria macroblephora*, both of which have shallow roots and form the main diet for the ecosystem's abundant grazers. Another common species in some areas is *Themeda triandra*, a taller grass that turns dark red when dry, and is consumed by wildebeest when more nutritious shorter grasses are unavailable. Parts of the Serengeti – particularly in the north and west – support a denser cover of deciduous woodland dominated by the gum-bearing African myrrh (*Commiphora africana*) and acacia trees such as the iconic umbrella thorn (*Vachellia tortilis*) and shrubbier whistling thorn (*Vachellia drepanolobium*).

There is little permanent water in the Serengeti, though perennial rivers such as the Mara and Grumeti support narrow strips of evergreen woodland, usually comprising various palms and fruiting ficus trees, the yellow-barked fever-tree (*Vachellia xanthophloea*), and the sausage tree (*Kigelia africana*), which is named for its heavy (up to 5kg) elongated fruits much favoured by elephants. Many parts of the Serengeti are studded with *koppies* (a Dutch or Afrikaans word literally meaning 'little heads'), isolated granitic outcrops that rise above the surrounding blanket of flat volcanic soil. Two magnificent trees commonly associated with koppies are fruiting rock figs such as *Ficus abutilifolia*, whose strong roots have been known to split boulders, and the cactus-like candelabra tree (*Euphorbia candelabrum*), a succulent whose deadly white latex was once harvested as a poison by hunter-gatherers.

The most conspicuous and worrying of several invasive species found in the Serengeti is the Mexican gold poppy (*Argemone mexicana*), a yellow-flowered perennial introduced to the Crater Highlands a few years back as a stowaway in a shipment of wheat seeds. This aggressive weed has spread profusely in recent years, colonising large tracts of former grassland in the Ngorongoro-Serengeti border area, and is also starting to appear closer to Seronera, for instance in the vicinity of Moru Koppies. The exotic poppy's spread is difficult to curb, partly because it produces a poison that impedes the growth of naturally occurring grasses, and partly because it responds to burning by growing back even more

SERENGETI NATIONAL PARK
For listings, see pages 302–4, 305–8, 309–12, 312–13 & 314–18

🅗 **Where to stay and eat**

profusely. Ecologists are concerned that it might eventually replace large tracts of the grassland on which the Serengeti's immense ungulate biomass depends to survive.

FAUNA

The most recent full census figures for the Serengeti ecosystem date to the 1980s and indicate that the commonest large herbivore species are wildebeest (1,300,000), Thomson's gazelle (250,000), Burchell's zebra (200,000), impala (70,000), topi (50,000), Grant's gazelle (30,000), kongoni (15,000) and eland (10,000). Anecdotal sources and more recent partial surveys indicate that these figures are now on the low side for several species. The current population of wildebeest, for instance, might well exceed two million, while the total number of zebras probably stands at 500,000, with the two species often encountered together in immense mixed herds. Other antelope species include Kirk's dik-dik, klipspringer, and small numbers of roan, oryx, oribi and waterbuck. There are also significant numbers of giraffe and warthog. The most common and widespread diurnal primates are the olive baboon and vervet monkey, but an isolated and seldom-seen population of patas monkey is resident in the west, and a few troops of black-and-white colobus haunt the riparian woodland along the Grumeti River through the Western Corridor.

As recently as the turn of the millennium, elephants were quite scarce in the Serengeti, but an aerial survey undertaken in 2014 counted more than 8,000 individuals in the Serengeti-Mara ecosystem, as compared with the 1986 tally of around 2,000. Some sources attribute this massive increase to greater persecution outside protected areas, but whatever the cause, elephants are visibly more common than they were even ten years ago, with the greatest concentrations to be found in the north. The same survey indicated that the buffalo population of the Serengeti probably stands at around 50,000. The park's black rhino population today stands at fewer than 50 individuals, as compared with 700 in the mid 1970s, and is restricted to the vicinity of the Moru Koppies in the far southeast, and the Mara River area in the far north. Ultimately, the success of most first-time safaris lies in the number and quality of the big cat encounters. There is something infinitely compelling about these animals, a fascination that seems to affect even the most jaded of safari drivers – many of whom are leopard obsessives, content to drive up and down the Seronera Valley all day in the search for a tell-tale tail dangling from a tree. And when it comes to big cats, the Serengeti rarely disappoints. The Tanzanian side of the greater Serengeti ecosystem supports an estimated 2,500–3,000 individuals, probably the largest single population left anywhere in Africa, and hundreds of resident lions stalk the plains around Seronera, as well as the Simba, Moru and Gol koppies close to the main Ngorongoro road. Here, it's normal to see two or three prides in the course of one game drive. Sociable, languid and deceptively pussycat-like, lions are most often seen lying low in the grass or basking on rocks, though several Serengeti prides are increasingly given to languishing in the trees on hot days.

Leopard numbers are unknown, due to their secrecy, but they are probably quite common throughout the park, and are very often seen in the Seronera Valley. Cheetahs, too, are frequently sighted: the park's estimated population of 500–600 is densest in the open grasslands around Seronera and further east towards Ndutu. In direct contrast to their more languid cousins, these streamlined, solitary creatures are most normally seen pacing the plains with the air of an agitated greyhound.

Of the other predators that can be seen in the Serengeti, spotted hyenas are very common, perhaps more numerous than lions. Golden jackals and bat-eared foxes appear to be the most abundant canid species on the plains around Seronera, while black-backed jackals are reasonably common in the thicker vegetation towards Lobo. Driving at dusk or dawn, you stand the best chance of seeing nocturnal predators such as civet, serval, genet and African wildcat. The real rarity among the larger predators is the African wild dog, which was very common in the area until the 1970s, before the population dwindled to local extinction as a result of canid-borne diseases and persecution by farmers living on the park's periphery. Fortunately, wild dogs are very mobile and wide-ranging animals, and sightings have been reported with increased frequency over recent years, particularly in the far north and the adjacent Loliondo

THE GREAT MIGRATION

The annual migration of at least two million ungulates – predominantly wildebeest but also large concentrations of zebra and lesser numbers of Thomson's gazelle, Grant's gazelle and eland – through the greater Serengeti ecosystem is the greatest spectacle of its type in Africa. Dictated by local rainfall patterns, the Serengeti migration does follow a reasonably predictable annual cycle, although there is also a fair amount of variation from one year to the next, dependent mainly on the precise timing of the rainy seasons. The cycle breaks up into the following main periods:

DECEMBER–APRIL The plains that stretch southeast from Seronera into the Ngorongoro Conservation Area form the Serengeti's main wildebeest calving grounds, centred on the Ndutu area of the NCA–Serengeti border. The wildebeest typically disperse into this area during the short rains, which fall in late November or early December, and stay put until the end of the long rains, generally in early May. These southeastern plains are the most accessible part of the park, particularly for those on a budget safari, and this is a fantastic time to be on safari in the Serengeti thanks to the lush green scenery. The optimum time to visit this area is the peak calving season (usually centred on February) when hundreds, even thousands, of calves are dropped daily, and predator concentrations are also at their peak. In March and April, you won't see the migration itself, but it's not uncommon to encounter herds of 10,000-plus animals on the move, following the rain to greener pastures.

MAY–JULY Usually towards the end of April, the wildebeest and their entourage start to congregate on the southern plains in preparation for the 800km northward migration. The actual migration, regularly delayed in recent years due to late rain, might start any time from late April to early June, with a herd of more than a million migrating animals marching in a braying column of up to 40km long, one of the most impressive spectacles in the world. The major obstacle faced by the wildebeest on this migration is the crossing of the Grumeti River through the Western Corridor, which typically occurs from June into early July. A great many animals die in the crossing, many of them taken by the Grumeti's ravenous and prolific population of outsized crocodiles, and the first herds to cross are generally at the greatest risk. For this reason, it can take up to two weeks from when the first wildebeest arrive at the southern bank of the river for the actual crossing to begin, by which time thousands upon thousands of wildebeest are congregated in the Western Corridor.

concessions. Indeed, following a series of introductions to the Serengeti from elsewhere in Tanzania, the park's wild dog population might now be as high as 250 individuals.

FEES AND FURTHER INFORMATION

Several guides to the park are available locally. They include the official 72-page booklet *Serengeti National Park*, with good maps and introductory information, and the newer and glossier *Serengeti* published by African Publishing House. Far more detailed is Veronica Roodt's *Tourist Travel & Field Guide to the Serengeti*, which is strong on maps, photographs, GPS points and other information, making it especially useful to self-drivers (see also maps on www.tracks4africa.co.za).

AUGUST–NOVEMBER Following the great northward sweep across the Grumeti, the ungulates usually cross the Mara River in August, before dispersing across the plains of the northwest. Conventional wisdom has it that August–October is a bad time to visit the Serengeti, because the wildebeest have crossed the Kenyan border into the Maasai Mara National Reserve. In reality, however, about half of the wildebeest stay in the northwest Serengeti over these months, and game viewing can be excellent, assuming that you can afford to base yourself at one of the exclusive tented camps in the Mara River area. Here, relatively small herds of wildebeest – typically between 500 and a few thousand – frequently travel back and forth between the northern and southern banks of the Mara River in response to changes in the local rainfall pattern, a truly spectacular event. In October, sometimes earlier, the animals generally cross the Mara River one last time and start to plod back southward to the short-grass plains of the southeast, and there is a good chance of catching the southward migration in the Lobo area between late October and mid November. The wildebeest usually reach the short-grass plains around Ndutu in late November, when the cycle starts all over again.

WHEN SHOULD YOU VISIT? Whether it is worth planning your safari dates around the migration is a matter of choice. With the best will in the world, it would be practically impossible to ensure that a few days in the Serengeti will coincide with the exact date of a river crossing, which is the most spectacular event in the migration calendar. On the other hand, if you choose the right part of the Serengeti – the southeast from December–May, the Western Corridor from May–July, the Mara River area from July–October, and the Lobo area from October–November – large herds of grazers should be easy enough to locate and there's a fair chance of witnessing a more spectacular migrational movement or river crossing.

On the other hand, bearing in mind that most predators and ungulate species other than zebra and wildebeest are strongly territorial and do not stray far from their core territory over the course of any given year, there is a lot to be said for avoiding the migration. Most lodges and camps now charge substantially lower rates during April and May, with a knock-on effect on the rates offered by safari companies that suddenly become hungry for business. Furthermore, the safari circuit as a whole is far less crowded outside of peak seasons, and in our experience the Serengeti, irrespective of season, will still offer game viewing to equal that of any game reserve in Africa.

13

The park entrance fee of US$60 per person per 24 hours plus 18% VAT can be paid only by MasterCard, Visa or Tanapa smartcard. No other cards are accepted, and neither is cash. For more details, see box, page 92.

NDUTU AND THE SOUTHEASTERN PLAINS

The short-grass plains stretching from the western extreme of the Ngorongoro Conservation Area through the southeast of the national park might be termed the 'classic' Serengeti: a vast open expanse teeming with all manner of wild creatures ranging from the endearing bat-eared fox to the imperious lion, from flocks of habitually panicked ostrich to strutting pairs of secretary birds, and from the gigantic eland antelope to the diminutive mongooses. Except during the rainy season, it is a dry and thinly vegetated area, supporting only two notable lakes: the larger but rather seasonal Ndutu on the Ngorongoro–Serengeti border, and the perennial but somewhat smaller Masek set entirely within the NCA less than 2km further east. Both lakes are alkaline, but not so salty as to prevent Maasai watering their cattle in them, and form part of the same basin as the paleontologically renowned Oldupai Gorge a short distance further north (pages 287–90).

It's also worth bearing in mind that roads around Seronera tend to be busiest during peak game-viewing hours of 07.30–10.00 and 14.00–16.30. So instead of breakfasting in camp, take a packed breakfast and head out as early as possible – game drives are permitted from 06.00 onwards, and even if you ignore the crowding issue, the first hour of daylight is the best time to see predators on the move. Also, bearing in mind that drivers tend to place emphasis on seeking out big cats because they think it's what their clients want, travellers with different priorities should talk them through with the driver – more radically, ask him to switch off his radio, stop worrying about what everybody else might be seeing, and just enjoy what animals you happen to chance upon.

WALKING SAFARIS Wayo Africa (*www.wayoafrica.com*) now offers multi-day walking safaris in designated wilderness sectors of the Serengeti that are all but inaccessible to other tourists. These safaris usually take place out of a simple but well-equipped mobile camp – dome tents with mattresses and bedding, safari-style hot bucket shower, mess tent with food cooked by a trained chef – which serve as a base for long morning hikes and shorter afternoon walks with an experienced armed guide. Alternatively, they can also set up more elaborate four- to ten-night semi-portered itineraries using a moveable camp that relocates daily, though guests need to carry their own tent, blow-up mattress, sleeping bag, clothes and personal toiletries. Generally, the routes follow watercourses so there is no need to carry water. On either type of trek, close-up encounters with the Big Five are commonplace, birding is great, and the night sky dazzling – but the biggest attraction is the opportunity to experience Africa's greatest national park at its most raw and untrammelled, far away from the crowding that often characterises the busier road circuits. Rates start around US$450 per person per day inclusive of transport, guiding, park fees and gear.

The southern plains are interspersed with several clusters of rocky hills known as koppies, each of which forms a microhabitat inhabited by non-plains wildlife such as klipspringer, rock hyrax, leopard, rock agama, rock thrushes, mocking chat and various cliff-nesting raptors. As the name suggests, **Simba Koppies**, which straddles the main road between the NCA and Seronera, is particularly good for lion, while the grassland around the more easterly **Gol Koppies** is excellent for cheetah and lion. Although trees flourish on the sides of these koppies, a striking feature of the surrounding plains is its paucity of trees. The most likely explanation for this quirk is that the soil, which consists of volcanic deposits from an ancient eruption of Ngorongoro, is too hard for most roots to penetrate, except where it has been eroded by flowing water.

The southeastern Serengeti is well populated with wildlife all year through, but it's especially rewarding between December and April, when the rains act as a magnet to the migrant herds of wildebeest and zebra. At this time of year, the prime game-viewing area is usually around Lake Ndutu, which lies at the epicentre of the wildebeest dispersal, and offers truly dramatic game viewing during and after the calving season. The acacia woodland around the lakes also supports a quite different selection of birds from other parts of the Serengeti, with the brilliantly coloured Fischer's lovebird being particularly conspicuous in the vicinity of the dead trees where it roosts.

MAASAI ROCK ART

An unusual relic of the Serengeti's former Maasai inhabitants is to be found at Moru Koppies in the form of some well-preserved rock paintings of animals, shields and other traditional military regalia near the base of a small koppie. This is one of the few such sites associated with the Maasai, and the paintings, which are mostly red, black and white, may well have been inspired by the more ancient and more accomplished rock art of the Kondoa area (pages 233–42) – although it's anybody's guess whether they possess some sort of ritual significance, or are purely decorative. On another koppie not far from the rock paintings is an ancient rock gong thought to have been used by the Datoga predecessors of the Maasai – a short but steep scramble up a large boulder leads to the rock gong and a close-by rock whose face is decorated with carved cupolas. Both sites should be inspected carefully from below before you climb the rocks, as lions frequently rest up there.

WHERE TO STAY AND EAT It may cause some confusion that the listings below include all lodges and several seasonal camps based in the Ndutu area, even though some of these technically lie within Ngorongoro Conservation Area. This is because the Ndutu area is an ecological extension of the southern Serengeti Plains, and the experience it offers is essentially a 'Serengeti' one of open plains and large wildebeest herds (especially between December and April). Indeed, despite lying within the NCA, Ndutu isn't well positioned for visiting Ngorongoro Crater. It should be noted, however, that if you stay at a lodge on the NCA side of the border, then crossing over to the Serengeti will attract a separate national park entrance fee. That said, dedicated photographers might be quite happy to skip paying national park fees and stick within the NCA, since – unlike in most parts of the Serengeti – off-road driving is permitted.

Exclusive

Sanctuary Kusini Camp [295 E6] (12 tents) 027 250 9817 or (UK) +44 (0)20 7190 7728; e reservations.tanzania@sanctuaryretreats.com; www.sanctuaryretreats.com; ⊕ closed Apr & May. With its fantastic location among a set of tall black boulders, this spaciously laid-out camp is the most remote & exclusive place to stay in the southern Serengeti, especially over Feb & Mar when the area hosts immense herds of wildebeest & zebra. At other times of the year, elephant, giraffe & buffalo are quite common in the surrounding acacia woodland, while the open plains 30mins' drive away are renowned for cheetah sightings, & can be explored off-road east of the main Ndutu road (a real bonus for photographers). A pride of around 20 lions, resident in the koppies immediately around camp, provides an exciting nocturnal soundtrack & is often easy to locate on early-morning drives. There are plenty of birds around, including the striking secretary bird after which the camp is named. Full-day drives to Moru Koppies & Seronera are a possibility when the local wildlife is quiet. Accommodation is in very spacious & luxurious tents with wooden floor, en-suite hot shower & a wide balcony with a comfortable couch where you can rest up between game drives. The common area is a billowing tented construction divided into a bar, restaurant, lounge & first shop, while sundowners are usually taken on an adjacent rock offering views to Ngorongoro. Kusini lies about 2hrs' drive south of Ndutu or Moru Koppies, but most clients fly in to the eponymous airstrip. One of the best-value options in this price & quality range. *US$795/1,030 sgl/dbl full game package, substantial discounts for 3+ nights &/or Sep–early Dec.* **$$$$$$$**

Nomad Serengeti Safari Camp (6 tents) m 0787 595908; e info@nomad-tanzania.com; www.nomad-tanzania.com. The oldest mobile camp in the Serengeti, established in the early 1990s, this small & exclusive old-style camp offers an authentic bush experience in comfortable standing tents with dbl beds, a small dressing area, eco-flush toilets & safari-style bucket showers. The emphasis is on tracking the migration, so it relocates seasonally in accordance with the predicted movements of the wildebeest. It is generally located close to Ndutu from Dec to Apr. *US$1,150/1,630 sgl/dbl, with low-season discounts available mid Mar–mid May & Nov–mid Dec.* **$$$$$$$**

✱ ⌂ **Olakira Camp** (9 tents) (South Africa) +27 (0)21 418 0468; m 0736 500515; www.asiliaafrica.com. This wonderful mobile camp moves seasonally between the Ndutu & Mara regions. It is in the south from Dec to Mar, usually to the east of Ndutu, to coincide with the wildebeest calving season. It has a classic safari ambience & décor, consisting of attractively furnished standing tents with king-sized or twin beds, private veranda & en-suite flush toilet & hot shower. *US$1,010/1,590 sgl/dbl full game package, dropping to US$625pp Mar, early Nov & early Dec.* **$$$$$$$**

⌂ **Lemala Ndutu/Mara Tented Camp** (12 tents) m 0788 071035/0682 913045; e res@lemalacamp.com; www.lemalacamp.com. This luxury mobile tented camp is situated in the NCA about 5km from Ndutu airstrip from Dec to Mar, when it is well positioned to catch the migration as it disperses in the southeast for the calving season. The tents are very spacious & decorated in classic safari style, with a wooden floor & canvas top, & all have twin or king-sized beds, solar-powered lighting & hot water. *US$880/1,300 sgl/dbl FB inc drinks. Full game packages inc activities an additional US$80pp. Low-season discounts Mar & early Dec.* **$$$$$$$**

⌂ **Mwiba Lodge** [295 E6] (8 tents) (UK) +44 (0)207 096 1287; e hello@classic-portfolio.com; www.classic-portfolio.com. This luxury tented camp lies in a 200km² chunk of former Maasai land bordering the NCA & Maswa Game Reserve on the Eyasi Escarpment south of the Serengeti. It has exclusive traversing rights of the surrounding ranch, & is ideal for those seeking a private & holistic safari experience, rather than just ticking off the Big Five as quickly as possible. The ranch consists mainly of thick acacia woodland, but there are areas of more open grassland, as well as more than 30 permanent springs that attract large numbers of wildlife during the dry season. Most species associated with the Serengeti are present, although resident populations are less

dense, & wildlife tends to be shyer. It is the best place in northern Tanzania to see the handsome greater kudu. Because it lies outside the national parks, standard game drives are supplemented by expertly guided night drives & enjoyable game walks. *US$1,865pp FB inc drinks, activities & all park & camp fees. Low-season discounts Mar–May.* **$$$$$$$**

Upmarket

✱ ⌂ **Ndutu Safari Lodge** [295 E6] (35 rooms) 027 253 7015; m 0736 501045/6; e bookings@ndutu.com; www.ndutu.com. Set within the NCA, this low-key family-owned retreat lies in thick acacia woodland overlooking the seasonal Lake Ndutu. It has a distinct 'bush' atmosphere lacking from other comparably priced lodges in the Serengeti ecosystem. The rooms are in small & unfussy stone chalets with netting, hot water & private veranda offering a good view into the bush. The bar & restaurant are open-sided stone & thatch structures frequented by a legion of genets by night, while the spectacular Fischer's lovebird nests in the parking area. This is a great base over Dec–Apr, when the surrounding plains are teeming with wildebeest, but it also offers good general game viewing away from the crowds at other times of year. Exceptional value. *US$296/493 sgl/dbl FB Dec–Apr, US$190/309 May–Nov.* **$$$$$**

⌂ **Lake Masek Camp** [295 F6] (20 tents) m 0736 503471; e reservations@tanganyikawildernesscamps.com; www.tanganyikawildernesscamps.com. Blessed with a perfect location overlooking the perennial Lake Masek, this well-priced camp offers accommodation in spacious standing tents set on wooden decks, king-sized or twin bed, net & outdoor shower. Staff is friendly & attentive, & while the buffet meals are nothing special, photographers will appreciate the early b/fast (from 06.00), while the DIY buffet b/fast or lunch seems like a great idea. *US$630/970 FB inc drinks Dec–Mar, dropping to a bargain US$285/480 other months.* **$$$$$$**

⌂ **Ndutu Wilderness Camp** [295 E5] (10 tents) (South Africa) +27 (0)87 941 3892; m 0786 642466/0754 842466; e reservations@wildfrontiers.com; www.tanzaniawildernesscamps.com; ⊙ Dec–Mar only. This sensibly priced seasonal camp, set on the NCA

Serengeti Balloon Safaris is – no prizes for guessing – the name of the company that runs balloon safaris daily at 06.00 from three launch sites within the national park: one throughout the year close to Seronera Wildlife Lodge, and others in the Ndutu area from 25 December to 15 March and the Western Corridor over June to August. Although not cheap, a balloon safari is definitely worth the expense if you can afford it. Gliding serenely above the trees as the sun rises allows you to see the expansive plains from a new and quite thrilling angle. It also offers the chance to see secretive species such as bushbuck and reedbuck, and, because you leave so early in the morning, you are likely to spot a few nocturnal predators. That said, any images you have of sweeping above innumerable wildebeest and zebra may prove a little removed from reality. Launching from Seronera or the Western Corridor, you can only be confident of seeing large herds of ungulates during the exact week or two when animals concentrate in the immediate vicinity. Odds are a lot better from Ndutu as the large herds tend to congregate there throughout December to March.

The package costs US$539 per person booked in advance or US$569 booked on site, both rates being inclusive of a Tanapa ballooning fee of US$40. It includes the transfer from your lodge or camp to the balloon site, a balloon trip of roughly an hour's duration, and a champagne breakfast. The breakfast is set up at a different site every day, depending on which way the balloons are blown, and it's presented with some flourish by the immaculately uniformed waiters who conjure up images of the safaris of old.

Be prepared for a very early start (the transfer from Seronera leaves at 05.30 and from the other lodges at around 04.30), and take some warm clothing, as well as a bag in which you can secure cameras, binoculars, etc, during take-off and landing. There is a booking desk for the Seronera launch site at the Seronera Wildlife, Serengeti Sopa and Serengeti Serena, as well as at the Visitors Centre at Seronera. Balloon safaris can be arranged through most other lodges and camps in the central Serengeti and Western Corridor. If you want to be certain of a place, it is advisable to book in advance, particularly during high season. Reservations can be made through any safari company, or directly through Serengeti Balloon Safaris (↘ 027 254 8967; m 0732 972308/0784 308494; e info@balloonsafaris.com; www.balloonsafaris.com).

side of Lake Ndutu, consists of en-suite tents with solar lighting, eco-friendly toilets & comfortable but unpretentious furnishings. It's one of the few camps to offer day & overnight guided walks in the NCA, partially backed up by vehicle &/or donkeys. *US$435/600 sgl/dbl FB, full game packages cost an additional US$120pp.* **$$$$$**

🏠 **Savannah Ndutu Camp** (12 tents)
↘ 027 254 7066; m 0684 547066; e bookings@ serengetisavannahcamps.com; www. serengetisavannahcamps.com. This small mobile camp aims to offer safari-goers a genuine bush experience at a reasonable price. It sets up near Ndutu from Dec to mid Apr to catch the calving season. The tents are simply but comfortably furnished & all have a private veranda, chemical toilet & starlight shower. *US$370/590 sgl/dbl FB.* **$$$$$$**

SERONERA AND THE SOUTH-CENTRAL PLAINS

The main focal point in the southern Serengeti – indeed, anywhere in the national park – is the park headquarters at Seronera. It is also the site of its oldest tourist lodge, as well as a cluster of public and special campsites, the staff village, various research projects, and a visitor information centre that incorporates a small site museum, a picnic area, a coffee shop, and an elevated wooden walkway leading through an informative open-air display.

Ecologically, the plains running immediately southeast from Seronera form a continuum with the Ndutu and NCA border area described above, comprising open grassland interspersed with several clusters of koppies. Wildlife viewing here is superb throughout the year, but peaks from March to May, when the post-calving wildebeest herds can usually be found in the vicinity. As the name suggests, **Simba Koppies**, which straddles the main road between the NCA and Seronera, is particularly good for lion. Closer to Seronera, the scenic **Moru Koppies** often provide good lion and cheetah sightings, and the area is home to around 25 black rhinos, descended from a herd of seven that migrated across from the NCA in the mid 1990s.

The two main waterways in the region are the small but perennial Mbalageti and Seronera rivers, both of which support a thin strip of riparian woodland. The sausage trees and umbrella thorns of the Seronera River Valley rank among the best places in Africa to search for leopards – there are simply too few tall trees for these normally elusive creatures to be as well hidden as they tend to be in dense woodland. More surprisingly, several lion prides resident along the Seronera River have taken to the trees with increasing regularity in recent years, particularly during the rains, when arboreal lion sightings are possibly more frequent than terrestrial ones.

Fed by the Mbalageti River immediately northeast of Moru Koppies, the small, saline **Lake Magadi** (a common name for lakes, as 'magadi' just means soda or salt) often supports large numbers of aquatic birds, including thousands of flamingos when the water level is suitable. A small hippo pool lies on the Seronera River about 5km south of Seronera along the road back towards the NCA. Far more impressive, however, is the **Retima Hippo Pool**, where up to 100 of these aquatic animals can be seen basking near the confluence of the Seronera and Grumeti rivers about 15km north of the park headquarters.

WHERE TO STAY AND EAT The most central base for exploring this region is the (soon to reopen) Seronera Wildlife Lodge, or one of the nearby campsites at the park headquarters. A few other chain lodges, including the Serengeti Serena and Sopa, are also well positioned for exploring the southern plains, and have far better facilities, and several seasonal or semi-permanent tented camps are also found in the area.

In addition to the lodges listed below, a cluster of seven **campsites** lies about 5km from Seronera Wildlife Lodge (*US$30pp*; **$$$**).

Exclusive

✳ 🏠 **Dunia Camp** [295 E5] (8 tents) 📞(South Africa) +27 (0)21 418 0468; **m** 0736 500515; www.asiliaafrica.com. Boasting a location close to the Moru Koppies & only an hour's drive from Seronera, this unpretentious but stylish semi-permanent camp offers excellent game viewing all year round, peaking from Dec to Mar. The spacious & airy tents come with king-sized or twin beds, unobtrusive décor brightened up by

Maasai fabrics, en-suite hot bucket shower & a spacious semi-enclosed veranda with comfortable seating. As with other Asilia camps, the hospitality, food & guiding are to the highest standard. *US$1,250/1,790 sgl/dbl FB inc all drinks & activities Jan, Feb, Jun–Oct & late Dec. Low-season discounts available.* **$$$$$$$**

✳ 🏠 **Namiri Plains** [295 F4] (8 tents) 📞(South Africa) +27 (0)21 418 0468; **m** 0786 500515; www.asiliaafrica.com. Located a 90min drive east of Seronera, with the nearest neighbouring camp 45mins' drive away, Namiri Plains is one of the most remote camps in the Serengeti. This semi-permanent camp opened in 2014 in an area (Soit Le Motonyi) that had been closed to the public for more than 20 years & had been used for cheetah conservation. This is still a superb region for big cats & you're bound to see plenty of lions & cheetahs. The spacious tents are simply & tastefully decorated (the focus here is on the safari experience rather than modern comforts), but you can still expect the high-quality guiding, food & atmosphere for which Asilia is renowned. *US$1,390/1,980 sgl/dbl FB inc all drinks & activities Jan–Mar & Jun–Oct. Low-season discounts available.* $$$$$$$

✳ 🏠 **Sametu Camp** [294 C5]
(8 tents) m 0752 225552/0767 000053; e info@karibucampcollection.com; www.karibucampcollection.com. This semi-permanent tented camp has a wonderfully isolated location overlooking the seasonal Ngare Nanyuki River about an hour's drive east of Seronera & 30mins from the Barafu & Sametu koppies, both of which often host lions & leopards. The camp has a very exclusive atmosphere, with the large & comfortable en-suite tents strung out along a wooded ridge in an area with no other permanent camps. The proximity to Seronera allows you to do some game drives in this wildlife-rich but sometimes over-touristed area, but to split your time between there & more off-the-beaten-track circuits towards Moru Koppies. *US$905/1,230 sgl/dbl FB.* $$$$$$$

🏠 **Four Seasons Safari Lodge** [295 E3]
(77 rooms) m 0768 981981; www.fourseasons.com/serengeti. Set amidst rocky hills near the Lobo road about an hour's drive north of Seronera, this large & opulent hotel-style lodge has tended to divide opinions since it opened in 2013. It is arguably the most luxurious lodge anywhere in northern Tanzania, but lacks the low-key canvas-dominated bush atmosphere associated with most other similarly exclusive camps, while the use of AC in all rooms doesn't do much to boost its eco-credentials. Still, taken on its own sanitised terms it is a magnificent set-up, & ideally suited to 1st-time safari-goers terrified at the prospect of sharing a tent with lizards or having nothing but canvas separating them from passing lions & elephants. Rooms are luxurious & come with king-sized or

twin beds, walk-in net, fan, AC, flatscreen DSTV, laminate floor & natural stone-tiled bathroom with tub & shower. Other features include a large deck & infinity pool overlooking a waterhole that attracts a steady stream of elephants & other thirsty wildlife, a choice of 3 restaurants, good rooms & other facilities for travellers with disabilities, gym, massage & spa, & a superb exploration centre with cultural, geological & wildlife displays. The location isn't all that great for game viewing so most clients do all-day or long half-day drives to the Seronera area. The high level of staff professionalism is also striking. *From US$1,175/1,540 sgl/dbl FB inc all drinks. Pricier full game packages & suites are available as are low-season discounts.* $$$$$$$

🏠 **Serengeti Pioneer Camp** [295 E5]
(12 rooms) ☎ 027 254 0630; m 0784 250630; e info@elewana.com; www.elewana.com. Situated below a rocky outcrop on the wooded hills to the south of Moru Koppies, this smart & attentively staffed new camp is well placed for game drives in & around the Seronera Valley. The standing tents, decorated in an early colonial safari style, have queen-sized beds with walk-in netting, soft furnishings, private covered veranda & en-suite solar hot showers. Excellent views from the canvas restaurant/bar are complemented by top-notch food. *US$1,118/1,490 sgl/dbl FB incl all drinks Jan, Feb, Jul–Oct & early Dec. Low-season rates available other months. Game packages an additional US$100pp.* $$$$$$$

🏠 **Nomad Serengeti Safari Camp** See pages 302–3. This top mobile camp is usually located in the vicinity of Moru Koppies or Seronera over May, early Jun & Nov. $$$$$$$

Upmarket

✳ 🏠 **Seronera Wildlife Lodge** [294 A5]
(100 rooms) ☎ 027 254 4595; e res@hotelsandlodges-tanzania.com; www.hotelsandlodges-tanzania.com. The most central lodge in the Serengeti, Seronera Wildlife Lodge is situated only a couple of kilometres from the park HQ & boasts an unbeatable year-round location for game drives. The original lodge was built around a granite koppie in the early 1970s & utilised the natural features to create an individual & unmistakably African character. It was starting to look very dated & timeworn prior to being gutted by fire in 2013, but we expect – or at least hope – the reincarnated version will look a lot less

outmoded when it reopens, an occasion currently scheduled for 2017. Even if not, the lodge's brilliant location, at the heart of the superlative (but sometimes rather overcrowded) Seronera game-viewing circuit, makes it a great choice. *US$405/610 sgl/dbl FB, with low-season discounts Mar–May & Nov.* **$$$$$$**

✷ 🏠 **Serengeti Central Wilderness Camp** (10 tents) 📞 (South Africa) +27 (0)11 7092 2035; m 0786 642466/0754 842466; e reservations@wildfrontiers.com; www. tanzaniawildernesscamps.com. This down-to-earth & reasonably priced semi-permanent camp comprises en-suite tents with solar lighting, eco-friendly toilets & comfortable but unpretentious furnishings. The central location close to Seronera offers good game viewing all year round. It can be used as a base for multi-day wilderness trails. *US$435/600 sgl/dbl FB, dropping to US$307/500 Mar–Jun & Nov to mid Dec. Full game packages cost an additional US$120pp.* **$$$$$$**

🏠 **Kati Kati Tented Camp** [295 E5] (10 tents) m 0767 333223/0784 207727; e reservations@ tanganyikawildernesscamps.com; www. tanganyikawildernesscamps.com. This simple but well-run bush camp stands in an acacia forest about 40mins' drive from Seronera. The standing tents all have king-sized or twin beds, en-suite bathrooms with bucket showers & solar lighting. A good-value & convenient option for budget-conscious safari-goers who want to enjoy a no-frills bush camp in the heart of the action. *US$315/520 sgl/dbl FB, with low-season discount Mar–Jun & Dec.* **$$$$$$**

🏠 **Serengeti Serena Lodge** [295 E4] (66 rooms) 📞 027 254 5555; e reservations@ serena.co.tz; www.serenahotels.com. Situated on a hilltop roughly 20km west of Seronera, this is the most comfortable of the larger upmarket lodges in this part of the Serengeti. Accommodation is in a village-like cluster of Maasai-style dbl-storey rondawels, built with slate, wood & thatch to create a pleasing organic feel. The spacious self-contained rooms each have 1 sgl & 1 king-sized bed, nets & fans, & hot showers. There is a swimming pool, & the buffet meals are far superior to those in most East African safari lodges. The one negative is that game viewing in the thick scrub around the lodge is poor except for when the migration passes through, & it's a good half-hour drive before you reach the main game-viewing

circuit east of Seronera Wildlife Lodge. *US$510/855 sgl/dbl FB. Low-season discounts Mar–May, Nov & early Dec.* **$$$$$$**

🏠 **Savannah Seronera Camp** 📞 027 254 7066; m 0684 547066; e bookings@ serengetisavannahcamps.com; www. serengetisavannahcamps.com. This small & reasonably priced mobile camp relocates from Ndutu (page 304) to Seronera from Jun to mid Nov. The tents are simply but comfortably furnished & have a private veranda, chemical toilet & starlight shower. Good value. *US$280/500 sgl/dbl FB.* **$$$$$$**

🏠 **Mbuzi Mawe Tented Camp** [295 F3] (16 tents) 📞 027 254 5555; e reservations@serena. co.tz; www.serenahotels.com. This pleasant tented camp is set among a group of ancient granite koppies overlooking the Tagora Plains northeast of Seronera. There is quite a bit of wildlife resident in the immediate vicinity, notably elephants, the rock-dwelling klipspringer after which the camp is named, & habituated hyraxes that lounge like well-fed domestic cats on the footpaths between tents. This is supplemented by the wildebeest migration as it heads southwards in Nov or Dec. However, the camp is most often used as a base from which to explore the Seronera circuit, about an hour's drive to the south. Accommodation is in large, earthily decorated en-suite standing tents, each of which contains 2 dbl beds & has a private stone patio with a view towards the rocks. *US$570/915 sgl/dbl FB. Significant discounts Jan–May & Nov–early Dec.* **$$$$$$**

🏠 **Serengeti Sopa Lodge** [295 E4] (73 rooms) 📞 027 250 0630; e info@sopalodges. com; www.sopalodges.com. This large ostentatious lodge lies about 30mins' drive south of Seronera, on the side of the Nyarboro Hills, close to the Moru Koppies. The rooms here are practically suites: each has 2 dbl beds, a small sitting room, a large bathroom, a private balcony & a large window giving a grandstand view over the plains below, perfectly appointed to catch the sunset. The food is excellent & facilities include a swimming pool & internet café. Game viewing in the surrounding area is generally very good, with a high chance of encountering tree-climbing lions on the road north to Seronera, & there's much less traffic in the immediate vicinity than there is around the park HQ. *US$385/680/867 sgl/dbl/trpl FB, substantial low-season discounts Mar–May, Nov & early Dec.* **$$$$$$**

🏠 **Naona Moru Camp** [295 E5] (8 tents)
m 0732 930833/0712 682239; e info@
nasikiacamps.com; www.nasikiacamps.com. Set in
densely wooded hills 40mins' drive south of Moru
Koppies, this small semi-permanent camp has a
real bush atmosphere & offers accommodation in
massive standing tents each with 2 dbl beds, walk-
in nets, solar power & a large en-suite hot shower.
It is pleasant enough but lacks any semblance of
a view, & feels a bit understaffed & overpriced
compared with other camps of a similar standard.
*US$700/1,200 sgl/dbl FB or US$790/1,400 for
a full-game package; no low-season discounts.*
$$$$$$$

Moderate
🏠 **Ikoma Bush Camp** [295 E3] (17 tents)
☏ 027 250 6315; m 0754 324193; e reservations@
moivaro.com; www.moivaro.com. This refreshingly
unpretentious camp is situated on a concession
immediately outside of the national park, roughly
3km from Ikoma Gate by road, & about 40km
northwest of Seronera. The concession has been
granted to the lodge by the nearby village of
Robanda, which is paid a fee (used to fund the
local school, water pump & clinic) in exchange for
use of the land & assistance with anti-poaching
patrols. Set in a glade of acacias, accommodation
is in old-style no-frills dbl & twin tents with en-
suite showers & small verandas facing out towards
the bush. Because it lies outside the park, guided

game walks are on offer, as are night drives, which
come with a chance of encountering the likes of
leopard, genet & more occasionally the secretive
aardvark. It's a useful base at any time of year,
but especially in Jun when the migration passes
through. Very reasonably priced. *US$256/373 sgl/
dbl FB Jan, Feb, Jul, Aug & late Dec, US$216/318
Mar, Jun & Sep–early Dec. Low-season discount Apr
& May.* **$$$$$**
🏠 **Mapito Tented Camp** [295 E3]
(10 tents) m 0732 975210/0786 447852; e info@
mapito-camp-serengeti.com; www.mapito-camp-
serengeti.com. Similar in style & feel to Ikoma
Bush Camp & situated outside the same entrance
gate, this likeable & reasonably priced tented camp
has a bush feel, plenty of avian & mammal activity
in the immediate vicinity, & a variety of activities
on offer, including guided walks & night drives. Set
on stone platforms, the standing tents come with
twin or king-size beds, are furnished with a strong
African touch, & have a private veranda & en-suite
toilets & showers. The solar-lit mess tent serves
hearty home-style meals. *US$335/540 sgl/dbl FB,
dropping to US$160pp Apr & May.* **$$$$$**

Budget
🏠 **Tanapa Resthouse** [294 A5] (3 rooms)
☏ 028 262 1510/5; e serengeti@tanzaniaparks.
com. Situated at the Seronera park headquarters.
US$30pp B&B. **$$**

THE WESTERN CORRIDOR

The relatively narrow arm of the Serengeti that stretches westward from Seronera
almost as far as the shore of Lake Victoria is generally flatter than the more northerly
parts of the park, but moister and more densely vegetated than the southern plains.
Aside from a few small isolated mountain ranges, the dominant geographic feature
of the Western Corridor is a pair of rivers, the Grumeti and Mbalageti, whose
near-parallel west-flowing courses, which run less than 20km apart, support tall
ribbons of riparian forest before eventually they exit the national park to empty
into Lake Victoria. The characteristic vegetation of the Western Corridor is park-
like woodland, interspersed with areas of open grassland and dense stands of the
ghostly grey 'whistling thorn' (*Acacia drepanolobrium*).

Game viewing is pretty good here throughout the year. The broken savannah to
the south of the Grumeti River supports substantial resident populations of lion,
giraffe, elephant, wildebeest, zebra and other typical plains animals, while the little-
visited vistas of open grassland north of the river are especially good for cheetah.
The riverine forest along the two rivers harbours a few troops of the exquisite black-
and-white colobus monkey, and the Grumeti is also home to plenty of hippos,
crocodiles and water-associated birds. The side road to Mbalageti Serengeti is a

good place to look for the localised kongoni antelope, and the acacia woodland around the junction with the main road is the one place in Tanzania where the localised patas monkey is regularly seen.

Few camping safaris make it this far west, and permanent accommodation is limited to a handful of smallish lodges and camps, so tourist traffic tends to be low. The exception is from late May to July when the migration usually passes through the Western Corridor (although it may stick further east in years of heavy rain) and several mobile camps set up in the vicinity. The crossing of the Grumeti River, usually in late June or early July, is one of the most dramatic sequences in the annual wildebeest migration, and a positive bonanza for a dense population of gargantuan crocodiles.

WHERE TO STAY

Exclusive

✳ 🏠 **&Beyond Grumeti Serengeti Tented Camp** [294 B3] (10 tents) 📞 (South Africa) +27 (0)11 809 4300; e safaris@andbeyond.com; www. andbeyond.com/grumeti-serengeti-tented-camp; ⊕ closed Apr. Overlooking a small pool near the Grumeti River, this plush & stylish bush camp easily ranks as one of our favourite spots anywhere in the Serengeti. The mood here is pure in-your-face Africa: the oxbow lake in front of the bar supports a resident pod of hippos & attracts a steady stream of other large mammals coming to drink, while prolific birdlife – both at the water's edge & in the surrounding thickets – includes the iconic black-headed gonolek & very localised Karamoja apalis. At night, the place comes alive with a steady chorus of insects & frogs, & hippos & buffalo grazing noisily around the tents – not for the faint-hearted, & you shouldn't even think about walking around at night without an armed escort. Facilities include an outdoor boma, where evening meals are served (except when it rains), & a circular swimming pool from where you can watch hippos bathing while you do the same thing. The recently refurbished standing tents have a massive interior dominated by a king-sized bed with walk-in nets, as well as a minibar, a spectacular riverside balcony with sofa, en-suite toilets & outdoor showers. The common areas have also been revamped with eccentrically shaped blown-glass decorations from Arusha & other unusual but striking artefacts. The atmosphere is very informal, the good food is complemented by excellent house wines, & the service is world class. Expertly guided game drives, incorporated in the room price, offer a good chance of encounters with the locally based 60-strong Grumeti lion pride, & venture into other little-visited areas inhabited by large herds of elands,

topi & buffalo, as well as offering regular sightings of cheetah, spotted hyena & African wild dog. All in all, the last word in down-to-earth bush luxury. *US$1,340pp FB Jun–Aug & late Dec, inc drinks & activities, US$740 all other months.* **$$$$$$$$**

🏠 **Singita Grumeti Reserves** (24 rooms, tents across 3 lodges) 📞 (South Africa) +27 (0)21 683 3424; e enquiries@singita.com; www. singita.com. The legendary South African lodge operator Singita has exclusive traversing rights across the 1,400km² Grumeti Game Reserve, a northern extension of the Western Corridor, where it operates a trio of luxury upmarket lodges aimed at seriously affluent travellers seeking an exclusive safari experience. The flagship **Sasakwa Lodge** [294 D3] on the eponymous hill offers dramatic elevated views across the verdant plains of the Western Corridor, while the chic, minimalist **Faru Faru Lodge** [294 D3] lies in a wooded area noted for its high mammal & bird diversity, & the more earthy **Sabora Camp** [294 C3] is a tented camp set in the open plains. The wildlife in this formerly undeveloped corner of the greater Serengeti is similar to other parts of the vast ecosystem, but notable population increases have been recorded since 2003. The enterprise employs 600 people, mostly from surrounding communities, & it offers cultural visits to nearby villages. Although wildlife viewing is good all year through, it peaks during Jul–Sep, when the migration is in the area. *From US$1,550pp, dropping to US$1,260pp Feb–May, Nov & early Dec. Rates inc all meals, drinks & activities.* **$$$$$$$$**

🏠 **Kirawira Luxury Serena Camp** [294 C3] (25 tents) 📞 027 254 5555; e reservations@serena. co.tz; www.serenahotels.com. This plush tented camp, set on a small acacia-covered hill offering sweeping views over the Western Corridor, has

13

Edwardian décor that gives it a distinct *Out of Africa* feel. The atmosphere is neither as intimate nor as 'bush' as other camps in this range, but it will probably appeal more to nervous safari-goers who prefer not to have hippo & buffalo chomping around their tent. The standing tents are all set on a raised platform & comfortably decorated, with a netted king-sized bed & en-suite shower & toilet. Facilities include a large swimming pool complete with a small waterfall from a higher plunge pool – it's a lovely place to relax. *US$1,165/1,845 sgl/ dbl FB. Huge low-season discounts Mar–May, Nov & early Dec.* **$$$$$$$**

🏠 **Nomad Serengeti Safari Camp** See pages 302–3. This top mobile camp is usually located in the Western Corridor over late Jun & Jul.

Upmarket

🏠 **Mbalageti Serengeti** [294 D4] (40 rooms) 📞 028 262 2387/8; e info@mbalageti. com; www.mbalageti.com. Located in the Western Corridor, Mbalageti is perched on the northwestern slopes of Mwamnevi Hill, which lies 16km south of the main road through the Western Corridor, crossing the game-rich seasonal Dutwa floodplain & the Mbalageti River *en route*. The 3 room types are quite different, but all are secluded in the evergreen woodland running along the ridge of the hill & come with large wooden decks offering a superb view over the river to the Dutwa Plains. The 14 standard rooms are basic & close together, but comfortable & built in 2 blocks with shared verandas; the 24 luxury tented chalets are much larger & more stylish, & there are also 2 huge executive suites that are good for families. The dining area & bar are centred on a swimming pool, also offering breathtaking panoramic views, & the food – different theme buffets every night – is excellent. Overall, it's a very comfortable & relatively affordable alternative to the more exclusive lodges in the Western Corridor. *US$352/610 tented chalets, US$305/360 lodge*

SERENGETI BIRDS

The Serengeti National Park, although popularly associated with grassland and open savannah, is in fact a reasonably ecologically varied entity. The western part of the national park consists of broken savannah, interspersed with impenetrable stands of whistling thorns and other acacias, and run through by the perennial Grumeti River and an attendant ribbon of riparian forest. The north, abutting Kenya's Maasai Mara National Reserve, is unexpectedly hilly, particularly around Lobo, and it supports a variety of more-or-less wooded savannah habitats. So, while the actual Serengeti Plains in the southeast of the park do support the relatively limited avifauna you tend to associate with open grassland, the national park ranks with the best of them in terms of avian variety. A working Serengeti checklist compiled by Schmidt in the 1980s tallied 505 species, and at least 30 new species have been added since 1990.

The Serengeti-Mara ecosystem is one of Africa's Endemic Bird Areas (EBA), hosting five bird species found nowhere else, some of which are confined to the Tanzanian portion of the ecosystem. These 'Serengeti specials' are easy to locate and identify within their restricted range. The **grey-throated spurfowl**, a common roadside bird around the park headquarters at Seronera, is easily distinguished from the similar red-throated spurfowl by the white stripe below its red mask. In areas of woodland, parties of exquisite **Fischer's lovebird** draw attention to themselves by their incessant screeching and squawking as they flap energetically between trees. If the endemic spurfowl and lovebird are essentially local variations on a more widespread generic type, not so the **rufous-tailed weaver**, a fascinating bird placed in its own genus, but with nesting habits that indicate an affiliation to the sparrow-weavers. The rufous-tailed weaver is significantly larger and more sturdily built than most African ploceids, and its scaly feathering, pale eyes and habit of bouncing around

Hot-air balloon rides in the Serengeti are an unforgettable experience. Gliding serenely above the trees as the sun rises allows you to see the expansive plains from a new and quite thrilling angle page 304

above The Hadza are Tanzania's only remaining tribe of true hunter-gatherers, using poisoned arrows to hunt their food pages 254–5

left A traditional homestead in the traditional Wa-Arusha village of Ng'iresi, on the slopes of Mount Meru page 143

below A wedding celebration of the Barabaig, a tribe of traditional pastoralists who lives on the slopes of Mount Hanang pages 230–1

above The Maasai traditionally worship a dualistic deity, Engai, who resides in the volcanic crater of Ol Doinyo Lengai pages 274–5

right Colourfully dressed Shambaa women sell fresh fruit and vegetables at the vibrant Lushoto market page 196

below Seaweed farming is a vital source of income for coastal villagers on Zanzibar, and is one of the island's biggest exports page 370

above A cyclist overlooking Lake Manyara, Tanzania's finest spot for birdwatching pages 251–6

left The fascinating and myriad painted shelters around Kondoa allow you to explore this enigmatic facet of Tanzania's prehistory pages 233–42

below Approximately 30m high, the spectacular Kilasia Waterfall flows solidly throughout the year pages 173–4

rooms sgl/dbl, executive suite US$910 dbl over 21 Dec–7 Jan & Jun–Aug. All rates FB. Good low-season discounts late Jan, Feb–May, Oct–Nov & early Dec. **$$$$$$**

Moderate

✴ 🏠 **Speke Bay Lodge** [294 B4] (8 rooms, 12 tents)

📞 028 262 1236; e info@spekebay.com; www. spekebay.com. Set on the eastern shore of Lake Victoria, this lovely beachfront lodge has been under the same Dutch owner-managers since it was founded in the mid 1990s. It forms an excellent overnight stop for those coming to the Serengeti from western Kenya or the Lake Victoria region, as well as offering an opportunity for those on lengthy safaris to take a day or two's break from bouncing through the dusty bush to enjoy the moister environment alongside Africa's largest lake. Only 15mins' drive outside the Ndabaka Entrance Gate, the lodge lies in 40ha of lakeshore woodland close to the Mbalageti River mouth. It offers good birdwatching (250 species recorded, including red-chested sunbird, swamp flycatcher, black-headed gonolek, slender-billed weaver & other lake specials unlikely to be seen in the Serengeti proper) as well as cultural visits by dugout to a nearby fishing village. The en-suite cottages have a thatched roof, stone floor, king-size bed, lake-facing balcony & high-quality hardwood & wrought-iron furnishing & finishes, but there are also cheaper & more basic standing tents using common showers. US$270/215pp sgl/dbl en-suite thatched bungalow; US$110/100pp sgl/dbl safari tent with common showers & toilets. All rates FB. **$$$–$$$$**

Budget & camping

🏠 **Serengeti Stop Over** [294 C3] (10 rooms)

📞 028 262 2273; m 0784 406996/422359; e info@ serengetistopover.com. This low-key budget lodge lies alongside the main Mwanza–Musoma road,

---

boisterously in small flocks could lead to it being mistaken for a type of babbler – albeit one with an unusually large bill!

Of the two other Serengeti-Mara EBA endemics, the most visible and widespread is the **Usambiro barbet**, a close relative of the slightly smaller D'Arnaud's barbet, which also occurs in the region but lacks the full white-on-black spotted chest band. Altogether more elusive is the **grey-crested helmet-shrike**, which strongly resembles the white helmet-shrike but is larger, has a more upright grey crest, and lacks an eye wattle. Although this striking bird indulges in typically conspicuous helmet-shrike behaviour, with small parties streaming noisily from one tree to the next, it is absent from the southern Serengeti, and thinly distributed in the north, where it is often associated with stands of whistling thorns. Another localised species associated with whistling thorns, the Karamoja apalis is most likely to be seen in the Western Corridor.

Endemic chasing will be a priority of any serious birding visit to the Serengeti, but the mixed woodland and grassland offers consistently good birdwatching, including many species that will delight non-birders. The massive ostrich is common, as are other primarily terrestrial giants such as the kori bustard, secretary bird and southern ground hornbill. Perhaps the most distinctive of the smaller birds is the lilac-breasted roller, often seen perched on trees alongside the road. Highlights are inevitably subjective, but include a breeding colony of Jackson's golden-backed weaver at &Beyond Grumeti Serengeti Tented Camp, the magnificent black eagle soaring above the cliffs at Lobo, and up to six different vulture species squabbling over a kill. And there is always the chance of an exciting 'first'. Recent additions to the Tanzanian bird list from the Serengeti include European turtledove (1997), short-eared owl (1998), long-tailed nightjar, black-backed cisticola and swallow-tailed kite (2000). In 2001, close to the Grumeti River, we were fortunate enough to see (and photograph) the first golden pipit ever recorded in the national park.

about 1km south of the Ndabaka Entrance Gate & 18km south of Bunda. The bandas & campsite use communal hot showers & cooking shades. The lodge can arrange safaris to Serengeti National Park, which will work out cheaper than a safari out of Arusha, if only because it is a mere 1km from the entrance gate & 135km from Seronera so an overnight or day trip is a realistic possibility. Other activities on offer include a walking safari to Lake Victoria, traditional & game fishing trips, a visit to the Nyerere Museum, & dancing & other cultural activities. *US$35/65 sgl/dbl banda B&B, camping US$5pp. Rooms* **$$$**, *camping* **$**

LOBO, LOLIONDO AND THE NORTH-CENTRAL SERENGETI

Wildly beautiful, and refreshingly untrammelled by comparison to the southern Serengeti, the plains that stretch northwards from Seronera towards the Lobo Hills are characterised by green undulating hills capped by some spectacular granite outcrops, particularly in the vicinity of Lobo itself. A cover of dense acacia woodland is interspersed with tracts of more open grassland, bisected by the ribbons of lush riparian woodland that enclose the eastern Grumeti River and its various tributaries. Partially due to the relatively dense foliage, the area doesn't generally match up to the far south in terms of game viewing, but it is also relatively untrammelled by tourism, so much so that it's still possible to do an entire game drive without seeing another vehicle.

Wildlife viewing in the Lobo area generally comes into its own during September and October, when the wildebeest pass through the area on the southward migration from Kenya to the Serengeti Plains. It also sometimes hosts large numbers of wildebeest in July, normally in wetter years when the northward migration tends to use a more easterly route than normal. But even at other times of year, there is plenty to see. This area supports most of the park's elephant population, and the Lobo Hills are known for hosting several large lion prides. Cheetah, leopard, spotted hyena and bat-eared fox are also quite common, as is the exquisite serval, a small spotted cat most often seen darting through open grassland shortly after sunrise.

Extending over 4,000km² along the northeastern border of the Serengeti and northern border of the NCA, the **Loliondo Game Controlled Area (LGCA)**, reached via Klein's Gate 20km north of Lobo, is an integral part of the wildebeest migration route through the greater Serengeti. Inhabited by the pastoralist Maasai, it effectively functions as a buffer zone to the national park, where cattle herds are frequently seen grazing alongside wild animals. Several lodges lie within the LGCA, on concessions that range in extent from a few dozen to a few thousand hectares. The largest and best of these concessions – indeed, one of the finest game-viewing destinations anywhere in Tanzania – is Klein's Camp, which effectively functions as a exclusive private reserve, and offers superb game viewing as well as optional extras such as night drives and game walks.

WHERE TO STAY AND EAT In addition to the lodges listed, the **campsite** immediately outside the Lobo Wildlife Lodge is little used compared with those at Seronera and it also costs US$30 per person. Facilities are limited to an ablution block and a rubbish pit. If you decide to stay, you can pop into the neighbouring lodge for a drink or meal.

Exclusive

＊ ⌂ &Beyond Klein's Camp [294 B2] (10 rooms) ✆ (South Africa) +27 (0)11 809 4300; e safaris@andbeyond.com; www.andbeyond. com/kleins-camp. Set within the LGCA on a hilly private concession bordered by the Serengeti National Park & Grumeti River, this wonderful &Beyond lodge offers some of the finest & most exclusive wildlife viewing in northern Tanzania, with a maximum of 20 guests & 5 4x4s patrolling its 100km² of acacia-strewn grassland. Because it lies outside the national park, there are no restrictions prohibiting night drives or off-road driving, both of which add an extra dimension to a safari. The range of wildlife is similar to the neighbouring part of the Serengeti, with at least one pride of around 20 lions resident, & a good chance of encountering one of several very relaxed leopards. The camp has a stunning location, comprising 10 en-suite bandas with hot shower, king-sized beds with walk-in nets & a private balcony strung along a hilltop offering panoramic views in all directions. Facilities include a swimming pool, a computer with internet access, & a well-stocked gift shop. Food, service & guiding are all to the highest standard. *US$1,340pp FB Jun–Sep & late Dec, inc drinks & activities, US$840pp all other months.* $$$$$$$

🏠 **Serengeti Migration Camp** [295 F3] (20 rooms) ☎ 027 254 0630–9; e info@elewana.com; www.elewanacollection.com. Set in the Ndasiata Hills about 20km from Lobo, this now ranks as one of the most exclusive lodges within the Serengeti National Park. Accommodation is in spacious en-suite luxury 'tents' made of canvas & wood, complemented by stylish wooden décor evoking the Edwardian era, & with large balconies facing the perennial Grumeti River. The lushly wooded grounds are rustling with birds & lizards, & there is a hippo pool on the river, with larger mammals often passing through camp. The surrounding area supports resident populations of lion, leopard, elephant & buffalo, & is fantastic when the migration passes through. Facilities include a swimming pool, jacuzzi, cocktail bar, library, lounge & a viewing platform where sundowners & private meals are served. An unusual feature of the camp is that short, guided game walks can be undertaken along several trails leading out from it. *US$1,118/1,490 FB sgl/dbl inc all drinks Jul–Oct & late Dec–early Jan. Low-season rates available other*

months. Game packages an additional US$100pp. $$$$$$$

🏠 **Buffalo Luxury Camp** [295 F2] (15 rooms) m 0732 971771; e reservations@intimate-places.com; www.intimate-places.com. Situated within the LGCA about 4km from Klein's Gate, this pleasant tented camp offers good access for game drives in the Serengeti's Lobo Hills, & guided walks & night drives can be undertaken within the confines of the 30ha concession. The spacious accommodation is in canvas-sided suites with a split-level hardwood floor, king-sized bed, sitting room, & large en-suite hot showers. *US$880/1,230 sgl/dbl suite, or US$1,088/1,555 sgl/dbl FB Jul–Oct inc drinks, with an extra US$135pp charged for a full game package. Low-season discount available other months.* $$$$$$$

Upmarket

☀ 🏠 **Lobo Wildlife Lodge** [295 H2] (75 rooms) ☎ 027 254 4595; e sales@hotelsandlodges-tanzania.com; www.hotelsandlodges-tanzania.com. As with several other former government hotels in this chain, Lobo boasts a wonderful setting & interesting architecture compromised by a gradual decline in service & maintenance, indifferent buffet meals, & fittings that betray its age. It was built between 1968 & 1970, when most tourism to the Serengeti came directly from Kenya, & has waned in popularity now that visitors to the Serengeti come through Arusha. It is built around a koppie, spanning 4 floors & with a fantastic view over the plains. The surrounding hills can offer some wonderful game viewing & the grounds are crawling with hyraxes & colourful agama lizards. If you can live with the organisational flaws, the combination of innovative architecture, fabulous setting, relative isolation & excellent game viewing – not to mention lack of comparably priced competition in this part of the Serengeti – makes it a definite pick. *US$405/610 sgl/dbl FB, low-season discounts Mar–May & Nov.* $$$$$

THE MARA RIVER AND THE FAR NORTHWEST

The one part of the northern Serengeti to match the southern plains for general game viewing is the northwestern wedge of sloping grassland that divides the Mara River from the Kenyan border. Accessed from the south via a concrete causeway near Kogatende Rangers Post, this extension of the legendary Maasai Mara National Reserve supports prodigious herds of elephant, eland, topi, gazelle, zebra, wildebeest, buffalo, etc, throughout the year, as well as significant numbers of lion and cheetah, and a small but regularly seen population of black rhino.

Game viewing along the Mara River can be little short of mind-boggling when the migration moves into the vicinity between July and September. During this time, large herds of wildebeest frequently gather on one or other side of the river, sometimes milling around for hours, even days, before one brave or foolish individual initiates a sudden river crossing, often for no apparent reason – indeed, it's not unusual for the same group of wildebeest to cross back in the opposite direction within hours of the initial crossing, suggesting that these slow-witted beasts are firm adherents to the maxim that the grass is always greener on the other side.

Back in the days when most safaris entered the park from Kenya, the far north of the Serengeti was quite busy with tourist traffic. However, the closure of the border between the Serengeti and Maasai Mara to non-residents in the late 1970s led to a long lull in casual tourism to the region, partly due to its remoteness from any lodge, and partly due to a period of regular banditry and poaching. The area effectively reopened to tourism with the arrival of Sayari Camp in 2005, and it is now serviced by quite a number of small camps and lodges, most of which lie to the south of the Mara River near Kogatende and the causeway. Though not quite as remote in feel as it was ten years ago, it remains perhaps the most untrammelled and exciting part of the Serengeti, and particularly during the migration season it makes for a highly recommended (albeit rather expensive) addition to any Tanzanian safari itinerary.

WHERE TO STAY
Exclusive

* ⌂ Sayari Camp [295 E2] (15 tents) \(South Africa) +27 (0)21 418 0468; m 0736 500515; www.asiliaafrica.com. Established in 2005 but recently relocated to a new setting in the rocky hills 2km south of the Mara River, this stylish camp offers excellent access to the Mara Triangle, as well as being ideally placed to catch wildebeest crossings in migration season. It is divided into a 9-unit & 6-unit wing, each with its own sitting area & mess serving imaginative & tasty food. Amenities include Wi-Fi throughout & a well-stocked library. Both wings offer accommodation in spacious & stylishly decorated tents with hardwood floors, walk-in netted king-sized beds, private balconies & hot showers, & the units are spaced so widely that guests are usually transported to the mess by car after dark. The genuine wilderness atmosphere, the remoteness from other lodges & the high-quality guiding typical of Asilia make this a real gem. *US$1,230/1,930 sgl/dbl FB inc all drinks & game drives Jul–Oct & late Dec–early Jan. Substantial low-season discounts during other months.* **$$$$$$**

* ⌂ Lamai Serengeti [295 E2] (12 rooms) \027 254 3281; m 0784 734490; e info@nomad-tanzania.com; www.nomad-tanzania.com. This luxurious permanent lodge is situated on the lushly wooded slope of the Nyamarumbwa (literally 'Many animal') Hills, about 25km south of the Kogatende Rangers Post & Mara Causeway. There are grandstand views in all directions, & the camp itself supports plenty of gaudy agama lizards, hyraxes, & plentiful birds including several localised barbet species. The game-viewing circuit immediately around the camp passes through an impressive group of koppies, where a large pride of lions is often seen sprawled out on the granite boulders & leopards are also observed quite commonly. It is also well placed to explore the network of roads around the Mara River, home to a resident group of black rhino & site of frequent wildebeest crossings in migration season. The luxurious & well-lit chalets, all attractive pastel shades & minimalist décor, have king-sized beds with walk-in netting, massive en-suite bathrooms, & large balconies offering great in-house birding. The food & service are superb, & the large swimming pool is a welcome luxury on hot days. *US$1,625/2,260 sgl/dbl Jul–Oct & 20 Dec–7 Jan, dropping to US$853/1,270 sgl/dbl other months. Rates inc all meals, drinks & game activities.* **$$$$$$**

⌂ Mkombe's House [295 E2] (4 rooms) \027 254 3281; m 0784 734490; e info@ nomad-tanzania.com; www.nomad-tanzania. com. Situated a short distance from Lamai under the same management, this unique lodge, aimed

THE SERENGETI HIGHWAY

The most controversial conservation issue to afflict East Africa in recent years was a proposal by the Tanzanian government to commence construction of a new road linking Arusha to the Lake Victoria region via the northern Serengeti. The proposal came into being as a result of President Kikwete's 2005 election promise to stimulate economic development in the isolated and impoverished region running west from the national park to the lake. The proposed road was to follow the Rift Valley north from Mto wa Mbu to Lake Natron, then ascend westward into the Loliondo Game Controlled Area, crossing through the Serengeti for about 53km between Klein's Gate and Tabora B Gate, before connecting with the main road along the east shore of Lake Victoria close to Musoma.

The proposed highway was universally condemned by ecologists and the tourism sector. There are two main arguments against its construction. The first is that it would bisect the northward and southward routes followed by the annual wildebeest migration, thereby disrupting this unique natural phenomenon. The second is that, if the existing asphalt road through Mikumi National Park serves as an indicator, regular truck traffic through the park would result in a huge number of road kills. Other concerns are that the road would improve access for poachers, provide an avenue for the spread of diseases and invasive weeds, and impact negatively on a globally important carbon sink through disruption to grazing patterns. It would also jeopardise the Serengeti's status as a UNESCO World Heritage Site, while a decrease in tourism to not only the Serengeti but also to Tanzania as a whole would cause a great loss of revenue and employment.

The proposal stood in limbo for several years. In June 2011, Tanzania's Minister for Natural Resources and Tourism wrote a letter to the UNESCO World Heritage Centre stating that if the proposed northern route did go ahead, the stretch running through the Loliondo Game Controlled Area and the Serengeti National Park would remain unpaved, strict speed limits would be imposed by Tanapa, and it would be illegal to drive at night (when wildlife is at most risk of being killed in a collision). Rather ambiguously, the same letter also stated that the government was considering an alternative southern route connecting Arusha to the Lake Victoria region, but bypassing the Serengeti ecosystem entirely. Meanwhile, the African Network for Animal Welfare decided to bring a case against the proposed Serengeti Highway to the East African Court of Justice (EACJ), which issued an injunction against the paved road in June 2014. The decision was appealed by the Tanzanian government, which questioned whether the matter fell under the jurisdiction of the EACJ. The appeal was rejected in August 2015, and for now the matter seems to be resolved, though there is still some talk of constructing a proper unpaved road along the same route. For updates, and information about other threats to the Serengeti, visit www.serengetiwatch.org.

at families or other parties, comprises a large 4-bedroom house offering expansive views across the distant Mara River into Kenya. With the look of a stylish beach house transplanted to the bush, the house has a cool & airy feel complemented by the predominant use of light pastel shades offset by splashes of bright African colours. All rooms are en suite with king-sized or twin beds & walk-in nets, & some offer an optional star-bed where you can sleep outside on the veranda below a glittering

13

Placed by some authorities in the same family as the closely related sparrows, the weavers of the family Ploceidae are a quintessential part of Africa's natural landscape, common and highly visible in virtually every habitat from rainforest to desert. The name of the family derives from the intricate and elaborate nests – typically but not always a roughly oval ball of dried grass, reeds and twigs – that are built by the dextrous males of most species.

It can be fascinating to watch a male weaver at work. First, a nest site is chosen, usually at the end of a thin hanging branch or frond, which is immediately stripped of leaves, probably to prevent snakes from reaching the nest undetected. The weaver then flies back and forth to the site, carrying the building material blade by blade in his heavy beak, first using a few thick strands to hang a skeletal nest from the end of a branch, then gradually completing the structure by interweaving numerous thinner blades of grass into the main frame. Once completed, the nest is subjected to the attention of his chosen partner, who will tear it apart if the result is less than satisfactory, and so the process starts all over again.

All but 12 of the 113 described weaver species are resident on the African mainland or associated islands, with at least 45 represented within Tanzania, all but six of which have a range extending into the north of the country. A full 20 of these Tanzanian species are placed in the genus *Ploceus* (true weavers), which is surely the most characteristic of all African bird genera. Most of the *Ploceus* weavers are slightly larger than a sparrow, and display a strong sexual dimorphism. Females are with few exceptions drab buff- or olive-brown birds, with some streaking on the back, and perhaps a hint of yellow on the belly.

Most male *Ploceus* weavers conform to the basic colour pattern of the 'masked weaver' – predominantly yellow, with streaky back and wings, and a distinct black facial mask, often bordered with orange. Seven Tanzanian weaver species fit this masked weaver prototype more or less absolutely, and a similar number approximate it rather less exactly, for instance by having a chestnut-brown mask, or a full black head, or a black back, or being more chestnut than yellow on the belly. Identification of the masked weavers can be tricky without experience – useful clues are the exact shape of the mask, the presence and extent of the fringing orange, and the colour of the eye and the back.

The golden weavers, of which only four species are present in Tanzania, are also brilliant yellow and/or light orange with some light streaking on the back, but they lack a mask or any other strong distinguishing features. Forest-associated *Ploceus* weavers, by contrast, tend to have quite different and very striking colour patterns, and although sexually dimorphic, the female is often as boldly marked as the

night sky. Amenities include a swimming pool, Wi-Fi, TV/DVD room, library & plentiful seating in the lounge & veranda. *US$1,625/2,260 sgl/dbl Jul–Oct & 20 Dec–7 Jan, dropping to US$853/1,270 sgl/dbl other months. Rates inc all meals, drinks & game activities.* **$$$$$$**

🏠 Lemala Kuria Hills [295 E2] (15 tents) m 0788 071035/0682 913045; e res@lemalacamp. com; www.lemalacamp.com; ⊕ closed Apr & May. This permanent tented camp has a great location in the Kuria Hills about 30mins' drive south of the Mara River. The glass-fronted tented suites are very spacious & all have twin or king-sized beds & 24hr electricity, plunge pools, Wi-Fi & hot water. It is a modern, hotel-like option in the northern Serengeti perfect for those who want to feel separated from the natural world around them. *US$1,110/1,700 FB sgl/dbl inc drinks Jul–Oct. Full game packages inc activities an additional US$80pp. Low-season discounts other months.* **$$$$$$**

male. The most aberrant among these is Vieillot's black weaver, the males of which are totally black except for their eyes, while the extralimital black-billed weaver reverses the prototype by being all black with a yellow face-mask. Among the more conspicuous *Ploceus* species in northern Tanzania are the Baglafecht, spectacled, vitelline masked, lesser masked and black-headed weavers – for the most part gregarious breeders forming single- or mixed-species colonies of hundreds, sometimes thousands, of pairs, often in reed beds and waterside vegetation. Most weavers don't have a distinctive song, but they compensate with a rowdy jumble of harsh swizzles, rattles and nasal notes that can reach deafening proportions near large colonies. One more cohesive song you will often hear seasonally around weaver colonies is a cyclic 'dee-dee-dee-Diederik', often accelerating to a hysterical crescendo when several birds call at once. This is the call of the Diederik cuckoo, a handsome green-and-white cuckoo that lays its eggs in weaver nests.

Oddly, while most East African *Ploceus* weavers are common, even abundant, in suitable habitats, seven highly localised species are listed as range-restricted, and three are regarded to be of global conservation concern. These include the Taveta palm weaver, which is restricted to the plains immediately below Kilimanjaro and is most common in the West Kilimanjaro–Amboseli area and around Lake Jipe, and the Usambara and Kilombero weavers, both endemic to a limited number of sites in eastern Tanzania.

Most of the colonial weavers, perhaps relying on safety in numbers, build relatively plain nests with a roughly oval shape and an unadorned entrance hole. The nests of certain more solitary weavers, by contrast, are far more elaborate. Several weavers, for instance, protect their nests from egg-eating invaders by attaching tubular entrance tunnels to the base – in the case of the spectacled weaver, sometimes twice as long as the nest itself. The grosbeak weaver (a peculiar larger-than-average, brown-and-white weaver of reed beds, distinguished by its outsized bill and placed in the monospecific genus *Amblyospiza*), constructs a large and distinctive domed nest, which is supported by a pair of reeds, and woven as precisely as the finest basketwork, with a neat raised entrance hole at the front.

By contrast, the scruffiest nests are built by the various species of sparrow- and buffalo-weaver, relatively drab but highly gregarious dry-country birds that occur throughout northern Tanzania. The most striking bird in the group is the white-headed buffalo-weaver, which despite its name is most easily identified by its unique bright-red rump. The endemic rufous-tailed weaver, a close relative of the buffalo-weavers, is a common resident of Tarangire, Serengeti and the Ngorongoro Conservation Area.

✳ ⌂ **Olakira Camp** See page 303. Over Jun–Nov, this wonderful mobile camp is set close to the confluence of the Mara & Bolongonja rivers, close to a frequently used wildebeest crossing point. **$$$$$$$**

⌂ **Nomad Serengeti Safari Camp** See pages 302–3. This top mobile camp is usually located in the Mara River region over late Jul–Nov. **$$$$$$$**

⌂ **Lemala Ndutu/Mara Tented Camp** See page 303. This luxury mobile tented camp relocates from Ndutu to the Mara River area over Jul–Oct, when it is close to 2 major crossing points. **$$$$$$$**

Upmarket

⌂ **Savannah North Camp** ☏ 027 254 7066; m 0684 547066; e bookings@ serengetisavannahcamps.com; www.

serengetisavannahcamps.com. This small & reasonably priced mobile camp operates close to the Mara River from Aug to Oct only. The tents are simply but comfortably furnished & have a private veranda, chemical toilet & starlight shower. Good value. *US$380/640 sgl/dbl FB. Full game packages cost an additional US$120pp.* **$$$$$**

Serengeti North Wilderness Camp (10 tents) (South Africa) +27 (0)87 941 3892; m 0786 642466/0754 842466; e reservations@wildfrontiers.com; www. tanzaniawildernesscamps.com. This down-to-earth & reasonably priced mobile camp moves from Ndutu to a location north of the Mara River from Jul to Oct. The en-suite tents have solar lighting, eco-friendly toilets & comfortable but unpretentious furnishings. *US$492/700 FB.* **$$$$$**

14

Rubondo Island National Park

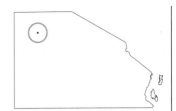

Although it practically borders the western Serengeti, Lake Victoria – the largest freshwater body in Africa – has never featured prominently on Tanzania's tourist circuit. The region's one significant wildlife attraction, gazetted in 1977, is the pedestrian-friendly Rubondo Island National Park, which stands in the lake's far southwest corner, 200km from the Serengeti as the crow flies, and forms a potential extension to a standard northern Tanzania safari package. Few tourists actually do make it to Rubondo, partly because the island's attractions are more low key and esoteric than those of Tanzania's high-profile savannah reserves. But a greater factor in Rubondo's obscurity is quite simply that its relative inaccessibility and limited tourist infrastructure make it an unrealistic goal for any but the most intrepid or wealthy of travellers.

This is a real shame, because Rubondo is a lovely retreat, offering the combination of a near-perfect climate, atmospheric jungle-fringed beaches, some unusual wildlife viewing, and the opportunity to explore it all on foot or by boat. Rubondo may not be to everybody's taste, but the island can be recommended without reservation to anybody with a strong interest in birds, walking or game fishing – or simply a yen to escape to an uncrowded and blissfully peaceful tropical paradise. It is to be hoped, however, that the recent acquisition of Rubondo's only private camp by the highly regarded Asilia group, and the likely reintroduction of scheduled flights from the Serengeti, will attract renewed interest in this unheralded gem of a park.

Rubondo has a remarkably pleasant climate all year round, with temperatures rarely falling outside a range of 20–25°C by day or by night. The average annual rainfall is around 1,200mm, with the driest months being June to September, and January and February. These dry months are the perfect time to visit Rubondo, but the park and lodge are open all year, and there is no serious obstacle to visiting during the rains. The entrance fee is US$30 per 24 hours plus 18% VAT. A national park fishing licence costs US$25 daily plus 18% VAT.

GEOGRAPHY AND VEGETATION

The 457km² national park is dominated by the green and undulating 240km² island for which it is named, but it does protect another 11 islets, none much larger than 2km², and there is talk of extending the boundary eastward to incorporate the forested west of Maisome Island. Rubondo Island itself essentially consists of a partially submerged rift of four volcanically formed hills, linked by three flatter isthmuses. It measures 28km from north to south but is nowhere more than 10km wide. The highest point on Rubondo is the Msasa Hills in the far south, which reach an elevation of 1,486m (350m above the level of the lake). The park headquarters, airstrip and various accommodation facilities lie within 2km of one another at Kageye, on the central isthmus, about 10km from the northern tip at the narrowest part of the island.

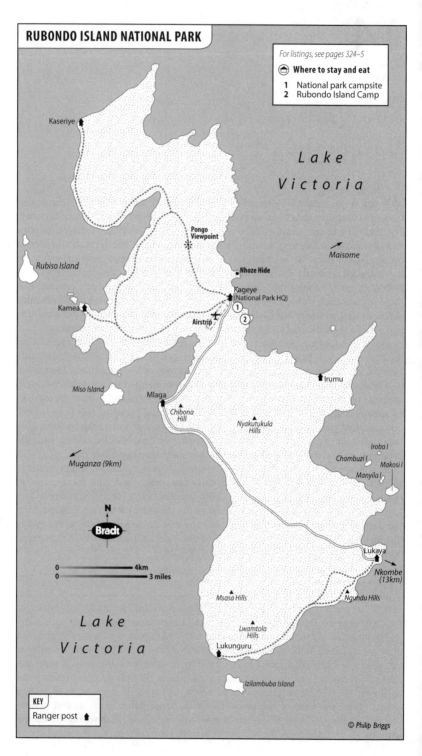

RUBONDO ISLAND NATIONAL PARK

For listings, see pages 324–5
⊖ **Where to stay and eat**
1   National park campsite
2   Rubondo Island Camp

Lake

Victoria

Kaseriye

Rubiso Island

Pongo
Viewpoint

Maisome

Nhoze Hide

Kageye
(National Park HQ)
1
2

Kamea

Airstrip

Miso Island

Irumu

Mlaga

*Chibona
Hill*

*Nyakutukula
Hills*

Muganza (9km)

Iroba I
Chambuzi I
Makosi I
Manyila I

N

Bradt

Łukaya

0   4km
0   3 miles

*Nkombe
(13km)*

Msasa Hills

Ngundu Hills

Lake

Victoria

*Lwamtola
Hills*

Lukunguru

Izilambuba Island

KEY
Ranger post ▲

© Philip Briggs

The dominant vegetation type is closed-canopy lowland forest, which covers about 80% of the island's surface area. This is interspersed with patches of open grassland and, all but restricted to the Lukaya area, acacia woodland. The eastern lakeshore is characterised by rocky areas and sandy beaches (such as those in front of the lodge and camp), while the western shore supports extensive papyrus swamps, often lined with wild date palms. Between December and March, an estimated 40 terrestrial and epiphytic orchid species come into bloom, as do gloriosa and fireball lilies. The red coral tree, which flowers almost all year round, is also a spectacular sight.

WILDLIFE

MAMMALS Rubondo's wildlife doesn't offer the easy thrills of many savannah reserves, but many large mammals are present, most alluring perhaps the introduced populations of chimpanzee and elephant (see box, pages 324–5). However, the presence of these glamour boys shouldn't shift the focus away from the island's interesting assemblage of naturally occurring residents, including the aquatic sitatunga antelope (see box, page 328), hippopotamus, crocodile and water monitor.

Vervet monkeys are numerous and easily seen all over Rubondo, but no other primate species occurs here naturally. This is difficult to explain, given the variety of primates that are present in similar island habitats on the Ugandan part of the lake, and given that the lake dried up fully in the biologically recent past, which would have allowed a free flow of species between the island and mainland forests.

There is no better place in Africa to observe the spot-necked otter, a widespread but elusive diurnal predator that feeds mainly on fish and frogs. A few pairs of otter are resident in the rocky bay around the lodge and camp – they regularly swim past camp, and the den can sometimes be seen through binoculars during the breeding season. The only terrestrial predators that occur on the island are the marsh mongoose and large-spotted genet, the latter regularly coming to feed around the lodge at dinnertime.

BIRDS With its combination of aquatic and forested habitats, Rubondo Island is an alluring destination for birdwatchers, especially as it can so easily be explored on foot. Oddly, the park's avifauna has never been properly studied, with the result that the only checklist, compiled from reported sightings by the Frankfurt Zoological Society and available at the Rubondo Island Camp, tallies up at a relatively low 225 species. It is likely that a substantial number of forest species that are resident on the island, or regular visitors, have thus far gone unrecorded.

The main avian attraction for casual visitors will be the concentrations of large water birds that occur along the island's swampy shores. Rubondo hosts Lake Victoria's densest fish eagle population – 638 individuals were recorded in a 1995 census – as well as large numbers of open-billed and yellow-billed storks. An excellent spot for varied water birds (as well as aquatic mammals and reptiles) is Mlaga Bay on the western side of the island, where some of the more prominent species are Goliath, purple and squacco heron, long-toed plover, blue-headed coucal, swamp flycatcher and various weavers. Of interest less for their variety than for their high number of birds are the so-called Bird Islands, a pair of tiny rocky islets that lie about 1km off the southeast shore of Rubondo, and support breeding colonies of various cormorants, egrets and ibises.

Dedicated birders are likely to be more interested in the forest and other terrestrial species. Two common birds on the island – Vieillot's black weaver and black-and-white casqued hornbill – are Guinea–Congo biome species with a very limited range in

14

Straddling the border with Kenya and Uganda, Lake Victoria is the world's second-largest freshwater body (after North America's Lake Superior) and some 51% of its 70,000km² surface area falls within Tanzania. Nowhere more than 75m deep, it fills an elevated depression between the two major forks of the Rift Valley, and much of the shoreline is shallow and marshy, while the open water laps four of the world's 20 largest freshwater islands (including Rubondo). At least 30 million people across the three countries are dependent on Lake Victoria as a primary source of water and/or food, and main population centres include the Tanzanian port of Mwanza, Kisumu in Kenya, and Kampala, Entebbe and Jinja in Uganda. The Kagera River, rising in the highlands of Rwanda and emptying into Lake Victoria in Tanzania, is the most remote source of the Nile, the world's longest river, which exits the lake near Jinja in Uganda.

Lake Victoria has been afflicted by a series of manmade ecological disasters over the past century. The degradation started in the early colonial era, with the clearing of large tracts of indigenous vegetation and drainage of natural swamps to make way for plantations of tea, coffee and sugar. One result of this was an increase in the amount of topsoil washed into the lake, so that the water became progressively muddier and murkier during the 20th century. More serious was the wash-off of toxic pesticides and other agricultural chemicals, which in addition to polluting the water contain nutrients that promote algae growth, in turn tending to decrease oxygenation levels. The foundation of several large lakeshore cities and plantations attracted migrant labourers from around the region, many of whom settled at the lake, leading to a disproportionate population increase and heavy overfishing.

By the early 1950s, the above factors had conspired to create a noticeable drop in yields of popular indigenous fish, in particular the Lake Victoria tilapia (ngege), which had been fished close to extinction. The colonial authorities introduced the similar Nile tilapia, which restored the diminishing yield without seriously affecting the ecological balance of the lake. More disastrous, however, was the gradual infiltration of the Nile perch, a voracious predator that feeds almost exclusively on smaller fish, and frequently reaches a length of 2m and a weight exceeding 100kg. How the perch initially ended up in Lake Victoria in the 1950s is a matter of conjecture, but by the 1960s, the colonial authorities, who favoured large eating fish over the smaller tilapia and cichlids, decided to ensure the survival of these alien predators with an active programme of introductions in the early 1960s.

It would be 20 years before the full impact of this misguided policy hit home. In a UN survey undertaken in 1971, indigenous haplochromine cichlids still constituted 80% of Lake Victoria's fish biomass, while the introduced perch and tilapia had effectively displaced the indigenous tilapia without otherwise altering the ecological balance. A similar survey undertaken ten years later revealed that the perch population comprised 80% of the lake's fish biomass, while the haplochromine cichlids – the favoured prey of the rapacious perch – accounted for a mere 1%. Lake Victoria's estimated 150–300 endemic cichlid species, all of which have evolved from a mere five ancestral species since the lake dried out 10,000–15,000 years ago, are regarded as representing the most recent comparable explosion of vertebrate adaptive radiation in the world. Ironically, these fish have also now been subject to what Boston University's Les Kauffman described as 'the greatest vertebrate mass extinction in recorded history'.

For all this, the introduction of perch could be considered a superficial success within its own terms. The perch now form the basis of the lake's thriving fishing industry, with up to 500 tonnes being exported annually by commercial fishing concerns in the three lakeshore countries. The tanned perch hide is used as a substitute for leather to make shoes, belts and purses, and the dried swim bladders, used to filter beer and make fish stock, are also exported commercially. The flip side of this is that as fish exports increase, local fishing communities are forced to compete against large commercial companies with better equipment and more economic clout. Furthermore, since the perch is too large to roast on a fire and too fatty to dry in the sun, it does not really meet local needs.

The introduction of perch is not the only damaging factor to have affected Lake Victoria's ecology. The amount of agricultural chemicals being washed into the lake has more than doubled since the 1950s, and large quantities of untreated sewage and industrial waste are dumped into the lake daily. This has led to an increase in the volume of chemical nutrients that promote the growth of plankton and algae. At the same time, the cichlids that once fed on these microscopic organisms have been severely depleted by the predatory perch.

The lake's algae levels have increased fivefold in the last four decades, with a corresponding decrease in oxygen levels. The lower level of the lake now consists of dead water – lacking any oxygenation or fish activity below about 30m – and the quality of the water closer to the surface has deteriorated markedly since the 1960s. Long-term residents of the Mwanza area say that the water was once so clear that you could see the lake floor from the surface to depths of 6m or more; today visibility near the surface is more like 1m.

A clear indicator of this deterioration has been the rapid spread of water hyacinth, an exotic South American species that thrives in polluted conditions, leading to high phosphate and nitrogen levels, and then tends to further deplete oxygen levels by forming an impenetrable mat over the water's surface. Unknown on the lake prior to 1989, the water hyacinth has subsequently colonised vast tracts of the lake's surface and clogged up several harbours, where it is barely kept under control by constant harvesting. To complete this grim vicious circle, Nile perch, arguably the main cause of the problem, are known to be vulnerable to the conditions created by hyacinth matting, high algae levels and decreased oxygenation in the water.

As is so often the case with ecological issues, what might at first be dismissed by some as an esoteric concern for bunny-huggers in fact has wider implications for the 30-plus million people resident in the Lake Victoria basin. The infestation of hyacinth and rapid decrease in indigenous snail-eating fish has led to a rapid growth in the number of bilharzia-carrying snails. The deterioration in water quality, exacerbated by the pumping of sewage, has increased the risk of sanitary-related diseases such as cholera spreading around the lake. The change in the fish biomass has encouraged commercial fishing for export outside of the region, in the process depressing the local semi-subsistence fishing economy, leading to an increase in unemployment and in protein deficiency. And there is an ever-growing risk that Africa's largest lake will eventually be reduced to a vast expanse of dead water, with no fish in it at all – with ecological, economic and humanitarian ramifications that scarcely bear thinking about.

THE FLOATING ZOO

Rubondo Island is unique among Tanzania's national parks not only in its aquatic location, but also in that it was conceived less as a game reserve than as a sort of 'floating zoo'. Proclaimed a forest reserve in German times, the island was upgraded to a game reserve in 1966, at the behest of Professor Bernhard Grzimek of the Frankfurt Zoological Society. Grzimek, best known for his tireless efforts to protect the Serengeti, believed that the forested island would make an ideal sanctuary for the breeding and protection of introduced populations of endangered Congolese rainforest species such as golden cat, okapi, bongo and lowland gorilla.

This plan never quite attained fruition, even though several chimpanzees were introduced to the island along with small numbers of elephant, giraffe, roan antelope, suni, black-and-white colobus monkey and black rhinoceros – most of which would not normally be regarded as forest-specific species. This arbitrary introduction programme was abandoned in 1973, only to be resurrected briefly in July 2000, when a flock of 37 grey parrots – captured in Cameroon for sale in Asia and confiscated in transit at Nairobi – were released on to the island.

Not all of the mammal reintroductions were a success. The 16 black rhinoceros that were relocated from the Serengeti in 1965 were poached in the 1970s, while the five roan antelope introduced in 1967 evidently died of natural causes before producing any offspring. By contrast, the six sub-adult elephants that were released on to the island between 1972 and 1973 have bred up to a population of greater than 40, with the larger herds concentrated in the south and lone bulls ranging all over the island – they are quite regularly seen around the park headquarters and lodge. Some concern has been expressed that an overpopulation of elephants could lead to the destruction of the natural forest, but the herd would probably

Tanzania. The lodge grounds and adjacent road and forest loop – where it is permitted to walk unguided – are as good a place as any to seek out other forest birds. Among the more interesting species recorded in this area are the blue-breasted kingfisher, grey-winged akalat, snowy-headed robin-chat, paradise flycatcher, common wattle-eye and green twinspot. The area around the lodge is also the main stomping – and screeching – ground for the recently introduced flock of African grey parrots.

GETTING THERE AND AWAY

Within the time constraints of a normal safari, the only realistic way to get to Rubondo is by air. **Coastal Aviation** (*www.coastal.co.tz*) operates daily flights (with a minimum inducement of two seats) from Arusha via the Kogatende and Grumeti airstrips in the Serengeti, and the lake port of Mwanza. The one-way fare is around US$550 per person from Arusha or US$330 from the Serengeti, and since flights land in the late afternoon and depart on the morning, the minimum stay – assuming you want to see much of the island in daylight – is two nights.

 WHERE TO STAY AND EAT *Map, page 320*

UPMARKET

Rubondo Island Camp (8 rooms) (South Africa) +27 (0)21 418 0468; **m** 0736 500515; www.asiliaafrica.com; ⊕ closed Apr & May.

Reopened in 2013 following extensive renovations, this attractive & immensely tranquil tented lodge comprises 8 luxury suites similar in standard to Asilia's other Tanzanian camps & lodges. It has a need to grow to 200 before this became a real threat, and contraception can be used to keep numbers in check.

The introduced black-and-white colobus also occasionally roam close to the lodge, but the main population of about 30 is concentrated in the far south of the island, and their normal territory can be reached by boat or car, followed by a 10-minute walk. The giraffe herd, estimated at around 100 individuals, is most likely to be encountered in the restricted area of acacia woodland around Lukaya, some distance south of the lodge and park headquarters. The suni are the most elusive of the introduced species, because they are so small, and secretive by nature.

Between 1966 and 1969, eight male and nine female chimpanzees were released on to the island, all of them born wild in the Guinean rainforest belt but captured when young to be taken to European zoos and circuses. Some had been held in good zoos where they had the company of other chimpanzees, while others were caged inadequately or in solitary confinement. Several individuals were regarded as troublesome and had regularly attacked or bitten their keepers, and two of the males were shot after their release because they had attacked people living on the island. The others appeared to settle down quickly. Two newborn chimps were observed in 1968, and it is now estimated that the total community numbers around 40, most of them at least second generation, but it is possible though unlikely that a couple of the original individuals survive. The chimps are normally resident in the central and northern parts of the island, near the Kamea and Irumu ranger posts, which respectively lie about 5km northwest and a similar distance southeast of the park headquarters at Kageye.

truly fabulous lakeshore location, with a tall forest gallery rising high behind & a sandy palm-lined beach fringed by rocky outcrops directly in front. The open-sided communal areas stand on one of the rocky outcrops, offering a pretty view over the lake. This leads down to a secluded beachfront platform where a variety of large water birds have taken up more-or-less permanent residence. Pied & malachite kingfishers hawk for food, paradise flycatchers flutter in the trees & the occasional pair of otters swims past. The swimming pool is built in a natural rock outcrop. A good selection of boat & foot excursions is offered, including chimp tracking (page 328) & fishing trips. *US$1,060/1,590 FB sgl/*

dbl inc all drinks & activities, dropping to US$690pp in the low season. **$$$$$$$**

BUDGET & CAMPING

⋀ **National park campsite** The national park camping site lies on a lovely forest-fringed beach about 1km north of Rubondo Island Camp, & a similar distance from park headquarters. No meals are available, & it's advisable to bring most of what you will need with you, but a shop in the park headquarters does sell a few basic foodstuffs (essentially what the national park staff would eat), as well as warm beers & sodas. A cook can be arranged on request. *US$30pp.* **$$**

WHAT TO SEE AND DO

A wide variety of activities can be arranged on the spot either through Rubondo Island Camp or the national park staff at the campsite. A good, inexpensive (*US$20pp*) introduction to the park, taking 2–4 hours depending on how often you stop, is the **guided trail** to Pongo Viewpoint and Nhoze Hide, the latter a good place to see sitatunga, a variety of birds and – very occasionally – elephant. Another popular activity is **a forest walk** from either Kamea or Irumu ranger posts

The first European to see Lake Victoria was John Hanning Speke, who marched from Tabora to the site of present-day Mwanza in 1858 following his joint 'discovery' of Lake Tanganyika with Richard Burton the previous year. Speke named the lake for Queen Victoria, but prior to that Arab slave traders called it Ukerewe (still the name of its largest island). It is unclear what name was in local use, since the only one used by Speke is Nyanza, which simply means lake.

A major goal of the Burton–Speke expedition had been to solve the great geographical enigma of the age, the source of the White Nile. Speke, based on his brief glimpse of the southeast corner of Lake Victoria, somewhat whimsically proclaimed his 'discovery' to be the answer to that riddle. Burton, with a comparable lack of compelling evidence, was convinced that the great river flowed out of Lake Tanganyika. The dispute between the former travelling companions erupted bitterly on their return to Britain, where Burton – the more persuasive writer and respected traveller – gained the backing of the scientific establishment.

Over 1862–63, Speke and Captain James Grant returned to Lake Victoria, hoping to prove Speke's theory correct. They looped inland around the western shore of the lake, arriving at the court of King Mutesa of Buganda, then continued east to the site of present-day Jinja, where a substantial river flowed out of the lake after tumbling over the cataract that Speke named Ripon Falls. From here, the two explorers headed north, sporadically crossing paths with the river throughout what is today Uganda, before following the Nile to Khartoum and Cairo.

Speke's declaration that 'The Nile is settled' met with mixed support back home. Burton and other sceptics pointed out that Speke had bypassed the entire western shore of his purported great lake, had visited only a couple of points on the northern shore, and had not attempted to explore the east. Nor, for that matter, had he followed the course of the Nile in its entirety. Speke, claimed his detractors, had seen several different lakes and different stretches of river, connected only in Speke's deluded mind. The sceptics had a point, but Speke had nevertheless gathered sufficient geographical evidence to render his claim highly plausible, and his notion of one great lake, far from being mere whimsy, was backed by anecdotal information gathered from local sources along the way.

Matters were scheduled to reach a head on 16 September 1864, when an eagerly awaited debate between Burton and Speke – in the words of the former, 'what silly tongues called the "Nile Duel"' – was due to take place at the Royal Geographic Society (RGS). And reach a head they did, but in circumstances more tragic than anybody could have anticipated. On the afternoon of the debate, Speke went out shooting with a cousin, only to stumble while crossing a wall, in the process discharging a barrel of his shotgun into his heart. The subsequent inquest recorded a verdict of accidental death, but it has often been suggested – purely on the basis of the curious timing – that Speke deliberately took his life rather than face up to Burton in public. Burton, who had seen Speke less than 3 hours earlier, was by all accounts deeply troubled by Speke's death, and years later he was quoted as stating 'the uncharitable [say] that I shot him' – an accusation that seems to have been aired only in Burton's imagination.

Speke was dead, but the 'Nile debate' would keep kicking for several years. In 1864, Sir Stanley and Lady Baker were the first Europeans to reach Lake Albert and nearby Murchison Falls in present-day Uganda. The Bakers, much to the delight of the anti-Speke lobby, were convinced that this newly named lake was a source of the Nile, although they openly admitted it might not be the only one. Following the Bakers' announcement, Burton put forward a revised theory, namely that the most remote source of the Nile was the Rusizi River, which he believed flowed out of the northern head of Lake Tanganyika and emptied into Lake Albert.

In 1865, the RGS followed up on Burton's theory by sending Dr David Livingstone to Lake Tanganyika. Livingstone, however, was of the opinion that the Nile's source lay further south than Burton supposed, and so he struck out towards the lake along a previously unexplored route. Leaving from Mikindani in the far south of present-day Tanzania, Livingstone followed the Rovuma River inland, continuing westward to the southern tip of Lake Tanganyika. From there, he ranged southward into present-day Zambia, where he came across a new candidate for the source of the Nile, the swampy Lake Bangweulu and its major outlet, the Lualaba River. It was only after his famous meeting with Henry Stanley at Ujiji, in November 1871, that Livingstone (in the company of Stanley) visited the north of Lake Tanganyika and Burton's cherished Rusizi River, which, it transpired, flowed into the lake. Burton, nevertheless, still regarded Lake Tanganyika to be the most likely source of the Nile, while Livingstone was convinced that the answer lay with the Lualaba River. In August 1872, Livingstone headed back to the Lake Bangweulu region, where he fell ill and died six months later, the great question still unanswered.

In August 1874, ten years after Speke's death, Stanley embarked on a three-year expedition every bit as remarkable and arduous as those undertaken by his predecessors, yet one whose significance is often overlooked. Partly, this is because Stanley cuts such an unsympathetic figure, the grim caricature of the murderous pre-colonial White Man blasting and blustering his way through territories where Burton, Speke and Livingstone had relied largely on diplomacy. It is also the case, however, that Stanley set out with no intention of seeking out headline-making fresh discoveries. Instead, he determined to test out the various theories that had been advocated by Speke, Burton and Livingstone about the Nile's source. First, Stanley sailed around the circumference of Lake Victoria, establishing that it was indeed as vast as Speke had claimed. Stanley's next step was to circumnavigate Lake Tanganyika, which, contrary to Burton's long-held theories, clearly boasted no outlet sufficiently large to be the source of the Nile. Finally, and most remarkably, Stanley took a boat along Livingstone's Lualaba River to its confluence with an even larger river, which he followed for months with no idea as to where he might end up.

When, exactly 999 days after he left Zanzibar, Stanley emerged at the Congo mouth, the shortlist of plausible theories relating to the source of the Nile had been reduced to one. Clearly, the Nile did flow out of Lake Victoria at Ripon Falls, before entering and exiting Lake Albert at its northern tip to start its long course through the sands of the Sahara. Stanley's achievement in putting to rest decades of speculation about how the main rivers and lakes of East Africa linked together is estimable indeed. He was nevertheless generous enough to concede that: 'Speke now has the full glory of having discovered the largest inland sea on the continent of Africa, also its principal affluent as well as its outlet. I must also give him credit for having understood the geography of the countries we travelled through far better than any of us who so persistently opposed his hypothesis.'

Two closely related antelope species occur naturally on Rubondo Island: the swamp-dwelling sitatunga and forest-dwelling bushbuck. Of these, the more interesting is the sitatunga – a widespread but localised species with uniquely splayed hooves that allow it to manoeuvre through swampy habitats – since Rubondo is one of only two East African parks where it is easily observed (the other being Saiwa Swamp in Kenya). The males of both these antelopes are very handsome, with large spiralled horns, but the sitatunga is larger, shaggier in appearance, and grey where the bushbuck is chestnut brown. The females of both species are smaller and less striking, but easily distinguished from one another, since the bushbuck is striped on its sides, whereas the sitatunga is unmarked.

Rubondo's sitatunga population probably exceeds ten individuals per km^2, and is not so habitat-specific as elsewhere, apparently – and unexpectedly – outnumbering bushbuck even in the forest. Researchers have noted that the sitatunga of Rubondo's forests are more diurnal than is normally the case, and have less-splayed feet and darker coats than those resident in the swamps – whether this is genetically influenced, or a function of wear and sun bleaching, is difficult to say. A possible explanation for this anomalous situation is that sitatunga colonised the island and expanded into forested habitats before there were any bushbuck around.

(ask at headquarters which of the two currently offers the better chance of seeing chimpanzees). This generally takes about 6 hours, and it costs US$25 per person inclusive of a guide and transport to the ranger post. Other options include **boat trips** to the swampy Mlaga Bay or Bird Island, **fishing expeditions** (the record catch is a 108kg Nile perch), and **walks** on more remote parts of the island to look for colobus monkeys or giraffes.

As for unguided activities, quite a bit of wildlife and lots of birds can be seen in the grounds of Rubondo Island Camp and the national park campsite, while the roughly 1km footpath and road between the two can be walked unaccompanied as a loop. **Swimming** is reputedly safe, at least at the beaches in front of the lodge and camp. The lake water is regularly tested for bilharzia, thus far always with a negative result, and – bearing in mind that human beings form an integral part of the bacteria's life cycle – all residents of the island take the bilharzia cure as a precautionary routine every six months. Do be aware that crocs occasionally swim past the beaches, so far without incident – still, you might want to look before you leap in!

The **chimp community** on Rubondo is currently being habituated by researchers, with the long-term aim of providing a tracking experience comparable to Mahale Mountains or Gombe Stream national parks on Lake Victoria. In the meantime, as of September 2016, the three-night Rubondo Chimp Habituation Experience, exclusive to Asilia, offers visitors a rare chance to join a habituation team as they gradually accustom the island's 40 chimpanzees to the presence of humans. This involves two nights at Rubondo Island Camp, split by a night at a fly-camp from where you can join the habituation team. The full three-night chimpanzee habituation experience starts at US$1,380 per person inclusive of all meals, drinks and activities, but excluding flights.

15

15

Zanzibar

Chris and Susan McIntyre

Zanzibar is one of those magical travel names, richly evocative even to the many Westerners who would have no idea where to start looking for it on a global map. Steeped in history, and blessed with a sultry tropical climate – warm to hot all year round and often very humid; it receives more rainfall and is windier than the mainland – and a multitude of idyllic beaches, Zanzibar is also that rare travel destination that genuinely does live up to every expectation. Whether it's a quick cultural fix you're after, scintillating diving, or just a palm-lined beach where you can laze away the day, some time on Zanzibar is the perfect way to round off a dusty safari on the Tanzanian mainland.

A separate state within Tanzania, Zanzibar consists of two large islands, Unguja or Zanzibar Island and Pemba, plus several smaller islets. Zanzibar Island is about 85km long and between 20km and 30km wide; Pemba is about 75km long and between 15km and 20km wide. Both are flat and low-lying, surrounded by coasts of rocky inlets or sandy beaches, with lagoons and mangrove swamps, and coral reefs beyond the shoreline. Farming and fishing are the main occupations, and most people live in small villages. Cloves are a major export, along with coconut products and other spices. The capital, and by far the largest settlement, is Zanzibar Town (usually known as Stone Town) on the west coast.

For many, the highlight of a stay is the old Stone Town, with its traditional Swahili atmosphere and wealth of fascinating buildings. For others, it is the sea and the coral reefs, which offer diving, snorkelling and game fishing to compare with anywhere in East Africa. And then there are the clove and coconut plantations that cover the interior of the 'Spice Island'; the dolphins of Kizimkazi; the colobus monkeys of Jozani; and the giant sea turtles of Nungwi. And above all, some will say, those seemingly endless tropical beaches.

For a detailed and dedicated guide to these incredible islands, see our comprehensive *Zanzibar, Pemba & Mafia: The Bradt Travel Guide* (9th edition), 2017.

HISTORY

Zanzibar has been trading with ships from Persia, Arabia and India for approximately 2,000 years. From about the 10th century AD, groups of immigrants from Shiraz (Persia) settled on Zanzibar and mingled with the local Swahili. The Portuguese established a trading station on the site of Zanzibar Town in the early 16th century. At the end of the 17th century, the Sultan of Oman's navy ousted the Portuguese from the island.

In 1840, Sultan Said of Oman relocated his capital in Muscat to Zanzibar. Many Omani Arabs settled on Zanzibar as rulers and landowners, forming an elite group, while Indian settlers formed a merchant class. The island became an Arab state, an important centre of regional politics, and the focus of a booming slave trade.

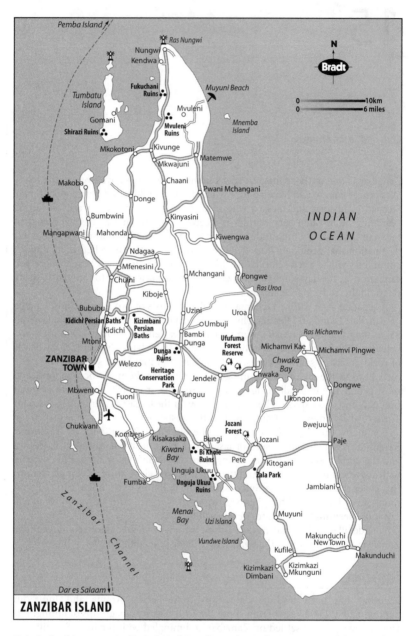

ZANZIBAR ISLAND

Britain had interests in Zanzibar throughout the 19th century; explorers such as Livingstone, Speke and Burton began their expeditions into the African interior from there. In 1890, Zanzibar became a British protectorate.

Zanzibar gained independence from Britain in December 1963. In 1964, the sultan was overthrown in a revolution and nearly all Arabs and Indians were expelled. Later the same year, Zanzibar and Tanganyika combined to form the United Republic of Tanzania.

Today, the distinctions between Shirazi and Swahili are often blurred. The islanders fall into three groups: the Hadimu of southern and central Zanzibar, the Tumbatu of Tumbatu Island and northern Zanzibar, and the Pemba of Pemba Island. Many people of mainland origin live on Zanzibar, some the descendants of freed slaves, others more recent immigrants. Many of the Arab, Asian and Goan people expelled in 1964 have since returned.

GETTING THERE AND AWAY

BY AIR An ever-increasing number of airlines offer direct flights between Zanzibar and Dar es Salaam, a 30-minute trip that costs around US$80. There are also regular flights to Zanzibar from Kilimanjaro International Airport (between Moshi and Arusha), some of which are direct, taking roughly an hour, while others require a change of plane at Dar and might take 3–4 hours depending on your connection. The main established airlines covering these routes are listed below, all of which offer a range of other domestic flights, while some also fly to Kenya, so the best choice will depend largely on your other travel plans. Any reliable tour operator will be able to advise you about this. Private charters are also available from the main safari spots.

Airlines
✈ **Air Tanzania** `022 117 500; m 0782 737730/737732; e info@airtanzania.co.tz; www. airtanzania.co.tz
✈ **Coastal Aviation** `024 223 3112; m 0785 500009 (Zanzibar Airport); e reservations@coastal. co.tz (scheduled flights) or aviation@coastal.co.tz (air charters); www.coastal.co.tz

✈ **Precision Air** `024 223 5126; m 0786 300418; e contactcentre@precisionairtz.com; www.precisionairtz.com
✈ **ZanAir** `024 223 3670/3768; e reservations@zanair.com; www.zanair.com

BY BOAT A number of hydrofoils and catamarans run daily between Dar es Salaam and Zanzibar, with prices determined largely by the efficiency and speed of the service. The booking kiosks for all these boats are clustered together at the ports on Zanzibar and in Dar. There's a lot to be said for asking around before you make any firm arrangements, or for using a tour operator to make your booking (this won't cost much more and saves a lot of hassle). Do be wary of the hustlers who hang around both ports – many are con artists and some are thieves. Tickets must be paid for in hard currency, as must the port tax of US$5. There have been two major ferry disasters in recent years, resulting in several hundred deaths, so it is imperative that you choose your carrier carefully.

Note that it is both unsafe and illegal to travel between Zanzibar and the mainland by dhow.

Passenger ships and ferries
🚢 **Azam Marine & Coastal Fast Ferries** `022 212 3324; e info@azammarine.com; www. azammarine.com. These operate the best of the commercial passenger boats between Zanzibar, Pemba & Dar es Salaam.
🚢 **MV Flying Horse** `022 212 4507 (Dar); m 0784 472497/606177 (Zanzibar); e asc@raha.

com. This large catamaran, run by the African Shipping Corporation, has a capacity of more than 400 passengers.
🚢 **Sea Star Services** `022 213 9996. This large catamaran runs daily between Dar es Salaam & Zanzibar.

ORGANISED TOURS Most international tour operators (pages 82–4) offering safaris to Tanzania can append a flight to Zanzibar (or a full travel package to the island) to your safari arrangements. Likewise, most safari companies based in Arusha are able to set up excursions to Zanzibar. If you are booking a safari in advance, there is a lot to be said for making all your travel arrangements through the same company.

VISAS AND TAXES Visitors who fly in to Zanzibar from mainland Tanzania do not need to complete an immigration card or show their passport and visa, but they may still be asked to produce a yellow fever certificate. All documentation must be shown, however, and an immigration card completed if you arrive by ferry from the mainland.

Travellers flying into Zanzibar from outside Tanzania can now buy a **visa on arrival** at the airport. A visa costs between US$20 and US$100 depending on your nationality and should be paid for in US dollars cash (travellers' cheques and other currencies are not accepted, though either can be converted into cash at a bureau de change at a poor rate). The **airport tax** of US$40 for international flights out of Zanzibar should be incorporated into the price of a ticket but, if not, it must also be paid in US dollars cash (not by credit card or travellers' cheque). Flights within Tanzania attract a US$9 airport tax, payable in Tanzanian shillings.

If you lose your passport while on Zanzibar, you will need to have an Emergency Travel Document issued at the Ministry of Home Affairs (% *024 223 9148*). This will allow you to travel back to the mainland (where nationals of most countries will find diplomatic representation in Dar es Salaam) or directly to your home country.

GETTING AROUND

PUBLIC MINIBUSES AND DALLA DALLAS Local minibuses and dalla dallas cover many routes around Zanzibar Island. These are faster than buses and fares are cheap, typically about US$0.50 around Zanzibar Town and a few dollars to cross the island.

Buses and dalla dallas from outlying villages heading for Zanzibar Town tend to leave very early in the morning but, apart from that, most vehicles simply leave when they're full. Be aware that the last buses to some coastal villages will leave Zanzibar Town by mid afternoon. The dalla dalla destinations are written on the front of the vehicle, but it's also worth telling the driver where you're going.

There are three **main terminals** in Zanzibar Town: Darajani Station on Creek Road (opposite the market), Mwembe Ladu, and Mwana Kwerekwe. The latter two locations are a few kilometres from town and are best accessed by a short hop on a dalla dalla from Darajani.

BUSES It is possible to reach many parts of Zanzibar Island by public bus, although most visitors use tourist minibuses or dalla dallas. All buses leave from **Darajani Bus Station** [337 H4] on Creek Road in Zanzibar Town. Generally you can expect to pay only a few dollars to travel half the length of the island between Zanzibar Town and Bwejuu. Note though, that journeys can be very slow.

On many routes, especially the longer ones, there is only one daily bus. It will usually leave Zanzibar Town around midday, in order to reach its destination in the evening and return in time for the morning market. Destinations are often written on the front of the bus but always check before boarding that the bus is going to the destination you think it should be.

Some of the bus routes are also covered by public minibuses or dalla dallas. These are usually slightly more expensive than the buses, but tend to be quicker.

CAR HIRE To hire a car, SUV or scooter, contact one of the island's tour operators (see below). A car or SUV for a day will cost US$60–100, excluding fuel. **Insurance cover** is in theory comprehensive, but check this thoroughly. Note that driving standards on Zanzibar are not good, and the roads can be pot-holed, so think very carefully before hiring a car. You should be aware that, unlike on the mainland, you need an **international driving licence** and a **local permit** to drive a vehicle on Zanzibar. Your tour operator can help organise a local permit (best to give 24 hours' notice), and insist that they do to avoid roadside police fines. Petrol is readily available island-wide nowadays.

TAXIS Taxis are fairly widely available. A short hop within Zanzibar Town costs just over US$3, while the trip to Mtoni costs around US$7–10 one-way; to Jozani or the east coast US$20–25 one-way or US$30–35 return. The going rate for transfers between the airport and Zanzibar Town is US$10–15.

BICYCLE HIRE Most of the tour operators in Zanzibar Town can arrange bicycle hire. The current rate for a heavy Chinese bike is from US$10 per day, while mountain bikes go for around US$15.

ZANZIBAR TOWN

Zanzibar's old quarter, usually called Stone Town, is a fascinating maze of narrow streets and alleyways that lead the visitor past numerous old houses and mosques, ornate palaces, and shops and bazaars. Many buildings in Stone Town date from the 19th-century slave boom. Houses reflect their builder's wealth: Arab houses have plain outer walls and large front doors leading to an inner courtyard; Indian houses have a more open façade and large balconies decorated with railings and balustrades. Most are still occupied.

A striking feature of many houses is the brass-studded doors with their elaborately carved frames. The size of a door and the intricacy of its design was an indication of the owner's wealth and status. The use of studs probably originated in Persia or India, where they helped prevent doors being knocked down by war-elephants. In Zanzibar, studs were purely decorative.

The area outside Stone Town used to be called Ng'ambo ('The Other Side'), and is still often referred to as such, though its official name is actually Michenzani (New City). Attempts have been made to modernise it and at the centre of Michenzani are some ugly apartment blocks, built by East German engineers as part of an international aid scheme.

TOUR OPERATORS A number of tour companies operate out of Zanzibar Town, offering tours, as well as transfers and general tourist information. The better companies can set up bespoke excursions, as well as make hotel reservations and onward travel arrangements. For straightforward day trips and transfers, there is no real need to make bookings before you arrive in Zanzibar, as they can easily be set up at the last minute. If, however, you want to have all your travel arrangements organised in advance through one company, or you have severe time restrictions, then it would be sensible to make advance contact with one of the companies with good international connections, such as those shortlisted on page 335.

While prices vary greatly depending on standard of service, season and group size, typical costs per person for the most popular outings are: City Tour (*US$20*);

15

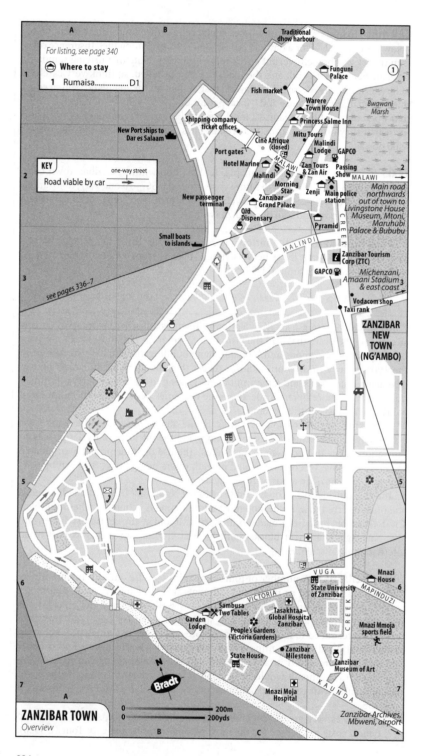

For listing, see page 340

🏠 **Where to stay**

1   Rumaisa..................D1

KEY

Road viable by car   one-way street ➡

Traditional
dhow harbour

🏠 Funguni
    Palace

Fish market •

Bwawani
Marsh

Warere
Town House

Shipping company
ticket offices

🏠 Princess Salme Inn

New Port ships to
Dar es Salaam

Ciné Afrique
(closed)

Mitu Tours •

Malindi
Lodge

GAPCO

Port gates

Zan Tours
& Zan Air

Passing
Show

Hotel Marine

Malindi

Morning
Star

Zenji

Main police
station

MALAWI

Main road
northwards
out of town to
Livingstone House
Museum, Mtoni,
Maruhubi
Palace & Bububu

New passenger
terminal

Zanzibar
Grand Palace

Old
Dispensary

Pyramid

Small boats
to islands

MALINDI

Zanzibar Tourism
Corp (ZTC)

GAPCO

Michenzani,
Amaani Stadium
& east coast

see pages 336–7

Vodacom shop

Taxi rank

**ZANZIBAR
NEW
TOWN
(NG'AMBO)**

V U G A

Mnazi
House

State University
of Zanzibar

MAPINDUZI

Sambusa
Two Tables

Garden
Lodge

Tasakhtaa–
Global Hospital
Zanzibar

Mnazi Mmoja
sports field

People's Gardens
(Victoria Gardens)

VICTORIA

Zanzibar
Milestone

State House

Zanzibar
Museum of Art

Mnazi Moja
Hospital

KAUNDA

N

Bradt

Zanzibar Archives,
Mbweni, airport

ZANZIBAR TOWN
Overview

0 ———— 200m
0 ———— 200yds

Prison Island Tour (*US$30*); Dolphin Tour (*US$40*); Spice Tour (*US$28*); Jozani Forest Tour (*US$35*). All these rates are per person (based on four people sharing), but for the tour only, and do not include extras like entrance fees (ie: for the Palace Museum this is US$2, for Prison Island US$4, for Jozani Forest US$4). Prices are negotiable, particularly out of season, but do be wary of unregistered companies and individuals offering substandard trips at very low rates.

It's also possible to arrange many of the standard tours more cheaply through taxi drivers or independent guides (nicknamed *papaasi* after a type of insect). With spice tours, this may often turn out to be a false economy, in that the guide will lack any botanical knowledge and may cut the excursion short, rendering the whole exercise somewhat pointless.

Recommended and well-established tour companies include:

✳ Eco+Culture Tours [337 F3]
☏024 223 3731; m 0755 873066/0777 410873; e ecoculturetours@gmail.com; www.ecoculture-zanzibar.org. A respected, ethically minded operator offering slightly more expensive, but excellent, day trips for those who want to avoid the more established circuits & contribute to community development. See also page 374.
Island Express Safaris & Tours ☏024 223 4375/64; m 0774 111222/111888; e info@islandexpress.co.tz; www.islandexpress.co.tz. A smart, efficient operation offering a more personal service than most operators. Tours & transfers are never for groups, but are only ever arranged on a private basis. This does make them slightly more expensive, though not prohibitively so, & of course gives complete flexibility for your trip.

Sama Tours [337 E4] m 0777 430385/431665; e samatours@zitec.org; www.samatours.com. Trips include 'special' spice tours with a knowledgeable local naturalist, plus boat trips & tailor-made tours, with guides who speak English, French, German or Italian.
✳ Zanzibar Different [336 D5] m 0777 430177; e info@zanzibardifferent.com; www.zanzibardifferent.com. Owned by the delightful Stefanie Schoetz of Mrembo Traditional Spa (see box, page 351) & creator of the Princess Salme Tour (see box, page 353), this ethical operation has put a new spin on some classic Zanzibari tours, as well as adding original offerings in music, cookery & the arts, including fabulously atmospheric dinner concerts at Mtoni Palace (usually Fri). Very flexible, all tours can be adapted for children.

⌂ WHERE TO STAY The last decade has seen a mushrooming of new hotels in Zanzibar Town, as well as around the island, and there are now numerous options at every level, from basic guesthouses to smart upmarket hotels. The following selection of places to stay is not exhaustive, as new places continually open and existing ones change name, location and ownership, but is a selection of our favourites in each price range. As a rule, room rates are quoted in US dollars, and at the top end of the range the management will probably insist that you pay in hard currency. Hotels at the lower end of the price bracket generally accept local currency at an exchange rate similar to those given at forex bureaux. Rates may be negotiable at budget hotels depending on how busy they are and the intended duration of your stay. It is advisable to make an advance reservation for any upmarket, moderate or popular budget hotel during peak seasons. Most prices include breakfast, though at budget hotels this may amount to little more than a slice of bread and a banana.

Travellers who arrive on Zanzibar by boat can expect to be met by a group of hotel touts. Some are quite aggressive and likely to take you to whichever hotel gives them the largest commission, while others are friendly and will find you a suitable hotel if you tell them what you want. Either way, the service shouldn't cost you anything, since the tout will get a commission from the hotel, and it may save a lot of walking in the confusing alleys of Stone Town. Given the difficulty of getting past the touts and the general aura of chaos around the ferry port, there is probably

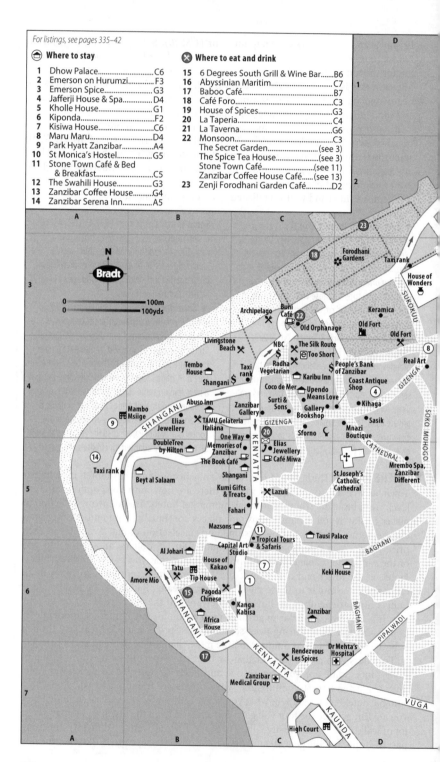

For listings, see pages 335–42

🛏 **Where to stay**

1	Dhow Palace	C6
2	Emerson on Hurumzi	F3
3	Emerson Spice	G3
4	Jafferji House & Spa	D4
5	Kholle House	G1
6	Kiponda	F2
7	Kisiwa House	C6
8	Maru Maru	D4
9	Park Hyatt Zanzibar	A4
10	St Monica's Hostel	G5
11	Stone Town Café & Bed	
	& Breakfast	C5
12	The Swahili House	G3
13	Zanzibar Coffee House	G4
14	Zanzibar Serena Inn	A5

❌ **Where to eat and drink**

15	6 Degrees South Grill & Wine Bar	B6
16	Abyssinian Maritim	C7
17	Baboo Café	B7
18	Café Foro	C3
19	House of Spices	G3
20	La Taperia	C4
21	La Taverna	G6
22	Monsoon	C3
	The Secret Garden	(see 3)
	The Spice Tea House	(see 3)
	Stone Town Café	(see 11)
	Zanzibar Coffee House Café	(see 13)
23	Zenji Forodhani Garden Café	D2

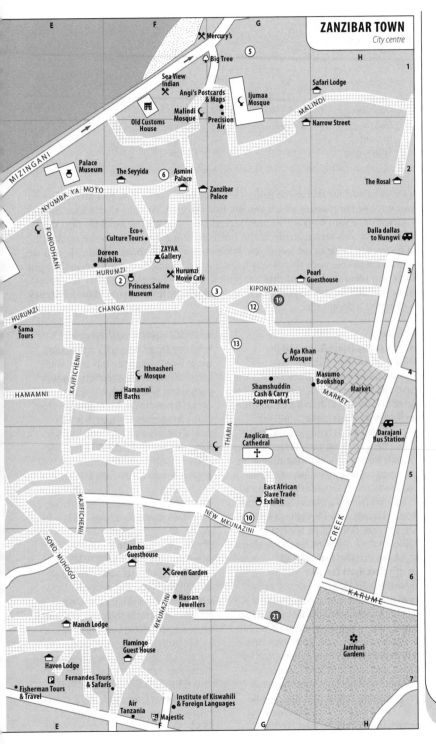

ACCOMMODATION PRICE CODES

Rates quoted in this chapter are for rooms in high season:

Exclusive	♔	US$300+
Luxury	$$$$$	US$200–300
Upmarket	$$$$	US$100–200
Mid range	$$$	US$50–100
Budget	$$	US$25–50
Shoestring	$	Below US$25

a lot to be said for taking the path of least resistance when you first arrive. Should you not like the place to which you are first directed, you can always look around yourself once your bags are securely locked away, and change hotel the next day.

However you arrive, many of the hotels in Stone Town cannot be reached by taxi. You are liable to get lost if you strike out on foot without a guide, though we found that people were always very helpful when it came to pointing us in the right direction (bearing in mind that the right direction may change every few paces). Most taxi drivers will be prepared to walk you to the hotel of your choice, but they will expect a decent tip.

Exclusive

✴ 🏠 **Jafferji House & Spa** [336 D4] (10 rooms) m 0774 078442/1; e info@ jafferjihouse.net; www.jafferjihouse.net. This hotel has the wow factor: an artistic blend of old & new. Zanzibari doors, old wall clocks & gramophones are reminiscent of days gone by, while warm colours & a top-quality finish give a modern feel. The 8 suites & 2 standard rooms all have AC, baths, exquisite furniture & traditional fabrics. Up on the rooftop is a tiny but gorgeous outpost of Amani Spa. Downstairs, the Mistress of Spices restaurant ($$$$) offers freshly prepared international food from an à la carte menu. There's also an internet café & TV room. Despite all the opulence, the hotel still feels warm & welcoming, like a home, albeit a stylish one! *US$130–590 dbl, B&B.* ♔

✴ 🏠 **Park Hyatt Zanzibar** [336 A4] (67 rooms) ☏ 024 550 1234; e zanzibar.park@ hyatt.com; www.zanzibar.park.hyatt.com. For location, grandeur & elegance, the imposing Park Hyatt Zanzibar is hard to beat. Opened in Mar 2015, in arguably Stone Town's most prestigious location, it has brought a luxury brand & international levels of hotel sophistication to the city. Sandwiched between leafy Kelele Sq & the Indian Ocean, & just mins on foot from the city hustle, this hotel offers calm & pampering to its high-end, image-conscious guests. The hotel spans 2 buildings:

the UNESCO-listed Mambo Msiige mansion & the brand-new Zamani Residence, a contemporary take on Swahili architecture, with strong Middle Eastern influences. Here, Modernist minimalism meets historic Swahili. Stark, whitewashed interiors & formidably high ceilings sit alongside soaring Omani arches, cool courtyards, wide marbled corridors & intricate timber latticework. Rooms are extremely comfortable & the public areas are equally grand. The atmosphere is fairly formal & the service is slick, with a distinct air of wealth permeating both the building & its guests. From its breezy seafront terrace, the Park Hyatt is Stone Town's ultimate hotel haven. *US$315–560 dbl, B&B.* ♔

🏠 **Zanzibar Serena Inn** [336 A5] (51 rooms) ☏ 024 223 1015/3051/3587; e zanzibar@serena.co.tz; www.serenahotels. com. This large, impressive, decidedly African hotel, converted from 2 historic buildings, overlooks the sea in the Shangani area. The staff are excellent & the hotel boasts all the in-room & public facilities that you would expect of an international-class establishment, including an inviting pool, 2 excellent restaurants (or a porter escort to the public food market), coffee shop, AC, Wi-Fi, satellite TV & reasonably priced, in-house massage treatments. *US$150–900 dbl, B&B.* $$$$–♔

Luxury

🏠 **Kisiwa House** [336 C6] (11 rooms)
📞 024 223 5654; e info@kisiwahouse.com; www.
kisiwahouse.com. Neighbouring Dhow Palace,
Kisiwa House opened in 2009 as an elegant &
welcoming hotel. Rooms are decorated in pure
white with splashes of sea blue & most are simply
huge (perfect for families). With a cheery, light-
filled reception, sunny rooftop restaurant & a
dbl-storey courtyard lounge for chilling, this place
displays calm, class & imagination throughout.
US$140–210 dbl, B&B. **$$$$$**

🏠 **Maru Maru** [336 D4] (50 rooms) 📞 024 223
8516/7/8; e reservations@marumaruzanzibar.
com; www.marumaruzanzibar.com. On the site of
an old Hindu temple, Maru Maru is a spotless, well-
finished & bright hotel. Modern rooms all have en
suites (some with traditional hammam baths),
powerful AC, Wi-Fi, fridge & a safe. In-room tea &
coffee facilities are provided as well as a flatscreen
TV. There's a choice of 2 dining areas – The Bakery,
in the fountain courtyard, for snacks & afternoon
teas, & the rooftop Terrace Restaurant, popular
for sunset laughter & cocktails, followed by spicy
Indian suppers (**$$$–$$$$**). One of the few
hotels in Stone Town with a lift. Parking provided.
US$115–324 dbl, B&B. **$$$$–**🍴

🏠 **Emerson on Hurumzi** [337 F3] (22 rooms)
📞 024 223 2784; e reception@emersononhurumzi.
com; www.emersononhurumzi.com. Reincarnated
many times, this hotel grande dame is a Stone
Town institution. The hotel itself sprawls across 3
venerable buildings dating from 1840, decorated
with antique Zanzibari furniture & carpets. Each
room is different, but each, very deliberately, is
without phone, TV or fridge. Some have AC, others
natural cooling – shutters, shades, deep balconies
& a sea breeze. The hotel's Tea House Restaurant
(🕐 *lunch & dinner; reservations essential*), the 2nd-
highest building in Zanzibar Town, has fine views.
US$175–250 dbl, B&B. **$$$$–$$$$$**

✳ 🏠 **Emerson Spice** [337 G3] (6 rooms)
📞 024 223 2776; m 0774 483483; e reservation@
emersonspice.com; www.emersonspice.com.
This exotic hotel has striking theatrical rooms,
each with a colourful twist on traditional Swahili
design. Ceilings are immense; vibrant colours
adorn the walls, & potted plants, stained-glass
windows & intricately carved wooden doors add
to the atmosphere. Rooms are kitted out with
open-plan en suites, fans & AC, fridges & mosquito

nets, & some even have dramatic hand-painted
murals. There's an interior courtyard complete with
twinkling blue pool reminiscent of a Moroccan
riad, a terrific rooftop restaurant offering a
5-course tasting experience, & a magical, open-air
courtyard restaurant (page 341). One of the best
choices for an atmospheric stay in Stone Town.
US$200–250 dbl, B&B. **$$$$–$$$$$**

Upmarket

🏠 **The Swahili House** [337 G3] (20 rooms)
m 0777 510209; e info@theswahilihouse.com;
www.theswahilihouse.com. This towering 19th-
century Indian merchant's house, built around a
central roofed courtyard, is today a traditionally
elegant hotel with an authentic Zanzibari feel &
good management. Rooms are decked out in locally
produced furniture & antiques, with polished stone
floors, narrow wooden balconies (some rooms) &
a touch of modernity thrown in in the form of AC &
fans. Spread over 4 floors, rooms nearest the top offer
excellent views of Stone Town's alleyways. But for
the best panorama head for the rooftop restaurant,
with its long bar, cushion-covered benches & even a
jacuzzi. *US$240–325 dbl, B&B.* **$$$$–**🍴

🏠 **Kholle House** [337 G1] (10 rooms)
m 0772 161033; e info@khollehouse.com;
www.khollehouse.com. Kholle is a favourite with
those seeking a traditionally inspired boutique
bolthole. It's beautiful & great thought has gone
into the high-quality furnishings, with antique
chests, French ceramics, glass lanterns & Zanzibari
beds complementing a warm ochre colour scheme.
Rooms are split into 3 categories, varying in size,
but all with Zanzibari beds, mosquito nets, fans
& AC. B/fast is à la carte overlooking the small
garden, where loungers & cushions surround the
swimming pool – a precious rarity in Stone Town
& a welcome relief after a hot day's sightseeing.
If arriving by taxi, ask your driver for 'holy house'
(the Swahili pronunciation). *US$100–200 dbl, B&B.*
$$$$

🏠 **Dhow Palace Hotel** [336 C6] (31 rooms)
📞 024 223 3012; e reservations@dhowpalace-
hotel.com; www.dhowpalace-hotel.com. This
excellent hotel in the Shangani area is a renovated
old house built around 2 central courtyards. Newer
rooms have private balconies, while larger original
rooms access a private section of shared balcony;
all are en suite (complete with Persian baths),
& are furnished with Zanzibari beds & antiques,

15

plus mod-cons including AC. The stylised Indian restaurant overlooks the pool courtyard (no alcohol served). All is spotlessly clean, the staff are friendly & the atmosphere tranquil. *US$100–150 dbl, B&B.* **$$$–$$$$**

🏠 **Zanzibar Coffee House** [337 G4] (8 rooms) 📞 024 223 9319; m 0773 061532; e coffeehouse@ zanlink.com; www.riftvalley-zanzibar.com. Housed in an 1885 Arabic home, this unpretentious haven is above the excellent café of the same name (page 342). Most of the rooms, with traditional Zanzibari 4-poster beds & AC, are en suite, though a few share facilities. Gracious staff provide a friendly service, the tower-top terrace offers one of Stone Town's best b/fast views, & rates remain great value. *US$110–185 dbl, B&B.* **$$$–$$$$**

Mid range

🏠 **Rumaisa Hotel** [334 D1] (7 rooms) m 0777 410695; e inforumaisa@yahoo.com; www.rumaisahotel.blogspot.co.uk. This funky little place is frequently recommended by 'flashpackers'. Located in the Funguni area of Stone Town, it's quite a walk from the centre but prices are lower than they otherwise would be for the room standard. Simple rooms are well-finished & furnished in different vivid colours in Zanzibar style. The decoration is pretty, with Indian furniture giving a homely feel. Staff are helpful & friendly. The blustery rooftop bar is filled with music in the evenings, when the owner's father plays the guitar & drums for guests. At the front, a communal balcony has a sea view with Prison Island in the distance. Remarkably, there is also a 52-seat cinema within the hotel, showing an array of family, Bollywood & Hollywood action movies for around US$3. *US$55 dbl, B&B.* **$$$**

🏠 **Stone Town Café & Bed & Breakfast** [336 C5] (8 rooms) m 0778 373737; e baraka@ zanlink.com; www.stonetowncafe.com. Above the bustling Stone Town Café (page 342) on Kenyatta Rd, this family-owned & run B&B offers delightful modern rooms with dbl polished wooden Zanzibari

beds, AC, fans & fridges. Each room has a small seating area with a TV, & en-suite shower rooms with hot water are standard. Cool floors & warm colours make this a cosy place to spend a night or 2, while high-quality accessories & sturdy furniture raise the standard above the average Stone Town B&B. B/fast is included at the café downstairs, where guests can order what they want from the menu up to a value of US$7, with anything over this costing extra. A top choice in this budget. *US$70 dbl, B&B.* **$$$**

Budget

🏠 **Kiponda Hotel** [337 F2] (15 rooms) 📞 024 223 3052; m 0777 431665; e info@kiponda.com; www.kiponda.com. On Nyumba ya Moto St, not far from the main seafront, this is a small, quiet hotel in a building that used to house part of a sultan's harem. It has been renovated in local style & still has an original carved wooden entrance door. The Zanzibari management team, headed up by the very helpful Salma, give the place a relaxed & friendly atmosphere, & although it's a touch more expensive than other hotels in this bracket, it is also a lot quieter & better value. The newer rooms are cleaner with simple furnishings & efficient fans; there is even a deep sink for washing laundry. Some rooms have AC, & 2 have their own bathroom located outside the room. Good b/fasts included. *US$60–75 dbl, B&B.* **$$–$$$**

🏠 **St Monica's Hostel** [337 G5] (16 rooms) Sultan Ahmed Mugheiri Rd; 📞 024 223 0773; e monicaszanzibar@hotmail.com; www. zanzibarhostel.com. Built in the 1890s to house workers at the UMCA mission, St Monica's now welcomes both church guests & younger backpackers. Cool thick walls, wide staircases & Arabesque arches form the backdrop for simple & very clean rooms with wide balconies overlooking the cathedral or gardens. The restaurant, run by the Mother's Union, offers fresh Swahili cuisine (no alcohol); there's also an art shop & an airy lounge area. *US$40–50 dbl, B&B.* **$$**

✕ WHERE TO EAT AND DRINK

The dining experience in Stone Town has recently taken a dramatic turn for the better, with the opening of some stylish evening eateries and a burgeoning selection of cool cafés.

We have only listed a selection here; there are plenty more to choose from, and the level of competition for custom means that standards are generally reflected by prices.

The cheapest place to eat in Stone Town is at the night market in **Forodhani Gardens** [336 D3], along the seafront, where dozens of vendors serve freshly grilled meat, chicken, fish, calamari and prawns with salad and chips or naan bread. This is far and away the best street food we've come across anywhere in southern and East Africa, and offers excellent value. The stalls cater primarily to locals and travellers, and many return night after night. Even if you aren't hungry or an adventurous eater, it's worth visiting for the spectacle.

Gastronomic

Top-end options, with main courses from around US$10, include:

✖ **Abyssinian Maritim** [336 C7] **m** 0772 940556/0713 359054/0752 940556; (noon–16.00 & 18.00–22.00 daily. This great little Ethiopian place is easy to find on the corner opposite the High Court in Vuga, serving authentic cuisine (*US$3–12*), great coffee & shisha pipes amid a north African décor. Receiving consistently enthusiastic praise & popular with Zanzibari expats & visitors alike, this culinary departure from Swahili curries is a very welcome addition to the restaurant scene. $$$$$

✱ ✖ **The Secret Garden** [337 G3] ✆024 223 2776; **e** reservations@emersonspice.com; www.emersonspice.com; ⊕ closed Wed. The newly opened Secret Garden is simply magical. Part of Emerson Spice (page 339), this tumbledown, former Swahili marketplace has been transformed into an utterly enchanting open-air restaurant. The flickering light of candles illuminate the crumbling windows & arches & help create the impression of a grand opera set. And here, an impeccable experience awaits: efficient waiters serve chilled glasses of wine at neat triangular tables & aromatic waves of spiced Swahili dishes (*US$8–15*) drift from an open *braai* (BBQ). It feels very James Bond & comes highly recommended. $$$$$

✱ ✖ **The Spice Tea House** [337 G3] ✆024 223 2776; **m** 0775 046395; **e** reservation@emersonspice.com; www.emersonspice.com; ⊕ 17.30–23.00; closed Thu. On the rooftop of

Emerson Spice (page 339), this intimate dining experience offers a lovely bird's-eye vista over town, a buzzing atmosphere & an impressive 5-course degustation menu. Open every night for a single sitting (*cocktails from 18.00; dinner 19.00*), the US$40pp set menu is excellent value, consistently delicious & worth booking to avoid disappointment. It's highly personal & the food is utterly delicious Swahili fusion cuisine. A real treat! $$$$$

Mid range

✱ ✖ **6 Degrees South Grill & Wine Bar** [336 B6] **m** 0620 644611; **e** info@6degreessouth.co.tz; www.6degreessouth.co.tz; ⊕ 10.00–01.00 daily. 'Quirky. Imaginative. Breezy. This culinary hotspot is all degrees of cool': a claim many of the cocktail-sipping diners would concur. This expansive restaurant & bar overlooks the Shangani Waterfront from 3 levels. The striking street-level restaurant, complete with soaring arched glass roof, serves a selection of Zanzibari favourites (*US$9–11*), while upstairs is the popular 2-storey cocktail bar Up North @ 6 Degrees, a perfect sundowner & late-night hangout. $$$–$$$$

✖ **House of Spices** [337 G3] ✆024 223 1264; **m** 0773 573727; **e** info@houseofspiceszanzibar.com; www.houseofspiceszanzibar.com. Offering tempting fusions of local & Mediterranean cuisine from the top floor of an attentively renovated Zanzibari house, House of Spices is justifiably popular. Most diners sit up on the lantern-lit roof terrace, where there's also a bar, while on the ground floor is a small spice shop selling tea &

Zanzibar ZANZIBAR TOWN

15

coffee. The varied menu includes curries & salads (*US$6–9*), as well as tapas & pizza (*US$8.50*). $$$–$$$$

✗ **Monsoon Restaurant** [336 C3] m 0777 410410; e monsoon@zanzinet.com; www. monsoon-zanzibar.com; ⏲ 11.30–22.30 daily. Facing Forodhani Gardens, this is a good place for traditional Zanzibari & Mediterranean food (*US$7+*), accompanied by live *taarab* or *ngoma* music on Wed, Fri & Sat nights. Aside from its bar, & a shady terrace with tables, Monsoon is a place to lounge around, kasbah style. Thick walls & good ventilation mean it's always cool, & so are most of the clients. You can even enjoy a shisha pipe with your Arabic coffee or cocktail (*US$5*). 3-course dinners with a glass of wine are great value at around US$16. $$$–$$$$

✳ ✗ **La Taverna** [337 G6] m 0776 650301; www.latavernazanzibar.com; ⏲ 11.00–23.00 Mon–Sat. A little off the main tourist trail, towards the market, this is a gem of a restaurant with a host of happy regular customers, delightful young Italian owners & consistently tasty, homemade pasta/pizza. Wine is inexpensive & free-flowing, which adds to the relaxed, casual vibe. $$$

✗ **La Taperia** [336 C4] e lataperiazanzibar@ gmail.com; ⏲ 10.00–22.00 daily (deli shop ⏲ 10.00–18.00). On one end of the balcony above the Shangani Post Office, La Taperia offers – as its name suggests – tasty tapas. There's a well-stocked bar, casual indoor dining area & popular tables & bar stools on the terrace. It's a buzzy place to grab a bite above the bustle, & uniquely in Stone Town, there is also a separate, glass-fronted delicatessen where you can buy imported cheese, a wide selection of cold-cut meats, olive oil, wine & fresh bread. $$$

Cheap & cheerful

🖵 **Baboo Café** [336 B7] m 0777 499297. Tucked under 2 sweet almond trees, with a terrace overlooking the sea, this tiny little café is a friendly, unpretentious hangout. Engaging service, under the guidance of owner Baboo, & tasty Swahili food, courtesy of his wife Mariam, both make for happy customers. Iced coffees, freshly squeezed juices, salads (*US$3.50–5*), seafood platters (*US$7.50*) & curries (*US$4*) are all on offer. Find it on the southern end of the beach behind Africa House Hotel, where sunset views are particularly good. $$–$$$

🖵 **Cafés of Forodhani Gardens** In the revamped Forodhani Gardens, there are now 3 small waterfront cafés, the best of which are **Café Foro** [336 C3] (nearest the children's playground) & **Zenji Forodhani Garden Café** [336 D2] (*www. zenjiforodhani.com*). Each has an identical pavilion building by the sea & shaded outdoor seating. Selling a selection of cold drinks & with varying menus of fish, burgers, wraps, salads & sweet treats, they are all open for b/fast, lunch & snacks, & offer a very pleasant sense of calm & green space. $$–$$$

🖵 **Stone Town Café** [336 C5] m 0778 373737; e baraka@zanlink.com; www. stonetowncafe.com; ⏲ 08.00–22.00 daily. The scents of spiced tea & falafel waft from this buzzing Aussie–Zanzibari-run café. Marked out by lush potted plants, passers-by queue for unfussy, tasty dishes served by friendly staff. All-day b/fasts (*US$5*), cheesy pizzas (*US$6*), fresh fruit shakes & smoothies, & tasty teatime treats (*US$3*) are recommended. $$

🖵 **Zanzibar Coffee House Café** [337 G4] ⏲ 08.00–18.00 daily. This friendly café behind Creek Rd market is an excellent place for a strong cup of freshly ground coffee & a light snack – the glass cabinet boasts a deliciously tempting array of fresh cakes, pies, pastries, croissants & sandwiches. The café is filled with heavy wooden kitchen-style tables that are perfect for gossiping groups, as well as intimate tables for 2. $$

ENTERTAINMENT AND NIGHTLIFE Although a largely Muslim island, most tourist restaurants serve African beers and many of the larger hotels have separate bars. Their atmosphere and quality vary considerably.

For cocktails the current top picks are the **Terrace Bar** at the Park Hyatt (page 338) and **Up North @ 6 Degrees** (page 341). **Mercury's** [337 F1] (m *0777 413081*; e *mercurys.zanzibar@gmail.com*), **Tatu** [336 B6] (m *0778 672772*; f *tatuzanzibar*), **Lulu** at the Seyyida [337 F2] (☎ *024 223 8352; www.theseyyida-zanzibar.com*), **Baboo Café** (see above) and the **Forodhani Gardens' cafés** (see above) all have a sea view and a decidedly more low-key vibe. For the ultimate

If you're heading to Stone Town in early February, be sure to buy tickets for Sauti Za Busara. Centred on Stone Town's atmospheric Old Fort, this four-day extravaganza celebrates the best of African music, traditional and modern. Over 200 musicians and artists take to the stage during this highly successful festival, which also includes screenings of documentaries and music videos. An electric atmosphere of African beats and friendly festival-goers from all over the world, plus a variety of souvenirs and street food, make this eclectic festival one of Africa's best. Tickets can be purchased through the festival's website, (*www.busaramusic.org*), or bought on the door, but expect to queue. Do bear in mind that city accommodation sells out fast around festival time, so book early for a guaranteed room.

sundowners though, try a dhow cruise with **The Original Dhow Safaris** (m *0772 007090;* e *info@dhowsafaris.net; www.dhowsafaris.net*).

If **live music** is of interest, the **Dhow Countries Music Academy** (DCMA) [337 F1] (*www.zanzibarmusic.org*) is based in the Old Customs House on Mizingani Street and hosts weekly concerts in their building and other venues: check out the jam sessions at **Livingstone** [336 C4] (⊕ *21.00–midnight Tue & Fri*) or listen over a glass of wine at **La Taperia** (page 342) on the first and third Friday of every month (⊕ *19.30–22.00*). They also host public workshops, often free of charge, and visiting musicians are welcomed with open arms. **The Old Fort** [336 D3] and **Mtoni Ruins** (page 353) are atmospheric venues, hosting mostly traditional musicians and dancers, but occasionally contemporary performances, too. A couple of times each week a 'night at the fort' evening is organised, which includes at least two performances plus a barbecue dinner. There are often performances on other nights, too. The best thing to do is visit the fort during the day, and ask the staff at the desk what's happening during your stay. On a larger scale, Zanzibar Town also plays host to the annual Sauti Za Busara festival (see box, above), and this is certainly the time to visit, if African music appeals.

For **movies**, the only real option for big-screen films is during the annual **Zanzibar International Film Festival** in June/July, when screenings are held in the atmospheric Old Fort amphitheatre. Otherwise, the little cinemas attached to the **Rumaisa Hotel** (page 340) and **Hurumzi Movie Café** [337 F3] (m *0659 921121;* f *hurumzini;* ⊕ *11.00–22.00 Mon–Sat*) have weekly film schedules for movie-lovers to get their fix.

SHOPPING Zanzibar Town is something of an Aladdin's cave for shoppers, with a vast array of shops catering for the ever-growing tourist influx. A selection of both favourites and perennials are listed here, though particularly worth checking out are those mentioned in the box on page 344; aside from their positive credentials, their products are some of the best quality and most original around.

In the larger tourist shops, prices are fixed and payable in Tanzanian shillings or US dollars, or by credit card (surcharges are usual), but in the market and at smaller, locally run outlets, cash is necessary and bargaining is part of the experience. There are no hard and fast rules to the latter, and sensible judgement is required, but a basic rule of thumb is to start negotiations at half the asking price; if you ultimately pay around 75% of the initial price, then it's likely that both parties will walk away happy.

Souvenirs For souvenirs without the bargaining, the best options are **Zanzibar Gallery** [336 C4] (*zanzibargallery.net*), which sells a range of carvings, clothes, maps, antiques and good selection of books, and **Memories of Zanzibar** [336 C5] (*www.memories-zanzibar.com*), where you can pick up anything from beaded flip-flops and silver bracelets to carvings and CDs.

Gizenga Street and **Hurumzi Street** are the hub of tiny local souvenir shops and pavement traders, where you'll find carvings, Tingatinga paintings, assorted jewellery, packets of spices, coconut-shell mobiles, twisted wire bikes and much more at every turn.

Antiques Around Zanzibar Town there are also several shops selling antiques from Arabia and India, dating from Omani and British colonial times. **Coast Antique Shop** [336 D4] on Gizenga Street has a particularly good selection of Zanzibar clocks, whilst the enthusiastic staff at **Zanzibar Curio Shop** have a great range of timber souvenirs from doors to carvings. Beside St Joseph's Cathedral, Abeid and Tamin Curio Shops are good places for genuinely hand-crafted chests.

Art and local crafts ZAYAA Gallery (Zanzibar Young Artist Association) at the eastern end of Hurumzi Street [337 F3] showcases young artists and has some especially lovely women's art, inspired by henna patterns. **Real Art [336 D4]** (**m** *0784 460419*) on Gizenga Street offers a good, if more expensive, selection of genuine Tanzanian and Zanzibari art. Inside the **Old Fort** [336 D3], seek out the small art shop beside the restaurant for original watercolours, oil paintings and well-observed pen-and-ink drawings. The friendly artists are on site and many of their works are impressive.

Tailors and clothes The current best bet for reliable, well-made bespoke clothing is **Kihaga** [336 D4] on Gizenga Street. On the same street, the tailor at **Mnazi Boutique** [336 D4] can copy any shirt, skirt or trousers you like, from material you

---

MADE IN ZANZIBAR – FAIR-TRADE AND HIGH QUALITY

There has been a welcome trend recently towards training members of the local community, especially women, to produce high-quality, well-designed clothing and accessories for sale to tourists. The women benefit from a new skill and a fair price for their efforts. Several of the brands belong to the 'Made in Zanzibar' producers' network (*madeinzanzibar.com*), a collective aiming to cross-promote quality products from Zanzibar to support the local 'economy', and provide an identifiable brand for visitors.

Currently, the best projects, products and shopping outlets are: **Fahari** [336 C5] (*www.fahari-zanzibar.com*) for stylish leatherwork; **Kanga Kabisa** [336 B6] (*www.kangakabisa.com;* ⊕ *09.00–19.00 daily*) for Nordic fashion in kanga print; **Dada** (*dadazanzibar.wordpress.com*) for wholesome tropical preserves and cosmetics; **Moto** (*motozanzibar.wordpress.com*) for basketry; **Malkia** (several hotel shops) for funky fashion; **Sasik** [336 D4] (*sasikzanzibar.blogspot.co.uk*) for appliqué; **Surti & Sons** [336 C4] (*surtiandsons.wordpress.com;* ⊕ *09.00–14.00 & 14.30–19.00 daily*) for bespoke leather sandals; **Upendo Means Love** [336 C4] (*upendomeanslove.com;* ⊕ *09.00–17.00 Mon–Sat*) for gorgeous island kidswear; and **Zenji Boutique** [336 C2] (*zenjicafeboutique.com*) for a pan-African craft selection.

buy in the shop or elsewhere in town. Prices start at US$10, and go up to US$25 for a complicated dress. Alternatively, **Osman** [337 F3], the tailor opposite ZAYAA Gallery at the end of Hurumzi Street, is highly recommended (in spite of his tiny, fabric-strewn workplace). For off-the-peg essentials, **One Way** [336 C4] sells piles of T-shirts embroidered with giraffes and elephants or emblazoned with Kenyan and Tanzanian slogans and logos.

Postcards, newspapers and books For postcards you can't go wrong at **Angi's Postcards & Maps** [337 G1] near the Big Tree; there's a truly massive selection here, all at good prices. African newspapers, some international magazines and a reasonable range of books are available from the **Masumo Bookshop** [337 G4], off Creek Road, and from some of the souvenir shops along Kenyatta Road near the old post office. Coffee-table books, fact and fiction can all be purchased from the well-stocked **Gallery Bookshop** [336 C4] (⊕ *from 09.00 daily*) on Gizenga Street, or their sister shop **The Book Café** [336 C5] on Kenyatta Road.

The best bookshop is the **Zanzibar Gallery** on Kenyatta Road (page 344), which has a good selection of fiction, field guides and coffee-table books on Zanzibar and other parts of Africa.

Jewellery If a more precious purchase is what you're after, **Hassan Jewellers** [337 F6] (*Mkunazini St;* m *0773 453575*), close to the market, is reliable and reputable. The family team here stocks a good range of tanzanite and is able to supply authentication certificates. Be aware that tanzanite is a soft stone that scratches easily; better to have it set as earrings or in a necklace than as a ring. For something more contemporary and unique, **Elias Jewellery** (m *0777 414686;* f *eliasjewellers*) is worth a look. It has two branches, one on Kenyatta Road [336 C5], above the post office and another opposite Tembo Hotel [336 B4]. A family business, you'll find tanzanite set in gold and silver, as well as some unusual pieces incorporating materials such as ebony wood and recycled rubber. For serious sparkle, with a dazzling price tag, **Lithos Africa** inside the Park Hyatt may fit the bill.

OTHER PRACTICALITIES
Banks and money changing A number of banks and forex bureaux are dotted around Stone Town, offering similar exchange rates against cash to their mainland counterparts. You can draw cash against Visa cards at the ATM outside the **National Bank of Commerce** on Kenyatta Road [336 C4], but the only place where you can draw against MasterCard is the ATM at Barclays Bank, a couple of kilometres out of town along the road towards the north coast. There are additional **ATMs** on Shangani [336 C6], near the Creek Road market [337 H6] and at Mwana Kwerekwe bus station. Currently, getting cash on a debit or credit card is virtually impossible anywhere else (although most upmarket hotels take card); however, the first bank outside Stone Town is currently under construction at Ce L'Hai shopping precinct in Kiwengwa. This branch of the People's Bank of Zanzibar will have an ATM as well as in-branch facilities.

These days, there isn't much to choose between banks and private bureaux in terms of rates, but you'll generally find the transaction takes a minute or two at a private bureau whereas changing money at banks often involves long queues and plenty of paperwork. Good private bureaux de change include the **Shangani Bureau de Change** [336 C4] and **Malindi Bureau de Change** [334 C2]. Most large hotels will also change money, although some deal only with their own guests, and they often offer poor rates.

Communications The **main post office** lies outside Stone Town towards the stadium [334 D2] (🕐 *08.00–12.30 & 14.00–16.30 Mon–Sat, 08.00–12.30 Sun*), but the **old post office** on Kenyatta Road [336 C4] (🕐 *08.00–13.00 & 14.00–16.30 Mon–Thu, 08.00–noon & 14.00–17.00 Fri, 09.00–noon Sat*) is the most convenient for tourists, and is also the place to collect poste restante mail addressed to Zanzibar.

For **international phone calls**, try the Tanzanian Telecommunications office [336 C5] (🕐 *08.00–21.00 daily*). Rates here are generally similar to those at some of the private bureaux around town, though it's as well to ask around. If you bring a mobile phone from home, it's emphatically worth the minor investment in a Tanzanian SIM card (which costs around US$2.50 and gives you a local number) and airtime cards (available in units of Tsh1,000 to 5,000). For the best coverage on the islands at present, purchase a Zantel SIM – visit Asko Tours and Travel [336 C4], next to the post office on Kenyatta Road, to purchase the relevant SIM card and ask them to help you set it up. Buy a reasonable amount of credit whilst in Stone Town as only tiny credit bundles are available once you leave the capital, and each one has to be loaded individually into your phone.

Wi-Fi is relatively easy to access in Zanzibar Town these days, and many a café, hotel and restaurant will advertise free Wi-Fi for customers. Speeds and reliability vary considerably, but connectivity is eminently possible! If you are a rare visitor without a mobile, tablet or laptop, you'll still find a few internet cafés around town. The cost of internet use from a PC is a pretty standard US$1 per hour across town, and most charge per 30-minute increment. **Shangani Internet Café** [336 C5] is one of the better places in Zanzibar Town.

Maps Aside from those in this book, the most accurate and attractive map of Stone Town (albeit somewhat out of date) is Giovanni Tombazzi's *Map of Zanzibar Stone Town*, which also has a useful map of the island on the flip side.

Medical facilities Zanzibar's private medical clinics, where staff speak English and drugs are more readily available, are usually a better option for visitors than the public Mnazi Mmoja General Hospital. There are pharmacies at the medical centres as well as in Stone Town.

✚ **Dr Mehta's Hospital** [336 D7] Pipalwadi St (opposite the High Court); ☏024 223 1566, emergency **m** 0777 419999, ambulance **m** 0656 959595; **e** drmehtashospital@gmail.com. For 24hr medical treatment.

✚ **Tasakhtaa – Global Hospital Zanzibar** [334 C6] ☏024 223 2341, emergency ☏024 223 2222/ **m** 0779 770577; **e** info@tasakhtaahospital. co.tz. Relatively new hospital open 24hrs for emergencies.

Police The main police station [334 D2] (☏ *112 or 024 223 0772*) is in the Malindi area, on the north side of Stone Town. Robberies can be reported here (travel insurance companies usually require you to provide a copy of the basic report on the incident from the local police if you are making a claim), but you should not expect any real action to be taken as the police are not particularly well motivated and corruption is rife.

Swahili lessons For experienced teachers and structured learning, the best place to start is the **Institute of Kiswahili and Foreign Languages** [337 F7] (☏ *024 223 0724/3337; e takiluki@zanlink.com; www.glcom.com/hassan/takiluki.html*). Inside the State University on Vuga Road, the institute offers individual lessons and courses. Classes cost US$4 per hour, or US$80 for a week's course.

Swimming pool The pool at the **Dhow Palace Hotel** [336 C6] (*www.dhowpalace-hotel.com*) is open to non-residents during quiet times (*US$5pp*). Just north of town, there's the option to swim at **Maruhubi Beach Villas** (*sites.google.com/site/maruhubizanzibar*) for US$5 per day, and the new water park at **Mtoni Marine** will open its slides and wave pools in 2017.

WHAT TO SEE AND DO
Spice tours and other excursions A spice tour has long been one of Zanzibar's most popular excursions into the interior of the island, giving visitors a chance to experience familiar flavours from the kitchen growing naturally. A typical tour lasts about 1½ hours and in addition to visiting a few spice plantations, tours will often include a walk around a cultivated rural homestead, as well as a visit to one of the island's ruins and a traditional Swahili lunch. The Princess Salme Tour operated by Zanzibar Different (see box, page 353) is a particularly good example at around US$55 per person.

Other popular excursions from Stone Town include a boat trip to one or more of the nearby islands, a full-day trip snorkelling and sailing around Menai Bay, a visit to the dolphins at Kizimkazi, and a trip to Jozani Forest to see the endemic Kirk's red colobus. These trips can all be undertaken from anywhere on the island and organised through any of the tour operators (pages 333–5).

Stone Town walking tour You can spend many idle hours getting lost in the fascinating labyrinth of narrow streets and alleys of Stone Town, and will almost inevitably hit most of the main landmarks within a couple of days of arriving. However, the following roughly circular walking tour through Stone Town will allow those with limited time to do their sightseeing in a reasonably organised manner (though they are still bound to get lost), and should help those with more time to orientate themselves before they head out to explore Stone Town without a map or guidebook in hand.

The obvious starting point for any exploration of Zanzibar Town is **Forodhani Gardens** [336 C3] (see box, page 348), the open park between Mizingani Road and the main sea wall. Laid out in 1936 to mark the Silver Jubilee of Sultan Khalifa, the gardens are a popular eating and meeting point in the evening, and the staircase rising from the gardens to the arched bridge to the south offers a good view over the old town.

Three of the most significant buildings in Stone Town lie alongside each other overlooking the seafront behind the Forodhani Gardens. The **Palace Museum** [337 E2] (⏰ *08.30–18.00 daily; admission US$3*) is the most northerly of these, a large white building with castellated battlements dating from the late 1890s. The palace was the official residence of the Sultan of Zanzibar from 1911 until the 1964 revolution, after which it was renamed the People's Palace. For many years after this, it served as a government office and was closed to the public. Since 1994, however, it has housed an excellent museum, with a variety of displays relating to the early days of the sultanate, including a room devoted to artefacts belonging to Princess Salme. The graves of all the early sultans of Zanzibar are in the palace garden.

Next to the Palace Museum, the **House of Wonders** (**Beit al Ajaib**) [336 D3] (⏰ *09.00–18.00 daily; admission US$5*) is a perfect rectangle, rising over several storeys, surrounded by tiers of impressive pillars and balconies and topped by a clocktower. It was built as a ceremonial palace in 1883, and was the first building on Zanzibar to have electric lights. Until recently it was the CCM party headquarters, but it is now home to the Museum of History and Culture, which houses about half of the

The Forodhani Gardens [336 D2] (Jamituri Gardens on some maps) are between the Arab Fort and the sea, overlooked by the House of Wonders. They were first laid out in 1936 to commemorate the Silver Jubilee of Sultan Khalifa (who ruled 1911–60), and were called Jubilee Gardens until the 1964 revolution. In the centre stands a podium where the band of the sultan's army used to play for the public. Nearer the sea is a white concrete arabesque arch, built in 1956 for the visit of Princess Margaret (sister of Queen Elizabeth II of Britain), but never officially used as the princess arrived at the dhow harbour instead. She did visit the gardens, however, and planted a large tree, which can still be seen today.

Forodhani has long been a popular place for local people and visitors in the evenings, lured by the waterfront gathering of stalls serving drinks and hot snacks. Years of excessive overuse and poor maintenance took its toll, though, and for several years 'gardens' was a euphemism for an unattractive, parched wasteland.

Wonderfully, things have changed. On 17 January 2008, the Aga Khan Trust for Culture, with approval from the Zanzibar government, finally began a major rehabilitation of the gardens. They had been in discussion about the project with the government since 2002 when the organisation first proposed comprehensive seafront rehabilitation. The aims of the project were to improve the infrastructure and to restore and preserve the civic components of the gardens, none of which had happened in the past as a result of overuse, disrepair and limited private refurbishment.

The project was completed in 2010, and the changes are plain to see. Everyone agrees that the new Forodhani Gardens are a vast improvement, with the practical introduction of wheelie bins, lighting and waste collections, a new sea wall of salvaged stone, an organised food court for the evening stall holders, three inviting cafés (page 342), a bandstand, a dhow-shaped adventure playground and tropical planting amid manicured lawns. We, like the Aga Khan, hope that this project will prove a catalyst for urban upgrading and economic opportunity, as well as aesthetically improving the remaining waterfront area.

eight planned permanent exhibitions (dedicated to the history of the Swahili Coast, and Zanzibar in particular). Sadly, it's crumbling more as the years go by and suffered a partial balcony collapse in late 2012 and a partial roof collapse in 2016. The building is periodically closed now for repairs, and some of its exhibits have been moved to the Zanzibar Museum of Art (page 349). If it is open during your stay in Stone Town, it is well worth a visit – though a jumble of craft stalls fills much of the tree-shaded parking area in front of the building, making access somewhat confusing.

Moving along the road, and directly facing Forodhani Gardens, the **Old Fort** [336 D3] (⊕ *07.00–19.00 daily; admission free, donations welcome*) is probably the oldest extant building in Stone Town, built by Omani Arabs between 1698 and 1701 over the site of a Portuguese church constructed a century before that, remnants of which can still be seen in the inner wall. A large, squarish, brown building with castellated battlements, the fort ceased to serve any meaningful military role in the 19th century, since when it has served variously as prison, railway depot and women's tennis club. The interior of the fort is open to visitors, who can climb to the top of the battlements and enter some of the towers. There is a restaurant serving cold drinks ($\oplus$ *08.00–20.00 daily*), and traditional music and dancing shows take place there weekly (page 343).

Heading southwest from the fort, under an arched bridge, the fork to your right is **Shangani Road**, the site of notable important buildings. Just before following this fork, to your left, the **Upimaji Building** was the home of the German merchant Heinrich Ruete (later the husband of Princess Salme) in the 1860s. To the left of the fork is a block of government offices which served as the **British Consulate** [336 B4] from 1841 until 1874, and next to that the **Tembo Hotel** [336 B4], a restored 19th-century building. As you follow Shangani Road around a curve, alongside the Park Hyatt Zanzibar, whose main building is part of the UNESCO-listed **Mambo Msiige building** [336 A4], you'll come out to a leafy green corner, **Kelele Square** [336 A5], where the Zanzibar Shipping Corporation Building, dating to around 1850, stands to your left and the Zanzibar Serena Inn, formerly Extelcoms House, straight ahead.

Perhaps 100m past the Serena Inn, to your left, you'll see the rear of **Tip House** [336 B6], a tall brown building that once served as the residence of Tippu Tip, the notorious 19th-century slave trader who helped explorers such as Livingstone and Stanley with supplies and route planning. The building is privately owned and is closed to visitors, but if you follow the alley around the rear of the house, you can see its huge carved front door from the street. Residents will sometimes show visitors around, although some 'guides' here are heroin addicts and visitors are advised to exercise caution. From here, wander up another 50m to the **Africa House Hotel** [336 B6], which served as the English Club from 1888 onwards. Neighbouring 6 Degrees South (page 341) is a good place to punctuate your walk with a cold drink or bite to eat.

From here, a small alley leads to **Kenyatta Road**, an important thoroughfare dotted with hotels, shops and restaurants, as well as a number of old buildings with traditional Zanzibari doors. Follow this southeastwards for about 300m, passing the somewhat unkempt **People's Gardens** [334 C6], originally laid out under Sultan Barghash for the use of his harem, until you reach the **Zanzibar Milestone** [334 C7]. This octagonal marble pillar shows the distance from Zanzibar Town to various settlements on the island and further afield.

Cross the gardens in front of the milestone to the distinctive **Zanzibar Museum of Art** [334 D7] ($\oplus$ *06.00–18.00 daily; admission US$3*). Also known as the Peace Memorial Museum, this impressive edifice, with its distinctive dome, arabesque windows and whitewashed walls, looks like a mosque or basilica. For years 'museum' was something of a misnomer; however, with the closure and planned restoration of the House of Wonders (pages 347–8), many exhibits have been moved here. The Zanzibari door at the back of the building is reputedly the oldest in existence.

From the museum, follow Creek Road northwards for about 400m, and to your left you'll easily pick out the imposing **Anglican Cathedral** [337 G5] ($\oplus$ *daily; admission US$5 inc guide & access to St Monica's Hostel & Slave Trade Exhibit*), built by the Universities' Mission in Central Africa (UMCA) over the former slave market between 1873 and 1880. Tradition has it that the altar stands on the site of the market's whipping block, and the cellar of the nearby **St Monica's Hostel** [337 G5] is said to be the remains of a pit where slaves were kept before being sold. Sultan Barghash, who closed the slave market, is reputed to have asked Bishop Steere, leader of the mission, not to build the cathedral tower higher than the House of Wonders. When the bishop agreed, the sultan presented the cathedral with its clock. The foundation of the UMCA was inspired by Livingstone: a window is dedicated to his memory, and the church's crucifix is made from the tree under which his heart was buried in present-day Zambia. Several other missionaries are remembered on plaques around the cathedral wall, as are sailors killed fighting the slave trade and servicemen who died in action in East Africa during World War I. Also at the hostel, the newly opened **East African Slave Trade Exhibit** lays out the full economic and social history of East African slavery from its origins to the post-slavery Empire years. It's a truly engrossing, if often appalling, exhibition.

A short distance further along Creek Road lies the **covered market** [337 H4], built at around the turn of the 20th century, and worth a visit even if you don't want to buy anything. It's a vibrant place where you can buy anything from fish and bread to sewing machines and secondhand car spares. Once you've taken a look around the market, follow Creek Road back southwards for 100m or so, passing the cathedral, then turn into the first wide road to your right. This is New Mkunazini Road, and if you follow it until its end, then turn right into Kajificheni Street and right again into Hammani Street, you'll come out at the **Hammani Baths** [337 F4] (⊕ 09.00–17.30 daily; admission US$1.50), one of the most elaborate Persian baths on Zanzibar, built for Sultan Barghash; the caretaker will show you around for a small fee.

Barely 200m from the baths, on Cathedral Street, **St Joseph's Catholic Cathedral** [336 D5] is notable for its prominent twin spires, and was built between 1896 and 1898 by French missionaries and local converts. There are now few Catholics on Zanzibar, and the cathedral is infrequently used, but visitors are welcome when the doors are open. The best way to get here from the baths is to retrace your steps along Kajificheni Street, then turn right into the first alley (which boasts several good examples of traditional Zanzibari carved doors) until you reach an open area where several roads and alleys meet – Cathedral Street among them. If you're in this area, or indeed if you fancy some serious pampering, consider making an appointment at the nearby Mrembo Traditional Spa (see box, page 351).

From the cathedral, continue northwards along Cathedral Street for perhaps 50m, then turn right into Gizenga Street, a good place to check out the curios at any of numerous small shops. If you follow Gizenga Street until you see the Old Fort to your left, you can conclude your walk by wandering back out to Forodhani Gardens. Alternatively, if you want to keep going, turn right opposite the fort into Hurumzi Street and, after continuing straight for about 300m, you'll come to the open square close to the Zanzibar Coffee House Café (a good place to take a break for a tasty snack and a drink; page 342). A left turn as you enter this square takes you past the **Aga Khan Mosque** [337 G4] and on to Jamatini Road, which after about 200m will bring you out at the seafront opposite the **Big Tree** [337 G1]. Known locally as Mtini, this well-known landmark was planted in 1911 by Sultan Khalifa and now provides shade for traditional dhow builders.

On Mizingani Road, just south of the Big Tree, the **Old Customs House** [337 F1], a large, relatively plain building dating to the late 19th century, is where Sultan Hamoud was proclaimed sultan in 1896.

From the open area next to the Big Tree, a left turn along Mizingani Road will take you back to the Old Fort, passing the above-mentioned buildings. Turn right into Mizingani Road, however, and after about 100m you'll pass the **Old Dispensary** [334 C2] (⊕ 09.00–18.00 daily; admission free), an ornate three-storey building built in the 1890s. Restored to its former glory by the Aga Khan, the dispensary now also contains a small exhibition hall of old monochrome photographs of Stone Town.

If the above directions seem too complicated, or you want further insight into the historical buildings of Stone Town, most tour operators can arrange a guided

[336 D5] (*Call or visit to book appointments;* ☎ *024 223 0004;* m *0777 430117; mrembospa.com;* ⊕ *09.30–18.00 daily*) Recently, a number of 'spas' have sprung up around Zanzibar as the Western craze for 'wellness' treatments has descended on the island. Many are little more than a massage table, some lemongrass oil and a friendly, if untrained, local masseuse; a few, in the larger hotels, are more sophisticated and professional. All can prove an enjoyable distraction, but the most engaging and original by far is Mrembo Traditional Spa.

In an old antique store close to St Joseph's Cathedral, Mrembo is a small, wonderfully unassuming place offering the finest traditional treatments from Zanzibar and Pemba. Their flagship treatment, Singo, is a natural exfoliating scrub traditionally used when preparing Zanzibari girls for marriage. Prepared by hand with a pestle and mortar (*kinu*), the fresh jasmine, ylang ylang, rose petals, *mpompia* (geranium), *mrehani* (sweet basil) and *liwa* (sandalwood) combine to create the most wonderfully aromatic blend. For men, the clove-based scrub Vidonge is said by Pembans to increase libido and stamina, and is even offered in souvenir packages. Hot sand massages, authentic henna painting and beauty treatments are available too, with all the herbal products coming from the owner's garden and skilfully prepared in front of you.

Although not its *raison d'être*, Mrembo is also an impressively inclusive community project. Two of the four local therapists are disabled: one deaf, Ali, and one blind, Asha. Trained in therapeutic massage by professional therapists from The African Touch (a Canadian-funded, community-based organisation in Kenya), they have both benefited enormously in confidence and social standing from their practical education and employment. Each has an able-bodied assistant at Mrembo to ease understanding, though Ali will cheerfully encourage you to try a little KiSwahili sign-language, using the alphabet poster for guidance.

For a lazy afternoon, or a simple massage or manicure whilst the sun's at its peak, Mrembo Traditional Spa is a great place. It is a true oasis of calm in the centre of Stone Town, and an experience not to be hurried.

city tour for around US$15–20, but for something really special contact Anjam Hassan at Zanzibar Different for his utterly infectious enthusiasm and knowledge of this city, its culture and people (page 335).

AROUND ZANZIBAR TOWN

Along the coast north of Zanzibar Town, stretching over a distance of about 5km, are several palaces dating from the 19th century. Built for the various sultans who ruled Zanzibar during this period, it was commonplace for these wealthy families to retreat from the heat, smell and disease of the city in the hotter months to less populated corners. Some of the palaces and homes are in good condition and worth a visit; others will appeal only to keen fans of historical ruins and those with exceptionally good imaginations.

Most people visit this area as a day trip from Zanzibar Town, but it is perfectly possible to base yourself in the small town of Bububu, which served as the terminus of a light (36-inch gauge) railway used to connect the north coast to the Old Fort in

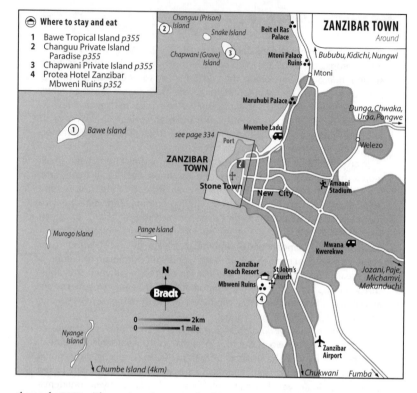

see page 334

Where to stay and eat

1 Bawe Tropical Island *p355*
2 Changuu Private Island
    Paradise *p355*
3 Chapwani Private Island *p355*
4 Protea Hotel Zanzibar
    Mbweni Ruins *p352*

ZANZIBAR TOWN
Around

Changuu (Prison) Island
Snake Island
Beit el Ras Palace
Chapwani (Grave) Island
Mtoni Palace Ruins
Bububu, Kidichi, Nungwi
Mtoni
Maruhubi Palace
Dunga, Chwaka, Uroa, Pongwe
Mwembe Ladu
Bawe Island
Port
Welezo
ZANZIBAR TOWN
Stone Town
Amaani Stadium
New City
Murogo Island
Pange Island
Mwana Kwerekwe
N
Bradt
Zanzibar Beach Resort
St John's Church
Mbweni Ruins
Jozani, Paje, Michamvi, Makunduchi
0   2km
0   1 mile
Nyange Island
Zanzibar Airport
Chumbe Island (4km)
Chukwani   Fumba

the early 1900s. The springs just outside the town supply most of Zanzibar Town's fresh water, and the name 'Bububu' presumably derives from the bubbling sound that they make. Of interest in town is a small, centuries-old mosque about 200m from the main crossroads, along the road back towards Zanzibar Town.

Between Zanzibar Town and Bububu lie the ruined palaces of Maruhubi and Mtoni, and Bububu is also the closest substantial settlement to the Persian baths at Kidichi and Kizimbani.

GETTING THERE AND AWAY Although some of the places mentioned below might be included in your spice tour, it is easy to visit most of them independently, using a combination of dalla dalla 502 or 534 (with frequent services to Bububu from the bus station on Creek Road) and your legs. Another possibility is to hire a car, scooter or bicycle from one of the tour operators (pages 333–5).

WHERE TO STAY AND EAT *Map, above, unless otherwise stated*

Protea Hotel Zanzibar Mbweni Ruins (13 rooms) 024 223 5478; www.marriott.com/hotels/travel/znzmr-protea-hotel-mbweni-ruins. This small hotel in the grounds of the Mbweni Ruins is rated as one of the best of its type in & around Zanzibar Town. Comfortable en-suite rooms with AC & private balconies are a short hop to the pool or beach. It's a relaxing spot, with a spa & waterside bar, & a popular restaurant

(*lunch US$10–20; dinner US$10–35*). The staff can advise visitors on local natural history. There's a free shuttle service to & from town, & port/airport transfers cost US$20 for 4 people. *US$160–250 dbl, B&B.* **$$$$–$$$$$**

Mangrove Lodge [map, page 357] (10 bungalows) m 0777 436954; e info@mangrovelodge.com; www.mangrovelodge.com. This peaceful, leafy & relaxed seaside retreat is located on a pretty slice of mangrove beach. The Zanzibari–Italian owners have taken admirable measures to reduce the environmental impact of the lodge: no energy-devouring AC, cooking over fire, locally sourced construction materials, furnishings by local tailors. Sandy pathways through tropical gardens & lawns link the pretty thatched bungalows, each with either a dbl or a sgl bed & a kitchenette. It's peaceful here – butterflies flutter around the orchard gardens, the restaurant looks over fishing boats bobbing on the bay, & sunbathers can choose between 2 secluded beaches. *US$80–180 dbl, B&B.* **$$$–$$$$**

WHAT TO SEE AND DO

Mtoni Palace (m *0782 500011;* ■ *mtonipalace*) The ruins of Mtoni Palace lie a short distance north of Maruhubi, and can be reached along the beach. The oldest palace on Zanzibar, Mtoni was built for Sultan Said in the 1840s. A book written by his daughter Salme describes the palace in the 1850s. At one end of the house was a large bathhouse, at the other the quarters where Said lived with his principal wife. Gazelles and peacocks wandered around the large courtyard until Mtoni was abandoned around 1885. Now, only the main walls, roof and bathhouses remain, but members of the resident Mtoni Palace Conservation Project are working hard to restore significant sections and offer interesting guided tours. The palace was used as a warehouse in World War I, with evidence of this alteration still visible.

Kidichi and Kizimbani Persian baths The Kidichi baths were built in 1850 for Sultan Said's wife, Binte Irich Mirza, the granddaughter of the Shah of Persia, and were decorated with Persian-style stucco. You can enter the bathhouse and see the bathing pool and toilets, but there is mould growing on much of the stucco. The baths lie about 3km east of Bububu; from the main crossroads follow the road

---

THE PRINCESS SALME TOUR

(✆ *024 223 0004;* m *0777 430117;* e *info@zanzibardifferent.com; www. zanzibardifferent.com; bookings must be made at least a day in advance*) Initiated by Stefanie Schoetz and the team at Mtoni Palace Conservation Project, this day trip combines a number of historical palaces and traditional ceremonies with an informative spice tour and delicious Swahili lunch. Escorted by a guide from the conservation project, small groups (approximately 4–6) are taken by boat from the evocative ruins of Mtoni Palace, Princess Salme's birthplace, to Bububu for a traditional coffee ceremony with tasty local treats (*kashata* – peanut brittle – and candy-like *halua*). After a short walk, perhaps into the grounds of Salme's cousin's home, visitors are transported by donkey and cart, Salme-style, to the Kidichi plantation area, where Mzee Yussuf guides a tour of his spice farm before his wife serves a deliciously fresh, homemade meal. Heading back down the hillside after lunch, there are great views towards the Indian Ocean and Stone Town before the cart arrives at the Persian baths, originally built in 1850 for Sultan Said's second wife Scheherazade. From here, visitors are whisked back to Mtoni Marine by minibus for a chilled drink in the bar. Thoroughly original and enjoyable.

The tour leaves Stone Town at 08.30, returning at 14.00, and costs US$55 per person, plus US$5 per person supplement for fewer than three people, including entrance fees, lunch, and a US$5 donation to Mtoni Palace Conservation Project. Reservations one day in advance essential.

heading inland (ie: turn right coming from Zanzibar Town) and you'll see the baths to your right after a walk of around 30 minutes. The Kizimbani baths are less attractive and less accessible on foot, lying a further 3km or so inland. The surrounding Kizimbani clove plantation, which is visited by many spice tours, was founded in the early 19th century by Saleh bin Haramil, the Arab trader who imported the first cloves to Zanzibar.

Mangapwani Slave Chamber Near the village of Mangapwani, some 10km north of Bububu, are a large natural cavern and a manmade slave chamber. This square cell cut into the coral was apparently built to hold slaves by one Muhammad bin Nassor Al-Alwi, an important slave trader. Boats from the mainland would unload their human cargo on the nearby beach, and the slaves would be kept here before being taken to Zanzibar Town for resale, or to plantations on the island. It is thought that some time after 1873, when slavery was officially abolished, the cave was used as a place to hide slaves, as an illicit trade continued for many years.

ISLANDS CLOSE TO ZANZIBAR TOWN

Several small islands lie between 2km and 6km offshore of Zanzibar, many of them within view of Zanzibar Town and easily visited from there as a day trip. Boat transport to Chumbe arranged with an independent guide will cost around US$20, but you will pay more to go on an organised tour (see pages 333–5 for tour operators). To cut the individual cost, it is worth getting a group together. Despite their individual attractions, these islands are quiet yet close to main shipping routes, so are not ideal overnight stays for those in search of either total isolation or entertainment and nightlife. Note that crossing to or from Zanzibar Town in an unlit boat at night is extremely dangerous.

CHUMBE ISLAND The coral island of Chumbe, along with several surrounding reefs, is gazetted as a nature reserve under the title of Chumbe Island Coral Park (CHICOP). The area is in near-pristine condition because it served as a military base for many years and visitors were not permitted. Snorkelling here is as good as anywhere around Zanzibar, with more than 350 reef fishes recorded, as well as dolphins and turtles. A walking trail circumnavigates the island, passing rock pools haunted by starfish, and beaches marched upon by legions of hermit crabs. Look out, too, for the giant coconut crab, an endangered nocturnal creature that weighs up to 4kg. Some 60 species of bird have been recorded on the island, including breeding pairs of the rare roseate tern, and the localised Ader's duiker, hunted out in the 1950s, has been reintroduced. Of historical interest are an ancient Swahili mosque and a British lighthouse built in 1904.

Day trips to the island (*US$95pp, inc transfers, guides, snorkelling equipment & lunch*) can be arranged only through reputable tour operators or from the Mbweni Ruins Hotel (pages 352–3). Alternatively, visitors can stay overnight.

⌂ **Where to stay and eat** *Map, page 375*

✳ ⌂ **Chumbe Island Lodge** (7 rooms) m 0777 413 232/0672 413 582/0777 413 582; e book@chumbeisland.com/ask@chumbeisland. com; www.chumbeisland.com; ⊕ mid Jun–mid Apr. Part of the Chumbe Island Coral Park (CHICOP), this superb, trail-blazing lodge is an example of truly eco-friendly accommodation. Bungalows are simple, clean, ingeniously designed & genuinely ecologically sensitive. The central area is a huge, star-shaped makuti structure – perfect for catching the sea breeze in the heat of the day. Fresh meals & drinks are served on the terrace (on the sounding of a gong), & there's a lovely upper deck of hammocks & chairs. Activities are all escorted & focus on learning about the surrounding environment & ecology, & include snorkelling (scuba diving is prohibited) on the nearby reefs; forest walks along the nature trail; & walks across the inter-tidal zone, with its plethora of rock pools. *US$520–560 dbl, Al.* 🐚

CHANGUU (PRISON) ISLAND Lying in the Zanzibar Channel, 6km northwest of Zanzibar Town, Changuu is a coral-rag islet, also known as Prison Island and at one time Kibandiko Island. It was originally owned by a wealthy Arab, who used it as a detention centre for disobedient slaves. A prison was built there in 1893, but never used; today it houses a café, library and boutique. The island is home to several giant tortoises, gifted from the Seychelles in the 18th century, though numbers remain severely threatened. An entrance fee of US$5 per person must be paid in hard currency. The island has a small beach and there's reasonable snorkelling on the nearby reef. Daily tours to see the historical ruins and tortoises are organised by many of Stone Town's operators (pages 333–5), invariably making the 20-minute crossing by dhow under sail. For a cheaper option, a local boat will take four people to the island for around US$30. There is a 27-room resort here too, **Changuu Private Island Paradise** (*www.privateislands-zanzibar.com*; 🐚; *map, page 352*), with beachfront cottages, swimming pool and a floodlit tennis court.

CHAPWANI (GRAVE) ISLAND This long, narrow and very pretty island has been the site of a Christian cemetery since 1879. Most of the graves belong to British sailors who were killed tackling Arab slave ships, while others date from World War I, when the British ship *Pegasus* was sunk in Zanzibar harbour. The island also has a small swimming beach – good at low and high tide – and faces Snake Island, where thousands of egrets roost overnight. The indigenous forest supports about 100 duikers, large numbers of fruit bats, and various coastal scrub birds. The giant coconut crab is often seen along the shore.

Between mid June and mid April, visitors can stay in one of the five semi-detached bungalows at **Chapwani Private Island** (*www.chapwaniisland.com*; **$$$$$**; *map, page 352*). There's a nice pool tucked among the trees or, for a more natural dip, a tidal outlet in a coral crevasse on the northeast of the island makes a pleasant place to swim at high tide, and a good place to explore the starfish and barnacle-clad rock pools otherwise.

BAWE ISLAND About 6km due west of Zanzibar Town, Bawe has broad sandy beaches and a densely vegetated centre. In 1879, it was given to the Eastern Telegraph Company by Sultan Barghash to be used as the operations station for the underwater telegraphic cable linking Cape Town with Zanzibar, the Seychelles and Aden in Yemen. A second line was run from Bawe Island to the External Telecommunications building in the Shangani area of Zanzibar Town. The old 'Extelcoms' building has now been converted into the Serena Inn, but the original phone line is largely redundant.

Lovely as the beach may be, it is firmly on the busy shipping route to Zanzibar Town and isn't visited as frequently as Changuu. In theory, it's possible to combine trips here with the tortoise excursions or simply arrange an out-and-back voyage with a boat captain in Zanzibar Town, though access prices do tend to be higher than those to Changuu. With the arrival of **Bawe Tropical Island** (*www.privateislands-zanzibar.com*; 🐚; *map, page 352*), visitors can retreat to this pretty beach spot overnight. Thatched cottages, with en-suite bathrooms and colourful interiors, line the sand, just a stone's throw from the warm, shallow sea.

15

Ageing hippies, cool dudes, gap-year students and bright young things escaping European city jobs are all drawn to the white sand, stage-set palm trees, turquoise sea and sparkling sunshine of northern Zanzibar. Burgeoning guesthouses and vast resort complexes; beachfront activity overload and vibrant nightlife; an ever-expanding community and immense pressure on natural resources: these are the things that now characterise northern Zanzibar above its pleasant, white-sand beaches, warm sea, nautical heritage and good diving opportunities. Less than 2 hours' drive from Stone Town on the fast tar road past increasingly rural villages, this area mixes backpacker budget tourism with an increasing number of large, luxurious resorts. Focused around Nungwi village on the northernmost tip, and spreading near-continuously along the golden sands of Kendwa, on the northwest coast, this bustling centre appears to offer every component of the perfect holiday: a wide range of accommodation, watersports galore, fresh seafood washed down with daily cocktails, and a lovely ocean vista.

Once-small backpackers' bolt-holes have grown from a handful of rooms to resort hotels, mid-range places have added literally dozens of rooms to their original quota, whilst large-scale luxury or all-inclusive resorts now sit cheek-by-jowl on vast tracts of land around the north coast. Quite literally every beachfront plot from Ras Nungwi to Kendwa now has some tourist accommodation, either operational or under construction, and that has come at an aesthetic, social and environmental cost, but to the holidaymakers who flock here, it's a vibrant ocean spot.

GETTING THERE AND AWAY Dalla dalla 116 runs between Zanzibar Town and Nungwi daily, while **bus** 14 operates half-hourly from north to south between 05.30 and 21.00. To reach Kendwa, it's a simple 20-minute walk along the beach from Nungwi. However, the vast majority of travellers prefer to be transferred by **private minibus**, which can cost up to US$15 per person depending on group size and your negotiating skills. The ideal is to get a group together in Zanzibar Town when you want to head out to Nungwi, then organise a transfer through a papaasi, a taxi driver or a tour company. Unless you have very rigid timings, there is no need to organise your transfer back to Zanzibar Town in advance, since several vehicles can be found waiting around for passengers in Nungwi, especially mid morning.

WHERE TO STAY Map, page 358

The number of hotels and guesthouses in this area has grown tremendously in recent years, with the busiest beach to the southwest of the peninsula. While there's no shortage of accommodation – new or old – finding something that is both good quality and good value is more of a challenge. Listed below are a handful of our favourites.

Nungwi
Exclusive

 Essque Zalu Zanzibar (40 rooms, 9 villas) m 0778 683960; e reservations@essquehotels. com; www.essquehotels.com. The imposing makuti construction that makes up Essque Zalu's central area is visible from quite a distance. The spacious suites are set in lush landscaped gardens, & are furnished beautifully using contemporary African fabrics, art & wallpapers. The resort is centred on the huge, saltwater pool, complete with a whirlpool, water jets & multi-coloured lighting. Looking out over the pool are the 2 restaurants: the deli-style Market Kitchen downstairs & the more upmarket à la carte Middle Eastern restaurant & shisha lounge upstairs. Sundowners can be enjoyed at the end of The Jetty for the ultimate sea view. There are also 9 vast 4-bedroom villas, a pampering spa, super-cool gym & a Petit VIP kids' club (*www.petitvip.com;* ⏰ 08.00–20.00). Facilities abound, rooms are top-notch & Essque Zalu is making a name as one of northern

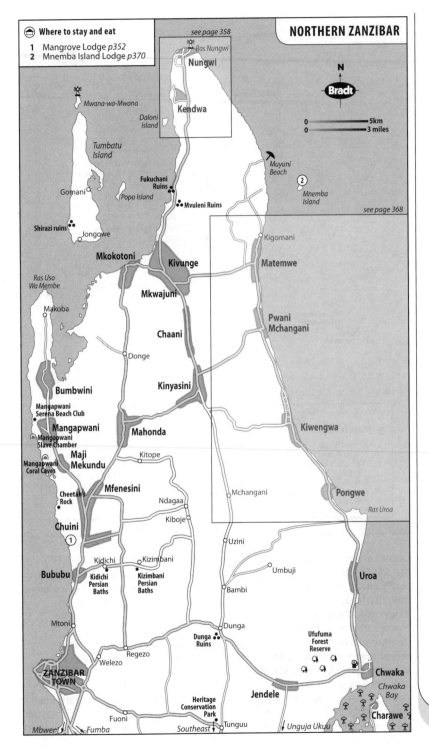

see page 358

NORTHERN ZANZIBAR

Where to stay and eat

1 Mangrove Lodge *p352*
2 Mnemba Island Lodge *p370*

N

Bradt

0   5km
0   3 miles

Ras Nungwi

Nungwi

Kendwa

Mwana-wa-Mwana

Daloni Island

Tumbatu Island

Muyuni Beach

2

Mnemba Island

see page 368

Gomani

Popo Island

Fukuchani Ruins

Mvuleni Ruins

Shirazi ruins

Jongowe

Kigomani

Mkokotoni

Kivunge

Matemwe

Ras Uso Wa Membe

Mkwajuni

Makoba

Chaani

Pwani Mchangani

Donge

Kinyasini

Bumbwini

Kiwengwa

Mangapwani Serena Beach Club

Mangapwani

Mahonda

Mangapwani Slave Chamber

Kitope

Maji Mekundu

Mangapwani Coral Caves

Mfenesini

Ndagaa

Mchangani

Pongwe

Cheetah's Rock

Kiboje

Ras Uroa

Chuini

1

Uzini

Kidichi

Kizimbani

Bububu

Kidichi Persian Baths

Kizimbani Persian Baths

Umbuji

Uroa

Bambi

Mtoni

Dunga

Regezo

Dunga Ruins

Ufufuma Forest Reserve

Welezo

Chwaka

ZANZIBAR TOWN

Chwaka Bay

Jendele

Charawe

Fuoni

Heritage Conservation Park

Mbweni

Fumba

Southeast

Tunguu

Unguja Ukuu

Zanzibar   NORTHERN ZANZIBAR

15

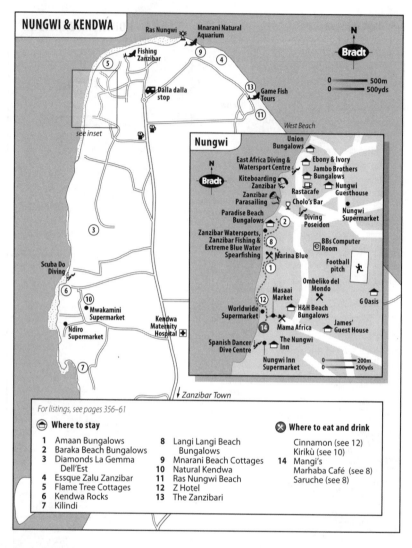

NUNGWI & KENDWA

Ras Nungwi
Mnarani Natural Aquarium
Fishing Zanzibar
Dalla dalla stop
Game Fish Tours
West Beach
see inset

Nungwi

Union Bungalows
East Africa Diving & Watersport Centre
Ebony & Ivory
Jambo Brothers Bungalows
Kiteboarding Zanzibar
Rastacafe
Nungwi Guesthouse
Zanzibar Parasailing
Cholo's Bar
Paradise Beach Bungalows
Diving Poseidon
Nungwi Supermarket
Zanzibar Watersports, Zanzibar Fishing & Extreme Blue Water Spearfishing
BBs Computer Room
Marina Blue
Football pitch
Masaai Market
Ombeliko del Mondo
G Oasis
Worldwide Supermarket
H&H Beach Bungalows
James' Guest House
Mama Africa
Scuba Do Diving
Mwakamini Supermarket
Kendwa Maternity Hospital
Ndiro Supermarket
Spanish Dancer Dive Centre
The Nungwi Inn
Nungwi Inn Supermarket

↓ Zanzibar Town

For listings, see pages 356–61

Where to stay

1 Amaan Bungalows
2 Baraka Beach Bungalows
3 Diamonds La Gemma Dell'Est
4 Essque Zalu Zanzibar
5 Flame Tree Cottages
6 Kendwa Rocks
7 Kilindi
8 Langi Langi Beach Bungalows
9 Mnarani Beach Cottages
10 Natural Kendwa
11 Ras Nungwi Beach
12 Z Hotel
13 The Zanzibari

Where to eat and drink

Cinnamon (see 12)
Kirikù (see 10)
14 Mangi's
Marhaba Café (see 8)
Saruche (see 8)

Zanzibar's premier resort options. *US$290–500 dbl, B&B.* **$$$$$–**

✴ 🏠 **Z Hotel** (35 rooms) m 0774 266266; e info@thezhotel.com; www.thezhotel.com; ⊕ Jun–mid Apr. Lording over South Beach & bringing a degree of city-boy bling to Nungwi, rooms here are divided into 6 levels of luxury, but all boast indulgences from iPod docking stations, AC & plasma TVs to White Company toiletries & stocked minibars. Every room has a balcony with a sea view of varying degrees. Elsewhere in the compact complex, the busy stone pool above the beach is a fine hangout, whilst the Cinnamon Bar

& Saruche Restaurant (page 361) are evening hotspots. The biggest issue for style-seekers may prove to be the less salubrious surrounding sprawl. *US$210–450 dbl, B&B.* **$$$$$–**

Upmarket

🏠 **Flame Tree Cottages** (16 rooms) ☎ 024 224 0100; e etgl@zanlink.com; www. flametreecottages.com. On the edge of Nungwi village, this lovely little place comprises a house & 15 red-roofed bungalows spread out in extensive gardens beside the beach. Some of the rooms are interconnecting making them perfect for families, though all offer homely comfort. Outside, the lovely raised pool is thoroughly inviting, & the surrounding gardens & space lend a refreshing feeling of space & peace – something increasingly difficult to find in Nungwi. Lounging in one of many hammocks around the garden, listening to the twittering birds & relaxing is lovely, & the quiet staff are happy to help with any requests. The activities on offer are gentle & range from lemongrass oil massage (*US$12/30mins*) to snorkelling trips aboard the owner's dhow; plus there's a Zanzi Yoga pavilion on site (page 362) offering popular beachside classes with Marisa. For culinary indulgence, chef Simai's delicious dishes can be enjoyed overlooking the dhows in the harbour. *US$170–440 dbl, B&B.* **$$$$–**🍲

✱ 🏠 **Ras Nungwi Beach Hotel** (33 rooms) 📞024 294 0125; **e** info@rasnungwi.com; www. rasnungwi.com. This perennially popular choice for honeymooners lies at the southern end of Nungwi's beach. Rooms of various categories are set in well-tended gardens & include AC, safes & neatly tiled bathrooms, though those situated further back have no sea view. Alongside the central bar & split-level dining room are a games area, a small swimming pool & a spa. Activities include snorkelling, diving, fishing & kayaking. The exceptional food & great wine list are highlights of any stay, with the occasional seafood BBQ featuring Swahili cuisine classics. *US$170–325 dbl, B&B.* **$$$$–**🍲

🏠 **The Zanzibari** (11 rooms) 📞024 550 0590; **m** 0772 222919; **e** info@thezanzibari.com; www. thezanzibari.com. Utterly transformed in the last decade, The Zanzibari is a lovely spot: friendly, tropical & independent. Amid extensive climbers & flowering shrubs, dbl rooms are set a distance back from the water's edge, but with cool, clean interiors. The 2 luxury villas, however, are right above the raised beach, & come complete with their own plunge pool – perfect for privacy-seeking families. There's a large pool with loungers dotted around the surrounding stone patio & bougainvillea shade for sunbathers. Everyone can enjoy the clifftop jacuzzi pools for dhow-spotting dips or relax in the thatched massage room. The restaurant menu is predominantly seasonal & Swahili in flavour, with many ingredients grown onsite, & there's a mezzanine chill-out zone & a friendly bar. *US$195–365 dbl, B&B.* **$$$$–**🍲

🏠 **Mnarani Beach Cottages** (31 rooms) 📞024 224 0494; **m** 0777 415551; **e** mnarani@

zanlink.com; www.lighthousezanzibar.com. Close to the northernmost tip of the island, Mnarani overlooks a beautiful stretch of beach, & is separated by dense vegetation from the lighthouse; unlike most other plots on this coast, it feels less boxed in by development. Some of its en-suite rooms have sea views; others are set in lush, tropical gardens close to the pool. Kayaks, windsurfers & surfboards can be hired, & the lagoon in front of the hotel is a great place for kitesurfing. The bar has a cool, relaxed vibe, & the staff are some of the friendliest on the north coast. *US$80–290 dbl, B&B.* **$$$$–$$$$$**

Mid range
🏠 **Langi Langi Beach Bungalows** (33 rooms) 📞024 224 0470; **e** reservations@ langilangizanzibar.com; www.langilangizanzibar. com. The hotel is divided into 2 sections by the main pedestrian footpath: the 3-storey blocks & restaurant on the seafront & the original rooms & swimming pool in the lush garden on the other. The 20 en-suite rooms are of a good standard, & sit right in the heart of Nungwi's tourist scene, with a densely tropical garden & refreshing pool. Set on a large cantilevered deck over the sea, is the Marhaba Café where the food, especially curries, is popular fare. Alongside this are 13 rooms including the Penthouse at the top, where tunnel-vision sea views are framed by the steep makuti thatch. The owners are friendly, employing only local staff, & are genuinely hospitable. *US$100–220 dbl, B&B.* **$$$–$$$$**

🏠 **Amaan Bungalows** (86 rooms) 📞024 550 1152; **m** 0775 044719; **e** info@ amaanbungalows.com; www.amaanbungalows. com. A Nungwi scene stalwart, Amaan's rooms are divided into 4 broad categories, with the premium sea-view selection perched on a coral-rock cliff above the sea. Regardless of category, all rooms are clean & well cared for with sgl to trpl occupancy, & 4 are interconnecting for groups & families. This is an ever-developing complex, popular with a young crowd seeking to be at the very centre of the action & older visitors on a budget. Bordering the main footpath through town, Amaan also has a practical grocery, a souvenir shop & a reliable internet café. Marina Blue & Infusion, immediately opposite on the seafront, are affiliated with Amaan & are good places to eat pizza & seafood, drink virtually anything & be merry at any hour of the day. *US$60–150 dbl, B&B.* **$$–$$$$**

🏠 **Baraka Beach Bungalows** (16 rooms) m 0777 422910/415569; e barakabungalow@hotmail.com; barakabungalow.atspace.com. These solid, makuti-thatched bungalows surround a small tropical garden beside West Beach. Rooms have undergone significant improvement of late, with AC, fans, electricity & hot water now standard. Interiors remain simple but very clean, with small terraces overlooking the palms, fuchsias & hibiscus – it's a perfectly pleasant corner. Rooms accommodate 2–6 people, so small groups of friends will be comfortable here. The affiliated restaurant is a tranquil, feet-in-the-sand place under brilliant blue umbrellas at the back of the beach. *US$50–100 dbl, B&B.* **$$–$$$**

Kendwa
Exclusive

✳ 🏠 **Kilindi** (15 rooms) m 0784 250630; e reservations@elewana.com; www.elewanacollection.com. Kilindi's unique design is a first for Zanzibar, & it's created quite a stir. Exclusive & upmarket without being pretentious, it offers bright white pavilions spread out over 20ha & overlooking a sweep of beach. Reminiscent of Greek Orthodox churches, the domed, 2-tier pavilions are dotted among the dense, indigenous shrubbery & each is accessed through heavy wooden Zanzibari doors, through which is a serene sanctuary shielded from the view of others by yet more luscious plants. With a personal butler to bring you whatever you may desire, including your meals, you may never wish to leave your pavilion. However, if you can be tempted away, there's an attractive, colonial chic restaurant & bar, a bijou spa & gorgeous infinity pool. For style, space & service, most definitely one of Zanzibar's top spots! *US$1,300–2,500 dbl, FB.* 👑

🏠 **Diamonds La Gemma Dell'Est** (138 rooms) ☎ 024 224 0125; e info.gemma@diamonds-resorts.com; lagemmadellest.diamondsresorts.com. This stylish resort at the northern end of Kendwa Beach is one of Zanzibar's best choices for families. Comfortable but contemporary rooms, with all mod-cons, are designed to give each a sea-view veranda, while remaining fairly unobtrusive. Exotic plants characterise the sloping gardens, & the beach is backed by an enormous pool with a children's area, jacuzzi & swim-up bar. Guests have the choice of several bars & restaurants, serving anything from pizza to Mediterranean buffets – although the seafood restaurant is charged extra. Activities range from diving (run by Scuba Do – page 363) & other watersports to quizzes & Swahili BBQs. *US$250–500 dbl, FB.* **$$$$$–**👑

Upmarket

✳ 🏠 **Natural Kendwa** (6 rooms) m 0778 579146; e naturalkendwavilla@yahoo.it; www.naturalkendwavilla.com. Some of the loveliest accommodation in Kendwa can now be found tucked behind the seafront resorts at this gem of a hotel. Amiable Italian owner, Andrea, has put his heart & considerable experience into the gorgeous rooms: original, contemporary & charming. The interiors are both simple in style & elaborate in detail, & all are blissfully spacious, whilst outside, manicured tropical gardens slope around the lovely free-form pool & jacuzzi that make for a beautiful setting & thoroughly enjoyable escape from the busy beach. Dining is in the adjoining restaurant (page 361), which is a highlight in itself; whilst beach days can be spent on the loungers at Kendwa Rocks (see below), where Natural Kendwa guests can enjoy free day passes. *US$135–200 dbl, B&B.* **$$$$–$$$$$**

Mid range

🏠 **Kendwa Rocks** (35 rooms) m 0774 415475; e booking@kendwarocks.com; www.kendwarocks.com. The 1st property to open on this stretch of beach, Kendwa Rocks celebrated its 22nd birthday in 2017. There's a range of accommodation, which gets booked up roughly in order of luxury: the best rooms go first! The all-new semi-detached Coconut Bungalows, spread out in a semicircle on a lovely stretch of sand, boast inviting batik hammocks & a shared plunge pool. At the other end of the scale, there's a 19-bed basic mixed dorm for groups of off-duty volunteers. On the beach, the Mermaid Bar is the epitome of beachside drinking dens: a hip DJ messes on decks in the corner, smiling staff stand behind a well-stocked bar festooned with lists of cocktails, while sun-kissed travellers recline, chat & drink. On Sat nights (*22.30 onwards*) & at Full Moon the bar hosts live music & a huge beach party (*US$7pp*): a messy affair that's often still in full swing at sunrise. Revellers come from all over the island to experience the cocktails, bonfires, dance beats & acrobatic shows here. *US$40–290 dbl, B&B.* **$$–$$$$$**

✕ WHERE TO EAT AND DRINK *Map, page 358*

Nearly all the hotels and guesthouses in Nungwi and Kendwa have attached restaurants, many of which are open to guests and non-guests alike. Others are standalone places that tend to close and spring up again as if with the tide. A few stand out as worth investigating in their own right, as listed below, but do ask around for the current culinary hotspots.

Nungwi

✕ **Marhaba Café** On Langi Langi's large seaside deck (page 359), this is a relaxed coffee shop by day & a Swahili restaurant by night. It's a popular place & worth booking for dinner (*US$8–12*), inside or out. Alcohol is not sold, but bring your own & it'll be chilled & served. **$$$–$$$$**

✕ **Saruche Restaurant** ⊕ dinner only daily. The formal restaurant at Z Hotel (page 358), Saruche serves an à la carte menu of African–European fusion food with a heavy emphasis on seafood (*main course US$8–15*). Accompanied by an international wine list, ocean views & island antiques, it's one of the smartest options currently in Nungwi. There are traditional music & entertainment nights throughout the week. **$$$–$$$$**

✴ ♀ **Cinnamon** ⊕ 07.00–late daily. Cinnamon is part of the Z Hotel complex (page 358) but welcomes non-residents, too. With its 1st-floor location overlooking the South Beach scene & sparkling sea, the young & beautiful are attracted by its contemporary décor & fabulous tropical cocktails (*US$5*), whilst late at night, the rooftop daybeds under the stars are a delight. Sipped at cushion-clad white baraza benches, surrounded by ever-changing mood lights & chilled tunes, this is a great pre-dinner drinks spot. Stay for sushi & tempting tasting platters (*US$5–15*) for lunch or dinner, or just work your way through the extensive cocktail list. There is a cool vibe here &

it's the only place by the beach where fashionable ladies won't feel out of place in high heels. **$$$–$$$$**

♀ **Mangi's Bar & Restaurant** ⊕ 08.00–22.00 daily. Long-running Mangi's is on a sandy, shaded spot beside Nungwi Inn Hotel. It's a relaxed hangout serving fresh juices, US$4 cocktails (the 'Zanzibar Mzungu' concoction of banana, rum, milk & vodka appearing popular), & snacks (*samosas US$4.50; chapattis US$5; baked potatoes US$6.50*). For US$15pp you can join the nightly BBQ buffet on the beach & indulge in the likes of king prawns in garlic butter, octopus in coconut curry & vegetable curry – just be sure to order before 16.00. **$$$**

Kendwa

✴ ♀ **Kirikù** m 0778 579146; e naturalkendwavilla@yahoo.it; www. naturalkendwavilla.com/ristorante; ⊕ 08.00–16.00 & 18.00–23.00 daily. This fabulous little restaurant adjoining Natural Kendwa (page 360) is a vibrant visual assault: a striking, multi-coloured Aztec mural covering every internal wall & ceiling. Guests are seated on the floor on red-&-green cushions at coconut-wood tables or at the bijou bar. It's quirky & fun, & a happy place to hang out. Food is equal part Italian (a testament to the owner's nationality) & part Swahili: biryani (*US$4*), linguini with mussels (*US$10*), pizza (*US$5–6.50*) & indulgent seafood platters (*US$20*). Come for any meal of the day, & you'll likely return for another. **$$–$$$**

HEALTH AND BEAUTY Temporary henna tattoos seem to be de rigueur in Nungwi, painted on to your skin by friendly local ladies as you lie under their makeshift palm shades on the beach. Be warned, however; the henna can badly mark bed linen, and hotel owners will charge for stains. It is also important to avoid black henna (pico): it is a synthetic dye and often results in bad allergic reactions, sometimes delayed by a few weeks, which requires medical treatment. For all-out African beach chic, hair-braiding services are also available, along with basic beach massages. For a less-public massage experience, try one of the following:

Baraka White House Spa In a small, immaculate room adjoining Baraka's Restaurant on West Beach, friendly therapists offer excellent local

treatments on kanga-covered massage tables. From deep muscle rubs to Indian head massage, foot treatments to facials, this little business offers them all. They are both professionally trained, so the standard is above that available on the beach; that said, this is not in any way a 'spa'. *Body treatments US$20/hr; manicures US$10*

Peponi Spa e info@rasnungwi.com. Set in the gardens of Ras Nungwi Beach Hotel (page 359), Peponi offers both guests & non-residents 'an array of rejuvenating, pampering & holistic treatments'. It is the area's best spa by far. Run by internationally qualified therapists & using natural oils & ingredients, this is a wonderfully relaxing place to spend a few hours, & who could resist the 90-min 'Nungwi Earth Soul Signature African Celebration'? *Body treatments US$40–115/45–75mins; manicures US$55/1hr; waxing & eyebrow tinting/threading US$20–37*

The Zalu Zanzibar Spa m 0778 683960; e ezz. retreat@essquehotels.com. Within the Essque Zalu Hotel (pages 356–8), this small spa pavilion fans out into sweet-smelling treatment rooms, a Vichy shower room, a sauna/steam & gym area. Using botanical healingEARTH products, the team of therapists offer a range of beauty treatments, massages, body polishes & finishing touches from waxing to manicures. *Facials US$120/90mins; body treatments US$80–280/1–3½hrs; manicures US$55/1hr*

Zanzi Yoga m 0776 310227; e info@ yogazanzibar.com; www.yogazanzibar.com. Founded in 2009, Yoga Zanzibar offers yoga classes & longer retreats. Based at Flame Tree Cottages (pages 358–9), individual yoga tuition & longer retreats are available year-round by registered teacher, Marisa. Relaxation, pranayama (breathing techniques), sun salutations, asanas (postures), & reiki available.

SHOPPING

Nungwi There are several small shops in Nungwi village, where you'll find an array of cheap souvenirs, including carvings, paintings and jewellery, as well as essential items. In the village itself, the well-equipped Nungwi School computer room has email and internet services (see below), and adjoining **Choices** sells souvenirs and swimwear. There's an ever-changing array of beauticians, barbers, local cafés, as well as the long-standing **Nungwi Supermarket**: a veritable Aladdin's cave of imported luxuries, from toothpaste and toiletries to chocolate and Pringles. There are also a couple of places on South Beach selling basics: **Nungwi Inn Supermarket** and **New Worldwide Supermarket**, beside the curio market. For artwork and souvenirs, a fairly contained **curio market** has grown on the alley running perpendicular to South Beach, alongside Z Hotel. Known locally as the Maasai Market, on account of the traders' tribal background, you'll find some entertainingly named shacks – IKEA Zanzibar, Leonardo da Vinci, Gucci – displaying an array of colourful paintings, carvings and beadwork.

Kendwa With the increase in accommodation and visitors, Kendwa now also has two small, local-style 'supermarkets': **Ndiro Supermarket** on the very edge of the coral cliff at the southern end of the beach and **Mwakamini Supermarket** on the village side of Kendwa Rocks. Both sell basic supplies of tinned food, crisps, sweets and water, but little else. For curios, the ever-increasing span of Maasai-manned stalls on the beach bordering La Gemma offers colourful paintings, beaded jewellery and occasionally carvings. Quality varies considerably so shop around and don't be blinded by the sun into making second-rate purchases.

OTHER PRACTICALITIES All of the larger hotels have internet facilities, almost all with Wi-Fi, and these days a reasonable number of the smaller backpacker places and cafes will also offer guest Wi-Fi. For access to a PC, we recommend the reliable **Nungwi School IT centre** as a first choice (⊕ *08.00–20.00 Mon–Fri, 08.30–19.30 holidays & w/ends; rates are very low at US$0.60/30min or US$1/hr*), as its income is used to reinvest in the school's computer initiative. It's clearly signposted beside the football field, on the right as you approach from the beach.

SPORTS AND ACTIVITIES If you want peace, quiet and fewer people, you will probably need to head to a different corner of the island. A whole raft of land and aquatic activities are available here.

Watersports The sweeping cape on which Nungwi is sited is surrounded by sparkling, warm, turquoise seas, making it a perfect spot to engage in countless water activities. Prices are all very similar; quality is highly variable. Listen to your instinct and other travellers' advice carefully when deciding who is currently offering the best trip.

Snorkelling and diving There are several competent dive operations on this stretch of coast. Divers are advised to talk seriously to the individual operators about safety, experience and ethos before signing up for courses or sub-aqua excursions. Knowledgeable, reliable operations include:

East Africa Diving & Watersport Centre m 0777 416425/420588; e info@sansibar-tauchen.de; www.diving-zanzibar.com. The oldest dive centre on the north coast & highly respected. On the beach in front of Jambo Brothers Guesthouse, it's an excellent & highly efficient PADI 5* Gold Palm Resort offering well-priced courses to Dive Master & a host of scuba trips. EADC also has bases within Essque Zalu, Z Hotel & Ras Nungwi Beach Hotel. *US$100/190/420 (plus US$30 to Mnemba Atoll) for 2/4/10 dives; Discover Scuba US$130; Open Water US$500; Advanced US$450; Nitrox US$300*

Scuba Do Diving (UK) +44 (0)1326 250773; m 0777 417157; e do-scuba@scuba-do-zanzibar.com; www.scuba-zanzibar.com. For many years, Scuba Do was Kendwa's only dive operation, & it remains a superb establishment. Owned & operated by a British couple, Christian & Tammy, it is a highly professional & well-equipped dive centre, based at Kendwa Beach. When out of the water, the team are also involved in extensive community work, most notably their commitment to training Zanzibaris & Tanzanians to become qualified dive masters & instructors, & the annual beach & underwater clean-up project. *Snorkelling trips US$45–85 Tumbatu/Mnemba; US$120/230/330/420 for 2/4/6/8 dives; Discover*

Scuba US$110; Open Water US$575; Advanced US$370

Spanish Dancer Dive Centre 024 224 0091; m 0777 417717/430005; e contact@spanishdancerdivers.com; www.divinginzanzibar.com. Based in an open rondavel on South Beach, Spanish Dancer is run by an impressive team. The dive centre is PADI 5* accredited & teaches in German, French, Spanish, Hebrew, English & Swahili, with confined water sessions in the lagoon off the beach or at Zanzibar Star. *US$110/205/295/445 (plus US$30 for Mnemba) for 2/4/6/10 dives; Discover Scuba US$155; Open Water US$495; Advanced US$395*

Zanzibar Watersports 024 223 3309; m 0773 165862; e info@zanzibarwatersports.com; www.zanzibarwatersports.com. With PADI 5* Gold Palm Instructor Development Centre status, offering all PADI qualifications to instructor level, Zanzibar Watersports has 2 bases: Paradise Beach Bungalows in Nungwi & Kendwa Rocks, Kendwa. There are also 1- & 2-man kayaks & wakeboarding equipment available & sunset dhow cruises for the more sedentary visitor. *US$65/115/310/460 (plus US$45 for Mnemba) for 1/2/6/10 dives exc equipment; Refresher US$30; Open Water US$499; Advanced US$450; kayaks US$10pp/hr; waterskiing US$50/15mins*

Sailing Aside from local sunset dhow trips, there are few opportunities to sail on board more modern vessels on this stretch of coast. For live-aboard diving and 'learn-to-sail' options, *Julia*, listed below, is the only real option.

Dive 'n' Sail Zanzibar m 0774 441234; e info@dive-n-sail.com/yachtjulia@hotmail.com; www.dive-n-sail.com. If sailing appeals, Dive 'n' Sail

operates a lovely 50ft Admiral catamaran, *Julia*, specialising in live-aboard dive trips & fishing excursions to Pemba & Mafia. Available for charter, the boat is fully equipped for diving & deep-sea fishing. With some notice, dive courses can be taught on board. All rates are subject to periodic change. *US$1,320/day private boat charter (1–5 persons) for min 4 days, excluding dives.*

Fishing

Nungwi's proximity to some of Africa's best deep-sea fishing grounds – Leven Bank and the deep Pemba Channel – offers serious anglers outstanding fishing opportunities. In addition to the weather-beaten local dhows that plough the coastal waters, the following operators currently offer game fishing in fully equipped, custom-built boats.

Fishing Zanzibar e info@fishingzanzibar. com; www.fishingzanzibar.com. Operated by Gerry Hallam (owner of Gerry's Bar), Fishing Zanzibar have 4 sport-fishing boats based in Nungwi, as well as a 50ft sailing yacht, *Walkabout*. The sport-fishing boats are kitted out with a stand-up fishing chair, outriggers, downriggers, Shimano fishing gear (line classes 25–80lb) & a full selection of lures, & take small charter groups (max 4 anglers) to Leven Bank & the Pemba Channel. Night fishing for broadbills is an option, as are live-aboard trips. *US$500–1,000 ½ day; US$1,000–2,000 full day, inc lunch; live-aboard US$1,300–2,500/day for 4 persons; rates vary by boat.*

Game Fish Tours m 0772 074766; e gamefishlodge@gmail.com; www. gamefishlodgezanzibar.wordpress.com. Based out of Game Fish Lodge in Nungwi, this South African operation runs half-day, night fishing & 2-day Pemba tours for reef & bottom fishing. They have 2 boats: a 14ft fibreglass Super Dolphin ski boat kitted out with a fish-finder & Penn & Scarborough tackle, & a Magnum 25ft game-fishing vessel offering plenty of deck space & a harness chair for fighting fish. Firmly focused on the serious game-fishing market. *US$900/day charter (3 persons). US$1,800–2,700 for 3–5 day Zanzibar package (inc fishing & lodge accommodation; 1–3 anglers).*

Zanzibar Fishing m 0773 235030; e info@ zanzibarwatersports.com; www.zanzibarfishing.

com. One of the best game-fishing operations on Zanzibar, & certainly the longest established, Zanzibar Fishing is a division of Zanzibar Watersports (page 363). They are extremely well kitted out for both professional fishermen & have-a-go holidaymakers, with 3 sport-fishing boats, professional tackle & international safety equipment. ½-day (*5hr*) outings depart at either 06.30 or 13.30; whole days (*8hrs*) depart 06.30. Rates include charter of boat, skipper, bait, tackle, equipment & lunch or snacks. *US$450/600 half/full day on Suli Suli; US$600/850 half/full day on Timimi; US$750/950 half/full day on Baloo.*

Extreme Blue Water Spearfishing m 0787 138642/0689 138642/0777 138642/0778 138642; e info@extremebluewaterspearfishing. com; www.extremebluewaterspearfishing.com. Based at Paradise Beach Bungalows in Nungwi, Extreme Blue offers beginner to advanced courses in free diving & spearfishing from both Nungwi & Paje. Day & live-aboard trips are both possible with trophy fish all being hunted. In so far as is possible with this activity, the team here appear to support 'ethical spearfishing' by varying hunting grounds, selecting fish carefully, only spearfishing whilst free diving (no underwater breathing kit allowed) & minimising waste by selling excess catch (profits to a village project fund). *US$180/280 half-/full-day spearfishing; US$700–1,000 ½-/full-day sport fishing. Live-aboard trips available with advance booking.*

Kiteboarding

In recent years, kiteboarding has grown in popularity and Nungwi is no exception. Steady winds (approximately 15–20 knots) for most of the year, level beaches, warm clear water and protected, shallow lagoons make it a great place for both beginners and more experienced kiters. Check centres are certified by the International Kiteboarding Organisation (IKO) if you are interested in quality assurance and training courses.

Kiteboarding Zanzibar e kiteboardingzanzibar@gmail.com; www. kiteboardingzanzibar.com. Kiteboarding Zanzibar

is IKO certified, using up-to-date Cabrinha, NPX & Dakine equipment, with qualified, experienced staff on hand for safety & lessons. Their Nungwi base is in a small but neat, thatched chalet alongside Zanzibar Parasailing, whilst a kite-mobile is used to transfer kit & kiters to selected beaches in Nungwi & Matemwe (season dependent – Nungwi Jun–end Sep; Matemwe end Dec–Mar), & perform on-the-spot maintenance & repairs. Under the management of Seif Hassan, there are usually 2–4 instructors based here, approx 15 kites, & with proof of certification you can hire equipment here, as well as sign up for lessons.

Motorised watersports

Nungwi now has several companies offering increasingly thrilling, motorised watersports. From stunt wakeboarding to sedate parasailing, and jet-ski safaris to fast-paced banana boats, the coastal waters are significantly busier and the range of activities vastly increased. Please consider carefully your own skill level, safety and the environmental impact of using powerful motorised machines, like jet skis.

Zanzibar Parasailing m 0779 073078; e hello@zanzibarparasailing.com; www.zanzibarparasailing.com. Parasailing flights arrived in Nungwi about 5 years ago and they are a popular diversion; it's unquestionably thrilling & offers spectacular island panoramas. Solo or tandem 'flights' are possible, as is an optional dip in the sea on your descent. The flight itself is 10mins long, though several people may be on your boat, resulting in a trip lasting up to an hour. In spite of the company's name, parasailing is only one of the thrill-seeking water activities available. Escorted Tumbatu jet-ski safaris, stereo or mono waterskiing with lessons are available too, & wake-boarding, knee-boarding, fly-boarding & an 8-person banana boat or ringos are also on offer. On a practical note, jet-ski drivers must be over 16, though no experience is necessary; parasailing is open to anyone over 8. *Parasailing US$100/130 solo/tandem; jet-ski safari US$220/250 1/2 riders/bike; jet-ski rental US$60/15mins; waterskiing US$45/10mins; wake-boarding US$45/10mins; banana boat US$20pp/15mins; ringos US$30pp/10mins; fly-boarding US$100/20mins.*

Zanzibar Watersports See page 363 for full details. Escorted jet-ski safaris (*75mins*) head from the Paradise Beach base in Nungwi to Tumbatu, where riders can have a quick swim before pushing on to Kendwa and back around the coast to the watersports centre. Drivers must be over 16 & no experience is necessary; passengers can be as young as 8. 2011 Yamaha 110 HP 4-Stroke jet-skis can also be hired for individual use. Parasailing, kite-surfing & waterskiing can also been arranged. *Jet-ski safari US$180/200 1/2 riders/bike; jet-ski rental US$50/15mins.*

WHAT TO SEE AND DO

Most visitors come to this area to relax on the beach, swim in the sea and perhaps party at night. For local attractions, the small turtle sanctuary and terrific local coral reefs are still a draw. If you want a more cultural experience, head down the coast to the 16th-century Swahili ruins at Fukuchani and Mvuleni, the bustling, ramshackle market at Mkokotoni, or venture across the water to Tumbatu Island. Note that the lighthouse at Ras Nungwi is still in operation and, although it is not open to visitors anyway, no photography is allowed.

Mnarani Natural Aquarium (*www.mnarani.com*; ⊕ *09.00–18.00 daily; admission US$5, 50% discount for children*) Hawksbill turtles have traditionally been hunted around Zanzibar for their attractive shells, and green turtles for their meat. In 1993, with encouragement and assistance from various conservation bodies and some dedicated marine biologists, the local community opened the Mnarani Natural Aquarium.

In the shadow of the lighthouse (Mnarani meaning 'place of the lighthouse' in Swahili), at the northernmost tip of Zanzibar Island, the aquarium was created around a large, natural, tidal pool in the coral rock behind the beach. Originally set up to rehabilitate and study turtles that had been caught in fishing nets, the aquarium project expanded to ensure that local baby turtles were also protected.

Turtles used to nest frequently on Nungwi Beach, though sadly, in some part due to hotel lighting and visitor volume, this is now a rare occurrence. If a nest is found, village volunteers now mark and monitor new nests, whilst local fishermen rescuing turtles caught in their nets receive a small fee. The resulting hatchlings are carried to small plastic basins and small concrete tanks at the aquarium where they remain for ten months. By this time, they have grown to 25cm and their chances of survival at sea are dramatically increased. All bar one of these turtles are then released into the sea, along with the largest turtle from the aquarium pool. The one remaining baby turtle is then added to the pool, ensuring a static population of 17 turtles.

Currently, this equates to four hawksbills (Swahili: *ng'amba*), identified by the jagged edge on their shell, sharper beak and sardine diet, and 13 seaweed-loving green turtles (Swahili: *kasakasa*). The aquarium manager keeps a log book detailing all eggs, hatchlings and releases.

In spite of the aquarium being little more than a glorified rock pool, it's fascinating to see the turtles at close quarters. Further, the money raised secures the project's future, and goes towards local community schemes – in a bid to demonstrate the tangible value of turtle conservation to the local population. With luck, this will lessen the trade in souvenir shell products and ensure the species' survival.

On a practical note, when timing your visit, the water is clearest about 2 hours before high tide (Swahili: *maji kujaa*).

Dhow-building and harbour activity Nungwi is the centre of Zanzibar's traditional dhow-building industry, where generations of skilled craftsmen have worked on the beach outside the village, turning planks of wood into strong ocean-going vessels, using only the simplest of tools. It is a fascinating place to see dhows in various stages of construction, but do show respect for the builders, who are generally indifferent towards visitors, and keep out of the way.

Fishing continues to employ many local men, who set out to sea in the late afternoon, returning at around 06.00 the following morning, taking their catch to the beach fish market. The spectacle is worth the early start, but if you don't make it, there's a smaller rerun at around 15.00 each day.

Cultural village tour (*US$15pp*) The base for the Nungwi Cultural Village Tours is adjacent to Mnarani Aquarium and run by the same volunteers. From the clearly marked bungalow, the 2-hour walks take in the aquarium, fish market (best visited early morning when the day's catches are landed), mosques, dhow-builders, basket-weavers and even touch on the uses of surrounding medicinal trees. A pleasant, guided trip, it offers visitors a different view of the community here, and gives photographers a great opportunity to capture the dhow-builders (always ask permission first). The money generated from these tours goes back into the community and is donated to a range of beneficiaries, from the kindergarten to the dhow-builders.

THE EAST COAST

The east coast of Zanzibar is where you will find the idyllic tropical beaches of which you've dreamed: clean white sand lined with palms and lapped by the warm blue waters of the Indian Ocean. Some travellers come here for a couple of days just to relax after seeing the sights of Zanzibar Town, and end up staying for a couple of weeks. Visitors on tighter time restrictions always wish they could stay for longer.

The east coast is divided in to two discrete stretches by Chwaka Bay, which lies at the same latitude as Zanzibar Town on the west coast. Traditionally, the most popular stretch of coast is to the south of this bay, between Bwejuu and Makunduchi, but recent years have seen an increasing number of developments further north, between Matemwe and Chwaka. Most hotels have restaurants, and you can usually buy fish and vegetables in the villages, but supplies are limited. If you are self-catering, stock up in Zanzibar Town.

GETTING THERE AND AWAY The east coast can be easily reached by bus or dalla dalla from Zanzibar Town. North of Chwaka Bay, bus 6 goes to Chwaka (some continue to Uroa and Pongwe), 13 goes to Uroa (via Chwaka), 15 goes to Kiwengwa and 16 to Matemwe. South of the bay, bus 9 goes to Paje (sometimes continuing to Bwejuu or Jambiani) and 10 to Makunduchi. Chwaka Bay can sometimes be crossed by boat between Chwaka and Michamvi, with the help of local octopus fishermen. Most travellers prefer to use private transport to the east coast: several tour companies and some independent guides arrange minibuses (*US$5–8pp each way*). Unless you specify where you want to stay, minibus drivers are likely to take you to a hotel that gives them commission.

NORTHEASTERN ZANZIBAR Stretching from Nungwi on the northernmost tip of the island to the mangrove swamps of Chwaka Bay, the sand beaches of the northeastern coastline are breathtaking in length and beauty. Less than 1km offshore, waves break along the fringe reef that runs the length of the island, and the warm, turquoise waters of the Indian Ocean attract divers, swimmers and fishermen. Bordering the sand, an almost unbroken strip of picturesque coconut palms provides shade for traditional fishing villages and sunbathing honeymooners, and completes many people's vision of paradise.

The beaches along Zanzibar's east coast slope very little. Consequently, when the tide is out, the water retreats a long way, making swimming from the beach difficult. It does, however, allow for fascinating exploration along the top of the exposed reef. For diving in the area, One Ocean (*www.zanzibaroneocean.com*) have offices in Kiwengwa and Matemwe, as well as at a number of hotels.

🏠 **Where to stay and eat** *Map, page 368*
The roughly 40km of coastline north of Chwaka Bay is lined with numerous lovely beaches and punctuated by a number of small traditional fishing villages, the most important of which – running from north to south – are Matemwe, Pwani Mchangani, Kiwengwa, Uroa and Chwaka. Hotels along this stretch of coast mostly fall into the mid-range to upmarket bracket, though good budget accommodation is available at Kiwengwa.

Exclusive
✴ 🏠 **Tulia Zanzibar Unique Beach Resort** (17 rooms) m 0773 409377; e reservation@tuliazanzibar.com; www. tuliazanzibar.com; ⊕ closed May. Tulia opened its imposing timber gates in Pongwe in 2015 to reveal an unexpectedly beautiful resort. An oasis of calm, beauty & luxury modern design, it boasts beautiful indigenous botanical gardens, stylish sgl-storey suites with classic interiors blending European elegance with natural materials. The restaurant serves some of Zanzibar's finest food alongside the curvaceous swimming pool. Aside from sophisticated chilling, guests (big & small) can giggle their way down the curvy water slide. One of the island's smartest & more sophisticated boutique hotels, with the benefit of a quiet, seafront (if not beach) & top-notch staff. *US$420–870 dbl, B&B.* 🍽

✴ 🏠 **Green & Blue** (14 rooms) m 0772 390086; e reservation@greenandblue-zanzibar. com; www.greenandblue-zanzibar.com. On a curved beach, this terrific lodge lies on a pleasantly large & strikingly landscaped plot in Matemwe.

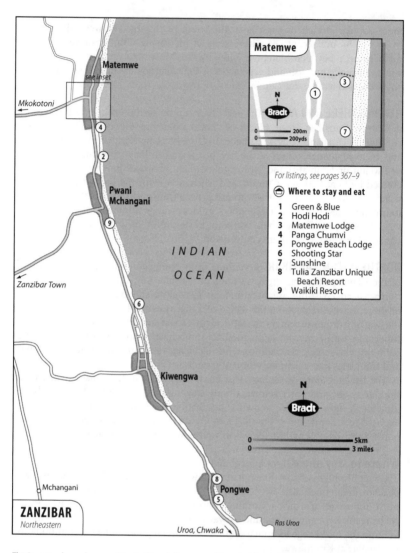

Matemwe

N

Bradt

| 0 | 200m |
| 0 | 200yds |

For listings, see pages 367–9

 Where to stay and eat

1 Green & Blue
2 Hodi Hodi
3 Matemwe Lodge
4 Panga Chumvi
5 Pongwe Beach Lodge
6 Shooting Star
7 Sunshine
8 Tulia Zanzibar Unique
   Beach Resort
9 Waikiki Resort

Matemwe
see inset

Mkokotoni

Pwani
Mchangani

INDIAN

OCEAN

Zanzibar Town

Kiwengwa

N

Bradt

| 0 | 5km |
| 0 | 3 miles |

Mchangani

Pongwe

ZANZIBAR
Northeastern

Uroa, Chwaka

Ras Uroa

The 2-person bungalows are identical bar their view, with well-designed interiors & a veranda, shaded by banana trees & palms. The beachfront public areas are the real draw though: a bar/restaurant cantilevered over the beach, 2 inviting pools & the Tulia Spa in the centre of the gardens. *US$235–330pp; FB.* **$$$$$**–🛏

✳ 🏠 **Matemwe Lodge** (12 rooms)
e reservations@asiliaafrica.com; www.asiliaafrica.com; 🕐 Jun–Mar. Smart yet informal, the quiet Matemwe Lodge is popular with couples. Each of its thatched cottages is perched on the edge of a low coral cliff, with a superb view across to

Mnemba Island. All have been upgraded into stylish suites, with electricity, mosquito nets, fan (on request), a day bed & an area to chill out as standard. Lush tropical gardens lead to the swimming pools, dining area & sandy beach. Activities include snorkelling & sailing in dhows, fishing, diving, & escorted reef walks. The lodge supports the local community through the provision of fresh water, a primary school, 2 deep-sea dhows for fishing, & teaching English. Neighbouring **Matemwe Retreat** (🛏), offers 4 exclusive villas under the same management. *US$220–440, AI.* **$$$$$**–🛏

Luxury

✳ 🏠 **Hodi Hodi** (7 rooms) m 0779 412603; e info@hodihodizanzibar.com; www. hodihodizanzibar.com. Situated between Matemwe & Pwani Mchangani, Hodi Hodi is small, smart, welcoming & personal. Owner Julia Bishop's love of Africa, the sea & the environment are distilled in this little piece of crafted beach-chic. It is all very low key, just as a homely beach retreat should be. On a tiny, picture-postcard little plot of coconut palms & ocean views, it consists of 3 houses: Poa, Toto & Dua, each with lovely open rooms & neat terraces overlooking the small garden & little oval pool. An honesty bar, daily cocktail hour & seasonal menu all make this a great spot for a quiet, chilled-out stay. *US$200–275 dbl, B&B.* **$$$$$**

🏠 **Shooting Star** (16 rooms) m 0777 414166; e shootingstarlodge@gmail.com; shootingstarlodge.com. Above Kiwengwa Beach, about 8km south of Matemwe, this is a social place where garden rooms, sea-view cottages & suites all feature Zanzibari beds & colourful Tingatinga pictures. An infinity pool & sundeck afford views over the ocean, reef & beach below. Dining is split across 3 shady areas, offering simple & filling meals, but it's the lively bar & relaxed lounge area that are the true heart of Shooting Star – & especially the lobster beach BBQ (*extra US$45pp*). Diving, snorkelling & fishing trips can be organised. *US$160–500 dbl, B&B.* **$$$$**–🍴

✳ 🏠 **Pongwe Beach Lodge** (20 rooms) e info@pongwe.com; www.pongwe.com; ⊕ closed May. Standing within its own quiet cove, under a shady oasis of coconut palms, this is a simple little lodge in a lovely location. It is a well-managed, good-value haven for relaxing on a beautiful beach, & is justifiably popular. There are airy, whitewashed bungalows in the garden, furnished simply, & 4 new en-suite rooms with huge spaces & a private sapphire swimming pool, There are plenty of inviting hammocks & loungers, a small library, a kite for seaside entertainment, free kayak hire & an array of other individual & group beach games, or there's a lovely infinity pool. Pongwe is especially proud of its food with tasty set-menu dinners, & there's an intimate tiered baraza lounge. *US$175–250 dbl, HB.* **$$$$**–**$$$$$**

Upmarket

🏠 **Sunshine Hotel** (16 rooms) m 0773 236578; e office@sunshinezanzibar.com; www.

sunshinezanzibar.com; ⊕ Jun–Apr. On a sweeping curve of white sand, this vibrant hotel occupies a relatively small plot of land in Matemwe. The immaculate gardens of raked stones & tropical trees, stylish architectural touches & calm efficiency lend this place a cool intimacy & prevent it from feeling claustrophobic. Light rooms are set in 2-storey chalets, some with private plunge pools & beach bandas, On the beach front, the 2-tier main area houses the restaurant, lounge & overlooks a small, sail cloth-shaded infinity pool. Sunshine has a lively buzz, which would appeal to sociable young couples as much as urban escapists. *US$150–350 dbl, B&B.* **$$$$**–**$$$$$**

Mid range

🏠 **Panga Chumvi** (15 rooms) m 0777 862899; e info@pangachumvi.com; www. pangachumvi.com. This small locally owned place just south of Matemwe offers surprisingly good, genuinely eco-friendly accommodation, just a stone's throw from a pretty quiet stretch of beach. The layout is somewhat unusual, but the selection of room types & tranquility make it well worth a look. There is a small onsite restaurant & bar, complete with pizza oven, offering the usual Swahili fare, but otherwise it's quite a private place to be. Community support is strong, with the owners heavily involved in Matemwe life & some interesting projects. Equally impressive is their real commitment to environmental awareness – an aspiration that many others on the island should embrace. *US$80–160 dbl, B&B.* **$$$**–**$$$$**

🏠 **Waikiki Resort & Restaurant** (27 rooms) m 0779 401603; e waikikibooking@hotmail. com; www.waikikiafrica.com. This delightful hotel in Pwani Mchangani is refreshingly small & personal, run by an enthusiastic Italian–English team. Life here focuses on the buzzing central restaurant, & the funky beached dhow bar Cassiopeia, with its chilled cocktail-drinking crew. Original bungalows are individually decorated with striking tropical murals, whilst at the back of the resort, 12 new rooms were built in 2016 around a welcome swimming pool. There is some basic activity equipment, free Wi-Fi, & a small massage zone. Onsite operator Kite Zanzibar can organise lessons (*US$140/260/375 beginner/intermediate/advanced*). *US$70–109 dbl, B&B.* **$$$**–**$$$$**

Mnemba Island The tiny island of Mnemba, officially titled Mnemba Island Marine Conservation Area (MIMCA), lies some 2.5km off the northeastern coast of Zanzibar, and forms part of the much larger submerged Mnemba Atoll. It is now privately leased by &Beyond (formerly Conservation Corporation Africa, or CCAfrica) and has become one of Africa's ultimate beach retreats. It cannot be visited without a reservation.

The island itself boasts wide beaches of white coral sand, fine and cool underfoot, backed by patches of tangled coastal bush and a small forest of casuarina trees. The small reefs immediately offshore offer a great introduction to the fishes of the reef for snorkellers, while diving excursions further afield allow you to explore the 40m-deep coral cliffs, a good place to see larger fish including the whale shark, the world's largest fish. The bird checklist for the island, though short, includes several unusual waders and other marine birds.

🏠 *Where to stay and eat* Map, page 357

✳ 🏠 **Mnemba Island Lodge** (12 bandas) ☏(South Africa) +27 (0)11 809 4300; e contactus@andbeyond.com; www.andbeyond. com; ⏲ Jun–Mar. The crème de la crème of &Beyond's impressive portfolio, Mnemba Island Lodge is the height of rustic exclusivity. Overlooking the beach from the forest's edge, its secluded, split-level bandas are constructed entirely of local timber & hand-woven palm fronds. Large, airy & open-plan, each has a huge bed & solid wooden furniture, softened with natural-coloured fabrics. A 'butler' is assigned to each room to ensure that everyone is content. The cuisine is excellent, with plenty of fresh seafood, fruit & vegetables, though guests may choose what, when & where to eat. A number of superb dive sites are within 15mins of the lodge. Up to 2 dives a day are included for qualified PADI divers, though courses are charged extra. There's also snorkelling, dbl kayaks, windsurfing, power-kiting, sailing, & fly or deep-sea fishing. Hot stone, aromatherapy, deep-tissue massage & reiki are all available, too. Mnemba is unquestionably expensive, but its flexibility & service levels are second to none, & its idyllic location & proximity to outstanding marine experiences are very hard to match. *US$1,270–1,760pp, AI.* 🐚

SOUTHEASTERN ZANZIBAR The coastline south of Chwaka Bay caters better to budget travellers than the coast further north, though a few relatively upmarket hotels are also found in the area. Until a few years ago, the southeast stretch of coast had the most crowded beaches on Zanzibar, but these days the area is quieter than Nungwi on the north coast.

Coming from Zanzibar Town along the main road through Jozani Forest, the first coastal settlement you'll hit is **Paje**, a small fishing village situated at a junction, from where minor roads run north and south along the coast. The most important settlement north of Paje and south of Chwaka Bay is **Bwejuu**, a fishing village whose livelihood is linked to the gathering and production of seaweed. Several resorts catering to all budgets lie within a few kilometres' radius of Bwejuu. South of Paje, **Jambiani** is a substantial village that runs for several kilometres along the beach, while the more southerly town of **Makunduchi** lacks any real tourist development.

The **Michamvi Peninsula**, which demarcates Chwaka Bay, is very similar to the northeast of the island, with the same stunning powder-white beaches, barrier reef, palm trees and a significant tidal change.

🏠 **Where to stay** Map, page 371
Exclusive

🏠 **The Palms** (6 villas) m 0774 440882; e info@palms-zanzibar.com; www.palms-zanzibar. com. Adjacent to Breezes in Dongwe & owned by the same family, The Palms is small & stylish, with a colonial feel, attracting affluent honeymooners

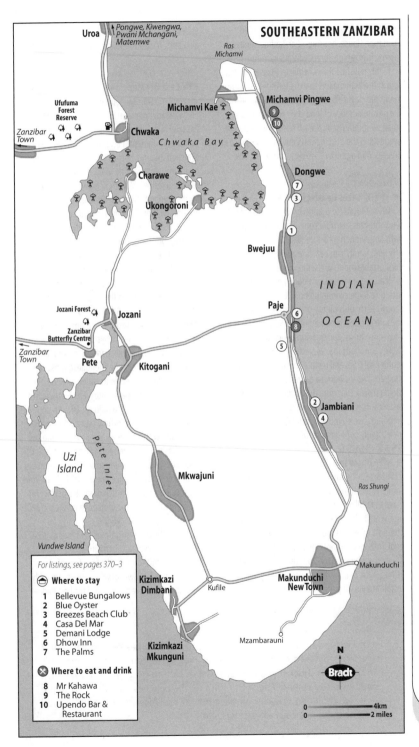

SOUTHEASTERN ZANZIBAR

Uroa
→ Pongwe, Kiwengwa, Pwani Mchangani, Matemwe

Ras Michamvi

Michamvi Kae
Michamvi Pingwe
9
10

Ufufuma Forest Reserve

Zanzibar Town

Chwaka

Chwaka Bay

Dongwe
7
3

Charawe

Ukongoroni

1

Bwejuu

INDIAN

Jozani Forest

Jozani

Zanzibar Butterfly Centre

Zanzibar Town

Pete

Kitogani

Paje
6
8
OCEAN

5

2 Jambiani
4

Uzi Island

Mkwajuni

Ras Shungi

Vundwe Island

For listings, see pages 370–3

🏠 Where to stay
1 Bellevue Bungalows
2 Blue Oyster
3 Breezes Beach Club
4 Casa Del Mar
5 Demani Lodge
6 Dhow Inn
7 The Palms

❌ Where to eat and drink
8 Mr Kahawa
9 The Rock
10 Upendo Bar & Restaurant

Kizimkazi Dimbani

Kufile

Makunduchi New Town

Makunduchi

Kizimkazi Mkunguni

Mzambarauni

N

Bradt

0   4km
0   2 miles

lured by image & intimacy. In the colonnaded Plantation House, housing a bar/lounge, dining room & mezzanine library, antique furniture rests on highly polished floors, while old-fashioned fans spin in the high makuti thatch. In the villas, huge rooms are classically elegant but with all mod-cons & a private outdoor plunge pool. They share a small swimming pool, & each has a private banda overlooking the beach. Most activities take place at Breezes. Min age 16. *US$670–1,060 dbl, AI.* 👑

Upmarket
☀ 🏠 **Breezes Beach Club & Spa** (74 rooms) m 0774 440883/5; e info@breezes-zanzibar.com; www.breezes-zanzibar.com. A perennial favourite with honeymooners & families, Breezes is a large, efficient, family-run beach resort in Dongwe. Comfortable rooms are set in whitewashed villas with all the amenities of a good hotel. Facilities include a large swimming pool & a great stretch of sandy beach, plus plenty of watersports, including the independently owned Rising Sun Dive Centre (*www.risingsun-zanzibar.com*). For landlubbers, there's a modern spa, yoga studio, fitness centre & tennis court. Several restaurants & bars complete the package, including a carved beach hut for dining *à deux* (but note that dinner at the smaller restaurants is not included in HB rates). Beach weddings, which must be arranged in advance, are increasingly popular here. *US$160–550 dbl, HB.* **$$$$–$$$$$**
☀ 🏠 **Dhow Inn** (28 rooms) m 0777 525828; e info@dhowinn.com; www.dhowinn. com. In Paje, Dhow Inn's motto 'come as a guest, leave as family' rings true. The lovely, modern rooms are built in 2 neighbouring circles, each around a whitewashed courtyard & swimming pool. Interiors are contemporary & thoughtfully finished, albeit set back from the water's edge. The atmospheric bar, Swahili charcoal grill & formal restaurant are all popular. Bike rental, beach

volleyball, kitesurfing & massage treatments all available. *US$200–450 dbl, B&B.* **$$$$$–**👑

Mid range
🏠 **Casa Del Mar** (14 rooms) m 0778 067510; e reservation@casa-delmar-zanzibar.com; www.casadelmar-zanzibar.com; 🕐 Jun–Mar. Casa del Mar is run with impressive enthusiasm, skill & environmental awareness. Rooms are in thatched 2-storey houses, made almost entirely of organic material. The majority of the staff are Jambiani residents, & the school & clinic receive regular support. These credentials aside, the accommodation & friendly vibe are good reasons to stay, too. En-suite rooms are either 1- or 2-storey, both with balconies & the latter with a galleried bedroom high in the thatch, & a lounge (or children's room). Food is served in the shady restaurant, there's a new pool & the lodge has its own boat for snorkelling trips (*US$15pp/day*). *US$75–120 dbl, B&B.* **$$$–$$$$**
🏠 **Blue Oyster Hotel** (14 rooms) m 0783 045796; e booking@blueoysterhotel.com; www. zanzibar.de. Set in lovely gardens in Jambiani, Blue Oyster remains one of the friendliest, most cared for & best-value hotels in its range. Ground-floor rooms are around a palm courtyard & others in a trio of smaller 2-storey buildings, all with en suites & balconies. The wonderfully breezy 1st-floor restaurant, with a wide veranda overlooking the sea, offers snacks (*around US$5*), delicious salads (*US$6*) or pizzas & evening meals like coconut-infused octopus with rice (*around US$10*). In front of the hotel a raised stretch of sand is perfect for sunbathing, or for a coconut-oil massage (*US$20*). *US$75–150 dbl, B&B.* **$$$**
☀ 🏠 **Bellevue Bungalows** (13 rooms) m 0777 209576; e bellevuezanzibar@gmail.com; www. bellevuezanzibar.com. On the top of a high rise of coral rock north of Bwejuu village, this thoroughly relaxed, gentle place offers one of the best budget

---

BEACHED SEAWEED

From December to mid February, some of the beaches on the east coast have large patches of brown seaweed washed ashore by the wind. This can be quite a shock if you expect pristine, picture-postcard tropical beach conditions. The seaweed normally stays on the beaches until the start of the rainy season, when it is carried back out to sea. After March, and up until November, the beaches are mostly clear.

deals on the island. Bellevue has evolved & flourished over the last decade. There are lush terraced gardens; the restaurant is an unassuming hotspot for fresh, healthy food; there's a super swimming pool & rooms filled with vibrant colour. It's a 50m walk down to the beach, but this is the only possible negative here. Bellevue is consistently brilliant & always improving to stay on top of its game, & offers super value. The owner, Dim, also owns Kite Centre Zanzibar on the beach (www.kitecentrezanzibar.com). US$48–100 dbl, B&B. $$$

Budget
☀ 🏠 **Demani Lodge** (20 rooms) m 0772 263115/0777 460079; e demanilodge@gmail.

com; www.demanilodge.com. Situated on the road between Paje & Jambiani, delightful Demani is a top choice for anyone on a tight budget who still wants a decent standard. Chill-out music, good vibes & interesting character added to a great recent renovation make it hard to beat for value. Rooms are in friendly circles around well-screened grounds & by far the island's most immaculate dorm is here. A swimming pool, rainbow hammocks, a fire pit & a terrific all-you-can-eat Swahili night (Thu) make the 10min walk to the beach acceptable. Value for money, the island's best budget deal. Dorm US$16pp, B&B; rooms US$36–40 dbl, B&B. $–$$

✖ Where to eat and drink Map, page 371
✖ **The Rock Restaurant** m 0777 835515; e info@therockrestaurantzanzibar.com; www.therockrestaurantzanzibar.com; ☺ lunch daily. Probably the most remarkable location of any Zanzibar restaurant, The Rock is perched on top of a marooned, seriously undercut coral-rock outcrop, just off the shore of the Michamvi Peninsula. Accessed by wandering across the sand at low tide, or by boat or breaststroke at high tide, the local team in this dilapidated building serve up a simple 'catch of the day' & seafood pasta dishes. It's very basic & quirky, but the views are terrific, the staff friendly & the experience unique. Call in advance or book online, especially if you're coming a distance. $$$

☀ ✖ **Upendo Bar & Restaurant** m 0777 244492; e info@upendozanzibar.com; www.upendozanzibar.com; ☺ 10.00 until last customer leaves daily. On a gorgeous sweep of beach, this is the perfect place to while away an afternoon, where gentle bar staff mix tantalising cocktails & exotic mocktails: try the Upendo signature drink (Sky vodka shaken with guava juice & honey, then topped with sparkling wine) or the Apple Virgin Mojito. London lounge music is piped into the

shady, cushion-covered beach barazas, & tasty treats are cooked to order. Delights range from salt-&-pepper squid (US$5) to loaded beef tacos (US$9) to the 'So Loaded' seafood fiesta sharing platter (US$100), comprising 1kg rock lobster, slipper lobster, crab, prawns, octopus, calamari & catch of the day. If you're too comfortable (or full) to move, there are even service bells provided. Sun brunches are an island institution, but it's worth a trip any time. Understated beach chic: a perfect place to just lose time. $$$

☀ 🖵 **Mr Kahawa** m 0776 038288; e mrkahawa@gmail.com; ☺ 08.00–17.00 daily. Opened in 2014 by the delightful Dutch owners behind Bellevue Bungalows & neighbouring kite centre (pages 372–3), Mr Kahawa (meaning Mr Coffee) has brought much-needed style & quality beachfront refreshment to Paje. Offers some of the best coffee on the east coast, plus delicious homemade baguettes, salads, cakes & smoothies. They also host a weekly cinema night on the beach, plus fortnightly fair-trade curio markets held here that are well worth supporting for your souvenir shopping. $$–$$$

THE WEST COAST

SOUTHWESTERN ZANZIBAR For most overseas visitors, Zanzibar's southwest corner holds little more than day-trip opportunities to see dolphins from Kizimkazi or troops of red colobus monkeys in Jozani Forest. As a result, few people stay in this area, with most opting instead for the endless beaches of the east coast or the buzz of Zanzibar's Stone Town. Away from the main tourist attractions, the villagers in these parts rarely encounter visitors, and their welcome is one of genuine friendliness and

Probably the island's best insight into genuine rural life is afforded by Eco+Culture's village tours (\024 223 3731; m 0777 410873; e info@ecoculture-zanzibar.org; www.ecoculture-zanzibar.org). Meet in the small, signposted hut in the centre of Jambiani (opposite the school), or be collected on foot from your hotel for these well-run, enlightening community-focused walks, organised and guided by resident Kassim Mande and his colleagues. A percentage of your fee goes directly towards community development initiatives, a direct result of the organisation's original NGO status.

Depending on your enthusiasm and heat tolerance, tours last anything from a few hours to the best part of a day and take in many aspects of everyday life. Spend time helping the women make coconut paste, reciting the alphabet in unison at the efficient kindergarten and meeting the *mganga* (traditional healer). Kassim's presence, reputation within the community and ability to translate allow for genuine interaction with the Jambiani residents and a thoroughly engaging time.

The trip can be arranged directly through Kassim or in advance through Eco+Culture's Stone Town office (page 335). Do be aware that of late there are a few villagers operating apparently copycat walks. It is well worth taking the time to seek out Kassim or the Eco+Culture office, not only for his knowledge and friendliness, but also to be sure that your money is directed back into vital village projects.

interest. It's a refreshing contrast to the more crowded and visitor-centric feeling taking over significant parts of the island's north and east coasts.

Where to stay and eat *Map, page 375*

Fumba Beach Lodge (26 rooms) m 0777 876298; e info@fumbabeachlodge.co.tz; www. fumbabeachlodge.com. Fumba was created in line with contemporary safari camps & the result is a fabulously original place, with clean lines & bold colour. Beach-chic rooms & suites are understated & spacious with lovely vistas. A large infinity pool lies next to the lounge & open-sided restaurant, while an African spa & efficient onsite dive centre keep guests entertained. The full-day picnic sailing trip around Menai Bay's islands makes for one of Zanzibar's most beautiful & indulgent outings. *US$220–360 dbl, HB/FB.* $$$$$–☀

 Karamba (24 rooms) m 0773 166406; e info@karambazanzibar.com; www.

karambazanzibar.com. This attractive clifftop lodge remains one of this coast's most appealing places to stay. Rooms all have individual interiors & are thoughtfully decorated in nautical blues & whites, boasting outdoor baths or blissful open-air showers hewn into coral rock. There are also 4 new duplex bungalows for up to 6 people & a honeymoon villa for rustic luxury. All rooms enjoy a sea view from their veranda though the harbour vista from the cushioned lounge/restaurant is arguably the finest of them all, with cocktails overlooking the sunset dhow activity making for a quintessentially Zanzibari experience. A Tanga-stone swimming pool, yoga, reiki & Ayurvedic therapies are also available. *US$240–320 dbl, B&B.* $$$$$–☀

Jozani–Chwaka Bay National Park (◷ *07.30–17.00 daily; admission US$10*)

This national park incorporates Jozani Forest, protecting the last substantial remnant of the indigenous forest that once covered much of central Zanzibar. It stands on the isthmus of low-lying land that links the northern and southern parts of the island, to the south of Chwaka Bay. The water table is very high and the area is prone to flooding in the rainy season, giving rise to this unique 'swamp-forest'

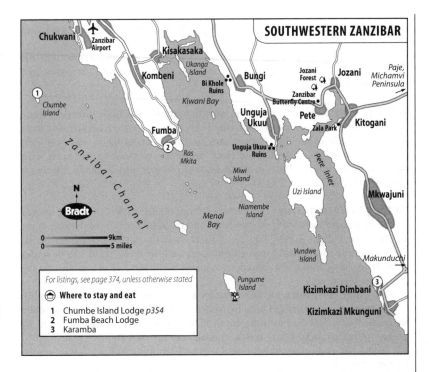

For listings, see page 374, unless otherwise stated

SOUTHWESTERN ZANZIBAR

Where to stay and eat

1 Chumbe Island Lodge *p354*
2 Fumba Beach Lodge
3 Karamba

environment. The large moisture-loving trees, the stands of palm and fern, and the humid air give the forest a cool, 'tropical' feel.

Jozani's main attraction is Kirk's red colobus, a beautiful and cryptically coloured monkey with an outrageous pale tufted crown. Unique to Zanzibar, Kirk's red colobus was reduced to a population of around 1,500 individuals in the mid 1990s, but recent researchers estimate between 1,600 and 3,000 individuals remain, whilst the IUCN (International Union for Conservation of Nature) has the number at under 2,000.

The forest used to be the main haunt of the Zanzibar leopard, a race that is found nowhere else, but which recent research suggests may well be extinct. The forest is also home to Ader's duiker, a small antelope that effectively may now be a Zanzibar endemic, as it is probably extinct and certainly very rare in Kenya's Sokoke Forest, the only other place where it has ever been recorded. Several other mammal species live in Jozani, and the forest is one of the best birding sites on the island, hosting a good range of coastal forest birds, including an endemic race of the lovely Fischer's turaco.

A network of nature trails has been established. The main one takes about an hour to follow at a leisurely pace, with numbered points of interest that relate to a well-written information sheet you can buy for a nominal cost at the reception desk. There are also several shorter loops. As you walk around the nature trails, it's possible to see lots of birds and probably a few colobus and Sykes monkeys, but these animals are shy, and will leap through the trees as soon as they hear people approaching. On the south side of the main road live two groups of monkeys that are more used to humans and with a guide you can watch these at close quarters. This is ideal animal viewing – the monkeys are aware of your presence but not disturbed. Some visitors have been tempted to try to stroke the monkeys or give them sweets, which is not only bad for the monkeys, but can be bad for tourists too – several people have been given a nasty nip or scratch.

South of the forest, a long thin creek juts in from the sea, and is lined with mangrove trees.

A new development in the area, based in the village of Pete, 1km from the entrance to the forest, is a mangrove boardwalk, allowing visitors a rare view into the unique mangrove habitat.

When to visit Keen naturalists who want to watch wildlife undisturbed, or those who just like a bit of peace and quiet, should try to visit the reserve either very early or in the middle of the day, as most groups come at about 09.00–10.00 on their way to the coast, or 15.00–16.00 on their way back. The monkeys and birds seem subdued in the midday heat, so about 14.00–15.00 seems to be the best time for watching their behaviour.

Getting there and away The entrance to the national park is clearly signposted on the main road between Zanzibar Town and the southern part of the east coast, north of the village of Pete. You can visit at most times of the year, but in the rainy season the water table rises considerably and the forest paths can be under more than 1m of water. The entrance fee includes the services of a guide and the mangrove boardwalk.

Many **tour companies** include Jozani on their east-coast tours or dolphin tours, but you can easily get here by frequent **public bus** (routes 9 or 10), **dalla dalla** (nos 309, 310, 324 or 326), hired **bike** or **car**. This road is well used by tourist minibuses and other traffic throughout the day, so after your visit to the forest you could flag something down and continue to the coast or return to Zanzibar Town.

Around Jozani
Neighbouring Jozani Forest is the Zanzibar Butterfly Centre, well worth combining if you're in the area.

Zanzibar Butterfly Centre (*ZBC;* e *mail@zanzibarbutterflies.com; www. zanzibarbutterflies.com;* ⊕ *09.00–17.00 daily; admission US$6*) The Zanzibar Butterfly Centre aims to show visitors the forest's fluttering friends close up, as well as generating an income for local villagers and preserving the forest. Twenty-six local farmers have been taught to identify butterfly species, gently capture female butterflies, net small areas for breeding, harvest eggs, plant appropriate caterpillar fodder, and ultimately collect the resulting pupae for breeding the next generation. The pupae are then sold on to overseas zoos and live exhibits, or displayed for visitors to this centre in the large, netted tropical garden. Here, 200–300 colourful butterflies can be seen in the enclosure, making for a fascinating diversion and one of Africa's largest butterfly exhibits. There are good guides and clear informative signs to explain the project and butterfly lifecycle, and experienced photographers can get some wonderful shots. The income generated from visitors to ZBC is channelled back into further funding local conservation and poverty-alleviation projects, whilst the message is made clear to the communities that protecting the natural habitat of these insects provides much-needed income. The centre is a fun, worthwhile, 30-minute stop, and its location, just outside Jozani Forest, makes it a convenient addition to a forest trip.

Kizimkazi
The small town of Kizimkazi lies on the southwestern end of the island, and is best known to tourists as the place to see humpback and bottlenose dolphins, both of which are resident in the area.

Getting there and away Most tourists visit Kizimkazi on an **organised day tour** out of Zanzibar Town, which costs US$25–100 per person, depending on group size, season and trip quality, including transport to/from Kizimkazi, the boat, all snorkelling gear and lunch. Alternatively, the town can be reached independently in a **hired car**, or with **dalla dalla** 326 from Zanzibar Town.

Dolphin watching The best time of year to see the dolphins is between October and February. From June to September, the southerly winds can make the seas rough, while during the rainy season (March to May), conditions in the boat can be unpleasant. However, out at sea you're likely to get wet anyway. You should also protect yourself against the sun. Sightings used to be almost guaranteed, but it's not unusual now for groups to return without having seen a single dolphin. Sadly, as the disturbances from too many boats and people increasingly outweigh the benefits of food and shelter, this trend is likely to continue, with fewer and fewer dolphins appearing in Kizimkazi's waters.

Never encourage your pilot to chase the dolphins or try to approach them too closely yourself. With up to 100 people visiting Kizimkazi daily in the high season, there is genuine cause to fear that tourism may be detrimental to the animals. If you do get close enough and you want to try your luck swimming with the dolphins, slip (rather than dive) into the water next to the boat, and try to excite their interest by diving frequently and holding your arms along your body to imitate their streamlined shape.

Kizimkazi Mosque Hidden behind its new plain walls and protective corrugated-iron roof, the mosque at Kizimkazi Dimbani is believed to be the oldest Islamic building on the East African coast. The floriate Kufic inscription to the left of the *mihrab* (the interior niche indicating the direction of Mecca) dates the original mosque construction to AD1107 and identifies it as the work of Persian settlers. The silver pillars on either side of the niche are decorated with pounded mullet shells from the island of Mafia, and the two decorative clocks, which show Swahili time (6 hours' difference from European time), were presented by local dignitaries. However, though the fine-quality coral detailing and columns date from this time, most of the building actually dates from an 18th-century reconstruction. The more recent additions of electrical sockets and flex have not been installed with a comparable degree of style or decoration.

Outside the mosque are some old tombs, a few decorated with pillars and one covered by a small makuti roof. The pieces of cloth tied to the edge of the tomb are prayer flags. The raised aqueduct that carried water from the well to the basin where hands and feet were washed is no longer used: running water is piped straight into a more recently built ablution area at the back of the mosque.

Archaeological evidence suggests that when the mosque was built, Kizimkazi was a large walled city. Tradition holds that it was founded and ruled by King Kizi, and that the architect of the mosque itself was called Kazi.

Today, very little of the old city remains, but non-Muslims, both men and women, are welcome to visit the mosque and its surrounding tombs. It's normally locked, and you'll probably have to find the caretaker with the key (he lives nearby, but is usually under the trees near the beach a few hundred metres further down the road). Show respect by removing your shoes and covering bare arms and legs, if they aren't already. On leaving you'll be shown the collection box for donations.

Menai Bay excursions The Menai Bay Conservation Area has a number of picturesque, uninhabited islands and sandbanks to explore, as well as some fascinating marine life. It's well worth taking a full-day excursion, either through Fumba Beach Lodge (page 374) if you're a guest, or with one of the two operators running trips: **Safari Blue** (m *0777 423162;* e *adventure@zanlink.com; www. safariblue.net*) or **Eco+Culture** (see box, page 374). Take towels and waterproof shoes for wading out to the boat across coral rock.

PEMBA ISLAND

Lying to the northeast of the larger island of Zanzibar and directly east of the mainland port of Tanga, Pemba is visited by few travellers. While tourist facilities on Zanzibar have mushroomed in recent years, Pemba has changed little over the last decade, making it a particularly attractive destination for those seeking to 'get away from it all'.

Pemba has a more undulating landscape than Zanzibar, and is more densely vegetated with both natural forest and plantation. The main agricultural product is cloves, which Pemba produces in far greater abundance than Zanzibar, with the attendant heady aroma permeating much of the island.

There is nothing on Pemba to compare with Zanzibar's Stone Town, but it does boast a number of attractive beaches, as well as some absorbing ruins dating to the Shirazi era. During holidays, traditional bullfights are sometimes held, presumably introduced during the years of Portuguese occupation. The island is also a centre for traditional medicine and witchcraft, and it is said that people seeking cures for spiritual or physical afflictions come from as far away as Uganda and the Congo to see Pemba's doctors.

Accommodation is limited to just a handful of lodges, hotels and guesthouses. Most are geared to the diver in search of the island's renowned underwater attractions, including some exciting drift dives and the possibility of seeing some of the larger pelagics.

The island's largest town is Chake Chake. To the north lies the port of Wete, while to the southwest is the port of Mkoani, used by most passenger ferries. There are banks and post offices in Chake Chake, Wete and Mkoani, but none have ATMs, so taking cash is advisable. The main hospital is in Chake Chake, where there is also a ZTC office.

GETTING THERE AND AWAY
By air

✈ **Auric Air** www.auricair.com. 3 daily flights from Dar to Pemba via Zanzibar, departing 07.45, 13.30 & 15.30 (*1hr 5mins; US$140 one-way*). There are also 2 daily flights from Tanga, departing 09.40 & 15.25 (*20mins; US$100 one-way*), plus 3 flights daily from Zanzibar, departing 08.20, 14.05 & 16.05 (*30mins; US$140 one-way*).

✈ **Coastal Aviation** www.coastal.co.tz. 2 daily flights from Dar to Pemba via Zanzibar (*1hr 5mins; US$140 one-way excl tax*), departing Dar at 07.30 & 14.00, with the later flight waiting for earlier connections from Selous & Ruaha. Return flights leave Pemba at 08.45 & 15.15.

✈ **Tropical Air** www.tropicalair.co.tz. 1 daily flight from Zanzibar to Pemba (*30mins; US$90 one-way excl tax*), departing at 14.00; returns from Pemba at 15.00. These can be used to connect with flights to/from Tanga & Dar.

✈ **ZanAir** www.zanair.com. 2 daily flights between Dar & Pemba via Zanzibar (*1hr 15mins; US$300 return inc tax*), departing 08.45 & 14.00 from Dar, returning 10.15 & 14.15.

By sea The main ferry port on Pemba is at Mkoani in the south.

🚢 **Azam Marine & Coastal Fast Ferries** ☎022 212 3324; e info@azammarine.com; www. azammarine.com. The best of the commercial passenger boats to Pemba from Zanzibar. It's a twice-weekly service (*Wed & Sat; US$35/45 economy/1st class*), departing at 07.00 from

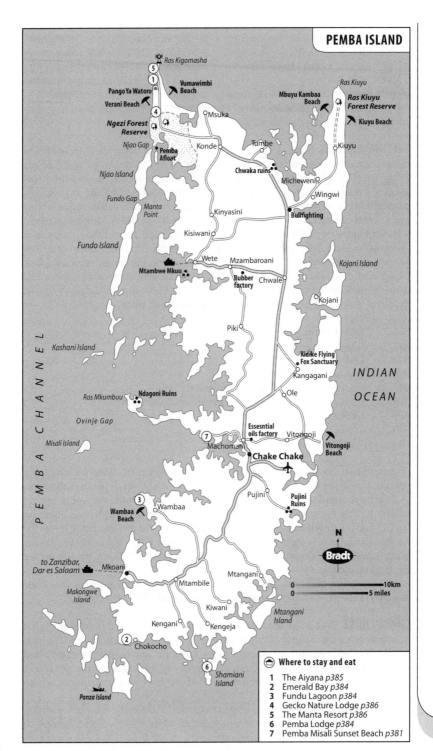

PEMBA ISLAND

Ras Kigomasha
5
1
Pango Ya Watoro
Verani Beach
Vumawimbi Beach
4
Ngezi Forest Reserve
Njao Gap
Pemba Afloat
Njao Island
Fundo Gap
Manta Point
Fundo Island
Msuka
Konde
Tumbe
Chwaka ruins
Micheweni
Wingwi
Kinyasini
Kisiwani
Bullfighting
Mtambwe Mkuu
Wete
Mzambaroani
Rubber factory
Chwale
Kojani Island
Piki
Kojani

Mbuyu Kambaa Beach
Ras Kiuyu Forest Reserve
Ras Kiuyu
Kiuyu Beach
Kiuyu

PEMBA CHANNEL
Kashani Island
Ras Mkumbuu
Ndagoni Ruins
Ovinje Gap
Misali Island

Kidike Flying Fox Sanctuary
Kangagani
Ole

INDIAN OCEAN

Esssential oils factory
Vitongoji
7
Machomani
Vitongoji Beach
Chake Chake
Pujini
Pujini Ruins

3
Wambaa
Wambaa Beach

N
Bradt

to Zanzibar, Dar es Salaam
Mkoani
Makongwe Island
Mtambile
Mtangani
Kiwani
Kengani
Kengeja
Mtangani Island

0 ———————— 10km
0 ———————— 5 miles

2
Chokocho
6
Shamiani Island
Panza Island

Where to stay and eat

1 The Aiyana *p385*
2 Emerald Bay *p384*
3 Fundu Lagoon *p384*
4 Gecko Nature Lodge *p386*
5 The Manta Resort *p386*
6 Pemba Lodge *p384*
7 Pemba Misali Sunset Beach *p381*

Zanzibar & arriving around 10.00. There is no direct service from Dar, but it is possible to leave from Dar at 18.00 the previous evening & travel via Zanzibar to Pemba, albeit a lengthy trip.

🚢 **MV *Mapinduzi II*** m 0777 438739; e znz@ shipco.go.tz; www.shipco.website/shipco.go.tz/ index.php. Zanzibar Shipping Corporation (ZSC),

the state-owned line, runs the new MV *Mapinduzi II* ('Revolution'). This Korean-built, cargo-passenger ship is generally used by local people because it is cheap (*Mon & Fri; US$25/35 economy/1st class one-way*), but some travellers on a tight budget also travel this way. Although slow, the cabins are quite airy & comfortable.

GETTING AROUND Pemba's road system was given a boost in 2005 with the completion of the tarred road across the island from Mkoani to Konde, paid for by the World Bank. North of Konde, and elsewhere, however, most of the roads are pretty poor, with access to some of the outlying villages requiring **4x4** vehicles, particularly in the rainy season. A network of inexpensive **dalla dallas** connects most main points of interest on Pemba, starting up at 06.00 (or 04.00 during Ramadan), with the regularity of the service depending on the popularity of the route; one of the most frequent is the No 606, with several buses each day. Services to and from Mkoani are tied in closely with ship arrivals. Fares on the longer routes, such as Chake Chake to Mkoani, are around US$1 one-way, with shorter trips about half that. The most useful routes are listed below (though note that dalla dallas will stop to collect or drop off passengers at any point along their route).

601	Wete to Konde
602	Chake Chake to Konde
603	Chake Chake to Mkoani
606	Chake Chake to Wete
305	Chake Chake to Wesha (Chake's port)
316	Chake Chake to Vitongoji (5km east of Chake Chake)
319	Chake Chake to Pujini
330	Chake Chake to Wambaa
10	Wete to Wingwi/Micheweni

Other **buses** connect Chake Chake and, to a lesser extent, Wete, with outlying villages; for details, check with the station manager at the bus depot in each town.

Most **tour companies** on the island can arrange car hire with a driver at around US$70 per day. Recommended drivers include Said (**m** *0777 430201*) and Suleiman (**m** *0777 431793*). **Self-drive** would cost around Tsh45,000 per day, but it is rare for tourists to hire cars in Pemba, and it's not the easiest thing to organise. With some effort it can be done through a few tour companies in Chake Chake, but it is not for the faint-hearted.

It's normally possible to arrange **bicycle hire** through your hotel reception for around US$10 per day, and **motorbike hire** for around US$22 per day.

CHAKE CHAKE This is the largest town on Pemba, and several centuries old, but it has never achieved a degree of importance comparable to Zanzibar Town. The busy market area and old port are pleasant to walk around, and seem very relaxed and untouristy after Zanzibar, but sightseeing is pretty much limited to the remains of an Omani fort near the modern hospital, part of which is now a good little museum.

Tour operators The tourist who arrives in Chake Chake in the hope of organising something on the fly could well be disappointed, since the town is less geared to visitors than in the past. The best bets are:

Coral Tours ✆024 245 2045; m 0777 437397; e coralnasa@yahoo.com; ⏰ 08.00–16.00 daily. Enthusiastic & incredibly helpful Pemban manager Nassor has extensive local knowledge & can book all manner of accommodation, tours & tickets, plus car, motorbike & bicycle hire.

Imara Tours & Travel ✆024 245 2648; m 0777 842084; e info@imaratours.com; ◼ Imaratours; ⏰ 08.00–15.30 Mon–Fri, 08.00–14.00 Sat, 09.00–13.00 Sun. Located on Chachani St, next door to the People's Bank of Zanzibar, Imara offers a range of tours & water-based activities

on Pemba as well as ferry & flight bookings, car hire & bike hire (*US$20/day*). They try hard to be environmentally aware & community focused.

Msewe Travel m 024 245 2774; e msewetours@gmail.com; ◼ MseweTravelLtd. Managed by the very friendly & enthusiastic Kassim, Msewe is down a tiny side street just across the road from Barclays Bank. The office provides lots of information on excursions, flights, ferries, diving, bullfighting & transfers. Other offices in Arusha & at Pemba Airport.

🏠 Where to stay *Map, page 382, unless otherwise stated*

There are a few central options, of which the Samail or Hifadhi are probably your best bet. Sadly, one by one, the small collection of clean and basic guesthouses just north of town have closed down. Alternatively, there are a handful of options to the north of the town, reached by taking dalla dalla 606 towards Wete.

In town

🏠 **Pemba Island Hotel** (16 rooms) ✆024 245 2215; e pembaislandhotel@yahoo.com. Run by strict Muslims, this welcoming & pleasant place is in the centre of town, just down the hill from the People's Bank of Zanzibar. En-suite rooms have dbl beds with AC/fans, nets, TV & fridge. In keeping with the hotel's Muslim ethos, no alcohol is permitted on the premises, & a marriage certificate is required for a couple to share a room. There's a rooftop restaurant. *US$50 dbl, B&B.* **$$$**

🏠 **Samail Modern Hotel & Restaurant** (16 rooms) m 0776 627619/0718 010960; e samailmodernhotel@yahoo.com. Samail opened in 2012 in a 3-storey building next door to Le Tavern. The bright restaurant serves a selection of spiced chicken & fish dishes with rice or biriyani (*US$3.50*). Cakes, bread & fresh fruit juices make for quick snacks & there's even an ice-cream machine. Upstairs, spacious rooms have AC, fans & TVs; bathrooms are fine & functional. *US$50 dbl, B&B.* **$$$**

🏠 **Hifadhi Hotel & Conference Centre** (14 rooms) m 0654 473772; e reservation@ hifadhihotel.com; ◼ HifadhiHotel. In pale blue & white, with banks of mirrored windows, this has the look of a hospital yet offers 'comfortable modern chick accommodation'. 15mins from the airport, it's certainly one of Chake Chake's better options, if not exactly glamorous. Clean rooms all have Zanzibari beds with heavy bedspreads & en-suite bathrooms, & it does benefit from a swimming pool. With self-proclaimed '5* luxury at 3* prices without cutting

corners', it's worth a try if you have to stay in town. *US$70–100 dbl, B&B.* **$$–$$$**

🏠 **Hotel Le Tavern** (8 rooms) ✆024 245 2660. On the main street, opposite the People's Bank of Zanzibar, Le Tavern is above a small row of shops. If you're asking for directions; it's pronounced 'lay' Tavern. Clean, en-suite rooms with sgl beds have mosquito nets, fans & crackling TVs, but are in desperate need of a fresh coat of paint. *Meals to order around US$5. US$40 dbl, B&B.* **$$**

Out of town

🏠 **Pemba Misali Sunset Beach** [map, page 379] (20 villas) ✆024 223 3882; m 0775 044717; e pembabeach@oceangrouphotel.com; ◼ misalisunset. North of Chake Chake, near the village of Wesha, Pemba Misali Sunset Beach's row of pea-green villas occupies a pretty waterfront spot, with sea views for all. Despite the bright exterior, a neutral colour scheme runs through the pleasant rooms. There's plenty of privacy & space, & outside a small terrace faces the sunset. Cantilevered over the sea, the restaurant serves up an eclectic mix of Indian, Arabic, Swahili & European meals along with the fisherman's daily catch. Diving is arranged through the onsite Pemba Misali Divers. Camping facilities are available. *US$95–150 dbl, B&B.* **$$$–$$$$**

🏠 **Pattaya Guesthouse** (6 rooms) m 0773 172445. This simple local guesthouse is fine if you want a feel of Pemba-style suburban living. Simple suppers of chicken & rice cost US$4 & must be ordered in advance. *US$30 dbl, B&B.* **$–$$**

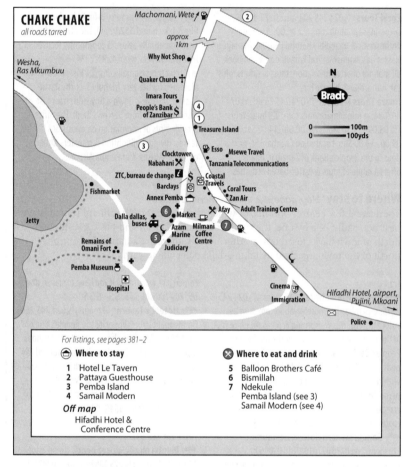

CHAKE CHAKE
all roads tarred

Machomani, Wete

Wesha,
Ras Mkumbuu

approx
1km

Why Not Shop

Quaker Church

Imara Tours

People's Bank
of Zanzibar

Treasure Island

Clocktower
Nabahani
ZTC, bureau de change
Barclays
Fishmarket
Annex Pemba

Esso
Msewe Travel
Tanzania Telecommunications

Coastal
Travels
Coral Tours
Zan Air

Jetty

Dalla dallas,
buses

Market
Afay
Adult Training Centre

Azam
Marine
Milmani
Coffee
Centre

Remains of
Omani Fort

Judiciary

Pemba Museum

Hospital

Cinema

Immigration

Hifadhi Hotel, airport,
Pujini, Mkoani

Police

N

0 — 100m
0 — 100yds

For listings, see pages 381–2

Where to stay

1 Hotel Le Tavern
2 Pattaya Guesthouse
3 Pemba Island
4 Samail Modern

Off map

Hifadhi Hotel &
Conference Centre

Where to eat and drink

5 Balloon Brothers Café
6 Bismillah
7 Ndekule
Pemba Island (see 3)
Samail Modern (see 4)

✗ Where to eat and drink *Map, above*

Both the **Samail Modern Hotel & Restaurant** and **Pemba Island Hotel** offer some of the better dining options for Chake Chake visitors, with simple Swahili meals coming in at around US$3–6. Other reliable options in town are: **Balloon Brothers Café** serving up tasty *mishkaki* (marinated meat skewers) on Market Street; **Bismillah** for its no-frills lunch by the market; and local-style **Ndekule Restaurant** for simple chicken or fish and rice dishes, set among the shops in the town centre.

What to see and do Chake Chake has a dusty charm that repays a walk through its small market and around its narrow streets and alleys crowded with shops selling a wide range of goods. Worth a visit is the **Pemba Museum** (⏰ *08.30–16.30 Mon–Fri, 09.00–16.00 Sat & Sun; admission US$3*). Located in part of the town's 18th-century Arab Fort, it retains the original wooden door, but other features were lost during restoration, and the cannons at the entrance came from Wete. Clearly laid-out exhibits cover every aspect of Pemba's history, economy and culture and of particular interest is the display on the ruins of Pemba, and the room on the island's maritime history and boatbuilding. Also, several rooms are set out to represent the interior of a Swahili house, while related displays focus on individual aspects of Swahili culture, from initiation and burial rituals to the use of herbal plants and traditional musical instruments. Visitors are accompanied around the exhibitions by a guide.

Excursions

Kidike Flying Fox Sanctuary (m *0777 472941;* ⌚ *09.00–18.00 daily; admission US$5/1 adult/child*) Just 7km north of Chake Chake is Kidike, home to more than half of Pemba's flying foxes. At the reserve, a local guide will show you the pathways through the forest to see the 4,000 flying foxes that roost in the treetops, feeding and, of course, flying overhead with their distinctive silhouette. Several tour operators run trips here, and individual drivers charge around US$25 from Chake Chake, including entrance. Alternatively, you can take a dalla dalla from Chake Chake, then walk the 45 minutes or so along the 3.5km track to the reserve.

Misali Island This small island west of Chake Chake, an easy boat ride from the main island, is surrounded by a coral reef. Its idyllic beach is good for swimming, whether at high or low tide, and it's worth bringing a mask and snorkel for the excellent reef fish. The waters are also a favourite with divers.

The forested interior of the island, criss-crossed by a network of clear walking trails, harbours a rich variety of birds including the endemic Pemba white-eye and sunbird.

The notorious pirate Captain Kidd is reputed to have had a hideout here in the 17th century, but today the island and the surrounding reef are incorporated within the Misali Island Marine Conservation Area. To get here, hire a boat from Chake Chake or Mkoani, or speak to one of the local tour operators.

Ras Mkumbuu Ruins About 14km west of Chake Chake, these well-preserved ruins lie at the tip of a long peninsula. Thought to have been one of the largest towns on the coast during the 11th century, Ras Mkumbuu may also have been the site of the earlier port of Qanbalu. Today, the remains of a mosque are visible, albeit overgrown, along with several pillar tombs.

The most enjoyable way to reach Ras Mkumbuu is by boat, perhaps combined with a visit to Misali Island. While there is a road from Chake Chake, the final 5km is negotiable only on foot or by bike.

Pujini Ruins This site is about 10km southeast of Chake Chake. You can walk there and back in a day, but it is easier to travel by hired bike or car. The ruins are the remains of a 13th-century Swahili town, known locally as Mkame Ndume ('milker of men'), after a despotic king who forced the inhabitants to carry large stones for the town walls while shuffling on their buttocks. The overgrown remains of the walls and ditches can be seen, as can a walkway which joined the town to the shore, some wide stairways that presumably allowed access to the defensive ramparts, and the site of the town's well.

Chwaka Ruins More ruins can be found on the island's northeast coast, close to the village of Tumbe (whose fish market is worth a visit in itself). Dating from as early as the 9th century, the town of Chwaka, or Harouni, was active as a port in the 15th century. In addition to the ruins of two small mosques, there are also remains of houses and tombs.

Ngezi Forest Reserve (⌚ *07.30–15.30 daily; admission short tour US$5pp, longer tour or birdwatching US$10; transit fee US$2; night walks by prior arrangement*) This small reserve in the north protects the last of the indigenous forest that used to cover much of the island. The forest supports an interesting range of vegetation, including the most substantial patch of tropical moist forest on Pemba. It is a good place for birders, who can seek out the Pemba white-eye, green pigeon, scops owl and sunbird, all of which are endemic to the island. Mammals include the endemic Pemba flying fox, Kirk's red colobus, vervet monkey, blue duiker, marsh mongoose and a feral population of European boars, introduced by the Portuguese and left untouched by their Muslim successors, who don't eat pork. A short nature trail runs through the forest. Not far from here, the open sandy beach at Vumawimbi is a great place to chill out.

MKOANI AND THE SOUTH The smallest of the three main towns on Pemba, Mkoani is also the busiest tourist centre, thanks to the boat services connecting it to Zanzibar and Dar es Salaam.

🏠 **Where to stay and eat** *Map, page 379*

✳ 🏠 **Fundu Lagoon** (18 rooms) 📞 +44 (0)870 240 6008 (UK); m 0774 438668; e reservations@ fundulagoon.com; www.fundulagoon.com; 🕐 mid Jun–mid Apr. In the south of the island, this upmarket & romantic hideaway is accessed by boat from Mkoani, & is extremely popular with honeymooners. En-suite tented rooms, with verandas overlooking the sea, nestle among the trees. Meals, predominantly seafood, are served in the restaurant or at the end of the jetty, with regular BBQ & Swahili nights. Snorkelling, kayaking & fishing are on offer, & there's a fully equipped dive centre; less strenuous are sunset dhow cruises, boat trips to Misali Island, & village excursions. There's also a treatment room, & a games room with satellite TV. *US$750–1,800 dbl, FB.* 🍽

🏠 **Emerald Bay** (7 rooms) m 0789 759698/0777 979667; e info@emeraldbay.co.tz; www.emeraldbay.co.tz. Through forested hills southwest of the main tar road, Chokocho is a remote valley village, beside a natural harbour, and the stepping-off point for Emerald Bay: a friendly, low-key resort. The 3-storey central area, complete with its castellated roof terrace, is traditionally built with white Omani arches & red concrete floors, with spacious, dbl-storey makuti-roof rooms either side. Inside, they are plainly decorated;

outside each has a small veranda. There is a new mosaic swimming pool, along with a few simple makuti umbrellas & coir loungers. Sea swimming is not possible directly in front of the hotel, which is predominantly mangrove, but complimentary sandbank trips are offered daily to nearby picture-perfect sandbanks. Meals receive regular praise, & the terrace dining area offers lovely bay views. This is a quiet, remote spot & not a place for jam-packed days of activities or long beach walks. *US$100–115 dbl, HB/FB.* **$$$**

🏠 **Pemba Lodge** (5 bungalows) 📞 024 224 0494; m 0777 415551/0655 417070; e info@ pembalodge.com; www.pembalodge.com; 🕐 May–Mar. With an emphasis on the 'eco', this is the vision of enthusiastic Pemban Nassor Ali. The 4 dbl & 1 family timber-frame bungalows are constructed from natural materials, featuring solar-powered lighting & composting toilets, but also a building design that harnesses the breeze from the Pemba Channel. Access to the lodge is an adventure by traditional (though motorised) boat through the beautiful mangroves, dinner is 'catch of the day' cooked over a gas flame, & there's an honesty bar. Come for ecological sensibility & peace on a deserted beach, not luxury. *US$440 dbl, FB.* 🍽

WETE AND THE NORTH The quiet and pleasant town of Wete, the second largest on the island, lies on a large inlet on the northwest coast.

🏠 **Where to stay and eat** Wete itself has several small guesthouses, as well as the run-down Wete Hotel, but most visitors head north to one of the beach lodges. All the hotels and guesthouses serve food with advance notice, and Wete also has a choice of local eating houses, most open until the last buses have left at 16.00. The pick of the eateries are: **Green Garden Refreshments**, a pleasant open-air café selling

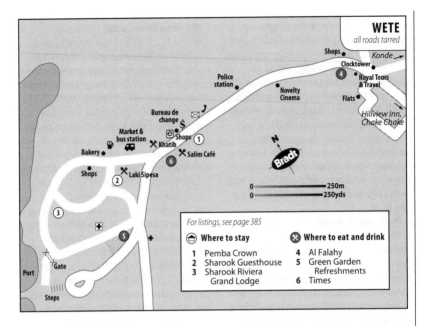

For listings, see page 385

WETE
all roads tarred

🛏 **Where to stay**
1 Pemba Crown
2 Sharook Guesthouse
3 Sharook Riviera
  Grand Lodge

✖ **Where to eat and drink**
4 Al Falahy
5 Green Garden
  Refreshments
6 Times

omelette and chips or beans and rice for around US$1; **Times Restaurant** is worth going to for the air-conditioning alone, but it also serves up good pizza, curries and grilled meats (*all US$4*) accompanied by English-language newspapers; and up towards the clocktower, the **Al Falahy Hotel**, serves tasty snacks and fried bread.

In town Map, above
🛏 **Pemba Crown Hotel** (12 rooms) ☎024 245 4191; m 0777 4936667; e sales@pembacrown. com; www.pembacrown.com. This 3-storey hotel is Wete's best accommodation, above a row of shops on the main street right in the centre. Rooms are clean & comfortable & the staff smiley & helpful. Spotless bedrooms come with AC, fans & TVs, plus a large balcony looking out over a busy street, which may not be the most attractive of views, but it's interesting to see townsfolk going about their everyday business. B/fast is the only meal served, but it's central enough to walk to any of the local cafés for a bite. *US$32–65 dbl, B&B.* **$$**
🛏 **Sharook Guesthouse** (4 rooms) ☎024 245 4386; e sharookguest@yahoo.com; www. pembaliving.com/sharook_guesthouse.html. Sharook is in the lower part of town, on a quiet side street near the market & bus station. It's a small, clean, family-run place with a peaceful & friendly atmosphere. With its own generator, the guesthouse offers constant running water & functioning TV. Dinner, with local dishes, must be ordered well in advance. Bike hire (*US$10/day*) can

be arranged, as can a range of tours around the island. Dinner US$10. *US$40 dbl, B&B.* **$$**
🛏 **Sharook Riviera Grand Lodge** (8 rooms) www.pembaliving.com/annex_to_sharook.html. Located in a sleepy, residential area overlooking the harbour, this is the annexe to the above & is not nearly as magnificent as the name suggests. The building is newly constructed, & inside are 8 sgl & dbl rooms plus a dorm. The communal space is made up of the b/fast room & a lounge with a computer & TV. Meals can be ordered in advance & are prepared fresh; juices, water & soft drinks are served but no alcohol. There are plans for a roof-top restaurant. *US$40 dbl, B&B.* **$$**

North of Wete Map, page 379
🛏 **The Aiyana** (30 villas) m 0777 006341/0772 833263; e reservations@theaiyana. com; theaiyana.com. A recent addition to the Pemba boutique hotel scene, the Aiyana is a collection of 30 luxury, thatched villas in lush gardens. Located on a picture-perfect crescent at the north of the island, each traditionally influenced, whitewashed villa boasts a gorgeous

Zanzibar PEMBA ISLAND

15

385

view across the powder sand to the turquoise ocean waters, with private outdoor space & stylish, contemporary interiors to match. The surrounding courtyards & gardens are filled with palms, tinkling fountains, bougainvillea-covered pergolas & fragrant frangipani & lily beds; the seafront is idyllic. So given the setting & views, simply chilling comes highly recommended here. For the more active, diving & snorkelling are good, the usual range of island excursions are on offer, & there's a beautiful spa. Meals are served either in the colonnade restaurant or around the resort & beach, with a variety of cuisine on offer. *US$380–1,267 dbl, AI.* 🍽

🏠 **The Manta Resort** (17 rooms) m 0776 718852; e sales@themantaresort.com; www. themantaresort.com; ⏲ Jun–Apr. Overlooking the northern end of Verani Beach, in a truly stunning location, The Manta Resort is a smart beach resort catering to divers & landlubbers alike. There are 6 seafront villas built on stilts affording a panoramic view across the Pemba Channel, plus garden rooms, some family-friendly, some basic. A central area serves as dining room, bar, lounge & lobby, with a big terrace looking out to sea & steps leading down to a powder-sand beach, with a 2-tiered beach bar: beware sea urchins. There is a spa, pool & a PADI dive centre, plus floating in the Indian Ocean in front of the hotel, a timber cube, boasting a dbl room 3m below the surface of the sea! Guests benefit from a location that boasts a wide range of birdlife & some interesting walks to the lighthouse, Vumawimbi Beach & Ngezi Forest (5km). *US$500 dbl, FB.* 🍽

🏠 **Gecko Nature Lodge** (22 rooms) m 0773 176737/0778 661489; e swahilidivers@ outlook.com; 📘 swahili.divers. Formerly Kervan Saray Beach, Gecko Nature Lodge came under new ownership in early 2017, & though it has undergone some renovations since, it remains a simple & unpretentious affair. Located close to the small village of Makangale, its thatched cottages are just above a sand-&-rock beach that is excellent for swimming at high tide. Bungalows contain cool & spacious rooms, with a dbl bed raised up on a plinth, complete with colourful bedding & mosquito nets, an en-suite bathroom & a solar-heated outdoor shower (warm water on sunny days only!). There is generator power 18.00–06.00 for light, but laptops & cameras can be charged in the office at other times. The rooms are lovely, with fresh flowers, slatted windows & oodles of colour. The lodge boasts a PADI 5* Resort Dive Centre with a team who are experienced in the surrounding reefs & sometimes challenging waters. Snorkellers, sunbathers & cruisers are more than welcome to hop on board, too. Birdwatching tours can be arranged to see Pemba's 4 endemic species, & trips are free for guests who pre-book as birders, but park fees are extra (see below). Kayaking (*US$70pp/½-day*), fishing, yoga, paddleboarding, local hikes & trips to the Ngezi Forest are also on offer. Aside from making sure everyone has a good time, the lodge is trying hard to maintain a low carbon footprint & to work with the local community. From backpackers to chilled families & hardcore divers, this is a super spot for a low-key beach break. *US$110–240 dbl, FB.* **$$$$–$$$$$**

Appendix 1

LANGUAGE

SWAHILI Swahili, the official language of Tanzania, is a Bantu language that developed on the East African coast about 1,000 years ago and has since adopted several words from Arabic, Portuguese, Indian, German and English. It spread into the Tanzanian interior along with the 19th-century slave caravans and is now the lingua franca in Tanzania and Kenya, and is also spoken in parts of Uganda, Malawi, Rwanda, Burundi, Congo, Zambia and Mozambique.

In Dar es Salaam, Zanzibar, Arusha, Moshi and the northern game reserves, you can get by with English well enough. If you travel in other parts of the country, you will need to understand some Swahili. And even if you are sticking to tourist areas, it is polite and can be useful to know a bit of Swahili.

There are numerous Swahili–English dictionaries on the market, as well as phrasebooks and grammar books, and most can be ordered from online sellers such as Amazon. For anybody serious about learning Swahili, Joan Russell's long-standing but recently upgraded *Teach Yourself Swahili* (TY Complete Courses, 2010) is the best choice, and the book comes with two invaluable CDs, though it is quite pricey at around US$40. A useful dictionary for travellers is Nicholas Awde's *Swahili-English/English-Swahili Practical Dictionary* (Hippocrene Books, 2000), which costs around US$30.

For short-stay visitors, all these books have practical limitations. Wading through a phrasebook to find the expression you want can take ages, while trying to piece together a sentence from a dictionary is virtually impossible. In addition, most books available are in Kenyan Swahili, which often differs greatly from the purer version spoken in Tanzania.

The following introduction is not a substitute for a dictionary or phrasebook. It is not so much an introduction to Swahili as an introduction to communicating with Swahili-speakers. Before researching this guide, my East African travels had mainly been in Kenya, Uganda and parts of Tanzania where English is relatively widely spoken. We learnt the hard way how little English is spoken in most of Tanzania. I hope this section will help anyone in a similar position to get around a great deal more easily than we did at first.

Pronunciation Vowel sounds are pronounced as follows:

a	like the a in *father*
e	like the e in *wet*
i	like the ee in *free*, but less drawn out
o	somewhere between the o in *no* and the word *awe*
u	similar to the oo in *food*

The double vowel in words like *choo* or *saa* is pronounced like the single vowel, but drawn out for longer. Consonants are in general pronounced as they are in English. *L* and *r* are often interchangeable, so that *Kalema* is just as often spelt or pronounced *Karema*. The same is true of *b* and *v*.

You will be better understood if you speak slowly and thus avoid the common English-speaking habit of clipping vowel sounds – listen to how Swahili-speakers pronounce their vowels. In most Swahili words there is a slight emphasis on the second-last syllable.

Basic grammar
Swahili is a simple language in so far as most words are built from a root word using prefixes. To go into all of the prefixes here would probably confuse people new to Swahili – and it would certainly stretch my knowledge of the language. They are covered in depth in most Swahili grammar books and dictionaries. The following are some of the most important:

Pronouns
ni	me	*wa*	they
u	you	*a*	he or she
tu	us		

Tenses
na	present
ta	future
li	past
ku	infinitive

Tenses (negative)
si	present
sita	future
siku	past
haku	negative, infinitive

From a root word such as *taka* (want) you might build the following phrases:

Unataka soda	You want a soda
Tutataka soda	We will want a soda
Alitaka soda	He/she wanted a soda

In practice, *ni* and *tu* are often dropped from simple statements. It would be more normal to say *nataka soda* than *ninataka soda*.

In many situations there is no interrogative mode in Swahili; the difference between a question and a statement lies in the intonation.

Greetings
There are several common greetings in Swahili. Although allowances are made for tourists, it is rude to start talking to someone without first using one or another formal greeting. The first greeting you will hear is *Jambo*. This is reserved for tourists, and a perfectly adequate greeting, but it is never used between Tanzanians (the more correct *Hujambo*, to which the reply is *Sijambo*, is used in some areas).

The most widely used greeting is *Habari?*, which more-or-less means *What news?* The normal reply is *Nzuri* (good). *Habari* is rarely used by Tanzanians on its own; you might well be asked *Habari ya safari?*, *Habari yako?* or *Habari gani?* (very loosely, *How is your journey?*, *How are you?* and *How are things?* respectively). *Nzuri* is the polite reply to any such request.

A more fashionable greeting among younger people is *Mambo*, especially on the coast and in large towns. Few tourists recognise this greeting; reply *Safi* or *Poa* and you've made a friend.

In Tanzanian society it is polite to greet elders with the expression *Shikamu*. To the best of my knowledge this means *I hold your feet*. In many parts of rural Tanzania, children will greet you in this way, often with their heads bowed and so quietly it sounds like *Sh ... oo*. Don't misinterpret this by European standards (or other parts of Africa where *Mzungu give me shilling* is the phrase most likely to be offered up by children); most Tanzanian children are far too polite to swear at you. The polite answer is *Marahaba* (I'm delighted).

Another word often used in greeting is *Salama*, which means peace. When you enter a shop or hotel reception, you will often be greeted by a friendly *Karibu*, which means *Welcome*. *Asante sana* (thank you very much) seems an appropriate response.

If you want to enter someone's house, shout *Hodi!* It basically means *Can I come in?* but would be used in the same situation as *Anyone home?* would in English. The normal response will be *Karibu* or *Hodi*.

It is respectful to address an old man as *Mzee*. *Bwana*, which means *Mister*, might be used as a polite form of address to a male who is equal or senior to you in age or rank, but who is not a *Mzee*. Older women can be addressed as *Mama*.

The following phrases will come in handy for small talk:

Where have you just come from?	*(U)natoka wapi?*
I have come from Moshi	*(Ni)natoka Moshi*
Where are you going?	*(U)nakwenda wapi?*
We are going to Arusha	*(Tu)nakwenda Arusha*
What is your name?	*Jina lako nani?*
My name is Philip	*Jina langu ni Philip*
Do you speak English?	*Unasema KiEngereze?*
I speak a little Swahili	*Ninasema KiSwahili kidigo*
Sleep peacefully	*Lala salama*
Bye for now	*Kwaheri sasa*
Have a safe journey	*Safari njema*
Come again (welcome again)	*Karibu tena*
I don't understand	*Sielewi*
Say that again	*Sema tena*

Numbers

1	*moja*	30	*thelathini*
2	*mbili*	40	*arobaini*
3	*tatu*	50	*hamsini*
4	*nne*	60	*sitini*
5	*tano*	70	*sabini*
6	*sita*	80	*themanini*
7	*saba*	90	*tisini*
8	*nane*	100	*mia (moja)*
9	*tisa*	150	*mia moja na hamsini*
10	*kumi*	155	*mia moja hamsini na tano*
11	*kumi na moja*	200	*mia mbili*
20	*ishirini*	1,000	*elfu (moja)* or *mia kumi*

Swahili time Many travellers to Tanzania fail to come to grips with Swahili time. It is essential to be aware of it, especially if you are catching buses in remote areas. The Swahili clock starts at the equivalent of 06.00, so that *saa moja asubuhi* (hour one in the morning) is 07.00, *saa mbili jioni* (hour two in the evening) is 20.00, etc. To ask the time in Swahili, say *Saa ngapi?*

Always check whether times are standard or Swahili. If you are told a bus leaves at nine, ask whether the person means *saa tatu* or *saa tisa*. Some English-speakers will convert to standard time, others won't. This does not apply so much where people are used to tourists, but it's advisable to get in the habit of checking.

Day-to-day queries
The following covers such activities as shopping, finding a room, etc. It's worth remembering that most Swahili words for modern objects, or things for which there would not have been a pre-colonial word, are often similar to the English. Examples are *resiti* (receipt), *gari* (car), *polisi* (police), *posta* (post office) and – my favourite – *stesheni masta* (station master). In desperation, it's always worth trying the English word with an *ee* sound on the end.

Shopping
The normal way of asking for something is *Ipo?* or *Zipo?*, which roughly means *Is there?*, so if you want a cold drink you would ask *Soda baridi zipo?* The response will normally be *Ipo* or *Kuna* (there is) or *Hamna* or *Hakuna* (there isn't). Once you've established the shop has what you want, you might say *Nataka koka mbili* (I want two Cokes). To check the price, ask *Shillingi ngape?* It may be simpler to ask for a brand name: Omo (washing powder) or Blue Band (margarine), for instance.

Accommodation
The Swahili for guesthouse is *nyumba ya wageni*. In my experience *gesti* works as well, if not better. If you are looking for something a bit more upmarket, bear in mind *hoteli* means restaurant. We found self-contained (*self-contendi*) to be a good keyword in communicating this need. To find out whether there is a vacant room, ask *Nafasi zipo?*

Getting around
The following expressions are useful for getting around:

Where is there a guesthouse?	*Ipo wapi gesti?*
Is there a bus to Moshi?	*Ipo basi kwenda Moshi?*
When does the bus depart?	*Basi itaondoka saa ngapi?*
When will the vehicle arrive?	*Gari litafika saa ngapi?*
How far is it?	*Bale gani?*
I want to pay now	*Ninataka kulipa sasa*

Foodstuffs

avocado	*parachichi*	maize porridge	
bananas	*ndizi*	(thick, eaten as	
bananas (cooked)	*matoke/batoke*	staple with	
beef	*(mnyama ya) ngombe*	relish)	*ugali*
bread (loaf)	*mkate*	mango(es)	*(ma)embe*
bread (slice)	*tosti*	meat	*mnyama*
coconuts	*nazi*	milk	*maziwa*
coffee	*kahawa*	onions	*vitungu*
chicken	*kuku*	orange(s)	*(ma)chungwa*
egg(s)	*(ma)yai*	pawpaw	*papai*
fish	*samaki*	pineapple	*nanasi*
food	*chakula*	potatoes	*viazi*
fruit(s)	*(ma)tunda*	rice	*pilau*
goat	*(mnyama ya) mbuzi*	rice (cooked plain)	*wali*
maize porridge		rice (uncooked)	*mchele*
(thin, eaten at		salt	*chumvi*
breakfast)	*uji*	sauce	*mchuzi/supu*
		sugar	*sukari*

tea	*chai*	vegetable	*mboga*
(black/milky)	*(ya rangi/maziwa)*	water	*maji*

Days of the week

Monday	*Jumatatu*	Friday	*Ijumaa*
Tuesday	*Jumanne*	Saturday	*Jumamosi*
Wednesday	*Jumatano*	Sunday	*Jumapili*
Thursday	*Alhamisi*		

Useful words and phrases

afternoon	*alasiri*	night	*usiku*
again	*tena*	no	*hapana*
and	*na*	no problem	*hakuna matata*
ask (I am		now	*sasa*
asking for …)	*omba (ninaomba …)*	OK or fine	*sawa*
big	*kubwa*	only	*tu*
boat	*meli*	passenger	*abiria*
brother	*kaka*	pay	*kulipa*
bus	*basi*	person (people)	*mtu (watu)*
car (or any		please	*tafadhali*
vehicle)	*gari*	road/street	*barabara/mtaa*
child (children)	*mtoto (watoto)*	shop	*duka*
cold	*baridi*	sister	*dada*
come here	*njoo*	sleep	*kulala*
European(s)	*mzungu (wazungu)*	slowly	*polepole*
evening	*jioni*	small	*kidogo*
excuse me	*samahani*	soon	*bado kidogo*
far away	*mbale kubwa*	sorry	*pole*
father	*baba*	station	*stesheni*
friend	*rafiki*	stop	*simama*
good	*mzuri*	straight or direct	*moja kwa moja*
(very good)	*(mzuri sana)*	thank you	*asante*
goodbye	*kwaheri*	(very much)	*(sana)*
here	*hapa*	there is	*iko/kuna*
hot	*moto*	there is not	*hamna/hakuna*
later	*bado*	thief (thieves)	*mwizi (wawizi)*
like	*penda*	time	*saa*
(I would like …)	*(ninapenda …)*	today	*leo*
many	*sana*	toilet	*choo*
me	*mimi*	tomorrow	*kesho*
money	*pesa/shillingi*	want	*taka*
more	*ingine/tena*	(I want …)	*(ninataka …)*
morning	*asubuhi*	where	*(iko) wapi*
mother	*mama*	yes	*ndiyo*
nearby	*karibu/mbale*	yesterday	*jana*
	kidogo	you	*wewe*

Useful conjunctions include *ya* (of) and *kwa* (to or by). Many expressions are created using these; for instance *stesheni ya basi* is a bus station and *barabara kwa Mbale* is the road to Mbale.

Health

flu	*mafua*	recover	*pona*
fever	*homa*	treatment	*tiba*
malaria	*malaria*	cure	*ponyesha*
cough	*kikohozi*	injection	*sindano*
vomit	*kutapika*	bone	*mfupa*
swollen	*uvimbe*	death	*mauti*
injure	*jeraha*	to examine	*vipimo*
weak	*dhaifu*	to fall down	*kuanguka*
pain	*maumizu*	to bleed	*kutokwa na damu*

MAA *Emma Thomson*

Maa is the language of the Maasai. It does not exist in written form, so the spellings below are approximate.

Greetings

Father/elderly man, I greet you	*Papa … supai*
Warrior/middle-aged man, I greet you	*Apaayia … supai*
Young woman, I greet you	*Siangiki … supai*
Boy, I greet you	*Ero … supai*
Girl, I greet you	*Nairo … supai*
Mother/middle-aged woman, I greet you	*Yeyio … takwenya*
Grandmother/elder woman, I greet you	*Koko … takwenya*
How are you?	*Koree indae?*
Are you fine/healthy?	*Kira sedan/kira biot?*
My name is …	*Aji …*
What is your name?	*Kekijaa enkarna?*
I come from …	*Aingwaa …*
Where do you come from?	*Kaingwaa?*
Goodbye	*Serae*

Numbers

1	*nabo*	13	*tomon ok ooni*
2	*are*	14	*tomon o ongwan*
3	*ooni*	15	*tomon o imiet*
4	*ongwan*	16	*tomon o ille*
5	*imiet*	17	*tomon o opishana*
6	*ille*	18	*tomon o isiet*
7	*naapishana*	19	*tomon o odo*
8	*isiet*	20	*tikitam*
9	*naudo*	100	*iip nabo*
10	*tomon*	1,000	*enchata nabo*
11	*tomon o obo*	2,000	*inkeek are*
12	*tomon o are*	3,000	*inkeek ooni*

Shopping

How much does it cost?	*Empesai aja?*
I want/need it	*Ayieu*
I don't want/need it today	*Mayieu taata*
I will buy this one	*Ainyang ena*
I will buy these	*Ainyang kuna*

| I won't buy anything today | *Mainyang onyo taata* |
| I haven't got any money | *Maata empesai* |

Useful words and phrases

Thank you	*Ashe*
Thank you very much	*Ashe naleng*
Take it (used when giving a gift)	*Ngo*
I receive it (used when accepting a gift)	*Au*
Leave me/it alone (to children)	*Tapala*
Go outside (to children)	*Shomo boo*
May I take a picture?	*Aosh empicha?*
Yes	*Ee*
OK	*Ayia*
No, I don't want you to	*A-a, mayieu*
Stop it	*Tapala*
Expression of sympathy (like '*pole*' in Swahili)	*Kwa adei*

AFRICAN ENGLISH Although many Tanzanians speak a little English, not all speak it fluently. Africans who speak English tend to structure their sentences in a similar way to how they would in their own language: they speak English with Bantu grammar.

For a traveller, knowing how to communicate in African English is as important as speaking a bit of Swahili, if not more so. It is noticeable that travellers who speak English as a second language often communicate with Africans more easily than first-language English-speakers.

The following ground rules should prove useful when you speak English to Africans:

- *Unasema KiEngereze?* (Do you speak English?). This small but important question may seem obvious. It isn't.
- Greet in Swahili then ask in English. It is advisable to go through the Swahili greetings (even *Jambo* will do) before you plough ahead and ask a question. Firstly, it is rude to do otherwise; secondly, most Westerners feel uncomfortable asking a stranger a straight question. If you have already greeted the person, you'll feel less need to preface a question with phrases like 'I'm terribly sorry' and 'Would you mind telling me' which will confuse someone who speaks limited English.
- Speak slowly and clearly. There is no need, as some travellers do, to speak as if you are talking to a three-year-old; just speak naturally.
- Phrase questions simply and with Swahili inflections. 'This bus goes to Dodoma?' is better than 'Could you tell me whether this bus is going to Dodoma?'; 'You have a room?' is better than 'Is there a vacant room?' If you are not understood, don't keep repeating the same question; find a different way of phrasing it.
- Listen to how people talk to you, and not only for their inflections. Some English words are in wide use, others are not. For instance, lodging is more likely to be understood than accommodation.
- Make sure the person you are talking to understands you. Try to avoid asking questions that can be answered with a yes or no. People may well agree with you simply to be polite.
- Keep calm. No-one is at their best when they arrive at a crowded bus station after an all-day bus ride; it is easy to be short-tempered when someone cannot understand you. Be patient and polite; it's you who doesn't speak the language.

Appendix 2

GLOSSARY

Acacia woodland	type of woodland dominated by thorny, thin-leafed trees of the genus *Acacia*
AICC	Arusha International Conference Centre
banda	a hut, often used to refer to hutted accommodation at hotels and lodges
boda-boda	motorcycle taxi
boma	traditional enclosure or homestead; administration building of the colonial era
brachystegia woodland	type of woodland dominated by broad-leaved trees of the genus *brachystegia*
bui-bui	black cloth worn veil-like by women, mainly in Islamic parts of the coast
bwana	mister (polite term of address to an adult man)
Chama Cha Mapinduzi	ruling party of Tanzania since independence (CCM)
cichlid	family of colourful fish found in the Rift Valley lakes
closed canopy forest	true forest in which the trees have an interlocking canopy
dalla-dalla	light vehicle, especially minibus, serving as public transport
dhow	traditional wooden seafaring vessel
duka	kiosk
endemic	unique to a specific country or biome
exotic	not indigenous; for instance plantation trees such as pines and eucalyptus
fly-camping	temporary private camp set up remotely from a permanent lodge
forex bureau	bureau de change
guesthouse	cheap local hotel
hoteli	local restaurant
indigenous	naturally occurring
kanga	colourful printed cloth worn by most Tanzanian women
KIA	Kilimanjaro International Airport
kitenge (pl *vitenge*)	similar to *kanga*
koppie (or *kopje*)	Afrikaans word used to refer to a small hill such as those on the Serengeti
mandazi	deep-fried doughball, essentially the local variant on a doughnut
mishkaki	meat (usually beef) kebab
mzungu (pl *wazungu*)	white person
NCA	Ngorongoro Conservation Area

ngoma	Swahili dance
Omani era	period when the coast was ruled by the Sultan of Oman, especially 19th century
savannah	grassland studded with trees
self-contained room	room with en-suite shower and toilet
Shirazi era	medieval period during which settlers from Shiraz (Iran) dominated coastal trade
taarab	Swahili music and dance form associated particularly with Zanzibar
Tanapa	Tanzania National Parks
ugali	stodgy porridge-like staple made with ground maize meal
woodland	area of trees lacking a closed canopy

Appendix 3

ENDEMIC AND NEAR-ENDEMIC BIRDS OF TANZANIA

ENDEMICS Full list of confirmed and probable species confined to Tanzania:

Grey-breasted spurfowl (*Pternistis rufopictus*) Serengeti & vicinity; common in scattered woodlands around Seronera.

Udzungwa forest partridge (*Xenoperdix udzungwensis*) Discovered 1991 in Udzungwa. Estimated population 3,500–4,000.

Rubeho forest partridge (*Xenoperdix obscurata*) Discovered in Rubeho Highlands 2003, proposed as new species 2005. Population may be <1,000.

Pemba green pigeon (*Treron pembaensis*) Confined to Pemba Island, greyer underneath than the mainland equivalent, but unmistakable in its limited range.

Fischer's lovebird (*Agapornis fischeri*) Feral population exists in Kenya, but naturally endemic to Serengeti & vicinity, where common.

Yellow-collared lovebird (*Agapornis personatus*) Feral population exists in Kenya. Common in Tarangire & semi-arid parts of central Tanzania.

Tanzanian red-billed hornbill (*Tockus ruahae*) Recently described, range centred on Ruaha National Park, where common.

Pemba scops-owl (*Otus pembaensis*) Very rare. Confined to Pemba Island.

Nduk Usambara eagle-owl (*Bubo vosseleri*) Eastern Arc forests including Usambara, Uluguru & Udzungwa.

Usambara nightjar (*Caprimulgus guttifer*) Recent debatable split from mountain nightjar. Usambara Mountains & possibly other Eastern Arc ranges.

Beesley's lark (*Chersomanes beesleyi*) Recent split from the spike-heeled lark. Population <1,000 in short grasslands west of Kilimanjaro.

Neumann's mountain greenbul (*Andropadus neumanni*) Recent split from mountain greenbul. Uluguru forests.

Yellow-throated mountain greenbul (*Andropadus chlorigula*) Recent split from mountain greenbul. Forests of Udzungwa, Ukaguru & Nguru.

Usambara thrush (*Turdus roehli*) Recent split from olive thrush. Usambara & Pare forests.

Usambara akalat (*Sheppardia montana*) Forests of western Usambara.

Iringa akalat (*Sheppardia lowei*) Udzungwa & other Eastern Arc ranges.

Rubeho akalat (*Sheppardia aurantiithorax*) Recently discovered in Rubeho Mountains.

Ruaha chat (*Myrmecocichla collaris*) Proposed new species. Present Ruaha & Katavi.

Mrs Moreau's Winifred's warbler (*Bathmocercus winifredae*) Udzungwa, Rubeho, Uluguru & some other Eastern Arc ranges.

Usambara hyliota (*Hyliota usambara*) East Usambara.

Kilombero cisticola (*Cisticola* sp) Recently discovered & undescribed. Kilombero Valley.

White-tailed cisticola (*Cisticola* sp) Recently discovered & undescribed. Kilombero Valley.

Reichenow's batis (*Batis reichenowi*) Eastern Arc forest canopies.
Banded green sunbird (*Anthreptes rubritorques*) Udzungwa, Nguru, Uluguru & Usambara.
Rufous-winged sunbird (*Cinnyris rufipennis*) Discovered in 1981. Udzungwa Mountains.
Rubeho sunbird (*Cinnyris sp*) Recently discovered in Rubeho Mountains.
Moreau's sunbird (*Cinnyris moreaui*) East Usambara, Udzungwa & other Eastern Arc ranges.
Loveridge's sunbird (*Cinnyris loveridgei*) Uluguru Mountains.
Usambara double-collared sunbird (*Cinnyris usambaricus*) Usambara & Pare mountains.
Pemba sunbird (*Cinnyris pembae*) Confined to Pemba Island.
Pemba white-eye (*Zosterops vaughani*) Confined to Pemba Island.
South Pare white-eye (*Zosterops winifredae*) Controversial split from mountain white-eye. South Pare Mountains.
Uhehe fiscal (*Lanius marwitzi*) Confined to highlands around Iringa.
Uluguru bush-shrike (*Malaconotus alius*) Rare. Forest canopies in Uluguru.
Ashy starling (*Cosmopsarus unicolor*) Central plains. Common in Tarangire & Ruaha.
Rufous-tailed weaver (*Histurgops ruficauda*) Serengeti, Ngorongoro & Tarangire national parks.
Kilombero weaver (*Ploceus burnieri*) Recently described. Kilombero Valley.
Usambara weaver (*Ploceus nicolli*) West Usambara, Uluguru & Udzungwa mountains.
Kipengere seedeater (*Serinus melanochrous*) Southern highlands.

NEAR ENDEMICS Several species have a range confined to Tanzania and one neighbouring country:

Fischer's turaco (*Tauraco fischeri*) Coastal Tanzania & Kenya.
Sokoke scops-owl (*Otus ireneae*) Eastern Usambara & one locale in Kenya.
Red-faced barbet (*Lybius rubrifacies*) Kagera region, nudging into Uganda & possibly Rwanda.
Friedmann's lark (*Mirafra pulpa*) Grassland at base of Kilimanjaro, Tanzania & Kenya.
Athi short-toed lark (*Calandrella athensis*) Grassland in Tanzanian–Kenyan border between Rift Valley & Lake Victoria.
Sokoke pipit (*Anthus sokokensis*) Coastal forest; Kenya & northern Tanzania.
Red-throated tit (*Parus fringillinus*) Serengeti–Mara ecosystem.
Dappled mountain robin (*Modulatrix orostruthus*) Udzungwa, East Usambara & one locale in Mozambique.
Spot-throat (*Modulatrix stictigula*) Eastern Arc, nudging into Malawi.
Stripe-faced greenbul (*Arizelocichla milanjensis*) Eastern Arc, nudging into Kenya.
Sharpe's akalat (*Sheppardia sharpei*) Eastern Arc, nudging into Malawi.
Swynnerton's robin (*Swynnertonia swynnertoni*) Montane forests of Eastern Arc, Mozambique & Zimbabwe.
Schalow's wheatear (*Oenanthe schalowi*) Rocky grassland, southern Kenya & northern Tanzania.
Black-lored cisticola (*Cisticola nigriloris*) Southern highlands, extending into Malawi.
Kungwe apalis (*Apalis argentea*) Albertine Rift endemic; isolated & racially discrete population in Mahale Mountains.
Karamoja apalis (*Apalis karamojae*) Serengeti Plains & northeast Uganda.
Moreau's tailorbird (*Artisornis moreaui*) Eastern Usambara & one locale in Mozambique.
African tailorbird (*Artisornis metopias*) Eastern Arc through to north Mozambique.
Fulleborne's black boubou (*Laniarius fuelleborni*) Eastern Tanzania, nudging into Malawi.
Grey-crested helmet-shrike (*Prionops poliolophus*) Serengeti–Mara ecosystem, into Kenya.
Hildebrandt's starling (*Lamprotornis hildebrandti*) South Kenya & north Tanzania.

Abbott's starling (*Pholia femoralis*) Pare Mountains, other forested locales in Kenya.
Kenrick's starling (*Poeoptera kenricki*) Montane forests in Tanzania & Kenya.
Amani sunbird (*Hedydipna pallidigaster*) Coastal forests, Tanzania & Kenya.
Taveta weaver (*Ploceus castaneiceps*) North Tanzania & south Kenya.
Tanzania masked weaver (*Ploceus reichardi*) Swamps in Tanzanian–Zambian border region.
Montane marsh widowbird (*Euplectes psammocromius*) Southern highlands, extending into Malawi.

Appendix 4

FURTHER INFORMATION

BOOKS
History and biography A limited number of single-volume histories covering East Africa and/or Tanzania are in print, but many are rather dated and textbook-like in tone. About the best bet is Robert Maxon's very readable and recently revised *East Africa: An Introductory History* (West Virginia University Press; 3rd edition 2009). Also highly recommended is Richard Hall's *Empires of the Monsoon: A History of the Indian Ocean and its Invaders* (HarperCollins, 1996), a highly focused and reasonably concise book that conveys a strong historical perspective thanks to the author's storytelling touch and his largely successful attempt to place the last 1,000 years of East and southern African history in an international framework. A more concise and modern book covering similar ground is Charles Cornelius's *History of the East African Coast* (CreateSpace, 2015). Considerably more bulky, and working an even broader canvas, John Reader's *Africa: A Biography of the Continent* (Penguin, 1998) has met with universal praise as perhaps the most readable and accurate attempt yet to capture the sweep of African history for the general reader.

Several books document specific periods and/or regions in African history. Good coverage of the coastal Swahili, who facilitated the medieval trade between the gold fields of Zimbabwe and the Arab world, is provided in J de Vere Allen's *Swahili Origins* (James Currey, 1992). Among the better popular works on the early era of European exploration are Hibbert's *Africa Explored: Europeans in the Dark Continent* (Penguin, 1982) and two excellent biographies by Tim Jeal: *Livingstone* (Yale University Press, revised and expanded edition 2013) and *Stanley: The Impossible Life of Africa's Greatest Explorer* (Faber & Faber, 2007), the latter voted *Sunday Times* 'Biography of the Year' in 2007. For an erudite, compelling and panoramic account of the decade that turned Africa on its head, Thomas Pakenham's gripping 600-page tome *The Scramble for Africa* (Abacus, 1992) was aptly described by one reviewer as '*Heart of Darkness* with the lights switched on'. For a glimpse into the colonial era itself, just about everybody who sets foot in East Africa ends up reading Karen Blixen's autobiographical *Out of Africa* (Penguin, 1937).

Field guides and natural history
General *East African Wildlife* by Philip Briggs and Ariadne Van Zandbergen (Bradt, 2nd edition, 2015) is a handy and lavishly illustrated one-stop handbook to the fauna of East Africa, with detailed sections on the region's main habitats, varied mammals, birds, reptiles and insects. It's the ideal companion for first-time visitors whose interest in wildlife extends beyond the Big Five but who don't want to carry a library of reference books.

Mammals The pick of the field guides, especially if your interest extends to bats and other small mammals, is Jonathan Kingdon's *Field Guide to African Mammals* (Bloomsbury

Natural History; 2nd revised edition, 2015), which also contains a goldmine of information about the evolutionary relationships of modern species. Its more compact counterpart is the same author's *Kingdon Pocket Guide to African Mammals* (Bloomsbury Natural History, 2016). Chris and Tilde Stuart's *Field Guide to the Larger Mammals of Africa* (Struik Publishers, 2006) is well suited to space-conscious travellers who are serious about putting a name to all the large mammals they see.

Not a field guide in the conventional sense so much as a guide to mammalian behaviour, Richard Estes's superb *The Safari Companion* (Green Books UK, Chelsea Green USA, Russell Friedman Books South Africa, 1999) is well organised and informative but rather bulky for casual safari-goers.

Birds Zimmerman, Turner, Pearson, Willet and Pratt's *Birds of Kenya and Northern Tanzania* (Christopher Helm, 3rd edition, 2005) is a contender for the best single-volume field guide available to any African country or region. I would recommend it to any serious birder sticking to northern Tanzania, since it provides complete coverage for the northern safari circuit, the Usambara and Pare mountains and Pemba Island, and although it stops short of Dar es Salaam and Zanzibar, this wouldn't be a major limitation. Unfortunately, the gaps in its coverage would limit its usefulness south of Dar es Salaam or in the Lake Victoria and Lake Tanganyika region.

For any birding itinerary extending to parts of Tanzania west of the Serengeti or south of the Usambara, the best option is the *Field Guide to the Birds of East Africa* by Stevenson and Fanshawe (Christopher Helm Publishers, 2002), which provides comprehensive coverage for the whole of Tanzania, as well as Kenya, Rwanda and Burundi, and contains very accurate plates, good distribution maps and adequately detailed text descriptions.

Another quality field guide that provides full coverage of East Africa is *Birds of Africa: South of the Sahara* by Ian Sinclair and Peter Ryan (Struik Publishers, 2nd edition, 2010), which describes and illustrates the 2,100-plus species recorded in the region. Should you already own it, or be planning more extensive travels in Africa, then this guide will more than suffice for Tanzania. But if your African travels will be restricted to East Africa, you are probably better off buying a more focused field guide.

Other field guides The past few years have seen the publication of a spate of high-quality field guides to other more specialised aspects of East Africa's fauna and flora. Among the more interesting of these titles are Najma Dharani's *Field Guide to Common Trees and Shrubs of East Africa* (Struik, 2nd edition, 2011), and a simply magnificent *Field Guide to the Reptiles of East Africa* by Stephen Spawls, Kim Howell, Robert Drewes and James Ashe (A & C Black, 2004). Alan Channing and Kim Howell's *Amphibians of East Africa* (Comstock Books in Herpetology, 2006) is also highly worthwhile. Matt Richmond and Irene Kamau's *East African Marine Ecoregion* (World Wide Fund for Nature USA, 2005) examines the whole of the East African coast.

National parks An excellent introductory handbook to all Tanzania's national parks and other major conservation areas is Olli Marttila's misleadingly named *The Great Savanna* (Auris Publishers, Finland, 2011). This includes a very useful overview of conservation in Tanzania, and detailed (20–30-page) description of each park and reserve, including lesser-known ones such as Rubondo Island, Mkomazi and Amani. There is also a useful pocket field guide to mammals and select birds at the back. The only place where it seems to be sold in northern Tanzania is the branch of A Novel Idea in the TFA Centre (page 134), where it costs US$50.

In the early 1990s, Jeanette Hanby and David Bygott wrote a series of excellent booklets covering Serengeti National Park, Tarangire National Park and Lake Manyara

National Park. These were published by Tanapa and can still be bought for US$5–10 from street vendors and bookshops in Arusha, and possibly at some safari lodges. The same authors have written an equally informative and widely available self-published booklet covering the Ngorongoro Conservation Area. These older guides have now been formally superseded by a series of glossier booklets covering each of the four major reserves, published by the African Publishing House in association with Tanapa. However, while these newer booklets are more up to date and colourful than the older ones, they are also pricier and not substantially more informative.

Bernhard Grzimek's renowned book *Serengeti Shall Not Die* (Collins, 1959) remains a classic evocation of the magic of the Serengeti, and its original publication was instrumental in making this reserve better known to the outside world. Iain Douglas-Hamilton's *Amongst the Elephants* (Penguin, 1978) did much the same for publicising Lake Manyara National Park, although the vast herds of elephants it describes have since been greatly reduced by poaching.

Those with an interest in ape behaviour would do well to read Jane Goodall's books about chimpanzee behaviour, *In the Shadow of Man* (Collins, 1971) and *Through a Window* (Weidenfield & Nicolson, 1990), based on her acclaimed research in Tanzania's Gombe Stream National Park. Also available is Nishida's *Chimpanzees of Mahale* (University of Tokyo, 1990), based on the similarly long-standing research project in Mahale Mountains National Park. A more visually attractive alternative is the coffee-table book *Mahale: A Photographic Encounter with Chimpanzees*, by Angelika Hofer, Michael Huffman and Gunter Ziesler (Sterling Publishing, New York, 2000).

Coffee-table books The best book of this sort to cover Tanzania as a whole is Paul Joynson-Hicks's *Tanzania: Portrait of a Nation* (Quiller Press, 2001), which contains some great down-to-earth cultural photography and lively anecdotal captions. It is stronger on cultural, landmark and scenic photography than on wildlife photography, for which M Iwago's superb *Serengeti* (Thames and Hudson, 1987) has few peers, although Reinhard Kunkel's stunning *Ngorongoro* (Welcome Enterprises, 2006) is certainly one, while Boyd Norton's more recent *Serengeti: The Eternal Beginning* (Fulcrim, 2011) is also very handsome and has better text. Javed Jafferji's atmospheric photographs are highlighted in *Images of Zanzibar*, while *Zanzibar – Romance of the Ages* makes extensive use of archive photographs dating to before the turn of the century. Both were originally published by HSP Publications in 1996, and are readily available on the island. For more wide-ranging pictorial coverage of Africa, look no further than the comprehensive *Africa: Continent of Contrasts*, with text by Philip Briggs and photography by Martin Harvey and Ariadne Van Zandbergen (Struik Publishers, 2005).

Health Self-prescribing has its hazards so if you are going anywhere very remote consider taking a health book. For adults there is *The Essential Guide To Travel Health* by Jane Wilson-Howarth (Cadogan, 2009); if travelling with the family look at *Your Child Abroad: A Travel Health Guide* by Jane Wilson-Howarth and Matthew Ellis, (Bradt, 2nd edition, 2014).

Fiction Surprisingly few novels have been written by Tanzanians or about Tanzania. An excellent novel set in World War I Tanzania is William Boyd's *An Ice-cream War*, while the same author's *Brazzaville Beach*, though not overtly set in Tanzania, devotes attention to aspects of chimpanzee behaviour first noted at Gombe Stream.

A Tanzanian of Asian extraction now living in Canada, M G Vassanji is the author of at least one novel set in Tanzania and the Kenyan border area, the prize-winning *Book of Secrets* (Macmillan, 1994). This is an atmospheric tale, with much interesting period detail, revolving around a diary written by a British administrator in pre-war Kenya and

TANZANIA ON CD

From traditional percussion and chants to Congolese-style guitar pop and a home-grown style of contemporary hip hop called bongo flava, Tanzania has a rich and varied musical culture, and – unlike a few years back – it is increasingly well represented on CD and on download sites such as emusic and iTunes. The following short list includes some of the most interesting material on offer:

Bi Kidude: Zanzibar (Retroafric, 2007) The first solo recordings by the gravel-voiced Queen of Taarab, a centurion who first performed in the 1920s and it still an active member of the Zanzibari music scene today.

Lady Jaydee: Ya 5 – The Best of Lady Jaydee (Machozi, 2012) The cream of the four studio CDs recorded by this very popular and multiple award-winning artist, one of the few to have given international exposure to bongo flava.

Mohamed Ilyas: Taarab (Chitu-Taku, 2009) A soulful modern taarab recording by one of Zanzibar's most legendary singers backed by a 16-piece orchestra.

Various Artists: Bongo Flava – Swahili Rap from Tanzania (Out Here, 2006) A rare international release featuring 70 minutes of modern Swahili hip-hop by 14 artists, mostly recorded in Dar Es Salaam.

Various Artists: Rough Guide to the Music of Tanzania (Rough Guides, 2009) Traditional music, 80s guitar pop and bongo flava all get an airing on this genre-spanning and highly recommended introduction to Tanzania's musical heritage.

Various Artists: Taarab 3 – Music of Zanzibar (Globestyle 1989) Excellent and well-annotated introduction to Zanzibar's distinctive taarab music, mostly played by small bands and recorded in the 1980s, also featuring one of the best recordings by the legendary Bi Kidude.

Various Artists: Tanzania Instruments (SWP, 2009) A fascinating countrywide tour of traditional instrumentals performances – ranging from Lake Victoria to Zanzibar – recorded by the legendary Hugh Tracey in 1950.

Various Artists: Tanzania Vocals (SWP, 2009) Another culture-hopping rerelease of material recorded by Hugh Tracey in 1950, this *a capella* selection includes atmospheric Maasai chants and a 600-strong mixed-sex Chagga choir recorded on the footslopes of Kilimanjaro.

Various Artists: Zanzibara Vol. 3 – The 1960s Sound of Tanzania (Buda, 2007) Highlife-influenced and infectiously poppy guitar-driven *muziki wa dansi* (dance music) recorded by the likes of the Jamhuri Jazz Band and Atomic Jazz Band in the late 1960s and early 1970s.

Vijana Jazz Band: The Koka Koka Sex Battalion (Sterns Africa, 2011) Showcasing one of the most exciting and popular purveyors of East African rumba-style *muziki wa dansi*, this includes a great selection of toe-tappers recorded in the 1970s and 1980s.

discovered in a flat in Dar es Salaam in the 1980s. Vassanji is also the author of *Uhuru Street*, a collection of short stories set in Dar es Salaam. The most prominent Tanzanian-born novelist is Abdulrazak Gurnah, a Zanzibari now living in the UK whose books are mostly set in East Africa. His best-known novels are *The Last Gift* (Bloomsbury, 2012), *Desertion* (Bloomsbury, 2005) and *Paradise* (Bloomsbury, 1994), which was shortlisted for the Booker and the Whitbread Prize.

Other Africa guides For a full list of Bradt titles, see www.bradtguides.com/shop.

Briggs, Philip *Kenya Highlights* Bradt Travel Guides, 2010.
Briggs, Philip *Malawi* Bradt Travel Guides, 2016.
Briggs, Philip *Mozambique* Bradt Travel Guides, 2015.
Briggs, Philip *Rwanda* Bradt Travel Guides, 2015.
Briggs, Philip and McIntyre, Chris *Tanzania Safari Guide* Bradt Travel Guides, 2017.
Briggs, Philip and Roberts, Andrew *Uganda* Bradt Travel Guides, 2016.
McIntyre, Chris *Zambia* Bradt Travel Guides, 2016.
McIntyre, Chris and Susan *Zanzibar* Bradt Travel Guides, 2017.

Travel literature
Jackman, Brian *Savannah Diaries* Bradt Travel Guides, 2014.
Jackman, Brian, Scott, Jonathan and Scott, Angela *The Marsh Lions* Bradt Travel Guides, 2012.
Scott, Jonathan *The Big Cat Man* Bradt Travel Guides, 2016.
Scott, Jonathan and Angela *The Leopard's Tale* Bradt Travel Guides, 2013.

MAPS A number of maps covering East Africa are available. The best is the Austrian-published Freytag-Berndt 1:2,000,000 map. By far the most accurate and up-to-date dedicated map of Tanzania is the 1:400,000 *Tanzania Travel Map* published by Harms Verlag (*www.harms-ic-verlag.de*). Electronic maps can be downloaded from www.tracks4africa.co.za on to some GPS receivers and smartphones.

A series of excellent maps by Giovanni Tombazzi covers most of the northern reserves, as well as Kilimanjaro, Mount Meru and Zanzibar. Colourful, lively and accurate, these maps are widely available throughout northern Tanzania, and are probably the most user-friendly maps I've seen in East Africa. Each map shows details of the appropriate conservation area in both the dry and wet seasons, and is liberally dotted with illustrations of common trees and other points of interest. Giovanni has also produced a map covering the whole northern safari circuit, useful to those who don't want to splash out on the whole series of more detailed maps. Also recommended are the new Harms Verlag maps to Ngorongoro Conservation Area, Lake Manyara National Park and Zanzibar Island.

WEBSITES The following offer information on Tanzania and Zanzibar:

www.dailynews.co.tz Current news.
www.thecitizen.co.tz Current news.
www.ntz.info Wide-ranging archive of material about northern Tanzania.
www.tanzaniatourism.com Tourist board website.
www.tanzaniaparks.com Current information and entrance fees for all the country's national parks.

Index

Page numbers in **bold** indicate main entries; those in *italics* indicate maps

INDEX OF ADVERTISERS